MATHPOWER™12

WESTERN EDITION

MATHPOWER™ 12

WESTERN EDITION

MATHPOWER™ 10–12,
Western Edition, **Authors**

George Knill, B.Sc., M.S.Ed.
Hamilton, Ontario

Stella Ablett, B.Sc.
Vancouver, British Columbia

Cynthia Ballheim, B.Sc., M.A.
Calgary, Alberta

John Carter, B.Sc., M.Sc.
Toronto, Ontario

Eileen Collins, B.A., M.Ed.
Hamilton, Ontario

Eleanor Conrad, B.Sc.
Pugwash, Nova Scotia

Russel Donnelly, B.Sc., M.A.
Calgary, Alberta

Michael Hamilton, B.Sc., M.Sc.
St. Catharines, Ontario

Rosemary Miller, B.A.
Hamilton, Ontario

Alan Sarna, B.A.
Vancouver, British Columbia

Harold Wardrop, B.Sc.
Surrey, British Columbia

MATHPOWER™ 12,
Western Edition,
Contributing Authors

Bruce Cload, Ph.D.
Toronto, Ontario

Louis Lim, B.Sc.
Belleville, Ontario

Blair Madore, Ph.D.
Toronto, Ontario

Darryl Smith, B.Sc.
Edmonton, Alberta

MATHPOWER™ 12
Western Edition, **Consultants**

John Caranci
Toronto, Ontario

John Chapman
Oliver, British Columbia

Terry Clifford
Winnipeg, Manitoba

John Crowley
North Vancouver
British Columbia

Bob Hart
Calgary, Alberta

Ken Mayson
North Vancouver
British Columbia

Petra Menz
Richmond, British Columbia

Sandy Orsten
Calgary, Alberta

Garry Phillips
Vancouver, British Columbia

Connie Shaver
Winnipeg, Manitoba

Darryl Smith
Edmonton, Alberta

Paula Thompson
Whitehorse, Yukon

**McGraw-Hill
Ryerson**

Toronto Montréal New York Burr Ridge Bangkok Bogotá Caracas
Lisbon London Madrid Mexico City Milan New Delhi
Seoul Singapore Sydney Taipei

McGraw-Hill
Ryerson Limited

A Subsidiary of The **McGraw·Hill** Companies

MATHPOWER™ 12
Western Edition

ISBN 0-07-552600-X

http://www.mcgrawhill.ca

6 7 8 9 0 TRI 0 9 8 7 6 5 4 3

Printed and bound in Canada

Canadian Cataloguing in Publication Data

Main entry under title:

Mathpower 12

Western ed.
Includes index.
ISBN 0-07-552600-X

1. Mathematics. I. Knill, George, date. II. Title: Mathpower twelve

| QA107.M376493 2000 | 510 | C99-932800-X |

PUBLISHER: Diane Wyman
EDITORIAL CONSULTING: Michael J. Webb Consulting Inc.
ASSOCIATE EDITORS: Mary Agnes Challoner, Maggie Cheverie, Jean Ford, Jackie Lacoursiere, Janice Nixon
SENIOR SUPERVISING EDITOR: Carol Altilia
COPY EDITOR: Carol Fordyce
PERMISSIONS EDITORS: Ann Ludbrook, Jacqueline Donovan
EDITORIAL ASSISTANT: Joanne Murray
SENIOR PRODUCTION COORDINATOR: Yolanda Pigden
PRODUCTION COORDINATOR: Brad Madill
ART DIRECTION: Wycliffe Smith Design, Inc.
COVER DESIGN: Wycliffe Smith Design, Inc., Dianna Little
INTERIOR DESIGN: Wycliffe Smith Design, Inc.
ELECTRONIC PAGE MAKE-UP: Tom Dart, Bruce Krever/First Folio Resource Group, Inc.
COVER ILLUSTRATIONS: Clarence Porter
COVER IMAGE: Benelux Press/Masterfile

COPIES OF THIS BOOK
MAY BE OBTAINED BY
CONTACTING:

McGraw-Hill Ryerson Ltd.

WEBSITE:
http://www.mcgrawhill.ca

E-MAIL:
Orders@mcgrawhill.ca

TOLL FREE FAX:
1-800-463-5885

TOLL FREE CALL:
1-800-565-5758

OR BY MAILING
YOUR ORDER TO:

McGraw-Hill Ryerson
Order Department,
300 Water Street
Whitby, ON L1N 9B6

Please quote the ISBN and title when placing your order.

CONTENTS

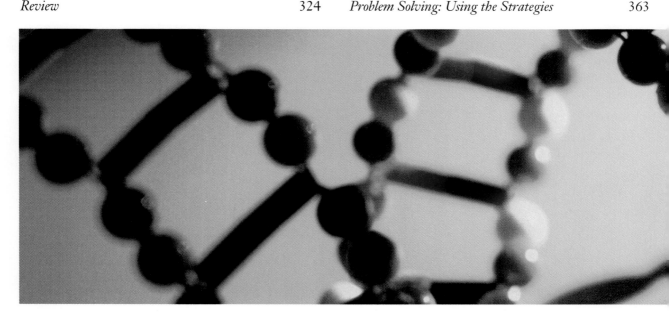

Using *MATHPOWER™ 12, Western Edition*

Each chapter contains several numbered sections.
In a typical numbered section, you find the following features.

2 **3**

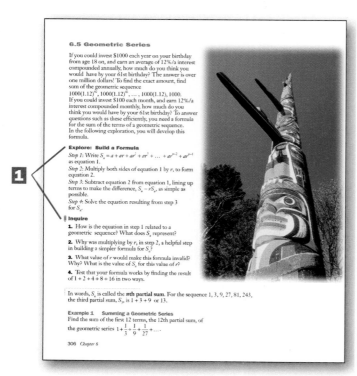

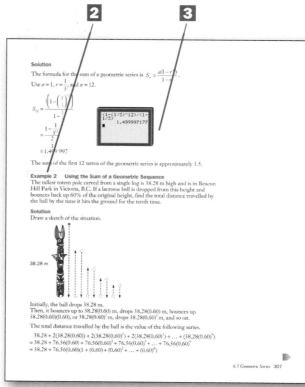

1 Explore and Inquire

You start with an exploration, followed by a set of inquire questions. The exploration and the inquire questions allow you to construct your own learning. Many explorations show how mathematics is applied in the world.

2 Examples

The examples show you how to use what you have learned.

3 Graphing Calculator Displays

These displays show you how technology can be used to solve problems.

4 Practice

By completing these questions, you practise what you have learned, so that you can stabilize your learning.

4

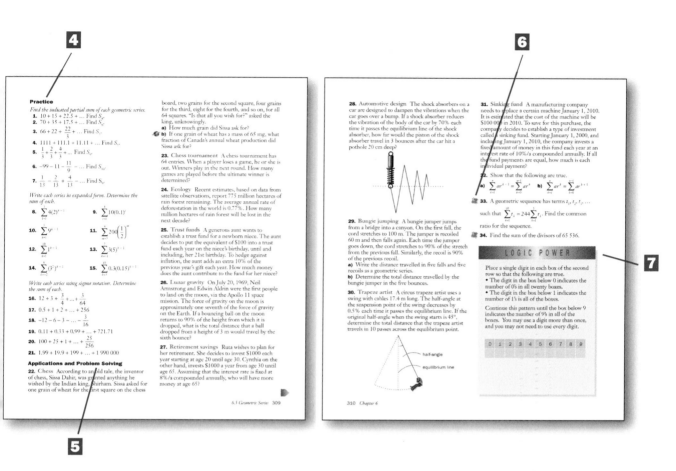

Practice

Find the indicated partial sum of each geometric series.
1. $10 + 15 + 22.5 + ...$ Find S_6.
2. $70 + 35 + 17.5 + ...$ Find S_9.
3. $66 + 22 + \frac{22}{3} + ...$ Find S_7.
4. $1111 + 111.1 + 11.11 + ...$ Find S_5.
5. $\frac{1}{3} + \frac{2}{3} + \frac{4}{3} + ...$ Find S_9.
6. $-99 - 11 - \frac{11}{9} - ...$ Find S_{10}.
7. $\frac{1}{13} - \frac{2}{13} + \frac{4}{13} + ...$ Find S_9.

Write each series in expanded form. Determine the sum of each.
8. $\sum_{i=1}^{8} 4(2)^{i-1}$
9. $\sum_{i=1}^{6} 10(0.1)^{i}$
10. $\sum_{i=1}^{10} 9^{i-1}$
11. $\sum_{i=1}^{n} 200\left(\frac{1}{2}\right)^{n}$
12. $\sum_{i=1}^{8} 1^{i-1}$
13. $\sum_{i=1}^{6} 3(5)^{i-1}$
14. $\sum_{i=1}^{5} (3^2)^{i-1}$
15. $\sum_{i=1}^{10} 0.3(0.15)^{i-1}$

Write each series using sigma notation. Determine the sum of each.
16. $12 + 3 + \frac{3}{4} + ... + \frac{3}{64}$
17. $0.5 + 1 + 2 + ... + 256$
18. $-12 - 6 - 3 - ... - \frac{3}{16}$
19. $0.11 + 0.33 + 0.99 + ... + 721.71$
20. $100 + 25 + 1 + ... + \frac{25}{256}$
21. $1.99 + 19.9 + 199 + ... + 1\,990\,000$

Applications and Problem Solving

22. **Chess** According to an old tale, the inventor of chess, Sissa Dahir, was granted anything he wished by the Indian king, Shirham. Sissa asked for one grain of wheat for the first square on the chess board, two grains for the second square, four grains for the third, eight for the fourth, and so on, for all 64 squares. "Is that all you wish for?" asked the king, unknowingly.
a) How much grain did Sissa ask for?
b) If one grain of wheat has a mass of 65 mg, what fraction of Canada's annual wheat production did Sissa ask for?

23. **Chess tournament** A chess tournament has 64 entries. When a player loses a game, he or she is out. Winners play in the next round. How many games are played before the ultimate winner is determined?

24. **Ecology** Recent estimates, based on data from satellite observations, report 775 million hectares of rain forest remaining. The average annual rate of deforestation in the world is 0.77%. How many million hectares of rain forest will be lost in the next decade?

25. **Trust funds** A generous aunt wants to establish a trust fund for a newborn niece. The aunt decides to put the equivalent of $100 into a trust fund each year on the niece's birthday, until and including, her 21st birthday. To hedge against inflation, the aunt adds an extra 10% of the previous year's gift each year. How much money does the aunt contribute to the fund for her niece?

26. **Lunar gravity** On July 20, 1969, Neil Armstrong and Edwin Aldrin were the first people to land on the moon, via the Apollo 11 space mission. The force of gravity on the moon is approximately one seventh of the force of gravity on the Earth. If a bouncing ball on the moon returns to 90% of the height from which it is dropped, what is the total distance that a ball dropped from a height of 3 m would travel by the sixth bounce?

27. **Retirement savings** Ruta wishes to plan for her retirement. She decides to invest $1000 each year starting at age 20 until age 30. Cynthia on the other hand, invests $1000 a year from age 30 until age 65. Assuming that the interest rate is fixed at 8%/a compounded annually, who will have more money at age 65?

6.5 Geometric Series 309

5

6

28. **Automotive design** The shock absorbers on a car are designed to dampen the vibrations when the car goes over a bump. If a shock absorber reduces the vibration of the body of the car by 70% each time it passes the equilibrium line of the shock absorber, how far would the piston of the shock absorber travel in 3 bounces after the car hit a pothole 20 cm deep?

29. **Bungie jumping** A bungie jumper jumps from a bridge into a canyon. On the first fall, the cord stretches to 100 m. The jumper is recoiled 60 m and then falls again. Each time the jumper goes down, the cord stretches to 90% of the stretch from the previous fall. Similarly, the recoil is 90% of the previous recoil.
a) Write the distance travelled in five falls and five recoils as a geometric series.
b) Determine the total distance travelled by the bungie jumper in the five bounces.

30. **Trapeze artist** A circus trapeze artist uses a swing with cables 17.4 m long. The half-angle at the suspension point of the swing decreases by 0.5% each time it passes the equilibrium line. If the original half-angle when the swing starts is 45°, determine the total distance that the trapeze artist travels in 10 passes across the equilibrium point.

half-angle

equilibrium line

310 *Chapter 6*

31. **Sinking fund** A manufacturing company needs to replace a certain machine January 1, 2010. It is estimated that the cost of the machine will be $100 000 in 2010. To save for this purchase, the company decides to establish a type of investment called a sinking fund. Starting January 1, 2000, and including January 1, 2010, the company invests a fixed amount of money in this fund each year at an interest rate of 10%/a compounded annually. If all the fund payments are equal, how much is each individual payment?

32. Show that the following are true.
a) $\sum_{i=1}^{n} ar^{i-1} = \sum_{i=0}^{n-1} ar^{i}$
b) $\sum_{i=1}^{n} ar^{i} = \sum_{i=0}^{n-1} ar^{i+1}$

33. A geometric sequence has terms $t_1, t_2, t_3, ...$ such that $\sum_{i=1}^{10} t_i = 244 \sum_{i=1}^{5} t_i$. Find the common ratio for the sequence.

34. Find the sum of the divisors of 65 536.

LOGIC POWER

Place a single digit in each box of the second row so that the following are true.
• The digit in the box below 0 indicates the number of 0's in all twenty boxes.
• The digit in the box below 1 indicates the number of 1's in all of the boxes.
Continue this pattern until the box below 9 indicates the number of 9's in all of the boxes. You may use a digit more than once, and you may not need to use every digit.

0	1	2	3	4	5	6	7	8	9

7

---

5 Applications and Problem Solving

These questions let you use what you have learned to solve problems, and to apply and extend your skills. The descriptors on many of the problems show connections to other disciplines, to other topics in mathematics, and to people's daily experiences.

6 Logos

The four logos indicate special kinds of problems or opportunities for research.

When you see this logo, you will be asked to demonstrate an understanding of what you have learned by writing about it in a meaningful way.

This logo signals that you will need to think critically when you answer a question.

This logo indicates an opportunity to work with a classmate or in a larger group to solve a problem.

For a problem with this logo, you will need to use your research skills to find information from the Internet, a print data bank, or some other source.

7 Power Problems

These problems are challenging and fun. They encourage you to reason mathematically.

Special Features of
MATHPOWER™ 12, Western Edition

Math Standard
There are 10 Math Standard pages before Chapter 1. By working through these pages, you will explore the mathematical concepts that citizens of the twenty-first century will need to understand.

Getting Started
A Getting Started section begins each chapter. This section reviews the mathematics that you will need to use in the chapter.

Mental Math
The Mental Math column in each Getting Started section includes a strategy for completing mental math calculations.

Problem Solving
The numerous ways in which problem solving is integrated throughout the book are described on pages xiv–xv.

Technology
Most chapters include one or more Technology sections. These sections allow you to explore the use of graphing calculators, geometry software, spreadsheets, and the Internet to solve problems. The use of technology is also integrated into many numbered sections and feature pages. The graphing calculator displays were generated using a TI-83 Plus calculator. The geometry software displays were generated using The Geometer's Sketchpad software.

Investigating Math
The explorations in the Investigating Math sections will actively involve you in learning mathematics, either individually or with your classmates.

Connecting Math and …
Each chapter includes a Connecting Math section. In these feature pages, you will apply mathematics to other subject areas, such as design, communications, history, and astronomy.

Computer Data Bank
The Computer Data Bank sections are to be used in conjunction with the *MATHPOWER™ 12, Western Edition, Computer Data Bank*. In these sections, you will explore the power of a computer database program in solving problems. The explorations in these sections use ClarisWorks 4.0 and 5.0, Microsoft 4.0, and Microsoft Access 97 for Windows 95, and ClarisWorks 5.0 for Macintosh OS 7.0.

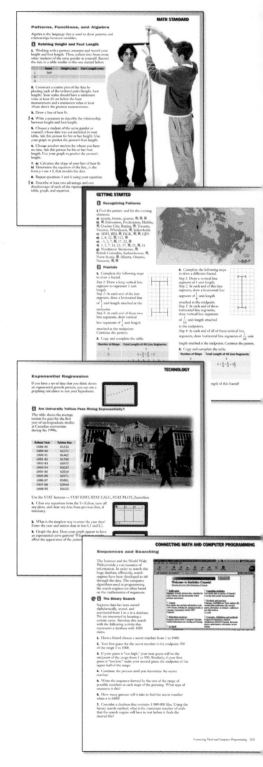

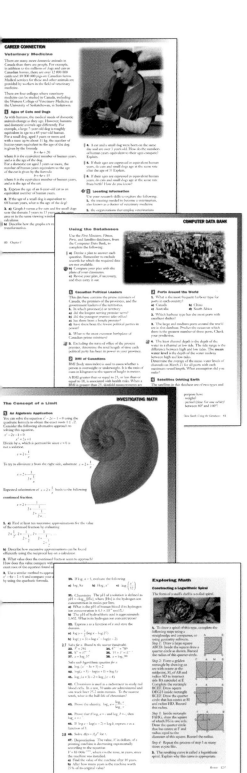

Career Connection

The explorations on the Career Connection pages show you some applications of mathematics to the world of work.

Review/Chapter Check

Near the end of each chapter are sections headed Review and Chapter Check, which allow you to test your progress. The questions in each Review are keyed to section numbers in the chapter, so that you can identify any sections that require further study.

Exploring Math

At the end of the Review section in each chapter, the Exploring Math column includes an enrichment activity designed as a problem solving challenge.

Cumulative Review

Chapter 3, Chapter 6, and Chapter 9 end with cumulative reviews. The cumulative review at the end of Chapter 3 covers the work you did in Chapters 1–3. The cumulative review at the end of Chapter 6 covers Chapters 4–6, and the cumulative review at the end of Chapter 9 covers Chapters 7–9. This is followed by a cumulative review of all the chapters.

Answers

On pages 450–493, there are answers to most of the questions in this book.

Glossary

The illustrated glossary on pages 494–508 explains mathematical terms.

Indexes

The book includes three indexes — an applications index, a technology index, and a general index.

Problem Solving in *MATHPOWER*™ *12, Western Edition*

In whatever career you choose, and in other parts of your daily life, you will be required to solve problems. An important goal of mathematics education is to help you become a good problem solver.

George Polya was one of the world's best teachers of problem solving. The problem solving model he developed has been adapted for use in this book. The model is a guide. It will help you decide what to do when you "don't know what to do."

The problem solving model has the following four steps.

Understand the Problem

Read the problem and ask yourself these questions.
- What am I asked to find?
- Do I need an exact or an approximate answer?
- What information am I given?
- What are the conditions or requirements?
- Is enough information given?
- Is there too much information?
- Have I solved a similar problem?

Think of a Plan

The main challenge in solving a problem is to devise a plan, or an outline of how to proceed. Organize the information and plan how to use it by deciding on a problem solving strategy. The following list of strategies, some of which you have used in previous grades, may help.

- Act out the problem.
- Look for a pattern.
- Work backward.
- Use a formula.
- Use logic.
- Draw and read graphs.
- Make an assumption.
- Guess and check.

- Use manipulatives.
- Solve a simpler problem.
- Use a diagram or flowchart.
- Sequence the operations.
- Use a data bank.
- Change your point of view.
- Use a table or spreadsheet.
- Identify extra information.

Carry Out the Plan

Estimate the answer to the problem. Choose the calculation method you will use to solve the problem. Then, carry out your plan, using paper and pencil, a calculator, a computer, or manipulatives. After solving the problem, write a final statement that gives the solution.

Look Back

Check your calculations in each step of the solution. Then, ask yourself these questions.
- Have I solved the problem I was asked to solve?
- Does the answer seem reasonable?
- Does the answer agree with my estimate?
- Is there another way to solve the problem?

Opportunities for you to develop your problem solving skills appear throughout this book.

In the first three chapters, there are nine numbered problem solving sections. Each section focusses on one strategy. The section provides an example of how the strategy can be used and includes problems that can be solved using the strategy.

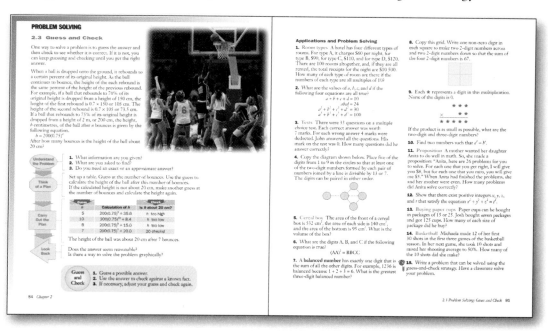

At the end of each chapter, you will find a section headed Problem Solving: Using the Strategies. Each of these sections includes a variety of problems that can be solved using different strategies.

Every numbered section of the book includes the subheading Applications and Problem Solving. The problems under this subheading are related to that section and provide you with many opportunities to apply problem solving strategies.

Many numbered sections include Power Problems, which have been grouped into three types — Logic Power, Number Power, and Word Power. These problems are challenging and fun.

Further problem solving opportunities are to be found in the Exploring Math columns. Each of these columns allows you to explore challenging mathematical ideas.

As described on pages xii–xiii, many special features in the book involve explorations. These features — including Math Standard, Technology, Investigating Math, Connecting Math, Computer Data Bank, and Career Connection sections — are filled with opportunities for you to refine your problem solving skills.

MATH STANDARD

Number and Operation

Every citizen in the 21st century should be competent working with numbers. This competency is necessary to analyze patterns, work with various number systems, and understand the relationships of numbers and operations.

1 Coin Collecting

1. The 1948 Canadian silver dollar is one of the coins most prized by coin collectors. Suppose that you find one of these coins, which is valued at $6000 in mint condition, at an auction. At the auction, you are the successful bidder, and purchase the coin for two thirds of the catalogue price. How much do you pay for the coin if there is an additional 10% buyer's fee and 7% GST both calculated on the bid price?

2. You predict that the 1948 silver dollar will increase in value by 15% each year. How much will the coin be worth in five years?

3. The price of silver changes daily, and is priced according to one troy ounce.
a) One troy ounce has a mass of 31.103 g. How many troy ounces are there in a 23.3 g silver dollar?
b) If the coin were melted for its silver content, how much would it be worth in Canadian currency, if silver is priced at $5.16 US per troy ounce, and the Canadian dollar is worth $0.6847 US?

2 Palindrome Bank Notes

1. Palindrome (or radar) bank notes are much sought after by paper money collectors. Finding such a bank note in uncirculated condition could mean that it is worth more than double its catalogue value. Study the dollar bill shown, and define what is meant by a palindrome bank note.

2. a) Choose any sequence of consecutive digits from the serial number. Reverse the digits of this number. Add these two numbers. What do you notice about the sum?
b) Repeat the process in a).

3. a) Does the serial number contain a two-digit prime number?
b) If yes, reverse the digits of the two-digit prime number. Is this new number also prime?
c) List all the two-digit prime numbers that are also prime when their digits are reversed.

4. In our present issue of bank notes, each series is numbered from 0000000 to 9999999. A maximum of ten thousand notes may have palindrome serial numbers. What is the probability of getting such a bank note? Express the answer as a fraction and as a percent.

Patterns, Functions, and Algebra

Algebra is the language that is used to show patterns and relationships between variables.

1 Relating Height and Foot Length

1. Working with a partner, measure and record your height and foot length. Then, collect data from seven other students of the same gender as yourself. Record the data in a table similar to the one started below.

	Name	Height (cm)	Foot Length (cm)
1	Self		
2			
3			

2. Construct a scatter plot of the data by plotting each of the ordered pairs (height, foot length). Your scales should have a minimum value at least 10 cm below the least measurement and a maximum value at least 10 cm above the greatest measurement.

3. Draw a line of best fit.

4. Write a sentence to describe the relationship between height and foot length.

5. Choose a student of the same gender as yourself, whose data was not included in your table. Ask this person for his or her height. Use your graph to predict the person's foot length.

6. Choose another student for whom you have no data. Ask this person for his or her foot length. Use your graph to predict the person's height.

7. a) Calculate the slope of your line of best fit.
b) Determine the equation of the line, in the form $y = mx + b$, that models the data.

8. Repeat questions 5 and 6 using your equation.

9. Describe at least one advantage and one disadvantage of each of the representations— table, graph, and equation.

MATH STANDARD

Geometry and Spatial Sense

Geometry involves inductive and deductive reasoning, and develops our ability to reason abstractly. Different branches of geometry include euclidean, analytic, transformational, and fractal.

1 Euler's Formula

Platonic solids are three-dimensional figures with congruent regular polygon-shaped faces. The Greek philosopher Plato believed that matter is made up of four elements and he associated each element with a platonic solid: fire (tetrahedron), earth (cube), air (octahedron), and water (icosahedron). The fifth platonic solid, the dodecahedron, represents the universe.

1. Copy and complete the table.

Platonic Solid	Number of Vertices	Number of Faces	Number of Edges
tetrahedron			
cube			
octahedron			
icosahedron			
dodecahedron			

2. Write a formula that relates the number of vertices and faces to the number of edges for all the platonic solids. This formula is known as Euler's formula.

3. Euler's formula holds true for any polyhedron. Show that it is true for a square-based pyramid and for a triangular prism.

2 Fractal Geometry

1. Stages 0, 1, and 2 of a Sierpinski triangle are shown. To obtain stage 1 from stage 0, the midpoints of each side of the equilateral triangle are joined and the triangle formed is removed. This process is repeated on each remaining smaller equilateral triangle to obtain stage 2. Draw stage 3 of a Sierpinski triangle.

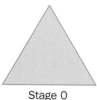

Stage 0　　　　Stage 1　　　　Stage 2

2. How many shaded triangles will there be in the nth stage?

3. Describe two instances in everyday life where you find geometric shapes with repeating patterns that get smaller.

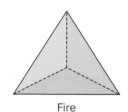

Fire

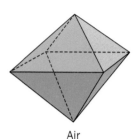

Air

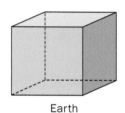

Earth

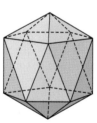

Water

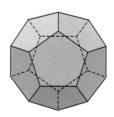

Universe

Measurement

Measurement involves many tools and formulas.

1 Counting Crowds

Have you ever wondered how crowds are counted at events? The following procedure describes how the police calculate crowd numbers.

Step 1: The site where the crowd is expected is measured and mapped on a grid.
Step 2: The area is calculated making allowances for objects such as trees, speakers and other technical equipment, vehicles, and so on.
Step 3: During the event, the scene is eyeballed and the crowd density is estimated.
· At 100% density there are four people per square metre, standing shoulder to shoulder.
· At 150% density there are six people per square metre, pressing against each other.
· People sitting are judged to be 25% density.
· People walking freely are considered to be 10% density.
Step 4: The estimate obtained using the previous steps is refined using video footage of the event.

1. Mark off one square metre on the floor using masking tape. Have four students stand inside the square. Do you think that this is a reasonable estimate to model 100% density? Give reasons why or why not.

2. What is the maximum number of people you can get to stand, with both feet on the ground, inside the square? Would this number be a more accurate reflection of 100% density in your opinion?

3. Use the first three steps of the above crowd-counting method to determine the number of people your classroom can hold at 100% density if everyone is standing.

4. Describe two events in your community for which the organizers would be particularly interested in the attendance. Suggest reasons why.

2 Maximizing Area

1. A farmer has 30 m of fencing with which he plans to enclose a rectangular pen for his three potbelly pigs. The pen needs fencing only on three sides as the fourth side is a wall.
a) What is the maximum area that each pig can be given?
b) If the amount of fencing is halved, is each pig's area also halved? Justify your answer.

2. If the farmer decides that the pen does not have to be rectangular, what shape would provide the greatest area for the pigs? Draw a scale drawing of this pen.

MATH STANDARD

Data Analysis, Statistics, and Probability

Statistics is the science of collecting, recording, organizing, analyzing, and interpreting data. Probability is the study of chance or uncertainty. Probability is classified as either experimental or theoretical, and is used to model and predict situations.

1 Human Demographics

Canada's population in 1951 was approximately 14 000 000. By 1997 it had grown to 30 300 000. The double bar graph compares the population in each of these years according to age groups.

1. a) Approximately what percent of the population was in the 5–19 age group in 1997?

b) Describe how the population under five years of age changed between 1951 and 1997. Give reasons for this change.

c) Explain the change in the population aged 65 years and over.

2. a) Draw a circle graph to show your prediction of the percent make-up of Canada's population in the year 2010, using the same age groups.

b) Suppose you are responsible for allocating the budget for your province in the year 2010. What areas might need increased funding? In what areas might funding be decreased?

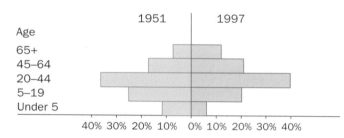

Canadian Population by Age

2 A Fair Game?

1. In a dice game, if you roll a prime number, you win $5; otherwise, you lose $3.

a) Roll a regular six-sided die 50 times, recording your results in a table. Do you think the game is fair?

b) Use theoretical probability to determine whether the game is fair.

c) If you think the game is unfair, how might the amount given for rolling a prime number, and the amount for any other roll, be changed so that the game is fair?

Problem Solving

The ability to solve problems is a skill needed in daily life and in a career. We strengthen our problem solving abilities through practice.

1 Solving Problems

1. What is the least number of moves needed to make the white knights and the black knights change places? The squares are numbered so you can keep track of your moves. (A knight can move diagonally to the opposite corner of a 3×2 rectangle of which it is in the corner. For example, the black knight on square 7 can move to square 2 or square 6.)

2. Must each calendar year have at least one Friday the thirteenth? Justify your answer.

3. a) What base do cartoon characters probably count in?
b) What answer would your favourite cartoon character probably give for $1 + 2 + 3 + 4$?

4. In 1997, Kanada and Takahashi used a computer to calculate π to 51.5 billion digits. Suppose each digit was written on banner paper, with each digit using a 10 cm width.
a) How long would the banner be?
b) How long would it take to complete the banner? Describe the assumptions you made in obtaining your answer.

5. In the sum, each different letter represents a different digit. What is the sum?

$$
\begin{array}{r}
W\,I\,.\,R\,E \\
+\quad M\,O\,.\,R\,E \\
\hline
\$M\,O\,N\,.\,E\,Y
\end{array}
$$

6. During their summer vacation, a family from Saskatoon plan to visit relatives in Vancouver and Prince Rupert. If the highway from Saskatoon to Calgary is closed for construction, determine the route they should take to minimize their total driving distance.

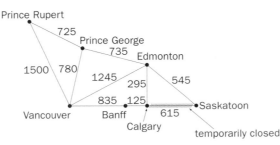

Driving Distances in Kilometres

MATH STANDARD

Reasoning and Proof

The ability to reason logically and abstractly is strengthened through studying mathematics. The beauty of mathematics comes alive through making conjectures and formalizing arguments through proofs.

1 Stay or Switch? That is the Question!

On a game show, a contestant is given the choice of three doors. Behind one door is a car, behind the other two doors are goats. The contestant chooses the door numbered 1, and the show host, who knows what is behind each door, opens the door numbered 3, behind which is a goat. Then the host asks the contestant "Do you want to switch to door number 2"?

1. Should the contestant stay with door number 1 or switch? Give reasons for your answer.

2. Write "goat," "goat," and "car" on slips of paper. With a partner, simulate the game at least thirty times. Change roles so that each person has turns being the host and the contestant. Record whether the contestant chooses to stay or to switch, and the outcome.
Based on your simulation, is it best for the contestant to stay or to switch? Explain.

2 Using Logic

1. At lunch time four friends, Anna, Pat, Petra, and Bonnie, are each eating a different type of fruit. The fruits are an apple, a pear, a peach, and a banana. None of the girls is eating a type of fruit that begins with the same initial as her name. If Anna does not like pears, who is eating what?

2. A guitar is on sale at 10% off. Which method of calculating the total price gives the lower price to the customer? Justify your choice.
A: discounting the regular price and then applying the taxes
B: applying the taxes on the regular price and then taking 10% off the total

3 True of False?

1. Determine whether each conditional statement is true or false. Then, write the converse statement for each and determine if it is true or false.
a) If $x > 0$ and $y > 0$, then $xy > 0$.
b) If n is an odd integer, then $n + 2$ is an odd integer.

MATH STANDARD

Communication

Mathematics is a universal language that needs to be communicated clearly in both written and oral forms.

1 Giving Detailed Instructions

1. With a partner, decide on four design elements: a single-digit number, a letter of the alphabet, a closed shape, and a simple easily-drawn picture. Without letting the other person see your work, create a full-page design or pattern using the four elements.

2. Give detailed instructions, either verbal or written, to your partner so that he or she can reproduce your design. Your partner may not say anything or peek at your design during this activity.

3. Compare your original design with your partner's attempt to duplicate it based on your instructions. Write your thoughts and reflections about your successes or difficulties in communicating your design to your partner.

4. Switch roles and repeat the activity.

2 Interpreting Graphs

1. Write a paragraph describing in detail the information that each graph portrays.

a)
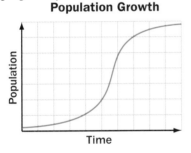
Population Growth

b)
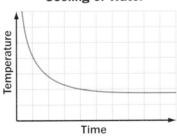
Cooling of Water

c)
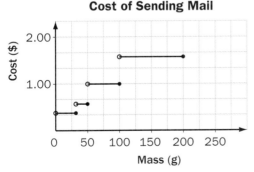
Cost of Sending Mail

2. Sketch a graph to represent each situation.
a) The number of customers in a fast-food restaurant throughout the day
b) The speed of a plane on a flight from Vancouver to Winnipeg

MATH STANDARD

Connections

Mathematics is used to solve problems in many other areas, such as the sciences, the social sciences, the arts, business, and sports. By connecting mathematics to applications, you learn how to use mathematical concepts and skills to solve problems.

1 Cryptography

The Rosetta Stone is a large basalt tablet engraved with three types of writing: ancient Egyptian hieroglyphs, Demotic, and Greek. It was made in Egypt around 200 B.C. and when it was found near the mouth of the Nile in 1799 A.D., it provided the key to decoding the ancient Egyptian hieroglyphs.

Mathematics is often used as the key in cryptography to encode and decode information. One such method is explored below.

1. To encode a message, replace each letter by its numerical position in the alphabet and write the numbers in 2×2 matrices (two rows, two columns). For example, MEET ME TODAY would be written

as $\begin{bmatrix} 13 & 5 \\ 5 & 20 \end{bmatrix}, \begin{bmatrix} 13 & 5 \\ 20 & 15 \end{bmatrix}, \begin{bmatrix} 4 & 1 \\ 25 & 24 \end{bmatrix}.$

How are any missing entries in the last matrix filled in?

2. Choose any 2×2 matrix and encrypt the message by adding each number in this matrix to the corresponding number in the message. For example, if the encrypting matrix is $\begin{bmatrix} 2 & -1 \\ 3 & 30 \end{bmatrix}$, the first part of the message above

becomes $\begin{bmatrix} 15 & 4 \\ 8 & 50 \end{bmatrix}$. Write the encrypted form of the other two parts of the message.

3. Send the message as a sequence of numbers. For the given example, the numbers would be 15, 4, 8, 50, …. The person receiving the message follows the steps backward to decode the message. Using the same encrypting matrix, decode the message 11, 19, 22, 33, 17, 11, 7, 54.

4. Use the steps above to send messages and receive messages from a partner.

5. Describe five applications of cryptography in our daily lives.

Representation

Mathematical problems can be solved by modelling and interpreting them using various representations. Representations may be algebraic, graphic, or numeric.

1 Königsberg Bridges Problem

About 200 years ago the small German town of Königsberg had seven bridges over the River Pregel that flows through the town. Many people in the town enjoyed taking walks across the bridges. A famous problem was posed. Is it possible to cross all seven bridges exactly once, without retracing one's path at some point?

Leonhard Euler (1707–1783), the famous Swiss mathematician, studied the question. He represented the problem as a graph, using vertices to represent the land and edges to represent bridges connecting those parts of the land.

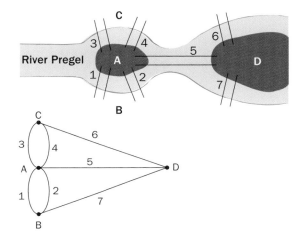

1. Euler found, after analyzing this and many other similar graphs, that it is possible to trace a path crossing each edge exactly once if the graph either has all even degree vertices, or has exactly two odd degree vertices. The degree of a vertex is the number of edges meeting at it. Is it possible to solve the Königsberg Bridges Problem? Justify your answer.

2. a) Suppose you were an engineer, hired by the town of Königsberg to add or remove one bridge so that the people can make their walk crossing each bridge exactly once. What plan would you present to the town?
b) Represent your plan as a graph, using vertices and edges.
c) Without lifting your pencil, show that your graph can be traced, crossing each bridge exactly once.

3. a) Copy the graph shown. Using Euler's rule, explain why it should be possible to trace a path that goes along each edge exactly once.
b) Trace one such path.
c) Copy the graph again, omitting any two of the edges. Can you draw a path that goes along each edge exactly once for this graph? Explain why or why not.

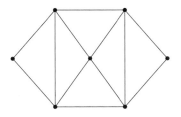

Transformations

1. For the set of footprints shown, which pairs of footprints are related by
a) a translation?
b) a translation followed by a reflection?
c) a reflection followed by a translation?

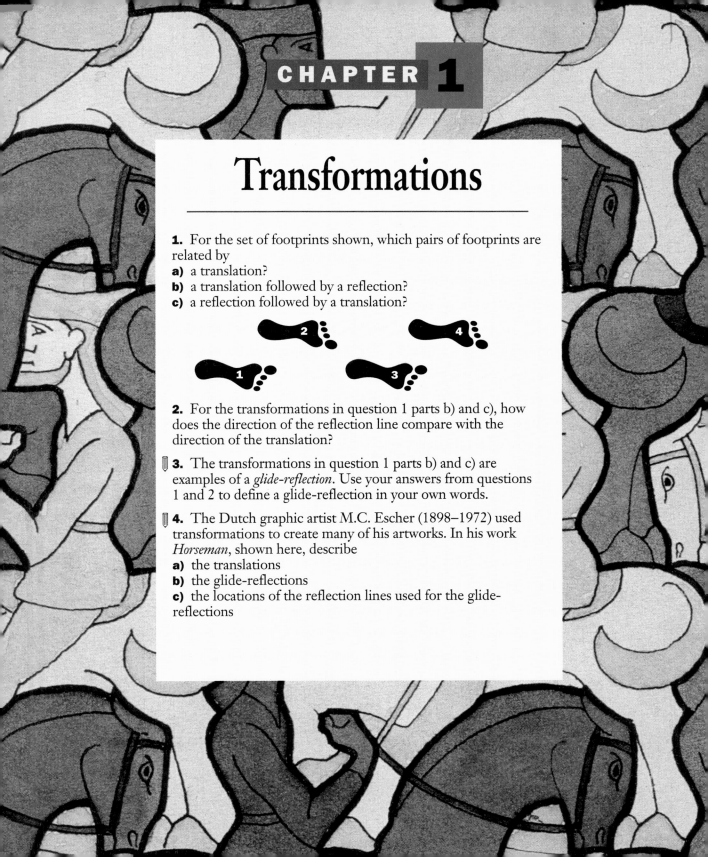

2. For the transformations in question 1 parts b) and c), how does the direction of the reflection line compare with the direction of the translation?

3. The transformations in question 1 parts b) and c) are examples of a *glide-reflection*. Use your answers from questions 1 and 2 to define a glide-reflection in your own words.

4. The Dutch graphic artist M.C. Escher (1898–1972) used transformations to create many of his artworks. In his work *Horseman*, shown here, describe
a) the translations
b) the glide-reflections
c) the locations of the reflection lines used for the glide-reflections

GETTING STARTED

Human Physiology

1 The Heart

1. For the average person at rest, the heart pumps blood at a rate of about 5 L/min. Therefore, the volume, V litres, pumped over a period of time, t minutes, is given by the function $V = 5t$.
a) Let $V = y$ and $t = x$, complete a table of values, and graph the function. Use the same scale on each axis.
b) Which quadrant did you use? Explain.

2. For top athletes in competition, the heart can pump blood at 30 L/min, so $V = 30t$.
a) Let $V = y$ and $t = x$, and graph this function on the same axes as the graph from question 1.
b) For points with the same non-zero x-coordinate, how do the y-coordinates compare for the two graphs?
c) Do the two graphs have any points in common?

3. a) Interchange the x- and y-coordinates in the table from question 1, so that a point (x, y) becomes the point (y, x). Graph the resulting coordinates on the same axes as the graph from question 1.
b) Describe what the graph with the interchanged coordinates represents.

4. a) Graph the line $y = x$ on the same set of axes you used in question 3.
b) Reflect the graph from question 1 in the line $y = x$. How does the result compare with the graph from question 3? Explain why.

2 Breathing

1. At rest, the average person breathes about 12 times per minute.
a) Write an equation that expresses the number of breaths in terms of the time, in minutes.
b) Graph the equation.

2. Use the graph from question 1 to graph an equation that expresses the time, in minutes, in terms of the number of breaths. Explain your reasoning.

Warm Up

1. If $f(x) = |2x - 3|$, find

a) $f(0)$ **b)** $f(2)$ **c)** $f(-1)$ **d)** $f\left(\dfrac{1}{2}\right)$

e) $f(-0.5)$ **f)** $f(1.5)$ **g)** $f(-4)$ **h)** $f(0.25)$

2. If $g(x) = \sqrt{x+1}$, find

a) $g(0)$ **b)** $g(3)$ **c)** $g(8)$ **d)** $g(-1)$

e) $g(0.21)$ **f)** $g(1.25)$ **g)** $g(-0.75)$ **h)** $g(-2)$

3. If $k(x) = (x-1)^3 + 2$, find

a) $k(0)$ **b)** $k(1)$ **c)** $k(-1)$ **d)** $k(4)$

e) $k(-2)$ **f)** $k(0.5)$ **g)** $k(1.5)$ **h)** $k(0.9)$

 4. Describe the transformation that maps the function $y = x^2$ onto each of the following functions.

a) $y = x^2 + 2$ **b)** $y = x^2 - 5$

c) $y = (x-1)^2$ **d)** $y = (x+3)^2$

e) $y = (x+2)^2 - 1$ **f)** $y = (x-3)^2 + 4$

5. a) Translate the graph $y = x$ upward by 1 unit.

b) Translate the graph $y = x$ to the left by 1 unit.

c) Compare the results from parts a) and b).

d) Translate the graph $y = x^2$ upward by 1 unit.

e) Translate the graph $y = x^2$ to the left by 1 unit.

f) Compare the results from parts d) and e).

g) Explain any differences in your answers to parts c) and f).

Determine the x- and y-intercepts of each of the following.

6. $x + 2y = 2$ **7.** $3x - 4y = 12$

8. $y = x - 1$ **9.** $y = 2x + 3$

10. $y = |x - 1|$ **11.** $y = (x+1)(x-2)$

For each graph,
a) *explain whether it represents a function*
b) *write the domain and range*

12.   **13.**

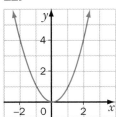   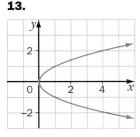

Write the domain and range of each function.

14. $y = x^2 - 1$ **15.** $y = |x + 3|$

16. $y = \dfrac{1}{x - 2}$ **17.** $y = \sqrt{x + 4}$

Mental Math

Find the image of the point (−2, 5) under each of the following translations.

1. 3 units upward

2. 6 units downward

3. 3 units to the left

4. 4 units to the right

5. 2 units downward and 1 unit to the right

6. 2 units upward and 5 units to the left

Name the translation that transforms the first point onto the second.

7. (2, 0) onto (4, 0)

8. (1, 3) onto (1, −1)

9. (6, −2) onto (0, −2)

10. (−1, −2) onto (−1, 3)

11. (1, 2) onto (5, 3)

12. (2, −2) onto (−1, −4)

Find the reciprocal of each of the following.

13. 0.1   **14.** 0.01   **15.** 0.5   **16.** −0.25

Express the reciprocal of each of the following as a decimal.

17. 5   **18.** 2.5   **19.** 0.4   **20.** −20

Evaluate each of the following expressions for
a) $x = 2$ **b)** $x = -3$

21. $3x - 1$ **22.** $|x + 1|$

23. $x^2 + 1$ **24.** $x^3 - 3$

25. $\sqrt{3x + 10}$ **26.** $\dfrac{1}{x^2 + 1}$

State the value(s) of x for which each of the following expressions is undefined.

27. $\dfrac{1}{x - 1}$ **28.** $\dfrac{x}{2x + 1}$

29. $\dfrac{5}{x(x + 1)}$ **30.** $\dfrac{3x}{x^2 - 1}$

Solve for x.

31. $3x = -6$ **32.** $\dfrac{x}{4} = 3$

33. $x - 3 = -1$ **34.** $x + 8 = 2$

35. $2x + 9 = 0$ **36.** $3x - 1 = 5$

37. $\dfrac{x}{3} + 1 = 0$ **38.** $2(x - 1) = 3$

TECHNOLOGY

Reviewing Graphs of Functions

1 Linear Functions

A **linear function** is a function of the form $y = mx + b$.

1. Graph each of the following in the standard viewing window of your graphing calculator. Sketch each graph in your notebook.

a) $y = 2x$ **b)** $y = 2x + 5$ **c)** $y = 2x - 6$
d) $y = -2x$ **e)** $y = -2x + 5$ **f)** $y = -2x - 6$

2. How are the graphs in question 1 the same? How are they different?

3. a) In question 1, the coefficient of x is either 2 or -2.
What does this coefficient represent?
b) How are the graphs related to the sign of this coefficient?

4. For each function in question 1, what is the x-intercept? the y-intercept?

5. Rewrite each of the following linear functions in the form $y = mx + b$.
Repeat question 1 for each function.

a) $2x + 3y = 6$ **b)** $x + 5y = 15$
c) $3x - y = 14$ **d)** $6x - 2y = -9$

6. For each graph in question 5, state the slope and y-intercept.

2 Absolute Value Functions

1. Graph each of the following pairs of functions in the standard viewing window of your graphing calculator. Sketch each graph in your notebook.

a) $y = x - 5$ **b)** $y = -2x + 1$ **c)** $y = -x - 3$
    $y = |x - 5|$ $y = |-2x + 1|$ $y = |-x - 3|$

2. How are the graphs in each pair the same? How are they different?

3. Use your answer to question 2 to explain the meaning of an absolute value function.

4. Graph each of the following functions in the standard viewing window of your graphing calculator. Sketch each graph in your notebook.

a) $y = |x|$ **b)** $y = 3|x|$ **c)** $y = -3|x|$

d) $y = -|x + 1|$ **e)** $y = -0.5|x - 2|$ **f)** $y = 0.5|x - 2|$

5. a) Which graphs in question 4 open up? open down?
b) What determines the direction of opening?

6. For each graph in question 4, write
a) the coordinates of the vertex
b) the domain and range
c) the equation of the axis of symmetry

3 Quadratic Functions

A **quadratic function** is a function of degree 2.

1. Graph each of the following in the standard viewing window of your graphing calculator. Sketch each graph in your notebook.

a) $y = x^2 + 4$ **b)** $y = -x^2 + 9$

c) $y = 0.5x^2 - 9$ **d)** $y = -3x^2 + 8$

e) $y = x^2 + 4x - 5$ **f)** $y = -2x^2 - 3x + 9$

2. Use your graphs to explain how the graphs are affected by

a) the sign of the coefficient of x^2

b) the magnitude of the coefficient of x^2

3. Use the Maximum or Minimum operation to find the vertex of each graph in question 1.

4. Use the Zero operation to find the x-intercepts for each graph in question 1, if possible.

5. Use the Value operation to determine the y-intercept for each graph in question 1.

4 Cubic Functions

A **cubic function** is a function of degree 3. The peaks and valleys, or turning points, of a cubic function are known as relative maximums and relative minimums.

1. Graph each of the following in the standard viewing window of your graphing calculator. Sketch each graph in your notebook.

a) $y = x^3 - 2x$ **b)** $y = x^3 - 3x + 4$

c) $y = -x^3 + 2$ **d)** $y = -3x^3 + 4x - 3$

e) $y = 2x^3 - 5x^2 - 3x + 2$ **f)** $y = (x + 1)(x - 2)(x + 3)$

2. For each graph in question 1, determine

a) the domain and range

b) any real zeros, to the nearest tenth, if necessary

c) the y-intercept

d) the coordinates of any relative maximums and relative minimums, rounded to the nearest tenth, if necessary.

3. What is the maximum possible number of turning points of a cubic function?

5 Rational Functions

A **rational function** is a function of the form $f(x) = \dfrac{g(x)}{h(x)}$, where $g(x)$ and $h(x)$ are polynomials and $h(x) \neq 0$.

The graph of the rational function $y = \dfrac{3}{x-2}$ is shown. The line $x = 2$ is a vertical asymptote of the graph. The line $y = 0$ is a horizontal asymptote of the graph. When the calculator is in the connected mode, the line, in the standard viewing window, that connects the two parts of the graph approximates the vertical asymptote. The line does not appear in the standard viewing window when the calculator is in the dot mode. The line does not appear in connected mode when the decimal viewing window or another "friendly" viewing window is used.

Standard Connected Mode   *Standard Dot Mode*   *Decimal Connected Mode*

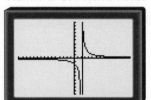 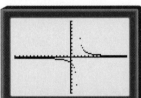 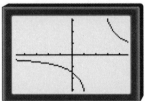

1. Graph each of the following in the standard viewing window of your graphing calculator. Sketch each graph in your notebook.

a) $y = \dfrac{4}{x+3}$

b) $y = \dfrac{x}{x-3}$

c) $y = \dfrac{-2x}{x+1}$

d) $y = \dfrac{3}{x^2-1}$

e) $y = \dfrac{x^2-x-6}{x-2}$

f) $y = \dfrac{1-x^2}{x-1}$

2. For each graph in question 1,
a) determine the equations of any horizontal or vertical asymptotes
b) state the domain and range

6 Radical Functions

A function such as $y = \sqrt{x} + 1$, which has a variable in the radicand, is called a **radical function**. To ensure that the range of a radical function is real, ensure that the radicand is not negative.

1. Graph each of the following in the standard viewing window of your graphing calculator. Sketch each graph in your notebook.

a) $y = \sqrt{x+2}$

b) $y = -\sqrt{x-3}$

c) $y = \sqrt{3x-2}$

d) $y = \sqrt{4-3x}$

e) $y = \sqrt{0.5x+1}$

f) $y = -\sqrt{-0.5x-2}$

2. Determine the domain and range for each graph in question 1.

3. What does the sign in front of the radical sign tell you about the graph?

4. What does the sign of the coefficient of x tell you about the graph?

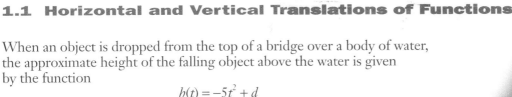

1.1 Horizontal and Vertical Translations of Functions

When an object is dropped from the top of a bridge over a body of water, the approximate height of the falling object above the water is given by the function

$$h(t) = -5t^2 + d$$

where $h(t)$ metres is the height of the object t seconds after it is dropped, and d metres is the height of the bridge.

Explore: Graph the Functions

The table includes the approximate heights, in metres, of three famous Canadian bridges.

Bridge	Height (m)
Ambassador Bridge	45
Confederation Bridge	60
Capilano Canyon Suspension Bridge	70

a) Write the function that describes the height of a falling object above the water t seconds after it is dropped from the top of each bridge.

b) Graph $h(t)$ versus t for the three functions on the same set of axes or in the same viewing window of a graphing calculator.

Inquire

1. In what quadrant do the three graphs appear? Explain why.

2. On the graphs for the Ambassador Bridge and the Confederation Bridge, how do the h-coordinates of any two points that have the same t-coordinate compare? Explain why.

3. On the graphs for the Ambassador Bridge and the Capilano Bridge, how do the h-coordinates of any two points that have the same t-coordinate compare? Explain why.

4. Graph the three functions $y = -5x^2 + b$ for $b = 45$, $b = 60$, and $b = 70$ on the same set of axes or in the same viewing window of a graphing calculator. If the domain of the three functions is the set of real numbers, how do the three graphs compare with the three graphs of $h(t)$ versus t from the Explore section, above? Explain why.

5. How do the three graphs from question 4 compare with the graph of $y = x^2$ over the same domain? Explain why.

Example 1 Positive Vertical Translation

a) Graph the functions $y = x^2$ and $y = x^2 + 2$ on the same set of axes.

b) How does the graph of $y = x^2$ compare to the graph of $y = x^2 + 2$?

Solution

a)

$y = x^2$

x	y
3	9
2	4
1	1
0	0
−1	1
−2	4
−3	9

$y = x^2 + 2$

x	y
3	11
2	6
1	3
0	2
−1	3
−2	6
−3	11

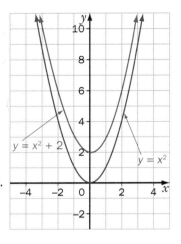

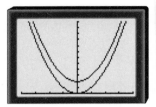

b) The graphs of $y = x^2$ and $y = x^2 + 2$ are congruent. The graph of the function $y = x^2 + 2$ is obtained when the graph of the function $y = x^2$ undergoes a vertical translation of 2 units in the positive direction, that is, upward.

The graph of the function $y = x^2 + 2$ can also be obtained from the graph of $y = x^2$ by adding 2 to each y-value on the graph of $y = x^2$. The point (x, y) on the graph of $y = x^2$ is transformed to become the point $(x, y + 2)$ on the graph of $y = x^2 + 2$.

Example 2 Vertical Translations

How do the graphs of $y = \sqrt{x} + 3$ and $y = \sqrt{x} - 2$ compare with the graph of $y = \sqrt{x}$, where $x \geq 0$.

Solution

$y = \sqrt{x}$

x	y
0	0
1	1
4	2
9	3
16	4

$y = \sqrt{x} + 3$

x	y
0	3
1	4
4	5
9	6
16	7

$y = \sqrt{x} - 2$

x	y
0	−2
1	−1
4	0
9	1
16	2

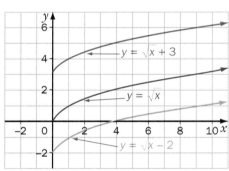

The graph of the function $y = \sqrt{x} + 3$ is the graph of the function $y = \sqrt{x}$ with a vertical translation of 3 units upward. The point (x, y) on the graph of $y = \sqrt{x}$ is transformed to become the point $(x, y + 3)$ on the graph of $y = \sqrt{x} + 3$.

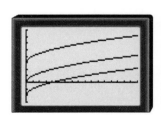

Similarly, the graph of the function $y = \sqrt{x} - 2$ is the graph of the function $y = \sqrt{x}$ with a vertical translation of 2 units downward. The point (x, y) on the graph of $y = \sqrt{x}$ is transformed to become the point $(x, y - 2)$ on the graph of $y = \sqrt{x} - 2$.

All three graphs are congruent and have domain $x \geq 0$.

The results from Examples 1 and 2 can be generalized for all functions as follows.

The graph of $y = f(x) + k$, or $y - k = f(x)$, is congruent to the graph of $y = f(x)$.
If $k > 0$, the graph of $y = f(x) + k$, or $y - k = f(x)$, is the graph of $y = f(x)$ translated upward by k units.
If $k < 0$, the graph of $y = f(x) + k$, or $y - k = f(x)$, is the graph of $y = f(x)$ translated downward by k units.

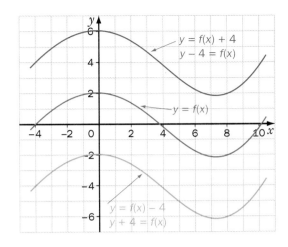

Example 3   Horizontal Translations

How do the graphs of $y = |x + 2|$ and $y = |x - 2|$ compare to the graph of $y = |x|$?

Solution

$y = |x|$		$y = |x + 2|$		$y = |x - 2|$	
x	**y**	**x**	**y**	**x**	**y**
6	6	6	8	6	4
4	4	4	6	4	2
2	2	2	4	2	0
0	0	0	2	0	2
-2	2	-2	0	-2	4
-4	4	-4	2	-4	6
-6	6	-6	4	-6	8

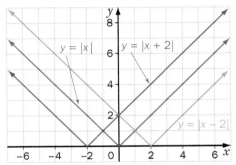

The graphs of $y = |x|$, $y = |x + 2|$, and $y = |x - 2|$ are congruent.
The graph of $y = |x + 2|$ is obtained when the graph of $y = |x|$ is translated horizontally 2 units to the left.
The graph of $y = |x + 2|$ is also obtained from the graph of $y = |x|$ by subtracting 2 from each x-value on the graph of $y = |x|$.
The point (x, y) on the graph of $y = |x|$ is transformed to become the point $(x - 2, y)$ on the graph of $y = |x + 2|$.
Similarly, the graph of $y = |x - 2|$ is obtained when the graph of $y = |x|$ is translated horizontally 2 units to the right.
The graph of $y = |x - 2|$ is also obtained from the graph of $y = |x|$ by adding 2 to each x-value on the graph of $y = |x|$.
The point (x, y) on the graph of $y = |x|$ is transformed to become the point $(x + 2, y)$ on the graph of $y = |x - 2|$.

The results from Example 3 can be generalized for all functions as follows.

The graph of $y = f(x - h)$ is congruent to the graph of $y = f(x)$.
If $h > 0$, the graph of $y = f(x - h)$ is the graph of $y = f(x)$ translated to the right by h units.
If $h < 0$, the graph of $y = f(x - h)$ is the graph of $y = f(x)$ translated to the left by h units.

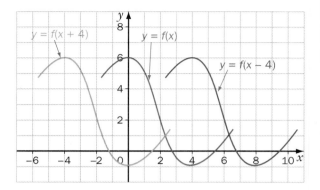

Example 4   Horizontal and Vertical Translations
Sketch the graph of $y = (x - 3)^3 + 4$.

Solution
Sketch the graph of $y = x^3$.
Translate the graph of $y = x^3$ three units to the right to obtain the graph of $y = (x - 3)^3$.
Translate the graph of $y = (x - 3)^3$ four units upward to obtain the graph of $y = (x - 3)^3 + 4$.
The point (x, y) on the function $y = x^3$ is transformed to become the point $(x + 3, y + 4)$. For example, $(0, 0)$ becomes $(3, 4)$.

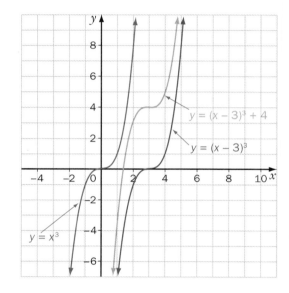

Note that, in Example 4, you could graph the three functions using a graphing calculator. However, it is not necessary to graph $y = x^3$ or $y = (x - 3)^3$ before graphing $y = (x - 3)^3 + 4$.

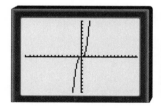 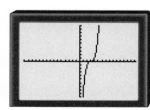 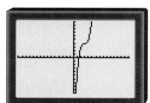

Practice

The function $y = f(x)$ is given. Describe how the graphs of the following functions can be obtained from the graph of $y = f(x)$.

1. $y = f(x) + 5$ **2.** $y = f(x) - 6$
3. $y = f(x - 4)$ **4.** $y = f(x + 8)$
5. $y - 3 = f(x)$ **6.** $y + 7 = f(x)$
7. $y = f(x + 3) - 5$ **8.** $y = f(x - 6) + 2$
9. $y = f(x - 5) - 7$ **10.** $y = f(x + 2) + 9$

The function $y = f(x)$ has been transformed to $y = f(x - h) + k$. Determine the values of h and k for each of the following transformations.

11. 6 units upward
12. 8 units downward
13. 3 units to the right
14. 5 units to the left
15. 2 units to the left and 4 units downward
16. 7 units to the right and 7 units upward

The graphs of four functions $y = f(x)$ are shown. For each of the four functions, sketch the graph of each of the following.

a) $y = f(x) - 4$ b) $y = f(x) + 2$
c) $y = f(x - 4)$ d) $y = f(x + 2)$
e) $y = f(x - 3) - 2$ f) $y = f(x + 4) + 3$

17.

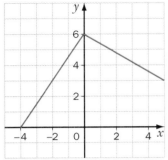

18.

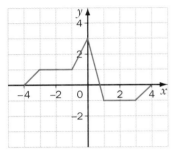

19.

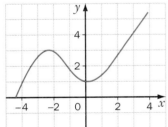

20.

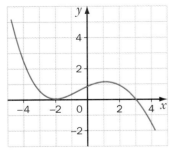

The graph of the function drawn in blue is a translation of the function drawn in red. Write an equation for each function drawn in blue. Check each equation using a graphing calculator.

21.

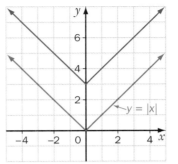

22.

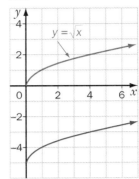

23.

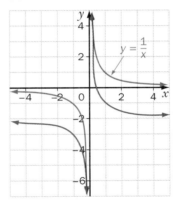

24.

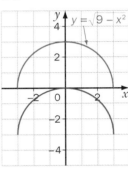

25.

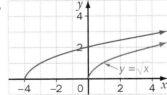

26.

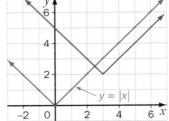

27.

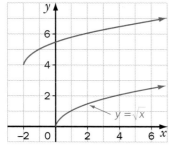

28.

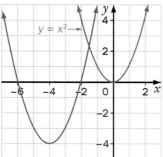

29.

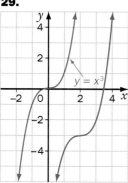

30.

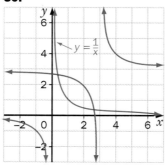

31. Use transformations to sketch the graph of each of the following functions, starting with the graph of $y = x$.
a) $y = x + 4$ **b)** $y = x - 5$
c) $y = (x - 4)$ **d)** $y = (x + 2)$
e) $y = (x + 5) - 2$ **f)** $y = (x - 1) + 6$

32. Use transformations to sketch the graph of each of the following functions, starting with the graph of $y = |x|$.
a) $y = |x| + 6$ **b)** $y = |x| - 4$
c) $y - 7 = |x|$ **d)** $y = |x - 2|$
e) $y = |x + 4|$ **f)** $y = |x - 3| - 3$

33. Use transformations to sketch the graph of each of the following functions, starting with the graph of $y = \sqrt{x}$.
a) $y = \sqrt{x} + 7$ **b)** $y + 3 = \sqrt{x}$
c) $y = \sqrt{x + 3}$ **d)** $y = \sqrt{x - 4}$
e) $y = \sqrt{x - 6} + 3$ **f)** $y = \sqrt{x + 5} + 4$

34. Use transformations to sketch the graph of each of the following functions, starting with the graph of $y = x^2$.
a) $y = x^2 + 3$ **b)** $y + 2 = x^2$
c) $y = (x - 7)^2$ **d)** $y = (x + 6)^2$
e) $y = (x + 4)^2 - 3$ **f)** $y = (x - 5)^2 + 5$

35. Use transformations to sketch the graph of each of the following functions, starting with the graph of $y = x^3$.
a) $y = x^3 - 1$ **b)** $y - 4 = x^3$
c) $y = (x - 3)^3$ **d)** $y = (x + 2)^3$
e) $y = (x + 3)^3 + 2$ **f)** $y = (x - 4)^3 - 3$

36. Use transformations to sketch the graph of each of the following functions, starting with the graph of $y = \dfrac{1}{x}$.

a) $y = \dfrac{1}{x} + 3$ **b)** $y = \dfrac{1}{x} - 2$

c) $y = \dfrac{1}{x - 4}$ **d)** $y = \dfrac{1}{x + 5}$

e) $y = \dfrac{1}{x + 6} + 2$ **f)** $y = \dfrac{1}{x - 3} - 4$

Applications and Problem Solving

37. Falling objects The approximate height above the ground of a falling object dropped from the top of a building is given by the function
$$h(t) = -5t^2 + d$$
where $h(t)$ metres is the height of the object t seconds after it is dropped, and d is the height from which it is dropped.

The table shows the heights of three buildings.

Building	Height (m)
Petro-Canada 1, Calgary	210
Park Place, Vancouver	137
Commerce Place, Edmonton	125

a) Write the three functions, f(P-C1), f(PP), and f(CP), that describe the height of a falling object above the ground t seconds after it is dropped from the top of each building.
b) Graph $h(t)$ versus t for the three functions on the same set of axes or in the same viewing window of a graphing calculator.
c) What transformation maps the graph of f(P-C1) onto the graph of f(PP)?
d) What transformation maps the graph of f(CP) onto the graph of f(PP)?
e) What transformation maps the graph of f(P-C1) onto the graph of f(CP)?

38. Service calls Elena and Mario both repair kitchen appliances. Elena charges $45 for a service call, plus $35/h for labour. Mario charges $40 for a service call, plus $35/h for labour. Write an equation for the cost, C dollars, of a service call in terms of the number of hours worked, t
a) for Elena   **b)** for Mario
c) How are the graphs of the two equations related? Explain.

39. When the graph of $y = 2x + 3$ is translated 1 unit to the right and 2 units upward, how is the resulting graph related to the graph of $y = 2x + 3$? Explain.

40. Greatest integer function The greatest integer function is defined by $[x] =$ the greatest integer that is less than or equal to x. For example, $[4] = 4$, $[4.83] = 4$, and $[-5.3] = -6$. The graph of $y = [x]$ is shown.

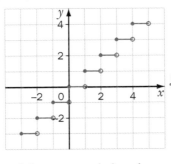

a) Explain the meanings of the open and closed dots on the graph of $y = [x]$.
b) Use transformations to sketch the graph of $y = [x] + 2$; $y = [x - 3]$; $y = [x + 4] - 1$.

41. Parking costs EZ-Park determines its parking charges based on the greatest integer function $f(x) = [x + 2] + 3$, where $f(x)$ is the parking charge and x is the number of hours that a vehicle is in the parking garage.
a) Sketch the graph of $f(x)$.
b) How much would a driver pay to park for 30 min? for 1 h? for 1 h 25 min? for 3 h 1 min?

42. Describe a vertical translation that could be applied to the graph of $y = \sqrt{x}$ so that the translation image passes through the point $(4, 0)$.

43. The function $f(x) = x + 3$ could be a vertical translation of $f(x) = x$ three units upward or a horizontal translation of $f(x) = x$ three units to the left. Explain why.

44. Chemistry a) One way to describe the concentration of an acid is as a percent by volume. For example, in 40 mL of a 30% acid solution, the volume of pure acid is $40 \times \dfrac{30}{100}$ or 12 mL, and the volume of water is $40 - 12$ or 28 mL. If 5 mL of pure acid is mixed with 20 mL of water to give 25 mL of acid solution, the concentration of the solution is given by $\dfrac{5}{25} \times 100\% = 20\%$. If water is mixed with 50 mL of 40% acid solution, write an equation that describes the acid concentration, $C(x)$, as a function of the volume of water added, x.
b) Graph $C(x)$ versus x.
c) What is the acid concentration after 10 mL of water have been added?
d) Write an equation that describes the acid concentration as a function of the volume of water added to 40 mL of 50% acid solution.
e) Graph $C(x)$ versus x for the function from part d).
f) What transformation maps the graph from part e) onto the graph from part b)?

45. a) Sketch the graph of $y = |x| + x$. Check your solution using a graphing calculator. Explain the result.
b) Sketch the graph of $y = |x| + x + 2$. Check your solution using a graphing calculator. Explain the result.

46. a) Sketch the graph of $y = x - |x|$. Check your solution using a graphing calculator. Explain the result.
b) Sketch the graph of $y = x - |x| + 2$. Check your solution using a graphing calculator. Explain the result.

47. a) Sketch the graph of $y = |x| - x$. Check using a graphing calculator. Explain the result.
b) Sketch the graph of $y = |x| - x + 2$. Check using a graphing calculator. Explain the result.

PROBLEM SOLVING

1.2 Use a Diagram

Diagrams can be useful for solving many types of problems, including geometry problems.

A monument commemorating Terry Fox and his Marathon of Hope stands just outside Thunder Bay. The statue of Terry Fox is 2.7 m tall, and stands on a base that is 2.1 m high. A statue is best viewed when the angle formed by the lines of sight to the bottom and the top of the statue is a maximum. Calculate the distance a person whose eyes are 1.6 m from the ground should stand from the base in order to view the statue of Terry Fox at the greatest angle. Round your answer to the nearest tenth of a metre.

Understand the Problem

1. What information are you given?
2. What are you asked to find?
3. Do you need an exact or an approximate answer?

Think of a Plan

Draw a circle through the top and bottom of the statue so that the height of the statue, AB, is a chord of the circle, and DE is a tangent to the circle. DE is parallel to the ground and is at a height equal to the height of the viewer's eyes from the ground. DE intersects the circle at the point of tangency, P.
Verify that when the viewer's eyes are at point P, ∠APB is the greatest viewing angle. Then, use similar triangles to find the distance of the viewer from the base.

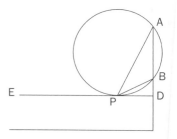

Carry Out the Plan

Suppose that the viewer's eyes are at M, and that M is farther away from the statue than P.
The viewing angle is ∠AMB.
Locate point P_1 where AM intersects the circle.
$\angle AP_1B = \angle APB$ (Angles in a Circle Theorem)
$\angle AP_1B$ is an exterior angle of $\triangle P_1MB$.
∴ $\angle AP_1B = \angle AMB + \angle P_1BM$ (Exterior Angle Theorem)
∴ $\angle AP_1B > \angle AMB$
∴ $\angle APB > \angle AMB$

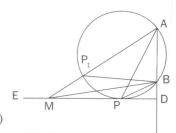

Similarly, it can be proved that, if the viewer's eyes are at M, and M is closer to the statue than P, ∠APB is the greatest viewing angle.

In $\triangle BDP$ and $\triangle PDA$,
$\qquad \angle BDP = \angle PDA$ (Same 90° angle)
$\qquad \angle DPB = \angle DAP$ (Tangent Chord Theorem)
∴ $\angle DBP = \angle DPA$ (Third Angle Theorem)
∴ $\triangle BDP \sim \triangle PDA$

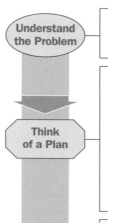

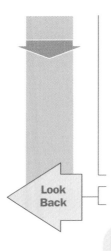

Since the triangles are similar, the ratios of the corresponding sides are equal.
In $\triangle BDP$ and $\triangle PDA$,

$$\frac{DP}{DA} = \frac{DB}{DP}$$

$$\frac{DP}{3.2} = \frac{0.5}{DP} \qquad DB = 2.1\ m - 1.6\ m$$

$$(DP)^2 = 1.6$$

$$DP \doteq 1.3$$

So, a person whose eyes are 1.6 m from the ground should stand about 1.3 m from the base in order to view the statue of Terry Fox at the greatest angle.

Look Back Does the answer seem reasonable?

Use a Diagram
1. Draw a diagram to represent the situation.
2. Use the diagram to solve the problem.
3. Check that the answer is reasonable.

Applications and Problem Solving

1. Statue of Liberty The Statue of Liberty is 47.7 m tall. It stands on a base that is 46.5 m high. Calculate the distance you should stand from the base in order to view the statue at the greatest angle.

2. Runners Two runners, Samara and Jennifer, start at opposite ends of an oval track. They start running at constant speeds at the same time, but in opposite directions. From her starting point to the time she passes Jennifer, Samara runs 200 m. From the first time they pass until the second time they pass, Jennifer runs 100 m. How long is the track?

3. Measurement A regular hexagon and an equilateral triangle each have a perimeter of 12 cm. What is the ratio of the area of the hexagon to the area of the triangle?

4. Overlapping squares Eight square sheets of paper overlap as shown in the diagram. Copy the diagram into your notebook and number the sheets from the top layer to the bottom.

5. Cheese cube Suppose you had a cube made of cheese. How could you make one cut of the cube to produce a face in the shape of a hexagon?

6. Bridge crossing Four people need to cross a footbridge at night to catch a train, which leaves in more than 15 min but less than 16 min. The bridge can hold only two people at a time. The group has one flashlight, which must be used for each crossing of the bridge. The flashlight must be carried by hand and cannot be thrown back. Because of their different degrees of nervousness, the people take different times to cross the bridge. Juan can cross in 1 min. Sue can cross in 2 min. It takes Alicia 5 min to cross, and it takes Larry 8 min. If they cross in pairs, they cross at the speed of the slower person. How can they cross and all catch the train?

7. Stack of cubes Three thousand cubes, each having a volume of $1\ cm^3$, are arranged to form a rectangular block measuring 10 cm by 15 cm by 20 cm. The 15 cm by 20 cm base of the rectangular block sits on a table. The block is spray painted green on all outside faces other than the base. For how many of the cubes is the number of faces painted green exactly

a) 3? **b)** 2? **c)** 1?

8. Write a problem that can be solved using a diagram. Have a classmate solve your problem.

1.3 Reflections

Like many other pyramids in Egypt, the
Bent Pyramid has a square base.
For a square-based pyramid, the area,
A, of the base can be expressed in
terms of the side length, s, of
the base.

$$A = s^2$$

Also, the side length of
the base can be expressed
in terms of the area of
the base.

$$s = \sqrt{A}$$

Explore: Graph the Functions

To compare the shapes of $A = s^2$ and $s = \sqrt{A}$, copy and complete
the tables, and graph $y = x^2$ and $y = \sqrt{x}$ on the same set of axes.

$y = x^2$

x	y
0	
1	
2	
3	
4	

$y = \sqrt{x}$

x	y
0	
1	
4	
9	
16	

Inquire

1. Why are the graphs drawn in the first quadrant?

2. Reverse the coordinates of the five points in the table for $y = x^2$. Where are the
points with the reversed coordinates located?

3. Reverse the coordinates of the five points in the table for $y = \sqrt{x}$. Where are the
points with the reversed coordinates located?

4. Draw the graph of $y = x$ on the same set of axes as the graphs of $y = x^2$ and $y = \sqrt{x}$.

5. Using the points in the tables, determine how the distances from the line $y = x$
compare for two points whose coordinates are the reverse of eachother.

6. For the graphs of $y = x^2$ and $y = \sqrt{x}$, what type of line is the line $y = x$? Explain.

7. The area of the base of the Bent Pyramid is about 35 300 m^2. What is the side
length of the base, to the nearest metre?

Example 1   Comparing y = f(x) and y = –f(x)

a) Given the graph of $y = f(x)$, as shown, graph $y = -f(x)$ on the same axes.

b) Describe how the graph of $y = -f(x)$ is related to the graph of $y = f(x)$.

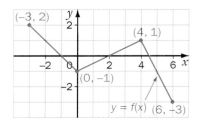

Solution

a) Use the given graph to complete a table of values for the function $y = f(x)$. Then, complete a table of values for the function $y = -f(x)$, and draw the graph.

$y = f(x)$

x	y
–3	f(–3) = 2
0	f(0) = –1
4	f(4) = 1
6	f(6) = –3

$y = -f(x)$

x	y
–3	–f(–3) = –2
0	–f(0) = 1
4	–f(4) = –1
6	–f(6) = 3

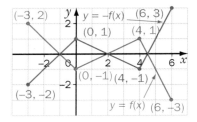

b) If $y = -f(x)$, then $y = -1f(x)$, so each y-value on the graph of $y = -f(x)$ is the corresponding y-value on the graph of $y = f(x)$ multiplied by -1. The point (x, y) on the graph of the function $y = f(x)$ becomes the point $(x, -y)$ on the graph of $y = -f(x)$. For example, $(-3, 2)$ becomes $(-3, -2)$, and $(6, -3)$ becomes $(6, 3)$. The graphs have the same x-intercepts. The graph of $y = -f(x)$ is a reflection of the graph of $y = f(x)$ in the x-axis.

As noted in Example 1, the two graphs have the same x-intercepts. Points that lie on the x-axis have a y-coordinate of 0, so they are unaltered by the transformation of $y = f(x)$ to $y = -f(x)$. Points that are unaltered by a transformation are said to be **invariant**.

In general, the point (x, y) on the graph of the function $y = f(x)$ becomes the point $(x, -y)$ on the graph of $y = -f(x)$. The graph of $y = -f(x)$ is a reflection of the graph of $y = f(x)$ in the x-axis. Points that lie on the x-axis are invariant, because their y-coordinate is 0.

If, in Example 1, $y = f(x)$ were defined by an equation, such as $f(x) = x - 1$, then $y = -f(x)$ would be defined by the equation $y = -(x - 1)$ or $y = -x + 1$. The graph of $y = -f(x)$ would be a reflection of the graph of $y = f(x)$ in the x-axis. The x-intercepts of the two graphs would be the same.

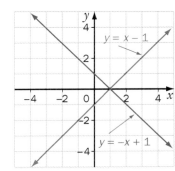

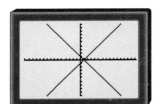

Example 2 Comparing y = f(x) and y = f(–x)

Let $f(x) = 2x + 1$.
a) Write an equation for $f(-x)$.
b) Graph $y = f(x)$ and $y = f(-x)$ on the same axes or in the same viewing window of a graphing calculator.
c) Describe how the graph of $y = f(-x)$ is related to the graph of $y = f(x)$.

Solution
a) Substitute $-x$ for x in $2x + 1$.
$2(-x) + 1 = -2x + 1$
so $f(-x) = -2x + 1$

b) Graph both functions using paper and pencil or a graphing calculator.

$y = 2x + 1$

x	y
-2	-3
-1	-1
0	1
1	3
2	5

$y = -2x + 1$

x	y
2	-3
1	-1
0	1
-1	3
-2	5

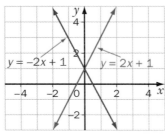

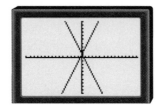

c) The point (x, y) on the graph of $y = 2x + 1$ becomes the point $(-x, y)$ on the graph of $y = -2x + 1$. For example, the point $(2, 5)$ becomes the point $(-2, 5)$. The point $(-1, -1)$ becomes the point $(1, -1)$. The graphs have the same y-intercept. The graph of $y = -2x + 1$ is the graph of $y = 2x + 1$ reflected in the y-axis.

In general, the point (x, y) on the graph of the function $y = f(x)$ becomes the point $(-x, y)$ on the graph of $y = f(-x)$. The graph $y = f(-x)$ is a reflection of the graph of $y = f(x)$ in the y-axis. Points that lie on the y-axis are invariant, because their x-coordinate is 0.

Example 3 Comparing y = f(x) and x = f(y)

Let $f(x) = 3x - 2$.
a) Write an equation for the inverse of $f(x)$.
b) Graph $y = f(x)$ and its inverse, $x = f(y)$, on the same axes or in the same viewing window of a graphing calculator.
c) Describe how the graphs of $y = f(x)$ and its inverse are related.

Solution
a) The inverse of the function $f(x) = 3x - 2$ can be found as follows.
$$f(x) = 3x - 2$$
Replace $f(x)$ with y: $\quad y = 3x - 2$
Interchange x and y: $\quad x = 3y - 2$
Solve for y: $\quad y = \dfrac{x + 2}{3}$

So, the inverse is $y = \dfrac{x + 2}{3}$.

b) Graph both functions using paper and pencil or a graphing calculator.

$$y = 3x - 2 \qquad y = \frac{x+2}{3}$$

x	y
-2	-8
-1	-5
0	-2
1	1
2	4

x	y
-8	-2
-5	-1
-2	0
1	1
4	2

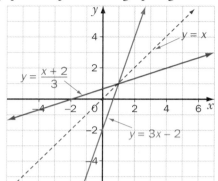

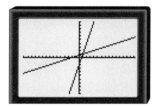

c) For the point (x, y) on the graph of $y = f(x)$, there is a corresponding point (y, x) on the graph of its inverse, $x = f(y)$. For example, the point $(-2, 0)$ becomes the point $(0, -2)$. The point $(2, 4)$ becomes the point $(4, 2)$. The point $(1, 1)$ is invariant. The graph of $x = f(y)$ is a reflection of the graph of $y = f(x)$ in the line $y = x$.

In general, for the point (x, y) on the graph of $y = f(x)$, there is a corresponding point (y, x) on the graph of its inverse, $x = f(y)$. The graph of $x = f(y)$ is a reflection of the graph of $y = f(x)$ in the line $y = x$. Points that lie on the line $y = x$ are invariant, because their x- and y-coordinates are equal.

Note that, in Example 3, $y = f(x)$ and its inverse, $x = f(y)$, are both functions. When the inverse is a function, it is called the inverse function of $f(x)$ and is denoted by $f^{-1}(x)$. Therefore, in Example 3, $f(x) = 3x - 2$ and $f^{-1}(x) = \frac{x+2}{3}$.

The results for reflecting the graphs of functions can be summarized as follows.

Reflection in the x-axis	**Reflection in the y-axis**	**Reflection in $y = x$**
The graph of $y = -f(x)$ is the graph of $y = f(x)$ reflected in the x-axis.	The graph of $y = f(-x)$ is the graph of $y = f(x)$ reflected in the y-axis.	The graph of $x = f(y)$ is the graph of $y = f(x)$ reflected in the line $y = x$.

Recall that a relation is a set of ordered pairs and that the inverse of a relation can be found by interchanging the domain and range of the relation.

Relation
(−2, 5), (0, 4), (3, 7)

Inverse Relation
(5, −2), (4, 0), (7, 3)

Recall that a function is a relation in which, for each element in the domain, there is exactly one element in the range.

Example 4   Reflecting Absolute Value Functions

If $f(x) = |x + 2|$, sketch each of the following graphs and state whether each graph represents a function.

a) $g(x)$, the reflection of $f(x)$ in the x-axis
b) $h(x)$, the reflection of $f(x)$ in the y-axis
c) $k(x)$, the reflection of $f(x)$ in the line $y = x$

Solution

a)

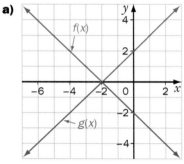

The graph of $g(x)$ is a function because there is one element in the range for each element in the domain.

b)

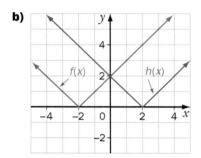

The graph of $h(x)$ is a function because there is one element in the range for each element in the domain.

c)

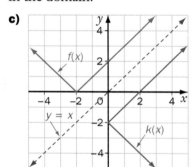

You can graph the inverse on a graphing calculator using the DrawInv instruction.

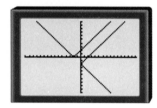

The graph of $k(x)$ is a not function because, for each element, except 0, in the domain, there are two elements in the range.

Recall the **vertical line test** for visualizing whether a relation is a function. In parts a) and b) of Example 4, it is not possible to draw a vertical line that intersects the graph of $g(x)$ or the graph of $h(x)$ in more than one point. These graphs represent functions. In part c) of Example 4, a vertical line can be drawn to intersect the graph of $k(x)$ in more than one point. The graph of $k(x)$ does not represent a function.

Example 5   Reflecting a Cubic Function

If $f(x) = x^3 - 1$, write an equation to represent each of the following functions, describe how the graph of each function is related to the graph of $y = f(x)$, and sketch each graph.

a) $y = -f(x)$ **b)** $y = f(-x)$ **c)** $y = f^{-1}(x)$

Solution

a) For $y = f(x)$ For $y = -f(x)$

$\qquad y = x^3 - 1$ $\qquad\qquad y = -x^3 + 1$

The graph of $y = -f(x)$ is the graph of $y = f(x)$ reflected in the x-axis.

Both graphs have the same x-intercept, 1.

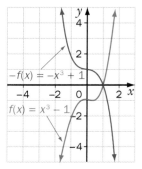
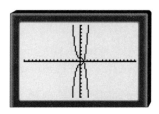

b) For $y = f(x)$ For $y = f(-x)$

$\qquad y = x^3 - 1$ $\qquad\qquad y = (-x)^3 - 1$

$\qquad\qquad\qquad\qquad\qquad y = -x^3 - 1$

The graph of $y = f(-x)$ is the graph of $y = f(x)$ reflected in the y-axis.

Both graphs have the same y-intercept, -1.

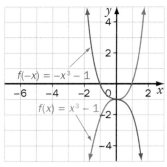
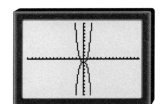

c) To find $f^{-1}(x)$, interchange x and y in the defining equation for $y = f(x)$.

For $y = f(x)$, $y = x^3 - 1$

For $x = f(y)$, $x = y^3 - 1$

so $\qquad\qquad y^3 = x + 1$

$\qquad\qquad y = \sqrt[3]{x+1}$

$\therefore \qquad f^{-1}(x) = \sqrt[3]{x+1}$

The graph of $y = f^{-1}(x)$ is the graph of $y = f(x)$ reflected in the line $y = x$.

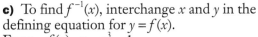
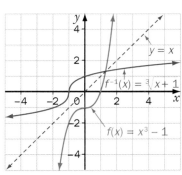
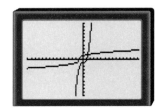

Example 6   Reflecting a Radical Function

If $f(x) = \sqrt{x-2}$, write an equation to represent each of the following functions, describe how the graph of each function is related to the graph of $y = f(x)$, sketch each graph, and identify any invariant points.

a) $y = -f(x)$ **b)** $y = f(-x)$ **c)** $y = f^{-1}(x)$

Solution

a) For $y = f(x)$ For $y = -f(x)$

$\qquad y = \sqrt{x-2}$ $y = -\sqrt{x-2}$

The graph of $y = -f(x)$ is the graph of $y = f(x)$ reflected in the x-axis.
Both graphs have the same x-intercept, 2.
There is one invariant point, $(2, 0)$.

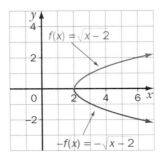

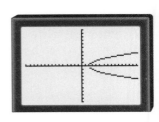

b) For $y = f(x)$ For $y = f(-x)$

$\qquad y = \sqrt{x-2}$ $y = \sqrt{-x-2}$

The graph of $y = f(-x)$ is the graph of $y = f(x)$ reflected in the y-axis.
There are no invariant points.

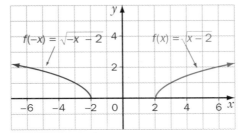

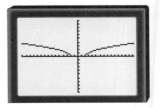

c) To find $f^{-1}(x)$, interchange x and y in the defining equation for $y = f(x)$.

For $y = f(x)$, $y = \sqrt{x-2}$, $x \geq 2$, $y \geq 0$

For $x = f(y)$, $x = \sqrt{y-2}$

and $x^2 = y - 2$

$\qquad y = x^2 + 2$

$\qquad y = x^2 + 2$, $x \geq 0$, $y \geq 2$ **Note the change in the**
$\therefore\ f^{-1}(x) = x^2 + 2$, $x \geq 0$, $y \geq 2$ **restrictions when x and y**
were interchanged.

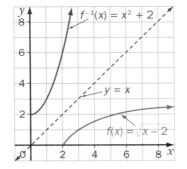

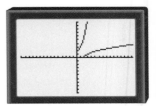

The graph of $y = f^{-1}(x)$ is the graph of $y = f(x)$ reflected in the line $y = x$.
There are no invariant points.

Example 7   Reflecting a Quadratic Function

If $f(x) = x^2 + 1$,
a) write an equation for $y = -f(x)$, $y = f(-x)$, and $x = f(y)$
b) describe how the graph of each equation from part a) is related to the graph of $y = f(x)$, and sketch the four graphs on the same axes

Solution

a) For $y = f(x)$ For $y = -f(x)$

$\qquad y = x^2 + 1$ $y = -x^2 - 1$

For $y = f(x)$ For $y = f(-x)$

$\qquad y = x^2 + 1$ $y = (-x)^2 + 1$

$\qquad\qquad\qquad\qquad\quad y = x^2 + 1$

For $f(x) = x^2 + 1$, the inverse relation can be obtained by interchanging x and y, and then solving for y.

$$y = x^2 + 1$$
$$x = y^2 + 1$$
$$x - 1 = y^2$$
$$\pm\sqrt{x-1} = y$$

So, solving $x = f(y)$ for y gives the equation $y = \pm\sqrt{x-1}$.

b) The graph of $y = -f(x)$ is the graph of $y = f(x)$ reflected in the x-axis.

Since the graph of $y = x^2 + 1$ is symmetrical about the y-axis, replacing x with $-x$ has no effect on the graph. So, the graphs of $y = f(x)$ and $y = f(-x)$ are the same.

The graph of $x = f(y)$ is the graph of $y = f(x)$ reflected in the line $y = x$.

Note that $x = f(y)$ is not a function.

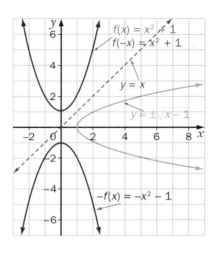

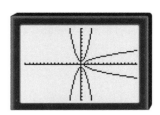

Example 8   Reflecting a Rational Function

a) Graph the function $f(x) = \dfrac{5}{x^2 + 1}$. Describe the graph.

b) Write an equation for $y = -f(x)$, $y = f(-x)$, and $x = f(y)$.

c) Describe how the graphs of $y = -f(x)$, $y = f(-x)$, and $x = f(y)$ are related to the graph of $y = f(x)$. Sketch the graphs.

Solution

a) For $f(x) = \dfrac{5}{x^2 + 1}$, $y = \dfrac{5}{x^2 + 1}$.

x	y
-3	0.5
-2	1
-1	2.5
0	5
1	2.5
2	1
3	0.5

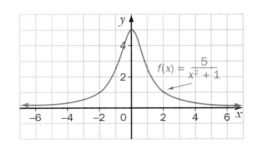

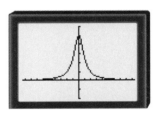

Since $x^2 \geq 0$, y is positive for all real values of x.
The graph is symmetrical about the y-axis.
It has a maximum value of 5 when $x = 0$.
As the value of x increases or decreases from 0, the value of y approaches 0 but never reaches it. For example, when $x = \pm 7$, $y = 0.1$. Therefore, the graph approaches the x-axis but never reaches it. The x-axis is a horizontal asymptote of the graph.

b) For $y = f(x)$

$$y = \frac{5}{x^2+1}$$

For $y = f(x)$

$$y = \frac{5}{x^2+1}$$

For $y = -f(x)$

$$y = -\frac{5}{x^2+1}$$

For $y = f(-x)$

$$y = \frac{5}{(-x)^2+1}$$

$$y = \frac{5}{x^2+1}$$

To find the inverse, $x = f(y)$, interchange x and y.

$$y = \frac{5}{x^2+1}$$

$$x = \frac{5}{y^2+1}$$

$$y^2+1 = \frac{5}{x}$$

$$y^2 = \frac{5}{x}-1$$

$$y = \pm\sqrt{\frac{5}{x}-1}$$

The inverse is $y = \pm\sqrt{\dfrac{5}{x}-1}$. This is not a function.

c) The graph of $y = -f(x)$ is the graph of $y = f(x)$ reflected in the x-axis.

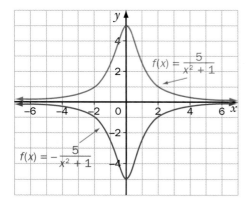

Since the graph of $y = \dfrac{5}{x^2+1}$ is symmetrical about the y-axis, replacing x with $-x$ has no effect on the graph. So, the graph of $y = f(-x)$ is the same as the graph of $y = f(x)$.

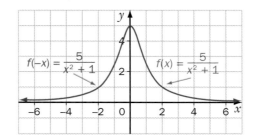

The graph of $x = f(y)$ is the graph of $y = f(x)$ reflected in the line $y = x$.

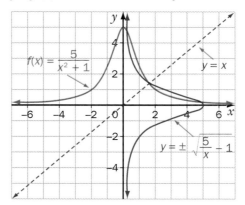

Practice

Copy the graph of y = f(x) and draw the graph of y = −f(x) on the same axes.

1.

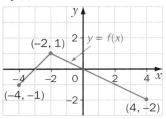

2.

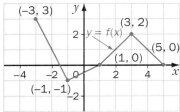

Copy the graph of y = f(x) and draw the graph of y = f(−x) on the same axes.

3.

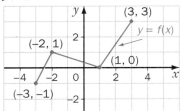

4.

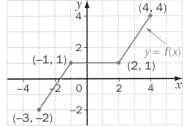

Copy the graph of y = f(x) and draw the graph of x = f(y) on the same axes.

5.

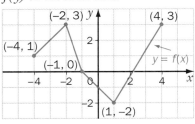

6.

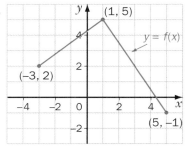

The blue graph is a reflection of the red graph in the y-axis. The equation of the red graph is given. Write the equation of the blue graph.

7.

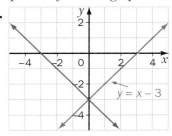

8.

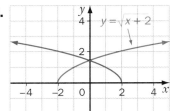

9.

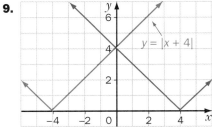

10.

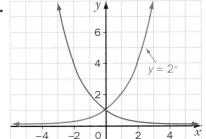

The blue graph is a reflection of the red graph in the x-axis. The equation of the red graph is given. Write the equation of the blue graph.

The blue graph is a reflection of the red graph in the line y = x. The equation of the red graph is given. Write the equation of the blue graph.

11.

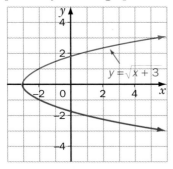

$y = \sqrt{x} + 3$

12.

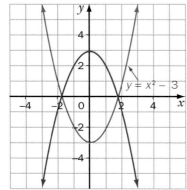

$y = x^2 - 3$

13.

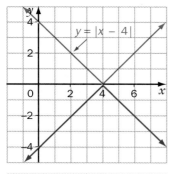

$y = |x - 4|$

14.

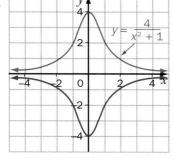

$y = \dfrac{4}{x^2 + 1}$

15.

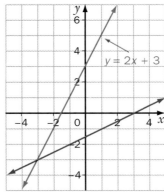

$y = 2x + 3$

16.

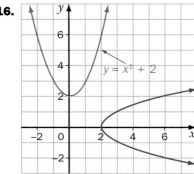

$y = x^2 + 2$

17.

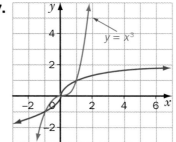

$y = x^3$

18.

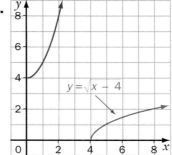

$y = \sqrt{x} - 4$

Graph f(x) and sketch the specified reflection image. State whether each reflection image represents a function.

19. $g(x)$, the reflection of $f(x) = |x - 1|$ in the y-axis

20. $h(x)$, the reflection of $f(x) = x^3 - 2$ in the x-axis

21. $k(x)$, the reflection of $f(x) = x^2 + 3$ in the line $y = x$

22. $g(x)$, the reflection of $f(x) = \sqrt{x - 3}$ in the y-axis

23. $k(x)$, the reflection of $f(x) = \dfrac{10}{x^2 + 1}$ in the x-axis

24. $h(x)$, the reflection of $f(x) = -2x - 1$ in the line $y = x$

25. $k(x)$, the reflection of $f(x) = |x + 1|$ in the line $y = x$

26. a) Given $f(x) = 2x - 4$, write equations for $-f(x), f(-x),$ and $f^{-1}(x)$.
b) Sketch the four graphs on the same set of axes.
c) Determine any points that are invariant for each reflection.

27. a) Given $f(x) = -3x + 2$, write equations for $-f(x), f(-x),$ and $f^{-1}(x)$.
b) Sketch the four graphs on the same set of axes.
c) Determine any points that are invariant for each reflection.

28. a) Given $f(x) = x^3 - 3$, write equations for $-f(x), f(-x),$ and $f^{-1}(x)$.
b) Sketch the four graphs on the same set of axes.

29. a) Given $f(x) = \sqrt{x + 3}$, write equations for $-f(x), f(-x),$ and $f^{-1}(x)$.
b) Sketch the four graphs on the same set of axes.

30. a) Given $f(x) = x^2 - 2$, write equations for $y = -f(x), y = f(-x),$ and $x = f(y)$.
b) Sketch the four graphs on the same set of axes.

31. a) Given $f(x) = \dfrac{6}{x^2 + 2}$, write the equations for $y = -f(x), y = f(-x),$ and $x = f(y)$.
b) Sketch each of the four graphs.
c) Describe each graph, identifying any asymptotes.

Applications and Problem Solving

32. Great Pyramid A coordinate grid is superimposed on a cross section of the Great Pyramid, so that the y-axis passes through the vertex of the pyramid, and the x-axis bisects two opposite sides of the base. The two sloping lines in the cross section are altitudes of two triangular faces of the pyramid. If one altitude can be represented by the equation $y = 1.27x + 146$, what is the equation of the other altitude? Explain why.

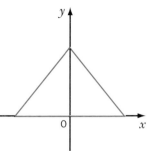

33. Write an equation for the line obtained by reflecting the line $x = 2$ in the line $y = x$.

34. How are the graphs of $y = x^2 - 2x$ and $y = 2x - x^2$ related? Explain.

35. a) Given $f(x) = \sqrt{25 - x^2}$, write the equations for $y = -f(x), y = f(-x),$ and $x = f(y)$.
b) Sketch the four graphs.
c) State which of the graphs represent functions.
d) Determine any points that are invariant for each reflection.

36. a) Given $f(x) = x^2 - x - 6$, determine the coordinates of the points at which the graph crosses the y-axis and the x-axis.
b) Use the points you found in part a) to sketch the graphs of $y = -f(x), y = f(-x),$ and $x = f(y)$.

37. Car rental The cost of renting a car for a day is a $40 rental fee, plus $0.15 for each kilometre driven.
a) Write an equation that expresses the total cost, y dollars, in terms of the distance driven, x kilometres.
b) Graph the equation over a reasonable domain and range.
c) Find the equation of the reflection of the graph in the line $y = x$.
d) Explain the meaning of the equation from part c).

38. Measurement The circumference, C, of a circle, can be modelled algebraically in terms of the radius, r, by the function
$$C = 2\pi r, \ r > 0$$
a) Use $C = y$ and $r = x$ to graph this function.
b) How did you show on the graph that r cannot equal 0?
c) Write an equation that expresses r in terms of C. What does this function model?
d) Use $r = y$ and $C = x$ to graph the function found in part c) on the same set of axes as the function in part a).
e) How are the two functions related? Explain.

39. Measurement The area, A, of a circle can be modelled algebraically in terms of the radius, r, by the function
$$A = \pi r^2, \ r > 0$$
a) Use $A = y$ and $r = x$ to graph this function.
b) Write an equation that expresses r in terms of A. What does this function model?
c) Use $r = y$ and $A = x$ to graph the function found in part b) on the same set of axes as the function in part a).
d) How are the two functions related? Explain.

40. Measurement The volume, V, of a cube can be modelled algebraically by the formula
$$V = l^3, \ l > 0$$
where l is the length of each edge.
a) Use $V = y$ and $l = x$ to graph this function.
b) Write an equation that expresses l in terms of V. What does this function model?
c) Use $l = y$ and $V = x$ to graph the function found in part b) on the same set of axes as the function in part a).
d) How are the two functions related? Explain.
e) What is the meaning of the point of intersection of the two graphs, in terms of volume and edge length?

41. Measurement The area, A, of an equilateral triangle can be modelled algebraically by the formula $A = \dfrac{\sqrt{3}}{4}s^2$, where s is the side length.

a) Use $A = y$ and $s = x$ to graph this function.
b) Write an equation that expresses s in terms of A. What does this function model?

c) Use $s = y$ and $A = x$ to graph the function found in part b) on the same set of axes as the function in part a).
d) How are the two functions related? Explain.
e) What is the meaning of the point of intersection of the two graphs, in terms of area and side length?

42. Sequencing reflections Copy the graph of $y = f(x)$, as shown. Sketch the graph of each relation obtained after a reflection in the y-axis, followed by a reflection in the x-axis, followed by a reflection in the line $y = x$.

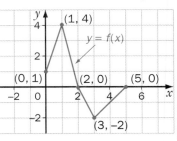

43. Combining transformations Write an equation for the function obtained as indicated.
a) Translate the graph of $y = x$ two units downward and then reflect it in the y-axis.
b) Reflect the graph of $y = x^2$ in the x-axis and then translate it two units upward.

44. a) Sketch the graph of the function $y = \sqrt{x}$.
b) On the same set of axes, graph $y = f^{-1}(x)$, $y = f^{-1}(-x)$, and $y = -f^{-1}(-x)$.
c) Compare the graphs of $y = f(x)$ and $y = -f^{-1}(-x)$. If the graph of $y = -f^{-1}(-x)$ is drawn from the graph of $y = f(x)$ by a single reflection, what is the equation of the reflection line?

45. If the graph of $f(x) = x^2 - 3$ is transformed into the graph of $f(-x)$, how many points are invariant? Explain.

46. If a line is not horizontal or vertical, how is the slope of the line related to the slope of its reflection image in each of the following? Explain.
a) x-axis   **b)** y-axis   **c)** the line $y = x$

47. Explain why $f(f^{-1}(x)) = x$ and $f^{-1}(f(x)) = x$.

48. If $f(x) = \dfrac{ax + b}{cx + d}$, $ad - bc \neq 0$, find an equation for $f^{-1}(x)$.

Exploring Even and Odd Functions

An **even function** satisfies $f(x) = f(-x)$ for all values of x in its domain.
An **odd function** satisfies $f(-x) = -f(x)$ for all values of x in its domain.

1 Classifying Functions

The above definitions can be used to classify functions as even, odd, or neither.
For example:

If $f(x) = x^2$
$f(-x) = (-x)^2$
$= x^2$
$= f(x)$
Since $f(x) = f(-x)$,
$f(x)$ is even.

If $g(x) = \dfrac{1}{x}$
$g(-x) = \dfrac{1}{-x}$
$= -\dfrac{1}{x}$
$= -g(x)$
Since $g(-x) = -g(x)$,
$g(x)$ is odd.

If $h(x) = x^2 - x$
$h(-x) = (-x)^2 - (-x)$
$= x^2 + x$
$-h(x) = -(x^2 - x)$
$= -x^2 + x$
Since $h(x) \neq h(-x)$,
and $h(-x) \neq -h(x)$,
$h(x)$ is neither even nor odd.

Classify each of the following functions as even, odd, or neither. Sketch each graph.

1. $f(x) = x$
2. $g(x) = x^4$
3. $h(x) = x^3$
4. $k(x) = x^2 + 3x$
5. $F(x) = |x|$

6. $G(x) = \dfrac{1}{x^2}$
7. $H(x) = \sqrt{x+1}$
8. $K(x) = 3x - x^3$
9. $f(x) = -2x^2$
10. $g(x) = -\dfrac{x^4}{2}$

2 Exploring Symmetry

1. Use your findings from Exploration 1 to answer the following.
a) About which axis are even functions symmetrical? Explain why.
b) Are odd functions symmetrical about either axis?
c) Do odd functions have rotational symmetry about a point? If so, name
the point and describe a rotation that maps an odd function onto itself.
d) Describe a sequence of two reflections that maps an odd function onto itself.

2. State whether the functions with the following graphs are odd, even, or neither.

a)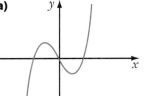

b)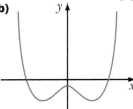

c)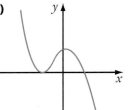

d)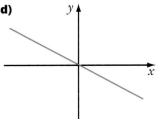

3. Determine whether each function is even or odd. Then, sketch the
graph for $x \geq 0$ and use symmetry to sketch the entire graph.

a) $f(x) = x^5$
b) $g(x) = 5 - 2x^2$
c) $h(x) = |-2x|$
d) $k(x) = \dfrac{1}{x^3}$

4. A function of the form $f(x) = ax^n$, where $a \neq 0$ and n is a positive
integer, is called a **power function**. How is the exponent in the equation
of a power function related to the symmetry of its graph?

1.4 Stretches of Functions

The clock in the Heritage Hall clock tower, in Vancouver, is known as Little Ben. It was built by the same company that built Big Ben in London, England. Little Ben is a mechanical clock with a pendulum.

On the Earth, the period of a pendulum is approximately represented by the function $T = 2\sqrt{l}$, where T is the period, in seconds, and l is the length of the pendulum, in metres. Since the force of gravity varies from one location to another in the solar system, the function for the period of a pendulum also varies. On the moon, the function is $T = 5\sqrt{l}$. On Pluto, the function is $T = 8\sqrt{l}$.

Explore: Graph the Functions

Let $y = T$ and $x = l$, and graph the three functions above, plus the function $y = \sqrt{x}$, on the same set of axes or in the same viewing window of a graphing calculator.

\$y = \sqrt{x}\$		\$y = 2\sqrt{x}\$		\$y = 5\sqrt{x}\$		\$y = 8\sqrt{x}\$	
x	y	x	y	x	y	x	y
0		0		0		0	
1		1		1		1	
4		4		4		4	
9		9		9		9	
16		16		16		16	

Inquire

1. For the functions $y = \sqrt{x}$ and $y = 2\sqrt{x}$, how do the y-coordinates of any two points that have the same non-zero x-coordinate compare? Explain why.

2. For the functions $y = \sqrt{x}$ and $y = 5\sqrt{x}$, how do the y-coordinates of any two points that have the same non-zero x-coordinate compare? Explain why.

3. For the functions $y = \sqrt{x}$ and $y = 8\sqrt{x}$, how do the y-coordinates of any two points that have the same non-zero x-coordinate compare? Explain why.

4. a) If Little Ben were placed on Pluto, the period of its pendulum would be 9.8 s. What is the length of the pendulum, to the nearest tenth of a metre?
b) If Little Ben were placed on the moon, what would the period of its pendulum be, to the nearest tenth of a second?

Example 1 Vertical Stretching of Quadratic Functions

a) Graph the functions $y = x^2$, $y = 2x^2$ and $y = \dfrac{2}{3}x^2$ on the same coordinate axes.

b) Describe how the graphs of $y = 2x^2$ and $y = \dfrac{2}{3}x^2$ are related to the graph of $y = x^2$.

Solution

a) Complete tables of values using convenient values of x, or use a graphing calculator.

$y = x^2$

x	y
3	9
2	4
1	1
0	0
−1	1
−2	4
−3	9

$y = 2x^2$

x	y
3	18
2	8
1	2
0	0
−1	2
−2	8
−3	18

$y = \dfrac{2}{3}x^2$

x	y
6	24
3	6
0	0
−3	6
−6	24

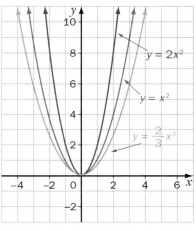

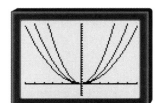

b) Given $y = 2x^2$, then $y = 2(x^2)$. The point (x, y) on the graph of the function $y = x^2$ is transformed to the point $(x, 2y)$ on the graph of $y = 2x^2$. The graph of $y = 2x^2$ is the graph of $y = x^2$ expanded vertically by a factor of 2.

Given $y = \dfrac{2}{3}x^2$, then $y = \dfrac{2}{3}(x^2)$. The point (x, y) on the graph of the function $y = x^2$ is transformed to the point $(x, \dfrac{2}{3}y)$ on the graph of $y = \dfrac{2}{3}x^2$. The graph of $y = \dfrac{2}{3}x^2$ is the graph of $y = x^2$ compressed vertically by a factor of $\dfrac{2}{3}$.

In Example 1, the point $(0, 0)$ is the only point that is on the graph of all three functions. Recall that this point is said to be invariant, because it is unaltered by the transformations.

Note from Example 1 that a stretch may be an expansion or a compression. An **expansion** is a stretch by a factor greater than 1. A **compression** is a stretch by a factor less than 1.

Example 2 Vertical Stretching and Reflecting

a) Copy the graph of $y = f(x)$, as shown.

On the same set of axes, graph $y = -3f(x)$ and $y = -\dfrac{1}{2}f(x)$.

b) Describe how the graphs of $y = -3f(x)$ and $y = -\dfrac{1}{2}f(x)$

are related to the graph of $y = f(x)$.

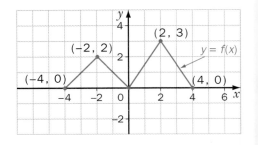

Solution

a) Use the given graph to complete a table of values for the function $y = f(x)$.
Then, complete tables of values for the functions $y = -3f(x)$
and $y = -\dfrac{1}{2}f(x)$, and draw the graphs.

$y = f(x)$ $\qquad\qquad$ $y = -3f(x)$ $\qquad\qquad$ $y = -\dfrac{1}{2}f(x)$

x	y
4	0
2	3
0	0
-2	2
-4	0

x	y
4	$-3(0) = 0$
2	$-3(3) = -9$
0	$-3(0) = 0$
-2	$-3(2) = -6$
-4	$-3(0) = 0$

x	y
4	$-\dfrac{1}{2}(0) = 0$
2	$-\dfrac{1}{2}(3) = -1.5$
0	$-\dfrac{1}{2}(0) = 0$
-2	$-\dfrac{1}{2}(2) = -1$
-4	$-\dfrac{1}{2}(0) = 0$

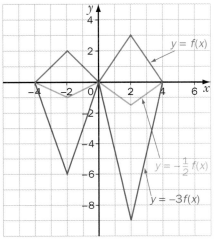

b) The point (x, y) on the graph of the function $y = f(x)$
becomes the point $(x, -3y)$ on the graph of $y = -3f(x)$.
The graph of $y = -3f(x)$ is the graph of $y = f(x)$ expanded
vertically by a factor of 3 and reflected in the x-axis.

The point (x, y) on the graph of the function $y = f(x)$ becomes the point $\left(x, -\dfrac{1}{2}y\right)$

on the graph of $y = -\dfrac{1}{2}f(x)$. The graph of $y = -\dfrac{1}{2}f(x)$ is the graph of $y = f(x)$

compressed vertically by a factor of $\dfrac{1}{2}$ and reflected in the x-axis.

In general, for any function $y = f(x)$, the graph of a function $y = af(x)$, where
a is any real number, is obtained by multiplying the y-value at each point on
the graph of $y = f(x)$ by a.
The point (x, y) on the graph of the function $y = f(x)$ is transformed into the
point (x, ay) on the graph of $y = af(x)$.
If $a > 1$, the graph of $y = f(x)$ expands vertically by a factor of a.
If $0 < a < 1$, the graph of $y = f(x)$ compresses vertically by a factor of a.
If $a < 0$, the graph is also reflected in the x-axis, since all non-zero y-values
for the function $y = f(x)$ change sign to give the graph of $y = af(x)$.
Any points of $y = f(x)$ that lie on the x-axis are invariant under the
transformation to $y = af(x)$.

Example 3 Vertical Stretching of Absolute Value Functions

Sketch the graphs of $y = |x + 2|$, $y = 4|x + 2|$, and $y = -\dfrac{1}{3}|x + 2|$, or graph them using a graphing calculator. How do the graphs compare?

Solution

If you graph using pencil and paper, use $y = |x|$ as the reference function.

The graph of $y = |x + 2|$ is congruent to $y = |x|$, with a horizontal shift of two units to the left.

The graph of $y = 4|x + 2|$ is the graph of $y = |x + 2|$ with a vertical expansion by a factor of 4.

The graph of $y = -\dfrac{1}{3}|x + 2|$ is the

graph of $y = |x + 2|$ with a vertical compression by a factor of $\dfrac{1}{3}$ and a reflection in the x-axis.

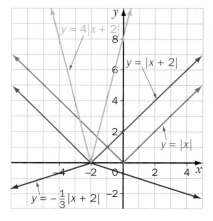

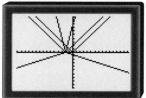

The point $(-2, 0)$ is invariant for $y = |x + 2|$, $y = 4|x + 2|$, and $y = -\dfrac{1}{3}|x + 2|$, because this point lies on the x-axis.

Example 4 Horizontal Stretching

Given the graph of $y = f(x)$, compare it to the graphs of

a) $y = f(2x)$ **b)** $y = f\left(\dfrac{1}{2}x\right)$

Solution

a) Use the given graph to complete a table of values for $y = f(x)$.

Then, complete a table of values for $y = f(2x)$. Use convenient values for x.

$y = f(x)$

x	y
-2	0
-1	2
0	4
1	3
2	2
3	1
4	0

$y = f(2x)$

x	y
-1	$f(2 \times (-1)) = f(-2) = 0$
-0.5	$f(2 \times (-0.5)) = f(-1) = 2$
0	$f(2 \times 0) = f(0) = 4$
0.5	$f(2 \times 0.5) = f(1) = 3$
1	$f(2 \times 1) = f(2) = 2$
1.5	$f(2 \times 1.5) = f(3) = 1$
2	$f(2 \times 2) = f(4) = 0$

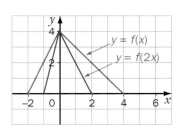

Note that, in the table for $y = f(2x)$, x-values such as -2 and 4 are not convenient, because $f(2 \times (-2)) = f(-4)$ and $f(2 \times 4) = f(8)$. Both $f(-4)$ and $f(8)$ are undefined.

For non-zero values of x, each point on $y = f(2x)$ is half as far from the y-axis as the equivalent point on $y = f(x)$.
The point (x, y) on the graph of the function $y = f(x)$ is transformed to the point $\left(\dfrac{x}{2}, y\right)$ on the graph of $y = f(2x)$. The graph of $y = f(2x)$ is a horizontal compression of the graph of $y = f(x)$ by a factor of $\dfrac{1}{2}$.

b) Use the table of values from part a) for $y = f(x)$.

Then, complete a table of values for $y = f\left(\dfrac{1}{2}x\right)$. Use convenient values for x.

$y = f(x)$

x	y
-2	0
-1	2
0	4
1	3
2	2
3	1
4	0

$y = f\left(\dfrac{1}{2}x\right)$

x	y
-2	$f\left(\dfrac{1}{2} \times (-4)\right) = f(-2) = 0$
-1	$f\left(\dfrac{1}{2} \times (-2)\right) = f(-1) = 2$
0	$f\left(\dfrac{1}{2} \times (0)\right) = f(0) = 4$
1	$f\left(\dfrac{1}{2} \times (2)\right) = f(1) = 3$
2	$f\left(\dfrac{1}{2} \times (4)\right) = f(2) = 2$
3	$f\left(\dfrac{1}{2} \times (6)\right) = f(3) = 1$
4	$f\left(\dfrac{1}{2} \times (8)\right) = f(4) = 0$

For non-zero values of x, each point on the graph of $y = f\left(\dfrac{1}{2}x\right)$ is twice as far from the y-axis as the equivalent point on $y = f(x)$.
The point (x, y) on the graph of the function $y = f(x)$ is transformed to the point $(2x, y)$ on the graph of $y = f\left(\dfrac{1}{2}x\right)$.

The graph of $y = f\left(\dfrac{1}{2}x\right)$ is a horizontal expansion of the graph of $y = f(x)$ by a factor of 2.

Note that the point $(0, 4)$ is invariant under both transformations in Example 4, because this point lies on the y-axis.

Example 5　Horizontal Stretching of Absolute Value Functions

a) Graph the functions $y = |x|$, $y = |3x|$, and $y = \left|\frac{1}{3}x\right|$.

b) Describe how the graphs of $y = |3x|$ and $y = \left|\frac{1}{3}x\right|$ are related to the graph of $y = |x|$.

Solution
a) Complete a table of values using convenient values for x, or use a graphing calculator.

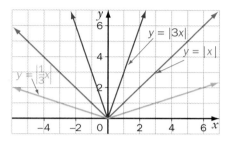

$y = |x|$

x	y
3	3
2	2
1	1
0	0
−1	1
−2	2
−3	3

$y = |3x|$

x	y
3	9
2	6
1	3
0	0
−1	3
−2	6
−3	9

$y = \left|\frac{1}{3}x\right|$

x	y
9	3
6	2
3	1
0	0
−3	1
−6	2
−9	3

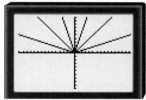

b) The three graphs are symmetrical about the y-axis.

The point (x, y) on the graph of $y = |x|$ becomes the point $\left(\frac{x}{3}, y\right)$

on the graph of $y = |3x|$. The graph of $y = |3x|$ is the graph of $y = |x|$

compressed horizontally by a factor of $\frac{1}{3}$.

The point (x, y) on the graph of $y = |x|$ becomes the point $(3x, y)$ on the

graph of $y = \left|\frac{1}{3}x\right|$. The graph of $y = \left|\frac{1}{3}x\right|$ is the graph of $y = |x|$

expanded horizontally by a factor of 3.

Note that the point (0, 0) is invariant, because it lies on the *y*-axis.

Example 6　Horizontal Stretching and Reflecting of Radical Functions

Compare the graphs of $y = \sqrt{-x}$, $y = \sqrt{-2x}$, and $y = \sqrt{-\frac{1}{2}x}$ to the graph of $y = \sqrt{x}$.

Solution

Complete tables of values using convenient values for x, or use a graphing calculator.

$y = \sqrt{x}$

x	y
0	0
1	1
4	2
9	3
16	4

$y = \sqrt{-x}$

x	y
0	0
−1	1
−4	2
−9	3
−16	4

$y = \sqrt{-2x}$

x	y
0	0
$-\dfrac{1}{2}$	1
−2	2
$-\dfrac{9}{2}$	3
−8	4

$y = \sqrt{-\dfrac{1}{2}x}$

x	y
0	0
−2	1
−8	2
−18	3
−32	4

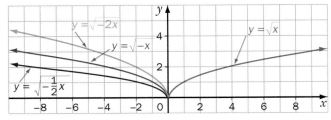
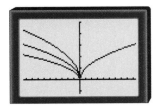

The graph of $y = \sqrt{-x}$ is the graph of $y = \sqrt{x}$ reflected in the y-axis.

The graph of $y = \sqrt{-2x}$ is the graph of $y = \sqrt{x}$ compressed horizontally by a factor of $\dfrac{1}{2}$ and reflected in the y-axis.

The graph of $y = \sqrt{-\dfrac{1}{2}x}$ is the graph of $y = \sqrt{x}$ expanded horizontally by a factor of 2 and reflected in the y-axis.

In general, for any function $y = f(x)$, the graph of a function $y = f(kx)$, where k is any real number, is obtained by dividing the x-value at each point on the graph of $y = f(x)$ by k.

The point (x, y) on the graph of the function $y = f(x)$ is transformed into the point $\left(\dfrac{x}{k}, y\right)$ on the graph of $y = f(kx)$.

If $k > 1$, the graph of $y = f(x)$ is compressed horizontally by a factor of $\dfrac{1}{k}$.

If $0 < k < 1$, the graph of $y = f(x)$ is expanded horizontally by a factor of $\dfrac{1}{k}$.

If $k < 0$, then the graph is also reflected in the y-axis, since all non-zero x-values for the function $y = f(x)$ change sign to give the graph of $y = f(kx)$. Any points of $y = f(x)$ that lie on the y-axis are invariant under the transformation to $y = f(kx)$.

Example 7 Vertical and Horizontal Stretches

Compare the graphs of $y = 3(4 - x^3)$, $y = 4 - (2x)^3$, and $y = 3(4 - (2x)^3)$ to the graph of $y = 4 - x^3$.

Solution

The graph of $y = 3(4 - x^3)$ is the graph of $y = 4 - x^3$ expanded vertically by a factor of 3.

The graph of $y = 4 - (2x)^3$ is the graph of $y = 4 - x^3$ compressed horizontally by a factor of $\frac{1}{2}$.

The graph of $y = 3(4 - (2x)^3)$ is the graph of $y = 4 - x^3$ expanded vertically by a factor of 3 and compressed horizontally by a factor of $\frac{1}{2}$.

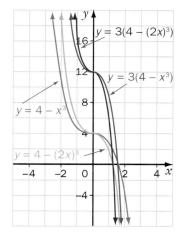

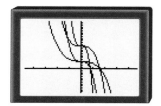

Example 8 Zeros of Functions

The polynomial function $P(x) = (x + 2)(x - 1)(x - 3)$, shown on the graph, has three zeros, at -2, 1, and 3. Use transformations to determine the zeros of the following functions.

a) $y = -2P(x)$

b) $y = P\left(\frac{1}{3}x\right)$

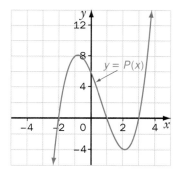

Solution

a) The zeros of $y = -2P(x)$ are identical to those of $y = P(x)$. Multiplying the function by -2 causes a stretch by a factor of 2 in the y-direction and a reflection in the x-axis, but points on the x-axis are invariant.
Therefore, the zeros of $y = -2P(x)$ are -2, 1, and 3.

The solution can be visualized graphically.

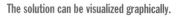

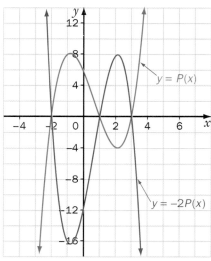

b) Multiplying the x-values by $\dfrac{1}{3}$ causes a horizontal expansion by a factor of 3.

Any points on the y-axis are invariant, but points on the x-axis are transformed.

Therefore, the zeros of $y = P\left(\dfrac{1}{3}x\right)$ are three times those of $P(x)$, that is, -6, 3, and 9.

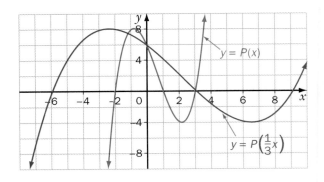

Practice

The graph of function $y = f(x)$ is shown.

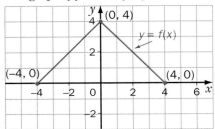

Sketch the graphs of the following functions.

1. $y = 2f(x)$

2. $y = \dfrac{1}{2}f(x)$

3. $y = f(2x)$

4. $y = f\left(\dfrac{1}{2}x\right)$

5. $y = 2f\left(\dfrac{1}{2}x\right)$

6. $y = \dfrac{1}{2}f\left(\dfrac{1}{2}x\right)$

The graph of $y = f(x)$ is shown. Sketch the graphs of the following functions.

7. $y = -2f(x)$

8. $y = \dfrac{1}{3}f(x)$

9. $y = f(3x)$

10. $y = f\left(\dfrac{1}{3}x\right)$

11. $y = -f\left(\dfrac{1}{2}x\right)$

12. $y = -\dfrac{1}{3}f(-3x)$

For each of the following sets of three functions,
a) *sketch them on the same grid, or graph them in the same viewing window of a graphing calculator*
b) *describe how the graphs of the second and third functions are related to the graph of the first function*
c) *identify any invariant points*

13. $y = x, y = 2x, y = \dfrac{1}{2}x$

14. $y = x^2, y = 3x^2,$ and $y = -\dfrac{1}{2}x^2$

15. $y = |x - 1|, y = -2|x - 1|,$ and $y = \dfrac{2}{3}|x - 1|$

16. $y = \sqrt{x + 4},\ y = -3\sqrt{x + 4},$ and $y = -\dfrac{3}{2}\sqrt{x + 4}$

17. $y = x^2, y = (2x)^2,$ and $y = \left(\dfrac{1}{2}x\right)^2$

18. $y = x^3,\ y = \left(-\dfrac{1}{2}x\right)^3,$ and $y = (2x)^3$

Describe how the graphs of the following functions can be obtained from the graph of the function $y = f(x)$.

19. $y = 3f(x)$

20. $y = \dfrac{1}{2}f(x)$

21. $y = -2f(x)$

22. $y = -\dfrac{1}{3}f(x)$

23. $y = f(2x)$

24. $y = f\left(\dfrac{1}{2}x\right)$

25. $y = f(-4x)$

26. $y = f\left(-\dfrac{1}{2}x\right)$

Describe how the graphs of the following functions can be obtained from the graph of the function $y = f(x)$.

27. $y = 3f(2x)$

28. $y = \dfrac{1}{2}f\left(\dfrac{1}{3}x\right)$

29. $y = 4f\left(\dfrac{1}{2}x\right)$

30. $y = \dfrac{1}{3}f(3x)$

31. $y = -2f(4x)$

32. $y = 5f\left(-\dfrac{1}{2}x\right)$

The blue graph is a stretch of the red graph. The equation of the red graph is given. Write an equation for the blue graph. Check each equation using a graphing calculator.

33.

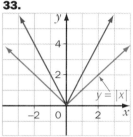

34.

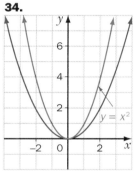

35.

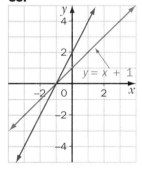

36.

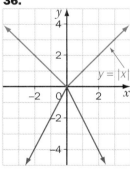

37.

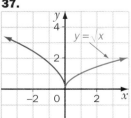

38.

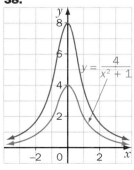

39.

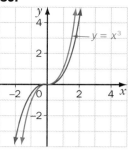

40.

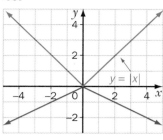

41. Use transformations and the zeros of the quadratic function $f(x) = (x + 4)(x - 2)$ to determine the zeros of each of the following functions.

a) $y = 3f(x)$
b) $y = f\left(\dfrac{1}{2}x\right)$
c) $y = f(-x)$

d) $y = -f(x)$
e) $y = f(2x)$
f) $y = f\left(-\dfrac{1}{2}x\right)$

42. Use transformations and the zeros of the polynomial function $f(x) = x(x + 3)(x - 6)$ to determine the zeros of each of the following functions.

a) $y = f(3x)$
b) $y = f(-x)$
c) $y = -2f(x)$

d) $y = f\left(\dfrac{1}{2}x\right)$
e) $y = -f(-x)$
f) $y = f(-2x)$

Applications and Problem Solving

43. Stopping distances The distance required to stop a car is directly proportional to the square of the speed of the car. The stopping distance for a car on dry asphalt can be approximated using the function $d(s) = 0.006s^2$, where $d(s)$ is the stopping distance, in metres, and s is the speed of the car, in kilometres per hour. The stopping distance for a car on wet asphalt can be approximated using the function $d(s) = 0.009s^2$. The stopping distance for a car on black ice can be approximated using the function $d(s) = 0.04s^2$.

a) For each of the three surfaces, what is the stopping distance for a car travelling at 80 km/h?

b) Write a reasonable domain and range for each of the functions $d(s) = 0.006s^2$, $d(s) = 0.009s^2$, and $d(s) = 0.04s^2$.

c) Let $y = d(s)$ and $x = s$. Graph the three functions, plus the function $y = x^2$, in the same viewing window of a graphing calculator.

d) Compare the graphs of $y = 0.006x^2$, $y = 0.009x^2$, and $y = 0.04x^2$ to the graph of $y = x^2$.

The function y = f(x) has been transformed to y = af(kx). Determine the values of a and k for each of the transformations in questions 44 to 49.

44. A vertical expansion by a factor of 4.

45. A vertical expansion by a factor of 3 and a reflection in the x-axis.

46. A horizontal compression by a factor of $\frac{1}{3}$.

47. A horizontal expansion by a factor of 2 and a reflection in the y-axis.

48. A vertical compression by a factor of $\frac{1}{2}$ and a horizontal expansion by a factor of 3.

49. A vertical expansion by a factor of 2 and a horizontal compression by a factor of $\frac{1}{4}$.

50. Use transformations to sketch the graphs of the following functions, starting with the graph of $y = \frac{1}{x}$.

a) $y = \frac{1}{2x}$ **b)** $y = \frac{1}{-x}$ **c)** $y = \frac{2}{x}$

51. The graph of $f(x) = \sqrt{16 - x^2}$ is shown.

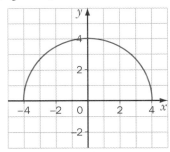

Use transformations to sketch the graph of each of the following functions.

a) $y = 3f(x)$ **b)** $y = \frac{1}{2}f(x)$

c) $y = f(2x)$ **d)** $y = f\left(\frac{1}{2}x\right)$

e) $y = -2f(x)$ **f)** $y = f(-2x)$

52. Equations of functions The functions $y = f(x)$ and $y = h(x)$ are both polynomials of degree three, and they have the same three x-intercepts, as shown. Determine the equation of each function.

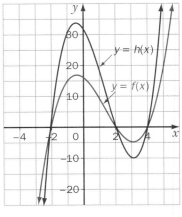

53. a) Sketch the graphs of $y = x + |x|$, $y = 2x + |x|$, and $y = 0.5x + |x|$ on the same set of axes. Check your solution using a graphing calculator.
b) Explain the differences in the graphs.

54. a) Sketch the graphs of $y = x + |x|$, $y = x + |2x|$, and $y = x + |0.5x|$ on the same set of axes. Check your solution using a graphing calculator.
b) Explain the differences in the graphs.

55. Greatest integer function Sketch the graph of $y = [x]$. Then, use transformations to sketch the graphs of the following functions. Check your solutions using a graphing calculator.
a) $y = [2x]$ **b)** $y = [0.5x]$ **c)** $y = 2[x]$

56. a) Describe the horizontal stretch that transforms $y = \sqrt{x}$ to $y = \sqrt{4x}$.
b) Describe the vertical stretch that transforms $y = \sqrt{x}$ to $y = 2\sqrt{x}$.
c) How do the graphs of $y = \sqrt{4x}$ and $y = 2\sqrt{x}$ compare?
d) How do the transformations in parts a) and b) compare? Explain why they compare in this way.
e) Do the horizontal stretch that transforms $y = \sqrt{x+1}$ to $y = \sqrt{4x+1}$ and the vertical stretch that transforms $y = \sqrt{x+1}$ to $y = 2\sqrt{x+1}$ compare in the same way as the transformations in parts a) and b)? Explain.

Using the Databases

Use the *First Ministers*, *Fitness*, *Ports*, and *Satellites* databases, from the Computer Data Bank, to complete the following.

a) Devise a plan to answer each question. Remember to exclude records for which the required data are not available.

b) Compare your plan with the plans of your classmates.

c) Revise your plan, if necessary, and then carry it out.

1 Canadian Political Leaders

This database contains the prime ministers of Canada, the premiers of the provinces, and the government leaders of the territories.

1. In which province(s) or territory

a) did the longest serving premier serve?

b) did the youngest premier take office?

c) has there been a female premier?

d) have there been the fewest political parties in power?

2. What is the most common birthplace of Canadian prime ministers?

3. Excluding the term of office of the present premier, determine the total length of time each political party has been in power in your province.

2 BMI of Canadians

BMI (body mass index) is used to assess whether a person is overweight or underweight. It is the ratio of mass in kilograms to the square of height in metres.

A BMI greater than or equal to 25, or less than or equal to 18, is associated with health risks. When a BMI is greater than 25, skinfold measurements are analyzed to determine whether the high BMI is a result of excess fat, and WHR (waist girth to hip girth ratio) is analyzed to assess the fat distribution.

1. What percent of the participants in this database have a BMI that is associated with health risks?

3 Ports Around the World

1. What is the most frequent harbour type for ports in each country?

a) Canada   **b)** China

c) Australia   **d)** South Africa

2. Which harbour type has the most ports with excellent shelter?

3. The large and medium ports around the world are in this database. Predict the ocean on which there is the greatest number of these ports. Check your prediction.

4. The least channel depth is the depth of the water in a channel at low tide. The tide range is the difference between high and low tides. The **mean water level** is the depth of the water midway between high and low tides.

Determine the average of the mean water levels of channels on March 21 for all ports with each maximum vessel length. What assumption did you make?

4 Satellites Orbiting Earth

The satellites in this database are of two types and have eight purposes.

1. Satellites for which purpose have

a) the greatest average weight?

b) the shortest average period (time for one orbit)?

c) average inclinations between 80° and 100°?

PROBLEM SOLVING

1.5 Use Logic

The ability to think logically is an important skill that you will use in any profession you choose and in everyday life. This skill can be improved with practice. Most counterfeit coin problems include a balance scale with two pans. In the present problem, there is a scale with a single pan. There are three large bags of gold coins, with an unknown number of coins in each bag. Two of the bags contain only real coins that have masses of 60 g each. The other bag contains only counterfeit coins that have masses of 61 g each. You can remove coins from the bags, but since the mass of a real coin and the mass of a counterfeit coin are almost the same, you cannot tell a real coin from a counterfeit coin without using the scale.

What is the minimum number of times you can use the scale in order to be certain which bag contains the counterfeit coins?

Understand the Problem
1. What information are you given?
2. What are you asked to find?
3. Do you need an exact or an approximate answer?

Think of a Plan
Think of different ways of removing coins from the bags and finding the masses of the coins.

Carry Out the Plan
Label the bags A, B, and C.
You could remove and find the mass of one coin from each bag.
This method requires using the scale three times, unless you are lucky enough to find that the first coin has a mass of 61 g or the second coin has a mass of 61 g. Another method is to take one coin from each of two bags and find the total mass of the two coins by using the scale only once. If you are lucky, and the total mass is 120 g, you know that the two coins came from the bags of real coins. However, if the total mass is 121 g, you do not know which coin is counterfeit.

One way to use the scale only once, and to be certain which bag contains the counterfeit coins, is to remove 1 coin from bag A, 2 coins from bag B, and 3 coins from bag C. Then, find the total mass of the 6 coins.
If the total mass is 361 g, bag A has the counterfeit coins, since $61 + 120 + 180 = 361$.
If the total mass is 362 g, bag B has the counterfeit coins, since $60 + 122 + 180 = 362$.
If the total mass is 363 g, bag C has the counterfeit coins, since $60 + 120 + 183 = 363$.
So, the minimum number of times you can use the scale in order to be certain which bag contains the counterfeit coins is one.

Look Back
Is there another method that will give the same answer?

Use Logic
1. Organize the information.
2. Draw conclusions from the information.
3. Check that your answer is reasonable.

Applications and Problem Solving

1. Cards There are four cards on a table, as shown in the diagram. Each card is coloured red or blue on one side, and has a circle or square on the other side.

To determine whether every red card has a square on its other side, what is the minimum number of cards you must turn over, and which cards are they?

2. Number grid Copy the grid into your notebook. Arrange the numbers 1, 2, 3, and 4 on a 4 by 4 grid so that
• each row and each column includes the numbers 1, 2, 3, and 4
• no identical numbers are next to each other in a row, a column, or a diagonal from corner to corner
Two numbers have been placed for you. Find three solutions.

1			
		1	

3. Months You are given the following information.

January = 2	June = 1
February = 3	July = 0
March = 1	August = 2
April = 2	September = 5
May = 1	October = 4

Find the values of November and December.

4. Hockey games The chart gives the standings in a four-team hockey league after each team played every other team.

Team	Won	Lost	Tied	Goals For	Goals Against
Lions	3	0	0	7	0
Tigers	1	1	1	1	1
Bears	0	1	2	2	7
Rams	0	2	1	2	4

Determine the score of each game.

5. Car speed A circular track is 1 km long. A car makes one lap of the track at 30 km/h. Is there a speed that the car can travel on the second lap to average 60 km/h for the two laps? Explain.

6. Probability There are four balls in a bag. One is yellow, one is green, and two are white. Someone takes two balls from the bag, looks at them, and states that one of them is white. What is the probability that the second ball taken from the bag is also white?

7. Puppies Max and Sheba belong to a litter of puppies. Max has as many sisters as he has brothers. Sheba has twice as many brothers as she has sisters. How many females and how many males are in the litter?

8. Coordinate geometry The coordinates of the endpoints of one diagonal of a square are (8, 11) and (4, 5). Determine the coordinates of the endpoints of the other diagonal without graphing.

9. What is the largest list of whole numbers less than 100 such that no number in the list is the sum of two other numbers in the list?

10. Cube faces Three faces of a cube are shown. Each face of the cube has been divided into four squares. Each square is coloured red, blue, or yellow. No two squares of the same colour touch along an edge anywhere on the cube. How many squares of each colour are on the cube?

11. The sum of 17 consecutive whole numbers is 306. Find the greatest of the 17 whole numbers.

12. a) Using only the odd digits, how many different three-digit numbers can be made?
b) Determine the sum of these three-digit numbers without adding them.

13. Write a problem that can be solved using logic. Have a classmate solve your problem.

1.6 Combinations of Transformations

Because of its mathematical simplicity, the 3-4-5 right triangle has as much appeal today as it did thousands of years ago. In architecture, a 3-4-5 right triangle, with 4 as the base, has a hypotenuse with the slope of a comfortable stairway.

Some buildings have A-frame roofs. An example can be seen at the Alexander Graham Bell National Historic Site in Baddeck, Nova Scotia. For many A-frame roofs, a cross section is an isosceles triangle.

In some cases, the isosceles triangle can be formed by attaching two 3-4-5 right triangles Two different isosceles triangles can be formed in this way.

Explore: Graph the Functions

Show the two isosceles triangles formed between the following functions and the x-axis by graphing each function using a table of values or a graphing calculator.

a) $y = -\frac{3}{4}|x| + 3, y \geq 0$ **b)** $y = -\frac{4}{3}|x| + 4, y \geq 0$

x	y
4	
3	
2	
1	
0	
−1	
−2	
−3	
−4	

x	y
3	
2	
1	
0	
−1	
−2	
−3	

Inquire

1. What are the side lengths and the height of triangle a)?

2. What is the slope of the roof formed by triangle a)?

3. What are the side lengths and the height of triangle b)?

4. What is the slope of the roof formed by triangle b)?

5. What transformations must be applied to $y = |x|$ to give the function $y = -\frac{3}{4}|x| + 3$?

6. What transformations must be applied to $y = |x|$ to give the function $y = -\frac{4}{3}|x| + 4$?

7. In questions 5 and 6, must the transformations be applied in a particular order, or does the order have no effect on the result? Explain.

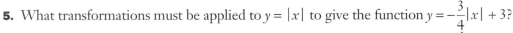

In this section, translations, expansions, compressions, and reflections will be used to perform combinations of transformations on functions. To simplify the procedure and give the desired results, perform the transformations in the following order.
• expansions and compressions
• reflections
• translations

In other words, perform multiplications (expansions, compressions, and reflections) before additions and subtractions (translations).

Example 1   Transforming Quadratic Functions

Sketch the graph of $y = x^2$ and the graph of $y = \frac{1}{2}(x + 4)^2 - 5$.

Solution
Sketch the graph of $y = x^2$.

To sketch the graph of $y = \frac{1}{2}(x + 4)^2 - 5$, first sketch the graph of $y = \frac{1}{2}x^2$. This graph is a vertical compression of $y = x^2$ by a factor of $\frac{1}{2}$.

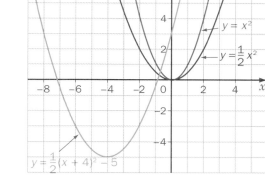

The transformed function can be graphed directly using a graphing calculator.

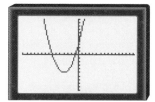

Then, apply the horizontal translation of 4 units to the left and the vertical translation of 5 units downward.

The result is the graph of $y = \frac{1}{2}(x + 4)^2 - 5$.

Example 2   Transforming Quadratic Functions
Given $f(x) = x^2$, sketch the graph of $y = f(x)$ and the graph of $y = -f(2(x - 5)) + 6$.

Solution
Sketch the graph of $y = x^2$.
The graph of $y = -f(2(x - 5)) + 6$ is the graph of $y = -(2(x - 5))^2 + 6$.
To sketch the graph of $y = -(2(x - 5))^2 + 6$, first sketch the graph of $y = (2x)^2$. This graph is a horizontal compression of the graph of $y = x^2$ by a factor of $\frac{1}{2}$.

Then, sketch the graph of $y = -(2x)^2$, which is a reflection of the graph of $y = (2x)^2$ in the x-axis.
Then, apply the horizontal translation of 5 units to the right and the vertical translation of 6 units upward.

The result is the graph of $y = -f(2(x - 5)) + 6$ or $y = -(2(x - 5))^2 + 6$.

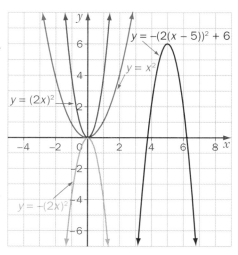

For such functions as $y = |3x + 6|$ and $y = \sqrt{-x + 5}$, factor the coefficient of the x term to identify the characteristics of the function more easily.

$y = |3x + 6|$ becomes $y = |3(x + 2)|$

$y = \sqrt{-x + 5}$ becomes $y = \sqrt{-(x - 5)}$

Example 3 Transforming Absolute Value Functions

Sketch the graph of $y = |x|$ and the graph of $y = 3|2x - 6| - 4$.

Solution

Sketch the graph of $y = |x|$.

Rewrite the function $y = 3|2x - 6| - 4$ as $y = 3|2(x - 3)| - 4$.

To sketch the graph of $y = 3|2(x - 3)| - 4$, first sketch the graph of $y = |2x|$, which is a horizontal compression of $y = |x|$ by a factor of $\frac{1}{2}$.

Then, sketch the graph of $y = 3|2x|$, which is a vertical expansion of the graph of $y = |2x|$ by a factor of 3. Then, apply the horizontal translation of 3 units to the right and the vertical translation of 4 units downward. The result is the graph of $y = 3|2x - 6| - 4$.

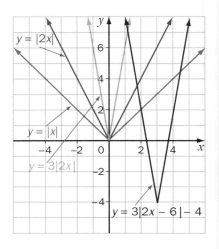

Example 4 Transforming Radical Functions

Given $f(x) = \sqrt{x}$, sketch the graph of $y = f(x)$ and the graph of $y = 2f(-x - 3) + 4$.

Solution

Sketch the graph of $y = \sqrt{x}$.

The graph of $y = 2f(-x - 3) + 4$ is the graph of $y = 2\sqrt{-x - 3} + 4$.

Rewrite $y = 2\sqrt{-x - 3} + 4$ as $y = 2\sqrt{-(x + 3)} + 4$.

To sketch the graph of $y = 2\sqrt{-(x + 3)} + 4$, first sketch the graph of $y = 2\sqrt{x}$. This graph is a vertical expansion of the graph of $y = \sqrt{x}$ by a factor of 2.

Then, sketch the graph of $y = 2\sqrt{-x}$, which is a reflection of the graph of $y = 2\sqrt{x}$ in the y-axis.

Then, apply the horizontal translation of 3 units to the left and the vertical translation of 4 units upward.

The result is the graph of $y = 2f(-x - 3) + 4$ or $y = 2\sqrt{-x - 3} + 4$.

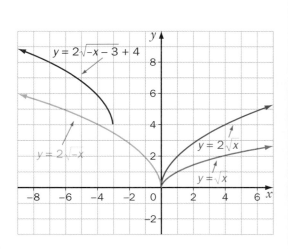

Example 5　Writing Equations

The graph of $f(x) = \sqrt{x}$ is expanded vertically by a factor of 5, reflected in the x-axis, translated 6 units to the right, and translated 3 units downward. Write the equation of the transformed function, $g(x)$.

Solution

When $y = f(x)$ is expanded vertically by a factor of 5, the function becomes $y = 5\sqrt{x}$. This function is reflected in the x-axis, becoming $y = -5\sqrt{x}$.

The function $y = -5\sqrt{x}$ is then translated 6 units to the right to give $y = -5\sqrt{x-6}$.

Finally, the function is translated 3 units downward to give $y = -5\sqrt{x-6} - 3$.

The solution can be visualized graphically.

Practice

Describe how the graph of each of the following functions can be obtained from the graph of $y = f(x)$.

1. $y = 2f(x) + 3$　　　**2.** $y = \dfrac{1}{2}f(x) - 2$

3. $y = f(x + 4) + 1$　　**4.** $y = 3f(x - 5)$

5. $y = f\left(\dfrac{1}{2}x\right) - 6$　　**6.** $y = f(2(x - 4))$

Describe how the graph of each of the following functions can be obtained from the graph of $y = f(x)$.

7. $y = 4f(x - 6) + 2$　　**8.** $y = -2f(x) - 3$
9. $y = f(-(x + 1)) - 1$　**10.** $y = -f(x - 3) + 1$
11. $y = 3f(2x) - 6$　　　**12.** $y = f(3(x + 4)) + 5$
13. $y = \dfrac{1}{2}f\left(\dfrac{1}{2}x\right) - 4$　**14.** $y = -2f(4(x - 2))$

Describe how the graph of each of the following functions can be obtained from the graph of $y = f(x)$.

15. $y = f(-x + 2)$　　**16.** $y = f(2x + 8) - 4$
17. $y = f(4 - x) + 5$　**18.** $y = f(3x - 6) + 8$

19. The graph of $y = f(x)$ is shown.

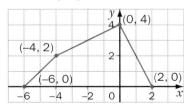

Sketch the graph of each of the following functions.

a) $y = f(x - 4) + 2$　　**b)** $y = f(x + 2) - 4$

c) $y = \dfrac{1}{2}f(x) - 3$　　**d)** $y = f(2x) + 3$

e) $y = -2f(x)$　　　　**f)** $y = f(-x) - 2$

Sketch each set of functions on the same set of axes in the given order.

20. $y = x$
　　$y = 3x$
　　$y = 3(x - 2) + 10$

21. $y = x^2$
　　$y = 2x^2$
　　$y = 2(x + 2)^2 - 3$

22. $y = |x|$
　　$y = \dfrac{1}{2}|x|$
　　$y = \dfrac{1}{2}|x - 4| + 2$

23. $y = x^2$
　　$y = \left(\dfrac{1}{2}x\right)^2$
　　$y = \left(\dfrac{1}{2}(x + 3)\right)^2 + 3$

24. $y = |x|$
　　$y = 3|x|$
　　$y = -3|x|$
　　$y = -3|x + 4| - 2$

25. $y = \sqrt{x}$
　　$y = 2\sqrt{x}$
　　$y = 2\sqrt{-x}$
　　$y = 2\sqrt{-(x - 3)} + 5$

Given $f(x) = x^2$, sketch the graph of each of the following.

26. $y = f(x - 3) + 1$　　**27.** $y = 2f(x + 5) - 4$

28. $y = \dfrac{1}{2}f\left(\dfrac{1}{2}x\right) + 3$　**29.** $y = -f(2(x - 2)) - 3$

30. $y = f(3 - x) + 2$　　**31.** $y = -\dfrac{1}{2}f(2x + 6) - 2$

Given $f(x) = |x|$, sketch the graph of each of the following.

32. $y = f(x+2) - 7$

33. $y = \dfrac{2}{3} f(x-4) + 3$

34. $y = 2f\left(\dfrac{1}{2}x\right) - 2$

35. $y = -f(2(x-3)) + 2$

36. $y = -\dfrac{1}{2} f(2-x) - 3$

37. $y = \dfrac{1}{3} f(4x-4) + 6$

Given $f(x) = \sqrt{x}$, sketch the graph of each of the following.

38. $y = f(x-5) - 4$

39. $y = 3f(x+3) + 2$

40. $y = \dfrac{1}{2} f(2(x-1))$

41. $y = 2f(3x-9) + 1$

42. $y = -f(-x) + 5$

43. $y = -2f(4-x) - 3$

44. Technology The calculator display shows the graph of $y = (x+2)^2 + 3$ and its image after a reflection in the x-axis and a reflection in the y-axis. Write the equation of the image.

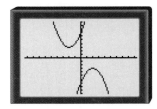

45. Technology The graph of $f(x) = x^2$ is expanded vertically by a factor of 3, translated 4 units to the right, and translated 2 units downward. Write the equation of the transformed function, $k(x)$. Check your solution using a graphing calculator.

46. Technology The graph $f(x) = |x|$ is compressed horizontally by a factor of $\dfrac{1}{3}$, translated 5 units to the left, and translated 1 unit upward. Write the equation of the transformed function, $h(x)$. Check your solution using a graphing calculator.

47. Technology The graph $f(x) = x^3$ is compressed vertically by a factor of $\dfrac{1}{3}$, reflected in the x-axis, translated 4 units to the right, and translated 5 units downward. Write the equation of the transformed function, $g(x)$. Check your solution using a graphing calculator.

48. Technology The graph $f(x) = \sqrt{x}$ is expanded horizontally by a factor of 2, reflected in the y-axis, and translated 6 units to the right. Write the equation of the transformed function, $g(x)$. Check your solution using a graphing calculator.

Applications and Problem Solving

49. Ski chalet A cross section of the roof of a ski chalet can be modelled by the function
$$y = -\dfrac{5}{3}|x-3| + 5, \quad y \geq 0.$$
a) Graph the function.
b) Find the side lengths and the height of the isosceles triangle. Round to the nearest tenth of a unit, if necessary.
c) What is the slope of the roof?
d) What transformations must be applied to $y = |x|$ to give the function $y = -\dfrac{5}{3}|x-3| + 5$, $y \geq 0$.

50. Emergency flare The height, y metres, of an emergency flare fired upward from a small boat can be modelled by the function
$$y = -5(x-4)^2 + 80$$
where x seconds is the time since the flare was fired.
a) Describe how the graph of $y = -5(x-4)^2 + 80$ can be obtained by transforming the graph of $y = x^2$.
b) Interpret the equation of the transformed function to find the maximum height reached by the flare and the time it takes to reach this height.

51. The graph of $f(x) = \sqrt{16 - x^2}$ is shown.

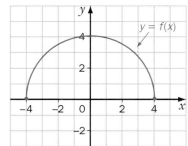

Sketch the graph of each of the following functions.
a) $y = \dfrac{1}{2} f(x) + 5$

b) $y = -\dfrac{1}{2} f(x) - 3$

c) $y = (f(x) - 3) - 2$

d) $y = -2f(x+6) + 5$

52. Technology Write the equations of the functions that result from the following transformations on $f(x) = \dfrac{x}{x^2 + 1}$.

Use a graphing calculator to check your equations.
a) reflected in the x-axis and translated 3 units to the left

b) compressed vertically by a factor of $\frac{1}{2}$, translated 4 units to the right, and translated 7 units downward

c) expanded horizontally by a factor of 2, translated 5 units to the right, and translated 2 units upward

53. Technology Write the equations of the functions that result from the following transformations on $f(x) = 2^x$. Use a graphing calculator to check your equations.

a) a reflection in the y-axis and a translation of 6 units downward

b) a horizontal compression by a factor of $\frac{1}{2}$, a translation of 4 units to the right, and a translation of 5 units upward

54. The function $y = f(x)$ has been transformed to $y = af(k(x - h)) + q$. Determine the values of a, k, h, and q for each of the following transformations.

a) a vertical expansion by a factor of 3 and a reflection in the y-axis

b) a vertical compression by a factor of $\frac{1}{3}$, a horizontal expansion by a factor of 2, a translation of 6 units to the right, and a translation of 1 unit downward

c) a vertical expansion by a factor of 2, a horizontal compression by a factor of $\frac{1}{2}$, a reflection in the x-axis, a reflection in the y-axis, a translation of 7 units to the left, and a translation of 4 units upward

55. Gravity If an object is dropped from an initial height of x metres, its approximate height above the ground, h metres, after t seconds is given by $h = x - 5t^2$ on the Earth and by $h = x - 0.8t^2$ on the moon. So, for objects dropped from an initial height of 20 m, the functions are $h = 20 - 5t^2$ and $h = 20 - 0.8t^2$.

a) Graph h versus t for $h = 20 - 5t^2$ and $h = 20 - 0.8t^2$ on the same axes.

b) Explain the meaning of the point that the two graphs have in common.

c) Describe a stretch that transforms $h = 20 - 0.8t^2$ into $h = 20 - 5t^2$. Justify your reasoning.

d) On the same axes that you used in part a), translate the graph of $h = 20 - 5t^2$ upward by 105 units. Explain the meaning of the point that the resulting graph and the graph of $h = 20 - 0.8t^2$ have in common.

e) The approximate height of an object dropped on Jupiter is given by $h = x - 12.8t^2$. So, for an initial height of 320 m, the function is $h = 320 - 12.8t^2$. Graph $h = 320 - 12.8t^2$ and $h = 20 - 0.8t^2$ on the same axes. Explain the meaning of the point that the graphs have in common.

f) Describe how the graph of $h = 20 - 0.8t^2$ can be transformed into the graph of $h = 320 - 12.8t^2$.

56. Describe how the graph of the function $y = \sqrt[3]{x + 1} - 2$ can be obtained from the graph of $y = x^3$.

57. Describe how the graph of the function $y = -\sqrt{x + 2} - 3$ can be obtained from the graph of $y = x^2$, $x \le 0$.

58. a) Expand the graph of $y = x$ vertically by a factor of 2. Then, translate the result 3 units to the left and 5 units downward. Compare the result to the graph of $y = 2x + 1$. Explain your findings.

b) If the same transformations are performed on the graph of $y = x^2$, instead of $y = x$, is the result the same as the graph of $y = 2x^2 + 1$? Explain.

NUMBER POWER

A positive integer is a *happy number* if the sum of the squares of its digits is 1, or if, when this process is continued until the sum is one digit, the result is 1.

32 is a happy number:
$3^2 + 2^2 = 13 \rightarrow 1^2 + 3^2 = 10 \rightarrow 1^2 + 0^2 = 1$

42 is not a happy number:
$4^2 + 2^2 = 20 \rightarrow 2^2 + 0^2 = 4$

- Is 23 a happy number? Explain.
- Find all the happy numbers less than 100. Use patterns to minimize the work.
- What pattern(s) do you see in the final sum for numbers that are not happy?

1.7 Reciprocal Functions and Absolute Value Functions

For thousands of years, gold has been regarded as a symbol of wealth. Many people have searched for deposits of this valuable metal. There have been several gold rushes in Western Canada, the largest being the Klondike Gold Rush, which began in 1897. This gold rush attracted 100 000 people to the Yukon and affected every Western Canadian community from Winnipeg to Victoria.

Gold is one of the heaviest metals, as shown by its density of 18.9 g/cm^3. Since density is defined as $\dfrac{\text{mass}}{\text{volume}}$, the density value shows that a 1-cm^3 block of gold has a mass of 18.9 g.

A related quantity is the specific volume, which is defined as $\dfrac{\text{volume}}{\text{mass}}$.

The specific volume of gold is about 0.0529 cm^3/g.
Thus, 1 g of gold has a volume of 0.0529 cm^3.
Notice that, since $\text{density} = \dfrac{\text{mass}}{\text{volume}}$, and

$\text{specific volume} = \dfrac{\text{volume}}{\text{mass}}$, the density, D, and the specific volume, v, are reciprocals of each other.

$$D = \frac{1}{v}$$

Explore: Graph the Function

a) Graph density versus specific volume on a graphing calculator, using the window variables Xmin=0, Xmax=1, Ymin=0, Ymax=20.
b) Why is the graph in the first quadrant?
c) The density of silver is 10.5 g/cm^3. What is the specific volume of silver?
d) The specific volume of diamond is 0.285 cm^3/g. What is the density of diamond?

Inquire

1. a) Graph $y = \dfrac{1}{x}$ over the real numbers.

b) Describe how the graph is different from the graph of density versus specific volume.

2. Graph $y = x$ over the real numbers on the same axes or in the same viewing window as $y = \dfrac{1}{x}$.

3. When the value of x is 0, what is the value of $\dfrac{1}{x}$? Explain.

4. What values of x and $\dfrac{1}{x}$ are the same? Explain.

5. a) When x is positive, is $\dfrac{1}{x}$ positive or negative?

b) When x is negative, is $\dfrac{1}{x}$ positive or negative?

6. What happens to the value of $\dfrac{1}{x}$

a) as x increases? **b)** as x decreases?

7. What happens to the absolute value of $\dfrac{1}{x}$

a) as the absolute value of x approaches zero?
b) as the absolute value of x gets very large?

If $f(x) = x$, then $\dfrac{1}{f(x)} = \dfrac{1}{x}$, where $\dfrac{1}{f(x)}$ denotes a **reciprocal function**.

Note that $\dfrac{1}{f(x)}$ does not mean $f^{-1}(x)$.

↑   ↑
reciprocal function   inverse function

The graph of $y = \dfrac{1}{f(x)}$ can be obtained from the graph of $y = f(x)$ using the following general rules.

• Where the value of the original function is zero, the value of the reciprocal function is undefined, and a vertical asymptote exists on the graph of the reciprocal function.

• Where the value of the original function is 1, the value of the reciprocal function is 1. Where the value of the original function is −1, the value of the reciprocal function is −1.

• Where the value of the original function is positive, the value of the reciprocal function is positive. Where the value of the original function is negative, the value of the reciprocal function is negative.

• If the value of the original function increases over an interval, the value of the reciprocal function decreases over the same interval. If the value of the original function decreases over an interval, the value of the reciprocal function increases over the same interval.

• As the absolute value of the original function approaches zero, the absolute value of the reciprocal function gets very large. As the absolute value of the original function gets very large, the absolute value of the reciprocal function approaches zero.

Example 1   Reciprocal of a Linear Function

Given that $f(x) = x - 2$, sketch the graphs of $y = f(x)$ and $y = \dfrac{1}{f(x)}$
on the same set of axes.

Solution

Sketch the graph of $f(x) = x - 2$ or $y = x - 2$.
The function has a zero at $x = 2$.

The graph of $y = \dfrac{1}{f(x)}$ is the graph of $y = \dfrac{1}{x - 2}$.

The function $y = \dfrac{1}{x - 2}$ is undefined when $x - 2 = 0$,
that is, when $x = 2$.

Draw a vertical asymptote at $x = 2$.

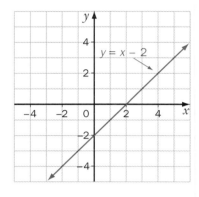

For both functions, determine the coordinates of points on both sides
of the asymptote, and then use the general rules to sketch the graph
of the reciprocal function.

x	4	3	2.1	2.01	1	1.9	1.99
x − 2	2	1	0.1	0.01	−1	−0.1	−0.01
$\dfrac{1}{x-2}$	$\dfrac{1}{2}$	1	10	100	−1	−10	−100

Plot the points $(3, 1)$ and $(1, -1)$, which are on both graphs.
The value of $y = x - 2$ is positive when $x > 2$, so the value of
$y = \dfrac{1}{x - 2}$ is positive when $x > 2$.

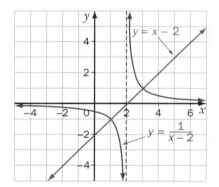

The value of $y = x - 2$ is negative when $x < 2$, so the value of
$y = \dfrac{1}{x - 2}$ is negative when $x < 2$.

The table shows that, as $|x|$ approaches 2, $|x - 2|$ approaches 0,
so $\dfrac{1}{|x - 2|}$ gets large.

As $|x|$ gets large, $|x - 2|$ also gets large, and $\dfrac{1}{|x - 2|}$ approaches 0.

The line $y = 0$ is a horizontal asymptote of $y = \dfrac{1}{x - 2}$.

The reciprocal function can be graphed
directly using a graphing calculator.

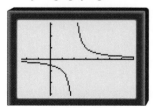

Example 2 Reciprocal of a Quadratic Function

Sketch the graphs of $f(x) = x^2 + 2$ and $\dfrac{1}{f(x)} = \dfrac{1}{x^2 + 2}$ on the same set of axes.

Solution

The graph of $f(x) = x^2 + 2$ or $y = x^2 + 2$ is a parabola that opens up and has vertex $(0, 2)$.

Note that, since $y = x^2 + 2$ does not intersect the x-axis, this function has no real zeros. So, $\dfrac{1}{x^2 + 2}$ is defined for all real numbers. Therefore, the graph

of $\dfrac{1}{f(x)} = \dfrac{1}{x^2 + 2}$ or $y = \dfrac{1}{x^2 + 2}$ has no vertical asymptotes.

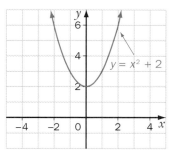

Since $f(x)$ is always positive, $\dfrac{1}{f(x)}$ is always positive.

When $f(x) = 2$, $\dfrac{1}{f(x)} = \dfrac{1}{2}$.

As $|x|$ gets large, $f(x)$ gets large and $\dfrac{1}{f(x)}$ approaches 0.

The line $y = 0$ is a horizontal asymptote of $y = \dfrac{1}{x^2 + 2}$.

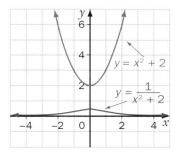

Example 3 Reciprocal of a Given Graph

The graph of $y = f(x)$ is shown.

Sketch the graph of $y = \dfrac{1}{f(x)}$.

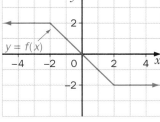

Solution

Since $f(0) = 0$, the function $y = \dfrac{1}{f(x)}$ is undefined when $x = 0$.

There is a vertical asymptote at $x = 0$.

When $x \geq 2$, $f(x) = -2$, so $\dfrac{1}{f(x)} = -\dfrac{1}{2}$.

When $x \leq -2$, $f(x) = 2$, so $\dfrac{1}{f(x)} = \dfrac{1}{2}$.

When $x < 0$, $f(x)$ is positive, so $\dfrac{1}{f(x)}$ is positive.

When $x > 0$, $f(x)$ is negative, so $\dfrac{1}{f(x)}$ is negative.

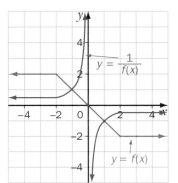

For $-2 < x < 2$, $x \neq 0$, as $|x|$ approaches 0, $\dfrac{1}{|f(x)|}$ gets large.

Recall that, for any real number x, $|x| = x$, if $x \geq 0$, and $|x| = -x$, if $x < 0$.
This definition is used to graph the absolute value function $y = |f(x)|$.

Example 4   Absolute Value of a Linear Function
Given $f(x) = 2x + 3$, sketch the graphs of $y = f(x)$ and $y = |f(x)|$ on the same set of axes.

Solution
First sketch the graph of $f(x) = 2x + 3$ or $y = 2x + 3$, which is a straight line with a slope of 2 and a y-intercept of 3. The x-intercept is $-\frac{3}{2}$.

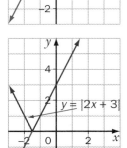

Consider the x-intercept and points on both sides of the x-intercept.

x	3	2	1	0	–1	$-\frac{3}{2}$	–2	–3	–4
$2x + 3$	9	7	5	3	1	0	–1	–3	–5
$|2x + 3|$	9	7	5	3	1	0	1	3	5

Use the graph of $y = 2x + 3$ to sketch the graph of $y = |f(x)|$ or $y = |2x + 3|$.
Where $2x + 3$ is zero or positive, the graph of $y = |2x + 3|$ is identical to the graph of $y = 2x + 3$. Where $2x + 3$ is negative, sketch the graph of $y = |2x + 3|$ by reflecting the graph of $y = 2x + 3$ in the x-axis.

From Example 4, note the following generalizations.
• When $f(x) \geq 0$, the graph of $y = |f(x)|$ is identical to the graph of $y = f(x)$.
• When $f(x) < 0$, the graph of $y = |f(x)|$ is the graph of $y = f(x)$ reflected in the x-axis.

Example 5   Absolute Value of a Quadratic Function
a) Sketch the graph of $f(x) = |x^2 - 4|$.
b) Given that the graph of $f(x) = -4(x - 2)^2 + 4$ has x-intercepts of 1 and 3, sketch the graph of $g(x) = |-4(x - 2)^2 + 4|$.

Solution
a) First sketch $y = x^2 - 4$.
The graph is a parabola that opens up, with zeros at 2 and –2, and a vertex at $(0, -4)$.
Now sketch the graph of $f(x) = |x^2 - 4|$ or $y = |x^2 - 4|$ by reflecting in the x-axis the part of $y = x^2 - 4$ that is below the x-axis.

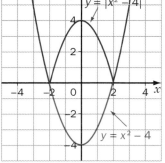

b) Sketch the graph of $y = -4(x - 2)^2 + 4$, which has the given zeros of 1 and 3 and has vertex $(2, 4)$. Sketch the graph of $g(x) = |-4(x - 2)^2 + 4|$ or $y = |-4(x - 2)^2 + 4|$ by reflecting in the x-axis the part of $y = -4(x - 2)^2 + 4$ that is below the x-axis.

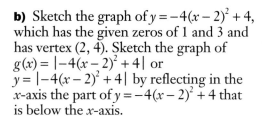

The absolute value function can be graphed directly using a graphing calculator.

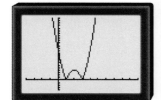

Example 6   Reciprocal of an Absolute Value Function

Sketch the graph of $f(x) = \dfrac{1}{|x^2 - 4|}$.

Solution

Consider the function as a quadratic function, $y = x^2 - 4$, a reciprocal function, and an absolute value function.

Sketch the graph of $y = x^2 - 4$.
The graph of $y = x^2 - 4$ has zeros at 2 and −2, so the reciprocal of $x^2 - 4$ is undefined at $x = 2$ and −2.

Sketch the graph of $y = \dfrac{1}{x^2 - 4}$.

The graph of $y = \dfrac{1}{|x^2 - 4|}$ can now be obtained by reflecting in the x-axis the part of $y = \dfrac{1}{x^2 - 4}$ below the x-axis.

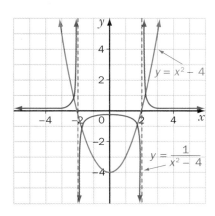

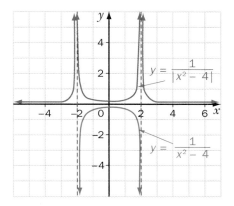

Example 7   Absolute Value of a Cubic Function

Sketch the graph of $y = |x(x + 3)(x - 2)|$.

Solution

Sketch the graph of $y = x(x + 3)(x - 2)$.

The zeros are $x = 0$, 2, and −3.

The left-most points are in the third quadrant and have negative y-values. The right-most points are in the first quadrant and have positive y-values.

The graph has a relative maximum at about $(-2, 8)$ and a relative minimum at about $(1, -4)$.

To sketch the graph of $y = |x(x + 3)(x - 2)|$, reflect in the x-axis the portion of the graph that is below the x-axis.

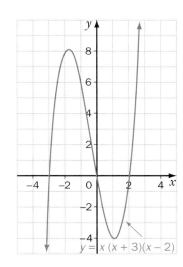

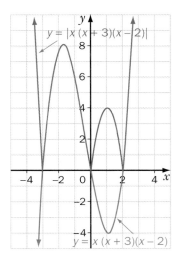

Practice

Sketch the following functions on the same set of axes in the given order.

1. $y = x$
   $y = 2x$
   $y = 2x - 6$
   $y = \dfrac{1}{2x - 6}$

2. $y = x^2$
   $y = (x + 3)^2$
   $y = (x + 3)^2 - 4$
   $y = \dfrac{1}{(x + 3)^2 - 4}$

Given the function f(x), sketch the graph of y = f(x) and the graph of $y = \dfrac{1}{f(x)}$ *on the same set of axes.*

3. $f(x) = x - 3$ **4.** $f(x) = x + 4$
5. $f(x) = 2x - 8$ **6.** $f(x) = 3x + 6$

Given the function f(x), sketch the graph of y = f(x) and the graph of $y = \dfrac{1}{f(x)}$ *on the same set of axes.*

7. $f(x) = x^2 + 1$ **8.** $f(x) = x^2 - 4$
9. $f(x) = x(x - 4)$ **10.** $f(x) = (x - 2)(x + 1)$

Given the function f(x), sketch the graph of y = f(x) and the graph of $y = \dfrac{1}{f(x)}$ *on the same set of axes.*

11. $f(x) = \sqrt{x}$ **12.** $f(x) = \sqrt{x} - 2$
13. $f(x) = \sqrt{x - 2}$ **14.** $f(x) = -\sqrt{x} + 1$

Given the function f(x), sketch the graph of y = f(x) and the graph of $y = \dfrac{1}{f(x)}$ *on the same set of axes.*

15. $f(x) = x^3$ **16.** $f(x) = (x - 1)^3$
17. $f(x) = x(x + 3)^2$ **18.** $f(x) = x(x + 2)(x - 2)$

Copy the graph of each function, y = f(x), and sketch the graph of $y = \dfrac{1}{f(x)}$.

19.

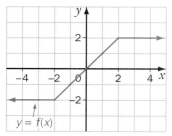

20.

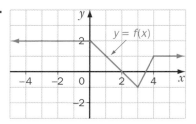

21.

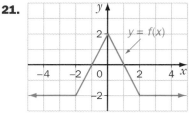

22.

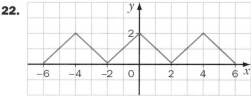

Sketch the following functions on the same set of axes in the given order.

23. $y = x$
   $y = 2x$
   $y = 2x + 6$
   $y = |2x + 6|$

24. $y = x^2$
   $y = (x - 2)^2$
   $y = (x - 2)^2 - 4$
   $y = |(x - 2)^2 - 4|$

Sketch the graphs of y = f(x) and y = | f(x)| on the same set of axes.

25. $f(x) = 2x + 1$ **26.** $f(x) = 3x - 6$
27. $f(x) = -x - 4$ **28.** $f(x) = 3 - 2x$

Sketch the graphs of y = f(x) and y = | f(x)| on the same set of axes.

29. $f(x) = x^2 - 4$ **30.** $f(x) = x(x + 5)$
31. $f(x) = -x(x - 4)$ **32.** $f(x) = (x - 1)(x + 3)$

Copy the graph of each function, y = f(x), and sketch the graph of y = | f(x)|.

33.

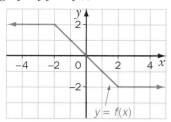

34.

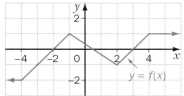

35.

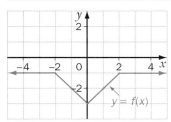

36. Given that the graph of $f(x) = (x+2)^2 - 9$ has x-intercepts of 1 and -5, sketch the graph of $k(x) = |(x+2)^2 - 9|$.

37. Given that the graph of $f(x) = -(x-3)^2 + 4$ has x-intercepts of 1 and 5, sketch the graph of $g(x) = |-(x-3)^2 + 4|$.

38. Given the function $y = -x^2 + 9$, sketch the graph of $y = |-x^2 + 9|$.

39. Sketch the graph of $\dfrac{1}{|x^2 - 9|}$.

40. Given the function $y = x(x+2)(x+5)$, sketch the graph of $y = |x(x+2)(x+5)|$.

41. Given the function $y = (x-1)(x+2)(x+4)$, sketch the graph of $y = |(x-1)(x+2)(x+4)|$.

Applications and Problem Solving

In questions 42–45, write an equation for each function. Check your solution with a graphing calculator.

42. Starting with $y = x$, expand it vertically by a factor of 5, shift it 4 units to the left, and take its reciprocal.

43. Starting with $y = x$, compress it vertically by a factor of $\dfrac{1}{2}$, shift it 5 units to the right, and take its absolute value.

44. Starting with $y = x^2$, compress it horizontally by a factor of $\dfrac{1}{2}$, shift it 4 units to the right and 3 units downward, and take its reciprocal.

45. Starting with $y = x^2$, expand it vertically by a factor of 2, shift it 3 units to the left and 5 units downward, and take its absolute value.

46. Given the function $f(x) = (x+3)^2 - 9$, sketch the graph of $g(x) = |(x+3)^2 - 9|$.

47. Given the function $f(x) = -2(x-1)^2 + 8$, sketch the graph of $h(x) = |-2(x-1)^2 + 8|$.

48. Given the function $f(x) = \dfrac{5}{x^2 + 1}$, sketch the graph of $y = \dfrac{1}{f(x)}$.

49. Sketch the graph of $f(x) = \dfrac{1}{|x(x-2)|}$.

50. Sketch the graph of $f(x) = \dfrac{1}{|(x+1)(x-2)|}$.

51. Graph $y = x^3 - 3$, $y = \dfrac{1}{x^3 - 3}$, and $y = |x^3 - 3|$ on the same set of axes.

52. Given the function $f(x) = 2^x - 4$, sketch the graphs of $y = \dfrac{1}{f(x)}$ and $y = |f(x)|$.

53. Given the function $f(x) = x(x-2)(x+2)^2$, sketch the graphs of $y = \dfrac{1}{f(x)}$ and $y = |f(x)|$.

54. For the function $f(x) = 2x + 4$, describe and explain the difference between $\dfrac{1}{f(x)}$ and $f^{-1}(x)$.

55. Given the function $y = \sqrt{x^2 - 16} - 4$, sketch the graph of $y = |\sqrt{x^2 - 16} - 4|$.

56. Given the function $y = \sqrt{49 - x^2} - 3$, sketch the graph of $y = |\sqrt{49 - x^2} - 3|$.

57. Greatest integer function Given the function $f(x) = [x]$, sketch the graphs of $y = \dfrac{1}{f(x)}$ and $y = |f(x)|$.

PROBLEM SOLVING

1.8 Solve Fermi Problems

About how many recordings are played by the radio stations in your province in a day?

Problems like this one, which involves estimation, are called **Fermi problems**. They are named after Enrico Fermi (1901–1954). He was a leading research scientist, who won the Nobel Prize for physics in 1938 and spent the last part of his career as a professor at the University of Chicago. He liked to show his students that they had the knowledge to answer seemingly impossible questions that he posed.

The importance of Fermi problems is to illustrate the difference between *guessing* and *estimation*. Although guessing may produce a reasonable answer to a problem, you do not know how much confidence to place in the answer. When estimating the answers to Fermi problems, you will need to make some assumptions. If the estimated answer seems to be unreasonable, go back and check the assumptions you have made.

About how many peanuts in the shell would be needed to fill a telephone booth?

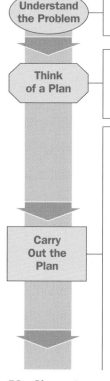

Understand the Problem

1. What information are you given?
2. What are you asked to find?
3. Do you need an exact or an approximate answer?

Think of a Plan

The problem is a volume problem, in which you are to estimate how many small objects are needed to fill a large object. The number of small objects, n, can be found using
$$n = (\text{large volume}) \div (\text{small volume})$$

Carry Out the Plan

You can use your research skills to find that the inside of a telephone booth approximates a square-based prism. The side length of the base is about 0.9 m, and the height is about 1.9 m.

Assume that peanuts in a shell approximate a cylinder with a diameter of about 1.5 cm and a height of about 4 cm.

The volume of a telephone booth, in cubic centimetres, is about $90 \times 90 \times 190$, or about 1 540 000 cm^3.

The volume of peanuts in the shell, in cubic centimetres, is about $\pi \times 0.75^2 \times 4$, or about 7 cm^3.

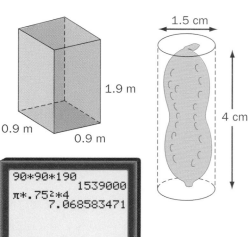

```
90*90*190
           1539000
π*.75²*4
        7.068583471
```

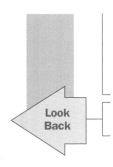

So, $n \doteq \dfrac{1\,540\,000}{7}$

$= 220\,000$

About 220 000 peanuts in the shell would be needed to fill a telephone booth.

Look Back

Does the answer seem reasonable?
Is there a way to improve the estimate?

Solve Fermi Problems

1. Locate the information you need.
2. Decide what assumption(s) to make.
3. Estimate the solution to the problem.
4. Check that your estimate is reasonable.

Applications and Problem Solving

Use your research skills to locate any missing information. You could use such sources as the Internet, a reference book, or an expert on the topic. For some problems, you may need to use a survey or measurement. Then, solve each problem.

1. Ten-dollar bills About how many ten-dollar bills would it take to paper the walls of all the classrooms in your school?

2. Toothpicks About how many flat toothpicks would be needed to cover the floor of your school gym?

3. Bananas Estimate the number of bananas it would take to fill all the lockers in your school.

4. Table tennis balls About how many table tennis balls would it take to fill a minivan?

5. Pianos Estimate the number of pianos in your province.

6. Pizza deliveries Estimate the number of pizzas that will be delivered in your province this year.

7. Phone calls About how many minutes will all the students in your school spend on the phone in a month?

8. Radio About how many recordings are played by all the radio stations in your province in a day?

9. Lake Winnipeg Estimate the number of drops of water in Lake Winnipeg.

10. Laughter About how many times does a grade 12 student laugh in a day?

11. Calculators Estimate the total number of times the students in your school press a calculator key in a school day.

12. Writing About how many Canadians make a living writing fiction novels?

13. Doughnut shops Estimate the number of doughnut shops in Canada.

14. Buildings About what percent of the land area in your city or town is covered by buildings?

15. Education Estimate the total number of hours all the college and university students in your province spend at lectures and laboratories in a year.

16. Write a problem similar to question 1, 2, or 3. Have a classmate solve your problem.

CAREER CONNECTION

Veterinary Medicine

There are many more domestic animals in Canada than there are people. For example, in addition to the millions of dogs and cats in Canadian homes, there are over 12 000 000 cattle and 10 000 000 pigs on Canadian farms. Medical services for these and other animals are provided by workers in the field of veterinary medicine.

There are four colleges where veterinary medicine can be studied in Canada, including the Western College of Veterinary Medicine at the University of Saskatchewan, in Saskatoon.

1 Ages of Cats and Dogs

As with humans, the medical needs of domestic animals change as they age. However, humans and domestic animals age differently. For example, a large 7-year-old dog is roughly equivalent in age to a 65-year-old human. For a small dog, aged 3 years or more and with a mass up to about 11 kg, the number of human years equivalent to the age of the dog is given by the formula

$$h = 4a + 20$$

where h is the equivalent number of human years, and a is the age of the dog.
For a domestic cat aged 3 years or more, the number of human years equivalent to the age of the cat is given by the formula

$$h = 4a + 15$$

where h is the equivalent number of human years, and a is the age of the cat.

1. Express the age of an 8-year-old cat as an equivalent number of human years.

2. If the age of a small dog is equivalent to 64 human years, what is the age of the dog?

3. a) Graph h versus a for cats and for small dogs over the domain 3 years to 15 years on the same axes or in the same viewing window of a graphing calculator.
b) Describe how the graphs are related by a transformation.

4. A cat and a small dog were born on the same day and are over 3 years old. How do the numbers of human years equivalent to their ages compare? Explain.

5. If their ages are expressed as equivalent human years, do cats and small dogs age at the same rate after the age of 3? Explain.

6. If their ages are expressed as equivalent human years, do cats and small dogs age at the same rate from birth? How do you know?

2 Locating Information

Use your research skills to explore the following.
1. the training needed to become a veterinarian, also known as a doctor of veterinary medicine

2. the organizations that employ veterinarians

3. other careers that involve animal care

4. the services provided by your local Humane Society

5. the purpose of Animal Health Week, when it is held, and the activities it includes

Frieze Patterns

A frieze pattern is a pattern that repeats in one direction. The patterns depend on the use of transformations. Many cultures have used frieze patterns to make decorative designs on buildings, textiles, pottery, and so on.

1 Using Transformations

One way of creating a frieze pattern is to make a basic design on a grid and then to transform the design. An example of a basic design is shown.

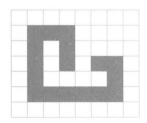

Describe how transformations have been used to create each of the following frieze patterns from the basic design.

Ukrainian pysanka

1.

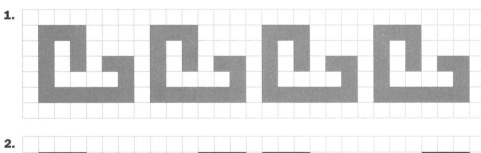

2.

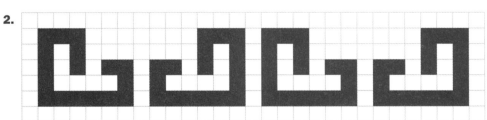

3.

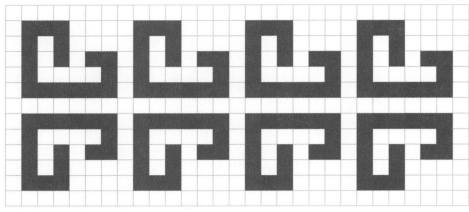

4.

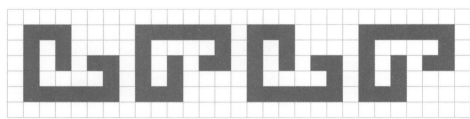

2 Transforming Triangles

The frieze pattern shown was created from equilateral triangles of side length 2 units.

1. What is the exact height of each triangle?

2. Suppose a coordinate grid is superimposed on the pattern as shown.

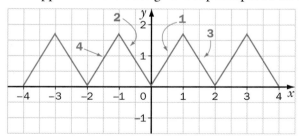

a) What is the exact slope of line segment 1?

b) Write an equation for line segment 1.

3. Use transformations to write an equation for
a) line segment 2
b) line segment 3
c) line segment 4

4. Use a different transformation, or combination of transformations, to create another frieze pattern from equilateral triangles. Superimpose a coordinate grid. Write a problem about your pattern and check that you can solve the problem. Then, have a classmate solve your problem.

3 Creating a Design

1. Design your own frieze pattern from a basic design of your choice.

2. Describe how you used transformations to create the pattern.

3. Suggest a possible use for your frieze pattern, and explain why you chose this use.

4 Locating Information

1. Use your research skills to investigate one of the following uses of frieze patterns.
a) pysankas (Ukrainian painted eggs)
b) First Nations designs
c) ancient Roman architecture
d) ancient Greek pottery
e) African designs
f) designs from an ancient or modern civilization of your choice

2. Use your research skills to determine how frieze patterns are classified and how many types of frieze patterns there are.

Geometric relief carvings – Mitla, Mixtec ruins

Review

1.1 *The function $y = f(x)$ is given. Describe how the graphs of the following functions can be obtained from the graph of $y = f(x)$.*

1. $y = f(x) - 3$ **2.** $y = f(x + 6)$
3. $y = f(x - 4) - 5$ **4.** $y + 5 = f(x)$

The graph of the function drawn in blue is a translation of the function drawn in red. Write an equation for each function drawn in blue. Check each equation using a graphing calculator.

5.

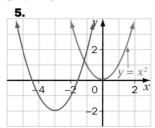

6.

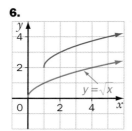

Use transformations to sketch the graphs of each of the following pairs of functions.

7. $y = |x|$
    $y = |x| + 5$

8. $y = \sqrt{x}$
    $y = \sqrt{x - 3}$

9. $y = x^2$
    $y = (x - 2)^2 - 4$

10. $y = \dfrac{1}{x}$

    $y = \dfrac{1}{x + 3} + 5$

1.3 *For each graph in questions 11 and 12, draw and label the following pairs of graphs.*
a) $y = f(x)$ and $y = -f(x)$ **b)** $y = f(x)$ and $y = f(-x)$
c) $y = f(x)$ and $x = f(y)$

11.

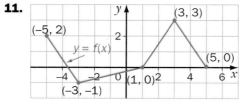

12.

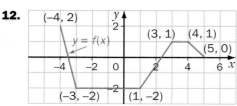

Graph $f(x)$ and sketch the specified reflection image. State whether each reflection image is a function.

13. $h(x)$, the reflection of $f(x) = \sqrt{x + 2}$ in the y-axis
14. $k(x)$, the reflection of $f(x) = -3x + 5$ in the line $y = x$
15. $g(x)$, the reflection of $f(x) = \dfrac{4}{x^2 - 2}$ in the x-axis
16. $g(x)$, the reflection of $f(x) = |x - 4|$ in the line $y = x$

17. a) Given $f(x) = x^3 + 3$, write the equations for $-f(x)$, $f(-x)$, and $f^{-1}(x)$.
b) Sketch the four graphs on the same set of axes.

1.4 *The graph of $y = f(x)$ is shown.*

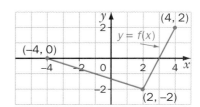

Sketch the graphs of the following functions.

18. $y = -3f(x)$ **19.** $y = 2f\left(\dfrac{1}{2}x\right)$ **20.** $y = -f(3x)$

Use transformations to sketch the graphs of the following pairs of functions.

21. $y = x - 4$
    $y = -(x - 4)$

22. $y = |x|$
    $y = \left|\dfrac{2}{3}x\right|$

23. $y = \sqrt{x + 2}$
    $y = -3\sqrt{x + 2}$

24. $y = x^3 + 4$
    $y = (2x)^3 + 4$

25. $y = (x - 3)^2$
    $y = -\dfrac{1}{4}(x - 3)^2$

26. $y = \dfrac{1}{x}$

    $y = \dfrac{1}{-3x}$

27. Given $f(x) = (x + 1)(x - 1)(x - 2)$, find the zeros of each of the following.
a) $y = f(2x)$ **b)** $y = f(-x)$ **c)** $y = -f(x)$

1.6 *Describe how the graph of each of the following functions can be obtained from the graph of $y = f(x)$.*

28. $y = f(2(x + 1))$ **29.** $y = 3f(x + 2) - 4$
30. $y = -3f(x) + 5$ **31.** $y = f(2(x - 3)) - 1$
32. $y = \dfrac{1}{2}f(4x) + 2$ **33.** $y = f(2x - 4) + 3$

34. Technology The graph of $f(x) = x^3$ is expanded vertically by a factor of 2, reflected in the y-axis, translated 3 units to the left, and translated 4 units downward. Write the equation of the transformed function, $g(x)$. Check using a graphing calculator.

7 *Sketch the graphs of $y = f(x)$ and $y = \dfrac{1}{f(x)}$ on the same set of axes.*

35. $f(x) = 2x + 4$ **36.** $f(x) = x(x - 9)$

37. $f(x) = \sqrt{x} + 1$ **38.** $f(x) = (x - 2)^3$

Copy the graph of each function, $y = f(x)$, and sketch the graph of $y = \dfrac{1}{f(x)}$.

39. 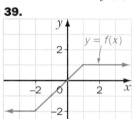   **40.**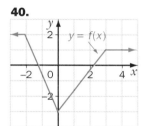

Sketch the graph of $y = f(x)$ and the graph of $y = |f(x)|$ on the same set of axes.

41. $f(x) = 3x - 4$ **42.** $f(x) = (x + 2)(x - 3)$

Copy the graph of each function, $y = f(x)$, and sketch the graph of $y = |f(x)|$.

43.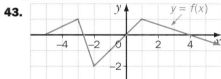

44.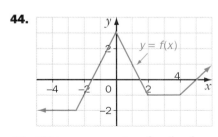

45. Write an equation for the function that results when you start with $y = x^2$, expand it horizontally by a factor of 2, translate it 3 units to the left and 4 units downward, and take its absolute value.

Exploring Math

Multiples and Divisors

Multiples and Divisors is a game for two players. The game is played using the whole numbers from 1 to 100.

In the following description of the game, we will call the players Amina and Bruno. An important rule of the game is that *the first number written must be an even number.*

1. Amina plays first by writing an *even* number, say 20.

2. Bruno then writes a number that is an exact multiple or an exact divisor of Amina's number. Suppose Bruno writes 40. He then draws a line through Amina's number, 20, so that this number cannot be used again.

3. Amina then writes a number that is an exact multiple or an exact divisor of Bruno's number, 40. Suppose Amina writes 5. She then draws a line through Bruno's number, 40, so that this number cannot be used again.

4. Now it is Bruno's turn, and he must write an exact multiple or exact divisor of Amina's previous number, 5. The two players continue to play until one player is unable to write a number. This player loses the game.

5. Play the game several times, taking turns to play first. Determine a winning strategy.

6. a) Describe the winning strategy.
b) Explain why the winning strategy works.
c) Explain why you think the game includes the rule that the first number must be an even number.

Chapter Check

Describe how the graph of each of the following functions can be obtained from the graph of y = f(x).

1. $y = f(x) + 4$

2. $y = f(x - 2) + 3$

3. $y = -2(f(x - 1))$

4. $y = \frac{1}{3}f(-3x) + 5$

The graph of y = f(x) is shown. Sketch the graphs of the following functions.

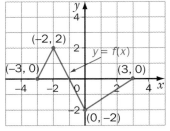

5. $y = f(x) + 3$

6. $y = \frac{1}{2}f(x)$

7. $y = f(3x)$

8. $y = -2f(-x)$

The blue graph is a transformation of the red graph. The equation of the red graph is given. Write the equation of the blue graph.

9.

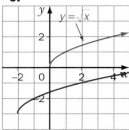

10.

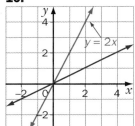

11.

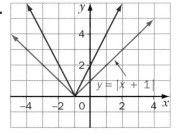

Sketch the graphs of each of the following pairs of functions on the same set of axes.

12. $y = x + 3$ and $y = -2(x + 3)$

13. $y = \sqrt{x}$ and $y = \sqrt{x} - 4$

14. $y = |x|$ and $y = |-x - 5| + 2$

15. $y = (x + 1)^2$ and $y = 2(x + 1)^2 - 3$

16. $y = x^3 - 2$ and $y = (3x^3) - 2$

17. $y = x - 2$ and $y = \frac{1}{x - 2}$

18. $y = |x - 1|$ and $y = |3x - 3| + 2$

In questions 19 to 21, graph f(x) and sketch the specified reflection image. State whether each reflection image represents a function.

19. $h(x)$, the reflection of $f(x) = |x + 1|$ in the y-axis

20. $g(x)$, the reflection of $f(x) = \sqrt{x - 6}$ in the x-axis

21. $k(x)$, the reflection of $f(x) = \frac{3}{x^2 + 1}$ in the line $y = x$

22. The graph of $f(x) = x^2$ is expanded vertically by a factor of 2, translated 3 units to the left, and translated 4 units upward. Write the equation of the transformed function, $h(x)$.

23. The graph of $f(x) = \sqrt{x}$ is compressed horizontally by a factor of $\frac{1}{2}$, reflected in the x-axis, and translated 4 units to the left. Write the equation of the transformed function, $g(x)$.

24. Write the equation that results when the function $f(x) = \frac{3}{x^2 - 4}$ is reflected in the x-axis and translated 3 units to the right.

25. Write the equation that results when you start with $y = x$, compress it horizontally by a factor of $\frac{1}{3}$, shift it 5 units to the right and 3 units downward, and take its absolute value.

26. Write the equation that results when you start with $y = x^2$, expand it vertically by a factor of 4, translate it 2 units to the left and 1 unit upward, and take its reciprocal.

27. Given $f(x) = x(x - 2)(x + 3)$, determine the zeros of each of the following.

a) $y = f(3x)$

b) $y = f(-2x)$

c) $y = 2f(x)$

d) $y = -\frac{1}{2}f(x)$

28. Sketch the graph of $f(x) = \frac{1}{|(x + 3)(x - 1)|}$.

Using the Strategies

1. Find two numbers whose quotient and difference both equal 3.

2. Find a positive number such that the product of $\frac{1}{5}$ of the number and $\frac{1}{9}$ of the number equals the number.

3. Water containers You have a 24-L container that is full of water. You also have three empty containers that can hold 5 L, 11 L, and 13 L. How can you use the containers to divide the water into three equal parts?

4. If you reduce a certain number by 8 and multiply the result by 8, you get the same answer as if you reduce the number by 9 and multiply the result by 9.
a) What is the number?
b) Use algebra to show why your answer is true.
c) Test your reasoning in part b) using different numbers.

5. People walking About how many people can walk past a point on a 4 m wide road in one hour?

6. Fenced field A rectangular field is half as wide as it is long and is completely enclosed by x metres of fencing. Express the area of the field in terms of x.

7. Hockey The chart gives the standings in a four-team hockey league after each team played every other team once.

Team	Won	Lost	Tied	Goals For	Goals Against
Spartans	2	0	1	5	2
Penguins	2	1	0	6	3
Ravens	1	2	0	1	3
Eagles	0	2	1	0	4

Determine the score of each game.

8. Find the number of solutions to the equation $2x + 3y = 715$, if x and y must be positive integers.

9. Evaluate $79\ 999\ 999\ 999^2$.

10. Geometry Prove that, in any parallelogram with side lengths x and y and diagonal lengths s and t, $\dfrac{s^2 + t^2}{x^2 + y^2} = 2$.

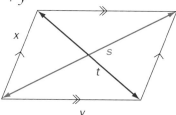

11. The sum of two numbers is 4 and their product is 6. What is the sum of the squares of the reciprocals of these numbers?

12. Solve the following system of equations.
$$a + b + c = 9$$
$$ab + bc + ac = 26$$
$$abc = 24$$

13. A four-digit number, whose digits are the same, is divided by the sum of the digits.

For example, $\dfrac{4444}{4+4+4+4} = \dfrac{4444}{16}$
$$= 277.75$$

Explain why the result is 277.75 for any four-digit number whose digits are the same.

14. Find n such that $\dfrac{n}{2}$ is a perfect square and $\dfrac{n}{3}$ is a perfect cube.

15. Geometry Express the length of the hypotenuse of a right triangle in terms of its area, A, and its perimeter, P.

16. Let $f_0(x) = \dfrac{1}{1-x}$ and $f_{n+1}(x) = f_0(f_n(x))$ for $n = 0, 1, 2, 3, \dots$. Find $f_{100}(100)$.

CHAPTER 2

Exponents and Logarithms

Loud noise can damage the eardrum. The power intensity of noise is measured in watts per square metre (W/m^2), and any noise above $10\ W/m^2$ is painful for the human eardrum. The table shows the power intensity of some noises.

Noise	Power Intensity
lowest level people can hear	$1 \times 10^{-12}\ W/m^2$
soft whisper from 5 m	$1 \times 10^{-9}\ W/m^2$
jet aircraft takeoff from 600 m	$1 \times 10^{-2}\ W/m^2$
light traffic from 15 m	$5 \times 10^{-7}\ W/m^2$
heavy traffic from 15 m	$1 \times 10^{-3}\ W/m^2$
jackhammer from 15 m	$5 \times 10^{-4}\ W/m^2$
loud discotheque	$0.7\ W/m^2$
vacuum cleaner	$1.2 \times 10^{-3}\ W/m^2$
jet aircraft takeoff from 30 m	$100\ W/m^2$

1. List the noises in ascending order of power intensity.

2. How many times as great is the power intensity of a soft whisper from 5 m away as with the lowest level people can hear?

3. How many times as great is the power intensity of a jackhammer as light traffic, both from 15 m away?

4. Is the noise of a jet aircraft taking off 600 m away likely to damage your eardrum? Why or why not? What if you were 30 m away from the plane?

GETTING STARTED

Depreciation

Most car dealers say that a car's trade-in value decreases by about 30% each year. This means that, if you buy a used car for $8000 now, it will be worth 70% of $8000 next year, and 70% of 70% of $8000 the following year.

Copy and complete the table to find the value of the car at various times. Estimate the values first, and then see how close you actually are to the values obtained using a calculator. You might choose to use a spreadsheet or the TABLE feature on a graphing calculator.

Time, t	Expression for the Value	Value in Dollars
3 years ago	8000×0.7^{-3}	
2 years ago		
1 year ago		
now	8000	
in 1 year	8000×0.7	
in 2 years		
in 3 years		
...		
in t years	8000×0.7^t	$V(t)$

1. Choose an appropriate scale and graph the relation between time, t, and value, $V(t)$.

2. Determine approximately how long it will be before the car is worth half of its present value.

3. How long will it be before the car is worth only 10% of its present value? How realistic is this answer?

4. a) Write a defining equation for the relation in the form "$V(t) =$".
b) Are there any restrictions on the value of t in the relation?
c) Are there practical limitations on the value of t in this context? Explain.

5. Does the zero exponent have any meaning in the equation $V(t) = 8000 \times 0.7^0$? Explain.

6. Compare the ratio of the car's value in two years' to its value two years ago. Does this surprise you? Explain.

7. If this particular used car was three years old when purchased, what was its value when new, to the nearest hundred dollars?

Warm Up

The formula for compound interest is
$$A = P(1 + i)^n$$
where A is the amount, P is the principal, i is the rate of interest per compounding period, and n is the number of compounding periods.

The rate of interest is 6% per annum. What is the value of i, in decimal form, if interest is compounded as follows?
1. annually
2. semi-annually
3. monthly
4. quarterly

How many interest periods are there in each of the following?
5. compounding monthly for 3 years
6. compounding quarterly for 5 years
7. compounding semi-annually for 10 years
8. compounding monthly for $1\frac{1}{2}$ years
9. compounding quarterly for 15 months
10. compounding annually for 12 months
11. compounding semi-annually for 30 months

What is the interest rate per period, expressed in decimal form, and the number of periods in each situation?
12. 11%/a compounded quarterly for 3 years
13. 6.5%/a compounded semi-annually for 2 years
14. 2.75%/a compounded annually for 7 years
15. 5.6%/a compounded quarterly for 12 months
16. 15.6%/a compounded monthly for 1 year

The rate of interest charged is 9.5% per annum. Find the amount owing on a loan of $5000 in each case.
17. interest compounded semi-annually for 3 years
18. interest compounded monthly for 2 years
19. interest compounded quarterly for $1\frac{1}{2}$ years
20. interest compounded monthly for 18 months

The rate of interest paid is 4.2%/a. Find the value of an initial investment of $2000 in each compound situation.
21. interest compounded annually for 8 years
22. interest compounded monthly for 2 years
23. interest compounded semi-annually for 5 years
24. interest compounded quarterly for 15 months
25. interest compounded quarterly for $2\frac{1}{2}$ years

Mental Math

Working with Exponents

Express each as a single power.
1. $a^5 \times a^3$
2. $(k^4)^2$
3. $m^6 \div m^2$
4. $t^{-2} \times t^7$
5. $h^0 \div h^{-3}$
6. $(n^{-3})^{-3}$
7. $p^8 \div p^{-1}$
8. $x^5 \times x^{-4} \times x$
9. $(y^{-2})^3 \div y^7$
10. $d^4 \div d^6 \times d^0$
11. $(k^2 \times k^3)^2$
12. $n^{\frac{1}{2}} \times n^{\frac{1}{2}}$

Evaluate.
13. 2^5
14. 3^3
15. 5^0
16. 7^{-1}
17. $4^{\frac{1}{2}}$
18. $(-8)^{\frac{1}{3}}$
19. $9^{-\frac{1}{2}}$
20. $8^{\frac{2}{3}}$
21. $6^{-2} \times 6^2$
22. $(5^5)^{\frac{2}{5}}$
23. $(-27)^{\frac{2}{3}}$
24. $16^{-\frac{1}{4}}$
25. $8^{\frac{1}{3}} \times 16^{-\frac{1}{4}}$
26. $7^0 \div \left(\frac{1}{4}\right)^{\frac{1}{2}}$
27. $100^{0.5} \times 8^{-\frac{1}{3}}$

Express each of the following as a power of 2.
28. 8^x
29. 32^x
30. 0.5^x
31. 4^{3x}
32. $\left(\frac{1}{4}\right)^x$
33. 64^{2x}
34. 16^{x+1}
35. 4^{-x}
36. $16^{\frac{x}{2}}$

Express each of the following as a power of 10.
37. 1000^x
38. 0.01^x
39. $100\,000^{-x}$
40. $0.0001^{\frac{x}{2}}$
41. 100^{2x-1}
42. $0.001^{-\frac{x}{2}}$

In each set, which expression has the least value? Which has the greatest?
43. $3^{-2}, 9^0, (0.5)^2, \left(\frac{1}{2}\right)^{-2}$

44. $125^{\frac{1}{3}}, 32^{\frac{1}{5}}, 100^{\frac{1}{2}}, 64^{\frac{2}{3}}$

45. $\dfrac{4}{8^{\frac{2}{3}}}, 100^{\frac{1}{3}}, 81^{\frac{1}{4}}, 0.5(121)^{\frac{1}{2}}$

INVESTIGATING MATH

Exploring Number Bases

The decimal numeration system in everyday use is also known as the Hindu-Arabic numeration system. The digits 1, 2, 3, 4, 5, 6, 7, 8, and 9 originated in India about 300 B.C., but there is no record of the 0 symbol until much later. In the decimal system, powers of 10 are used to show numbers larger than 9. Throughout history many other systems of numeration involving powers of different bases have been used. For example, the Yuki Indians used base 4, counting the spaces between fingers; in Babylonia, base 12, the duodecimal system, was used first, and then replaced by base 60.

In recent times, base 2, the **binary system**, has become central to the electronic storage of data. Computer programmers also use related systems: the **octal system**, which uses base 8, and the **hexadecimal system**, which uses base 16.

1 Exploring Numbers in Other Bases

The expanded form of the decimal number 34 567 is
$3 \times 10^4 + 4 \times 10^3 + 5 \times 10^2 + 6 \times 10^1 + 7 \times 10^0$.
To specify the base of a number, the base is written to the lower right of the number. The subscript is not used if the base is 10. To convert from some other base to base 10, use the expanded form as follows.
$$34\ 567_8 = 3 \times 8^4 + 4 \times 8^3 + 5 \times 8^2 + 6 \times 8^1 + 7 \times 8^0$$
$$= 14\ 711$$

1. Convert to base 10.
a) 257_8 **b)** 3108_{12} **c)** 3401_8
d) 8214_{16} **e)** 1111_2 **f)** 10111011_2

2. What is the expanded form of $14\ 823_b$?

3. If $75_b = 61$, what is the value of b?

4. For what values of b is $169_b = (13_b)^2$?

5. Copy and complete the table to show the equivalent binary numbers for decimal numbers from 0 to 16.

Decimal Number	Binary Number	Number of Digits in Binary Number
0	0	1
1	1	1
2	10	2

2 Converting From Base 10 to Another Base

To convert from base 10 to another base, divide the decimal number by descending powers of the desired base, as in the following example.

Convert 23 457 into base 8.
First, find the largest power of 8 that is less than or equal to 23 457.
Use $8^1 = 8$, $8^2 = 64$, $8^3 = 512$, $8^4 = 4096$, ... Then proceed as follows.

$$23\ 457 = 5(4096) + 2977$$
$$= 5(4096) + 5(512) + 417$$
$$= 5(4096) + 5(512) + 6(64) + 33$$
$$= 5(4096) + 5(512) + 6(64) + 4(8) + 1$$
$$= 5(8^4) + 5(8^3) + 6(8^2) + 4(8^1) + 1(8^0)$$

So, $23\ 457 = 55\ 641_8$.

There is another way of doing the conversion. See if you can justify why it works from the example shown.

$$8)\overline{23\ 457}$$
$$8)\overline{2\ 932} \rightarrow 1$$
$$8)\overline{366} \rightarrow 4$$
$$8)\overline{45} \rightarrow 6$$
$$5 \rightarrow 5$$

Starting from the bottom and going up gives $55\ 641_8$.

1. a) Convert 451 to base 8.
b) Convert 285 to base 2.

2. Predict how many digits each number will have in binary form. Then, check by doing the conversion.
a) 4013   **b)** 3456

3. Hexadecimal numbers use the digits 0, 1, 2, ... , 9, A, B, C, D, E, F, where A = 10, B = 11, ... , F = 15. Express each of the following in hexadecimal form.
a) 2541   **b)** 3456   **c)** 35 871

4. Programmers use the octal and hexadecimal forms of numbers because it is relatively easy to convert between them and binary numbers. Copy and complete the table to show the numbers in each system that are equivalent to the decimal numbers 0 to 16.

Decimal	Binary	Octal	Hexadecimal
0	000	00	0
1	001	01	

5. Hexadecimal numbers are used in HTML computer programs to code colours. Colour values have six digits in them. The first two digits give the intensity of red, the next two digits give the intensity of green, and the last two digits give the intensity of blue. The greatest two-digit hexadecimal is FF, so the code FF0000 describes full intensity red.
a) Describe the colour that would correspond to 00FF00.
b) How many different intensities of blue can be shown?

6. When a certain binary number is converted to hexadecimal form, it has three fewer digits. However, its decimal form and hexadecimal form have the same number of digits.
a) How many digits are in the binary representation of the original number?
b) Between which decimal numbers does the original number lie?
c) Repeat parts a) and b) if the hexadecimal form has six fewer digits than the binary form, but again the decimal and hexadecimal forms have the same number of digits.

PROBLEM SOLVING

2.1 Use a Data Bank

You must locate information to solve some problems. There are many sources of information, including the Internet, the media, print data banks, and experts.

The brightness of planets and stars as they appear from the Earth is described on a scale of apparent magnitudes. A lower apparent magnitude signifies a brighter object. A difference of 5 magnitudes corresponds to a factor of 100 times as bright. So, a star of magnitude 3 is 100 times as bright as a star of magnitude 8, and a star of magnitude 0 is 100 times as bright as a star of magnitude 5.

A difference of 1 magnitude corresponds to a factor of $\sqrt[5]{100}$ times as bright. A difference of 2 magnitudes corresponds to $\sqrt[5]{100} \times \sqrt[5]{100}$ or $\left(\sqrt[5]{100}\right)^2$ times as bright. A positive difference of d corresponds to $\left(\sqrt[5]{100}\right)^d$ times as bright.

Aside from our sun, the brightest star in the sky is Sirius. How many times as bright as the North Star, Polaris, is Sirius, to the nearest whole number?

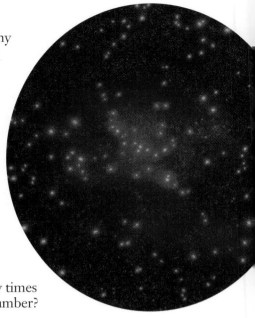

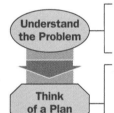
Understand the Problem

1. What information are you given?
2. What are you asked to find?
3. Do you need an exact or an approximate answer?

Think of a Plan

Locate values for the apparent magnitudes of Sirius and Polaris. Find the positive difference, d, between these magnitudes. Substitute the difference into the formula $\left(\sqrt[5]{100}\right)^d$ to find how many times as bright Sirius is as Polaris.

Carry Out the Plan

The apparent magnitude of Sirius is –1.5, and the apparent magnitude of Polaris is 2. The positive difference, $d = 2 - (-1.5)$
$$= 3.5$$
Substitute for d in the formula.
$$\left(\sqrt[5]{100}\right)^d = \left(\sqrt[5]{100}\right)^{3.5}$$
$$= (100^{\frac{1}{5}})^{3.5}$$
$$= 100^{0.7}$$
$$\doteq 25$$

So, Sirius is 25 times as bright as Polaris, to the nearest whole number.

Check by estimation.
A difference of 1 magnitude means a factor of $\sqrt[5]{100}$, which is about 2.5.
A difference of 3 magnitudes is a factor of about $2.5 \times 2.5 \times 2.5$, or about 15.
A difference of 4 magnitudes is a factor of about $2.5 \times 2.5 \times 2.5 \times 2.5$, or about 40.
So, a difference of 3.5 magnitudes is a factor between about 15 and 40.

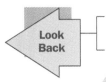

Look Back

Does the answer seem reasonable?
Is there a way to solve the problem graphically?

Use a Data Bank

1. Locate the information you need.
2. Solve the problem.
3. Check that the answer is reasonable.

Applications and Problem Solving

Locate the necessary information and solve the problems.

1. Moons Most planets in our solar system have moons. Which planets have moons that are larger than the planet Mercury?

2. Land area Suppose the land area of each province were divided equally among all the people living in that province. In which province would a person receive
a) the most land?   **b)** the least land?

3. Species at risk Species at risk are grouped into five categories: extinct, extirpated, endangered, threatened, or vulnerable.
a) What does each category mean?
b) What things are included when the word *species* is used?
c) What is the total number of species now at risk in Canada?
d) What is the average annual rate of increase in the species at risk in Canada?
e) What is the current estimate of the rate of extinction of species worldwide?

4. Astronomy Some objects in our solar system can be brighter than the brightest stars in the night sky. The moon and the planet Venus can be the brightest objects. How many times as bright is a full moon as the planet Venus, when Venus is at its brightest? Round your answer to the nearest whole number.

5. Driving distance a) What is the shortest driving distance from Edmonton to Brownsville, Texas?
b) How long would the trip take if you could average 100 km/h and you drove, at most, 10 h a day?

6. National debt If Canada's current national debt were divided equally among all Canadians, what would be each person's share?

7. Coastal communities What percent of Canadians live in coastal communities?

8. Identifying people Verification systems based on hand geometry have been developed to identify people. These systems are suited for applications that do not require extreme security.
a) How do these systems use hand measurements to identify people?
b) Where could these systems be used?

9. Renewable energy a) What percent of Canadian energy comes from renewable sources, such as solar and wind power?
b) What is the projected percent increase in renewable energy use over the next 25 years?
c) What country produces the most wind energy? What is Canada's wind energy production as a percent of that country's wind energy production?

10. Canada a) What percent of the world's population lives in Canada?
b) What percent of the world's energy consumption is used by Canadians?

11. Oil supply a) Graph the actual and projected annual world oil production for every tenth year from 1950 to 2050.
b) On the same set of axes or in the same viewing window, graph the actual and projected annual world oil consumption for every tenth year from 1950 to 2050.
c) Use the data to decide if oil consumption is projected to exceed oil production before the year 2051.

12. Write a problem using information from a data bank. Have a classmate locate the information and solve your problem.

INVESTIGATING MATH

Exploring Exponential Functions

In the following explorations, use a graphing calculator or draw the graphs manually.

1. a) Graph the function $y = 2^x$.
b) Describe the features of the graph, listing the domain, the range, the intercepts, and the equations of any asymptotes.
c) Is the function continuous? Explain.

2. Consider the function $y = 2^x - 1$.
a) Predict how the graph of this function will compare with the graph of $y = 2^x$. Describe any similarities and any differences that you expect.
b) Graph the function $y = 2^x - 1$. Give the domain, the range, the intercepts, and the equations of any asymptotes. Were your predictions correct?
c) How would you expect the graph of $y = 2^x + 1$ to compare to the graph of $y = 2^x$? Check by graphing.

3. a) Graph $y = 2^x$ and $y = 3(2^x)$ on the same graph. Describe the similarities and the differences between the two graphs.
b) Predict how the graph of $y = 4(2^x)$ would compare with the graphs in a). Check by graphing.
c) What transformation relates the graphs of $y = b^x$ and $y = Ab^x$, where $b > 1$, and $A \neq 0, 1$?

4. a) Graph $y = 2^x$ and $y = 3^x$ on the same graph. Describe the similarities and the differences between the two graphs.
b) Predict how the graph of $y = 5^x$ would compare with the graphs in a). Check by graphing.
c) Describe the features of the graph of $y = b^x$, where $b > 1$, listing the domain, the range, the intercepts, and the equations of any asymptotes.
d) At what point does the graph of $y = a^x$ intersect the graph of $y = b^x$, where $a, b > 1$?

5. a) Graph $y = 2^x$ and $y = 2^{-x}$ on the same graph. How are the graphs related? Describe their similarities and their differences.
b) Graph $y = 3^x$ and $y = 3^{-x}$ on the same graph. How are the graphs related? Describe their similarities and their differences.
c) What transformation relates the graphs of $y = b^x$ and of $y = b^{-x}$, where $b > 1$?
d) If the point (4, 2401) is on the graph of $y = b^x$, what point must be on the graph of $y = b^{-x}$?

6. Now consider the graph of the function $y = b^x$ for $0 < b \leq 1$.
a) Describe the graph of $y = b^x$ if $b = 1$.
b) Graph the function $y = \left(\dfrac{1}{2}\right)^x$. What do you notice? Explain why.
c) Predict the appearance of the graph of $y = \left(\dfrac{1}{3}\right)^x$. Give reasons for your answer.

7. Summarize the properties of exponential functions of the form $y = b^x$, where $b > 0$. Be sure to describe the difference between when $b < 1$ and when $b > 1$. What features are common to all such functions?

8. Consider the exponential function $y = b^x$, and the points (m, b^m) and (n, b^n) on the curve. If $b^m = b^n$, what can you conclude about the values of m and n? Explain why.

9. Exponential functions are defined as functions of the form $y = b^x$, where $b > 0$. Consider why the base is restricted to values greater than zero.
a) If $b = 0$, what happens to the equation?
b) What if $b < 0$? Try to obtain a graph of $y = (-2)^x$, either by making a table of values or by using a graphing calculator. If you use a graphing calculator, examine the TABLE. Describe at least two features of this graph that make it different from those of the exponential functions you have graphed.

2.2 Exponential Functions as Models of Growth or Decay

Exponential functions can be used to model many real world phenomena, such as population growth, the growth or decay of various substances, and the value of investments that are earning compound interest.

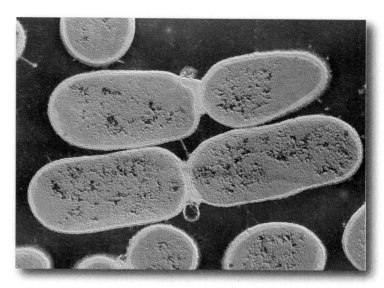

Bacteria and other unicellular organisms reproduce by the process of fission. The organism divides into two roughly equal halves. Under ideal conditions, bacteria can double every 20 to 30 min. From a single bacterial cell, after one doubling period there will be 2 cells, after two doubling periods there will be 2^2 or 4 cells, after three doubling periods there will be 2^3 or 8 cells, and so on. The number of bacteria grows exponentially as a power of 2.

Explore: Develop a Model

A type of bacteria is doubling every 30 min. Copy and complete the table to show the pattern in the growth of the number of bacteria. Then, graph the data. Write an equation that shows the number of bacteria, B, that a single bacterium will grow to in n doubling periods.

Number of Doubling Periods, n	Number of Bacteria, B
0	1
1	2
2	
3	
4	
5	
6	

Inquire

1. What type of equation relates B and n?

2. Does it make sense to join the data points in this situation? Explain.

3. After 2 h, how many bacteria will result from a single bacterium?

4. If there were 100 bacteria initially in a sample of the same type, how many bacteria would there be 2 h later? What equation would give the number of bacteria after n doubling periods, for this sample?

5. A culture has a bacterial count of 500 now. What equation would give the number of bacteria that are present t hours from now?

6. How could you use the equation from the previous question to find the number of bacteria that were present one hour before the count was done?

7. Consider a sample that doubles every k min and has an initial count of B_0. Write an equation to represent the number of bacteria, $B(t)$, present as a function of time, t, in hours, since the initial count.

Functions such as the one relating the number of bacteria to time are exponential functions. An **exponential function** is a function of the form
$$f(x) = Ab^x$$
where A is a constant and $b > 0$.

Example 1   Using an Exponential Function
A certain culture of bacteria, given suitable conditions, triples every 25 h. The initial count of a sample shows 1000 bacteria present.
a) Write an exponential function that models the given conditions.
b) Approximately how many bacteria will there be in 4 days?
c) How many bacteria were there 3 days prior to the count?

Solution
a) Let $B(t)$ represent the number of bacteria at any time, t, where t is in hours. Then, since the initial population is 1000 and the number is tripling every 25 h,

$$B(t) = 1000(3^{\frac{t}{25}})$$

b) 4 days is 4×24 hours. Use $t = 96$.

$$B(96) = 1000\left(3^{\frac{96}{25}}\right)$$
$$\doteq 67\ 943$$

In 4 days, approximately 68 000 bacteria will be present.

> **Estimate**
> $$1000(3)^{\frac{96}{25}} \doteq 1000(3^4)$$
> $$= 81\ 000$$

```
1000*3^(96/25)
        67943.14065
```

c) 3 days ago is (-3×24) hours. Use $t = -72$.

$$B(-3) = 1000\left(3^{-\frac{72}{25}}\right)$$
$$\doteq 42$$
Three days prior to the count, there were approximately 42 bacteria.

> **Estimate**
> $$1000\left(3^{-\frac{72}{25}}\right) \doteq 1000(3^{-3})$$
> $$= 1000 \times \frac{1}{27}$$
> $$\doteq \frac{1000}{25}$$
> $$= 40$$

```
1000*3^(-72/25)
        42.25623376
```

In the previous example, an exponential function was used to model a growth situation, and the equation was used to solve related problems. The next example shows how the graph of an exponential function can be used to solve related problems.

Example 2　Using the Graph of an Exponential Function

An investment of $500 is earning interest at 6%/a compounded semi-annually.
a) Write an exponential function that represents the amount of the investment, $A(t)$, in dollars, after t years.
b) Graph the function. Use the graph to determine approximately how many years it will take for the amount of the investment to double.

Solution

a) For compound interest, the amount, $A(t)$, is related to the principal, P, by the formula $A(t) = P(1 + i)^n$, where t is the time in years, i is the interest rate per compounding period, and n is the number of compounding periods.

$P = 500$, $i = \dfrac{6\%}{2}$ or 0.03, $n = 2t$

$\therefore A(t) = 500(1 + 0.03)^{2t}$
An exponential function for the amount of the investment after t years is
$A(t) = 500(1.03)^{2t}$

b) *Method 1:* Graph manually.

t in years	A(t)
0	500
1	530.45
2	562.75
5	671.96
10	903.06
15	1213.63

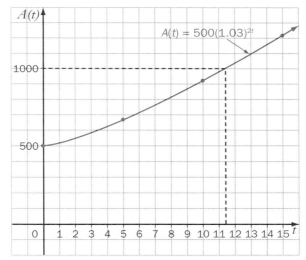

Interpolate the value of t when $A(t) = 1000$.

From the graph, $t \doteq 11\dfrac{1}{2}$.

The investment of $500 at 6%/a compounded semi-annually doubles after approximately 12 years.

Method 2: Use a graphing calculator.
Graph $y = 500(1.03)^{2x}$.
Adjust the domain and range so you can see when the exponential curve exceeds a y-value of 1000.
Then, use TRACE to find the value of x when $y = 1000$.
Alternatively, you can enter the line Y2 = 1000 and use INTERSECT to find the answer.

The investment of $500 at 6%/a compounded semi-annually doubles after approximately 12 years.

In some situations, instead of growth, exponential decay is occurring. The following example illustrates this type of situation.

Example 3   Working With Exponential Decay

The intensity of the light below the surface of a particular lake is reduced by 4% for every metre below the surface.

a) Write an exponential function that models the intensity of the light at any depth below the surface.

b) What percent of the original intensity of the light remains 10 m below the surface?

c) Use a graph to determine how far below the surface the light has to travel for its intensity to be 30% of the surface intensity. Round the answer to the nearest tenth of a metre.

Solution

a) Since the intensity is reduced by 4%, it is 100% − 4%, or 96%, of the intensity occurring one metre above, for every metre below the surface the light has to travel.

Let $I(d)$ represent the intensity at a depth of d metres, and I_0, the original intensity. Then,

$I(d) = I_0(0.96)^d$

b) When $d = 10$

$I(d) = I_0(0.96)^{10}$

$\doteq 0.6648\, I_0$

At a depth of 10 m, about 66% of the original intensity of the light remains.

c) *Method 1*: Graph manually.

At a depth d, the percent of the original intensity remaining is given by

$\dfrac{I(d)}{I_0} = 0.96^d$.

d in metres	$\dfrac{I(d)}{I_0} = 0.96^d$
0	1
2	0.9216
4	0.8493
8	0.7214
12	0.6127
16	0.5204
20	0.4420
24	0.3754
28	0.3189
32	0.2708

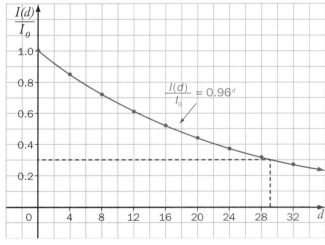

The light is reduced to 30% of the surface intensity at a depth of about 29.5 m.

Method 2: Use a graphing calculator.
If the intensity is 30% of the surface intensity, then $I(d) = 0.3I_0$.
$0.3I_0 = I_0(0.96)^d$
$\therefore\ 0.3 = 0.96^d$
Graph the function $y = 0.96^x$.
To find the value of x for which $y = 0.3$, either
use TRACE or graph the line $y = 0.3$ and use INTERSECT.

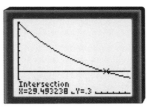

The light is reduced to 30% of the surface intensity at a depth of about 29.5 m.

Practice

*Use the graph of $y = 3^x$ to find the approximate value
of each power.*
1. $3^{1.5}$ **2.** $3^{0.5}$ **3.** $3^{-0.25}$

*Use the graph of $y = 3^x$ to find the approximate value
of x satisfying each equation.*
4. $3^x = 5$ **5.** $3^x = 7$ **6.** $3^x = -0.25$

*Use the graph of $y = \left(\dfrac{1}{3}\right)^x$ to find the approximate
value of each power.*
7. $\left(\dfrac{1}{3}\right)^{0.25}$ **8.** $\left(\dfrac{1}{3}\right)^{-1.25}$ **9.** $\left(\dfrac{1}{3}\right)^{-0.75}$

*Use the graph of $y = \left(\dfrac{1}{3}\right)^x$ to find the approximate
value of x satisfying each equation.*
10. $\left(\dfrac{1}{3}\right)^x = 0.5$ **11.** $\left(\dfrac{1}{3}\right)^x = 4$ **12.** $\left(\dfrac{1}{3}\right)^x = 6$

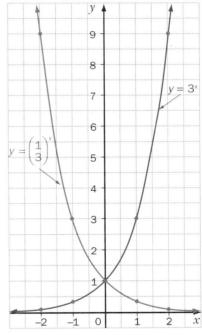

*Because of conservation efforts, the number of
bullfrogs in a marsh area is increasing by 15% each
year. Use the graph showing the growth of the
population for the first six years to answer the
following questions.*
13. How many bullfrogs were there at the initial
count?
14. How many years did it take for the
population to double?
15. After how many years were there over 100
bullfrogs in the area?

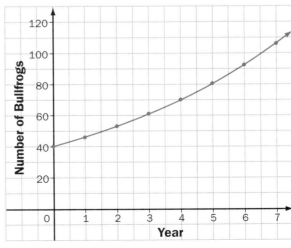

2.2 Exponential Functions as Models of Growth or Decay   81

The doubling period of a bacterium is 20 min. If there are 300 bacteria in a culture initially, how many bacteria will there be after each time period?
16. 40 min   **17.** 1 h   **18.** 2 h

The number of bacteria, N(t), in a culture is given by $N(t) = 9000 \times 2^{\frac{t}{4}}$, where t is the time elapsed in hours since the initial count.
19. How many bacteria were there at the initial count?
20. What is the doubling period, in minutes, for this type of bacterium?
21. After what time period would you expect there to be 36 000 bacteria?
22. How many bacteria will be present one day later?
23. How many bacteria, to the nearest ten, will be present 30 min after the initial count?

Applications and Problem Solving

24. Gopher population The summertime population of gophers in a field can be modelled by the equation $P(n) = 100(1.1)^n$, where *n* is measured in years from now. Plot the graph for the first 10-year period, and use the graph to find out approximately how long it will take for the gopher population to double.

25. Bacteria A type of bacterium doubles every 45 min and there are 5000 now.
a) Write an equation of the form $P(t) = P_0(2)^{kt}$, that will give the number of bacteria $P(t)$ at any time *t*, in minutes, where P_0 represents the original population.
b) How many bacteria will there be in 90 min? in 135 min? in 180 min?
c) How many bacteria were there 22.5 min ago?
d) How many bacteria will there be in 10 h?
e) How many bacteria were there 3 h ago?
f) Graph the function and use your graph to estimate how long it will take before there are ten times as many bacteria as there are now.

26. Population growth A country's population is growing at the rate of 3% annually. Assume that the population is now 30 million.
a) Write an exponential function that relates the population, $P(t)$, in millions, and the time *t* in years from now.

b) What will the population be in 15 years, to the nearest tenth of a million?
c) Approximately how many years will it take for the population to double?
d) What factors could cause your model to break down?

27. Population decrease The population of a rural community is 18 000 now but is decreasing by 13% each year.
a) Write an exponential function that relates the population $P(t)$ and the time *t* in years from now.
b) What will the population be in 4 years, to the nearest hundred?
c) In approximately how many years will only half of the current population remain?
d) What factors could cause this model to change?

28. Investment Suppose you have an investment that is earning 5%/a interest compounded annually and the investment is worth $1700 now.
a) Write an exponential function that will give the value of this investment at any time *t*.
b) How much will the investment be worth in 6 years?
c) How much was the investment worth 2 years ago?
d) Use a graph of the function to approximate how long it will take the current value of the investment to double.
e) Suppose you did not know the current value of the investment and simply called it P_0. Would the answer to d) change?

29. Light intensity In a particularly murky river, the intensity of light is reduced by 5% for every metre that the light travels below the surface of the water.
a) Set up an exponential model that gives the intensity of light as a function of the depth below the surface.
b) What percent of the original intensity remains at a depth of 7 m?
c) To the nearest metre, at what depth would there be only 10% of the original intensity of the light remaining?

30. Investments Laura has savings of $1200 on which she is earning 6.25% per annum interest compounded annually. Marco has $2000 that is earning 4.75% per annum interest compounded annually.
a) Write exponential functions for the amount that each person has after t years.
b) Graph both functions.
c) How long will it take Laura to double her money?
d) How long will it take Marco to double his money?
e) How long would it take for Laura to have the same amount of money as Marco and what is this amount?

31. Population An equation of the form $P = P_0(b^t)$ models a population that is changing exponentially with time.
a) What does each of the variables in this expression represent? State any restrictions on each variable.
b) How can you tell, from the equation, whether the population is increasing or decreasing?

32. World population The world's population is growing exponentially.
a) The world's population in 1970 was about 3.6 billion. If the population has increased at 2% per year since then, what will the world's population be in 2010?
b) How long will it take the population in the year 2000 to double?
c) What was the population in the year 1960? What assumption have you made?

33. World food supply It is generally assumed that about 0.824 ha of land is needed to provide food for one person. There are about 25 billion hectares of arable land in the world.
a) What is the maximum sustainable population, assuming that no other sources of food are available?
b) Using the growth rate and information from the previous question, determine in what year the maximum population will be reached.

34. Computer speeds In 1950 a computer could perform about 2700 calculations per second. The speed of computers became about 10 times as fast every 7 years.
a) Set up an exponential model for the number of calculations a computer could do at any time t, in years, since 1950.
b) Approximately how many calculations per second could a computer perform in 1990?
c) How many calculations per second will a computer be able to perform in the year 2009? Do you think this answer is realistic? Give reasons for your answer.

LOGIC POWER

Polyominoes are shapes made up of unit squares attached to each other along one or more edges. Polyominoes are considered to be distinct if there is no rotation or reflection that superimposes them. For example, two unit squares can be attached in only one way, along one edge to form a single domino. Pentominoes are formed by joining five unit squares. There are 12 distinct pentominoes as shown.

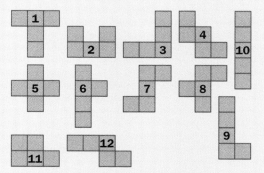

• Which of the pentominoes can be used, on their own, to tile the plane? In other words, which can be replicated to cover the plane with no spaces?
• Find a way of fitting all 12 pentominoes together to cover a 6 by 10 rectangle.
• Find a way of fitting all 12 pentominoes together to cover a 3 by 20 rectangle.

PROBLEM SOLVING

2.3 Guess and Check

One way to solve a problem is to guess the answer and then check to see whether it is correct. If it is not, you can keep guessing and checking until you get the right answer.

When a ball is dropped onto the ground, it rebounds to a certain percent of its original height. As the ball continues to bounce, the height of the each rebound is the same percent of the height of the previous rebound. For example, if a ball that rebounds to 70% of its original height is dropped from a height of 150 cm, the height of the first rebound is 0.7×150 or 105 cm. The height of the second rebound is 0.7×105 or 73.5 cm. If a ball that rebounds to 75% of its original height is dropped from a height of 2 m, or 200 cm, the height, h centimetres, of the ball after n bounces is given by the following equation.

$$h = 200(0.75)^n$$

After how many bounces is the height of the ball about 20 cm?

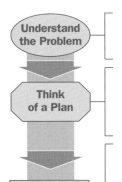

Understand the Problem

1. What information are you given?
2. What are you asked to find?
3. Do you need an exact or an approximate answer?

Think of a Plan

Set up a table. Guess at the number of bounces. Use the guess to calculate the height of the ball after this number of bounces.
If the calculated height is not about 20 cm, make another guess at the number of bounces and calculate the height again.

Carry Out the Plan

Guess		Check
n	Calculation of h	Is h about 20 cm?
5	$200(0.75)^5 \doteq 35.6$	h too high
10	$200(0.75)^{10} \doteq 8.4$	h too low
8	$200(0.75)^8 \doteq 15.0$	h too low
7	$200(0.75)^7 \doteq 20.0$	20 checks!

The height of the ball was about 20 cm after 7 bounces.

Look Back

Does the answer seem reasonable?
Is there a way to solve the problem graphically?

Guess and Check

1. Guess a possible answer.
2. Use the answer to check against a known fact.
3. If necessary, adjust your guess and check again.

Applications and Problem Solving

1. Room types A hotel has four different types of rooms. For type A, it charges $60 per night, for type B, $90, for type C, $110, and for type D, $120. There are 100 rooms altogether, and, if they are all rented, the total receipts for the night are $10 500. How many of each type of room are there if the numbers of each type are all multiples of 10?

2. What are the values of a, b, c, and d if the following four equations are all true?

$$a + b + c + d = 10$$
$$abcd = 24$$
$$a^2 + b^2 + c^2 + d^2 = 30$$
$$a^3 + b^3 + c^3 + d^3 = 100$$

3. Tests There were 33 questions on a multiple choice test. Each correct answer was worth 7 marks. For each wrong answer 4 marks were deducted. John answered all the questions. His mark on the test was 0. How many questions did he answer correctly?

4. Copy the diagram shown below. Place five of the digits from 1 to 9 in the circles so that at least one of the two-digit numbers formed by each pair of numbers joined by a line is divisible by 13 or 7. The digits can be paired in either order.

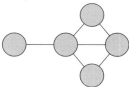

5. Cereal box The area of the front of a cereal box is 532 cm², the area of each side is 140 cm², and the area of the bottom is 95 cm². What is the volume of the box?

6. What are the digits A, B, and C if the following equation is true?

$$(AA)^2 = BBCC$$

7. A balanced number has exactly one digit that is the sum of all the other digits. For example, 1236 is balanced because $1 + 2 + 3 = 6$. What is the greatest three-digit balanced number?

8. Copy this grid. Write one non-zero digit in each square to make two 2-digit numbers across and two 2-digit numbers down so that the sum of the four 2-digit numbers is 67.

9. Each ✱ represents a digit in this multiplication. None of the digits is 0.

If the product is as small as possible, what are the two-digit and three-digit numbers?

10. Find two different numbers such that $a^b = b^a$.

11. Proposition A mother wanted her daughter Anita to do well in math. So, she made a proposition: "Anita, here are 26 problems for you to solve. For each one that you get right, I will give you $8, but for each one that you miss, you will give me $5." When Anita had finished the problems, she and her mother were even. How many problems did Anita solve correctly?

12. Show that there exist positive integers x, y, z, and t that satisfy the equation $x^2 + y^2 + z^2 = t^2$.

13. Buying paper cups Paper cups can be bought in packages of 15 or 25. Josh bought seven packages and got 125 cups. How many of each size of package did he buy?

14. Basketball Michaela made 12 of her first 30 shots in the first three games of the basketball season. In her next game, she took 10 shots and raised her shooting average to 50%. How many of the 10 shots did she make?

15. Write a problem that can be solved using the guess-and-check strategy. Have a classmate solve your problem.

2.4 Solving Exponential Equations

Viruses can spread quickly. If it is known that an infectious virus doubles every 9 min, and that a person will show symptoms of the infection when 8^{23} of the viruses are present in the person's body, how long will it take for the first symptoms to appear after initial infection?

When mathematicians encounter a new type of problem for which a method of solution is not immediately apparent, they will sometimes resort to a "guess and test" strategy. Often this approach leads to a more sophisticated method of solving the problem.

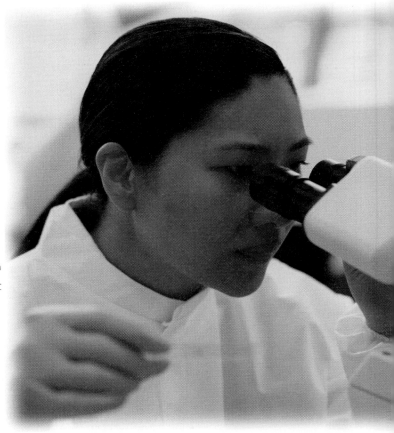

Explore: Use Trial and Error

If $8^{x-3} = (2^{x-2})^2$, then what is the value of x? Use a trial-and-error approach to find what value of x makes both sides of the equation have the same value, organizing your work in a table.

Value of x	L.S. $= 8^{x-3}$	R.S. $= (2^{x-2})^2$
2	$8^{2-3} = 8^{-1}$ $= \frac{1}{8}$	
3		

Inquire

1. Why do you think that the least value of x tested was 2?

2. The numbers 8 and 2 are both powers of a common base. What is this base? Rewrite the equation $8^{x-3} = (2^{x-2})^2$ using the common base. Use the properties of exponents to simplify the exponents.

3. Explain why you can now use a linear equation in x to solve the original equation.

4. Solve the linear equation. Did you obtain the same value for x as you did using trial and error?

5. Explain why this question would be more difficult to do if the 8 were changed to 25.

6. How could you have solved the equation $8^{x-3} = (2^{x-2})^2$ by graphing functions? Use a graphing calculator to verify the solution using this method.

One method of solving an exponential equation is based on the property that if $a^x = a^y$ then $x = y$, for $a \neq -1, 0, 1$.

Example 1   Solving Exponential Equations by Using a Common Base

Solve for x.

a) $8^{3x-2} = 16^{x+1}$

b) $27^{x+3} = \left(\dfrac{1}{9}\right)^{2x-5}$

c) $\dfrac{8^{x+6}}{16^{2x-1}} = 32^{3x-4}$

Solution

a)
$$8^{3x-2} = 16^{x+1}$$
$$(2^3)^{3x-2} = (2^4)^{x+1} \qquad \text{Since } 8 = 2^3 \text{ and } 16 = 2^4, \text{ rewrite using base 2.}$$
$$2^{9x-6} = 2^{4x+4} \qquad \text{Simplify the exponents using the power of a power property.}$$

Since both sides are single powers of the same base, the exponents must be equal. Equate exponents.
$$9x - 6 = 4x + 4$$
$$5x = 10$$
$$x = 2$$

b)
$$27^{x+3} = \left(\dfrac{1}{9}\right)^{2x-5}$$
$$(3^3)^{x+3} = (3^{-2})^{2x-5} \qquad \text{Express 27 and } \dfrac{1}{9} \text{ as powers of the same base, 3.}$$
$$3^{3x+9} = 3^{-4x+10} \qquad \text{Simplify exponents.}$$
$$3x + 9 = -4x + 10 \qquad \text{Equate exponents.}$$
$$7x = 1$$
$$x = \dfrac{1}{7}$$

c)
$$\dfrac{8^{x+6}}{16^{2x-1}} = 32^{3x-4}$$
$$\dfrac{(2^3)^{x+6}}{(2^4)^{2x-1}} = (2^5)^{3x-4} \qquad \text{Express 8, 16, and 32 as powers of their common base, 2.}$$
$$\dfrac{2^{3x+18}}{2^{8x-4}} = 2^{15x-20} \qquad \text{Simplify exponents.}$$
$$2^{3x+18-(8x-4)} = 2^{15x-20} \qquad \text{Simplify the left side using the quotient of powers law.}$$
$$2^{-5x+22} = 2^{15x-20}$$
$$-5x + 22 = 15x - 20 \qquad \text{Equate exponents.}$$
$$42 = 20x$$
$$x = 2.1$$

There are many exponential growth or decay situations in which skills with exponential equations can be used. The **half-life** of a substance is the length of time it takes for the substance to decay to half of its original amount. Analysis of half-lives is very important in some medical tests and in archaeology.

Example 2 Modelling Exponential Decay

To determine whether a person has a thyroid deficiency, a radioactive iodine with a half-life of 8.2 d is injected into the blood stream. A healthy thyroid gland absorbs all the radioactivity.

a) Determine an exponential function that models the amount of radioactive iodine that should be present in the thyroid gland of a healthy person after any number of days.

b) After how long should only 25% of the radioactive iodine be present in the thyroid gland of a healthy person? *Hint:* You do not need a calculator.

Solution

a) Let $A(d)$ represent the amount of radioactive iodine present in the thyroid gland after d days and A_0, the original amount injected into the blood stream. Since the substance is decreasing by one half every 8.2 d, the equation is

$$A(d) = A_0 \left(\frac{1}{2}\right)^{\frac{d}{8.2}} \quad \text{or} \quad A(d) = A_0 (0.5)^{\frac{d}{8.2}}.$$

b) $25\% = \dfrac{1}{4}$

In $A(d) = A_0 \left(\dfrac{1}{2}\right)^{\frac{d}{2}}$, use $A(d) = \dfrac{1}{4} A_0$.

$$\frac{1}{4} A_0 = A_0 \left(\frac{1}{2}\right)^{\frac{d}{8.2}}$$

$$\therefore \quad \left(\frac{1}{2}\right)^2 = \left(\frac{1}{2}\right)^{\frac{d}{8.2}}$$

Equate exponents. $\dfrac{d}{8.2} = 2$

$$d = 16.4$$

Only 25% of the radioactive iodine should be present in the thyroid gland of a healthy person after 16.4 d.

Example 3 Finding the Doubling Period

A bacterial culture starts with 3000 bacteria. After 3 h the estimated count is 48 000. What is the doubling period for this bacterial culture?

Solution

Let d represent the doubling period, in hours, for the bacterial culture.

So, in 3 h the number of bacteria will double $\dfrac{3}{d}$ times.

Let $N(t)$ represent the number of bacteria after t hours, so $N(0) = 3000$ and $N(3) = 48\ 000$.

An equation for the number of bacteria at any time is as follows:

$$N(t) = N(0) \times 2^{\frac{t}{d}}$$

Then,

$$48\,000 = 3000 \times 2^{\frac{3}{d}}$$

$$\frac{48\,000}{3000} = 2^{\frac{3}{d}}$$

$$16 = 2^{\frac{3}{d}}$$

$$2^4 = 2^{\frac{3}{d}}$$

Equate exponents.

$$4 = \frac{3}{d}$$

$$d = \frac{3}{4}$$

The doubling period for this bacterial culture is $\frac{3}{4}$ h.

Example 4   Finding the Time Elapsed

Once inside the human body, a particularly infectious virus doubles every 9 min. The first symptoms of infection occur when there are about 8^{23} of these viruses present in the body. If a person is infected with a single virus now, how long will it take for the first symptoms to appear?

Solution

The population, $P(t)$, of the virus at any time t is given by the relation,

$P(t) = P_0(2^{\frac{t}{9}})$, where P_0 represents the original population and t the time in minutes. Use $P_0 = 1$ and solve for t when $P(t) = 8^{23}$.

$$8^{23} = 2^{\frac{t}{9}}$$

$$(2^3)^{23} = 2^{\frac{t}{9}}$$

$$2^{69} = 2^{\frac{t}{9}}$$

Equate exponents.

$$\frac{t}{9} = 69$$

$$t = 621$$

The first symptoms will occur 621 min, or 10 h 21 min, after the person is infected.

Practice

Solve.

1. $27^x = 9^{2x-1}$

2. $4^{2x-1} = 64$

3. $6^{3x-6} = 1$

4. $2^{-x} = 128$

5. $5^{4-x} = \frac{1}{5}$

6. $32^{3x-2} = 64$

7. $2^{-2x} = 32$

8. $4^{8x} = \frac{1}{16}$

9. $3^{2x-1} + 1 = 2$

10. $3(5^{x+1}) = 15$

Solve.

11. $\dfrac{27^x}{9^{2x-1}} = 3^{x+4}$

12. $27^x(9^{2x-1}) = 3^{x+4}$

13. $\sqrt[5]{256} \div \sqrt[6]{64} = 2^x$

14. $\dfrac{(9^{2x-1})^3(3^{3x})^2}{(27^{x+2})^4} = 81^3$

15. $8(2x-1)^3 = 125$

16. $8^{\frac{1}{4}} \times \left(\dfrac{1}{4}\right)^{\frac{x}{2}} = 16^{\frac{3}{4}}$

Strontium-90 has a half-life of 25 years. How much time has elapsed if the following fraction remains in a sample?

17. $\dfrac{1}{4}$ **18.** 12.5% **19.** $\dfrac{1}{32}$

What is the half-life of each substance?

20. After 30 h, a sample of plutonium-243 decays to $\dfrac{1}{64}$ of its original amount.

21. In 40.8 years, a sample of lead-210 decays to 25% of its original amount.

22. In eight days, a sample of vanadium-48 decays to $\dfrac{1}{\sqrt{2}}$ of its original amount.

23. In 2 min, a sample of radium-221 decays to 6.25% of its original amount.

Applications and Problem Solving

24. Solve each equation.

a) $\sqrt[5]{\dfrac{4^{3x-2}}{8^{x+1}}} = 16$ **b)** $\left(\dfrac{3}{4}\right)^{3x-2} \times \left(\dfrac{4}{3}\right)^{1-x} = \dfrac{9}{16}$

c) $\left(\dfrac{9^{2x}}{27^{3x-1}}\right)^3 = \sqrt[3]{3^x}$ **d)** $(5^{x-1})^x = 25$

e) $2^{x-1} - 2^x = 2^{-3}$ **f)** $3^{x+1} + 3^x = 36$

25. Bacteria At the initial count, a bacteria culture contained 1250 bacteria. Another count, $1\frac{1}{2}$ h later, revealed approximately 80 000 bacteria. What is the doubling period for this bacterium?

26. Half-life The half-life of sodium-24 is 14.9 h. A hospital buys a 40-mg sample of sodium-24.
a) How many grams, to the nearest tenth, of sodium-24 will remain after 48 h?
b) After how long will only 2.5 mg remain?

27. Radiology Cobalt-60, which has a half-life of 5.3 years, is extensively used in medical radiology. The amount left at any time is given by the relationship $A(t) = A_0\left(\dfrac{1}{2}\right)^{\frac{t}{5.3}}$, where A_0 represents the initial amount and t, the time in years.
a) What fraction of the initial amount will remain after 10.6 years?

b) How long will it take until there is only 12.5% of the original amount remaining?

28. Bacteria A bacterium is quadrupling every seven days.
a) Write an exponential function that models the growth of the number of bacteria.
b) How many times as great will the number of bacteria be in three weeks as the number now?
c) How long will it take the number of bacteria to double?
d) How long ago was there only 25% of the current number of bacteria?
e) After how long will a single bacterium grow to 8^{24} bacteria?

29. Technology Describe how you might solve an equation of the form $a^{mx+b} = a^{nx+c}$ using a graphing calculator. Test your method by solving the equation $2^{5x-2} = 2^{3x+4}$ manually and by using the graphing calculator. Which method do you prefer and why?

30. Algebra Given that $f(x) = 3^x$, show that $f(x+2) - f(x) = 8f(x)$.

31. Number theory Given $f(x) = 2^{3x+1}$, show that $f(x+1) - f(x)$ is divisible by 7 if x is a non-negative integer.

32. Find x and y if $\dfrac{16^{x+2y}}{8^{x-y}} = 32$ and $\dfrac{32^{x+3y}}{16^{x+2y}} = \dfrac{1}{8}$.

33. a) Solve the following equation for x. Check your solution.
$$(8x)^{-\frac{1}{2}} = \dfrac{1}{4}$$
b) How is this equation different from the other exponential equations that you have solved in this section?

34. Solve for x.
a) $9^{2x} = 2(9^x) + 3$
b) $3(3^x) + 9(3^{-x}) = 28$

35. a) For what value(s) of x is $2^x = x^2$?
b) For what values of x is $2^x > x^2$?

36. a) For what value(s) of x is $2^x = x^3$?
b) For what values of x is $2^x < x^3$?

Exponential Regression

If you have a set of data that you think shows an exponential growth pattern, you can use a graphing calculator to test your hypothesis.

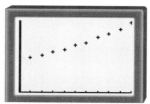

1 Are University Tuition Fees Rising Exponentially?

The table shows the average tuition fee paid for the first year of undergraduate studies at Canadian universities during the 1990s.

School Year	Tuition Fee
1988-89	$1232
1989-90	$1271
1990-91	$1462
1991-92	$1706
1992-93	$1872
1993-94	$2023
1994-95	$2214
1995-96	$2371
1996-97	$2601
1997-98	$2944
1998-99	$3155

Use the STAT features — STAT EDIT, STAT CALC, STAT PLOT, ZoomStat.

1. Clear any equations from the Y= Editor, turn off any plots, and clear any data from previous lists, if necessary.

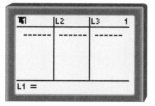

2. What is the simplest way to enter the year data? Enter the year and tuition data in lists L1 and L2.

3. Graph the data. Does your graph appear to have an exponential curve pattern? What factors might affect the appearance of the pattern?

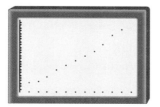

4. Determine the equation of the exponential function that is the best fit to the data by using the Exponential Regression instruction.

5. Graph the curve of best fit.

6. Use the Trace instruction to compare the curve of best fit with the data points. Are university tuition fees growing exponentially?

7. According to this exponential model, what will the average cost of first year university tuition be in the year 2009-10? What factors might cause the actual amount any one student has to pay to be different from the amount projected by this model?

2 Using Exponential Regression to Compare Growth Rates

1. Use a graphing calculator to determine the equation of the exponential function that is the best fit for how the average annual tuition fees for medical school and law school changed with time. Enter the fees for Medicine in L3 and for Law in L4, and modify the steps from the previous exploration to display the three sets of data on one screen.

| School Year | Tuition Fee | |
	Medicine	Law
1988-89	$1370	$1173
1989-90	$1453	$1243
1990-91	$1720	$1452
1991-92	$2074	$1680
1992-93	$2248	$1882
1993-94	$2380	$2021
1994-95	$2694	$2274
1995-96	$2868	$2428
1996-97	$3370	$2681
1997-98	$4010	$2985
1998-99	$4943	$3277

2. Can you tell, by looking at the graphs of the three data plots, whether there is any difference in their rates of increase? Explain.

3. Can you tell, by looking at the exponential equations, whether there is any difference in their rates of increase? Explain.

4. Graph $y = 1 + \dfrac{x}{2} + \dfrac{x^2}{4} + \dfrac{x^3}{8} + \dfrac{x^4}{16} + \dfrac{x^5}{32}$, where $0 \le x \le 3$. If $y = Ab^x$ approximates this curve, what are the values of A and of b?

Exploring the Inverse of an Exponential Function

In the previous chapter, you explored the inverse of various functions. You saw that, graphically, the inverse is obtained through a reflection in the line $y = x$, and that the equation for the inverse of $y = f(x)$ can be obtained by interchanging x and y. Here you will explore how these concepts apply to exponential functions.

1 Exploring the Inverse of $y = 2^x$

1. a) Copy and complete the table of values for $y = 2^x$.

x	y
−1	
0	
1	
2	
3	

b) Sketch the graph of the function $y = 2^x$.

2. a) How can you use the table of values from the previous question to determine points that are on the graph of the inverse of $y = 2^x$?
b) What transformation could you apply to the graph of $y = 2^x$ to obtain the graph of its inverse?
c) On the same graph on which you sketched $y = 2^x$, sketch the graph of its inverse.
d) What are the domain, the range, the intercepts, and the equation of any asymptotes for the inverse graph? Is the inverse a function?

3. a) Write an equation for the inverse of $y = 2^x$ by interchanging x and y.
b) If you try to write the equation for the inverse in the form "$y =$" there is a problem. What is it? Express the inverse in the form "$y =$" using words.

2 Exploring the Inverse of $y = 10^x$

1. Repeat the steps of Exploration 1 for the function $y = 10^x$.

2. To solve the problem encountered in trying to write the equation for the inverse of an exponential function, mathematicians created a new word, *logarithm*, which is shown on calculators as LOG.
a) Use a graphing calculator with a window [−2.35, 2.35, 1] by [−2, 2, 1]. Graph Y1 = 10^X and Y2 = log(X). What do you notice?
b) Examine the TABLE for the two functions. Describe how the y-values for $x = 1$ support your observation in a).
c) Now examine the entries for $x = 2$. Show that the value for Y2 also supports your observation about the meaning of LOG(X).
d) Write a sentence that defines LOG(X).
e) Write and evaluate an equivalent exponential expression to determine the value of log 1000. Check your answer by using the LOG key to find log 1000.
f) By examining the TABLE, or otherwise, describe the restriction on the domain of the function $y = \log x$.

2.5 Logarithms

For the function $y = 2^x$, the inverse is $x = 2^y$. The inverse equation cannot be solved for y using any operations that you have learned so far. A succinct way of writing "y is the exponent for base 2 that gives the result x" is needed. When mathematicians encounter a situation like this, they create a new operation. The inverse of an exponential function is called a **logarithmic function**.

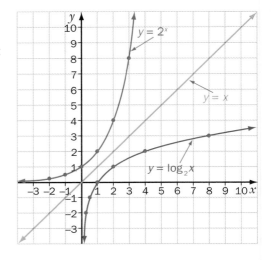

$y = \log_2 x$ Read "y is the logarithm in base 2 of x".

$y = \log_2 x$ means exactly the same as $x = 2^y$.

$y = \log_2 8$ means the same as $8 = 2^y$. Since $8 = 2^3$, $\log_2 8 = 3$.

Explore: Rewrite in Another Form

Copy and complete the table by converting each logarithmic form to exponential form and then finding the value of y.

Logarithmic Form	Exponential Form	Value of y
$y = \log_2 16$		
$y = \log_2 64$		
$y = \log_2 \dfrac{1}{2}$		
$y = \log_{10} 100$		
$y = \log_{10} 1000$		
$y = \log_{10} 0.1$		
$y = \log_3 81$		
$y = \log_5 125$		

Inquire

1. If $\log_2 n = 5$, what is the value of n?

2. If $\log_2 16 = k$, what is the value of k?

3. If $\log_b 49 = 2$, what is the value of b?

4. What is the range of the function $y = b^n$? What does this tell you about the domain of $\log_b n$? Explain.

5. a) Could the value of $\log_b n$ ever be a negative number? Explain.
b) Could the value of $\log_b n$ ever be zero? Explain.

6. Between which two integers must the value of $\log_3 59$ be? Explain.

As you have seen, a logarithm is an exponent. Since the exponential function $f(x) = b^x$ is defined for $b > 0$ and $b \neq 1$, and $f(x) > 0$ for all values of x, the following biconditional statement is true.

$\log_b n = x$ if and only if $b^x = n$, where $b > 0$ and $b \neq 1$.

exponent   exponent

$\log_b n = x \iff b^x = n$

base   base

Example 1   Changing From Exponential Form to Logarithmic Form

Express each in logarithmic form.

a) $n = 4^x$ **b)** $243 = 3^5$ **c)** $2^{-4} = \dfrac{1}{16}$

Solution

a) $n = 4^x$

$\therefore\ x = \log_4 n$

b) $243 = 3^5$

$\therefore\ 5 = \log_3 243$

c) $2^{-4} = \dfrac{1}{16}$

$\therefore\ -4 = \log_2 \dfrac{1}{16}$

Example 2   Changing From Logarithmic Form to Exponential Form

Express each in exponential form.

a) $\log_{10} 10\ 000 = 4$ **b)** $\log_5 \dfrac{1}{25} = -2$ **c)** $\log_k t = x$

Solution

a) $\log_{10} 10\ 000 = 4$

$\therefore\ 10^4 = 10\ 000$

b) $\log_5 \dfrac{1}{25} = -2$

$\therefore\ \ \ 5^{-2} = \dfrac{1}{25}$

c) $\log_k t = x$

$\therefore\ k^x = t$

Example 3   Evaluating Logarithms

Find the value of each logarithm.

a) $\log_2 64$ **b)** $\log_4 \dfrac{1}{16}$ **c)** $\log(0.001)$ **d)** $\log_4 4^5$

Solution

a) Let $x = \log_2 64$

Write in exponential form.

$2^x = 64$

$2^x = 2^6$

$x = 6$

$\therefore\ \log_2 64 = 6$

Alternatively, find the value of $\log_2$ 64 mentally.

Think: What exponent for base 2 gives the value 64?

b)   Let $x = \log_4 \dfrac{1}{16}$

$4^x = \dfrac{1}{16}$

$4^x = 4^{-2}$

$x = -2$

$\therefore\ \log_4 \dfrac{1}{16} = -2$

c)   Let $x = \log_{10} 0.001$

$$10^x = 0.001$$
$$10^x = 10^{-3}$$
$$x = -3$$
$$\therefore \log(0.001) = -3$$

Whenever no base is written, assume that the base is 10.
$\log x = \log_{10} x$

d)   Let $x = \log_4 4^5$

$$4^x = 4^5$$
$$x = 5$$
$$\therefore \log_4 4^5 = 5$$

Part d) of the example above illustrates a general property: $\log_b b^n = n$.
Proof:
   Let $x = \log_b b^n$
Then, expressing in exponential form,
   $$b^x = b^n$$
   $$\therefore x = n$$
$$\therefore \log_b b^n = n$$

Example 4   Graphing Logarithmic Functions
a) On the same set of coordinate axes, graph $y = \log_2 x$ and $y = \log_6 x$.
b) Predict the position of $y = \log_3 x$. Explain.

Solution
a) Make a small table of values for each function, using the exponential form
of each to help select convenient choices for x.

$y = \log_2 x$ $y = \log_6 x$
$x = 2^y$ $x = 6^y$

x	y
1	0
2	1
4	2
8	3

x	y
1	0
6	1
36	2

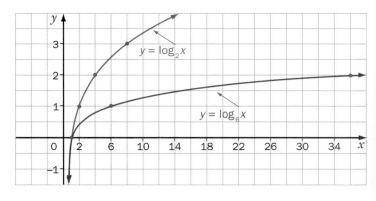

b) If $y = \log_3 x$, then $x = 3^y$.
For $x = 1$, $y = 0$ since $1 = 3^0$.
Every real number with an exponent of zero is equal to 1, so all three graphs
pass through the point (1, 0).
For $y = 2$,

in $y = \log_2 x$ in $y = \log_6 x$ in $y = \log_3 x$
  $2 = \log_2 x$ $2 = \log_6 x$ $2 = \log_3 x$
$\therefore x = 2^2$ $\therefore x = 6^2$ $\therefore x = 3^2$
  $= 4$ $= 36$ $= 9$

The value 9 is between 4 and 36; therefore the graph of $y = \log_3 x$ will be between the graphs of $y = \log_2 x$ and $y = \log_6 x$.
For any chosen y-value, the x-value of $y = \log_3 x$ can be found by dividing the corresponding x-value of $y = \log_6 x$ by that of $y = \log_2 x$. For example, when $y = 2$, $x = \dfrac{36}{4} = 9$.

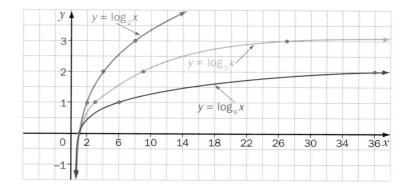

Exponential growth is a relatively rapid rate of growth. Therefore, in some applied situations where values are increasing exponentially, a logarithmic scale is used. One example is the Richter scale, which measures the intensity of earthquakes.

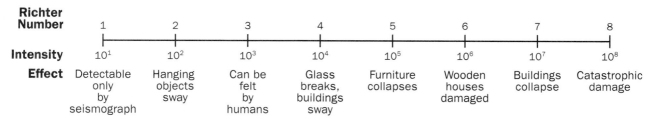

Richter Number	1	2	3	4	5	6	7	8
Intensity	10^1	10^2	10^3	10^4	10^5	10^6	10^7	10^8
Effect	Detectable only by seismograph	Hanging objects sway	Can be felt by humans	Glass breaks, buildings sway	Furniture collapses	Wooden houses damaged	Buildings collapse	Catastrophic damage

Example 5   Interpreting the Richter Scale

An earthquake in Turkey in 1999 measured 7.4 on the Richter scale. An earthquake in Seattle in 1996 measured 5.3. How many times as intense was the earthquake in Turkey as the one in Seattle?

Solution

7.4 on the Richter scale means an intensity of $10^{7.4}$.
5.3 on the Richter scale means an intensity of $10^{5.3}$.
Compare the intensities, I.

$$\dfrac{I_{\text{Turkey}}}{I_{\text{Seattle}}} = \dfrac{10^{7.4}}{10^{5.3}}$$
$$= 10^{2.1}$$
$$\doteq 126$$

Estimate

$10^2 = 100$ and $10^3 = 1000$

The earthquake in Turkey was approximately 126 times as intense as the earthquake in Seattle.

Logarithms also occur in some formulas. For example, the shade number of welding glasses is determined by a formula involving the logarithm of the fraction of visible light transmitted through the glass.

Example 6   Working With a Logarithmic Formula

The shade number of welding glasses is given by the formula

$$\text{shade \#} = \frac{7(-\log_{10} T)}{3} + 1$$

where T is the fraction of visible light transmitted through the glass. To view an eclipse of the sun, amateur astronomers must wear #14 welding glasses to protect their eyes. What fraction of the visible light is transmitted through #14 welding glasses? Express the answer, to three significant digits, in scientific notation and as a percent.

Solution

$$14 = \frac{7(-\log_{10} T)}{3} + 1$$

$$13 = \frac{7(-\log_{10} T)}{3}$$

$$\frac{13}{7} \times 3 = -\log_{10} T$$

$$-\frac{39}{7} = \log_{10} T$$

Express in exponential form.

$$T = 10^{-\frac{39}{7}}$$

$$= 2.68 \times 10^{-6}$$

#14 welding glasses transmit approximately 2.68×10^{-6}, or 0.000 268%, of the visible light.

Practice

Express in logarithmic form.

1. $3^2 = 9$ **2.** $6^3 = 216$

3. $4^5 = 1024$ **4.** $8^0 = 1$

5. $49^{\frac{1}{2}} = 7$ **6.** $5^{-2} = \frac{1}{25}$

7. $8^{\frac{2}{3}} = 4$ **8.** $9^{-1} = \frac{1}{9}$

9. $10^4 = 10\,000$ **10.** $a^b = c$

Express in exponential form.

11. $\log_5 5 = 1$ **12.** $\log_7 49 = 2$

13. $\log_3 729 = 6$ **14.** $\log_2 \frac{1}{16} = -4$

15. $\log_{10} 1 = 0$ **16.** $\log_{16} 4 = 0.5$

17. $\log_8 4 = \frac{2}{3}$ **18.** $\log_2 4096 = 12$

19. $\log 0.1 = -1$ **20.** $\log_3 \sqrt{3} = 0.5$

Evaluate.

21. $\log_2 32$ **22.** $\log_3 27$

23. $\log 1000$ **24.** $\log_7 7$

25. $\log_9 1$ **26.** $\log_5 625$

27. $\log_2 2^9$ **28.** $\log_6 \dfrac{1}{36}$

29. $\log_2 0.25$ **30.** $\log 0.0001$

31. $\log_6 \sqrt{6}$ **32.** $\log_2 8\sqrt{2}$

What is the value of x in each?

33. $\log_3 81 = x$ **34.** $\log_5 x = 2$

35. $\log_x 64 = 3$ **36.** $\log_x 49 = 2$

37. $\log_{\frac{1}{2}} 8 = x$ **38.** $\log_8 x = \dfrac{1}{3}$

39. $\log_x 16 = \dfrac{4}{3}$ **40.** $\log_9 3\sqrt{3} = x$

Applications and Problem Solving

41. If $b > 0$ and $b \neq 1$, then prove that each statement is true.

a) $\log_b 1 = 0$

b) $\log_b b = 1$

c) $b^{\log_b x} = x$

42. Determine the values of x for which $\log_4 x < 2$.

43. If $x = \log_3 100$, the value of x is between two consecutive integers. Give the two integers and explain why.

44. **Graphing a)** By choosing convenient values in the domain $0 \leq x \leq 100$, graph $y = \log_{10} x$ and $y = \log_2 x$ on the same set of coordinate axes.

b) Sketch the position of the graph of $y = \log_5 x$ by using the graphs from a).

45. **Graphing** Sketch the graphs of $y = \log x$ and $y = |\log x|$.

a) Describe the domain and range of each. What points, if any, do they have in common?

b) Check your work by graphing both functions using a graphing calculator using a window $[0, 2.35, 1]$ by $[-2, 2, 1]$.

46. **Richter scale** Consider the table of some earthquakes in the twentieth century.

Location and Date	Magnitude
Japan 1933	8.9
Alaska 1964	8.5
Guatemala 1976	7.5

a) How many times as intense was the earthquake in Japan as the one in Alaska?

b) How many times as intense was the earthquake in Japan as the one in Guatemala?

c) How many times as intense was the earthquake in Alaska as the one in Guatemala?

d) If a recent earthquake in the Pacific Ocean was half as intense as the one in Guatemala, then what was its approximate magnitude. *Hint:* Use trial and error with the exponent key.

47. **Chemistry** A logarithmic scale, in base 10, is used to express the pH of solutions. This scale measures relative acidity, compared with neutral water which has a pH of 7. A pH of less than 7 indicates an acidic solution, while a pH of more than 7 indicates a basic solution.

a) Acid rain has a pH of 4.2. How many times as acidic is acid rain as neutral water?

b) Tomato juice has a pH of 4.1. The pH of eggs is 7.8. How many times as acidic is tomato juice as eggs?

48. **Welding glasses** Health and safety codes give the shade number of welding glasses that must be worn for certain occupations. What percent of the visible light, correct to two significant digits, is transmitted through the glasses in each of the following?

a) For electric welding, shade #11 glasses must be worn.

b) For furnace operation, #9 welding glasses must be worn.

49. **Welding glasses** A worker who is doing metal arc-welding must wear shade #10 welding glasses. For soldering, a person must wear shade #2 welding glasses. How many times as much light is transmitted through #2 welding glasses as through #10s?

50. Earthquakes The Richter magnitude, R, is related to the energy, E in kilowatt-hours, released by the earthquake by the equation
$$R = 0.67 \log(0.37E) + 1.46.$$
How much energy was released by the following earthquakes? Express answers in scientific notation to three significant digits.
a) $R = 8.9$ in Japan in 1933
b) $R = 7.7$ in Peru in 1985
c) $R = 8.5$ in Alaska in 1964

51. Astronomy Johannes Kepler (1571-1630) kept a very accurate collection of astronomical data on planetary motion. In particular, he had data on the planet's average distance from the sun and the time, in days, it took the planet to revolve around the sun. If you graphed the data for the six planets known at the time as points (D, T) where D represents the average distance from the sun, in millions of kilometres, and T the time, in days, for the planet to revolve around the sun, you would find that the curve of best fit is the curve shown.

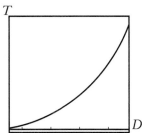

If you took the logarithm in base 10 of each coordinate and plotted these values, you would obtain a linear pattern of the form $y = mx + b$, as shown.

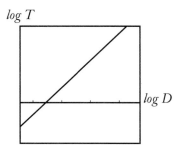

The ordered pairs (D, T) for the Earth and for Saturn are as follows.
Earth (150, 365)   Saturn (1430, 10 753)

a) By taking the logarithm of each of the coordinates, show that m is approximately 1.5.
b) Show that b is approximately -0.7.
c) The time for Venus is about 226 days. What is the approximate average distance of Venus from the sun?
d) Jupiter is, on average, about 780 million kilometres from the sun. Approximately how many days does Jupiter take to revolve around the sun?
e) Use the equation $\log T = m \log D + b$. Express T in terms of D, without logarithms by using integral exponents.

52. If $\log_4 x = a$, express each of the following in terms of a.
a) $\log_{16} x$
b) $\log_2 x$

53. Consider $y = \log x$ where $x > 0$.
a) Prove that $(x_1 x_2, y_1 + y_2)$ is on the graph of $y = \log x$ if (x_1, y_1) and (x_2, y_2) are on the graph.
b) Prove that $\left(\dfrac{x_1}{x_2}, y_1 - y_2 \right)$ is on the graph of $y = \log x$ if (x_1, y_1) and (x_2, y_2) are on the graph.

54. Prove that, for any chosen y-value, the x-value of $y = \log_3 x$ can be found by dividing the corresponding x-value of $y = \log_6 x$ by that of $y = \log_2 x$.

55. What is the domain of $y = \log \dfrac{x}{x-1} - x$?

56. Graph $\log_{|x|} y = \log_{|x|} 3 + \log_{|x|} 2^x$.

Exploring Graphs of Logarithmic Functions

The log key on the graphing calculator is programmed to work in base 10. In the following, assume that $f(x) = \log x$ means $f(x) = \log_{10} x$. Confirm your predictions for the properties of the functions by using the CALC operations, and/or the TABLE feature, as well as reviewing the graphs displayed together.

1 Logarithmic Functions of the Form $f(x) = \log(x + k)$

1. Graph $y = \log x$, using a window $[-2.35, 2.35, 1]$ by $[-2, 2, 1]$.
Identify the following characteristics of the function $f(x) = \log x$.
a) the domain
b) the range
c) the x-intercept
d) the y-intercept
e) the equation of any asymptote

2. a) Predict how the graph of $f(x) = \log(x + 1)$ will compare with the graph of $f(x) = \log x$. Describe any similarities and any differences that you expect.
b) Graph $y = \log(x + 1)$ in the same window as $y = \log x$ to check your predictions.

3. a) Predict how the graph of $f(x) = \log(x - 1)$ will compare with the graph of $f(x) = \log x$. Describe any similarities and any differences that you expect.
b) Graph $y = \log(x - 1)$ in the same viewing window as $y = \log x$ to check your predictions.

4. Generalize your observations. Describe the properties of the graph of the function $y = \log(x + k)$, where k is any real number. What transformation relates $y = \log x$ to $y = \log(x + k)$?

2 Logarithmic Functions of the Form $f(x) = \log ax$

1. a) Predict how the graph of $f(x) = \log 2x$ will compare with the graph of $f(x) = \log x$. Describe any similarities and any differences that you expect.
b) Graph $y = \log x$ and $y = \log(2x)$ in the same viewing window to check your predictions.

2. a) Predict how the graph of $f(x) = \log(0.5x)$ will compare with the graph of $f(x) = \log x$. Describe any similarities and any differences that you expect.
b) Graph $y = \log 0.5x$ in the same viewing window to check your predictions.

3. Generalize your observations. Describe the properties of the graph of the function $y = \log ax$, where $a > 0$. What transformation relates $y = \log x$ to $y = \log ax$?

3 Logarithmic Functions of the Form $f(x) = \log(ax + k)$

1. From your conclusions above, predict the following for the function $f(x) = \log(2x + 1)$.
a) the domain
b) the range
c) the x-intercept
d) the y-intercept
e) the equation of any asymptote
Graph $y = \log(2x + 1)$ to verify your predictions.

2. a) Describe the transformations that you would apply to the graph of $y = \log x$ to obtain a sketch graph of $y = \log(ax + k)$, where $a > 0$ and k is any real number.
b) Identify the properties of a function of the form $y = \log(ax + k)$, including the domain, the range, the x- and y-intercepts, and the equation of the asymptote.

3. Use your knowledge of transformations of functions to sketch the graph of each of the following, and state the domain, the range, the equation of the asymptote, and the intercepts. Describe how the graph compares with $y = \log x$. Use a graphing calculator to check your answers.
a) $y = \log x + 3$ **b)** $y = 2\log 2x$
c) $y = -\log x$ **d)** $y = \log(3x + 1)$
e) $y = \log(-x)$

2.6 Laws of Logarithms

John Napier (1550–1617) was a Scottish lord and a keen amateur mathematician. His greatest mathematical accomplishment was the invention of logarithms. When he first published his logarithmic tables in about 1594, he provided a highly useful tool for simplifying the process of long multiplication and division. In 1624, he applied his idea to inventing a tool that worked on the principle of logarithms, the slide rule. With the development of inexpensive hand-held calculators, logarithmic tables and slide rules are no longer used. However, the principles of logarithms are still important because they provide a useful method for solving some types of exponential equations. Logarithms also provide a helpful method for graphing certain types of relations between two variables, especially when the numbers involved become very large or very small but positive.

Explore: Use a Model

Use two strips of heavy paper at least 15 cm long. Mark 1-cm intervals and label the intervals as shown. Continue the scales to the right as far as you can by extending the pattern.

A	1	2	4	8	16	32	64	128	256	512	1024

B	1	2	4	8	16	32	64	128	256	512	1024

Slide ruler B below ruler A until the point 1 on its scale aligns with the 8 on the scale above. Now locate the number 32 on ruler B and read the number above it. This shows the product $8 \times 32 = 256$. Use your simple slide rule to find each of the following products.

a) 4×16 **b)** 16×16 **c)** 32×4

Inquire

1. Explain how your simple slide rule works. What property of exponents is it based on?

2. Describe the steps you would use to find the quotient $128 \div 8$ using your slide rule.

3. Describe how to use your slide rule to find an approximate value for 24×75. Explain why the result is not very accurate.

4. If the midpoint between 1 and 2 on your slide rule is x, what is the exact value of x?

5. Explain how you would construct a simple base 3 slide rule.

TABLE 2. Four-Place Logarithms o

N	0	1
10	0000	
11	0414	
12	079	
13		
14		
15		235
16		260
17		283
		30
		32
20	3010	3032
21	3222	3243
22	3424	
23		

Numbers	Logs
8.36	0.9222
15.84	1.1998
132.4	2.1220

8.36 × 15.84 ≐ 132.4

29	4472	4487
	4624	4639
30	4771	4786
31	4914	4928
32	5051	5065
33	5185	5198
34	5315	5328
35	5441	545
36	5563	557
37	5682	56
38	5798	58
39	5911	59
40	6021	
41	6128	
42	6232	
43	6335	
44	6435	
45	6532	
46	6628	
47	6721	
48	6812	
49	6902	
50	6990	
51	7076	
52	7160	
53	724	
54	732	

In working with powers of the same base, you often use the laws of exponents.

Product of powers: $b^x \times b^y = b^{x+y}$

Quotient of powers: $b^x \div b^y = b^{x-y}$

Power of a power: $(b^x)^y = b^{xy}$

Root of a power: $\sqrt[y]{b^x} = b^{\frac{x}{y}}$

Since logarithms are exponents, it is reasonable to assume that similar laws exist for logarithms.

To multiply two powers of the same base, you *add* the exponents. Is the logarithm of a product equal to the sum of the logarithms of the factors? First test a specific case.

Does $\log_2 (16 \times 64) = \log_2 16 + \log_2 64$?

$$
\begin{aligned}
\textbf{L.S.} &= \log_2 (16 \times 64) & \textbf{R.S.} &= \log_2 16 + \log_2 64 \\
&= \log_2 (2^4 \times 2^6) & &= \log_2 2^4 + \log_2 2^6 \\
&= \log_2 2^{10} & &= 4 + 6 \\
&= 10 & &= 10
\end{aligned}
$$

The property is true in this case.

Logarithm of a Product
$\log_b xy = \log_b x + \log_b y$

Proof:

Let $M = \log_b x$ and $N = \log_b y$

Then, by definition, $x = b^M$ and $y = b^N$.

So, $xy = b^M \times b^N$

$\qquad = b^{M+N}$

Express $xy = b^{M+N}$ in logarithmic form.

$\log_b xy = M + N$

$\qquad\quad = \log_b x + \log_b y$

Using very similar steps, the quotient property can be proved.

Logarithm of a Quotient
$\log_b \dfrac{x}{y} = \log_b x - \log_b y$

Example 1   Evaluating Logarithms Using the Product and Quotient Laws
Evaluate each expression.

a) $\log_5 100 + \log_5 \dfrac{1}{4}$ **b)** $\log_2 384 - \log_2 12$

Solution

a)

Use the logarithm of a product law.

$$
\begin{aligned}
&\log_5 100 + \log_5 \frac{1}{4} \\
&= \log_5 \left(100 \times \frac{1}{4}\right) \\
&= \log_5 25 \\
&= 2
\end{aligned}
$$

b)

Use the logarithm of a quotient law.

$$
\begin{aligned}
&\log_2 384 - \log_2 12 \\
&= \log_2 \frac{384}{12} \\
&= \log_2 32 \\
&= 5
\end{aligned}
$$

Logarithm of a Power

$\log_b x^n = n\log_b x$

Proof:
Let $M = \log_b x$
So, in exponential form, $x = b^M$.
Then, $x^n = (b^M)^n$
$\qquad = b^{Mn}$
Express $x^n = b^{Mn}$ in logarithmic form.
$\log_b x^n = Mn$
$\qquad = (\log_b x)n$
$\therefore \log_b x^n = n\log_b x$

Using similar steps, the root property can be proved.

Logarithm of a Root

$\log_b x^{\frac{1}{n}} = \frac{1}{n}\log_b x \ $ or $ \ \log_b \sqrt[n]{x} = \frac{\log_b x}{n}$

Example 2   Using the Logarithm of a Power and Logarithm of a Root Laws
Evaluate each expression.

a) $\log_7 49^5$ 　　　　　　**b)** $\log_3 \sqrt[5]{27}$

Solution

a)
Use the logarithm of
a power property.
$$\begin{aligned}&\log_7 49^5\\ &= 5\log_7 49\\ &= 5 \times 2\\ &= 10\end{aligned}$$

b)
Use the logarithm
of a root property.
$$\begin{aligned}&\log_3 \sqrt[5]{27}\\ &= \frac{\log_3 27}{5}\\ &= \frac{3}{5}\end{aligned}$$

Example 3   Simplifying Using the Laws of Logarithms
Write each expression as a single logarithm.

a) $\log(a + b) + \log(a - b)$ 　　**b)** $\log A - 3\log B + 5\log \sqrt[5]{C}$

Solution

a)
Use the logarithm
of a product law.
$$\begin{aligned}&\log(a + b) + \log(a - b)\\ &= \log(a + b)(a - b)\\ &= \log(a^2 - b^2)\end{aligned}$$

b)
$$\begin{aligned}&\log A - 3\log B + 5\log \sqrt[5]{C}\\ &= \log A - \log B^3 + 5\log C^{\frac{1}{5}}\\ &= \log \frac{A}{B^3} + \log C^{\frac{5}{5}}\\ &= \log \frac{AC}{B^3}\end{aligned}$$

Example 4 Working With the Laws of Logarithms

If $x = \log_4 5$ and $y = \log_4 3$, express $\log_4 225$ in terms of x and y.

Solution

Method 1:

$$\begin{aligned}
\log_4 225 &= \log_4 (25 \times 9) \\
&= \log_4 25 + \log_4 9 \\
&= \log_4 5^2 + \log_4 3^2 \\
&= 2\log_4 5 + 2\log_4 3 \\
&= 2x + 2y
\end{aligned}$$

Method 2:

$$\begin{aligned}
\log_4 225 &= \log_4 15^2 \\
&= 2\log_4 15 \\
&= 2\log_4 (5 \times 3) \\
&= 2[\log_4 5 + \log_4 3] \\
&= 2[x + y] \\
&= 2x + 2y
\end{aligned}$$

The pH of a solution is defined by

$$pH = -\log_{10}[\text{H+}]$$

where the [H+] is the hydrogen ion concentration in moles per litre (mol/L). The pH of pure water, which is acid-base neutral, is 7 because, in the ionization of pure water,

$[\text{H+}][\text{OH}^-] = 1.0 \times 10^{-14}$ (moles^2/litre^2) and $[\text{OH}^-] = [\text{H+}]$.

$$\begin{aligned}
\therefore \quad [\text{H+}]^2 &= 1.0 \times 10^{-14} \\
[\text{H+}] &= \sqrt{1.0 \times 10^{-14}} \\
&= 1.0 \times 10^{-7}
\end{aligned}$$

Then, $\quad \begin{aligned}[t] pH &= -\log_{10}(1.0 \times 10^{-7}) \\
&= -(0 + (-7)) \\
&= 7 \end{aligned}$

Example 5 Working With the pH Scale

The pH of a solution is given by $pH = -\log_{10}[\text{H+}]$, where [H+] is the hydrogen concentration in moles per litre.

a) Determine the pH of potato soil, to the nearest tenth, if its hydrogen ion concentration is 5×10^{-8} mol/L?

b) What is the hydrogen ion concentration of a weak vinegar solution if its pH is 3.1?

Solution

a)
$$\begin{aligned}
pH &= -\log_{10}[5 \times 10^{-8}] \\
&= -(\log_{10} 5 + (-8)\log_{10} 10) \\
&= -\log_{10} 5 + 8 \\
&\doteq -0.7 + 8 \\
&= 7.3
\end{aligned}$$

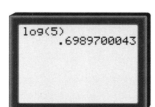

The pH of potato soil is approximately 7.3.

b) Use pH = 3.1 in $pH = -\log_{10}[\text{H+}]$.

$$\begin{aligned}
3.1 &= -\log_{10}[\text{H+}] \\
-3.1 &= \log_{10}[\text{H+}]
\end{aligned}$$

Express in exponential form.

$$\begin{aligned}
[\text{H+}] &= 10^{-3.1} \\
&= 10^{0.9} \times 10^{-4} \\
&\doteq 7.9 \times 10^{-4}
\end{aligned}$$

The hydrogen ion concentration in a weak vinegar solution is 7.9×10^{-4} mol/L.

Base 10 logarithms are called **common logarithms**. Mathematicians and scientists also frequently use **natural logarithms,** which have base e, where e is a special irrational number that has approximate value 2.718 28. On a calculator, these logarithms are found using the LN key. You know that $\log_{10} 10 = 1$, so $\ln e$ should similarly have value 1. Try it! In the last section of this chapter you will see how to work with e and $\ln e$.

Practice

Use the product and quotient laws to express each as a single logarithm and then evaluate.

1. $\log_{10} 8 + \log_{10} 1.25$

2. $\log_4 32 + \log_4 2$

3. $\log_3 108 - \log_3 4$

4. $\log_2 80 - \log_2 5$

5. $\log_6 4 + \log_6 9$

6. $\log_5 500 - \log_5 4$

7. $\log_3 8 - \log_3 24$

8. $\log_7 245 + \log_7 \dfrac{1}{5}$

9. $\log_8 6 - \log_8 3 + \log_8 2$

10. $\log_{10} 4 + \log_{10} 5 - \log_{10} 2$

Use the power and root laws to simplify and then evaluate each.

11. $\log_3 9^{20}$　　　　**12.** $\log_2 8^{25}$

13. $\log_{10} \sqrt{0.1}$　　　**14.** $\log_3 \sqrt[3]{9}$

15. $\log_5 5\sqrt{5}$　　　　**16.** $\log_7 49^{2.5}$

17. $\log_8 2^{\frac{3}{2}}$　　　　**18.** $\log_2 16^5$

If $\log 17 = k$, determine an expression for each of the following.

19. $\log 170$　　　　　**20.** $\log 17\ 000$

21. $\log 1.7$　　　　　**22.** $\log \sqrt{17}$

23. $\log 17^{10}$　　　　**24.** $\log \dfrac{17}{1000}$

If $\log_3 4 = x$, express each of the following in terms of x.

25. $\log_3 64$　　　　　**26.** $\log_3 2$

27. $\log_3 144$　　　　**28.** $\log_3 \sqrt[5]{4^7}$

If $\log_3 x = 8$, evaluate the following.

29. $\log_3 9x$　　　　　**30.** $\log_3 x^2$

31. $\log_3 \dfrac{x^4}{27}$　　　　**32.** $\log_3 \dfrac{3}{x}$

Evaluate.

33. $2 \log_3 12 - 2 \log_3 4$

34. $\log_4 6 + \log_4 \dfrac{64}{3} - \log_4 8$

35. $\log_3 (9 \times 27 \times 81)$

36. $\dfrac{1}{2} \log_3 144 - \log_3 4 + 2 \log_3 3$

37. $7^{\log_7 3}$

38. $\log_5 \sqrt{175} - \log_5 \sqrt{7}$

Write each expression as a single logarithm.

39. $\log_2 a + \log_2 b - \log_2 c$

40. $\log x^2 - 5\log y$

41. $\log A + \log \sqrt{B} - 3 \log C$

42. $\log_7 \sqrt[3]{x} - \log_7 y^3 + 2\log_7 y$

Applications and Problem Solving

43. Prove that $\log \dfrac{1}{x} = -\log x$, where $x > 0$.

44. In each, express y as a function of x and state the domain.
a) $\log y = \log x + \log 3$
b) $\log y = 3 \log x$
c) $\log y = \dfrac{1}{2}(\log x + \log 5)$

d) $\log_2 y = \log_2 x + \log_2 \dfrac{x}{4}$

45. Prove that $\log_b \dfrac{x}{y} = \log_b x - \log_b y$, by letting $\log_b x = M$ and $\log_b y = N$.

46. Prove the following.

a) $\log_b x^{\frac{1}{n}} = \dfrac{\log_b x}{n}$　　**b)** $\log_b \sqrt[n]{x^m} = \dfrac{m \log_b x}{n}$

47. Chemistry The pH of a solution is given by $pH = -\log_{10}[H+]$, where $[H+]$ is the hydrogen concentration in moles per litre.
a) Determine the pH of acid rain, to the nearest tenth, if its hydrogen ion concentration is 6.3×10^{-5} mol/L?
b) What is the hydrogen ion concentration of black coffee if its pH is 5.0?
c) What is the hydrogen ion concentration of eggs if their pH is 7.8?

48. Medicine The pH of a person's blood can be found using the Henderson-Hasselbach formula,

$$pH = 6.1 + \log_{10} \frac{B}{C}$$

where B represents the concentration of bicarbonate in the blood and C, the concentration of carbonic acid. Most people have a blood pH of about 7.4.
a) Rewrite the formula so that it does not contain the logarithm of a quotient.
b) In a blood sample, the concentration of bicarbonate is 25 and the concentration of carbonic acid is 2. Find the pH of this person's blood to the nearest tenth.

49. Biology The amount of energy, E, measured in kilocalories per gram molecule, needed to transport a substance from the outside of a living cell to the inside of that cell is given by

$$E = 1.4 \log_{10} \frac{C_2}{C_1}$$

where C_1 represents the concentration of the substance outside the cell and C_2, the concentration inside the cell. If the concentration of a substance inside a cell is twice the concentration outside it, find the energy needed to transport the substance into the cell.

50. Astronomy Kepler's third law of planetary motion is given by the relationship

$$\log T = \frac{\log k + 3\log r}{2}$$

where T is the period of a planet's revolution about the sun, r is the planet's mean distance from the sun, and k is a constant that can be determined from orbital data. Express the equation in exponential form.

51. Consider the following. Decide which step is incorrect, giving reasons.
a) $\log_3 0.1 < 2 \log_3 0.1$
$$2 \log_3 0.1 = \log_3 (0.1)^2$$
$$= \log_3 0.01$$
So, $\log_3 0.1 < \log_3 0.01$
∴ $0.1 < 0.01$
b) $\dfrac{1}{2} > \dfrac{1}{4}$

$$\frac{1}{2} > \left(\frac{1}{2}\right)^2$$

$$\log \frac{1}{2} > \log \left(\frac{1}{2}\right)^2$$

$$\log \frac{1}{2} > 2 \log \frac{1}{2}$$

∴ $1 > 2$

52. According to the law of powers, $\log x^2 = 2\log x$. However, the functions $y = \log x^2$ and $y = 2\log x$ are not the same. Explain the difference.

53. Evaluate.
a) $10^{\log 7 + \log 5}$ **b)** $3^{\log_3 7 - \log_3 5}$
c) $8^{\log_2 7}$ **d)** $2^{\log_4 9}$

54. Let $x = \log 196$, $y = \log 225$, and $z = \log 256$. Write an algebraic expression in x, y, and/or z for $\log 2$, $\log 3$, $\log 4$, $\log 5$, $\log 6$, $\log 7$, $\log 8$, and $\log 9$.

NUMBER POWER

The numbers 1 through 6 are arranged in a **difference triangle**. The absolute value of the difference between successive digits appears below them.

     6   2   5
        4   3
           1

Arrange the numbers 1 through 10 in a difference triangle.

2.7 Logarithms and Equation Solving

Logarithms provide an important tool for finding an unknown exponent in any exponential equation such as $A(t) = A_0 b^t$. As you have seen, these kinds of equations are useful for modelling real world situations such as population growth ($b > 1$) or decay ($0 < b < 1$). Compound interest, the intensity of light as it passes through water or glass, stopping distances for various speeds, and the time it takes a substance to cool are all examples of situations that can be modelled by exponential functions. You have solved problems of this type by using the graph of the exponential function. In this section you will see how, by using logarithms, solutions can be found algebraically.

Explore: Solve an Equation

Consider the equation $3^{x+2} = 5^{2x-3}$. First, use trial and error to find the value of x, to the nearest tenth, that satisfies the equation. Then, graph the exponential functions $y = 3^{x+2}$ and $y = 5^{2x-3}$, using a graphing calculator or manually. Use your graph to estimate the solution to the equation $3^{x+2} = 5^{2x-3}$, to the nearest tenth.

Inquire

1. What are the disadvantages of trying to solve the equation by trial and error?

2. What is the domain of each of the exponential functions that you graphed? What is the range?

3. What are the disadvantages of trying to solve the equation using a graph drawn manually?

4. What might the disadvantages be of trying to solve an equation of this type using a graph drawn with a graphing calculator?

5. Why can you *not* solve this exponential equation by equating exponents?

The following example shows how, by taking logarithms, an exponential equation can be converted to a linear equation and hence solved. The process of "taking logarithms" of both sides of an equation is valid because the logarithm is a one-to-one function, that is, $x = y$ if and only if $\log_b x = \log_b y$.

Example 1   Using Logarithms to Solve Exponential Equations
Solve for x. Round to the nearest tenth.

a) $2^x = 5$ **b)** $3^{x+2} = 5^{2x-3}$

Solution

a)

Take logarithms of both sides.
Use the power law.

$$2^x = 5$$
$$\log(2^x) = \log 5$$
$$x \log 2 = \log 5$$
$$x = \frac{\log 5}{\log 2}$$
$$x \doteq 2.3$$

Estimate

$2^2 = 4$ and $2^3 = 8$, so x is between 2 and 3, but closer to 2.

b)

Take logarithms of both sides.
Use the power law.
Expand.
Collect like terms.
Solve for x.

$$3^{x+2} = 5^{2x-3}$$
$$\log(3^{x+2}) = \log(5^{2x-3})$$
$$(x+2)\log 3 = (2x-3)\log 5$$
$$x \log 3 + 2\log 3 = 2x \log 5 - 3\log 5$$
$$3\log 5 + 2\log 3 = 2x \log 5 - x \log 3$$
$$3\log 5 + 2\log 3 = x(2\log 5 - \log 3)$$
$$x = \frac{3\log 5 + 2\log 3}{2\log 5 - \log 3}$$
$$\doteq 3.3$$

Example 2   Solving a Problem Involving Exponential Change

The intensity of sunlight below the ocean's surface decreases exponentially with depth below the surface. When the intensity at the surface is 100 units, the intensity at a depth of 3 m is 6 units.
a) Determine an equation for the exponential function.
b) What will the intensity be at a depth of 2 m, to the nearest tenth?
c) A particular plant cannot grow if the intensity of the sunlight is less than 0.001 unit. What is the maximum depth, to the nearest centimetre, at which this plant can grow?

Solution

a) Let $I(d)$ represent the intensity of sunlight at any depth d, in metres. Then,

$$I(d) = 100b^d$$

When $d = 3$, $I(d) = 6$.

$$6 = 100b^3$$
$$0.06 = b^3$$

Take logarithms of both sides.

$$\log 0.06 = 3\log b$$
$$\frac{\log 0.06}{3} = \log b$$
$$\log b \doteq -0.407$$
$$\therefore b = 10^{-0.407}$$
$$b \doteq 0.39$$

An equation for the exponential function is $I(d) = 100(0.39)^d$.

b) At a depth of 2 m, use $d = 2$.
$$I(d) = 100(0.39)^2$$
$$\doteq 15.2$$
The intensity of sunlight at a depth of 2 m is 15.2 units, to the nearest tenth.

c) Find d when $I(d) = 0.001$.

$$0.001 = 100(0.39)^d$$
$$0.00001 = 0.39^d$$
$$\text{or } 10^{-5} = 0.39^d$$

Take logarithms of both sides.

$$\log(10^{-5}) = d\log 0.39$$
$$-5 = d\log 0.39$$
$$\therefore d = \frac{-5}{\log 0.39}$$
$$\doteq 12.23$$

The maximum depth, to the nearest centimetre, at which this particular plant can grow is 12.23 m.

Example 3   Finding the Half-Life of a Substance

Lead-210 is a radioactive nuclide. If 8 g of it decays to 6.75 g in 5 years, then what is the half-life of lead-210? Round the answer to the nearest tenth.

Solution

The general equation is $A(t) = A_0\left(\dfrac{1}{2}\right)^{\frac{t}{H}}$ where $A(t)$ represents the amount present after t years, A_0 is the original amount, and H is the half-life of the substance. Substitute $A(t) = 6.75$, $A_0 = 8$, $t = 5$.

$$6.75 = 8\left(\frac{1}{2}\right)^{\frac{5}{H}}$$
$$6.75 = 8(0.5)^{\frac{5}{H}}$$
$$\frac{6.75}{8} = (0.5)^{\frac{5}{H}}$$

Take logs of both sides.

$$\log\frac{6.75}{8} = \frac{5}{H}\log 0.5$$
$$H = \frac{5\log 0.5}{\log 0.84375}$$
$$\doteq 20.4$$

Therefore, the half-life of lead-210 is about 20.4 years.

Notice that, in the previous solutions, base 10 logarithms and the *log* key on a calculator were used. What if you need to evaluate a logarithm in a base other than 10? The next example shows a method of converting from another base to base 10, so that the log key on a calculator can be used.

Example 4 Evaluating Logarithms in Any Base

Evaluate $\log_5 782$, rounded to the nearest hundredth.

Solution

Let

$$x = \log_5 782$$

Write in exponential form.

$$5^x = 782$$

Take the logarithm of each side.

$$\log 5^x = \log 782$$

Use the power law.

$$x \log 5 = \log 782$$

$$x = \frac{\log 782}{\log 5}$$

$$x \doteq 4.14$$

Estimate

Since $5^4 = 625$ and $5^5 = 3125$, x is between 4 and 5, and is closer to 4.

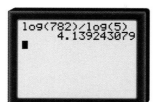

```
log(782)/log(5)
        4.139243079
■
```

Rounded to the nearest hundredth
$\log_5 782 = 4.14$.

The steps of the previous example can be used as a model for proving the general result, known as the change of base rule, which holds for $a > 0$, $b > 0$, $c > 0$, and $b \neq 1$, $c \neq 1$.

$$\log_b a = \frac{\log_c a}{\log_c b}$$

Proof:

Let

$$x = \log_b a$$

Write in exponential form.

$$b^x = a$$

Take the logarithm, in base c, of each side.

$$\log_c b^x = \log_c a$$

Use the power law.

$$x \log_c b = \log_c a$$

$$x = \frac{\log_c a}{\log_c b}$$

$$\therefore \quad \log_b a = \frac{\log_c a}{\log_c b}$$

The change of base property is a **logarithmic identity**. It is a statement that is true for all values of the variables for which the functions on both sides of the equation are defined. Other identities involving logarithms can be proved either directly, using the definition of a logarithm as was done in the proof above, or by using properties that have been previously proved.

Example 5 Proving a Logarithmic Identity

a) Prove that $\dfrac{1}{\log_5 8} + \dfrac{1}{\log_6 8} = \dfrac{1}{\log_{30} 8}$.

b) State a general property, or identity, that the previous result suggests.

c) Prove the identity by using properties already established.

Solution

a)

$$\text{L.S.} = \frac{1}{\log_5 8} + \frac{1}{\log_6 8}$$

$$= \frac{\log 5}{\log 8} + \frac{\log 6}{\log 8} \qquad \text{Use the change of base property.}$$

$$= \frac{\log 5 + \log 6}{\log 8}$$

$$= \frac{\log(5 \times 6)}{\log 8} \qquad \text{Use the log of a product property.}$$

$$= \frac{\log 30}{\log 8}$$

$$= \frac{1}{\log_{30} 8}$$

$$= \text{R.S.}$$

b) The general property suggested by the result in a) is $\dfrac{1}{\log_a x} + \dfrac{1}{\log_b x} = \dfrac{1}{\log_{ab} x}$.

c)

$$\text{L.S.} = \frac{1}{\log_a x} + \frac{1}{\log_b x} \qquad \text{Change } \log_a x \text{ to base } ab: \ \log_a x = \frac{\log_{ab} x}{\log_{ab} a},$$

$$= \frac{\log_{ab} a}{\log_{ab} x} + \frac{\log_{ab} b}{\log_{ab} x} \qquad\qquad \text{so, } \frac{1}{\log_a x} = \frac{\log_{ab} a}{\log_{ab} x}.$$

$$= \frac{\log_{ab} a + \log_{ab} b}{\log_{ab} x}$$

$$= \frac{\log_{ab} ab}{\log_{ab} x}$$

$$= \frac{1}{\log_{ab} x}$$

$$= \text{R.S.}$$

Example 6 Solving a Logarithmic Equation

Solve for x.

$$\log_5 (x - 6) = 1 - \log_5 (x - 2)$$

Solution

The conditions $b > 0$ and $b \neq 1$ are satisfied.

Since $\log_b n$ exists only for $n > 0$, there is a restriction $x > 6$.

Remember always to check that restrictions on $\log_b n$ are satisfied.

$$\log_5 (x - 6) = 1 - \log_5 (x - 2)$$
$$\log_5 (x - 6) + \log_5 (x - 2) = 1$$

Use the product law. $\log_5 (x - 6)(x - 2) = 1$

Express in exponential form. $(x - 6)(x - 2) = 5^1$

Solve the quadratic equation. $x^2 - 8x + 12 = 5$
$$x^2 - 8x + 7 = 0$$
$$(x - 7)(x - 1) = 0$$
$$\therefore x = 7 \text{ or } x = 1$$

The solution $x = 1$ must be rejected because of the restriction $x > 6$.
The solution is $x = 7$.

Practice

Find the value of x. Round to the nearest hundredth.

1. $3^x = 125$
2. $10^{x-4} = 7$
3. $4^{2x} = 15$
4. $9^{2x+3} = 568$
5. $(0.7)^{3x} = 2.08$
6. $2^{-x} = 6$
7. $8^{-\frac{x}{3}} = 20$
8. $2^{x^2} = 10$

Solve for x. Round to the nearest hundredth.

9. $2^{x+3} = 17^x$
10. $17^{x+4} = 196^{3x-2}$
11. $21^{2x+5} = 278^{3x-7}$
12. $0.63^{x-4} = 5^{2x}$
13. $7 \times 2^x = 5^{x-2}$
14. $485 \times 5^{x+2} = 12^{2x-1}$

First, estimate the value of each of the following. Then evaluate and round to the nearest hundredth.

15. $\log_3 88$
16. $\log_4 91$
17. $\log_5 1012$
18. $\log_6 250$
19. $\log_7 71$
20. $\log_8 567$

Solve for x.

21. $\log_2 x = \log_2 5 + \log_2 3$
22. $\log_2 x = \log_2 18 - \log_2 6$
23. $\log x + \log 12 = \log 8$
24. $\log x = 1 + \log 2$
25. $4 \log_5 x = \log_5 625$

An amount of money is invested at 12%/a interest. Write an equation and solve it to determine the length of time it will take for each of the following events to occur. Round answers to the nearest tenth of a year.

26. the original amount to double if interest is compounded annually

27. the original amount to double if interest is compounded monthly

28. the original amount to triple if interest is compounded annually

29. the original amount to triple if interest is compounded monthly

A photocopier was purchased for $12 500. The value of the machine each year is 85% of its value the preceding year.

30. Write an exponential equation that gives the value of the photocopier t years after it was purchase.

31. To the nearest tenth of a year, how long will it take for the photocopier to be worth half of what it cost new?

32. To the nearest tenth of a year, how long will it take before it is worth only $1500?

Prove each of the following identities
a) *using exponential functions*
b) *using logarithmic properties that you already know*

33. $(\log_a x)(\log_x a) = 1$

34. $\dfrac{\log_a x}{\log_a y} = \dfrac{\log_b x}{\log_b y}$

35. $(\log_a x)(\log_b a) = \log_b x$

36. $\log_{\frac{1}{a}} x = -\log_a x$

37. $\log_{b^n} (x^n) = \log_b x$

38. $\log_{\frac{1}{b}} \left(\dfrac{1}{x} \right) = \log_b x$

39. For the proofs in questions 33–38, which method of proof, a) or b), was easier? Why do you think this is the case?

Applications and Problem Solving

40. Find the roots of each equation. Remember to check for restrictions and reject inadmissible roots.

a) $\log_2(x-2) + \log_2 x = \log_2 3$

b) $\log_2(x-2) + \log_2 x = 3$

c) $\log_5(3x+1) + \log_5(x-3) = 3$

d) $\log_9(x-5) = 1 - \log_9(x+3)$

e) $\log_2(x^2+8) - \log_2 6 = \log_2 x$

f) $\log(2x+1) = 1 + \log(x-2)$

g) $\log_3(x-2) + \log_3 10 - \log_3(x^2+3x-10) = 0$

h) $(\log_3 x)^2 = \log_3 x^2 + 3$

41. Technology Use the change of base formula to rewrite $y = \log_4 x$ in a form in which you can graph the function using a graphing calculator. Graph the function. Explain how you could use the value at $x = 4$ to verify your graph. What other value of x might you choose to test?

42. Interest Find how long it will take, to the nearest month, for $12 500 to grow to $20 000, if it is invested at 10% compounded monthly.

43. Half-life How long will it take 20 mg of iodine-131 to decay to 16.85 mg if the half-life of iodine-131 is 8.1 days?

44. Bacterial growth The number of bacteria in a culture is a function of time according to the formula $P(t) = P_0(8)^{kt}$ where $P(t)$ represents the number of bacteria at time t, P_0 the original number of bacteria, t the time in hours, and k is a constant that depends on the type of bacterium.

a) If it takes 3 h for 20 bacteria to increase to 3200, then what is the value of k, to the nearest hundredth?

b) No matter what the value of P_0, how long will it take the bacteria population to triple? Answer to the nearest hundredth.

c) If there are P_0 bacteria now, how long ago were there half as many? Answer to the nearest hundredth.

45. Cheese A particular type of cheese will keep for 140 h at 0°C and for 20 h at 25°C.

a) Set up an exponential equation that expresses the number of hours the cheese will keep as a function of temperature.

b) How long will the cheese keep at 5°C, to the nearest hour?

46. Medicine An important advance in medical science has been the discovery and use of radiotracers. These are radioactive nuclides that can be taken orally and then traced throughout various biological systems to help diagnose and treat various illnesses or malfunctions in an organ.

a) Iodine-131 is used to study the thyroid. A sample contains 20 mg. Two days later 16.85 mg are present. What is the half-life of iodine-131, to the nearest tenth?

b) Phosphorus-32 is used to study the eyes, liver, and tumors. After 10 days, only 154 mg of a 250 mg sample remains. What is the half-life of phosphorus-32, to the nearest tenth?

c) Strontium-87 is used in the study of bones. After one hour, 78.1 mg remains of a 100 mg sample. What is the half-life of strontium-87, to the nearest tenth?

d) Sodium-24 is used in the study of the circulatory system. 500 units are taken orally. Four hours later, 414.6 units are present. What is the half-life of sodium-24, to the nearest tenth?

47. Radiation Contamination of the environment with strontium-90 from nuclear fall-out can pose some very serious health hazards because its chemistry is similar to that of calcium. The half-life of strontium-90 is 28.8 years. If it gets into grass and hay, it can be incorporated into cow's milk along with calcium, and is then passed on to humans where it will lodge in the bones. Since its half-life is so long, it can cause radiation damage that can lead to cancer.

a) Set up a function of time that gives the amount of strontium-90 at any time t.

b) How long will it be before there is only 10% of the original amount of strontium-90 remaining?

c) What percent remains after five years?

d) Without using a calculator, determine how long it will be before only 25% of the strontium-90 is remaining.

48. Given $a > 0$, $b > 0$ and $a \neq 1$, $b \neq 1$, prove that $\log_a b = \dfrac{1}{\log_b a}$.

49. If $\log_a n = x$ and $\log_c n = y$, $n \neq 1$, prove that $\dfrac{x-y}{x+y} = \dfrac{\log_b c - \log_b a}{\log_b c + \log_b a}$.

50. If $L = \log_x yz$, $M = \log_y xz$, and $N = \log_z xy$, prove that $L + M + N = LMN - 2$.

51. By using the properties of logarithms, show that

$$\left(\log\frac{a}{b}\right)\left(\log\frac{c}{d}\right) = \left(\log\frac{a}{c}\right)\left(\log\frac{b}{d}\right) + \left(\log\frac{a}{d}\right)\left(\log\frac{c}{b}\right).$$

52. Bacteria Show that the doubling time of a bacterium that
a) triples every H hours is given by the relationship $t \doteq 0.63H$
b) increases 5-fold every H hours is given by the relationship $t \doteq 0.43H$
c) increases n-fold every H hours is given by the relationship $t \doteq 0.301 \times \dfrac{H}{\log n}$

53. Light intensity The intensity of the sunlight below the surface of a river is reduced by 4.6% for every metre below the surface. Show that the depth that the sunlight can reach if the intensity is to be $I(d)$ is given by

$d \doteq -48.9\log\dfrac{I(d)}{I_0}$, where I_0 is the initial

intensity and d is the depth in metres.

54. Caribou population The caribou population of an area has been growing at an annual rate of 2%.
a) If there are 850 caribou now, how long will it take before there are 1000?
b) How long will it take for the population to double?
c) If there are P_0 now, show that the length of time, t, it will take the population to reach a population of $P(t)$ is given by the relationship
$t \doteq 116.28 \log \dfrac{P(t)}{P_0}$.

d) Use the relationship in c) to find how long it will take 900 caribou to grow to a population of 1400.

55. Population growth Show that, with an annual growth rate of r%, the time it will take an initial population of P_0 to reach a population of $P(t)$ is given by the relation $t = \dfrac{1}{\log(1+r)}\log\dfrac{P(t)}{P_0}$.

56. An exponential function is expressed in the form $\log y = m \log x + b$ to obtain a graph that is linear. Find the equation of the original function.

57. If $(2 \log b)^2 + 8(\log a)(\log b) = 0$, express b in terms of a.

58. Show that

$$2\log_a(x+y) = 2\log_a x + \log_a\left(1 + \frac{2y}{x} + \frac{y^2}{x^2}\right).$$

59. If $\log_a\left(1+\dfrac{1}{8}\right) = x$, $\log_a\left(1+\dfrac{1}{15}\right) = y$ and

$\log_a\left(1+\dfrac{1}{24}\right) = z$, show that

$\log_a\left(1+\dfrac{1}{80}\right) = x - y - z$.

60. If $2\log_8 x = A$, $\log_2 2x = B$, and $B - A = 4$, then find the value of x.

61. Solve for x if $\dfrac{7^x + 7^{-x}}{2} = t$.

62. Solve for x.
a) $x = 25^{1 + \log_5 x}$
b) $8^{\log_2 x} - 25^{\log_5 x} = 4x - 4$
c) $\log_{36}(x-2) + \log_{36}(x+1) + \log_{36}(x-3) = 4^{-\frac{1}{2}}$

63. Solve for x.
$\log_4(x+1) + \log_4 x = 2$

NUMBER POWER

What is the remainder of the division $5^{100} \div 7$?

2.8 Continuous Exponential Growth or Decay

As you read this sentence, the population of the world has increased. The population does not increase in jumps at the end of each year, but is growing continuously. When mothballs are exposed to the air, they gradually disintegrate. At each instant in time, the volume of the mothball is fractionally less than it was the instant before. As you will see below, this type of continuous increase or decrease can be defined by a special exponential function.

Explore: Use a Table

Suppose $1 is invested for one year in an unusual bank that pays interest at 100%/a. Imagine that the bank says you can have the interest compounded as often as you like. Is there a limit to the amount of the investment at the end of the year, no matter how frequently the interest is compounded? Copy and complete the following table to find out. Use a spreadsheet with appropriate formulas and increase the number of compounding periods if you wish.

Principal	Number of Compounding Periods	Rate of Interest Per Period	Amount in Dollars
$1	1	1.00	$1(1 + 1.00)^1 = 2$
$1	2	0.50	$1(1 + 0.50)^2 = ?$
$1	4		
$1	12		
$1	100		
$1	1000		
$1	10 000		
$1	...		

Inquire

1. As the frequency of compounding increases, what amount does the investment seem to approach, to the nearest cent?

2. If you could invest $500 for one year at 100%/a compounding every second, what amount would you expect at the end of the year?

3. If a person's investment amounted to $2125.70 after one year with interest at 100% compounding every second, how much must they have invested, to the nearest dollar?

4. Write a formula for the amount, A, of an investment, if $1 is invested at 100%/a compounding n times per year.

5. Compare the following two situations. Give reasons why one is an example of continuous exponential growth, while the other is not.
A The intensity of sound decreases as you move away from its source.
B The minimum hourly wage increases by 1% on April 1 of each year.

The value of the expression $\left(1+\dfrac{1}{n}\right)^n$ as n gets increasingly large

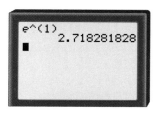

approaches 2.718 281 828 459 045 235 … . Like π, this is a special irrational number which occurs in a variety of situations in mathematics. Mathematicians named the number e, after the famous Swiss mathematician Leonard Euler. Because of its use in many areas, values of e^x are programmed into scientific calculators. The screen shows the value of e^1.

In any situation where continuous growth is occurring, at a rate of $r\%$ per year, the amount, A, at the end of t years is given by

$$A = A_0 e^{\left(\frac{r}{100}\right)t}$$

where A_0 is the initial amount.

Example 1   Population Growth
The population of Vancouver in 1981 was 1 380 000. Since then, the population has been growing continuously at an average rate of 1.7%/a. The population, P, can be modelled by the equation
$$P = 1.38 \times 10^6 \times e^{0.017t}$$
where t is the number of years since 1981.
a) Using this model, find the projected population of Vancouver in 2011, to the nearest tenth of a million.
b) Give reasons why the model might not accurately predict the population of Vancouver in 2011.

Solution
a) The year 2011 is 30 years after 1981, so, use $t = 30$.
$P = 1.38 \times 10^6 \times e^{0.017t}$
$\quad = 1.38 \times 10^6 \times e^{0.017 \times 30}$
$\quad \doteq 2.298 \times 10^6$

Using this model, the projected population of Vancouver in 2011 is about 2.3 million.
b) A number of factors could cause the model to break down. The rate of growth might increase because of a large wave of immigration, or it might decrease because of the expense of housing in the area. The city boundaries might be changed, causing an immediate change in the city's population at that single point in time, which the exponential growth would not reflect.

When continuous exponential decrease or decay is occurring, this is reflected in a negative exponent. If you need to find the value of an exponent in a situation involving continuous exponential growth or decay, two methods are possible. You can use a graphing calculator or you can use the method of taking logarithms of both sides of the equation. Logarithms in base e, which are called **natural logarithms,** are used.

Example 2 Continuous Exponential Decay

The main ingredient of mothballs is naphthalene, which is a white hydrocarbon made from coal tar. Because of its low boiling point, this chemical evaporates in air quite readily. The volume, $V(t)$, of a mothball after t weeks is given by

$$V(t) = V_0 e^{-0.35t}$$

where V_0 is the initial volume.

a) If a mothball with a diameter of 2 cm is exposed to the air, what volume will remain after three weeks?

b) Graph the function $V(t)$ and use the graph to determine after how many weeks only 10% of the original volume remains.

c) Use logarithms to find how long it will take, to the nearest week, for the mothball to reduce to half its original volume.

Solution

a) First find the original volume of the mothball.

The formula for the volume of a sphere is $V = \dfrac{4\pi r^3}{3}$.

$$\therefore\ V_0 = \frac{4\pi}{3}$$

Then, find the volume when $t = 3$.

$$V(t) = V_0 e^{-0.35t}$$

$$V(3) = \frac{4\pi}{3} \times e^{-0.35 \times 3}$$

$$\doteq 1.47$$

b) Graph $y = \dfrac{4\pi}{3} e^{-0.35x}$ and $y = 0.1\left(\dfrac{4\pi}{3}\right)$, and find

their point of intersection.

Only 10% of the original volume remains after about $6\dfrac{1}{2}$ weeks.

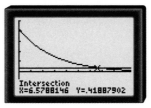

c) When the volume is reduced to half the original volume, $V(t) = 0.5V_0$.

$$V(t) = V_0 e^{-0.35t}$$

$$0.5V_0 = V_0 e^{-0.35t}$$

$$0.5 = e^{-0.35t}$$

Take natural logarithms of both sides.

$$\ln 0.5 = -0.35t$$

$$\therefore\quad t = \frac{\ln 0.5}{-0.35}$$

$$t \doteq 1.98$$

It will take about two weeks for the mothball to reduce to half its original size.

Practice

Use a calculator to find the value of ln x, rounded to three decimal places, for each value of x.

1. 2

2. 0.8

3. 0.3

4. 55

5. 12.5

6. π

Use a calculator to find the value of e^x, rounded to three decimal places, for each value of x.

7. 0.6

8. 0.8

9. 0.055

10. −0.5

11. −0.02

12. 0.25

Solve each equation, giving answers rounded to three decimal places.

13. $1500 = 5e^{0.045x}$

14. $2 = e^{5k}$

15. $65 = e^{7n}$

16. $45 = e^{0.075y}$

17. $\ln 3.6 = 0.034t$

18. $\ln 45.3 = 0.24k$

19. $\ln 1.5 = 0.002n$

20. $\ln 625 = 2.5x$

Predict the similarities and the differences that you would expect to see in the graphs of each pair of functions. Using a graphing calculator, or otherwise, graph each pair and check your predictions. Give the coordinates of the point of intersection, if any.

21. $y = 2^x$ and $y = e^x$

22. $y = e^x$ and $y = e^{-x}$

23. $y = e^x$ and $y = 2e^x$

24. $y = e^x$ and $y = e^x + 1$

25. $y = \log x$ and $y = \ln x$

Applications and Problem Solving

26. Demographics In 1997, the population of Calgary was 795 000. This was an increase of 3.06% from the previous year. Assuming that the population is growing continuously, the population P, in thousands, can be determined by the formula
$$P = 795e^{0.0306t}$$
where t is the time in years since 1997.
a) Using this model, what is the population of Calgary in the year 2000?
b) According to this model, in which year would the population of Calgary exceed one million?
c) Find the current population of Calgary. Does the model seem to be correct? If not, give possible reasons why not.

27. The temperature, T, in degrees Celsius, of a cup of coffee t minutes after it is poured is given by $T = 95e^{-0.05t}$.
a) How hot was the coffee when it was first poured?
b) Find the temperature of the coffee 10 min later.

28. Meteorology Atmospheric pressure varies with altitude above the surface of Earth. For altitudes up to 10 km, the pressure p, in kilopascals, is given by $p = 100e^{-0.139a}$, where a is the altitude in kilometres.
a) If you were going upward in a hot-air balloon, would the atmospheric pressure be increasing or decreasing? Explain.
b) What would the pressure be, to the nearest kilopascal, at 1500 m above the surface of Earth?
c) At what altitude, to the nearest tenth of a kilometre, is the pressure 45 kPa?

29. Physics The intensity of light, I, passing through a glass with an absorption coefficient of 0.2 is given by $I(t) = I_0 e^{-0.2t}$, where I_0 is the initial intensity, and t is the thickness of the glass in centimetres.
a) What thickness will reduce the intensity to half the initial intensity?
b) What effect does doubling the thickness of the glass have on the intensity of light passing through it?

30. Rule of 70 The rule of 70 says, if a population (or money) is growing at r% per year, then, the doubling time is approximately $70 \div r$. This rule works best for small values of r.
a) According to the rule of 70, about how long would it take an investment earning 5% per year to double?
b) Set up an exponential model for an investment earning 5% a year, and, by finding t, see how long it will take the investment to double. How close is this answer to the answer obtained using the rule of 70?
c) It can be shown that, if an amount is compounding continuously at r% for t years, $A(t) = A_0 e^{0.01rt}$. Solve this equation for t by taking the natural logarithm of both sides.
d) By letting $A(t) = 2A_0$ in the result of part c), show why the rule of 70 works.

31. Linguistics If two languages have evolved separately from a common ancestral language, the number of years since the split, $T(w)$, is given by
$$T(w) = -5000 \ln w$$
where w is the percent of words from the ancestral language that are still common to both languages. If two languages split 2000 years ago, what percent of the words from the ancestral language would you expect to find in both languages today?

32. Newton's Law of Cooling This law states that the difference between the temperature of a warm body and that of the cooler surroundings decreases exponentially. To determine the time of death, police will take the temperature of a body when they find it and again t min later. If T is the temperature of the body t min after they find it, then
$$T - T_0 = ae^{-kt}$$
where T_0 is the temperature of the surrounding air, and a and k are constants related to the cooling object.
a) At 1:30 a.m. the police discovered a body in the basement of a house. The temperature in the basement was 10°C and the temperature of the body when it was found was 32°C. The temperature of the body 90 min later was 28°C. Find the values of a and k.
b) Since normal body temperature is 37°C, this must be the value of T at the time of death. Using the results of part (a), determine the approximate time of death. What assumption have you made?
c) Solve $T - T_0 = ae^{-kt}$ for t.

33. Space travel A radioisotope is used as a power source for a satellite. The power output is given by the equation,
$$P = 50e^{-\frac{t}{250}}$$
where P is the power in watts, and t is the time in days.
a) How much power is available after 100 days?
b) The equipment in the satellite needs 10 W of power to function properly. For how long can the satellite operate?

34. For what values of x is $\ln x < 0$? Explain.

35. Engineering A flexible cable suspended between two points forms a curve known as a **catenary**. Its shape is given by the function
$$y = \frac{e^x + e^{-x}}{2}.$$
a) Graph the curve.
b) Describe the characteristics of the catenary. Give the domain, range, x- and y-intercepts, equation of the axis of symmetry, and equation of any asymptotes.

36. Change of base Rewrite $\log_{10} 5$ in base e.

37. Solve to the nearest hundredth.
$$e^{2x} - 2e^x + 1 = 0$$

LOGIC POWER

A tangram is an ancient Chinese puzzle in which a square is cut into seven pieces: five triangles, one square, and one parallelogram.

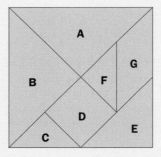

• If the original square has side length one unit, determine an exact expression for the area of each of the seven pieces.
• Make a set of tangram pieces. Fit all seven pieces together to form a rectangle.

Archaeology

Archaeologists use a process called radiological dating to determine how old a fossil is. This process compares the ratio of two radio-active isotopes and uses the known half-life to calculate the age of the artifact. For organic remains the general method used is carbon-14 dating. Since the action of cosmic rays on atmospheric nitrogen produces carbon-14, scientists know that it has been present in the atmosphere for thousands of years. As carbon-14 becomes oxidized to carbon dioxide, it is absorbed into plants and other living organisms by photosynthesis. As long as the organism is alive, the ratio of carbon-14 to carbon-12 is constant. When the organism dies, the carbon-14 starts to decay to carbon-12 and the ratio changes. The ratio of carbon-14 to carbon-12 in a living organism is approximately 1.2×10^{-12}.

1 Carbon-14 to Carbon-12 Ratio

1. Since the half-life of carbon-14 is about 5730 years, the ratio of carbon-14 to carbon-12 after t years can expressed as $1.2 \times 10^{-12} \times 2^{-\frac{t}{5730}}$. An ancient artifact is found to have a carbon-14 to carbon-12 ratio of 2.0×10^{-14}. What is the approximate age of this artifact?

2. A fossilized branch of a tree is found to have a ratio of carbon-14 to carbon-12 of 1.9×10^{-13}. What is the approximate age of the fossil?

3. If a fossilized shell is found to have a ratio of carbon-14 to carbon-12 of 2.4×10^{-15}, what is the approximate age of the shell?

4. Scientists prefer to use natural logarithms. Instead of base 2, they use e in the carbon-14 to carbon-12 ratio. If $(2)^{-\frac{t}{5730}} = e^{-\frac{t}{n}}$, what is the value of n, to the nearest ten?

2 Percent of Carbon-14

Sometimes the amount of carbon-14 is given as a percent of the amount normally found in the atmosphere. The age of the artifact can still be found, as the following example illustrates.

An animal bone contains only 10% of the carbon-14 normally found in the atmosphere. What is the approximate age of the bone?

To find how many half-lives elapse until only 10% of the carbon-14 remains, set up an exponential equation as follows.

$$C(H) = C_0 \left(\frac{1}{2}\right)^H = C_0 (2)^{-H}$$, where H is the *number*

of half-lives needed to have only $C(H)$ remaining. Then, for 10% remaining,

$$0.10 C_0 = C_0 (2)^{-H}$$
$$\log 0.10 = -H \log 2$$
$$H = -\frac{\log 0.10}{\log 2}$$
$$\doteq 3.322$$

Since about 3.322 half-lives have passed, the approximate age of the bone is 3.322×5730, or about 19 000 years.

1. A fossil contains 60% of the carbon-14 normally found in the atmosphere. Approximately how old is the fossil?

2. A piece of cloth is claimed to be from the first century A.D. If 35% of the carbon-14 normally found in the atmosphere is present in the remains, determine whether the claim could be true.

PROBLEM SOLVING

2.9 Solve a Simpler Problem

Some variations of chess do not use the familiar 64-square board. Capablanca's chess uses a board with 80 small squares. If the side length of each small square is 1 unit, then the dimensions of the board are 8 units by 10 units, and the area is 80 square units. The numbers 8 and 10 are factors of 80. Other rectangular boards could be made with the same area, using dimensions 5 by 16, 4 by 20, and so on. Finding the dimensions of all the possible rectangles would give all the factors of 80.

The factors of 360 have a sum of 1170.
What is the sum of the reciprocals of the factors?

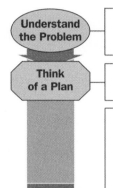

Understand the Problem

1. What information are you given?
2. What are you asked to find?
3. Do you need an exact or an approximate answer?

Think of a Plan

Start by calculating the sum of the factors, and the sum of the reciprocals of the factors, of small numbers.

Carry Out the Plan

Number	Factors	Sum of Factors	Reciprocals of Factors	Sum of Reciprocals
2	1, 2	3	$1, \frac{1}{2}$	$\frac{2}{2} + \frac{1}{2} = \frac{3}{2}$
3	1, 3	4	$1, \frac{1}{3}$	$\frac{3}{3} + \frac{1}{3} = \frac{4}{3}$
4	1, 2, 4	7	$1, \frac{1}{2}, \frac{1}{4}$	$\frac{4}{4} + \frac{2}{4} + \frac{1}{4} = \frac{7}{4}$
12	1, 2, 3, 4, 6, 12	28	$1, \frac{1}{2}, \frac{1}{3}, \frac{1}{4}, \frac{1}{6}, \frac{1}{12}$	$\frac{12}{12} + \frac{6}{12} + \frac{4}{12} + \frac{3}{12} + \frac{2}{12} + \frac{1}{12} = \frac{28}{12}$ or $\frac{7}{3}$

When finding the sum of the reciprocals of the factors of a number, the common denominator of the fractions is the number itself. The resulting numerator of the sum of the fractions is the sum of the divisors. Since the divisors of 360 have a sum of 1170, the sum of the reciprocals of the divisors is $\frac{1170}{360}$ or $\frac{13}{4}$.

Look Back

Does the answer seem reasonable?
How could you check that the answer is correct?

Solve a Simpler Problem

1. Break the problem into smaller parts.
2. Solve the problem.
3. Check that your answer is reasonable.

Applications and Problem Solving

1. Find the sum of the reciprocals of the factors of 180.

2. Systems of equations Solve the following system of equations.

$$v + w + x + y = 0$$
$$w + x + y + z = 1$$
$$x + y + z + v = 2$$
$$y + z + v + w = 4$$
$$z + v + w + x = 5$$

3. Jogging with the dog Marisa lives on a farm. She took her dog, on a leash, and jogged at a speed of 10 km/h. When they were 15 km from home, Marisa turned to go home. She let her dog off the leash. The dog ran towards home at a speed of 16 km/h. Once he got there, he turned and ran back to Marisa. Once he reached her, he turned and ran back to the house. The dog repeated this until Marisa arrived home. If Marisa had maintained her speed of 10 km/h, and the dog kept running at 16 km/h, how far did the dog run altogether?

4. Find the sum of the first 5000 multiples of 2.

5. What is the value of the following product?
$(99 - 9)(99 - 19)(99 - 29)...(99 - 189)(99 - 199)$

6. Ticket roll A total of 3001 digits are used to print the numbers on a roll of cloakroom tickets. The roll starts with number 1. How many tickets are in the roll?

7. Fencing Thirty-two posts are placed equal distances apart in a fence that is 400 m long. How far apart are the posts?

8. Page numbers What page of a book are you reading if the product of the page number on the page and on the facing right page is 15 006?

9. Welding A welder has 203 metal chains of 100 links each. His task is to combine them into one very long chain. How many links must be cut open and then welded shut to complete the task?

10. How many whole numbers less than 1000 do not contain the digit 5?

11. Measurement Four hundred regular hexagonal prisms are packed in a pattern with adjacent edges touching as shown. The length of each side of each hexagon is 4 cm. There are twenty prisms in each of twenty rows.

a) What is the perimeter of the shape formed?
b) What is the volume of the smallest box that would be needed to pack the prisms, if each is 15 cm tall?

12. Conveyor belt A heavy carton is placed on a conveyor belt. Each of the wheels under the conveyor belt has a circumference of 10 cm. If the wheels all begin turning clockwise at the same speed, how many turns does each wheel have to make to move the carton a distance of 30 cm along the conveyor belt?

13. Checkers How many ways are there to move the checker from square A to square B so that it can be made a king?

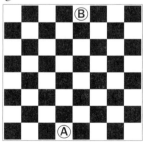

14. Write a problem that can be solved using the solve-a-simpler-problem strategy. Have a classmate solve your problem.

CONNECTING MATH AND PHYSICS

Sound Intensity and Decibels

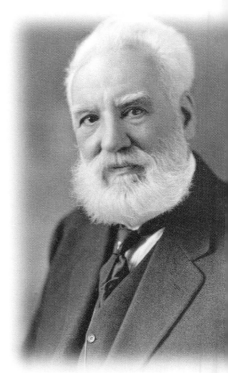

1 Comparing the Intensity of Sounds

The loudness of your voice, a piece of music, and a rock concert can all be measured mathematically. The original unit of measure is the *Bel*, named after Sir Alexander Graham Bell. For most practical purposes this turned out to be too large a unit so the more common unit, the *decibel* (dB), which is one tenth of a Bel, is used today. This scale is logarithmic in nature. For every Bel, or every ten decibels, there is a tenfold increase in the intensity, or loudness, of the sound. In fact, for any intensity, I, the decibel level is defined as follows:

$$dB = 10\log\frac{I}{I_0}$$ where I_0 is the intensity of a barely audible sound.

I_0 has a decibel level of 0.

The table shows some sound intensities and their decibel levels.

Sound	Decibel Level $dB = 10\log(\frac{I}{I_0})$	Intensity
barely audible	0 dB	I_0
whisper	30 dB	$10^3 I_0$
soft music	40 dB	$10^4 I_0$
2-person normal conversation	60 dB	$10^6 I_0$
loud stereo	80 dB	$10^8 I_0$
rock concert	120 dB	$10^{12} I_0$
pain level	130 dB	$10^{13} I_0$

How many times as loud is a normal conversation between two people as a whisper?

Since we are really comparing the intensities, we can proceed as follows:

$$\frac{I(\text{conversation})}{I(\text{whisper})} = \frac{10^6 I_0}{10^3 I_0} = 10^3$$

So a normal conversation between two people is 1000 times as loud, or as intense, as a whisper.

1. Use the definition of decibel level and the properties of logarithms to show that, if the decibel level of a sound is 45 dB, then the intensity is $10^{4.5} I_0$.

2. How many times as loud is a rock concert as a loud stereo?

3. A city ordinance says the maximum allowable traffic noise is 80 dB. How many times as great is the intensity of a "boom box" playing at 85 dB?

4. The smallest difference in sound that the human ear can detect is about 1 dB. What is the intensity of this difference in sound?

5. After complaints about working conditions, the employees' union convinced management to reduce the noise level from 100 dB to 95 dB. Is this a significant reduction? Explain.

6. The original unit, the Bel, turned out to be too large a unit for most practical purposes. Consider the table of sounds and their intensities and give a possible reason for wanting to use decibels instead of Bels.

2 The Effect of Combining Sounds

If two radios are both playing music at 50 dB each, then what is the total decibel level?

Let $10^x I_0$ represent the intensity of two radios. Then,

$$10^x I_0 = 2 \times 10^5 I_0$$
$$10^x = 2 \times 10^5$$
$$\therefore x = \log(2 \times 10^5)$$
$$= \log 2 + \log 10^5$$
$$= 0.3010 + 5$$
$$\doteq 5.3$$

Therefore, the decibel level of two radios playing at the same time at a level of 50 dB each is 53 dB.

1. The decibel level of a plane at takeoff is about 110 dB. What would the decibel level be if two planes took off at the same time?

2. A race car accelerating has a decibel level of about 85 dB. What would the decibel level be if three cars were accelerating simultaneously?

3. The noise of Niagara Falls is about 90 dB. The noise inside a ride at the Pacific National Exhibition was half as intense. What was its decibel level?

4. What is the decibel level of something that is one tenth as loud as the intensity of sound at the pain level?

Review

Graph each function and give its domain, range, intercepts, and equations of the asymptotes.

1. $y = 4^x$

2. $y = 4^x - 2$

3. $y = \left(\dfrac{1}{4}\right)^x$

4. $y = \left(\dfrac{1}{4}\right)^x + 3$

5. Bacteria The bacteria in a petri dish double every 3 h. There were 2500 at the initial count.
a) Write an equation of the form $P(t) = P_0(b)^{kt}$ that gives the population of bacteria, $P(t)$, at time t in hours.
b) How many bacteria will there be in 15 h?
c) How many bacteria were there 3 h ago?

6. Investment Suppose you have $1250 in a GIC that is paying 5%/a interest compounded annually.
a) Set up an exponential function that gives the amount of the investment at time t. Graph the function.
b) State the domain, range, intercept(s), and equations of the asymptote(s) of the function.
c) How much will the investment be worth in six years?
d) Use the graph to find out how many years it will take your money to triple.

7. Population The size of a decreasing population is given by $P(t) = P_0(2)^{-\frac{t}{7}}$ where $P(t)$ represents the population at time t, in years, and P_0 is the initial population. What percent of the original population will there be after
a) 7 years? **b)** 14 years? **c)** 32 years?
d) How does the population 7 years ago compare with the population 7 years in the future?

2.4 *Solve.*

8. $5^{2x+3} = 1$

9. $25^{13 - 8x} = \left(\dfrac{1}{125}\right)^x$

10. $(16^{2x+1})(8^{x-3}) = \left(\dfrac{1}{4}\right)^{x+2}$

11. $\dfrac{9^{2x}}{27^{x-2}} = 81^{3x-4}$

12. Bacteria At the initial count there were 280 bacteria in a culture. Ten hours later, there were 4480 bacteria. What is the doubling period for this type of bacteria?

13. Half-life In 15 days, a sample of bismuth-210 has decayed to $\dfrac{1}{8}$ of its original mass. What is the half-life of bismuth-210?

14. Radioactivity Iodine-131 has a half-life of 8 days. How long will it take for a 100 mg sample to decay to 12.5 mg?

15. Cream The number of hours, $H(t)$, that cream stays fresh decreases exponentially as the temperature of the surrounding air, t, in degrees Celsius, increases. The relationship is $H(t) = 160(0.1)^{0.038t}$.
a) If the cream is kept in a refrigerator at 0°C, how long will it stay fresh?
b) If the cream is left out of the refrigerator and stays fresh for only 16 h, what is the room temperature?
c) Show that the cream will keep approximately 3.7 times as long at 5°C as it will at 20°C.

2.5 *Find the value of x.*

16. $x = \log_3 243$

17. $x = \log 0.1$

18. $x = \log_7 7^5$

19. $x = \log_5 0.04$

20. $\log_4 \dfrac{1}{2} = x$

21. $\log_8 x = 2$

22. $\log_x 81 = 4$

23. $\log x = 0.01$

24. For what values of x is $\log_4 (x - 3) < 2$?

25. Earthquakes Richter magnitude, R, is defined by the equation $R = 0.67 \log 0.37E + 1.46$, where E is the energy, in kilowatt-hours, released by the earthquake. In scientific notation, to three significant digits, how much energy was released by the following earthquakes?
a) $R = 7.5$ in Guatemala in 1976
b) $R = 5.8$ in Morocco in 1960

2.6 *Write as a single logarithm.*

26. $\log x^4 - 2\log xy^3$

27. $3\log A + 2\log B - \left(\log \sqrt{A} - \log 2B\right)$

28. $\log \sqrt{a^2 - b^2} - \dfrac{1}{2}\log(a + b)$

29. If $\log_5 2 = x$, express each in terms of x.
a) $\log_5 16 - 3\log_5 4$
b) $\log_5 (8 \times 16 \times 32) - \log_5 \sqrt[3]{64}$

30. If $\log_2 x = 5$, evaluate the following.

a) $\log_2 8x$ **b)** $3\log_2 x^4$ **c)** $\log_2\left(\dfrac{x^5}{32}\right)$

31. Chemistry The pH of a solution is defined as pH $= -\log_{10}$ [H+], where [H+] is the hydrogen ion concentration in moles per litre.
a) What is the pH of human blood if its hydrogen ion concentration is 6.3×10^{-8} mol/L?
b) The pH of hydrochloric acid is approximately 1.602. What is its hydrogen ion concentration?

32. Express y as a function of x and state the domain.

a) $\log y = \dfrac{1}{3}(\log x - \log 27)$

b) $\log(y + 3) = \log x^3 - \log(x - 2)$

Solve for x. Round to the nearest hundredth.
33. $5^x = 241$ **34.** $4^{3x-2} = 789$
35. $8^{2x} = 37^{x-4}$ **36.** $35 \times 3^x = 11^{x-1}$
37. $x = \log_2 57$ **38.** $x = \log_3 99$

Solve each logarithmic equation for x.
39. $\log_3(x^2 - 3x + 5) = 2$
40. $\log(x + 5) - \log(x + 1) = \log 3x$
41. $\log_4(x + 3) - 2 = \log_4(x - 4)$

42. Chromium is used as a radiotracer to study red blood cells. In a test, 30 units are administered and one week later 25.2 units remain. To the nearest tenth, what is the half-life of chromium?

43. Prove the identity, $\log_b a = \dfrac{\log_b x}{\log_a x}$.

44. Prove that if $\log_b a = c$ and $\log_x b = c$, then $\log_a x = c^{-2}$.

45. If $\log x - \log(x - 2) = \log b$, express x as a function of b.

46. Solve $A(t) = A_0 e^{kt}$ for t.

47. Depreciation The value, V, in dollars, of a printing machine is decreasing exponentially according to the equation $V = 85\ 000e^{-0.14t}$, where t is the time, in years, since the machine was installed.
a) Find the value of the machine after 10 years.
b) After how many years is the machine worth 25% of its original value?

Exploring Math

Constructing a Logarithmic Spiral

The form of a snail's shell is a coiled spiral.

1. To draw a spiral of this type, complete the following steps using a straightedge and compasses, or using geometry software.
Step 1: Draw a large square ABCD. Inside the square draw a quarter circle as shown. Record the radius of this quarter circle.

Step 2: Form a golden rectangle by drawing an arc with centre at the midpoint, M, of AB and radius MD to intersect side BA extended at F. Complete the rectangle BCEF. Draw square DEGH inside rectangle BCEF. Draw the quarter circle that has centre at H and radius HD. Record this radius.

Step 3: Inside rectangle FAHG, draw the square of which FG is one side. Draw the quarter circle that has centre at F and radius equal to the diameter of this square. Record the radius.

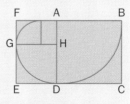

Step 4: Repeat the process of step 3 as many times as you like.

2. The resulting curve is called a logarithmic spiral. Explain why this name is appropriate.

Chapter Check

1. Appreciation A rare baseball card has been increasing in value at a rate of 12% per year. Its value, $V(t)$, is given by the relation $V(t) = 4.75(1.12)^t$, where t is in years and $t = 0$ is the year 1980.
a) How much will the card be worth in the year 2010?
b) If the card had been increasing at the same rate before 1980, what was its value in 1975?
c) In which year was the card worth $20?

2. Population The trout population in a lake has been doubling every five years. There were 200 trout at the initial count.
a) Write an equation of the form $P(t) = P_0(b)^{kt}$ that gives the population of the trout at time t, in years.
b) How many trout will there be in 12 years?
c) How many trout were there 3 years ago?

3. Depreciation An excavating company has a digger that was purchased for $140 000. It is depreciating at 12% per year.
a) Set up an exponential function that gives the value of the digger after t years.
b) Graph the function. Give the domain, range, intercept(s), and equation(s) of the asymptote(s).
c) How much will the digger be worth in 7 years?
d) How long it will take before the equipment is worth $70 000?

4. Solve for x.
a) $(9^{2x+1})(3^{x-3}) = \left(\dfrac{1}{27}\right)^{x-1}$ **b)** $\dfrac{16^{2x}}{8^{x+2}} = 32^{x-4}$

5. Radioactivity A radioactive substance decays according to the equation $A(t) = A_0(0.1)^{0.073t}$, where t is in years and A_0 is the original amount of the substance.
a) What percent of the original amount will be left after 5 years?
b) How long will it take until there is only 10% of the original amount left?

6. If $\log_3 4 = x$, express each of the following in terms of x.
a) $\log_3 16 - 2\log_3 32$ **b)** $\log_3 2$

7. If $\log_3 x = 7$, evaluate the following.
a) $\log_3 9x$ **b)** $\log_3 x^{10}$ **c)** $\log_3 \dfrac{\sqrt[4]{x}}{81}$

8. Express y as a function of x. State the domain.
a) $\log y = \log(1 - 3x)$
b) $\log(y + 3) = \log x^2 - \log(x + 3)$
c) $\log_2(y - 3) = 5 + \log_2(x - 4)$

9. Solve for x. Round to the nearest hundredth.
a) $3^x = 129$ **b)** $5^{2x+1} = 498$
c) $\left(\dfrac{2}{3}\right)^{3x} = 0.56^{x+2}$ **d)** $79 \times 2^{x+1} = 7^{3x-4}$
e) $\log_6 567 = x$ **f)** $x = \log_4 0.283$

10. Solve for x.
a) $\log_8 x - 1 = \log_8(x - 1)$
b) $\log_2(33x - 9) - \log_2(2x + 3) = 4$
c) $\log_2(2x + 5) + \log_2 x = \log_2 12$
d) $\log_6 3x + \log_6(x + 4) = 2$
e) $(\log x)^2 = \log x^2$

11. Population growth Show that the doubling time of a population that increases ten-fold every H hours is given by $t \doteq 0.3H$.

12. Light intensity On a foggy night the intensity of light from an approaching car is drastically reduced. The distance away, d, in metres, is related to the intensity, $I(d)$, by
$$d \doteq -166.67\log\dfrac{I(d)}{125}.$$
a) How far from you is an approaching car if the intensity is 50 lumens?
b) What is the maximum intensity of the light from an approaching car?
c) Solve the equation for $I(d)$.

13. Physics The intensity of light, in lumens, passing through a liquid with an absorption coefficient of 0.2 is given by
$$I(d) = 1000e^{-0.2d}$$
where d is the depth, in metres.
a) What is the intensity of light passing through 5 m of this liquid?
b) How many metres must the light travel before the intensity is reduced to 1% of the original intensity?

Using the Strategies

1. If $A \times B = 24$, $C \times D = 32$, $B \times D = 48$, and $B \times C = 24$, what is the value of $A \times B \times C \times D$?

2. Age Stan is twice as old as his sister Paula was when Stan was as old as Paula is now. The sum of their ages now is 49 years. How old are Stan and Paula now?

3. Measurement The diameter of the circle is the same as the radius of the semicircle. What fraction of the area of the semicircle is shaded?

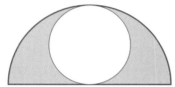

4. The number 153 has an interesting property.
$$1^3 + 5^3 + 3^3$$
$$= 1 + 125 + 27$$
$$= 153$$
There are two three-digit numbers that begin with 3 and also have this property. There is also one three-digit number, beginning with 4, that has the same property. Find these numbers.

5. If a, b, and c are three different real numbers whose sum is zero and whose product is two, what is the value of $a^3 + b^3 + c^3$?

6. Bacteria Two jars have the same capacity. One bacterium is placed in one jar, and two of the same bacterium are placed in the other jar. This bacterium doubles every 3 min. In 2 h, the jar that started with two bacteria is full. How long does it take for the other jar to fill?

7. The positive integers are arranged in the pattern shown. If this pattern is continued, what number will fall in the nineteenth column of the sixty-fifth row?

1				
2	3			
4	5	6		
7	8	9	10	
11	12	13	14	15

8. Place the fewest possible mathematical symbols between digits to make the following equation true.
$$1\ 2\ 3\ 4\ 5\ 6\ 7\ 8\ 9 = 100$$

9. Rolls of steel Three rolls of steel are held together with a band. The diameter of each roll of steel is 1 m. What is the length of the band?

10. Time If it is 9 a.m. now, what time will it be 99 999 999 999 h from now?

11. Two neighbouring houses are located near a straight section of a rural road as shown. The electric company plans to place a pole at the roadside and connect wires from there to the two houses. How far from the point X should the pole be located so that the minimum length of wire is needed?

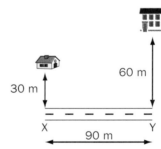

12. Each of the letters represents a different digit. There is only one possible number that, when multiplied by 4, has the property shown. What is the number?

$$\begin{array}{r} A\ B\ C\ D\ E \\ \times\ \qquad 4 \\ \hline E\ D\ C\ B\ A \end{array}$$

13. Population density If the entire population of Canada moved to Prince Edward Island, and each person was given an equal area of the land to live on, what area would each person have?

CHAPTER 3

Conics

The cone of water vapour formed when a jet breaks the sound barrier can be seen when captured on high-speed film.

An aircraft in flight produces air-pressure waves. These are similar to the water waves produced by the bow of a ship. When an aircraft breaks the sound barrier, these air-pressure waves combine to form a shock wave in the shape of a cone. You will hear a sonic boom if you are in the area where the conical shock wave intersects the ground.

If the conical shock wave intersects the ground when the jet is travelling parallel to the ground, the sonic boom is heard in an area that is the shape of one branch of a **hyperbola**.

shape where the sonic boom is heard
one branch of a hyperbola

Sketch the shape where the sonic boom is heard when the jet is
1. flying straight up vertically   **2.** climbing gently   **3.** climbing at a steep angle

Recognizing Conics Around Us

The early Greek mathematicians first studied conics. Around 200 B.C., Apollonius of Perga published a definitive work entitled *Conic Sections*. In eight books with around 400 propositions, he provided a comprehensive investigation of the subject, earning himself the title of "The Great Geometer."

Many mathematicians undertook further investigations of conics over the centuries. In the sixteenth century, Galilei Galileo used the mathematics of conic sections to derive laws for projectile motion. One of his contemporaries, Johannes Kepler, used the mathematics of conic sections to deduce laws for planetary motion.

In this chapter, the following four conic sections will be studied.

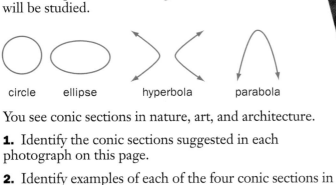

circle   ellipse   hyperbola   parabola

You see conic sections in nature, art, and architecture.

1. Identify the conic sections suggested in each photograph on this page.

2. Identify examples of each of the four conic sections in nature, art, and architecture in your local area. Which type of conic section did you find most often? least often?

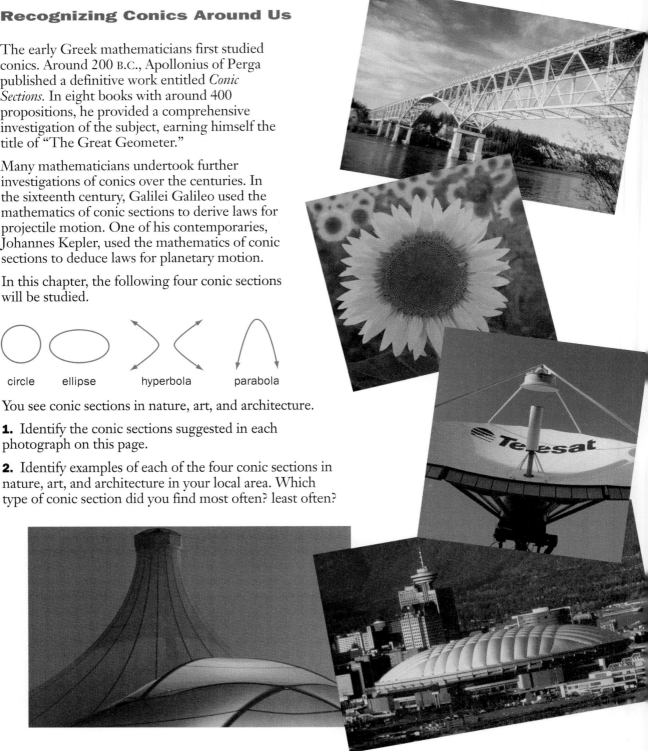

Warm Up

For each function,
a) *graph, using a graphing calculator, or sketch*
b) *find any x-intercepts*
  1. $f(x) = x^2 - 4$
  2. $f(x) = (x + 1)^2$
  3. $f(x) = -3x^2$
  4. $f(x) = (x - 2)^2 + 5$
  5. $f(x) = 0.5x^2 - 4.5$
  6. $f(x) = x^2 - 4x + 4$
  7. $f(x) = -x^2 + 10x - 12$
  8. $f(x) = x^2 + 7x + 1$
  9. $f(x) = 0.5x^2 - x + 3$
  10. $f(x) = 3x^2 - 18x - 5$
  11. $f(x) = 2 + 4x - 2.5x^2$

For each parabola,
a) *find the coordinates of the vertex*
b) *state whether the vertex is a maximum or minimum*
  12. $y = x^2 + 8x - 1$
  13. $y = 2x^2 - 6x + 3$
  14. $y = 0.5x^2 - x - 4$
  15. $y = -4x^2 + 12x - 2$
  16. $2y = -3x^2 - 6x - 9$

Given $d = \sqrt{(x_2 - x_1)^2 + (y_2 - y_1)^2}$, the formula for the distance between two points (x_1, y_1) and (x_2, y_2), find the distance between each pair of points.
  17. $(3, -2)$ and $(8, 10)$
  18. $(-1, 6)$ and $(2, 2)$
  19. $(-4, -9)$ and $(4, 6)$
  20. $(6, 2)$ and $(4, -5)$
  21. $(-2, 8)$ and $(-5, -1)$
  22. $(-1, -3)$ and $(-6, -9)$

Given $(x, y) = \left(\dfrac{x_1 + x_2}{2}, \dfrac{y_1 + y_2}{2} \right)$, the formula for the midpoint of a line segment with endpoints (x_1, y_1) and (x_2, y_2), find the midpoint of the line segment with each pair of endpoints.
  23. $(4, -1)$ and $(8, 11)$
  24. $(-1, 8)$ and $(2, 4)$
  25. $(-4, 7)$ and $(4, 6)$
  26. $(6, 2)$ and $(4, -5)$
  27. $(-2, 8)$ and $(-6, -1)$
  28. $(1, -3)$ and $(-6, -9)$

Mental Math

Find the square root of each number.
  1. 144   **2.** 16   **3.** 225   **4.** 25
  5. 441   **6.** 36   **7.** 289   **8.** 64
  9. 400   **10.** 81   **11.** 324   **12.** 169

Expand and simplify.
  13. $(x + 3)^2$ **14.** $(2x - 5)^2$
  15. $(3x + y)^2$ **16.** $(x - 6y)^2$
  17. $(4x - 7y)^2$ **18.** $(5x + 3y)^2$
  19. $(4x + 3y)^2$ **20.** $(11x - 2y)^2$

What constant needs be added to each polynomial to make it a perfect square trinomial?
  21. $x^2 + 12x$ **22.** $x^2 - 8x$
  23. $x^2 + 3x$ **24.** $x^2 - 6x$
  25. $x^2 + 5x$ **26.** $x^2 - 16x$
  27. $x^2 + x$ **28.** $4x^2 - 4x$
  29. $9x^2 + 12x$ **30.** $x^2 + 2x$
  31. $4x^2 - 8x$ **32.** $16x^2 + 8x$
  33. $x^2 + bx$ **34.** $ax^2 + bx$

For each parabola, state the
a) *coordinates of the vertex*
b) *direction of the opening*
c) *equation of the axis of symmetry*
d) *maximum or minimum value*
  35. $y = x^2 - 8$ **36.** $y = (x - 3)^2$
  37. $y = (x - 5)^2 + 2$ **38.** $y = -2x^2$
  39. $y = 3(x + 4)^2 + 5$ **40.** $y = 4(x - 1)^2 - 6$
  41. $y = -0.5(x + 3)^2 - 2$

Write the equation for each quadratic function.
  42. vertex at $(0, 0)$, passing through $(-5, 20)$
  43. vertex at $(3, -2)$, congruent to $y = 0.5x^2$
  44.

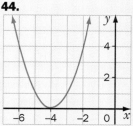

  45.

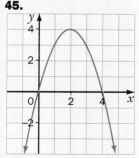

3.1 The Cone and Conic Sections

Circles, ellipses, hyperbolas, and parabolas are called conic sections because they are, in fact, sections of a cone.

Explore 1: Make a Model

Work with a partner.
Student 1: Hold one end of a piece of string about 30 cm long in your hand.
Student 2: Take the other end of the string in your hand and pull it straight out. Then, rotate your hand in a circular motion.

The solid that the path of the string delineates is a **cone**, similar to the shape of a party hat or an ice cream cone. The string is the **generator** of the cone.

Inquire

1. Modify the modelling you just did. This time:
Student 1: Hold the middle of the piece of string in one hand.
Take one end of the string in your other hand, and pull it straight out.
Student 2: Take the other end of the string in your hand and pull it straight out in the opposite direction.
Students 1 and 2: Rotate your hands holding the ends of the string in a circular motion.

The solid that the path of the string delineates is a double cone or a **double-napped cone**. Again, the string is called the **generator** of the cone. The middle point is the **vertex**. The open circular ends are the **bases**.

There are different types of cone depending on the shape of the base. The most common type, which you just generated, is the **right circular cone**. Its base is a circle and its **central axis** is perpendicular to the base.

By slicing this type of cone at different angles, the circle, the ellipse, the parabola, and the hyperbola can be generated. Apollonius of Perga was the first to realize that each conic section can be derived from the intersection of a double-napped right circular cone and a plane.

base
generator
central axis
vertex
generator
central axis
base

Explore 2: Make a Model

Use conical vegetables, such as carrots or parsnips, and some tempera paint. Make the following cuts in your vegetables.

a) parallel to the base

b) inclined to the base

c) parallel to the central axis

d) parallel to the cone's generator

Then, dip the sliced pieces into some paint and make prints of the plane figures.

Inquire

1. Identify the conic section in each print.

2. Which conic section can be generated only by using a double-napped cone?

3. Identify two characteristics of each conic section. Compare your results with those of your classmates.

Example

Describe the symmetry in a circle.

Solution

The circle has rotational symmetry about its centre point, which is on the cone's central axis.

Practice

1. Define the generator of a cone.

2. What is the difference between a cone and a double-napped cone?

3. Justify the name "right circular cone."

Applications and Problem Solving

4. Modelling Use a flashlight to generate a cone of light, and a table top as the plane that intersects the cone. Create each of the conic sections. Describe the orientation of the flashlight to the table top when each conic section is generated.

5. To which part of the cone, if any, is the plane parallel when each conic section is generated?

6. Symmetry Describe the symmetry in the parabola, the ellipse, and the hyperbola.

7. Which of the conic sections are closed figures? open figures?

8. Compare and contrast
a) the ellipse and the circle
b) the parabola and the hyperbola

9. Sonic shock waves Now that you have generated conic sections yourself, revisit the sonic shock waves in the chapter opener on page 131. Confirm the shape where the sonic boom is heard when the jet is
a) flying straight up vertically
b) climbing gently
c) climbing at a steep angle

10. Degenerate conic sections Some slices of a double-napped cone cut by a plane do not yield a circle, an ellipse, a parabola, or a hyperbola. Such slices yield degenerate conic sections. What slices would yield degenerate conic sections? What are the degenerate conic sections?

11. General form For all conic sections, $Ax^2 + Bxy + Cy^2 + Dx + Ey + F = 0$, where A, B, and C are not all 0, is the general form of the equation. The Bxy term does not appear when the axes of the conic section are parallel to the x- and/or y-axes. Most conic sections you will examine in this chapter have axes parallel to the x- and/or y-axes.
a) Why can A, B, and C not all equal 0?
b) Consider the shape, symmetry, and other properties that you have observed in the conic sections as slices of a cone cut by a plane, and use your previous knowledge about equations of parabolas to predict how to complete each statement.
i) In the general form of the equation for a(n) ▓▓▓▓ with its axes parallel to the x- and/or y-axes, either $A = 0$ or $C = 0$, and $B = 0$.
ii) In the general form of the equation for a(n) ▓▓▓▓ , $A = C$, and $B = 0$.
iii) In the general form of the equation for a(n) ▓▓▓▓ with its axes parallel to the x- and/or y-axes, A and C have opposite signs, and $B = 0$.
iv) In the general form of the equation for a(n) ▓▓▓▓ with its axes parallel to the x- and/or y-axes, A and C have the same sign, $A \neq C$, and $B = 0$.

PROBLEM SOLVING

3.2 Look for a Pattern

Dynamics is the branch of mathematics that deals with forces and their relations to patterns of motion. In meteorology, this relates especially to wind and precipitation patterns. To help predict when and where a tornado might occur, meteorologists look for horizontal wind shears which produce anvil-shaped clouds. Patterns found using Doppler radar, which measures the speed and direction of drops of precipitation, are also used. The ability to determine patterns is an important aspect of many careers.

Many whole numbers can be written as the difference of two squares. For example,

$$24 = 7^2 - 5^2$$
$$21 = 11^2 - 10^2$$

Which of the positive integers 1, 2, 3, … 20 can be expressed as the difference of two squares? Generalize the results for all whole numbers.

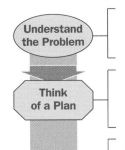

Understand the Problem
1. What information are you given?
2. What are you asked to find?
3. Do you need an exact or an approximate answer?

Think of a Plan

Set up a table and determine which numbers can be expressed as the difference of squares. Determine the patterns for odd and even numbers.

Carry Out the Plan

Number	Difference of Squares	Number	Difference of Squares
1	$1^2 - 0^2$	11	$6^2 - 5^2$
2	not possible	12	$4^2 - 2^2$
3	$2^2 - 1^2$	13	$7^2 - 6^2$
4	$2^2 - 0^2$	14	not possible
5	$3^2 - 2^2$	15	$8^2 - 7^2$
6	not possible	16	$5^2 - 3^2$
7	$4^2 - 3^2$	17	$9^2 - 8^2$
8	$3^2 - 1^2$	18	not possible
9	$5^2 - 4^2$	19	$10^2 - 9^2$
10	not possible	20	$6^2 - 4^2$

The numbers 1, 3, 4, 5, 7, 8, 9, 11, 12, 13, 15, 16, 17, 19, and 20 can be expressed as the difference of two squares.

Starting with 2, every fourth number in the list could not be expressed as the difference of two squares. There are different patterns for expressing odd numbers and even numbers as the difference of squares.

Odd Numbers
The bases of the squares are consecutive numbers whose sum is the number.

Even Numbers
The bases of the squares differ by two. The even numbers are also multiples of 4.

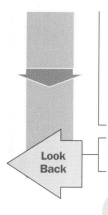

The odd numbers have the form
$$(n + 1)^2 - n^2$$
$$= n^2 + 2n + 1 - n^2$$
$$= 2n + 1$$

The even numbers have the form
$$(n + 1)^2 - (n - 1)^2$$
$$= (n^2 + 2n + 1) - (n^2 - 2n + 1)$$
$$= 4n$$

The whole numbers that can be expressed as the difference of two squares are all the odd numbers, and all even numbers that can be written in the form $4n$, where n is any natural number.

Look Back

Does the answer seem reasonable?
How could you check that the answer is correct?

Look for a Pattern

1. Use the given information to find a pattern.
2. Use the pattern to solve the problem.
3. Check that your answer is reasonable.

Applications and Problem Solving

1. Stair climbing If it is possible to climb stairs one step at a time or two steps at a time, then there are three different ways stairs with three steps can be climbed.

one step, then one step, then one step
two steps, then one step
one step, then two steps

In how many different ways can stairs with 20 steps be climbed?

2. Suppose, according to a certain set of rules, the number 2 can be written as the sum of one or more positive integers in the two ways shown.

$2 = 2$
$2 = 1 + 1$

Using the same rules, the number 3 can be written as the sum of one or more positive integers in four ways as follows.

$3 = 3$
$3 = 2 + 1$
$3 = 1 + 2$
$3 = 1 + 1 + 1$

Using the same rules, in how many ways can the number 17 be written as the sum of one or more positive integers?

3. If you wrote the numbers 1, 2, 3, ..., 999 000, how many digits would you write?

4. Units digit What is the units digit when 17^{133} is written in standard form?

5. Find the sum of
$$\frac{1}{2} + \left(\frac{1}{3} + \frac{2}{3}\right) + \left(\frac{1}{4} + \frac{2}{4} + \frac{3}{4}\right) + \left(\frac{1}{5} + \frac{2}{5} + \frac{3}{5} + \frac{4}{5}\right) + \dots$$
$$+ \left(\frac{1}{100} + \frac{2}{100} + \dots + \frac{99}{100}\right).$$

6. Factorial The value of $n!$, which is called n factorial, is defined as
$$n! = n \times (n - 1) \times (n - 2) \dots \times 3 \times 2 \times 1$$
For example, $6! = 6 \times 5 \times 4 \times 3 \times 2 \times 1$
$$= 720$$
What is the last digit of $1! + 2! + 3! + \dots + 99!$?

7. Sums Given that $S_1 = 1$, $S_2 = 2 + 3$, $S_3 = 4 + 5 + 6$, $S_4 = 7 + 8 + 9 + 10$, and so on, determine the value of S_{20}.

8. Write a problem that can be solved by looking for a pattern. Have a classmate solve your problem.

3.3 The Circle

The compact disc player is everywhere these days. Developed jointly by Philips and Sony, it first came on the market in 1983. By 1986, over one million CD players were being sold each year. Because of the low-cost laser components, the CD player has become one of the most successful electronic devices to date.

If you trace around the outside of a compact disc, the result is a circle.

A **circle** is the set or **locus** of all points in a plane which are equidistant from a fixed point. This fixed point is called the **centre**. The distance from this centre to any point on the circle is called the **radius**.

Explore 1: Use a Model

Use a CD or a cutout of a circle with its centre marked.
Draw a set of coordinate axes in the middle of a sheet of 0.5 cm grid paper.
Centre the CD at the origin. Trace around the outside of the CD.
Mark point P on the circle in the first quadrant.
Draw a radius from the origin to point P.
What are the coordinates of point P to the nearest millimetre?

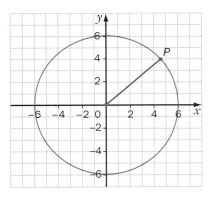

The radius can be calculated using $d = \sqrt{(x_2 - x_1)^2 + (y_2 - y_1)^2}$, the formula for the distance between two points (x_1, y_1) and (x_2, y_2). Create a right triangle by dropping a perpendicular from point P to the x-axis. Explain the distance formula in terms of the Pythagorean Theorem.

Inquire

1. Calculate the radius of the circle.
2. Measure the radius to the nearest millimetre. How does this compare with your calculated value?
3. In one of the other quadrants, mark a point on the circle. Repeat questions 1 and 2.
4. For a circle of radius r, centred at the origin and passing through (x, y), write an equation for r in terms of x and y.

Explore 2: Use a Model

Retrace the CD with its centre at (2, 3).
Mark point P on the circle.
Draw the radius from the centre of the circle to point P.
What are the coordinates of point P to the nearest millimetre?

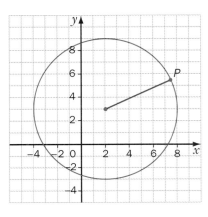

Again, the radius can be calculated using $d = \sqrt{(x_2 - x_1)^2 + (y_2 - y_1)^2}$, the formula for the distance between two points (x_1, y_1) and (x_2, y_2).

Inquire

1. Did the radius of the circle change when the CD was moved? What is the radius?

2. Calculate the radius of the circle. How does this compare with the value from question 1?

3. Retrace the CD with the centre in any other quadrant. Repeat questions 1 and 2.

4. For a circle of radius r, centred at (h, k) and passing through (x, y), write an equation for r in terms of x and y.

The **standard form** of a circle with centre (h, k) and radius r is
$$(x - h)^2 + (y - k)^2 = r^2.$$
When the centre of the circle is at the origin, (h, k) is $(0, 0)$ and the standard form is
$$x^2 + y^2 = r^2.$$

The **general form** of a circle can be obtained by expanding the standard form.
$$(x - h)^2 + (y - k)^2 = r^2$$
$$(x^2 - 2hx + h^2) + (y^2 - 2ky + k^2) = r^2$$
$$x^2 + y^2 + (-2h)x + (-2k)y + (h^2 + k^2) = r^2$$

Because h, k, and r are constants, $-2h$, $-2k$, $(h^2 + k^2)$, and r^2 are constants. So, the equation can be written as
$$x^2 + y^2 + Dx + Ey + F = 0.$$

Example 1   Finding the Equation of a Circle Given the Centre and Radius

Write the equation of the circle with centre $(-3, 5)$ and radius 6 in standard form and general form.

Solution

The centre and the radius are known.

Use $(x - h)^2 + (y - k)^2 = r^2$ and substitute $h = -3$, $k = 5$, $r = 6$.
$$(x - (-3))^2 + (y - 5)^2 = 6^2$$
$$(x + 3)^2 + (y - 5)^2 = 36 \qquad \text{standard form}$$
$$(x^2 + 6x + 9) + (y^2 - 10y + 25) = 36$$
$$x^2 + y^2 + 6x - 10y + 34 - 36 = 0$$
$$x^2 + y^2 + 6x - 10y - 2 = 0 \qquad \text{general form where } D = 6,\ E = -10,\ \text{and } F = -2$$

Example 2   Finding the Equation Given the Centre and a Point on the Circle

Write the equation of the circle with centre $(4, -1)$ and passing through $(3, 7)$ in standard form and general form.

Solution

The centre is known; the radius needs to be found.

Use $(x - h)^2 + (y - k)^2 = r^2$ and substitute $h = 4$, $k = -1$, $x = 3$, and $y = 7$.
$$(3 - 4)^2 + (7 - (-1))^2 = r^2$$
$$(-1)^2 + 8^2 = r^2$$
$$65 = r^2$$

Now, use $(x-h)^2 + (y-k)^2 = r^2$ and substitute $h = 4, k = -1, r^2 = 65$.

$$(x-4)^2 + (y-(-1))^2 = 65$$
$$(x-4)^2 + (y+1)^2 = 65 \qquad \text{standard form}$$
$$x^2 - 8x + 16 + y^2 + 2y + 1 = 65$$
$$x^2 + y^2 - 8x + 2y + 17 - 65 = 0$$
$$x^2 + y^2 - 8x + 2y - 48 = 0 \qquad \text{general form where } D = -8, E = 2, \text{ and } F = -48$$

Example 3   Finding the Centre and the Radius

Find the centre and radius of each circle.

a) $x^2 + y^2 + 14x - 72 = 0$

b) $x^2 + y^2 - x + 2y - 14.75 = 0$

Solution

The centre and radius can be read from the equation in standard form.
Complete the square to change each equation into the form $(x-h)^2 + (y-k)^2 = r^2$.

a)
$$x^2 + y^2 + 14x - 72 = 0$$
$$x^2 + 14x \qquad + y^2 = 72$$
$$(x^2 + 14x + 49 - 49) + y^2 = 72$$
$$(x+7)^2 + y^2 = 121$$
$h = -7, k = 0, \text{ and } r = 11$
So, the centre is at $(-7, \ 0)$ and the radius is 11.

b)
$$x^2 + y^2 - x + 2y - 14.75 = 0$$
$$x^2 - x + \qquad y^2 + 2y \qquad = 14.75$$
$$(x^2 - x + 0.25 - 0.25) + (y^2 + 2y + 1 - 1) = 14.75$$
$$(x - 0.5)^2 + (y + 1)^2 = 16$$
$h = 0.5, k = -1, \text{ and } r = 4$
So, the centre is at $(0.5, \ -1)$ and the radius is 4.

The Y = Editor of a graphing calculator can draw graphs only of equations
which are explicitly written as y is a function of x. Some calculators have a
draw instruction, the circle instruction, that can be used to graph a circle.

Example 4   Graphing a Circle Using a Graphing Calculator

Graph $(x-5)^2 + (y+1)^2 = 9$ using a graphing calculator.

Solution 1   Using the Y= Editor

Solve the equation for y in terms of x.
$$(x-5)^2 + (y+1)^2 = 9$$
$$(y+1)^2 = 9 - (x-5)^2$$
$$y + 1 = \pm\sqrt{9 - (x-5)^2}$$
$$y = \pm\sqrt{9 - (x-5)^2} - 1$$

Then, graph both equations in a square viewing window.
$$\text{Y1} = \sqrt{9 - (x-5)^2} - 1 \text{ and Y2} = -\sqrt{9 - (x-5)^2} - 1$$
Check. The centre is at $(5, -1)$ and the radius is 3.

Solution 2   Using the Circle Instruction

Enter the coordinates of the centre $(5, -1)$ and the
radius 3.

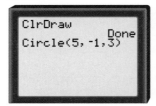
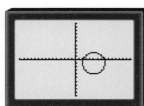

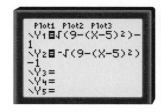
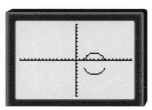

Practice

Write the equation for the circle centred at the origin and with the given radius in standard form.

1. 9   **2.** 4   **3.** 5   **4.** 8

5. 1.5   **6.** 6   **7.** $\sqrt{5}$ **8.** $2\sqrt{2}$

Write the equation for the circle with each centre and radius in standard form.

9. centre $(-2, 5)$, radius 3
10. centre $(-5, -1)$, radius 7
11. centre $(2, 8)$, radius 10
12. centre $(-3, 3)$, radius 12
13. centre $(-4, -5)$, radius 5
14. centre $(3, -4)$, radius 1.1
15. centre $(5, -4)$, radius $\sqrt{6}$
16. centre $(-6, 7)$, radius $3\sqrt{5}$

Find the centre and the radius of each circle.

17. $x^2 + y^2 = 121$ **18.** $x^2 + y^2 = 144$
19. $3x^2 + 3y^2 - 27 = 0$ **20.** $25x^2 + 25y^2 - 100 = 0$
21. $4x^2 + 4y^2 - 25 = 0$
22. $(x - 5)^2 + (y - 9)^2 = 16$
23. $(x + 3)^2 + (y - 1)^2 = 81$
24. $(x + 7)^2 + (y + 2)^2 - 64 = 0$
25. $(x - 6)^2 + (y + 4)^2 = 9.61$
26. $4(x + 1)^2 + 4(y - 3)^2 = 9$

Determine the equation in standard form for each circle. Then, expand it to find the general form.

27. centre $(8, 2)$, passing through $(5, 0)$
28. centre $(4, -6)$, passing through $(-8, 1)$
29. centre $(2, 3)$, passing through $(7, 2)$
30. centre $(-4, 5)$, tangent to the x-axis
31. centre $(-6, -5)$, tangent to the y-axis

Determine the equation in standard form for the circle with endpoints of a diameter at each pair of points.

32. $(3, -6)$ and $(3, 2)$ **33.** $(1, 4)$ and $(-3, -6)$
34. $(-3, 4)$ and $(5, 2)$ **35.** $(3, 10)$ and $(-7, -2)$

Find the centre and the radius of each circle.

36. $x^2 - 6x + y^2 - 8y - 39 = 0$
37. $x^2 - 7x + y^2 + 7y = 17.75$.
38. $x^2 + 8x + y^2 + 4y = 12$
39. $x^2 + 8 + y^2 - 8y = 0$

Use a graphing calculator to graph each circle.

40. $x^2 + y^2 = 40$
41. $5x^2 + 5y^2 - 100 = 0$

42. $(x - 4)^2 + (y + 6)^2 = 30$
43. $x^2 + 6x + y^2 - 4y = 37$
44. $2(x + 5)^2 + 2(y - 6)^2 = 48$
45. $x^2 + 8x + y^2 + 10y + 13 = 0$

Applications and Problem Solving

46. Locus definition a) Use geometry software and the *Circle by Center and Radius* construction to construct several circles.
b) Use compasses or a safety compass to construct several circles.
c) Explain why the constructions in parts a) and b) use the definition of a circle as a locus of points.

47. Coins More cost effective than bills, coins have, on average, twenty years in circulation compared with one year for a bill. The Royal Canadian Mint used a centimetre grid to design a frame to hold a set of coins.
Determine the equation of the outline for each coin in standard form.

Coin	Diameter (mm)	Centre
Toonie	28.00	(0, 5)
Loonie	26.50	(3.5, 3.5)
50¢	27.13	(−3.5, 3.5)
25¢	23.88	(1.5, −4.5)
10¢	18.03	(3.5, −3)
5¢	21.20	(−1.5, −4.5)
1¢	19.05	(−3.5, −3)

48. Toonie In early 1996, the Canadian two-dollar coin was introduced. Its inner core is aluminum-bronze and its outer ring is nickel. The diameter of the inner core is 17 mm. What is the equation that represents the circle separating the core and the ring of the toonie on the centimetre grid in question 47?

49. General form You have been using $x^2 + y^2 + Dx + Ey + F = 0$ as the general form of a circle in this section. But, in question 11 of Section 3.1, you were introduced to
$Ax^2 + Bxy + Cy^2 + Dx + Ey + F = 0$
as the general form of any conic section. Explain why A and C are 1 for circles and why the Bxy term never applies to circles.

50. Translations Another way of thinking about a circle not centred at the origin is as a translation of the circle centred at $(0, 0)$ with the same radius. Use diagrams and explanations to justify that the mapping of $x^2 + y^2 = 49$ to $(x - 4)^2 + (y + 1)^2 = 49$ is $(x, y) \rightarrow (x + 4, y - 1)$. Then, generalize to write the mapping of $x^2 + y^2 = r^2$ to $(x - h)^2 + (y - k)^2 = r^2$.

Use your results from the previous question to write the equation of the image of $x^2 + y^2 = 9$ under each translation.

51. $(x, y) \rightarrow (x + 4, y + 2)$
52. $(x, y) \rightarrow (x - 5, y - 7)$
53. $(x, y) \rightarrow (x - 3, y + 8)$
54. $(x, y) \rightarrow (x + 1, y - 6)$

55. The circle $x^2 + y^2 = 25$ is translated so its centre is at $(-3, 4)$. Let (m, n) be a point on the original circle. In terms of m and n, what are the coordinates of the corresponding point on the translated circle? Let (a, b) be a point on the translated circle. In terms of a and b, what are the coordinates of the corresponding point on the original circle?

56. In each of the four quadrants, a circle of radius 4 is drawn touching both axes. A smaller circle centred at the origin is drawn to touch each of the other circles. What is the equation of the smaller circle?

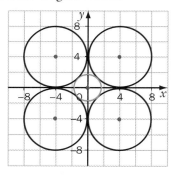

57. The points $(1, 0)$ and $(-1, -2)$ lie on a circle. The centre of the circle is on the line $y = -2x$. What is the equation of the circle?

58. Radio-controlled airplane Todd is flying his radio-controlled airplane 30 m above the ground in a circular path described by the equation $(x - 5)^2 + (y - 2)^2 = 36$. Emiko is flying her plane at the same height in a circular path described by the equation $(x + 1)^2 + (y - 4)^2 = 25$. Do the paths of the two planes intersect? If so, at how many points?

59. A circle centred at the origin with radius $\frac{1}{2}$ is translated. The translated circle passes through $\left(2, \frac{3}{2}\right)$ and $\left(2, \frac{1}{2}\right)$. By what was the original circle translated?

60. A circle of radius 2 centred at the origin intersects the axes at four points. Using these four intersection points as centres, four circles of radius 1 are drawn. At each of the two points where each of those four circles intersect the axes, a circle of radius $\frac{1}{2}$ is drawn.

What are the equations of the eight circles of radii $\frac{1}{2}$?

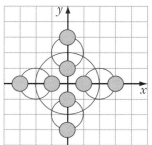

61. Four nested circles have radii 8, 4, 2, and 1 respectively. The line $y = x$ divides each circle exactly in half, and each circle touches the other circles only at the origin. The circle of radius 1 passes through the point $(\sqrt{2}, \sqrt{2})$. What is the equation of each circle? Sketch all four circles.

62. What is the equation of the largest circle that can be inscribed inside a square centred at $(-1, 3)$ with sides 9 units long?

63. Stone-circle monuments Certain ancient Western European peoples built stone-circle monuments. Most of these, dating between 5000 and 3000 years old, consist of between 6 and 60 stones enclosing a more or less circular area. The most famous, Stonehenge near Salisbury in England, is a circle 29.6 m in diameter. A 12-stone circle can be modelled by the equation $x^2 + y^2 = 1$ with stones at $(1, 0)$, $(0, 1)$, $(-1, 0)$, and $(0, -1)$. What are the coordinates of the other 8 stones?

3.4 The Ellipse

Comets are generally classified according to the type of orbit in which they move. Comets whose period can be calculated move in closed-curve elliptical orbits. Some comets are affected by the gravitational pull of large planets to the extent that they move off into space in hyperbolic orbits.

The orbit of Halley's comet is elliptical. It enters our solar system every 76 years. It returns next in the year 2061.

Explore: Use a Model

Draw a set of coordinate axes on a sheet of graph paper.
On the positive *x*-axis, insert a pushpin.
On the negative *x*-axis, the same distance from the origin as the first pushpin, insert another pushpin. Each pin represents a **focus** of an ellipse (plural **foci**).

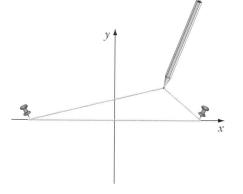

Tie together the ends of a piece of string that is more than twice as long as the distance between the pins so that the string forms a loop.
Place the loop of string around the pushpins.
Insert a pencil in the loop and pull the loop taut to form a triangle with the two pushpins and the pencil point as vertices.

Pull the pencil around the loop to draw a closed curve.

The shape is an **ellipse**. There are two axes of symmetry. Each intersects the ellipse in two places. The longer line segment between the intersection points of the ellipse and one axis of symmetry is the **major axis**. The shorter line segment between the intersection points of the ellipse and the other axis of symmetry is the **minor axis**.

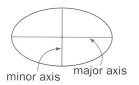

minor axis   major axis

Inquire

1. For your ellipse, along which axis is the major axis? If the foci were on the *y*-axis, along which axis would the major axis be?

2. Mark point P on the ellipse. Join point P to each focus with a line segment. These line segments are the **focal radii**.

3. Measure the focal radii. Then, sum the two lengths.

4. Repeat questions 2 and 3 for two other points.

5. How are the three sums related?

6. Measure the lengths of the major and minor axes.

7. What is the relationship between the sum of the focal radii and the lengths of the axes?

An **ellipse** is the locus of all points in a plane such that the sum of the distances from two given points in the plane, the foci, is constant.

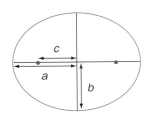

For an ellipse, half the length of the major axis is denoted by a, half the length of the minor axis by b, and half the length of the distance between the foci by c. Therefore, the major axis has length $2a$ units, the minor $2b$ units, and the distance between the foci $2c$ units.

Example 1 Showing a Relationship
Show that the constant that is the sum of the distances from the two foci to a point on the ellipse is the same as the length of the major axis, $2a$.

Solution
Mark point P where the major axis meets the ellipse.
Add the distances between this point and the foci, that is, sum the focal radii.

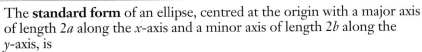

$$F_1P + F_2P = (a - c) + (a + c)$$
$$= 2a$$

So, the constant that is the sum of the distances from the two foci to a point on the ellipse is $2a$, which is the length of the major axis.

The **standard form** of an ellipse, centred at the origin with a major axis of length $2a$ along the x-axis and a minor axis of length $2b$ along the y-axis, is

$$\frac{x^2}{a^2} + \frac{y^2}{b^2} = 1.$$

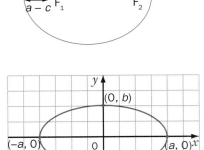

The standard form of an ellipse, centred at the origin with a major axis of length $2a$ along the y-axis and a minor axis of length $2b$ along the x-axis, is

$$\frac{y^2}{a^2} + \frac{x^2}{b^2} = 1 \text{ or } \frac{x^2}{b^2} + \frac{y^2}{a^2} = 1.$$

These standard forms can be derived using the locus definition and the distance formula. See question 29 on page 151.

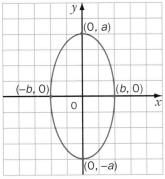

As in the case of the circle, the standard form of an ellipse, centred at any point (h, k) with a major axis of length $2a$ parallel to the x-axis and a minor axis of length $2b$ parallel to the y-axis, is

$$\frac{(x - h)^2}{a^2} + \frac{(y - k)^2}{b^2} = 1.$$

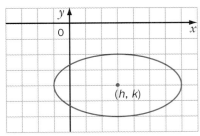

The standard form of an ellipse, centred at any point (h, k) with a major axis of length $2a$ parallel to the y-axis and a minor axis of length $2b$ parallel to the x-axis, is

$$\frac{(y-k)^2}{a^2}+\frac{(x-h)^2}{b^2}=1 \ \text{ or } \ \frac{(x-h)^2}{b^2}+\frac{(y-k)^2}{a^2}=1.$$

The **general form** of an ellipse with its axes parallel to the x- and y-axes is
$$Ax^2 + Cy^2 + Dx + Ey + F = 0,$$
where A and C have the same sign and $A \neq C$. Only ellipses with axes parallel to the x- and y-axes are considered in this chapter. The general form can be derived from the standard forms by expanding and simplifying. See question 30 on page 151.

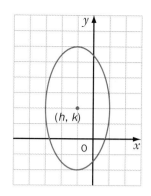

Example 2 Finding the Equations of Ellipses with Centre at (0, 0)

Write the equation for each ellipse in standard form and general form.

a) centre at $(0, 0)$, foci at $(3, 0)$ and $(-3, 0)$, length of major axis 10, and length of minor axis 8

b)

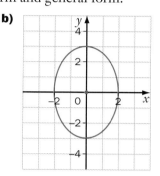

Solution

a) The centre is at $(0, 0)$.
The foci are on the x-axis. So, the major axis is along the x-axis.
The length of the major axis is 10 units. So, $a = 5$.
The length of the minor axis is 8 units. So, $b = 4$.

Use $\dfrac{x^2}{a^2}+\dfrac{y^2}{b^2}=1$ and substitute $a = 5$ and $b = 4$.

$$\frac{x^2}{5^2}+\frac{y^2}{4^2}=1$$

$$\frac{x^2}{25}+\frac{y^2}{16}=1 \qquad \text{standard form}$$

$$16x^2 + 25y^2 = 16\times 25$$

$$16x^2 + 25y^2 - 400 = 0 \qquad \text{general form where } A = 16,\ C = 25, \text{ and } F = -400$$

b) The centre is at (0, 0).
The major (longer) axis is along the y-axis. The ellipse intersects its major axis at (0, 3) and (0, –3). So, the length of the major axis is 6 units, and $a = 3$.
The minor (shorter) axis is along the x-axis. The ellipse intersects its minor axis at (2, 0) and (–2, 0). So, the length of the minor axis is 4 units, and $b = 2$.

Use $\dfrac{x^2}{b^2} + \dfrac{y^2}{a^2} = 1$ and substitute $a = 3$ and $b = 2$.

$$\frac{x^2}{2^2} + \frac{y^2}{3^2} = 1$$

$$\frac{x^2}{4} + \frac{y^2}{9} = 1 \qquad \text{standard form}$$

$$9x^2 + 4y^2 = 9 \times 4$$

$$9x^2 + 4y^2 - 36 = 0 \qquad \text{general form where } A = 9,\ C = 4,\text{ and } F = -36$$

Example 3 Finding the Equations of Ellipses with Centre at (*h*, *k*)

Write the equation for each ellipse in standard form and general form.

a)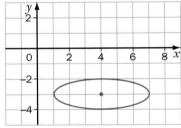

b) centre at (–2, 5), passing through (–5, 5), (1, 5), (–2, –2), and (–2, 12)

Solution

a) The centre is at (4, –3), so $h = 4$ and $k = -3$.
The major axis is parallel to the x-axis. Its length is 6 units. So, $a = 3$.
The minor axis is parallel to the y-axis. Its length is 2 units. So, $b = 1$.

Use $\dfrac{(x-h)^2}{a^2} + \dfrac{(y-k)^2}{b^2} = 1$ and substitute $h = 4$, $k = -3$, $a = 3$, and $b = 1$.

$$\frac{(x-4)^2}{3^2} + \frac{(y-(-3))^2}{1^2} = 1$$

$$\frac{(x-4)^2}{9} + \frac{(y+3)^2}{1} = 1 \qquad \text{standard form}$$

$$(x-4)^2 + 9(y+3)^2 = 9$$

$$(x^2 - 8x + 16) + 9(y^2 + 6y + 9) = 9$$

$$x^2 - 8x + 16 + 9y^2 + 54y + 81 - 9 = 0$$

$$x^2 + 9y^2 - 8x + 54y + 88 = 0 \qquad \text{general form where } A = 1,\ C = 9,\ D = -8,\ E = 54,\text{ and } F = 88$$

b) The centre is at $(-2, 5)$, so $h = -2$ and $k = 5$.
Plot the other points and sketch the ellipse.
The major axis is parallel to the y-axis and 14 units in length. So, $a = 7$.
The minor axis is parallel to the x-axis and 6 units in length. So, $b = 3$.

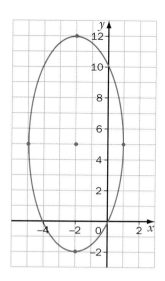

$$\text{Use } \frac{(x-h)^2}{b^2} + \frac{(y-k)^2}{a^2} = 1 \text{ and substitute } h = -2, k = 5, a = 7,$$
$$\text{and } b = 3.$$

$$\frac{(x-(-2))^2}{3^2} + \frac{(y-5)^2}{7^2} = 1$$

$$\frac{(x+2)^2}{9} + \frac{(y-5)^2}{49} = 1 \qquad \text{standard form}$$

$$49(x+2)^2 + 9(y-5)^2 = 49 \times 9$$
$$49(x^2 + 4x + 4) + 9(y^2 - 10y + 25) = 441$$
$$49x^2 + 196x + 196 + 9y^2 - 90y + 225 - 441 = 0$$
$$49x^2 + 9y^2 + 196x - 90y - 20 = 0 \qquad \begin{array}{l}\text{general form where } A = 49, C = 9,\\ D = 196, E = -90, \text{ and } F = -20\end{array}$$

Example 4 Finding the Relationship Between a, b, and c

For an ellipse with major axis of length $2a$ units, minor axis of length $2b$ units, and the distance between the foci of $2c$ units, show that $a^2 = b^2 + c^2$.

Solution
Draw a sketch to help visualize the situation.
Mark foci F_1 and F_2, and centre C.
Mark point P where the minor axis meets the ellipse.
Join foci F_1 and F_2 to point P.

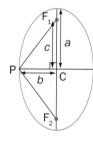

$F_1P + F_2P = 2a$ from Example 1
$F_1P = F_2P = a$ corresponding sides in congruent triangles
$a^2 = b^2 + c^2$ Pythagorean Theorem

Example 5 Finding the Centre, Axes, and Foci

Find the coordinates of the centre, the length of the major and minor axes, and the coordinates of the foci of each ellipse.
a) $x^2 + 2y^2 - 2x + 4y - 1 = 0$ **b)** $9x^2 + 4y^2 + 6x + 4y - 23 = 0$

Solution
The centre and lengths of the axes can be read from the standard form equation.
Complete the square to change each equation to standard form.

a)
$$x^2 + 2y^2 - 2x + 4y - 1 = 0$$
$$x^2 - 2x + 2y^2 + 4y = 1$$
$$x^2 - 2x \qquad + 2(y^2 + 2y) \qquad = 1$$
$$(x^2 - 2x + 1 - 1) + 2(y^2 + 2y + 1 - 1) = 1$$
$$(x-1)^2 - 1 + 2(y+1)^2 - 2 = 1$$
$$(x-1)^2 + 2(y+1)^2 = 4$$
$$\frac{(x-1)^2}{4} + \frac{(y+1)^2}{2} = 1$$

$h = 1, k = -1, a^2 = 4, b^2 = 2$

So, $c^2 = a^2 - b^2$
$= 4 - 2$
$= 2$

$a = 2, b = \sqrt{2}, c = \sqrt{2}$

The centre is at $(1, -1)$.

The major axis, parallel to the x-axis, has a length of $2(2)$ or 4 units.

The length of the minor axis is $2\sqrt{2}$ units.

The foci are at $(1 + \sqrt{2}, -1)$ and $(1 - \sqrt{2}, -1)$.

b)
$$9x^2 + 4y^2 + 6x + 4y - 23 = 0$$
$$9x^2 + 6x + 4y^2 + 4y = 23$$
$$9\left(x^2 + \frac{2}{3}x\right) + 4\left(y^2 + y\right) = 23$$
$$9\left(x^2 + \frac{2}{3}x + \frac{1}{9} - \frac{1}{9}\right) + 4\left(y^2 + y + \frac{1}{4} - \frac{1}{4}\right) = 23$$
$$9\left(x + \frac{1}{3}\right)^2 - 1 + 4\left(y + \frac{1}{2}\right)^2 - 1 = 23$$
$$9\left(x + \frac{1}{3}\right)^2 + 4\left(y + \frac{1}{2}\right)^2 = 25$$
$$\frac{9\left(x + \frac{1}{3}\right)^2}{25} + \frac{4\left(y + \frac{1}{2}\right)^2}{25} = 1$$
$$\frac{\left(x + \frac{1}{3}\right)^2}{\dfrac{25}{9}} + \frac{\left(y + \frac{1}{2}\right)^2}{\dfrac{25}{4}} = 1$$

$h = -\dfrac{1}{3}, k = -\dfrac{1}{2}, a^2 = \dfrac{25}{4}, b^2 = \dfrac{25}{9}$

So, $c^2 = a^2 - b^2$
$$= \frac{25}{4} - \frac{25}{9}$$
$$= \frac{9(25) - 4(25)}{36}$$
$$= \frac{125}{36}$$

$a = \dfrac{5}{2}, b = \dfrac{5}{3}, c = \dfrac{5\sqrt{5}}{6}$

The centre is at $\left(-\dfrac{1}{3}, -\dfrac{1}{2}\right)$. The major axis, parallel to the y-axis, has a length of $2\left(\dfrac{5}{2}\right)$ or 5 units.

The length of the minor axis is $2\left(\dfrac{5}{3}\right)$ or $\dfrac{10}{3}$ units. The foci are at $\left(-\dfrac{1}{3}, -\dfrac{1}{2} + \dfrac{5\sqrt{5}}{6}\right)$ and $\left(-\dfrac{1}{3}, -\dfrac{1}{2} - \dfrac{5\sqrt{5}}{6}\right)$.

Example 6   Graphing Ellipses Using a Graphing Calculator

Use a graphing calculator to graph.

a) $4x^2 + (y-1)^2 = 64$

b) $4(x+5)^2 + \dfrac{(y-1)^2}{4} = 1$

Solution

Express each equation in standard form to be able to visualize what the graph should look like.
Then, solve each equation for y in terms of x.

a)
$$4x^2 + (y-1)^2 = 64$$
$$\frac{4x^2}{64} + \frac{(y-1)^2}{64} = 1$$
$$\frac{x^2}{16} + \frac{(y-1)^2}{64} = 1$$

So, $h = 0$, $k = 1$, $a^2 = 64$, and $b^2 = 16$.
The centre is at $(0, 1)$.
The major axis, parallel to the y-axis, has a length of $2(8)$ or 16 units.
The minor axis has a length of $2(4)$ or 8 units.
$$4x^2 + (y-1)^2 = 64$$
$$(y-1)^2 = 64 - 4x^2$$
$$y - 1 = \pm\sqrt{64 - 4x^2}$$
$$y = \pm\sqrt{64 - 4x^2} + 1$$

Then, graph both equations in a square viewing window.

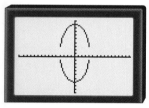

Check. The centre is at $(0, 1)$ and the lengths of the axes are 16 units and 8 units.

b)
$$4(x+5)^2 + \frac{(y-1)^2}{4} = 1$$
$$\frac{(x+5)^2}{\dfrac{1}{4}} + \frac{(y-1)^2}{4} = 1$$

So, $h = -5$, $k = 1$, $a^2 = 4$, and $b^2 = \dfrac{1}{4}$.
The centre is at $(-5, 1)$.
The major axis, parallel to the y-axis, has a length of $2(2)$ or 4 units.

The minor axis has a length of $2\left(\dfrac{1}{2}\right)$ or 1 unit.

$$4(x+5)^2 + \frac{(y-1)^2}{4} = 1$$
$$\frac{(y-1)^2}{4} = 1 - 4(x+5)^2$$
$$(y-1)^2 = 4(1 - 4(x+5)^2)$$
$$y - 1 = \pm\sqrt{4 - 16(x+5)^2}$$
$$y = \pm\sqrt{4 - 16(x+5)^2} + 1$$

Then, graph both equations in a square viewing window, adjusting to make the graph larger and squaring the viewing window again.

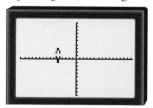 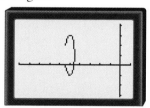

Check. The centre is at $(-5, 1)$ and the lengths of the axes are 4 units and 1 unit.

Practice

For each ellipse, determine the
a) coordinates of the centre
b) lengths of the major and minor axes
c) coordinates of the foci

1.

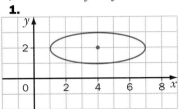

2.

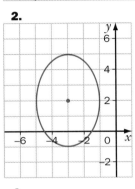

3.

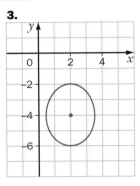

4.

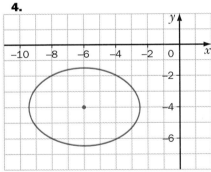

5. $\dfrac{x^2}{64} + \dfrac{y^2}{36} = 1$

6. $\dfrac{x^2}{16} + \dfrac{y^2}{49} = 1$

7. $\dfrac{(x-3)^2}{9} + \dfrac{(y-8)^2}{100} = 1$

8. $\dfrac{(x+7)^2}{4} + \dfrac{(y-5)^2}{25} = 1$

9. $9x^2 + 16y^2 = 144$

10. $49(x+12)^2 + 7(y-1)^2 = 49$

Sketch the graph of each ellipse. Then, graph any two, using a graphing calculator.

11. $\dfrac{x^2}{9} + \dfrac{y^2}{25} = 1$

12. $\dfrac{x^2}{36} + y^2 = 1$

13. $\dfrac{(x-3)^2}{16} + \dfrac{y^2}{4} = 1$

14. $\dfrac{(x+1)^2}{81} + \dfrac{(y-2)^2}{49} = 1$

15. $\dfrac{(x-5)^2}{4} + \dfrac{(y-6)^2}{25} = 1$

16. $\dfrac{x^2}{100} + (y+3)^2 = 1$

17. $9x^2 + 36y^2 = 144$

18. $(x+3)^2 + 4(y-2)^2 = 36$

19. $4x^2 + (y+1)^2 = 9$

20. $15(x+2)^2 + \dfrac{(y+3)^2}{4} = 4$

Write the equation for each ellipse in standard form and general form.
21. centre $(3, -2)$, passing through $(-4, -2)$, $(10, -2)$, $(3, 1)$, and $(3, -5)$
22. centre $(-1, -2)$, passing through $(-5, -2)$, $(3, -2)$, $(-1, 4)$, and $(-1, -8)$
23. foci at $(0, 0)$ and $(0, 8)$, sum of focal radii 10
24. foci at $(-1, -1)$ and $(9, -1)$, sum of focal radii 26

For each ellipse, determine the
a) coordinates of the centre
b) lengths of the major and minor axes
c) coordinates of the foci
25. $3x^2 + y^2 + 6x - 8y - 11 = 0$
26. $x^2 + 121y^2 - 726y + 968 = 0$
27. $9x^2 + 25y^2 - 9x - 50y - 197.75 = 0$

Applications and Problem Solving

28. Technology Use a graphing calculator.
a) Graph the circle $x^2 + y^2 = 16$.
b) Graph $Ax^2 + y^2 = 16$ for at least two values of $A > 1$.
c) Graph $Ax^2 + y^2 = 16$ for at least two values of $0 < A < 1$.

d) Graph $x^2 + Cy^2 = 16$ for at least two values of $C > 1$.

e) Graph $x^2 + Cy^2 = 16$ for at least two values of $0 < C < 1$.

f) How are the graphs alike? different? Explain the similarities and differences.

g) Graph $Ax^2 + y^2 = 16$ for $A = 0$.

h) Sketch the graph $x^2 + Cy^2 = 16$ for $C = 0$.

i) Explain the graphs in parts g) and h).

29. Standard form Consider an ellipse with its major axis along the x-axis, foci at $(-c, 0)$ and $(c, 0)$, x-intercepts at $(-a, 0)$ and $(a, 0)$, and y-intercepts at $(0, -b)$ and $(0, b)$.

a) Use the distance formula to show that for a point (x, y) on the ellipse,

$$\sqrt{(x-c)^2 + y^2} + \sqrt{(x+c)^2 + y^2} = 2a .$$

b) Isolate one radical term in the equation in part a) and derive $\dfrac{x^2}{a^2} + \dfrac{y^2}{a^2 - c^2} = 1$.

c) Use the relationship $a^2 = b^2 + c^2$ to derive $\dfrac{x^2}{a^2} + \dfrac{y^2}{b^2} = 1$, the standard form for the ellipse with its major axis along the x-axis.

30. General form Expand $\dfrac{(x-h)^2}{a^2} + \dfrac{(y-k)^2}{b^2} = 1$, the standard form of an ellipse, centred at (h, k) with a major axis of length $2a$ parallel to the x-axis and a minor axis of length $2b$ parallel to the y-axis, to derive the general form $Ax^2 + Cy^2 + Dx + Ey + F = 0$, where A and C have the same sign and $A \neq C$.

31. Technology Graph $2x^2 + y^2 - 12 = 0$ using a graphing calculator. Create two other equations of this type by changing one coefficient. Graph them.

32. Distortions Another way of thinking about an ellipse is as a distorted circle.

a) Sketch the graph of the unit circle $x^2 + y^2 = 1$ and the ellipse $\dfrac{x^2}{16} + y^2 = 1$.

b) What are the intercepts?

c) Describe the ellipse as an expansion or compression of the circle, giving the direction.

d) Complete this statement. The mapping of $x^2 + y^2 = 1$ to $\dfrac{x^2}{16} + y^2 = 1$ is $(x, y) \rightarrow (\blacksquare x, \blacksquare y)$.

e) Repeat parts a) to d) for the ellipse $x^2 + \dfrac{y^2}{9} = 1$.

f) Repeat parts a) to d) for the ellipse $\dfrac{x^2}{9} + \dfrac{y^2}{4} = 1$.

g) Generalize to write the mapping of $x^2 + y^2 = 1$ to $\dfrac{x^2}{a^2} + \dfrac{y^2}{b^2} = 1$.

Use your results from the previous question. Describe the transformations (translations and distortions) that have been applied to the unit circle $x^2 + y^2 = 1$ to produce each ellipse. Then, find the standard form equation of each ellipse.

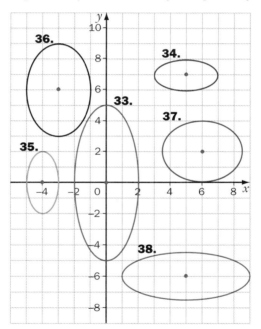

39. Covered entrance A semi-elliptical covering is to be built over an 8-m-wide road and the 2-m-wide sidewalks on either side of it that lead to an art centre. If there is a maximum clearance of 5 m over the road, what will be the minimum clearance over the road? What is the height of the tallest person that will be able to walk down the middle of the sidewalks? Are these numbers realistic?

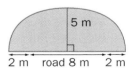

40. Domed stadium BC Place Stadium has an air-filled fabric dome roof that forms the shape of an ellipse when viewed from above. Its maximum length is approximately 230 m, its maximum width is approximately 190 m, and its maximum height is approximately 60 m.

a) Find an equation for the ellipse formed by the base of the roof.

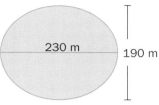

230 m 190 m

b) Taking a cross section of the roof at its greatest width results in a semi-ellipse. Find an equation for this semi-ellipse.

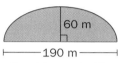

60 m 190 m

c) The promoters of a concert plan to send fireworks up from a point on the stage that is 30 m lower than the centre of the ellipse in part b), and 40 m along the major axis of this ellipse from its centre. How far is that point on the stage from the roof?

41. Design An ellipse is drawn with centre (0, 0) and major axis along the y-axis.
A second ellipse is drawn with centre (0, 0) and major axis equal to the minor axis of the first ellipse.
A third is drawn with centre (0, 0) and major axis equal to the minor axis of the second ellipse.
A fourth ellipse is drawn with centre (0, 0) and major axis equal to the minor axis of the third ellipse. The first ellipse passes through (0, 5).

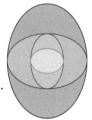

The second ellipse passes through $\left(2, \dfrac{3\sqrt{3}}{2}\right)$.

The third ellipse passes through (0, 3), (0, −3),

and $\left(\dfrac{4\sqrt{2}}{3}, 1\right)$. The fourth ellipse passes through

$\left(\sqrt{2}, 1\right)$. Find the standard equation of each ellipse.

42. Sign The shape of a sign can be modelled by the equation $x^2 + 1.96y^2 = 1.96$. (The measurements are in metres.) The four-letter company name is to be painted on the sign in large letters. Each letter will be 1.0 m high and 0.4 m wide, and there will be 0.2 m between the letters. Will the name fit, centred on the sign?

43. Whisper Chamber In the United States Capitol building, the Whisper Chamber was built in the shape of an ellipse. If you stood at one focus and a friend stood at the other, you would be able to hear your friend whisper, even though you would be much too far away to hear under normal conditions. This is possible because of a reflective property of the ellipse.

a) Draw an ellipse, centred at the origin. Mark foci F_1 and F_2 on the appropriate axis. Mark point P on the ellipse. Draw focal radii F_1P and F_2P. Draw the straight line that touches the ellipse only at point P. Measure the angle between this line and each focal radius. What do you observe? Repeat for two other points on the ellipse.

b) Other architects have used elliptical shapes to provide good acoustical environments because of this reflective property. Use your research skills to find other examples.

44. Find the area of the rectangle with the greatest area that can be inscribed in the ellipse

with the equation $\dfrac{x^2}{25} + \dfrac{y^2}{9} = 1$.

45. Prove that the area of a square inscribed in

the ellipse $\dfrac{x^2}{a^2} + \dfrac{y^2}{b^2} = 1$ is $\dfrac{4a^2b^2}{a^2 + b^2}$.

NUMBER POWER

Use each of the digits 1 through 9 once to make true equations.

■ − ■ + ■ = 6

■ − ■ − ■ = 6

■ ÷ ■ × ■ = 6

Orbiting Satellites

Use the *Satellites* database, from the Computer Data Bank, to complete the following.

1 Communications Satellites

The apogee of a satellite is the greatest distance that the orbit of the satellite takes the satellite from Earth. The perigee is the closest distance that the orbit takes the satellite to Earth.

Geosynchronous satellites are located almost directly above the equator because they orbit Earth at approximately the same speed as the speed of the surface of Earth in its movement in relation to the sun.

1. Devise a plan to check the validity of the following statement. Remember to exclude the records for which the required data are not available. Describe any calculation fields you would add.

> Communications satellites are usually geosychronous, with apogees and perigees almost equal, with inclinations close to 0°, and with periods close to 1440 min.

2. Compare your plan with the plans of classmates. Revise your plan, if necessary, and carry it out. Which satellites most closely match this description?

2 Weather Satellites

1. Devise a plan to check the validity of the following statements about weather satellites. Remember to exclude the records for which the required data are not available.

> Most weather satellites have apogees and perigees almost equal, have inclinations close to 90°, and have periods close to 90 min. Most are usually much less distant from Earth than communications satellites. But some have orbits that resemble those of communications satellites.

2. Compare your plan with the plans of classmates. Revise your plan, if necessary, and carry it out. Which satellites most closely match the first two statements? Which match the third statement?

3 Elliptical Orbits

Make the following assumptions about the satellites orbiting Earth.
- The orbits are elliptical.
- The ellipses are centred at the origin.
- The major axis is along the *x*-axis.
- The centre of Earth is one focus.
- The radius of Earth is 6337 km.

1. a) Which satellite has the greatest difference between its apogee and perigee?
b) What are its apogee and perigee?
c) Explain the following sketch of its orbit.

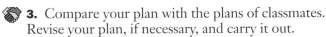

7493 km

45 536 km

d) How would you find the values of a and c?
e) What are their values?
f) Use the relationship between a^2, b^2, and c^2 to find b^2.
g) What is the equation of the elliptical orbit?

2. Devise a plan to model the orbit of each satellite using the equation of an ellipse in standard form. Remember to exclude the records for which the required data are not available. Describe any calculation fields you would add.

3. Compare your plan with the plans of classmates. Revise your plan, if necessary, and carry it out.

4. Justify the following statement.
> On the basis of the assumptions above, most satellite orbits are very close to circular.

3.5 The Hyperbola

The Concorde, a supersonic aircraft developed by Britain and France, first began passenger service in 1976. The Concorde cruises at twice the speed of sound at an altitude of 17 000 m. As a passenger on the Concorde on a flight from London to New York, you would cross five time zones in 3.5 h. Your arrival in New York time would be 1.5 h prior to your departure in London time.

As you saw in the chapter opener, at speeds greater than the speed of sound, air pressure disturbances accumulate in front of the aircraft and a conical shock wave forms. When the Concorde is flying parallel to the ground, this conical shock wave intersects the ground in the shape of one branch of a hyperbola.

Explore 1 Make a Table

In the diagram, the two points equidistant from the origin, F_1 and F_2, are the **foci** of the hyperbola. With each point as a centre, two sets of concentric circles were drawn.
A smooth curve was constructed through (3, 0) and certain intersection points of the circles in the right half-plane.
A smooth curve was constructed through (−3, 0) and certain intersection points of the circles in the left half-plane.

Copy this diagram onto centimetre grid paper.

Each curve is one **branch** of the hyperbola.
Mark point P_1 on the hyperbola. Join point P_1 to each focus with a line segment. These line segments are the **focal radii**. Measure the focal radii. Record your measurements in a table. Repeat for three other points on the hyperbola, P_2, P_3, and P_4.

Point	Focal Radius From F_1 (cm)	Focal Radius From F_2 (cm)
P_1		
P_2		
P_3		
P_4		

Inquire

1. Measure the distance between the two foci.

2. At which points did each branch of the hyperbola intersect the x-axis? These points are the **vertices** of the hyperbola.

3. What is the distance between the vertices?

4. Examine the data in your table. How are the focal radii and the distance between the vertices related?

5. If you drew the hyperbola with vertices at (2, 0) and (−2, 0) would your answer to question 4 still be true? Explain your reasoning. Then, test your prediction.

A **hyperbola** is the locus of all points in a plane such that the absolute value of the difference of the distances from any point on the hyperbola to two given points in the plane, the foci, is constant.

For a hyperbola, there are two axes of symmetry. One intersects the hyperbola at its vertices. The second is perpendicular to the first. The line segment between the vertices is the **transverse axis**. Half the length of the transverse axis is denoted by a, and half the distance between the foci is denoted by c. Therefore, the transverse axis has length $2a$ units and the distance between the foci $2c$ units.

By choosing one of the vertices as the point on the hyperbola and subtracting the distances between it and the foci, you see that the constant is $2a$.

$$|F_1P - F_2P| = |(c - a) - (2a + c - a)|$$
$$= |c - a - 2a - c + a|$$
$$= |-2a|$$
$$= 2a$$

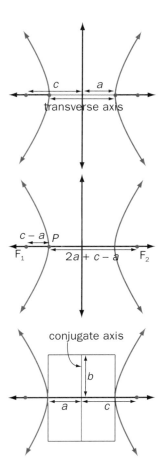

Explore 2 Use a Diagram

Copy the diagram from Explore 1 onto centimetre grid paper again. Then, construct the rectangle with vertices $(-3, 4)$, $(3, 4)$, $(3, -4)$, and $(-3, -4)$.
Draw the line segment from $(0, 4)$ to $(0, -4)$. This segment, perpendicular to the transverse axis, is the **conjugate axis**.
Half the length of the conjugate axis is denoted by b. Therefore, the conjugate axis has length $2b$ units.

For a hyperbola, the value of b is always chosen to satisfy $a^2 + b^2 = c^2$. With this value of b, the diagonals of the rectangle gain a particular property. What was the relationship between a, b, and c for ellipses?

Inquire

1. What are the values of a and b for this hyperbola?

2. Verify that $a^2 + b^2 = c^2$ for this hyperbola.

3. Draw the diagonals of the rectangle, extending them well beyond the rectangle.

4. How do these lines and the hyperbola interrelate? These lines are called the **asymptotes** of the hyperbola.

5. What is the slope of each asymptote? How are the slopes related?

6. Draw a rectangle with vertices $(-3, y_1)$, $(3, y_1)$, $(3, -y_1)$, and $(-3, -y_1)$ where $0 < y_1 < 4$. Draw the diagonals of the rectangle, extending them well beyond the rectangle. How do these lines and the hyperbola interrelate? Why is the line segment from $(0, y_1)$ to $(0, -y_1)$ not the conjugate axis?

7. Draw another rectangle with vertices $(-3, y_2)$, $(3, y_2)$, $(3, -y_2)$, and $(-3, -y_2)$ where $y_2 > 4$. Draw the diagonals of the rectangle, extending them well beyond the rectangle. How do these lines and the hyperbola interrelate? Why is the line segment from $(0, y_2)$ to $(0, -y_2)$ not the conjugate axis?

8. Recall the equation of an ellipse with its major axis along the x-axis in standard form. Using points on the hyperbola, determine a similar type of equation for the hyperbola.

9. How would the equation change if the centre were moved from $(0, 0)$ to (h, k)?

10. Rotate the hyperbola through $90°$ about the origin, either by tracing or by applying a transformation to selected coordinates. The foci and vertices should now be on the y-axis. How does this change the equation for the hyperbola? Check your prediction with specific points.

The **standard form** of a hyperbola, centred at the origin with a transverse axis of length $2a$ along the x-axis and a conjugate axis of length $2b$ along the y-axis, is

$$\frac{x^2}{a^2} - \frac{y^2}{b^2} = 1$$

and the slopes of the asymptotes are $\dfrac{b}{a}$ and $-\dfrac{b}{a}$.

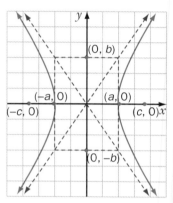

The standard form of a hyperbola, centred at the origin with a transverse axis of length $2a$ along the y-axis and a conjugate axis of length $2b$ along the x-axis, is

$$\frac{y^2}{a^2} - \frac{x^2}{b^2} = 1$$

and the slopes of the asymptotes are $\dfrac{a}{b}$ and $-\dfrac{a}{b}$.

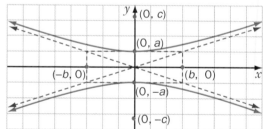

These standard forms can be derived using the locus definition and the distance formula. See question 37 on page 161.

As in the case of the ellipse, the standard form of a hyperbola, centred at any point (h, k) with a transverse axis of length $2a$ parallel to the x-axis and a conjugate axis of length $2b$ parallel to the y-axis, is

$$\frac{(x-h)^2}{a^2} - \frac{(y-k)^2}{b^2} = 1$$

and the slopes of the asymptotes are $\dfrac{b}{a}$ and $-\dfrac{b}{a}$.

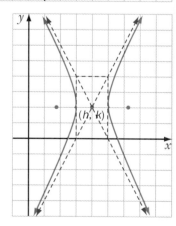

The standard form of a hyperbola, centred at any point (h, k) with a transverse axis of length $2a$ parallel to the y-axis and a conjugate axis of length $2b$ parallel to the x-axis, is

$$\frac{(y-k)^2}{a^2} - \frac{(x-h)^2}{b^2} = 1$$

and the slopes of the asymptotes are $\dfrac{a}{b}$ and $-\dfrac{a}{b}$.

The **general form** of a hyperbola with its axes parallel to the x- and y-axes is
$$Ax^2 + Cy^2 + Dx + Ey + F = 0,$$
where A and C have opposite signs. The general form equation can be derived from the standard forms by expanding and simplifying. See question 38 on page 161.

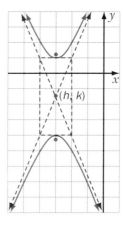

Example 1   Finding the Equation of a Hyperbola
Describe the properties of the hyperbola shown.
Then, write the equation in standard form and general form.

Solution
The centre is at $(2, 3)$. So, $h = 2$ and $k = 3$.
The transverse axis is parallel to the x-axis and of length 6 units. So, $a = 3$.
The vertices are at $(2 - 3, 3)$ or $(-1, 3)$ and $(2 + 3, 3)$ or $(5, 3)$.
The slopes of the asymptotes are 2 and -2.

Since $a = 3$, and the slope of one of the asymptotes $= \dfrac{b}{a}$, then $2 = \dfrac{b}{3}$. So, $b = 6$.

The conjugate axis is parallel to the y-axis and of length 12 units.

Use $\dfrac{(x-h)^2}{a^2} - \dfrac{(y-k)^2}{b^2} = 1$ and substitute $h = 2$, $k = 3$, $a = 3$, and $b = 6$.

$$\frac{(x-2)^2}{3^2} - \frac{(y-3)^2}{6^2} = 1$$

$$\frac{(x-2)^2}{9} - \frac{(y-3)^2}{36} = 1 \qquad \text{standard form}$$

$$36(x-2)^2 - 9(y-3)^2 = 9 \times 36$$
$$36(x^2 - 4x + 4) - 9(y^2 - 6y + 9) = 324$$
$$36x^2 - 144x + 144 - 9y^2 + 54y - 81 = 324$$
$$36x^2 - 9y^2 - 144x + 54y + 63 - 324 = 0$$
$$36x^2 - 9y^2 - 144x + 54y - 261 = 0 \qquad \text{general form where } A = 36, C = -9,$$
$$D = -144, E = 54, \text{ and } F = -261$$

Example 2 Finding the Centre, Vertices, and Asymptotes

Find the coordinates of the centre, the coordinates of the vertices, and the equations of the asymptotes of $4x^2 - y^2 - 16x - 14y - 34 = 0$.

Solution

Complete the square to change the equation to standard form.

$$4x^2 - y^2 - 16x - 14y - 34 = 0$$
$$4x^2 - 16x - y^2 - 14y - 34 = 0$$
$$4(x^2 - 4x \qquad) - (y^2 + 14y \qquad) - 34 = 0$$
$$4(x^2 - 4x + 4 - 4) - (y^2 + 14y + 49 - 49) - 34 = 0$$
$$4(x-2)^2 - 16 - (y+7)^2 + 49 - 34 = 0$$
$$4(x-2)^2 - (y+7)^2 = 1$$
$$\frac{(x-2)^2}{\frac{1}{4}} - (y+7)^2 = 1$$

$h = 2$, $k = -7$, $a^2 = \dfrac{1}{4}$, $b^2 = 1$

The centre is at $(2, -7)$.

Since $a^2 = \dfrac{1}{4}$, $a = \dfrac{1}{2}$ and the transverse axis is parallel to the x-axis and of length 1.

The vertices are located at $\left(2 - \dfrac{1}{2},\ -7\right)$ or $\left(1\dfrac{1}{2},\ -7\right)$ and $\left(2 + \dfrac{1}{2},\ -7\right)$ or $\left(2\dfrac{1}{2},\ -7\right)$.

Since $b = 1$, one asymptote has slope -2, and the other slope 2.
Both asymptotes pass through the centre $(2, -7)$.
Using the point-slope equation for a line, the equations of the asymptote are

$$y - y_1 = m(x - x_1) \quad \text{and} \quad y - y_1 = m(x - x_1)$$
$$y - (-7) = 2(x - 2) \qquad y - (-7) = -2(x - 2)$$
$$y + 7 = 2x - 4 \qquad\qquad y + 7 = -2x + 4$$
$$y = 2x - 11 \qquad\qquad\quad y = -2x - 3$$

Example 3 Graphing a Hyperbola Using a Graphing Calculator

Sketch the graph of $\dfrac{(y+2)^2}{4} - \dfrac{(x-1)^2}{25} = 1$.

Then, graph the hyperbola and its asymptotes, using a graphing calculator, and use the Trace function to see how the graph of the hyperbola approaches the graphs of the asymptotes.

Solution

The centre of the hyperbola is at $(1, -2)$.

The transverse axis is parallel to the y-axis.
Since $a^2 = 4$, $a = 2$ and the transverse axis has length $2(2)$ or 4 units.
The vertices are $(1, -2 - 2)$ or $(1, -4)$ and $(1, -2 + 2)$ or $(1, 0)$.
The conjugate axis is parallel to the x-axis.
Since $b^2 = 25$, $b = 5$ and the conjugate axis has length $2(5)$ or 10.

The slopes of the asymptotes are $\pm \dfrac{a}{b}$ or $\pm \dfrac{2}{5}$.

After plotting the centre, the vertices, and the asymptotes, sketch the hyperbola.

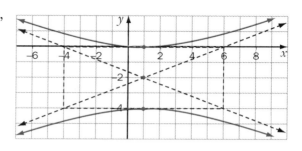

Solve the equation for y in terms of x.

$$\frac{(y+2)^2}{4} - \frac{(x-1)^2}{25} = 1$$

$$25(y+2)^2 - 4(x-1)^2 = 4 \times 25$$

$$(y+2)^2 = \frac{100 + 4(x-1)^2}{25}$$

$$y + 2 = \pm\sqrt{\frac{100 + 4(x-1)^2}{25}}$$

$$y = \pm\sqrt{\frac{100 + 4(x-1)^2}{25}} - 2$$

The slopes of the asymptotes are $\pm\frac{2}{5}$ and both pass through the centre $(1, -2)$.

Using the point-slope equation for a line, the equations of the asymptotes are

$$y - y_1 = m(x - x_1) \quad \text{and} \quad y - y_1 = m(x - x_1)$$

$$y - (-2) = \frac{2}{5}(x - 1) \qquad y - (-2) = -\frac{2}{5}(x - 1)$$

$$y = \frac{2}{5}(x - 1) - 2 \qquad y = -\frac{2}{5}(x - 1) - 2$$

Then, graph all four equations in a square viewing window.

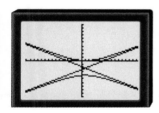 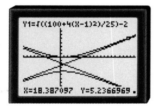 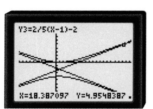

Practice

For each hyperbola, determine the
a) *coordinates of the centre*
b) *directions and lengths of both axes*
c) *coordinates of the vertices*
d) *slopes of the asymptotes*

1.

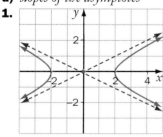

2.

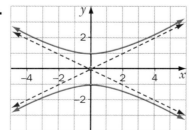

3.

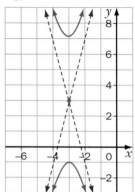

4.

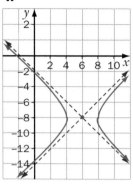

Determine the equation of each hyperbola in standard form and general form.

14.

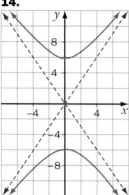

15.

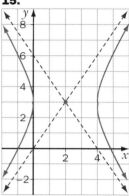

5.

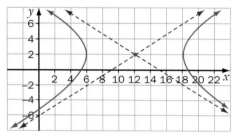

16.

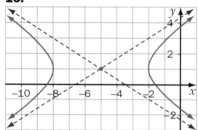

For each hyperbola, determine the
a) coordinates of the centre
b) directions and lengths of both axes
c) coordinates of the vertices
d) slopes of the asymptotes

6. $\dfrac{x^2}{121} - \dfrac{y^2}{225} = 1$

7. $\dfrac{(x-1)^2}{144} - \dfrac{y^2}{64} = 1$

8. $\dfrac{(x+3)^2}{81} - \dfrac{(y-5)^2}{16} = 1$

9. $\dfrac{(y+4)^2}{49} - \dfrac{x^2}{100} = 1$

10. $\dfrac{4(y-8)^2}{9} - \dfrac{(x-2)^2}{169} = 1$

11. $\dfrac{y^2}{196} - \dfrac{(x-3)^2}{64} = 1$

12. $25(x+10)^2 - 36(y+4)^2 = 900$

13. $\dfrac{(y+6)^2}{9} - \dfrac{(x+2)^2}{256} = 1$

17.

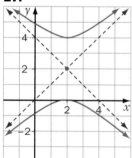

18.

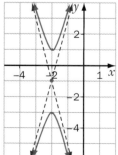

Write the equation for each hyperbola in standard form and general form.

19. centre $(4, 0)$, one vertex $(2, 0)$, slope of one asymptote $\dfrac{3}{2}$

20. centre $(0, 5)$, one focus $(5, 5)$, transverse axis 8
21. centre $(1, 2)$, one vertex $(1, 0)$, one focus $(1, 15)$
22. centre $(-1, 3)$, one focus $(-1, -2)$, difference of focal radii 6
23. centre $(6, -8)$, one vertex $(6, -20)$, slope of one asymptote 3

Sketch the graph of each hyperbola. Then, graph the hyperbola and its asymptotes, using a graphing calculator.

24. $\dfrac{x^2}{9} - \dfrac{y^2}{16} = 1$

25. $\dfrac{(x-1)^2}{25} - \dfrac{(y+2)^2}{4} = 1$

26. $\dfrac{(x+3)^2}{36} - \dfrac{(y+4)^2}{25} = 1$

27. $\dfrac{(y-2)^2}{9} - \dfrac{(x-2)^2}{4} = 1$

28. $\dfrac{(y+5)^2}{16} - \dfrac{(x+1)^2}{49} = 1$

29. $\dfrac{(x-1)^2}{25} - 4y^2 = 1$

30. $4x^2 - y^2 = 36$
31. $4y^2 - 25(x-2)^2 = 100$
32. $9x^2 - 16(y+3)^2 = 144$

For each hyperbola, find the
a) *coordinates of the centre*
b) *coordinates of the vertices*
c) *equations of the asymptotes*

33. $x^2 - 4y^2 - 6x - 8y - 11 = 0$
34. $(y-1)^2 - 36(x+5)^2 = 9$
35. $x^2 - 10x - 36y^2 + 216y = 335$
36. $25x^2 - 4y^2 + 100x + 24y = 36$

Applications and Problem Solving

37. Standard form Consider a hyperbola with its transverse axis parallel to the y-axis, foci at $(0, -c)$ and $(0, c)$, vertices at $(0, a)$ and $(0, -a)$, and the slope of one asymptote $\dfrac{a}{b}$ and the other $-\dfrac{a}{b}$.

a) Use the distance formula to show that for a point (x, y) on the hyperbola
$$\sqrt{(y+c)^2 + x^2} - \sqrt{(y-c)^2 + x^2} = 2a \text{ when } y > 0 \text{ and}$$
$$\sqrt{(y-c)^2 + x^2} - \sqrt{(y+c)^2 + x^2} = 2a \text{ when } y < 0.$$

b) From the equations in part a), derive
$$\dfrac{y^2}{a^2} - \dfrac{x^2}{c^2 - a^2} = 1.$$

c) Use the relationship $a^2 + b^2 = c^2$ to derive $\dfrac{y^2}{a^2} - \dfrac{x^2}{b^2} = 1$, the standard form for the hyperbola centred at $(0, 0)$ with transverse axis parallel to the y-axis.

38. General form Expand $\dfrac{(x-h)^2}{a^2} - \dfrac{(y-k)^2}{b^2} = 1$, the standard form of a hyperbola, centred at any point (h, k) with a transverse axis of length $2a$ parallel to the x-axis and a conjugate axis of length $2b$ parallel to the y-axis, to derive the general form $Ax^2 + Cy^2 + Dx + Ey + F = 0$, where A and C have opposite signs.

39. Rectangular hyperbolas The following are examples of rectangular hyperbolas.
i) $x^2 - y^2 = 5$ **ii)** $x^2 - y^2 = -4$
iii) $y^2 - x^2 = 8$ **iv)** $y^2 - x^2 = -2$
a) Examine the equations. What do they have in common?
b) Use a graphing calculator to graph each hyperbola and the equations of its asymptotes.
c) What do the graphs have in common that sets them apart from other hyperbolas that you have graphed?

40. Distortions Another way of thinking about a non-rectangular hyperbola is as a distorted rectangular hyperbola.

a) Use a graphing calculator to graph $y^2 - x^2 = 1$, the unit rectangular hyperbola with transverse axis along the y-axis, and the hyperbola $y^2 - \dfrac{x^2}{9} = 1$.

b) What are the intercepts?

c) Describe the second hyperbola as an expansion or compression of the rectangular hyperbola, giving the direction.

d) Complete this statement. The mapping of $y^2 - x^2 = 1$ to $y^2 - \dfrac{x^2}{9} = 1$ is $(x, y) \rightarrow (\blacksquare x, \blacksquare y)$.

e) Repeat parts a) to d) for the hyperbola $\dfrac{y^2}{16} - x^2 = 1$.

f) Repeat parts a) to d) for the hyperbola $\dfrac{y^2}{9} - \dfrac{x^2}{4} = 1$.

g) Generalize to write the mapping of $y^2 - x^2 = 1$ to $\dfrac{y^2}{a^2} - \dfrac{x^2}{b^2} = 1$.

h) Imagine the unit rectangular hyperbola with transverse axis along the x-axis $x^2 - y^2 = 1$, and write the mapping of $x^2 - y^2 = 1$ to $\dfrac{x^2}{a^2} - \dfrac{y^2}{b^2} = 1$.

41. The *xy* term a) Use a graphing calculator to graph each of the following equations.

i) $xy = 8$ **ii)** $xy = -5$ **iii)** $xy = 10$

b) What are the equations of the asymptotes of these equations?

c) What type of hyperbola are these?

42. Marine biology A ship is monitoring the movement of a pod of whales with its radarscope. The radarscope screen can be modelled as a coordinate grid with the ship at the centre $(0, 0)$. The pod appears to be moving along a curve such that the absolute value of the difference of its distances from $(2, 7)$ and $(2, -3)$ is always 6. What equation describes the path of the pod?

Use your results from questions 39 and 40. Describe the transformations (translations and expansions or compressions) that have been applied to one of the unit rectangular hyperbolas, indicating which, to produce each hyperbola. Then, find the equation of each hyperbola in standard form.

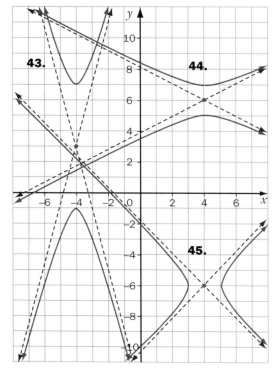

46. The points (m, n), $(m, -n)$, $(-m, n)$, and $(-m, -n)$ all lie on a hyperbola. Write a possible equation for this hyperbola.

47. Inverse variation Rectangular hyperbolas appear in many inverse relationships. For a fixed distance, the time required to travel the distance is inversely proportional to the speed travelled.

a) Use a graphing calculator to graph the inverse relationship between time and speed for a distance of 500 km.

b) What speed would be required if the time were 4 h?

48. Chemistry Boyle's Law, an important concept in chemistry, states that, if the temperature of a gas is constant, then the pressure exerted by the gas varies inversely as the volume of the gas.
a) The volume of a gas is 34.2 L when the pressure is 500 Pa (Pascals). Use a graphing calculator to graph the inverse relationship between pressure and volume.
b) What is the volume of the gas at the same temperature when the pressure is 800 Pa?

49. Technology Graph $4x^2 - 25y^2 - 100 = 0$ using a graphing calculator. Create two other equations of this type by changing one coefficient. Graph them.

50. Conjugate hyperbolas Two hyperbolas are centred at (1, 2). One has a transverse axis parallel to the x-axis and the other has a transverse axis parallel to the y-axis. They share the same pair of asymptotes and axis lengths. If the equation of one hyperbola is $\dfrac{(y-2)^2}{25} - \dfrac{(x-1)^2}{9} = 1$, what are the lengths of the conjugate and transverse axes of the other hyperbola?

51. Space shuttle In 1981, the United States launched the first reusable space shuttle, *Columbia*. When a small jet aircraft breaks the sound barrier, you hear one sonic boom. When the space shuttle breaks the sound barrier, you hear two sonic booms. Use your research skills to determine why.

52. Wedding arch A balloon arch in the shape of one branch of a hyperbola is being made for a wedding party. The arch is to span 4 m and have a maximum clearance of 2.2 m.
a) Find a possible equation for the hyperbola.
b) What would be the height of the arch 1.2 m from the centre, given your equation?

53. Technology Use a graphing calculator to graph Hyperbola I: $x^2 - y^2 = 1$. Consider the transformation of the hyperbola given by the mapping $(x, y) \rightarrow \left(\dfrac{x}{\sqrt{2}} - \dfrac{y}{\sqrt{2}}, \dfrac{x}{\sqrt{2}} + \dfrac{y}{\sqrt{2}} \right)$.

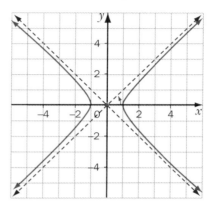

a) The image of $x^2 - y^2 = 1$ under this transformation is also a hyperbola, Hyperbola II. Find the equation in general form of Hyperbola II, the length of its axes, and the coordinates of its vertices. What is the value of the coefficient of the xy term, B, in this equation? Graph Hyperbola II on the same set of axes as Hyperbola I.
b) The image of Hyperbola II under the transformation is also a hyperbola, Hyperbola III. Find the equation in general form of Hyperbola III, the length of its axes, and the coordinates of its vertices. What is the value of the coefficient of the xy term, B, in this equation? Graph Hyperbola III on the same set of axes as Hyperbolas I and II.
c) Graph a circle of radius 1, centred at the origin on the same set of axes as the hyperbolas. What is the image of this circle under the transformation?
d) What is the transformation $(x, y) \rightarrow \left(\dfrac{x}{\sqrt{2}} - \dfrac{y}{\sqrt{2}}, \dfrac{x}{\sqrt{2}} + \dfrac{y}{\sqrt{2}} \right)$ doing to points in the plane?
e) What would be the image of the hyperbola $x^2 - y^2 = 1$ if this transformation were applied three times successively? applied eight times successively?

3.6 The Parabola

You have had a great deal of experience with parabolas in your study of quadratic functions and equations. Projectile motion, and the curves of bridges, arches, and satellite dishes can be modelled by the equation of a parabola.

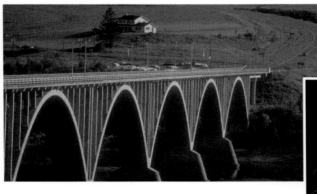

Explore: Make a Model

Draw a line segment about 12 cm long on a sheet of waxed paper.
Mark points along the line segment at about every centimetre.
Mark a point not on the line segment a couple of centimetres to one side.
The line segment is the **directrix** and the point not on it is the **focus**.
Fold one endpoint of the directrix over onto the focus and make a firm crease. Unfold the paper.
Fold the next point on the directrix over onto the focus and make a firm crease. Unfold the paper.
Continue until all the points on the directrix have been folded over onto the focus. Unfold the focus.
What shape have you created?

Inquire

1. Draw a perpendicular line segment from one of the points on the directrix to the curve.

2. Measure that perpendicular distance to the curve and measure the distance from the focus to the same point on the curve.

3. How do the distances compare?

4. Repeat questions 1 to 3 with three other points on the directrix.

This gives another way of looking at the parabola. It is the locus of all points in a plane that are the same distance from a line in the plane, the directrix, as from a fixed point in the plane not on the line, the focus.

A parabola has one **axis of symmetry** which intersects the parabola at its **vertex**. The focus, as well as the vertex, lies on the axis of symmetry. The distance between the focus and the vertex is $|p|$, as is the distance between the vertex and the point on the directrix that lies on the axis of symmetry.

For a parabola with axis of symmetry parallel to the y-axis and vertex at (h, k)
• the equation of the axis of symmetry is $x = h$
• the coordinates of the focus are $(h, k + p)$
• the equation of the directrix is $y = k - p$
• when p is positive, the parabola opens up
• when p is negative, the parabola opens down

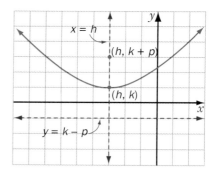

The **standard form** of these parabolas with axis of symmetry parallel to the y-axis and vertex at (h, k) is
$$(x - h)^2 = 4p(y - k).$$

For a parabola with axis of symmetry parallel to the x-axis and vertex at (h, k),
• the equation of the axis of symmetry is $y = k$
• the coordinates of the focus are $(h + p, k)$
• the equation of the directrix is $x = h - p$
• when p is positive, the parabola opens to the right
• when p is negative, the parabola opens to the left

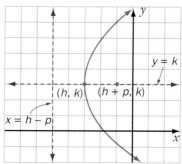

The standard form of these parabolas with axis of symmetry parallel to the x-axis and vertex at (h, k) is
$$(y - k)^2 = 4p(x - h).$$

These standard forms can be derived using the locus definition and the distance formula. See question 44 on page 169.

The **general form** of a parabola with its axis parallel to the x- or y-axis is
$$Ax^2 + Cy^2 + Dx + Ey + F = 0,$$
where either $A = 0$ or $C = 0$. Only parabolas with axes parallel to the x- or y-axis are considered in this chapter. The general form can be derived from the standard forms by expanding and simplifying. See question 45 on page 169.

Example 1 Finding the Equations of Parabolas

Write the equation for each parabola in standard form and general form.
a) focus at $(2, 5)$ and directrix $x = 6$
b) passes through $(5, 2)$, vertex at $(4, 3)$, and opens down

Solution

For each, sketch a graph of the given information.

a) The equation of the axis of symmetry, parallel to the x-axis, is $y = 5$.
The x-coordinate of the focus is 2 and the directrix is $x = 6$.
So, $2p = 2 - 6$
$$p = -2$$
The vertex is $(2 + 2, 5)$ or $(4, 5)$. So, $h = 4$ and $k = 5$.

$$\text{Use } (y - k)^2 = 4p(x - h) \text{ and substitute } h = 4, k = 5, \text{ and } p = -2.$$
$$(y - 5)^2 = 4(-2)(x - 4)$$
$$(y - 5)^2 = -8(x - 4) \quad \text{standard form}$$
$$y^2 - 10y + 25 = -8x + 32$$
$$y^2 - 10y + 8x + 25 - 32 = 0$$
$$y^2 + 8x - 10y - 7 = 0 \quad \text{general form where } A = 0, C = 1, D = 8,$$
$$E = -10, F = -7$$

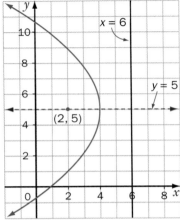

b) The axis of symmetry is parallel to the y-axis.
The vertex is $(4, 3)$. So, $h = 4$ and $k = 3$.
To find p, use $(x - h)^2 = 4p(y - k)$ and substitute $h = 4, k = 3, x = 5,$ and $y = 2$.
$$(5 - 4)^2 = 4p(2 - 3)$$
$$1 = -4p$$
$$-\frac{1}{4} = p$$

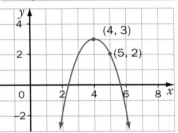

Now, use $(x - h)^2 = 4p(y - k)$ and substitute $h = 4, k = 3,$ and $p = -\frac{1}{4}$.

$$(x - 4)^2 = 4\left(-\frac{1}{4}\right)(y - 3)$$
$$(x - 4)^2 = -(y - 3) \quad \text{standard form}$$
$$x^2 - 8x + 16 = -y + 3$$
$$x^2 - 8x + y + 16 - 3 = 0$$
$$x^2 - 8x + y + 13 = 0 \quad \text{general form where } A = 1, C = 0, D = -8, E = 1, F = 13$$

Example 2 Finding the Focus, Vertex, Directrix, and Axis of Symmetry

Find the coordinates of the focus and the vertex, and the equations of the directrix and the axis of symmetry, and the direction of the opening of $y^2 - 4x + 2y + 5 = 0$.

Solution

Complete the square to change to standard form.
$$y^2 - 4x + 2y + 5 = 0$$
$$y^2 + 2y \qquad = 4x - 5$$
$$y^2 + 2y + 1 - 1 = 4x - 5$$
$$(y + 1)^2 = 4x - 5 + 1$$
$$(y + 1)^2 = 4x - 4$$
$$(y + 1)^2 = 4(x - 1)$$
$$h = 1, k = -1, p = 1$$

So, the vertex is (1, –1). The equation of the axis of symmetry is $y = -1$.
The parabola opens to the right. The focus is $(1 + 1, -1)$ or $(2, -1)$.
The equation of the directrix is $x = 1 - 1$ or $x = 0$.

You have graphed many parabolas that were functions, that is, with an x^2-term.
However, when a parabola is not a function and opens to the left or right with an
axis of symmetry parallel to the x-axis, that is, with a y^2-term, you must solve the
equation for y in terms of x and graph the two resulting equations as you graphed
the other conic sections using a graphing calculator.

Example 3   Graphing a Parabola Using a Graphing Calculator
Graph $y^2 - 6x - 6y + 39 = 0$.

Solution
To solve an equation with both a y^2-term and a y-term for y, complete the square.

$$y^2 - 6x - 6y + 39 = 0$$
$$y^2 - 6y \qquad\quad = 6x - 39$$
$$y^2 - 6y + 9 - 9 \quad = 6x - 39$$
$$(y - 3)^2 = 6x - 39 + 9$$
$$(y - 3)^2 = 6x - 30$$
$$y - 3 = \pm\sqrt{6x - 30}$$
$$y = \pm\sqrt{6x - 30} + 3$$

Graph both equations in a square viewing window.
Check. The vertex is at (5, 3) as in the standard form equation,
$(y - 3)^2 = 6(x - 5)$.

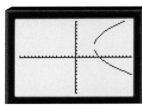

In the general form, $Ax^2 + Bxy + Cy^2 + Dx + Ey + F = 0$, where A, B, and C are
not all 0, for conic sections with axes parallel to the x- and/or y-axis, $B = 0$ and
• for a parabola, either $A = 0$ or $C = 0$
• for a hyperbola, A and C have opposite signs
• for an ellipse, A and C have the same sign and $A \neq C$
• for a circle, $A = C$

Example 4   Identifying a Conic Section From its Equation
Which type of conic section is $9x^2 - 54x = 4y^2 + 40y + 55$?

Solution
Express the equation in general form.
$$9x^2 - 54x = 4y^2 + 40y + 55$$
$$9x^2 - 4y^2 - 54x - 40y - 55 = 0$$
$A = 9$ and $C = -4$. They have opposite signs. So, the conic section is a hyperbola.

Practice
Write the equation of the parabola with each focus and directrix in standard form.
1. (0, 2), $y = -4$ **2.** (0, –3), $y = 2$ **3.** (4, 0), $x = 1$ **4.** (–3, 0), $x = 1$
5. (2, 2), $y = -1$ **6.** (–3, –2), $x = -1$ **7.** (–5, –1), $x = 5$ **8.** (–4, 4), $y = 5$

Write the equation for each parabola in standard form and general form.

9. vertex at (4, 2), focus 3 units to left of vertex
10. vertex at (−3, −1), directrix 2 units above vertex
11. vertex at origin, focus at (−3, 0)
12. passing through (2, −1), vertex at (−7, −5), opens to right
13. axis of symmetry $x = 2$, focus at (2, −6), $p = -2$
14. focus at (3, 0), $p = 2$, opens up

Find the coordinates of the focus and the vertex, the equations of the directrix and the axis of symmetry, and the direction of opening of each parabola.

15. $y^2 - 12x = 0$ **16.** $x^2 + 3y = 6x$
17. $x^2 + 4x = -2y - 10$ **18.** $2y^2 + 16x = 16y - 64$

Classify the conic section represented by each equation.

19. $4x^2 + y^2 - 8x - 6y = 0$ **20.** $x^2 + y^2 + 2x - 7 = 0$
21. $16x^2 - 12y^2 + 5y - 3 = 0$
22. $6x^2 + 3x - 10y = 0$ **23.** $7y^2 - 5x - 11y = 0$
24. $8x^2 + 8y^2 + 3x - 6y - 13 = 0$

Write the equation for each conic section in standard form and general form.

25.

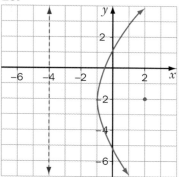

26.

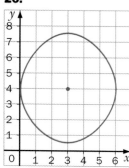

27.

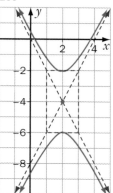

28.

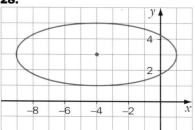

29.

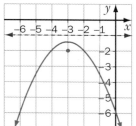

30.

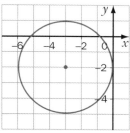

31.

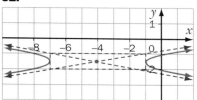

Express each equation in standard form. Then, graph the conic section, using a graphing calculator, or sketch it.

32. $x^2 + y^2 + 8x - 6y = 0$
33. $x^2 + y^2 + 10y + 9 = 0$
34. $16x^2 + 25y^2 - 400 = 0$
35. $9x^2 - 16y^2 = -1$
36. $x^2 - 4x - 2y - 6 = 0$
37. $y^2 - 2x - 8y + 22 = 0$
38. $x^2 - 4y^2 + 6x - 8y - 11 = 0$
39. $3x^2 + 24x + 2y + 54 = 0$
40. $16x^2 - 9y^2 - 32x + 36y + 124 = 0$
41. $4x^2 + 25y^2 - 24x + 200y + 336 = 0$
42. $4x^2 + 9y^2 - 16x + 18y - 11 = 0$
43. $64x^2 + 9y^2 - 384x - 36y + 468 = 0$

Applications and Problem Solving

44. Standard form Consider a parabola with its axis of symmetry parallel to the y-axis, focus at $(h, k + p)$, and the equation of the directrix $y = k - p$.
a) Use the distance formula to show that for a point (x, y) on the parabola $y^2 - 2y(k - p) + (k - p)^2 = (x - h)^2 + y^2 - 2y(k + p) + (k + p)^2$
b) From the equations in part a), derive $4p(y - k) = (x - h)^2$.

45. General form Expand $4p(y - k) = (x - h)^2$, the standard form of a parabola with vertex at (h, k) with its axis of symmetry parallel to the y-axis, to derive the general form $Ax^2 + Dx + Ey + F = 0$.

46. Football One of the best-known kickers from the Canadian Football League is Lui Passaglia. During his first 20 seasons with the B.C. Lions, Lui scored 3160 points. Consider this situation. Lui kicks the ball from the 42-yard line (38 m). Let the point on the ground where Lui's foot contacts the ball be the origin, and let the unit interval be 1 m. Suppose the football follows the path $10y = -x^2 + 39x$, and is kicked directly at the field goal posts, the bottoms of which are 3 m above the ground.

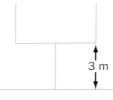

3 m

a) Sketch the path of the football.
b) Will Lui score the field goal?
c) If Lui were kicking from the 45-yard line (41.15 m), would he have scored the field goal?

47. Baseball In 1992, the Toronto Blue Jays became the first Canadian team to win the World Series. In 1993, the Toronto Blue Jays captured the title again, with Joe Carter hitting a 3-run homer to win it. Consider this situation. Joe hits the baseball from a point that is 110 m from the 2-m-high home run wall. Let the point where Joe hits the ball be modelled as the origin with the unit interval of length 1 m. If the ball travels in the path $x^2 - 115x + 95y = 0$, with a graphing calculator determine
a) whether the baseball will clear the wall
b) if it does clear the wall, whether a player standing at the wall could jump up and catch the ball

48. Suspension bridge A suspension bridge uses a long cable connected between pairs of towers to support the bridge deck. The cable is attached to the bridge deck at uniformly spaced intervals by shorter connecting cables. The Lions Gate Bridge, the longest suspension bridge in Western Canada, spans a total length of 1517.3 m, with the main span being 472.0 m. The height of each tower is 111.0 m. Suppose the cable of the main span of the bridge is approximated by a parabola, so that the bridge deck passes through the vertex of the parabola and the bridge deck is placed halfway up the supporting towers.

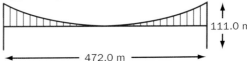

111.0 m

472.0 m

a) Determine an equation for the parabola.
b) Determine the length of the connecting cable needed to attach the bridge deck to the main cable at a point 30 m from the vertex.
c) Is it likely that the bridge deck passes through the vertex of the parabola? If not, what type of adjustment should be made to the equation?

49. Roof support arches Hyperbolic arches anchored to the ground support the roof of a sports complex. These arches span a distance of 60 m and have a maximum height of 20 m.
a) Find a possible equation for a hyperbola to model one of these arches.
b) What is the height of the arch at 25 m from the transverse axis, using your equation?
c) If the arches were parabolic, find the height at 25 m from the axis of symmetry of the parabola.
d) If the arches were semi-elliptical, find the height at 25 m from the major axis.
e) Discuss the relative merits of each shape for arched roofs.

TECHNOLOGY

Using the Locus Construction of Geometry Software to Construct Conic Sections

Complete the following explorations using geometry software. Points have been named to simplify the steps. The letters in the steps match the letters on the screens shown. You may have different letters in your constructions. Your letters do not have to match those used here.

1 The Parabola

1. Construct a parabola using the locus construction by following these steps:
a) Construct horizontal line segment AB across the bottom of the screen.
b) Construct point C on line segment AB.
c) Construct point D above line segment AB, but not directly above C.
d) Construct line segment DC.
e) Construct midpoint E of line segment DC.
f) Construct a line perpendicular to line segment DC through E.
g) Construct a line perpendicular to line segment AB through point C.
h) Construct the intersection point F of the two lines constructed in parts f) and g).
 i) Hide everything except line segment AB (the directrix), point D (the focus), and points C and F (needed for the locus construction).
 j) Select points C and F, and construct the locus.

2. a) Measure the distances CF and DF. What do you notice?
b) Move focus D closer to and farther from directrix AB. What do you notice?
c) Explain your results.

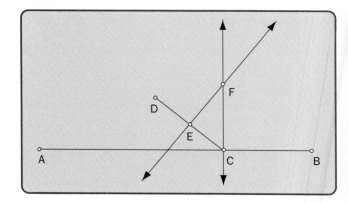

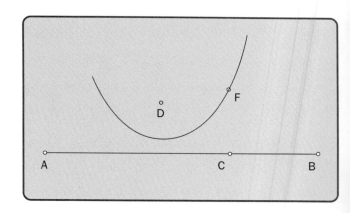

2 The Ellipse

1. Construct an ellipse using the locus
construction by following these steps:
a) Construct line AB across the top of the screen.
b) Construct point C on line AB. If point C is not
between points A and B, move it between them.
c) Hide the line.
d) Construct line segment AC and line
segment CB.
e) Construct point D in the centre of the screen
to one side.
f) Construct point E in the centre of the screen
to the other side.
g) Construct a circle with centre E and
radius CB.
h) Construct a circle with centre D and radius
AC. If the circles do not intersect, drag one centre
closer to the other.
i) Construct the intersection points F and G of
the two circles.
j) Hide the circles.
k) Select points C and F, and construct the locus.
l) Select points C and G, and construct the locus.
(Most, but not all, of the ellipse is constructed.)

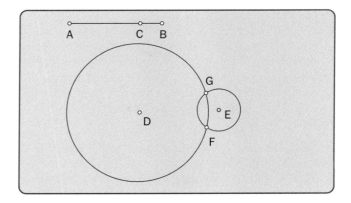

2. a) Measure the distances DF and EF. Calculate
the sum.
b) Measure the distances DG and EG. What is
their sum?
c) Move point F along the ellipse. Calculate the
sum of DF and EF at several locations. What do
you notice?
d) Explain your results.

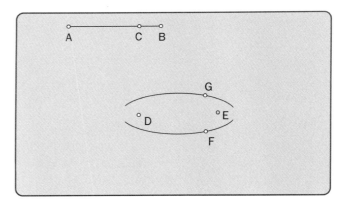

3 The Hyperbola

1. Based on the difference between the locus
definitions of a hyperbola and an ellipse, what one
step would be different in Exploration 2 if the
construction was for a hyperbola?

2. Construct a hyperbola using the locus
construction, and measure the appropriate
distances to check.

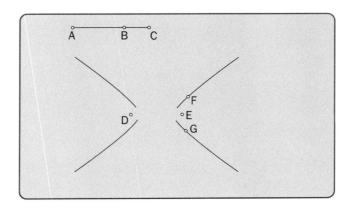

PROBLEM SOLVING

3.7 Work Backward

Reverse engineering is the process of analyzing a product, such as a cellular phone or a computer program, by taking the product and working backward to see how it was designed. Reverse engineering is also an indispensable part of software maintenance and cannot be performed without a complete understanding of the system. The ability to work backward is an important problem solving skill required in many professions.

In 1996, the population of Terrace, British Columbia, was twice the population of Crowsnest Pass, Alberta. From 1991 to 1996, the population of Terrace increased by 11.8%, and the population of Crowsnest Pass decreased by 4.9%. From 1981 to 1991, the population of Terrace increased by 4.8%, and the population of Crowsnest Pass decreased by 8.6%. Find the ratio of the population of Terrace to the population of Crowsnest Pass in 1981, to the nearest hundredth.

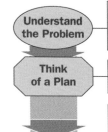

Understand the Problem

   1. What information are you given?
   2. What are you asked to find?
   3. Do you need an exact or an approximate answer?

Think of a Plan

   For each town, start in 1996 and work backward to find the 1981 population in terms of the 1996 population.

Let p represent the population of Crowsnest Pass in 1996.
Let x represent the population of Crowsnest Pass in 1991.
Since the population decreased by 4.9% from 1991 to 1996,

$$p = (100 - 4.9)\% \text{ of } x$$
$$p = 0.951x$$
$$x = \frac{p}{0.951}$$

So, the population of Crowsnest Pass in 1991 was $\frac{p}{0.951}$.

Since the population decreased by 8.6% from 1981 to 1991, the population of Crowsnest Pass in 1981 was

Carry Out the Plan

$$\frac{p}{(0.951)(0.914)} \doteq 1.15p$$

The population of Terrace in 1996 was $2p$.
Since the population increased by 11.8% from 1991 to 1996, the population of Terrace in 1991 was $\frac{2p}{1.118}$.

Since the population increased by 4.8% from 1991 to 1996, the population of Terrace in 1981 was $\frac{2p}{(1.118)(1.048)} \doteq 1.71p$.

The ratio of the population of Terrace to the population of Crowsnest Pass, in 1981, was $1.71p : 1.15p = 1.49 : 1$, to the nearest hundredth.

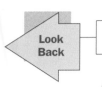

Look Back

Does the answer seem reasonable?
How could you check that the answer is correct?

Work Backward
1. Start with what you know.
2. Work backward to get an answer.
3. Check that your answer is reasonable.

Applications and Problem Solving

1. Employee discount Tamiko works part-time in a clothing store in Edmonton. She decides to buy a leather jacket which is on sale for 35% off. As an employee she receives a further 10% discount off the sale price. After the 7% GST was added to the discounted price, Tamiko paid $203.43 for the jacket. What was the original retail price of the jacket?

2. Playing cards Every Friday evening three friends get together and play cards. One evening they agreed that whenever one of them lost a game, that person would have to double the money of each of the others. After playing three games, and each person having lost once, the friends noticed that they each had $24. How much did each person have to start with?

3. Comic books Mario decided to give away his collection of comic books. He gave half of the books plus one extra to his sister Ella. Then, he gave half of the remainder plus one extra to his cousin Stephan. Then, he gave half of the comic books that were left plus one extra to a neighbour. Finally, he gave the remaining 74 to a charity shop. How many comic books did Mario have in his collection?

4. The arithmetic mean of a set of 100 numbers is 38. Two numbers of the set, 45 and 55, are discarded. What is the mean of the remaining set of numbers?

5. Population In 1996 the population of Mossport was a perfect square. By 1998 the population had increased by 100 and was 1 more than a perfect square. By 2000 the population had increased by a further 100 and was again a perfect square. What was the population of Mossport in 1996?

6. If the sum of two numbers is 4 and the product of the numbers is – 60, find the sum of the squares of the reciprocals of the numbers.

7. Badminton In a badminton tournament, Lena has won 12 games and lost 3 games. She has 9 games left to play. How many of the remaining games must she win to have an overall 50% average?

8. Survey A poll of 50 students reveals the following information.
   4 students are taking biology, English, and math.
   8 are taking biology and math.
   15 are taking English and math.
   12 are taking biology and English.
   25 are taking math.
   23 are taking biology.
   28 are taking English.
a) How many of the students polled are not taking any of English, biology, and math?
b) How many are taking biology and math, but not English?

9. Doublets Convert flour into bread by changing one letter at a time to make a new word each time.

$$FLOUR$$
$$\cdots$$
$$\cdots$$
$$BREAD$$

The best solution has the fewest steps.

10. What two whole numbers, neither containing any zeros, have a product of exactly one billion?

11. Write a problem that can be solved by working backward. Have a classmate solve your problem.

CONNECTING MATH AND HISTORY

Quadratures

Early Greek mathematicians were fascinated by geometrical constructions employing only the straightedge and compasses. With these two instruments, line segments and circles can be drawn. The straightedge is not a ruler; it does not have any marks on it. Arbitrary distances, therefore, cannot be measured.

Interest in these geometrical constructions is based in mythology. The Delian oracle prophesied that, to eradicate a certain plague, the cubical altar of Apollo must be doubled in size. The problem generalizes to doubling the volume of a solid while still maintaining its shape.

A similar geometrical-construction problem is to construct a square of exactly the same area as a figure in a plane, using only a straightedge and compasses. This is finding the **quadrature** of a plane figure.

You may wish to try the following quadrature constructions using only a straightedge and compasses, as they were originally done. Or you may wish to use geometry software.

1 Quadrature of a Rectangle

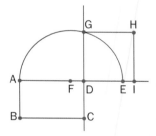

1. Construct rectangle ABCD.
2. Extend side AD beyond D.
3. Construct line segment DE on the extension equal to side CD.
4. Construct midpoint F of AE.
5. Construct a semicircle with centre F through A and E.
6. Construct the line perpendicular to AE at D, intersecting the semicircle at G.
7. Construct line segment DG on that perpendicular line.
8. DG is the side of the required square. Construct square DGHI.
9. Prove that the area of rectangle ABCD equals the area of square DGHI.

2 Quadrature of a Triangle

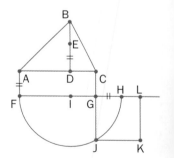

1. Construct △ABC.
2. Construct altitude BD.
3. Construct midpoint E of BD.
4. Construct rectangle ACGF where AF = DE.
5. Construct the quadrature of rectangle ACGF, following the same steps you used to construct the quadrature of rectangle ABCD in Exploration 1.
6. Prove that the area of △ABC is equal to the area of rectangle ACFG.

3 Quadrature of a Lune

In the fifth century B.C., Hippocrates of Chios was the first to construct a quadrature of certain special lunes. A lune is a crescent-shaped figure bounded by two circular arcs. Hippocrates' construction was based on the following.
• the Pythagorean Theorem
• the fact that an angle inscribed in a semicircle is always 90°
• the fact that the ratio of the areas of two semicircles is equal to the ratio of the squares of their diameters

Construct a lune by following these steps:
1. Construct a semicircle with centre O and diameter AB.
2. Construct the perpendicular bisector of AB, intersecting the semicircle at C.
3. Construct line segment OC on that perpendicular bisector.
4. Construct inscribed ∠ACB.
5. Construct the midpoint D of AC.
6. Construct a semicircle with centre D and diameter AC.
7. Construct point E on the smaller semicircle and point F on the larger semicircle between A and C. The lune is the region defined by AECF.

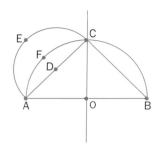

Let the length of the radius OA be r. Then, diameter AB of the larger semicircle, semicircle ACBO, is $2r$.
Since both line segment OC and line segment OA equal r, the diameter AC of the smaller semicircle, semicircle AECD, equals $\sqrt{2}r$ by the Pythagorean Theorem. The square of diameter AC equals $2r^2$ and the square of diameter AB equals $4r^2$. Since the ratio of the squares of the diameters is equal to the ratio of the areas of the semicircles,

$$\frac{AC^2}{AB^2} = \frac{1}{2}.$$

Therefore, the area of semicircle AECD is half the area of semicircle ACBO.
Bisector OC cuts semicircle ACBO in half.
Therefore, the area of semicircle AECD is equal to the area of quarter circle AFCO.

Semicircle AECD and quarter circle AFCO share the common region AFCD. Therefore, the area of semicircle AECD minus that of AFCD must equal the area of quarter circle AFCO minus that of AFCD.
To be specific, the area of the lune AECF equals the area of the △ACO.
Since a triangle is quadrable, a quadrature of lune AECF can be constructed.

8. Verify that the ratio of the areas of any two semicircles is equal to the ratio of the squares of their diameters.
9. Complete the construction of the quadrature of Hippocrates' lune.

Three great geometrical constructions were posed, but left unsolved, by the Greeks. With only a straightedge and compasses, is it possible to
• double the volume of a cube?
• trisect an angle?
• square a circle (construct the quadrature of a circle)?

Each of these constructions was proved to be mathematically impossible. The mathematics is highly sophisticated and represents one of the triumphs of abstract algebra. The ideas involved encompass the work of many mathematicians, but were initially based on that of Evariste Galois (1811–1832).

Review

3.1 **1.** Sketch the conic section created when a plane intersects a cone parallel to the cone's generator.

2. When the lamp is turned on, describe the conic section created by the light from it shining on a
a) vertical wall
b) horizontal ceiling
c) slanted ceiling

3.3 *Write the equation in standard form for the circle with each centre and radius.*
3. centre (2, −6), radius 4
4. centre (−1, −3), radius $\sqrt{7}$

Determine the equation in standard form for each circle. Then, expand it to find the general form.
5. centre (5, −2), passing through (8, 0)
6. centre (−5, 6), passing through (−2, 2)
7. endpoints of a diameter at (2, −1) and (2, 5)
8. endpoints of a diameter at (−4, 12) and (2, 0)

Find the centre and radius of each circle.
9. $x^2 + y^2 + 9x - 8y + 4 = 0$
10. $x^2 + y^2 + 4x - 8 = 0$

Use a graphing calculator to graph each circle.
11. $(x + 3)^2 + (y - 1)^2 = 10$
12. $x^2 + y^2 - 10x + 4y + 17 = 0$

Write the equation of the image of $x^2 + y^2 = 16$ under each translation.
13. $(x, y) \rightarrow (x - 1, y + 3)$
14. $(x, y) \rightarrow (x + 4, y - 6)$

15. Earthquake An earthquake observation centre is located at (−2, 5) on a kilometre grid. An earthquake epicentre is detected at a distance of 120 km from the observation centre. What is the equation of the circle that defines where the epicentre could be located?

3.4 **16.** Describe the difference between the equations in standard form for a circle and for an ellipse.

Find the coordinates of the centre, the lengths of the major and minor axes, and the coordinates of the foci of each ellipse.

17.

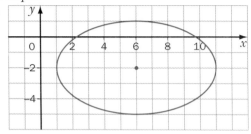

18.

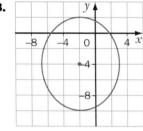

19. $\dfrac{(y + 7)^2}{16} + (x - 2)^2 = 1$ **20.** $4x^2 + 9y^2 = 36$

Write the equations for each ellipse in standard form and general form.
21. foci at (12, 0) and (−12, 0), endpoints of minor axis at (0, 5) and (0, −5)
22. centre (1, −3), passing through (1, −1), (1, −5), (2, −3), and (0, −3)

Find the coordinates of the centre, the lengths of both axes, and the coordinates of the foci of each ellipse.
23. $4x^2 + y^2 + 16x = 0$
24. $3x^2 + y^2 + 6x + 4y - 9 = 0$

Determine the equation of the image of $x^2 + 4y^2 = 9$ after each transformation.
25. translated 3 units to the left
26. translated 6 units to the right
27. stretched horizontally by a factor of 5

28. Satellite The first artificial Earth-orbiting satellite was *Sputnik I*, placed into elliptical orbit by the USSR in 1957. The orbit carried it to an apogee of 950 km and a perigee of 230 km. If one focus is the centre of Earth, the centre is at the origin, and the major axis is along the *x*-axis, find the equation for orbit. The radius of Earth is 6337 km at the equator.

29. Describe the difference between the equations in standard form for an ellipse and for a hyperbola.

For each hyperbola, determine the
a) *coordinates of the centre*
b) *directions and lengths of both axes*
c) *coordinates of the vertices*
d) *slopes of the asymptotes*

30. $\dfrac{y^2}{169} - \dfrac{x^2}{121} = 1$

31. $16(x+5)^2 - 25(y+3)^2 = 400$

Write the equation of each hyperbola in standard form and general form.

32. centre $(3, 1)$, one vertex $(1, 1)$, slope of one asymptote $\dfrac{2}{3}$

33. foci $(2, 5)$ and $(-4, 5)$, transverse axis 4

Sketch the graph of each hyperbola. Then, graph the hyperbola and its asymptotes, using a graphing calculator.

34. $xy = -25$ **35.** $(x-4)^2 - 16(x+5) = 4$

Find the coordinates of the centre and of the vertices of the hyperbola, and the equations of the asymptotes.

36. $x^2 - y^2 - 6 = 0$

37. $25y^2 - 9x^2 - 100y - 72x - 269 = 0$

Write the equations for each parabola in standard form and general form.

38. vertex at $(-4, 3)$, focus 2 units to the right of the vertex

39. vertex at $(5, -3)$, directrix 2 units below the vertex

40. passing through $(5, 2)$, vertex at $(4, 3)$, opens down

Find the coordinates of the focus and the vertex, the equations of the directrix and the axis of symmetry, and the direction of opening of each parabola.

41. $x^2 - 12y = -12$ **42.** $y^2 - 8x = 2y - 39$

43. For $Ax^2 + y^2 = 144$, describe the graph if
a) $A > 1$ **b)** $0 < A < 1$ **c)** $A = 0$ **d)** $A < 0$

44. Satellite communications A reflector dish has a diameter of 1.8 m and is 24 cm deep. Model the dish as a parabola opening up with its vertex at the origin. What is the equation of the parabola? What are the coordinates of the focus?

Exploring Math

Hyperbolas and Parabolas of Fermat

Pierre de Fermat (c.1601–1665) was the son of a leather merchant in France. Fermat, a lawyer, applied himself to the study of mathematics in his leisure time. He proposed what became one of the most well-known conjectures of all time, **Fermat's Last Theorem.** Andrew Wiles of Princeton University solved this conjecture in the mid-1990s.

Fermat investigated many new curves by generalizing known algebraic equations.

1. Equations of the form $y^n = ax^m$ are called the **parabolas of Fermat**.
a) Let $a = 1$. Create nine equations with three different values of n and three different values of m to graph using a graphing calculator.
b) Graph sets of three equations at a time to determine what happens when n is held fixed and m is changed.
c) Graph sets of three equations at a time to determine what happens when m is held fixed and n is changed.
d) What do you predict would happen to the graph of the equation if a were increased? decreased? Create equations, and graph to check.
e) How is $y^n = ax^m$ a generalization of a parabola?

2. Equations of the form $x^m y^n = b$ are called the **hyperbolas of Fermat**.
a) Let $b = 1$. Create nine equations with three different values of n and three different values of m to graph using a graphing calculator.
b) Graph sets of three equations at a time to determine what happens when n is held fixed and m is changed.
c) Graph sets of three equations at a time to determine what happens when m is held fixed and n is changed.
d) What do you predict would happen to the graph of the equation if b were increased? decreased? Create equations, and graph to check.
e) How is $x^m y^m = b$ a generalization of a rectangular hyperbola?

3. Use your research skills to investigate Fermat's Last Theorem, including Wiles' modern proof.

Chapter Check

1. Describe how you would shine a flashlight on a plane surface to obtain each conic section.

Identify each of the following conic sections and find its equation in standard form.

2. the set of all points 4 units from $(3, -2)$

3. foci at $(10, 0)$ and $(-10, 0)$, difference between focal radii 12

4. $2x^2 - 20x - y + 47 = 0$

5. unit circle translated 3 units left, 8 units downward, and expanded horizontally by a factor of 5

6. foci at $(4, 0)$ and $(-4, 0)$, sum of focal radii 10

7. $x^2 + 225y^2 - 4x - 5 = 0$

8. $x^2 + y^2 + 6x - 8y - 11 = 0$

9. $9x^2 - 4y^2 - 180x - 56y + 740 = 0$

10. centre at $(-2, -8)$, one vertex at $(-2, -20)$, slope of one asymptote 6

Write the equation for each conic section in standard form and general form.

11.

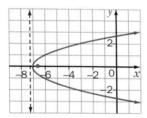

12.

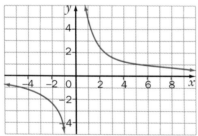

13.

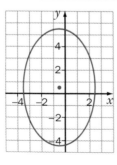

14.

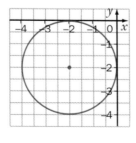

15.

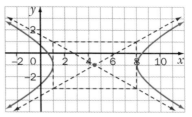

16.

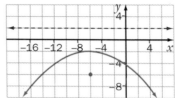

Express each equation in standard form and give the coordinates of the centre, or, in the case of a parabola, the vertex.

17. $9x^2 + y^2 + 36x = 9$

18. $x^2 + y^2 - 2x + 4y = 5$

19. $9x^2 - 4y^2 - 8y + 32 = 0$

20. $3x^2 + 12x - 4y - 12 = 0$

Express each equation in general form and give the values of A and C.

21. $\dfrac{(x+2)^2}{9} + \dfrac{(y-1)^2}{36} = 1$

22. $y - 6 = -\dfrac{9}{4}(x+2)^2 + 6$

23. $\dfrac{(y+4)^2}{16} - \dfrac{(x-2)^2}{9} = 1$

24. $\dfrac{x^2}{16} + \dfrac{(y+5)^2}{16} = 1$

25. Falling object A rock thrown horizontally from the top of a 40-m cliff follows a parabolic path and lands 30 m from the base of the cliff. What is the equation of the parabolic path if the vertex of the parabola is at the origin?

26. Stadium The domed roof of a stadium has a semi-elliptical cross section. The maximum height of the dome is 50 m and its span is 200 m. How high is the dome 30 m from one of its ends?

Using the Strategies

1. For the parabola $x = y^2$, an equilateral triangle can be formed by the vertex and two of its points. Find the coordinates of these two points.

2. Integers How many integers greater than one million and less than four million are perfect squares?

3. Surveys Periodically, surveys are mailed to households across the country to determine product use and buying patterns. In the latest survey, 1012 forms were returned, of which 937 forms were considered valid. One set of questions asked whether the respondents had purchased a VCR, a computer, a CD player, or a car in the past three years. 282 people answered yes to all four, 314 replied yes to at least three, 426 said yes to at least two, and all responded yes to at least one. How many had purchased exactly one, two, and three of these items in the past three years?

4. Sulphur A conical pile of sulphur is 6 m high and has a volume of 85 m³. If another 15 m³ is added to the pile, and the pile stays cone-shaped with the same radius, what will be the increase in the height of the cone?

5. Toothpicks Six toothpicks are used to form two equilateral triangles, as shown. Move three of the toothpicks to different positions so that four equilateral triangles are formed.

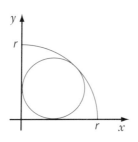

6. Geometry Find the equation of the largest circle that can be inscribed in a quadrant of a circle with centre at the origin and radius r.

7. Locus In a 2 by 2 square, find the locus of all points for which the sum of the squares of the distances from the four vertices is 16.

8. How many digits are in the standard form of the number 9^{9^9}?

9. Volunteer work At a school, each student does volunteer work at one of three hospitals, A, B, and C. At the end of each month, of those who work at A, 5% move to B and 10% move to C. Of those who work at B, 5% move to C and 10% move to A. Of those who work at C, 5% move to A and 10% move to B. If there are 1200 students at the school, and an equal number start at each hospital, how many will be working at hospital B at the end of six months?

10. Volume A right triangle has legs of 6 cm and 8 cm. The triangle is to be rotated in space about one of its three sides. What is the maximum possible volume of the resulting geometric solid?

11. If $n = 5^x + 5^x + 5^x + 5^x + 5^x$, find an expression for the value of n^5.

12. Geometry A circle is inscribed in an equilateral triangle, and a square is inscribed in the circle. Determine the exact value of the ratio of the area of the triangle to the area of the square.

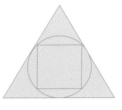

13. When an integer is divided by 15, the remainder is 7. What is the sum of the remainders when the same integer is divided by 3 and by 5?

14. Coins Place four coins tails up on the desk. Turn over three of the coins. Continue turning over any three of the coins at a time, until all the coins are heads up. What is the lowest number of such moves that results in all heads up?

15. Expansion If $n(n-1)(n-2)(n-3)(n-4) = 95\ 040$, what is the value of n?

16. In the sum, each different letter represents a different digit. What digits do A, B, and C represent?

$$
\begin{array}{r}
A\,B\,C \\
A\,B\,C \\
+\ A\,B\,C \\
\hline
B\,B\,B
\end{array}
$$

1. Given the graph of the function $y = f(x)$, sketch the graph of each of the following, and describe the translation taking place.

a) $y = f(x) + 2$ **b)** $y = f(x - 3)$
c) $y = f(x + 1) - 4$ **d)** $y = f(x - 2) + 5$

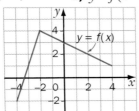

2. Given the graph of $y = f(x)$, draw and label the following pairs of graphs, and state the line of reflection.

a) $y = f(x)$ and $y = -f(x)$
b) $y = f(x)$ and $y = f(-x)$
c) $y = f(x)$ and $x = f(y)$

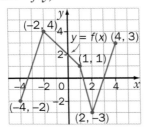

3. Graph $f(x)$ and sketch the specified reflection image. State whether the reflection image represents a function.

a) the reflection of $f(x) = \sqrt{x - 2}$ in the x-axis

b) the reflection of $f(x) = x^2 - 3$ in the line $y = x$
c) the reflection of $f(x) = -4x + 5$ in the y-axis

4. The graph of $y = f(x)$ is shown. Sketch the graphs of the following functions.

a) $-2f(x)$ **b)** $\dfrac{1}{2}f(x)$ **c)** $f(3x)$ **d)** $\dfrac{1}{2}f\left(\dfrac{1}{2}x\right)$

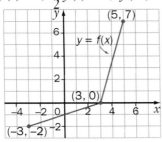

5. Describe how the graph of each of the following functions can be obtained from the graph of $y = f(x)$.

a) $y = -5f(x) + 3$ **b)** $y = 4f\left(\dfrac{1}{2}x\right) + 2$

c) $y = 2f(x + 3) - 4$ **d)** $y = f(7(x - 5)) + 1$

e) $y = f(8(x + 7))$ **f)** $y = \dfrac{1}{3}f(2x - 6) - 9$

6. Sketch the graphs of $y = f(x)$ and $y = \dfrac{1}{f(x)}$ on the same set of axes.

a) $f(x) = 3x - 2$ **b)** $f(x) = (x + 3)(x - 4)$
c) $f(x) = \sqrt{x} + 5$ **d)** $f(x) = x(x + 2)^2$

7. Sketch the graphs of $y = f(x)$ and $y = |f(x)|$ on the same set of axes.

a) $f(x) = -x + 6$ **b)** $f(x) = x(x - 7)$

8. Investment Marilyn earns 5.5% per annum compounded annually on her initial investment of $1500.
a) Write an exponential function that gives the amount of the investment at time t.
b) How much will the investment be worth in five years?
c) Approximately how many years will it take her money to double?

9. Population The population of a town is currently 12 000, but is decreasing by 7% each year.
a) Write an exponential function that relates the population, $P(t)$, and the time, t, in years from now.
b) What will the population be in three years, to the nearest hundred?
c) In approximately how many years will only half of the current population remain?

Solve.

10. $7^{4x + 1} = 1$ **11.** $2^{x^2 + 2x} - \dfrac{1}{2} = 0$

12. $9^{3x} = \left(\dfrac{1}{27}\right)^{x - 2}$ **13.** $8^{\frac{1}{3}}(4)^{x - 2} = \left(\dfrac{1}{16}\right)^{\frac{3}{4}}$

14. Half-life A radioactive substance decays to $\dfrac{1}{32}$ of its original amount after 40 h. What is the half-life of the substance?

15. Doubling period At the initial count there were 2240 bacteria in a culture. Fifteen hours later there were 71 680 bacteria. What is the doubling period for this type of bacterium?

Find the value of x.
16. $x = \log_4 1024$

17. $\log x = -2$

18. $\log_3 \dfrac{1}{27} = x$

19. $\log_x 243 = 5$

Write as a single logarithm.
20. $2\log_5 x - 3\log_5 x^2 z$
21. $\log_6 a + \log_6 b - 2\log_6 ac$
22. $\dfrac{1}{2}\log a + 4\log \sqrt{b} - \left(\log \sqrt[3]{a} - \log 5b\right)$
23. $\dfrac{1}{4}\log_2(x^2 - 2xy - 3y^2) - \log_2 \sqrt[4]{x - 3y}$

24. Given $\log_4 5 = a$ and $\log_4 3 = b$, write $\log_4 225$ in terms of a and b.

Find the value of x, to the nearest hundredth.
25. $4^x = 225$ **26.** $3^{5x-4} = 98$
27. $7^{2x} = 8^{5x-1}$ **28.** $x = \log_6 79$

Solve for x.
29. $\log(x + 4) + \log 3 = 0$
30. $\log_2(x - 2) + \log_2 12 = \log_2(x^2 + 4x - 12)$
31. $\log_3(3x - 4) - \log_3(x + 2) = \log_3 2$
32. $(\log_5 x^2)^2 = \log_5 x^4$

33. Bacteria A bacteria culture grows from 400 to 5000 bacteria in two hours.
a) Find the constant k for the growth formula $B(t) = 400e^{kt}$ where t is time in hours. Round your answer to the nearest ten thousandth.
b) Find the number of bacteria present after five hours, to the nearest ten.

34. a) Name the four conic sections that can be derived from the intersection of a double-napped right circular cone and a plane.
b) Sketch each of the conic sections.

Write the equation in standard form for the circle with each centre and radius.
35. centre (6, −2), radius 7
36. centre (−4, −5), radius $\sqrt{8}$

Determine the equation in standard form for each circle. Then, express the equation in general form.
37. centre (2, −5), passing through (5, 0)
38. centre (3, 2), passing through (2, −2)

Find the centre and radius of each circle.
39. $x^2 + 10x + y^2 - 18y + 90 = 0$
40. $x^2 + y^2 + 10y - 11 = 0$

Sketch the graph of each ellipse. Label the coordinates of the centre, the lengths of the major and minor axes, and the coordinates of the foci.
41. centre (−1, 2), passing through (3, 2), (−5, 2), (−1, 4), and (−1, 0)
42. centre (0, 3), passing through (5, 3), (−5, 3), (0, 13), and (0, −7)

For each hyperbola, determine the
a) coordinates of the centre
b) directions and lengths of the transverse and conjugate axes
c) coordinates of the vertices
d) slopes of the asymptotes
e) equations in standard form and general form

43.

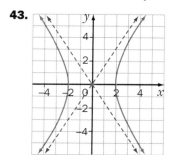

44.

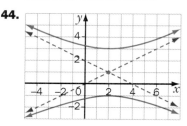

Sketch the graph of each parabola. Label the coordinates of the focus and the vertex, and the equations of the directrix and the axis of symmetry.
45. $y^2 - 2x = 0$ **46.** $x^2 + 4y = 8x$
47. $y = (x - 3)^2 - 4$ **48.** $y^2 + 6y = 3x - 12$

CHAPTER 4

Trigonometric Functions

Since the early 1600's, astronomers have been studying sunspots. Sunspots are relatively dark spots that occur individually or in groups on the surface of the sun. These areas represent magnetic storms and appear darker because the temperature in that region is lower than the temperature on the surrounding surface of the sun. Most sunspots have a distinct dark central portion called the umbra and a less dark outer region called the penumbra. The number of sunspots in any year seems to occur in a cycle.

The graph shows the annual mean number of sunspots for the period 1800–1900.

1. Analyze the graph.
a) Describe the general pattern of the graph. Is the pattern consistent over the time period shown?
b) How many peaks occurred between 1800 and 1900?
c) The mean length of time between successive low numbers of sunspots

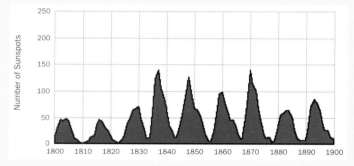

is referred to as the solar cycle. Estimate the number of years in the solar cycle.
d) If you found the mean length of time between successive peak numbers of sunspots, would you expect the same answer as in part c)? Explain.

2. Look at any one solar cycle. Is the cycle symmetrical about a vertical line drawn through the maximum of that cycle?

3. For the period shown on the graph, estimate the following values.
a) the maximum number of sunspots, to the nearest ten
b) the average maximum number of sunspots

Building a Trig Rule

The primary trigonometric ratios are defined in terms of the sides of a right triangle.

$$\sin A = \frac{\text{opposite}}{\text{hypotenuse}}$$

$$\cos A = \frac{\text{adjacent}}{\text{hypotenuse}}$$

$$\tan A = \frac{\text{opposite}}{\text{adjacent}}$$

1 Build a Trig Rule

You can build a device for obtaining approximate values of trigonometric ratios quickly. To make a "trig rule," accurately construct the following three parts.

Template 1
Draw a quarter circle on cardboard and label it as shown.

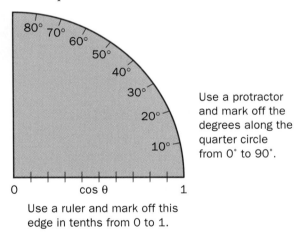

Use a protractor and mark off the degrees along the quarter circle from 0° to 90°.

Use a ruler and mark off this edge in tenths from 0 to 1.

Template 2
From a sheet of clear acetate, cut out a piece for the hypotenuse ruler. Use an overhead marker pen to draw and label the rule, using the same linear scale as in Template 1.

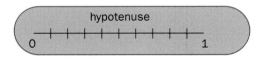

Template 3

Using the same scale as in Template 2, make and label a sine ruler.

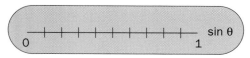

Assemble the trig rule by joining the templates with butterfly fasteners as shown.

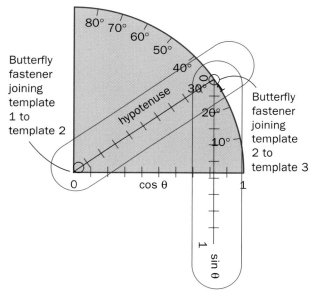

1. Use your trig rule to estimate the following trigonometric values.

a) sin 34°　　　　　　**b)** cos 65°
c) sin 5°　　　　　　　**d)** cos 79°
e) sin 88°　　　　　　**f)** sin 10°

2. Use your trig rule to estimate the measure of ∠A for each given trigonometric value.

a) sin A = 0.2　　　　**b)** cos A = 0.5
c) sin A = 0.9　　　　**d)** cos A = 0.3
e) sin A = 0.7　　　　**f)** sin A = 0.4

3. How does the trig rule work?

4. Could a trig rule be built to determine the sine and cosine values of the following range of angles? Explain.

a) 0° – 180°
b) 0° – 360°
c) negative angles

Mental Math

Right Triangles

Find the length of side x in each.

1.

2.

3.

4.
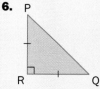

What is the measure of ∠P in each?

5.
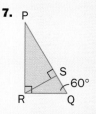

6.
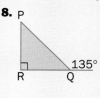

7. P

8. P

Give the other two primary trigonometric ratios for ∠θ in each.

9. $\sin \theta = \dfrac{4}{5}$

10. $\cos \theta = \dfrac{5}{13}$

11. $\tan \theta = \dfrac{\sqrt{3}}{1}$

Estimate the area of the shaded sector.

12.
13.

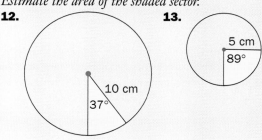

4.1 Angular Measure

Sundials tell time based on the position of the sun, with the premise that when the sun reaches its highest point, it is noon for that particular day. The actual elapsed time between successive noons varies, depending on the time of the year. Sometimes a day is more than 24 h and sometimes less. Telling the exact time on a sundial is difficult. Unlike a conventional clock that is able to display time in seconds, the angular measure of a sundial is, at best, capable of being read to the nearest minute. This is due to the fact that, from Earth, the angular measurement representing the radius of the sun is only $\frac{1}{4}^{\circ}$. The movement of Earth relative to the radius of the sun is equivalent to one minute of time. Discerning that $\frac{1}{4}^{\circ}$ change on a sundial is the difficult task.

Explore: Use a Model to Visualize

Draw a large circle. Mark and measure one radius, r. Cut a piece of string the same length as the radius of your circle. Carefully place the string around the circumference and mark off successive arcs of length r.

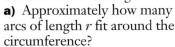

a) Approximately how many arcs of length r fit around the circumference?

b) What is the measure, to the nearest degree, of the sector angle of one sector with arc length r?

Inquire

1. What is the formula for the circumference, C, in terms of the radius, r?

2. Exactly how many arc lengths, each equal to the radius, fit around the circumference?

3. Exactly how many arc lengths, each equal to the radius, fit around a semicircle? Does your answer vary if the radius changes? Explain.

In your previous work with angular measure, you have used degrees as the unit of measure. In the late 1800's, mathematicians and physicists saw the need for another unit of angular measure to aid in simplifying calculations. This unit was called a radian.

One **radian** is the measure of the angle formed by rotating the radius of a circle through an arc equal in length to the radius.

Since the circumference of any circle is $2\pi r$, where r is the radius, there are 2π sectors with arc length r in one revolution.

$\therefore 2\pi$ rad $= 360°$ or π rad $= 180°$ Rad is the abbreviation for radians.

To convert from radians to degrees, or vice versa, solve the previous equation in terms of either unit.

$180° = \pi$ rad π rad $= 180°$

$1° = \dfrac{\pi}{180}$ rad 1 rad $= \dfrac{180°}{\pi}$

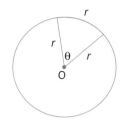

$\angle\theta$ measures one radian
$\angle\theta = 1$ rad

Example 1   Changing Degree Measure to Radian Measure

Express each angle measure in radians. Leave answers in terms of π.
a) 45°   **b)** 75°   **c)** 210°   **d)** −210°

Solution

a) $45° = 45\left(\dfrac{\pi}{180}\right)$ rad

$= \dfrac{\pi}{4}$ rad

b) $75° = 75\left(\dfrac{\pi}{180}\right)$ rad

$= \dfrac{5\pi}{12}$ rad

c) $210° = 210\left(\dfrac{\pi}{180}\right)$ rad

$= \dfrac{7\pi}{6}$ rad

d) $-120° = -120\left(\dfrac{\pi}{180}\right)$ rad

$= -\dfrac{2\pi}{3}$ rad

Example 2   Changing Radian Measure to Degree Measure

Express each angle measure in degrees. Round to two decimal places where necessary.
a) $\dfrac{4\pi}{3}$ rad   **b)** $-\dfrac{3\pi}{4}$ rad   **c)** 2.5 rad   **d)** −0.4 rad

Solution

a) $\dfrac{4\pi}{3}$ rad $= \dfrac{4\pi}{3}\left(\dfrac{180°}{\pi}\right)$

$= 240°$

b) $-\dfrac{3\pi}{4}$ rad $= -\dfrac{3\pi}{4}\left(\dfrac{180°}{\pi}\right)$

$= -135°$

c) 2.5 rad $= 2.5\left(\dfrac{180°}{\pi}\right)$

$\doteq 143.24°$

d) -0.4 rad $= -0.4\left(\dfrac{180°}{\pi}\right)$

$\doteq -22.92°$

Any angle measure given without a degree symbol is assumed to be in radians. For example, $\theta = 2\pi$ represents an angle measure of 2π radians.

When working with sectors of a circle, a proportion can be used to find an unknown arc length or sector angle.

$$\frac{\text{arc length}}{\text{circumference}} = \frac{\text{sector angle}}{\text{one revolution}}$$

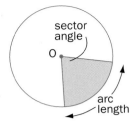

Example 3   Working with Radians to Find a Sector Angle or Arc Length

Find the indicated arc length or sector angle.

a)

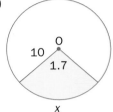

b)

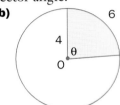

Solution

Since the question involves angle measures in radians, use one revolution $= 2\pi$.

a)
$$\frac{\text{arc length}}{2\pi r} = \frac{\text{sector angle}}{2\pi}$$
$$\frac{x}{2\pi(10)} = \frac{1.7}{2\pi}$$
$$x = 17$$

b)
$$\frac{\text{sector angle}}{2\pi} = \frac{\text{arc length}}{2\pi r}$$
$$\frac{\theta}{2\pi} = \frac{6}{2\pi(4)}$$
$$\theta = 1.5$$

An angle is in **standard position** when its vertex is at the origin and its initial ray is on the positive x-axis. The other ray forming the angle is called the **terminal arm**. If the angle of rotation is counterclockwise, the angle is positive. If the angle of rotation is clockwise, the angle is negative.

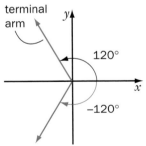

Angles that have the same terminal arm are called **coterminal angles**. The least of the non-negative coterminal angles is called the **principal angle**.

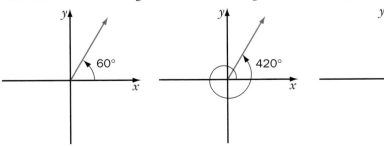

60° and 420° are coterminal angles.

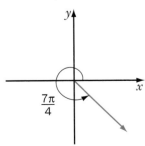

$-\dfrac{\pi}{4}$ and $\dfrac{7\pi}{4}$ are coterminal angles.

Angles having a difference of 360° or 2π radians, or any multiple of these amounts, are coterminal angles.

Example 4 Finding Coterminal Angles

Determine one positive and one negative coterminal angle for each of the following angles.

a) 210° **b)** $\dfrac{2\pi}{3}$

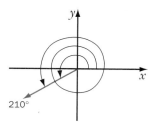
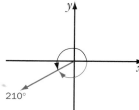

Solution

a) A positive angle that is coterminal with 210° is 210° + 360°, or 570°. A negative angle that is coterminal with 210° is 210° − 360°, or −150°.

b) A positive angle that is coterminal with $\dfrac{2\pi}{3}$ is $\dfrac{2\pi}{3} + 2\pi$, or $\dfrac{8\pi}{3}$. A negative angle that is coterminal with $\dfrac{2\pi}{3}$ is $\dfrac{2\pi}{3} - 2\pi$, or $-\dfrac{4\pi}{3}$.

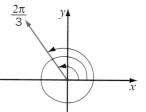
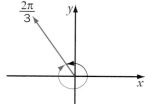

Radians are often used in applications involving **angular speed**, that is, the rate at which the central angle is changing.

Example 5 Expressing Angular Speed in Radians Per Second

A pottery wheel with radius 16 cm makes 30 revolutions in 10 s. Determine the average angular speed of the wheel in radians per second. Round your answer to the nearest hundredth.

Solution

Each time the wheel rotates, it turns through a central angle of 2π radians. So in 30 revolutions the wheel turns through 60π radians.

Use the relationship, angular speed = $\dfrac{\text{angle change}}{\text{time}}$.

$$\begin{aligned}\text{Average angular speed} &= \frac{60\pi}{10} \\ &= 6\pi \\ &\doteq 18.85\end{aligned}$$

The average angular speed of the wheel is 18.85 rad/s, to the nearest hundredth.

Practice

1. Copy and complete the table by changing each angle measure to radians. Express answers in terms of π.

degrees	0	30	45	60	90	120	135	150	180
radians									

2. Copy and complete the table by changing each angle measure to degrees.

degrees							
radians	$\dfrac{7\pi}{6}$	$\dfrac{5\pi}{4}$	$\dfrac{4\pi}{3}$	$\dfrac{3\pi}{2}$	$\dfrac{5\pi}{3}$	$\dfrac{7\pi}{4}$	$\dfrac{11\pi}{6}$

Determine the equivalent measure in degrees, to the nearest tenth, for each of the following radian measures.
3. 1   **4.** 0.4   **5.** −2.8
6. 4.25   **7.** −3.6   **8.** 0.63
9. −1.3   **10.** 3.14   **11.** 7.75

Find the equivalent measure in radians, to the nearest hundredth, for each of the following degree measures.
12. 40°   **13.** 63°   **14.** 145°
15. 19°   **16.** −100°   **17.** 32.8°
18. 205.8°   **19.** 27.5°   **20.** −112.3°

Determine the measure of each sector angle, θ, in radians, to the nearest tenth.

21. 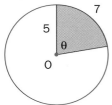   **22.**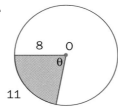

23. 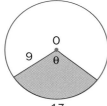   **24.**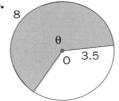

Determine the measure of each arc, x, to the nearest tenth.

25. 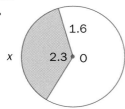   **26.**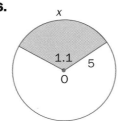

27. 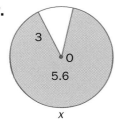   **28.**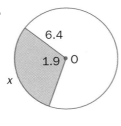

Find one positive and one negative coterminal angle for each given angle.
29. 40°   **30.** 270°   **31.** −60°
32. 155°   **33.** −200°   **34.** 312°

35. $\dfrac{3\pi}{4}$ **36.** $-\dfrac{\pi}{2}$ **37.** $\dfrac{\pi}{3}$

38. $-\dfrac{7\pi}{8}$ **39.** $\dfrac{11\pi}{6}$ **40.** $-\dfrac{6\pi}{5}$

Determine whether the angles in each pair are coterminal.

41. $\dfrac{11\pi}{3}, \dfrac{16\pi}{3}$ **42.** $\dfrac{\pi}{8}, \dfrac{33\pi}{8}$

43. $-\dfrac{5\pi}{9}, \dfrac{5\pi}{9}$ **44.** 440°, 80°

45. −11°, 371°   **46.** 9°, 681°

What is the measure of the principal angle that is coterminal with each given angle?
47. 760°   **48.** −205°   **49.** 1200°
50. −500°   **51.** 625°   **52.** −850°

53. 5π   **54.** $\dfrac{11\pi}{3}$ **55.** $-\dfrac{9\pi}{2}$

56. $-\dfrac{13\pi}{3}$ **57.** $\dfrac{15\pi}{8}$ **58.** $\dfrac{23\pi}{6}$

Give the greatest negative angle that is coterminal with each angle.
59. 305°   **60.** 118°   **61.** −420°
62. −950°   **63.** 212°   **64.** 700°

65. $\dfrac{2\pi}{3}$ **66.** $\dfrac{7\pi}{6}$ **67.** $\dfrac{13\pi}{8}$

68. $\dfrac{17\pi}{3}$ **69.** $-\dfrac{9\pi}{4}$ **70.** $-\dfrac{11\pi}{2}$

Applications and Problem Solving

71. Ferris wheel A Ferris wheel with a radius of 25.3 m makes two rotations every minute.
a) Find the average angular speed of the Ferris wheel in radians per second.
b) How far does a rider travel if the ride lasts 5 min?

72. Watch What is the angular speed, in radians per second, of the second hand on a watch?

73. Sports car The idling speed of a four-cylinder sports car is 850 rpm. Find the angular speed of the crankshaft in radians per second.

74. Saw blade A circular saw with diameter 18.4 cm rotates at 2400 rpm. What is the angular speed of a point on the edge of the saw blade in radians per second?

75. A point on the rim of a lathe pulley turns at 2.22×10^4 degrees per second.
a) Express the angular speed in revolutions per minute.
b) What is the angular speed in radians per minute, as a multiple of π?

76. Geography The easternmost point in Canada is Cape Spear, Newfoundland, at 82°40′ W. The westernmost point is the Yukon-Alaska border, at 141°00′ W. Express the angle between these two lines of longitude in radians, to the nearest tenth.

77. Geography The Earth rotates on its axis once every 24 h. Through how many radians does the Earth turn in one week?

78. Eyesight In good lighting, a person with normal eyesight can just distinguish two objects with an angular separation of 5×10^{-4} rad. What is this angle in degrees?

79. Tool and dye A machine can be set to cut equilateral triangles at regularly spaced intervals around the edge of a circular steel plate, thus creating a saw blade. The machine uses radian measure.
a) If the machine is to be set to cut 16 teeth around the circle, draw a sketch diagram to indicate the angle of rotation at each cut.
b) If the machine is reset to cut 24 teeth, draw a sketch to indicate the angle of rotation at each cut.
c) Describe how to find the angle of rotation of each cut if the machine is set to cut n teeth.

80. Tire speed A car is travelling at 100 km/h.
a) What is the angular speed of a tire which has a radius of 36 cm?
b) Through how many radians will the tire turn in 30 s at this speed?

81. Explain why the measurements of coterminal angles differ by a multiple of 360°.

82. Grads Some calculators work in three modes of angular measure: DEG, RAD, and GRAD. The third of these modes is grads. There are 400 grads in one revolution.
a) What are the values of the sine, cosine, and tangent of 100 grad?
b) Express 100 grad in degree measure and in radian measure.
c) Express 1 rad in grad measure.
d) Find out more about the grad. When was it first used? Where are grads used today?

83. There are infinitely many angles that are coterminal with any given angle.
a) Write an expression that represents all angles that are coterminal with 30°.
b) Write an equivalent expression for the same set of coterminal angles in radian measure.

LOGIC POWER

A hidden picture on the grid is made up of solid squares and blank squares. The numbers at the ends of rows and columns are clues that are read left to right and top to bottom, respectively. For example, 1.3.4 means that there is one solid square followed by a block of 3 solid squares followed by a block of 4 solid squares. The order is correct, but you must determine the number of blank squares in between the blocks of solid squares. Use a 10 by 10 grid to find the design.

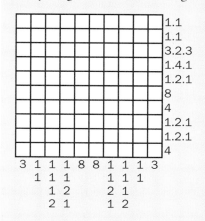

TECHNOLOGY

Investigating Snell's Law Using a Spreadsheet

When you look at a straw in a glass of water, the straw appears to bend at the surface of the water. This illusion is due to the refraction of light as it passes from one medium to another. According to the basic principle of Snell's Law, the angle of incidence is related to the angle of refraction as follows.

$$\text{Index of refraction} = \frac{\text{sine of the angle of incidence}}{\text{sine of the angle of refraction}}$$

The index of refraction is different for different substances. This fact is used by gemologists who use a refractometer to measure the index of refraction and thus identify a particular stone.

1 Finding the Index of Refraction of Water

In an experiment to verify the law of refraction for light passing from air to water, students made measurements of the angles of incidence and refraction. A spreadsheet was used to calculate the sines of both angles and then approximate the index of refraction. The results of the spreadsheet calculation are shown.

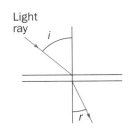

	A	B	C	D	E
	Angle of Incidence	Angle of Refraction			Index of Refraction
1					
2	i (degrees)	r (degrees)	sin i	sin r	n = sin i/sin r
3	10	7	−0.544	0.657	−0.83
4	20	13	0.913	0.420	2.17
5	30	19	−0.988	0.150	−6.59
6	40	25	0.745	−0.132	−5.63
7	50	30	−0.262	−0.988	0.27
8	60	35	−0.305	−0.428	0.71
9	70	38	0.744	0.296	2.61
10	80	40	−0.994	0.745	−1.33

1. According to Snell's Law, the index of refraction of a material should be a constant. Explain what error has been made by the students in obtaining the results shown.

2. a) Modify the spreadsheet to correct the error.
b) What is the approximate index of refraction of water, to two decimal places? Explain any differences in the value of n.

3. Is there any angle at which the light can enter the water and not appear to bend? Explain.

4. What would you expect the index of refraction to be for light passing from water to air? Explain.

2 Determining the Index of Refraction of Other Substances

1. In an experiment to determine the index of refraction of glass, measurements were made of the angles of incidence and refraction. The results are recorded in a table as shown.

Angle of Incidence, i	20°	30°	40°	50°	60°	70°
Angle of Refraction, r	13°	19°	24°	29°	34°	37°

a) Enter these results into a spreadsheet. Use the spreadsheet to calculate the value of $\dfrac{\sin i}{\sin r}$ for each pair of angles. What range of values is obtained for the index of refraction?

b) Use the spreadsheet to calculate the mean of the values of $\dfrac{\sin i}{\sin r}$. Explain why this value can be used as a fairly accurate value for the index of refraction of glass.

c) A ray of light strikes a sheet of glass that is 8 mm thick, at an angle of incidence of 45°. Draw a scale diagram to show the path of the ray of light as it passes through the glass and shines out the other side.

2. The index of refraction of diamond is 2.417. The angles of incidence and refraction of several crystals are measured and recorded. Which crystals are probably diamond?

	Angle of Incidence	Angle of Refraction
Crystal A	42.1°	16.1°
Crystal B	51.8°	16.7°
Crystal C	36.7°	14.3°

4.2 Trigonometric Ratios of Any Angle

When the Confederation Bridge linking Prince Edward Island with New Brunswick was being constructed, the world's largest floating catamaran crane, the Svanen, was brought from Europe to lift the heavy concrete sections into place.

Operating a crane is a highly skilled occupation. The responsibilities of a crane operator include the pre-operational inspection and maintenance of the crane, calculating the crane capacities and weights, and checking clearances so that buildings, hydro wires, and the crane itself will not be damaged. Training is available through apprenticeship programs that can take two to three years to complete. In judging the angles and positions of the crane arm, the operator is using concepts of trigonometry all the time.

Explore: Use a Diagram

△OAB has vertices at O(0, 0), A(3, 4), and B(3, 0). A unit circle intersects OA at P. C is located such that PC is perpendicular to OB.
a) Why is △OPC similar to △OAB?
b) Write a proportion that relates the sides of the similar triangles.

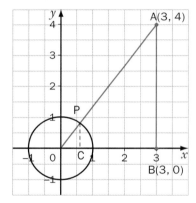

Inquire

1. What is the length of OB? of OA? of OP?

2. Use a proportion to determine the length of OC. Leave the answer in fraction form.

3. Find the length of PC, justifying your steps. Leave the answer in fraction form.

4. What are the coordinates of P?

5. Write the sine ratio and the cosine ratio for ∠AOB.

6. Compare the sine ratio and the cosine ratio for ∠AOB with the coordinates of P. What do you notice?

 7. If a point Q(x, y) lies on OA such that OQ = r, what are the coordinates of Q?

If θ is any angle in standard position, and $P(x, y)$ is any point on the terminal arm of $\angle\theta$, at a distance r from the origin, then by the Pythagorean Theorem $r = \sqrt{x^2 + y^2}$.

The three primary trigonometric ratios are defined in terms of x, y, and r as follows.

$$\sin\theta = \frac{y}{r} \qquad \cos\theta = \frac{x}{r} \qquad \tan\theta = \frac{y}{x}$$

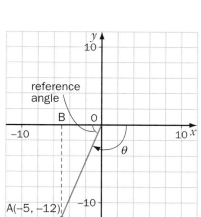

The three reciprocal trigonometric ratios are defined as follows.

$$\text{cosecant} = \frac{1}{\text{sine}} \qquad \text{secant} = \frac{1}{\text{cosine}} \qquad \text{cotangent} = \frac{1}{\text{tangent}}$$

$$\csc\theta = \frac{r}{y} \qquad \sec\theta = \frac{r}{x} \qquad \cot\theta = \frac{x}{y}$$

Example 1   Writing Trigonometric Ratios for Angles in Any Quadrant

The point $A(-5, -12)$ lies on the terminal arm of an $\angle\theta$ in standard position, where $\theta < 0$. Determine the exact value of the six trigonometric ratios for $\angle\theta$.

Solution

Recall that the reference angle is the acute angle formed by the terminal arm and the x-axis. Form $\triangle OAB$ by drawing a line perpendicular to the x-axis from the point $A(-5, -12)$.

In $\triangle OAB$,

$$OA = \sqrt{(-5)^2 + (-12)^2}$$
$$= 13$$

The primary trigonometric ratios can be written as follows.

$$\sin\theta = \frac{y}{r} \qquad \cos\theta = \frac{x}{r} \qquad \tan\theta = \frac{y}{x}$$

$$= \frac{-12}{13} \qquad = \frac{-5}{13} \qquad = \frac{-12}{-5}$$

$$= -\frac{12}{13} \qquad = -\frac{5}{13} \qquad = \frac{12}{5}$$

Then, the reciprocal ratios follow directly from the primary ratios.

$$\csc\theta = -\frac{13}{12} \qquad \sec\theta = -\frac{13}{5} \qquad \cot\theta = \frac{5}{12}$$

The trigonometric ratios of any angle in the first quadrant are always positive. However, as Example 1 shows, in the third quadrant the tangent ratio is positive but the sine and cosine ratios are negative. The following chart summarizes the signs of trigonometric ratios in each quadrant.

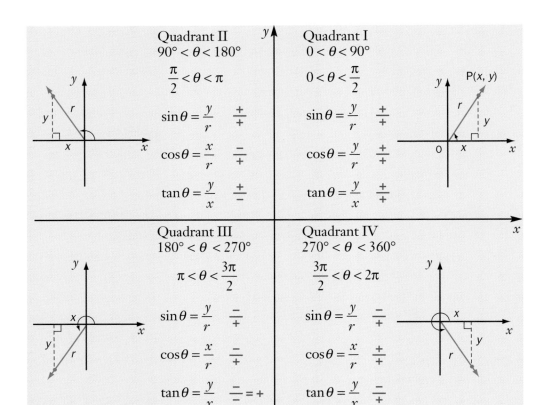

Quadrant II
$90° < \theta < 180°$

$\dfrac{\pi}{2} < \theta < \pi$

$\sin\theta = \dfrac{y}{r}$ $\dfrac{+}{+}$

$\cos\theta = \dfrac{x}{r}$ $\dfrac{-}{+}$

$\tan\theta = \dfrac{y}{x}$ $\dfrac{+}{-}$

Quadrant I
$0 < \theta < 90°$

$0 < \theta < \dfrac{\pi}{2}$

$\sin\theta = \dfrac{y}{r}$ $\dfrac{+}{+}$

$\cos\theta = \dfrac{y}{r}$ $\dfrac{+}{+}$

$\tan\theta = \dfrac{y}{x}$ $\dfrac{+}{+}$

P(x, y)

Quadrant III
$180° < \theta < 270°$

$\pi < \theta < \dfrac{3\pi}{2}$

$\sin\theta = \dfrac{y}{r}$ $\dfrac{-}{+}$

$\cos\theta = \dfrac{x}{r}$ $\dfrac{-}{+}$

$\tan\theta = \dfrac{y}{x}$ $\dfrac{-}{-} = +$

Quadrant IV
$270° < \theta < 360°$

$\dfrac{3\pi}{2} < \theta < 2\pi$

$\sin\theta = \dfrac{y}{r}$ $\dfrac{-}{+}$

$\cos\theta = \dfrac{x}{r}$ $\dfrac{+}{+}$

$\tan\theta = \dfrac{y}{x}$ $\dfrac{-}{+}$

The memory device ASTC can be used to determine which primary trigonometric ratios are positive in each quadrant.

S	A
Sine	All
T	C
Tangent	Cosine

In your previous work you have used the triangles shown to find the exact trigonometric ratios for angles measuring 30°, 45°, and 60°.

θ	30° or $\dfrac{\pi}{6}$	45° or $\dfrac{\pi}{2}$	60° or $\dfrac{\pi}{3}$
$\sin\theta$	$\dfrac{1}{2}$	$\dfrac{1}{\sqrt{2}}$	$\dfrac{\sqrt{3}}{2}$
$\cos\theta$	$\dfrac{\sqrt{3}}{2}$	$\dfrac{1}{\sqrt{2}}$	$\dfrac{1}{2}$

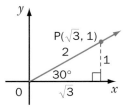

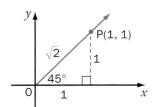

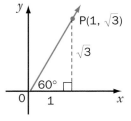

You can extend this method to find exact trigonometric ratios for any angle related to these special angles.

Example 2   Finding Exact Trigonometric Ratios

Find the exact primary trigonometric ratios for 120°.

Solution

120° is in the second quadrant. The reference angle is 60°.
Form a 30°-60°-90° triangle as shown. Then the coordinates
of a point P on the terminal arm of 120° are $(-1, \sqrt{3})$.

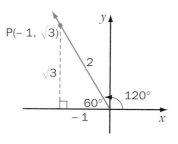

$$\sin\theta = \frac{y}{r} \qquad\qquad \cos\theta = \frac{x}{r} \qquad\qquad \tan\theta = \frac{y}{x}$$

$$\therefore \ \sin 120° = \frac{\sqrt{3}}{2} \qquad \cos 120° = \frac{-1}{2} \text{ or } -\frac{1}{2} \qquad \tan 120° = \frac{\sqrt{3}}{-1} \text{ or } -\sqrt{3}$$

In general, answers left in radical or fractional form are to be considered exact,
in comparison to an approximated decimal value.

Example 3   Finding Exact Trigonometric Ratios

Find the exact value of each trigonometric function.

a) $\cos\dfrac{5\pi}{4}$ 　　　　　　**b)** $\cot\left(-\dfrac{\pi}{6}\right)$

Solution

a) Since $\dfrac{5\pi}{4} = \pi + \dfrac{\pi}{4}$, the terminal arm of the angle is in the third quadrant.

The reference angle is $\dfrac{\pi}{4}$ or 45°. Form a 45°-45°-90° triangle as shown.

Then, the coordinates of a point P on the terminal arm are $(-1, -1)$.

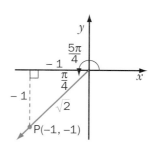

$$\cos\theta = \frac{x}{r}$$

$$\therefore \ \cos\frac{5\pi}{4} = \frac{-1}{\sqrt{2}} \text{ or } -\frac{1}{\sqrt{2}}$$

b) The terminal arm of a rotation of $-\dfrac{\pi}{6}$ is in the fourth quadrant.

Since $\dfrac{\pi}{6} = 30°$, form a 30°-60°-90° triangle as shown.

Then, the coordinates of a point P on the terminal arm are $(\sqrt{3}, -1)$.

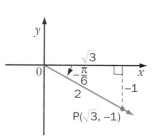

$$\cot\theta = \frac{x}{y}$$

$$\therefore \ \cot\left(-\frac{\pi}{6}\right) = \frac{\sqrt{3}}{-1} \text{ or } -\sqrt{3}$$

Example 4   Working Backward

For an angle θ in standard position, $\sin\theta = -\dfrac{1}{\sqrt{2}}$ and $\cos\theta = \dfrac{1}{\sqrt{2}}$.

a) In which quadrant must the terminal arm of $\angle\theta$ lie?
b) What is the exact value of $\tan\theta$?
c) What is the measure, in radians, of the principal angle that satisfies the given facts?
d) Write an expression for all angles θ that satisfy the given facts.

Solution

a) The cosine is positive in quadrants I and IV. Since $\sin\theta$ is negative, the terminal arm of $\angle\theta$ must lie in quadrant IV to satisfy both conditions.

b) Use $\sin\theta = -\dfrac{1}{\sqrt{2}} = \dfrac{y}{r}$ and $\cos\theta = \dfrac{1}{\sqrt{2}} = \dfrac{x}{r}$ to obtain
the coordinates of point P on the terminal arm. Notice that the triangle formed is a 45°-45°-90° triangle.

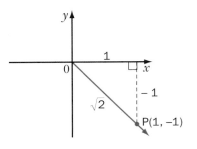

$$\begin{aligned} \tan\theta &= \frac{y}{x} \\ &= \frac{-1}{1} \\ &= -1 \end{aligned}$$

c) From part b), the reference angle is 45° or $\dfrac{\pi}{4}$ radians.

Since the terminal arm is in quadrant IV, the principal angle
is $2\pi - \dfrac{\pi}{4}$ or $\dfrac{7\pi}{4}$.

The measure of the principal angle that
satisfies the given facts is $\dfrac{7\pi}{4}$.

d) All angles that are coterminal with $\dfrac{7\pi}{4}$ satisfy the given facts.

Additional complete clockwise or counterclockwise rotations of 2π produce coterminal angles.

Thus, the set of all angles coterminal with $\angle\theta$ is given by the expression
$\dfrac{7\pi}{4} \pm 2k\pi$, where k is any integer.

Example 5   Applying Trigonometric Ratios

The arm of a crane used for lifting very heavy objects can move so that it has a minimum angle of inclination of 30° and a maximum of 60°. Use exact values to find an expression, in simplified form, for the change in the vertical displacement of the end of the arm, in terms of the length of the arm, a.

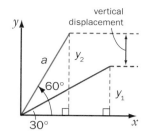

Solution

In the figure, the vertical displacement is $y_2 - y_1$. Using exact trigonometric ratios for 30° and 60°, find expressions for y_1 and y_2 as follows.

$$\sin 30° = \frac{y_1}{a} \qquad \sin 60° = \frac{y_2}{a}$$

$$\frac{1}{2} = \frac{y_1}{a} \qquad \frac{\sqrt{3}}{2} = \frac{y_2}{a}$$

$$\therefore y_1 = \frac{a}{2} \qquad \therefore y_2 = \frac{\sqrt{3}}{2}a$$

Then, the vertical displacement of the end of the arm is given by

$$y_2 - y_1 = \frac{\sqrt{3}}{2}a - \frac{a}{2}$$

$$= \frac{a}{2}\left(\sqrt{3} - 1\right)$$

The change in the vertical displacement of the end of the crane arm is given by the expression $\frac{a}{2}\left(\sqrt{3} - 1\right)$.

Practice

The coordinates of a point P on the terminal arm of each ∠θ are shown. Write the six exact trigonometric ratios for each ∠θ.

1.

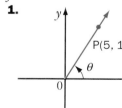

P(5, 12)

2.

P(−1, −√3)

3.

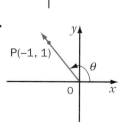

P(−1, 1)

4.

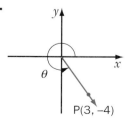

P(3, −4)

Find the exact values of sin θ, cos θ, and tan θ if the terminal arm of ∠θ in standard position contains the given point.

5. P(−8, 15)   **6.** P(5, −3)

7. P(−1, −8)   **8.** P(4, 4)

9. P(4, −3)   **10.** P(−2, 5)

11. P(−4, −2)   **12.** P(6, 3)

State whether the value of each function is positive or negative.

13. sin 100°   **14.** tan 315°

15. cos(−35°)   **16.** $\sin \dfrac{\pi}{8}$

17. $\cot \dfrac{7\pi}{5}$ **18.** $\sec\left(-\dfrac{\pi}{10}\right)$

19. tan 400°   **20.** $\sin \dfrac{3\pi}{4}$

Given $\angle\theta$ in standard position with its terminal arm in the stated quadrant, find the exact values of the remaining five trigonometric ratios for θ.

21. $\cos\theta = -\dfrac{2}{3}$, quadrant II

22. $\sin\theta = -\dfrac{1}{3}$, quadrant IV

23. $\tan\theta = \dfrac{3}{5}$, quadrant III

24. $\sec\theta = -\dfrac{8}{5}$, quadrant III

25. $\cot\theta = \dfrac{3}{4}$, quadrant I

26. $\csc\theta = \dfrac{12}{5}$, quadrant II

Write the exact value of each.

27. $\sin\dfrac{3\pi}{4}$

28. $\tan\dfrac{2\pi}{3}$

29. $\cos 150°$

30. $\cot\dfrac{7\pi}{6}$

31. $\sec(-60°)$

32. $\sin 135°$

33. $\csc\left(-\dfrac{5\pi}{6}\right)$

34. $\tan\dfrac{10\pi}{3}$

Write the approximate values of each, to four decimal places.

35. $\tan 240°$

36. $\cos\left(-\dfrac{5\pi}{4}\right)$

37. $\sec\dfrac{7\pi}{3}$

38. $\sin(-270°)$

39. $\cos(-120°)$

40. $\cos 150°$

41. $\sin\left(-\dfrac{\pi}{4}\right)$

42. $\csc 675°$

Applications and Problem Solving

43. θ is an angle in standard position such that $\sin\theta = \dfrac{5}{13}$.
a) Draw a diagram to show the two possible positions of $\angle\theta$.
b) What are the two possible values of $\cos\theta$?

44. a) The diagram shows a point on the terminal arm of an angle of $\dfrac{\pi}{2}$. Using this and similar figures, copy and complete a table for the trigonometric ratios of angles whose terminal arms are on the axes.

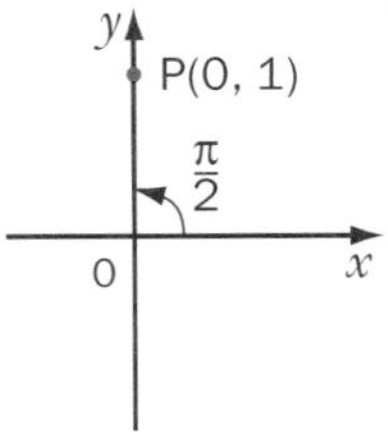

$\angle\theta$	0	90° or $\frac{\pi}{2}$	180° or π	270° or $\frac{3\pi}{2}$
$\sin\theta$				
$\cos\theta$				
$\tan\theta$		undefined		
$\csc\theta$				
$\sec\theta$				
$\cot\theta$				

b) Why is tan 90° undefined?

45. θ is a third quadrant angle and $\tan\theta = 1$.
a) Write the coordinates of a point on the terminal arm.
b) Write the other five trigonometric ratios for $\angle\theta$.

46. If $\sin\theta = \dfrac{2}{3}$, find all possible values of $\cos\theta$.

47. If $\sec\theta = -3$, find all possible values of $\cos\theta$ and of $\tan\theta$.

48. If θ is an angle in standard position such that $\tan\theta > 0$, in which quadrant or quadrants must the terminal arm of θ lie?

49. Docking A ship is tied up loosely at the dock. As the tide changes, the gangplank has a minimum angle of inclination of 30° and a maximum of 45°.
a) Write an exact expression for the minimum and maximum heights above the ship deck that the gangplank can reach in terms of its fixed length, a.
b) Write an expression for the minimum and maximum distance the lower end of the gangplank can be from the side of the ship in terms of its fixed length, a.

50. Given $0 \le \theta \le 2\pi$, for what values of θ is $\sin(-\theta) = \sin \theta$? For what values is $\sin(-\theta) = -\sin \theta$? Are the same results true for $\cos(-\theta)$ and $\tan(-\theta)$? Copy and complete a table similar to the one below to show your conclusions.

	Equivalent to	
$\sin(-\theta)$	$\sin \theta$ for $\theta = \pi$	$-\sin \theta$
$\cos(-\theta)$	$\cos \theta$	$-\cos \theta$
$\tan(-\theta)$	$\tan \theta$	$-\tan \theta$

51. You know that $\dfrac{1}{4} + \dfrac{1}{4} = \dfrac{1}{2}$ is a true statement. Is the following true?

$$\sin \frac{\pi}{4} + \sin \frac{\pi}{4} = \sin \frac{\pi}{2}$$

52. a) Prove the following relationship.

$$\frac{\sin \theta}{\cos \theta} = \tan \theta, \ \theta \ne \frac{\pi}{2} + k\pi, \text{ where } k \text{ is any integer.}$$

b) Why is the restriction $\theta \ne \dfrac{\pi}{2} + k\pi$ needed?

c) Write and prove a similar statement relating $\sin \theta$, $\cos \theta$, and $\cot \theta$.

d) Write and prove a similar statement relating $\csc \theta$, $\sec \theta$, and $\cot \theta$.

53. Determine the value of each of the following.

a) $\log_2 \left(\sin \dfrac{\pi}{4} \right)$ **b)** $\log_5(\cos 2\pi)$

54. Any non-vertical line can be defined by an equation of the form $y = mx + b$.
a) If the line contains the terminal arm of an angle θ in standard position, how can the equation $y = mx + b$ be simplified?
b) By considering a unit circle that intersects the line, explain how $\tan \theta$ is related to the equation $y = mx + b$.

55. If α is the central angle, measured in radians, of a sector of a circle with radius r, show that the area of the shaded segment, S, is given by

$$S = \frac{1}{2}r^2(\alpha - \sin \alpha).$$

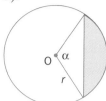

Each of the five houses on a street has a front door of different colour. Each home-owner is of a different nationality. Each owner drives a different type of vehicle, prefers a particular restaurant, and has a different type of pet. Use the clues below to determine who owns the fish.

The British person lives in the house with the red door. The Swede keeps dogs. The Dane drives a motorcycle. The house with the green door is on the left of the house with the white door.

The owner of the house with the green door drives a truck. The person who likes to eat at the Italian restaurant has a parrot. The owner of the house with the yellow door prefers the Chinese restaurant. The owner of the middle house drives a car. The Norwegian lives in the first house. The owner who prefers the Mexican restaurant lives next door to the person who has a cat.

The owner who keeps horses lives next door to the one who prefers the Chinese restaurant. The owner who prefers the Greek restaurant rides a bicycle. The German prefers the East Indian restaurant. The Norwegian lives next to the house with the blue door. The owner who prefers the Mexican restaurant has a neighbour who drives a van.

INVESTIGATING MATH

Period and Amplitude

Examples of a repeated cycle or pattern exist in a variety of everyday items such as wallpaper, fabric prints, flooring, quilts, lattice designs, cable sweaters, and computer graphic designs.

When working with functions, if a pattern repeats regularly over some interval of the domain, then the magnitude of the interval is called the **period** of the function. For a periodic function, half the distance between the greatest and least values of the function is called the **amplitude**. In the example below, the pattern repeats every 4 units in the domain, so the period is 4. The maximum value of the function is 3, and the minimum value is −3, so the amplitude is $\frac{3-(-3)}{2}$, or 3.

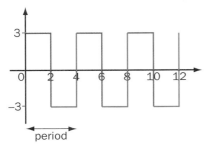

1. What are the period and the amplitude for each periodic function?

a)

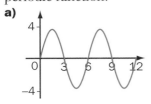

b)

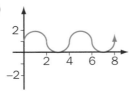

c)

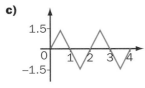

d)

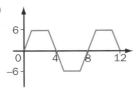

2. Draw a periodic function with amplitude 8 and period 3. Compare your diagram with a classmate's. Are your diagrams the same?

Sine and Cosine Functions on a Graphing Calculator

1 The Nature of a Sine Curve

1. Select degree mode. Plan how to graph $y = \sin x$ for $0° \leq x \leq 360°$.
a) What value will you use for Xmin? for Xmax? Choose an Xscl.
b) What is the maximum value of $\sin x$? the minimum? Use your answers to guide your choice of Ymin and Ymax. Choose a Yscl.
c) Graph $y = \sin x$. Describe the graph. What are its x-intercepts and y-intercepts? Where does the maximum value occur? the minimum value? For what values of x is the function positive? For what values is it negative? How does this relate to the ASTC rule?

2. a) If the domain is extended to $-360° \leq x \leq 360°$, predict how the graph of $y = \sin x$ will change. What will be the same? What are the amplitude and period of $y = \sin x$?
b) Alter the Xmin and graph $y = \sin x$ to check your prediction.

3. a) If the domain were extended to $-720° \leq x \leq 720°$, draw a sketch of the graph that you would expect to obtain.
b) Alter the Xmin and Xmax. Graph to confirm your sketch.

4. Repeat the previous three questions using radian mode.

2 The Nature of a Cosine Curve

1. Select radian mode. Plan how to graph $y = \cos x$ for $0 \leq x \leq 2\pi$.
a) What value will you use for Xmin? for Xmax? Choose an Xscl.
b) What is the maximum value of $\cos x$? the minimum? Use your answers to guide your choice of Ymin and Ymax. Choose a Yscl.
c) Graph $y = \cos x$. Describe the graph. What are its x-intercepts and y-intercepts? Where does the maximum value occur? the minimum value? For what values of x is the function positive? For what values is it negative?

2. a) If the domain is extended to $-2\pi \leq x \leq 2\pi$, predict how the graph of $y = \cos x$ will change. What will be the same? What are the amplitude and period of $y = \cos x$?
b) Alter the Xmin and graph $y = \cos x$ to check your prediction.

3. a) If the domain were extended to $-4\pi \leq x \leq 4\pi$, draw a sketch of the graph that you would expect to obtain.
b) Alter the Xmin and Xmax. Graph to confirm your sketch.

4. Repeat the previous three questions using degree mode.

3 Comparing Sine and Cosine Curves

1. Graph $y = \sin x$ as Y1 and $y = \cos x$ as Y2 for $-2\pi \leq x \leq 2\pi$.
a) How are the graphs similar? How do they differ?
b) Is there a single transformation that relates the graph of $\cos x$ to the graph of $\sin x$? If so, describe this transformation.

2. Repeat the previous question in degree mode.

4.3 Graphing Sine and Cosine Functions

Wind has been used as an energy source throughout history, first to power boats and grind grain, later to pump water and generate electricity. The windmill is known to have been in existence since about the seventh century, and is believed to have originated in Persia.

The blades of a windmill or wind turbine transfer the kinetic energy of the wind to another device capable of transforming the wind power into a useful form of energy. The wind generating plant on Cowley Ridge, Alberta, produces more than 55 000 000 kWh of electricity per year.

As the wind turbine turns, the height of a point on one of the blades, relative to its centre, can be shown as a function of time as follows.

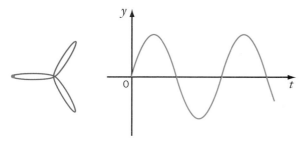

Explore: Draw a Graph

a) Copy and complete the table using exact values.

θ	0°	30°	45°	60°	90°	120°	135°	150°	180°
sin θ									

θ	210°	225°	240°	270°	300°	315°	330°	360°
sin θ								

b) Use your table of values to sketch a graph of $y = \sin \theta$, for $0 \le \theta \le 360°$.

Inquire

1. What is the maximum value of sin θ? the minimum value?

2. What are the x-intercepts of $y = \sin \theta$?

3. a) How would the y-values in your table change if the function were $y = 2 \sin \theta$? How would the answers to the previous two questions change? Explain why.
b) Verify your answers using a graphing calculator. Use degree mode. Set Xmin = 0, Xmax = 360, Xscl = 30, Ymin = −2.5, Ymax = 2.5, Yscl = 0.1. Graph $y = \sin \theta$ as Y1 and $y = 2 \sin \theta$ as Y2.

4. Refer to the information about a wind turbine presented above and the graph shown. How is the maximum value of this graph related to the dimensions of the blades? How do you think the graph would change if the turbine's rotational speed increased?

Functions that repeat themselves over a particular interval of their domain are **periodic functions**. The interval is called the **period** of the function. The graph of $y = \sin x$ shows that it is a periodic function.

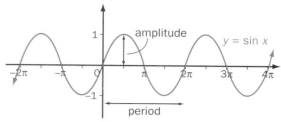

The portion of the curve for $0 \le x < 2\pi$ is repeated continuously in both directions. Therefore, the period of $\sin x$ is 2π.

In general, a function, $f(x)$, is considered periodic if $f(x) = f(x + p)$ for all x in the domain of the function. The least positive value of p is the period of the function. For example, $\sin x = \sin(x + 2\pi)$ or $\sin(x + 360°) = \sin x$.

The **amplitude** of a periodic function is one half the difference between the maximum value and minimum value.

$\text{Amplitude} = \dfrac{|max - min|}{2}$, where max and min represent the maximum and

minimum values of the function, respectively.

The graph of $y = \sin x$ has a maximum value of 1 and a minimum value of -1.

Therefore, the amplitude of $\sin x$ is $\dfrac{|1 - (-1)|}{2} = 1$.

Example 1   Comparing the Period and Amplitude of $y = \sin x$ and $y = \cos x$

Use a graphing calculator to graph $y = \sin x$ and $y = \cos x$ for $0 \le x \le 4\pi$.
a) Describe how the period and amplitude of the two graphs compare.
b) How is the graph of $y = \cos x$ related to the graph of $y = \sin x$?

Solution
a) Use radian mode. Set the window as follows.
Xmin = 0
Xmax = 4π [0, 4π, $\pi/2$] by [-2, 2, 1]
Xscl = $\pi/2$ is used to denote this
Ymin = -2 window setting.
Ymax = 2
Yscl = 1
Graph $y = \sin x$ as Y1 and $y = \cos x$ as Y2.
Two complete cycles of both functions occur in the domain $0 \le x \le 4\pi$.
The period of both functions is 2π.
Both functions have a maximum value of 1 and a minimum value of -1.
Each function has amplitude 1.
b) The y-intercept for the sine curve is 0 while the y-intercept for the cosine curve is 1. The graph of $y = \cos x$ is related to the graph of $y = \sin x$

by a shift of $\dfrac{\pi}{2}$ to the left.

So, $\cos x = \sin\left(x + \dfrac{\pi}{2}\right)$.

From your earlier work with functions, you know that $y = af(x)$ is related to $y = f(x)$ by a vertical stretch of a factor a. The following example shows how this principle applies to sine and cosine functions.

Example 2   Determining the Amplitude of y = a sin x

a) Graph $y = \sin x$, $y = 4 \sin x$, and $y = 0.5 \sin x$, for $0 \le x \le 2\pi$.
b) State the amplitude of each function.

Solution

a) *Method 1:* Graph manually
Step 1: Sketch the base sine curve, $y = \sin x$, for $0 \le x \le 2\pi$.

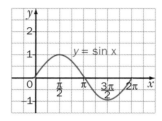

Step 2: Map selected points of the graph of $y = \sin x$ onto their image points.
The following table demonstrates the pattern.

x	y = sin x	y = 4 sin x	y = 0.5 sin x
0	0	0	0
$\frac{\pi}{2}$	1	4	0.5
π	0	0	0
$\frac{3\pi}{2}$	-1	-4	-0.5
2π	0	0	0

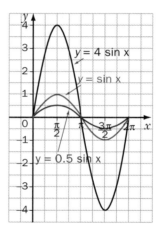

Method 2: Use a graphing calculator
Ensure that radian mode is selected.
Set the window to $[0, 2\pi, \pi/4]$ by $[-5, 5, 1]$.

[Xmin, Xmax, Xscl] by [Ymin, Ymax, Yscl]

Graph $y = \sin x$ as Y1, $y = 4 \sin x$ as Y2, and $y = 0.5 \sin x$ as Y3.

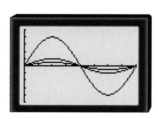

b) The amplitude of $y = \sin x$ is 1. The amplitude of $y = 4 \sin x$ is 4 and the amplitude of $y = 0.5 \sin x$ is 0.5.

Each of the sine and cosine curves examined so far has had a period of 360°, or 2π radians. The following example illustrates how a change in the period is reflected in the equation of the function.

Example 3   Determining the Period for y = cos bx, b > 1

a) Graph $y = \cos x$ and $y = \cos 2x$, for $0 \le x \le 360°$. State the period of each function.

b) Predict the period of $y = \cos 3x$. Check by graphing.

Solution

a) Select degree mode.
Set the window to [0, 360, 30] by [−2, 2, 1].
Graph $y = \cos x$ as Y1 and $y = \cos 2x$ as Y2.

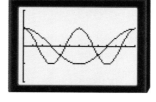

The period of $y = \cos x$ is 360°.
The graph of the function $y = \cos 2x$ has two complete cycles for $0 \le x \le 360°$. The period of $y = \cos 2x$ is 180°.

b) The graph of $y = f(x)$ is related to $y = f(kx)$ for $k > 1$ by a horizontal compression of factor $\frac{1}{k}$. So the graph of $y = \cos 3x$ is related to $y = \cos x$ by a horizontal compression of factor $\frac{1}{3}$. The period of $y = \cos x$ is 360°, so the period of $y = \cos 3x$ will be 120°. The graph of $y = \cos 3x$ will have three complete cycles for $0 \le x \le 360°$.

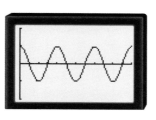

Example 4   Determining the Period for y = cos bx, b < 1

a) Graph $y = \cos x$ and $y = \cos\dfrac{x}{2}$, for $0 \le x \le 2\pi$. State the period of each function.

b) Predict the period of $y = \cos\dfrac{x}{4}$. Check by graphing.

Solution

a) Select radian mode.
Set the window [0, 2π, π/4] by [−2, 2, 1].

Graph $y = \cos x$ as Y1 and $y = \cos\dfrac{x}{2}$ as Y2.

The period of $y = \cos x$ is 2π radians.

The graph of the function $y = \cos\dfrac{x}{2}$ completes

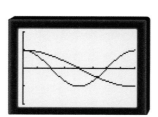
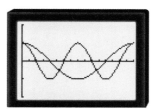

only one half of its cycle for $0 \le x \le 2\pi$. To see one full cycle, extend the domain to Xmax = 4π.

The period of $y = \cos\dfrac{x}{2}$ is 4π.

b) The graph of $y = \cos\dfrac{x}{4}$ will complete only one quarter of its cycle

for $0 \leq x \leq 2\pi$. So, the period of $y = \cos\dfrac{x}{4}$ is 8π. To check, extend the

domain to $Xmax = 8\pi$ and graph $y = \cos\dfrac{x}{4}$ as Y3.

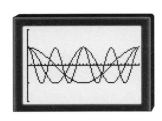

Example 5 Determining the Period and the Amplitude of $y = a \cos bx$

Consider the function $y = 2\cos\dfrac{x}{3}$.

a) Predict the amplitude and the period of the function.
b) Graph the function to check your answer.

Solution
a) Compared with $y = \cos x$, $y = 2\cos\dfrac{x}{3}$ will have a vertical stretch of factor 2

and will complete only one third of a full cycle for $0 \leq x \leq 2\pi$.

For the function $y = 2\cos\dfrac{x}{3}$, the amplitude, $|a|$, is 2 and the period is 6π.

b) Graph $y = 2\cos\dfrac{x}{3}$, using the viewing window

$[0, 6\pi, \pi/4]$ by $[-3, 3, 1]$.

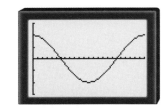

The graph confirms that the amplitude is 2
and the period is 6π.

The previous examples suggest the following generalization.

For functions of the form $y = a \sin b\theta$ and $y = a \cos b\theta$, where $a, b \neq 0$,

the amplitude is $|a|$, and the period is $\dfrac{360°}{|b|}$ or $\dfrac{2\pi}{|b|}$.

Example 6 Writing an Equation From the Graph
What is the equation of the sine function shown?

Solution

$$\text{Amplitude} = \frac{|max - min|}{2}$$
$$= \frac{|2.5 - (-2.5)|}{2}$$
$$= 2.5$$

The amplitude is 2.5.

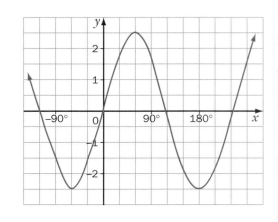

One complete cycle of the curve occurs in 240°, so the period is 240°.

$$\text{Period} = \frac{360°}{|b|}$$

$$240° = \frac{360°}{|b|}$$

$$b = 1.5$$

The equation for the sine function shown is $y = 2.5 \sin 1.5x$.

Example 7   Writing an Equation From the Graph

What is the equation of the cosine function shown?

Solution

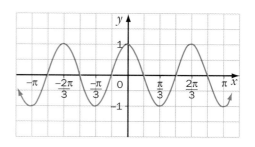

$$\text{Amplitude} = \frac{|max - min|}{2}$$

$$= \frac{|1 - (-1)|}{2}$$

$$= 1$$

The amplitude is 1.

One complete cycle of the curve occurs in $\frac{2\pi}{3}$, so the period is $\frac{2\pi}{3}$.

$$\text{Period} = \frac{2\pi}{|b|}$$

$$\frac{2\pi}{3} = \frac{2\pi}{|b|}$$

$$b = 3$$

The equation for the cosine function shown is $y = \cos 3x$.

Practice

What is the amplitude of each function?

1. $y = 5 \sin \theta$ **2.** $y = 3 \cos \theta$

3. $y = \frac{1}{2} \cos \theta$ **4.** $y = -3.5 \sin \theta$

5. $y = -\sin \theta$ **6.** $y = \frac{2}{3} \cos \theta$

7. $y = 12 \cos \theta$ **8.** $y = -6 \sin \theta$

9. $y = -0.4 \sin \theta$ **10.** $y = 120 \cos \theta$

Find the period, in degrees, of each function.

11. $y = \cos 2\theta$ **12.** $y = \sin 3\theta$

13. $y = \sin \frac{3\theta}{4}$ **14.** $y = \cos 0.5\theta$

15. $y = \sin 6\theta$ **16.** $y = -\sin 2.5\theta$

17. $y = 2 \cos \frac{\theta}{3}$ **18.** $y = 0.5 \cos \theta$

19. $y = -2 \sin 4\theta$ **20.** $y = 3 \sin \frac{3\theta}{10}$

Determine the amplitude and the period in radians of each function.

21. $y = 4 \sin \theta$ **22.** $y = -3 \cos 2\theta$

23. $y = 0.5 \cos \frac{3\theta}{5}$ **24.** $y = 2 \sin 0.5\theta$

25. $y = 3 \sin \frac{2\theta}{3}$ **26.** $y = 8 \cos \frac{4\theta}{5}$

27. $y = 2.5 \cos \frac{\theta}{6}$ **28.** $y = 75 \sin 12\theta$

29. $y = -6.8 \sin 7.2\theta$ **30.** $y = 1.4 \cos 0.6\theta$

Write an equation of the cosine function with the given characteristics.

31. amplitude $\frac{1}{3}$, period π

32. amplitude 3, period 2π

33. amplitude 7, period 150°

34. amplitude 0.5, period 720°

35. amplitude 2.8, period 90°

Write an equation of the sine function with the given characteristics.

36. amplitude 6, period 180°
37. amplitude 0.4, period 45°
38. amplitude 3.5, period 10π
39. amplitude 15, period $\dfrac{\pi}{3}$
40. amplitude 2.8, period 60°

Determine the equation for each sine function.

41.

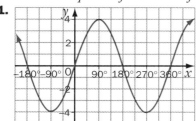

42.

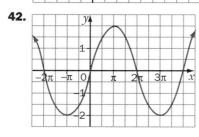

Determine the equation for each cosine function.

43.

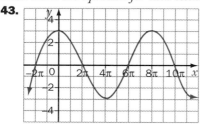

44.

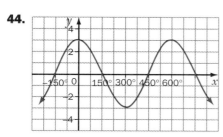

Determine the amplitude, and the period, in radians, of each function. Graph the function to verify your answers.

45. $y = -4 \cos x$
46. $y = \dfrac{1}{3} \sin 4x$
47. $y = 3 \cos 6x$
48. $y = \dfrac{1}{4} \sin \dfrac{x}{2}$
49. $y = 110 \sin 3x$
50. $y = 4.5 \cos \dfrac{x}{4}$

Applications and Problem Solving

51. a) Graph $y = \sin x$ and $y = -\sin x$. How are the graphs related?
b) Predict how the graphs of $y = \cos x$ and $y = -\cos x$ are related. Graph to check your prediction.
c) Generalize the property. How is the graph of $y = a \sin x$ related to the graph of $y = -a \sin x$? How is the graph of $y = a \cos x$ related to the graph of $y = -a \cos x$? Does the negative coefficient affect the amplitude or the period?

52. Graph $y = \sin x$ and $y = \cos x$, for $0 \le x \le 360°$.
a) For what values of x is $\sin x > \cos x$?
b) For what values of x is $\sin x < \cos x$?
c) For what values of x is $\sin x = \cos x$?
d) For what values of x is $\sin x = -\cos x$?

53. If the graphs of $y = A \cos x$ and $y = B \cos x$ are reflections of each other in the x-axis, how are A and B related?

54. Music On an oscilloscope, the note A above middle C appears as a sine curve with a period of $\dfrac{1}{440}$. If the amplitude is 10, write an equation for the curve.

55. Frequency The frequency of a periodic function is defined as the number of cycles completed in a second. This is the same as the reciprocal of the period of a periodic function and is typically measured in Hertz (Hz).
a) What is the frequency of $y = \sin t$? of $y = \cos t$?
b) Determine the frequency of $y = -\sin 2t$ and of $y = 4 \cos \dfrac{t}{2}$.

56. Sound A simple sound, such as that produced by a tuning fork, is made up of vibrations that produce a sinusoidal graphic image on an oscilloscope. Such sounds can be represented by a function of the form $S(t) = a \sin bt$, where t is the time in seconds after the sound was initiated. The loudness of the sound is related to the amplitude of the function. The frequency of the vibrations is given by $\dfrac{|b|}{2\pi}$. A tuning fork for middle C produces 264 vibrations per second.
a) Determine the equation of the function describing the oscilloscope image of a middle C tuning fork if the amplitude is 20.
b) Graph the function for the first $\dfrac{1}{60}$ s after the tuning fork is struck.

57. Electricity The voltage, V, in volts, of an ordinary household alternating current circuit is given by
$$V(t) = 170 \sin 120\pi t$$
where t is the time in seconds.
a) Determine the amplitude and the period for this function.
b) The average voltage in an alternating current circuit is given by $\dfrac{\text{amplitude}}{\sqrt{2}}$. Find the voltage to the nearest whole number.
c) The number of cycles completed in 1 s is the frequency of the current. Determine the frequency.
d) Find the change in the voltage between the time $t = 0.04$ and $t = 0.14$.
e) Graph two cycles of the function.

58. Electricity A generator produces a voltage, V, in volts, given by $V(t) = 120 \cos 30\pi t$, where t is the time in seconds. Graph the function for $0 \le t \le 0.5$.

59. FM radio A radio station sends out a signal having an equation of the form $y(t) = A \sin 2\pi ft$, where f is the number of periods through which the signal oscillates in 1 s, that is, its frequency, and t is the time in seconds. For a particular station, the equation has the form $y = A \sin(10^7 \times 2\pi t)$. What is the frequency of this station?

60. Biorhythms According to biorhythm theory, three cycles affect people's lives, giving them favourable and non-favourable days. The physical cycle has a 23-day period, the emotional cycle has a 28-day period, and the intellectual cycle has a 33-day period. The cycles can be shown graphically as sine curves with amplitude 1 and with the person's date of birth being considered as the start of each cycle.
a) Write a sine function to represent each type of cycle.
b) Graph the three cycles for the first 100 days of someone's life.
c) Neil Armstrong was born on August 5, 1930. On July 16, 1969, he was the first person to set foot on the moon. At what level were each of his three biorhythms on that historic day?

61. Pendulum For a simple pendulum, the angle θ between the pendulum and the vertical is given by
$$\theta(t) = 0.1\sin\sqrt{\frac{9.8}{l}}\,t$$
where l is the length of the pendulum in centimetres and t is the number of seconds that it has been in motion.
a) Graph the function to show how θ changes with time over the first 60 s of motion for a pendulum of length 49 cm. What is the maximum size of $\angle\theta$?
b) Predict how the graph and the maximum size of $\angle\theta$ would change if the pendulum were longer or shorter. Test your predictions. Write a paragraph describing your conclusions.

62. Even or odd functions A function is described as **even** if $f(-x) = f(x)$, and as **odd** if $f(-x) = -f(x)$.
a) Determine whether $y = \sin x$ is an odd or an even function. Justify your answer, including a description of the symmetry of the function. Is your conclusion true for all sine functions of the form $y = a \sin bx$? Explain.
b) Complete a similar analysis for $y = \cos x$.

63. Use the definition of a periodic function to prove that $\sin 2x$ has a period of π.

Knowledge about transformations is necessary for an artist to create an image similar to the one shown. Once a basic shape is drawn, the artist can use translations and stretches of the image to create an eye-catching piece of art.

Explore: Analyze a Graph

One period of each of five sine functions is shown on the graph.

a) How are the graphs similar? How are they different?

b) Describe the transformation that relates $f(x)$ and $g(x)$.

c) Describe the transformation that relates $f(x)$ and $h(x)$.

d) Describe the transformation that relates $f(x)$ and $j(x)$.

e) Describe the transformation that relates $f(x)$ and $k(x)$.

Inquire

1. Given that $f(x) = \sin x$, write the equation for each of the other sine functions.

2. What is the y-intercept of each of the graphs? How do these values relate to the equations?

3. For what values of k does the graph of $y = \sin x + k$ have no x-intercepts?

4. Graph $y = \sin x$ as Y1 and $y = \sin\left(x - \dfrac{\pi}{2}\right)$ as Y2 for $-2\pi \le x \le 2\pi$. Describe the transformation that relates Y1 and Y2.

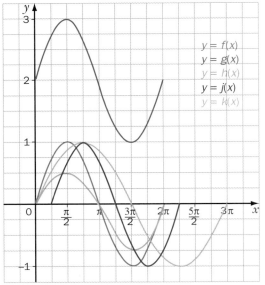

5. Predict how the graph of $y = \sin\left(x + \dfrac{\pi}{2}\right)$ would differ from the graph of $y = \sin x$. Graph both functions to check your prediction. What cosine function has the same graph as $y = \sin\left(x + \dfrac{\pi}{2}\right)$?

6. Predict how the graph of $y = 0.5\sin\dfrac{2}{3}\left(x - \dfrac{\pi}{4}\right) + 2$ would differ from the graph of $y = \sin x$. Graph both functions to check your prediction.

The principles of transformations that were established in Chapter 1 apply to trigonometric functions and can be summarized as follows.

vertical stretch	$y = af(x)$	$y = a \sin x$	changes the amplitude to $|a|$
horizontal stretch	$y = f(bx)$	$y = \sin bx$	changes the period to $\dfrac{2\pi}{|b|}$, $b \neq 0$
vertical translation	$y = f(x) + k$	$y = \sin x + k$	shifts the curve vertically k units upward if $k > 0$ k units downward if $k < 0$
horizontal translation	$y = f(x + h)$	$y = \sin(x + h)$	shifts the curve horizontally h units left if $h > 0$ h units right if $h < 0$

For trigonometric functions, the horizontal translation is sometimes called the **phase shift**.

Example 1   Using Transformations to Graph a Sine Function

a) Describe how the graph of $y = 3\sin\left(x - \dfrac{2\pi}{3}\right) - 2$ can be drawn by using transformations of the graph of $y = \sin x$. Sketch graphs to illustrate your analysis.

b) Check your prediction using a graphing calculator.

Solution
a) *Step 1:* Sketch two cycles of $y = \sin x$.

Step 2: The shift in the domain, $x - \dfrac{2\pi}{3}$,

indicates a phase shift of $\dfrac{2\pi}{3}$ units to the right.

Step 3: The numerical coefficient 3 indicates an amplitude of 3.

Step 4: The constant -2 indicates a downward vertical displacement of 2 units.

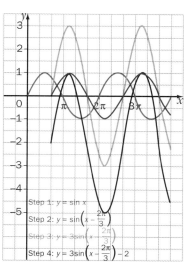

b) The analysis above helps in choosing an appropriate window on a graphing calculator. Use $[0, 4\pi, \pi/3]$ by $[-6, 2, 1]$.

Graph $y = \sin x$ as Y1 and $y = 3\sin\left(x - \dfrac{2\pi}{3}\right) - 2$ as Y2.

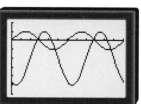

Any sine or cosine function can be expressed in the form

$$y = A \sin B(x + C) + D \text{ or } y = A \cos B(x + C) + D.$$

From this form the following features of the graph can be identified.
The amplitude is $|A|$.

The period is $\dfrac{360°}{|B|}$, or $\dfrac{2\pi}{|B|}$.

With respect to $y = \sin x$, or to $y = \cos x$, the phase shift is $-C$ units and the vertical displacement is D units.

Example 2   Analyzing a Sine Function

A sine function is given by the equation $y = 3\sin 2\left(x - \dfrac{\pi}{4}\right) + 2$.

a) Determine the domain, range, amplitude, period, y-intercept, phase shift, and vertical displacement with respect to $y = \sin x$.
b) Confirm your analysis using a graphing calculator.
c) Determine the x-intercepts for $0 \le x \le 2\pi$, using a graphing calculator.

Solution
a) Domain: x is any real number.
Sketching the transformations of $y = \sin x$ can help in visualizing the other properties.

From the equation, the amplitude is 3, the period is $\dfrac{2\pi}{|2|}$ or π, the phase shift is $\dfrac{\pi}{4}$ to the right, and the vertical displacement is 2 upward.

To find the range, consider the amplitude and vertical displacement, and apply these changes to the range of $y = \sin x$, that is, to $-1 \le y \le 1$.
So, the range is $3(-1) + 2 \le y \le 3(1) + 2$.
Range: $-1 \le y \le 5$

At the y-intercept, $x = 0$.

$$y = 3\sin 2\left(0 - \dfrac{\pi}{4}\right) + 2$$
$$= 3\sin\left(-\dfrac{\pi}{2}\right) + 2$$
$$= 3(-1) + 2$$
$$= -1$$

The y-intercept is at -1.

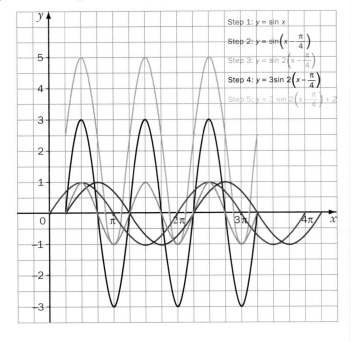

b) Set the window at $[-2\pi, 2\pi, \pi/2]$ by $[-1, 5, 1]$.

Graph $y = 3\sin 2\left(x - \dfrac{\pi}{4}\right) + 2$.

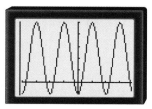

c) The x-intercepts occur when $y = 0$.
Use the ZERO operation on the graphing
calculator to find the x-intercepts.

In the interval $0 \le x \le 2\pi$, $x \doteq 0.4204$, 2.7210,
3.5621, 5.8627.

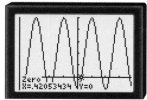

The following example shows an alternative approach to obtaining a sketch
graph of a sine or cosine function. Instead of marking horizontal and vertical
axes and then using transformations to place the curve, this second approach
starts with the basic function curve and then adjusts the axes to satisfy the
particular function.

Example 3   Graphing by Transforming the Axes

a) Sketch at least two periods of the function $y = 4\cos\dfrac{1}{3}(x - \pi) + 2$. Give the

domain, range, amplitude, phase shift, and vertical displacement with respect
to $y = \cos x$.
b) Verify your graph using a graphing calculator.

Solution

a) *Step 1:* Sketch two periods of a basic cosine
curve.

Step 2: Comparing $y = 4\cos\dfrac{1}{3}(x - \pi) + 2$

with $y = A \cos B(x + C) + D$, the value of A
is 4. Label the y-axis to show that the curve
reaches maximum value 4 and minimum
value -4.

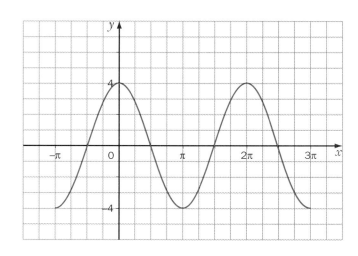

Step 3: i) The vertical displacement, *D*, is 2 units upward. Move the *x*-axis 2 units downward to show this.

ii) Since $B = \dfrac{1}{3}$, the period of this function is $\dfrac{2\pi}{\left|\dfrac{1}{3}\right|}$ or 6π radians.

Change the scale on the *x*-axis to show this.

iii) The amplitude is 4.

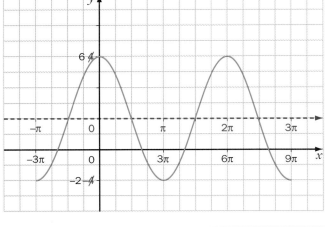

Step 4: The value *C* is $-\pi$, indicating a phase shift of π units to the right. Move the *y*-axis π units to the left to show this.

The domain is any real number. To find the range, consider the amplitude and vertical displacement, and apply these changes to the range of $y = \cos x$, that is, to $-1 \le y \le 1$.

So the range is $4(-1) + 2 \le y \le 4(1) + 2$.
Range: $-2 \le y \le 6$

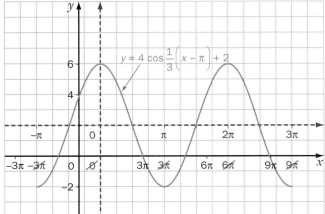

$$y = 4\cos\frac{1}{3}\left(x - \pi\right) + 2$$

b) Set the window to $[0, 8\pi, \pi/3]$ by $[-2, 6, 1]$.

Graph $y = 4\cos\dfrac{1}{3}(x - \pi) + 2$.

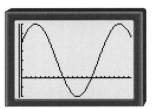

Example 4 Determining an Equation From the Graph

A partial graph of a cosine function is shown. Determine the equation of the function in the form $y = A \cos B(x + C) + D$.

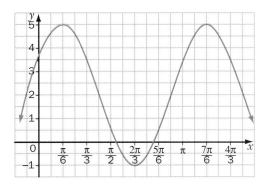

Solution

$$\text{Amplitude} = \frac{|max - min|}{2}$$

$$A = \frac{|5 - (-1)|}{2}$$

$$A = 3$$

One complete cycle occurs in the interval $\frac{\pi}{6} \le x \le \frac{7\pi}{6}$, so the period is π.

$$\text{Period} = \frac{2\pi}{|B|}$$

$$\pi = \frac{2\pi}{|B|}$$

$$B = 2$$

The first crest occurs at $x = \frac{\pi}{6}$. For $y = \cos x$, where $0 \le x \le 2\pi$, the first crest

occurs at $x = 0$, so the curve has a phase shift of $\frac{\pi}{6}$ to the right.

$$\therefore \ C = -\frac{\pi}{6}$$

The mid-line of the curve is the line $y = 2$, so the vertical shift is $+2$. This can be found by adding the amplitude to the minimum value on the graph or by subtracting the amplitude from the maximum. Using the former approach,

$$D = -1 + 3$$
$$\therefore D = 2$$

The equation of the given function, in the form $y = A \cos B(x + C) + D$, is

$$y = 3\cos 2\left(x - \frac{\pi}{6}\right) + 2.$$

Example 5   Graphing Sine as a Function of Time

The motion of a weight on a spring can be described by the equation

$y = 2\sin\left(\pi t - \frac{\pi}{3}\right)$, where y represents the displacement in centimetres and

t represents the time in seconds. Sketch the graph of this function over two periods.

Solution
Sketch two periods of a basic sine curve, letting 6 units represent one period horizontally.

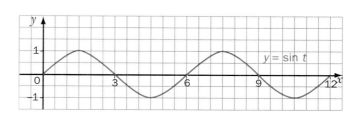

Rewrite $y = 2\sin\left(\pi t - \dfrac{\pi}{3}\right)$ in the form

$y = A \sin B(x + C) + D$.

$\therefore\ y = 2\sin \pi\left(t - \dfrac{1}{3}\right)$

The value of C is $-\dfrac{1}{3}$, indicating a

phase shift of $\dfrac{1}{3}$ unit to the right.

Since $B = \pi$, the period is $\dfrac{2\pi}{|\pi|}$ or 2 units.

The amplitude is 2, and there is no vertical displacement.

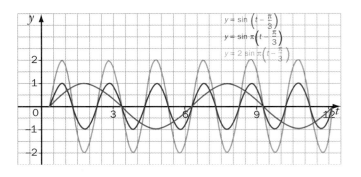

Practice

Determine the vertical displacement and the horizontal phase shift of each function with respect to $y = \sin x$.

1. $y = \sin x + 3$

2. $y = \sin x - 1$

3. $y = \sin(x - 45°)$

4. $y = \sin\left(x - \dfrac{3\pi}{4}\right)$

5. $y = \sin(x - 60°) + 1$

6. $y = \sin\left(x + \dfrac{\pi}{3}\right) + 4$

7. $y = \sin\left(x + \dfrac{3\pi}{8}\right) - 0.5$

8. $y = \sin(x - 15°) - 4.5$

Determine the vertical displacement and the horizontal phase shift of each function with respect to $y = \cos x$.

9. $y = \cos x + 6$

10. $y = \cos x - 3$

11. $y = \cos\left(x + \dfrac{\pi}{2}\right)$

12. $y = \cos(x + 72°)$

13. $y = \cos(x - 30°) - 2$

14. $y = \cos\left(x + \dfrac{\pi}{6}\right) + 1.5$

15. $y = \cos(x + 110°) + 25$

16. $y = \cos\left(x - \dfrac{5\pi}{12}\right) - 3.8$

Determine the amplitude, period, horizontal phase shift, and vertical displacement for each function with respect to $y = \sin x$ or $y = \cos x$.

17. $y = 2\sin x - 3$

18. $y = \cos x + 3$

19. $y = \cos 3(x - 90°)$

20. $y = 0.5\sin(2x) - 1$

21. $y = -3\cos 4\left(x - \dfrac{\pi}{4}\right) + 5$

22. $y = 6\sin 3(x - 20°)$

23. $y = -5\sin 2\left(x - \dfrac{\pi}{6}\right) + 1$

24. $y = 0.8\cos\dfrac{2}{3}\left(x - \dfrac{\pi}{3}\right) - 7$

Write an equation for the function with the given characteristics.

	Type of Function	Amplitude	Period	Phase Shift	Vertical Displacement
25.	sine	4	2π	none	none
26.	cosine	2	π	none	1 upward
27.	sine	1	360°	60° right	3 upward
28.	sine	5	720°	120° left	none
29.	cosine	0.5	2π	$\dfrac{3\pi}{4}$ left	2 downward
30.	cosine	1.5	3π	$\dfrac{\pi}{12}$ right	4 upward

Each graph shows part of a sine function of the form $y = A \sin B(x + C) + D$. Determine the values of A, B, C, and D. Graph the equation to check.

31

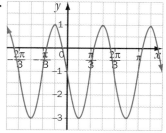

32.

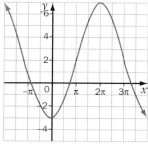

Applications and Problem Solving

33. Describe how the graph of $f(\theta) = 3 \sin\left(\theta - \dfrac{5\pi}{12}\right)$ differs from the graph of $y = \sin \theta$. Check your answer by graphing.

34. Sketch the graph of each function. Then, check your work using a graphing calculator. Give the amplitude, period, phase shift, and vertical displacement with respect to $y = \sin x$ or $y = \cos x$. Determine the x- and y-intercepts in the first positive period.

a) $y = 6 \sin\left(2x + \dfrac{\pi}{4}\right) + 3$

b) $y = 4 \cos 3\left(x - \dfrac{\pi}{2}\right) - 2$

c) $y = \dfrac{1}{2} \cos(2x - 90°) + 1$

d) $y = 2 \sin \dfrac{1}{2}(x + 45°)$

35. Springs An object attached to the end of a spring is oscillating up and down. The displacement of the object, y, in metres, is a function of the time, t, in seconds, and is given by

$$y = 2.4 \cos\left(12t + \dfrac{\pi}{6}\right).$$

a) Sketch two cycles of the function.
b) What is the maximum distance through which the object oscillates?

36. Electricity A particular electromagnetic wave can be described by $y = \cos\left(6\pi \times 10^{12} t - \dfrac{\pi}{3}\right)$, where y is the height of the wave, in centimetres, and t is the time in seconds. Graph two cycles of the function.

37. For a sine function expressed in the form $y = A \sin B(x + C) + D$, D represents the vertical displacement with respect to $y = \sin x$. Does the value of D affect the amplitude? the period? the maximum and minimum values of the function? Provide examples to illustrate your comments.

38. Under certain conditions, the graph $y = A \sin B(x + C) + D$ and the graph of $y = E \cos F(x + G) + H$ will be the same. What are the conditions?

39. The equation of a sine function can be expressed in the form $y = A \sin B(x + C) + D$. Describe what you know about A, B, C, or D for each of the following to be true.
a) The period is greater than 2π.
b) The amplitude is less than one unit.
c) The graph passes through the origin.
d) The graph has y-intercept at A.
e) The graph has no x-intercepts.

NUMBER POWER

If $\sqrt{\text{WONDERFUL}} = \text{OODDF}$, what number is wonderful?

TECHNOLOGY

Investigating Sound Waves

When a tuning fork vibrates, it disturbs nearby air molecules, changing the local air pressure. These pressure variations can be detected by a Vernier microphone, and the resulting digitized signal can be transferred to a graphing calculator and displayed on the screen as a sinusoidal curve.

1 Collecting Data

1. a) Download or enter the BEATS.83P and SOUND.83P programs into a graphing calculator. These programs are available with the CBL™ System-Experiment Workbook or at http://www.ti.com/calc/docs/cblwb1.htm.

b) Connect the graphing calculator, CBL™ unit, and microphone as shown.
c) Turn on the CBL™ unit and the calculator.
d) Start the program SOUND on the calculator.
e) Select a tuning fork whose frequency is between 200 Hz and 300 Hz (middle C = 262 Hz).

2. a) Strike the tuning fork and place it as close as possible to the microphone, without actually touching it . Immediately press ENTER on the calculator.
b) If the resulting plot on the calculator screen is not sinusoidal, press CLEAR ENTER and repeat step a) again.
c) When you are satisfied with your graph, you can save it as a PIC variable and print it later if you have a graph link to your computer. Otherwise, work with the image on your calculator screen.

2 Analyzing the Data

1. a) Determine the time values at the beginning and end of one complete cycle, to find the period, T, of the function.

b) The frequency of sound is the reciprocal of the period. Calculate the frequency, F, using your result from part a).

c) How does this experimental value compare with the frequency printed on the tuning fork? What percent is the error of the correct value?

2. a) Find the maximum and minimum pressure values displayed to determine the amplitude, A, of the function.

b) Write an equation that you think describes the pressure time curve, in the form $y = A \sin 2\pi F(x + D)$, where D is the horizontal displacement.

c) Enter your equation as the next available Y= on the graphing calculator. Then, press GRAPH to see how well it matches the tuning fork curve. Adjust the value of D until you have a reasonably accurate match. Record the equation or, if you are working with a graph-link, save the Y= and GRAPH screens.

3 Continue Investigating

1. Repeat parts 1 and 2 using different tuning forks.

2. Examine your results. Is there any correlation between the percent error that you found for the frequency and the actual frequency of the tuning fork? If so, explain why you think this may occur. What other factors might be affecting the accuracy of your results?

4.5 Applications of Sinusoidal Functions

The world's largest Ferris wheel is located in Yokohama, Japan. It is called the Cosmoclock 21 and has a clock with a minute hand that is 12.95 m long mounted on its hub. The Ferris wheel has a diameter of 100 m, with its hub being 55 m above the ground level. The ride has sixty 8-seat gondolas.

Explore: Draw a graph

Joy is the last to board a Ferris wheel at the county fair. The loading platform is 2 m above ground level. The Ferris wheel has a radius of 8 m and completes one revolution in 48 s. Sketch a graph to show Joy's height above the ground for the first 48 s of the ride.

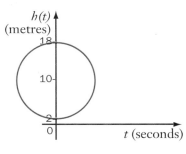

Inquire

1. What is the maximum height above the ground that Joy reaches? the minimum? What is the amplitude of the graph?

2. Explain why Joy's height above the ground can be represented by a periodic function. What is the period?

3. If the path is represented by a sine function of the form $y = A \sin B(x + C) + D$, use your answers to the previous two questions to give the values of A and B. Identify the phase shift and vertical displacement with respect to $y = \sin x$, to obtain the values of C and D. What is the equation of the function?

4. If the ride lasts for 6 min 13 s, at what height above the ground will Joy be when the ride stops?

5. Explain how you would use a graphing calculator to find Joy's height above the ground 63 s after the start of the ride.

6. Write a similar sine function to represent the height of one point on the Cosmoclock 21 Ferris wheel, if a ride lasts 4 min during which time the wheel turns twice.

An important application of trigonometry is the use of sinusoidal functions to model periodic data. However, judgements often must be made on how good the sine or cosine model is, and for what domain the model gives reasonable predictions.

Example 1 Modelling Temperature

The table shows the average monthly temperature, in degrees Celsius, for Winnipeg.
The plotted data have a maximum and a minimum value, and a pattern that might be
modelled by an equation of the form $y = A \cos B(x + C) + D$.

Month, m	1	2	3	4	5	6	7	8	9	10	11	12
Temperature, t	–19	–16	–8	3	11	17	20	18	12	6	–5	–14

a) What are the amplitude and the period of the function?
b) Determine the phase shift and the vertical displacement
with respect to $y = \cos x$.
c) Write the equation in the form $t = A \cos B(m + C) + D$.
d) Use the model to predict the average monthly
temperature for October. How does this value compare
with the actual recorded value?

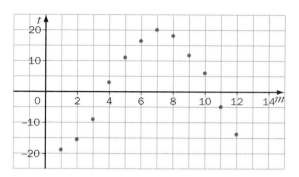

Solution

a) $\text{Amplitude} = \dfrac{|max - min|}{2}$

$A = \dfrac{|20 - (-19)|}{2}$

$A = 19.5$

The amplitude of the function is 19.5.
Since the cycle of average monthly temperatures repeats each 12 months,
the period is 12.

$12 = \dfrac{2\pi}{|B|}$

$\therefore \quad B = \dfrac{\pi}{6}$

b) The maximum occurs in July, when $m = 7$, so the phase shift, C, is –7.
The vertical displacement, D, can be found by adding the amplitude to the minimum
value on the graph.

$D = -19 + 19.5$

$\therefore D = 0.5$

c) Using the results of parts a) and b), the equation, in the form

$t = A \cos B(m + C) + D$, is $t = 19.5 \cos \dfrac{\pi}{6}(m - 7) + 0.5$.

d) For October, $m = 10$.

$t = 19.5 \cos \dfrac{\pi}{6}(m - 7) + 0.5$

$= 19.5 \cos \dfrac{\pi}{6}(10 - 7) + 0.5$

$= 0.5$

The model predicts the temperature for October to be 0.5°C, while the actual
temperature was 6°C. It appears that this model is not the "best fit" for the data.

Example 2   Modelling Tides

By using the averages of high and low tide levels, the depth of water, $d(t)$, in metres, in a seaport can be approximated by the sine function,
$$d(t) = 2.5 \sin 0.164\pi(t - 1.5) + 13.4$$
where t is the time in hours.
a) Graph the function.
b) What is the period of the tide, from one low tide to the next?
c) A cruise ship needs a depth of at least 12 m of water to dock safely. For how many hours per tide cycle can the ship dock safely?

Solution

a) Since there are 24 h in a day, using $0 \le t \le 24$ will show the tidal activity for one day.
From the equation, the amplitude is 2.5, and the vertical displacement is 13.4, so the range is 10.9 to 15.9. Use a window of [0, 24, 1] by [10, 16, 1]. Graph $d(t) = 2.5 \sin 0.164\pi(t - 1.5) + 13.4$.

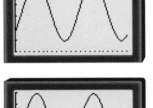

b) Using $B = 0.164\pi$ from the equation, the period is $\dfrac{2\pi}{|0.164\pi|}$, or 12.2 h, to the nearest tenth.

Also, by finding the time of successive minimums on the graph, the period of the tide, from one low tide to the next, is 22.841–10.646, or 12.2 h, to the nearest tenth.

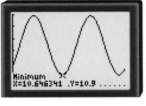
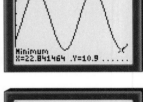

c) To find when the depth is at least 12 m, find the points of intersection of the curve and the line $y = 12$.

The depth is at least 12 m for 8.751 – 0.346 or 8.4 h, to the nearest tenth, each cycle.

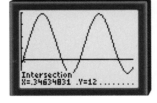
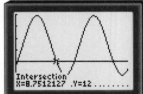

Example 3   Using Environmental Data

According to statistical data from Environment Canada, the greatest normal (average) daily maximum temperature in Edmonton is 23°C on July 28. The lowest normal daily maximum temperature is –14°C on Jan 6.
a) Write a sine or cosine function to approximate this variation in maximum temperatures.
b) Use the equation to predict the maximum temperature on November 10. Compare the predicted value with the normal daily maximum value from the graph.

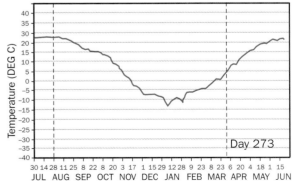

Normal Daily Maximum, Edmonton

Solution

a) Amplitude $= \dfrac{|max - min|}{2}$

$$A = \dfrac{|23 - (-14)|}{2}$$

$$A = 18.5$$

The amplitude is 18.5.

The period is 365 days, so $B = \dfrac{2\pi}{365}$.

Since the graph begins on June 30, the offset to the maximum on July 28 is 28 days. With respect to $y = \cos x$ the phase shift is -28. The mid-line is 18.5 below the maximum, or the line $y = 4.5$. So the vertical displacement, D, is 4.5.
A cosine function that describes the variation in maximum temperature is

$$t(d) = 18.5\cos\dfrac{2\pi}{365}(d - 28) + 4.5$$

where t represents the temperature and d, the day number.

If a sine function is used, the values for A, B, and D remain the same. On day 273 the graph crosses the mid line, so $C = -273$. A sine function that describes the variation in maximum temperature is

$$t(d) = 18.5\sin\dfrac{2\pi}{365}(d - 273) + 4.5.$$

b) On November 10, $d = 133$. For the cosine model,

$$t(d) = 18.5\cos\dfrac{2\pi}{365}(133 - 28) + 4.5$$

$$\doteq 0$$

For the sine model,

$$t(d) = 18.5\sin\dfrac{2\pi}{365}(133 - 273) + 4.5$$

$$\doteq -8$$

On November 10, the greatest temperature in Edmonton is predicted to be 0°C using the cosine model, or −8°C using the sine model. From the graph, the recorded normal daily maximum temperature for November 10 is approximately 3°C. Once again there is a discrepancy between this sinusoidal model and actual data.

Practice

Each graph represents a sine function in the form
$y = A \sin B(t + C) + D$ or a cosine function in the form
$y = A \cos B(t + C) + D$. Write both equations for each.

1.

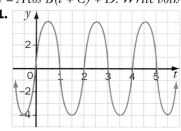

2.

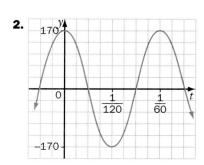

3.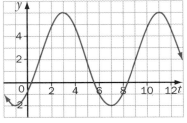

4.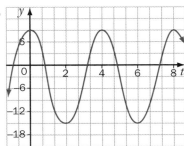

5.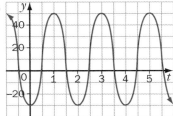

The graph below represents the rise and fall of sea level in part of the Bay of Fundy. The graph can be modelled by a sine function of the form h(t) = A sin B(t + C) + D, where t is the time, in hours, and h is the height relative to mean sea level, in metres.

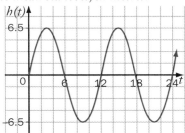

6. What is the range of the tide levels?

7. What is the value of A?

8. What is the period?

9. What is the value of B?

10. What are the values of C and D? Explain your answer.

11. What is the equation represented by the graph?

The temperature in an air-conditioned home on a hot day can be modelled by the function

$$t(x) = 20 + 1.5\cos\frac{\pi x}{12}$$

where x is the time, in minutes, after the air conditioning turns on and t(x) is the temperature, in degrees Celsius.

12. What are the maximum and minimum temperatures in the home?

13. Find the temperature 10 min after the air conditioning turns on.

14. What is the period of the function? How would you interpret this value in the context?

15. At what two times after the air conditioning turns on is the temperature in the home 19°C?

Applications and Problem Solving

16. Tidal wave The height of a tidal wave above mean sea level is related to time by the function

$$h(t) = 1.45\cos\frac{2\pi t}{12.4} + 1.45$$

where *h* represents the height, in metres, above sea level and *t* is the time, in hours.

a) What is the maximum height of the wave?

b) In the first cycle, at what times does the maximum occur?

c) What is the minimum height of the wave?

d) What is the period of the wave?

e) What is the height of the wave 2 h after high tide?

17. Predator-prey situations The rodent population in a region varies approximately according to the equation

$$r(t) = 1200 + 300\sin\frac{\pi t}{2}$$

where *t* is the number of years since 1970 and *r* is the number of rodents.

a) Find the maximum and minimum numbers of rodents and the years in which they occurred in the first cycle.

b) What is the period of the function?

c) How many rodents could be expected in 2010?

18. Ferris wheel A Ferris wheel of diameter 40 m has its centre 21 m above the ground. The wheel rotates once every 30 s.
a) Draw a graph to show a rider's height above the ground during a 4-min ride, starting at the lowest position.
b) Find an equation of the graph.

19. Paddle wheel The water wheel on a paddle steamer has a radius of 2 m. The wheel rotates at 5 rev/min and has 0.2 m submerged in the water.
a) Draw a graph to show the height, relative to the surface of the water, of a point on the edge of the wheel for two complete revolutions. Use a point that is touching the surface of the water at the start of motion.
b) Determine the equation for a sine function that describes the height of the point.

20. Tides At high tide, the average depth of water in a harbour is 22 m, and at low tide the average depth is 10 m. The tides in the harbour complete one cycle approximately every 12 h.
a) Write a sine function that relates the depth of the water in the harbour, y, to the time, t, in hours, after low tide.
b) Graph the function for a two-day period.

21. Climate The averages of mid-afternoon temperatures in Regina, over a thirty-year period, are shown.
a) Determine the equation of a sine or cosine function that approximates this data.
b) Use a graph of the function to estimate during what percent of the year the mid-afternoon temperatures are below freezing.
c) Graph the actual data and compare it with your equation from part a). Is your model a good approximation of the data? Why or why not?

Month	Temperature
Jan	−11.0°C
Feb	−7.4°C
Mar	−0.6°C
Apr	10.5°C
May	18.5°C
Jun	23.4°C
Jul	26.3°C
Aug	25.6°C
Sep	18.6°C
Oct	11.9°C
Nov	0.2°C
Dec	−8.4°C

22. Employment The number of people employed in a resort town can be modelled by the function

$$f(x) = 4.9 + 1.5\sin\left(\frac{\pi x}{6} + 1\right)$$

where x is the number of the month (Jan = 1) and $f(x)$ is the number of people in thousands.
a) What is the minimum value of the function? Interpret what this number means in terms of the model.
b) In which month is the maximum number of people employed?
c) What type of resort town might this be? Explain.
d) If a new large hotel were opened in the resort town, describe how the function might change. Give reasons for your answer.

23. Sunrise times At Estevan, Saskatchewan, the latest sunrise time is at 09:12 on December 21. The earliest sunrise time is at 03:12 on June 21. Sunrise times on other dates can be predicted from a sinusoidal equation. There is no daylight saving time in Saskatchewan, and the period is 365 days.
a) Write a sinusoidal equation that relates the sunrise time to the day of the year.
b) Use the equation to predict the time of sunrise on February 10.
c) What is the average time of sunrise throughout the year?

24. Using environmental data Refer back to Example 3 and these two models.

$$t(d) = 18.5\cos\frac{2\pi}{365}(d - 28) + 4.5$$

$$t(d) = 18.5\sin\frac{2\pi}{365}(d - 273) + 4.5$$

a) Graph the two models. How are they similar? How are they different? Explain.
b) Find a sine or cosine curve that better approximates the data. Explain why it is better. Is a sinusoidal function a good model for this data? Why or why not?

4.6 Other Trigonometric Functions

The robotic arm pictured can rotate 90° from horizontal to vertical. If a heavy object is placed in its hand, the arm is in danger of breaking when at positions close to horizontal. Tests indicate that, for a weight of 1 kg (9.8 N at the surface of Earth), the arm cannot have a slope less than $\frac{1}{4}$. For what angles is it safe for the arm to hold a weight of 1 kg?

Explore: Use Skills With Functions

Since $\sin\theta = \frac{y}{r}$, $\cos\theta = \frac{x}{r}$, and $\tan\theta = \frac{y}{x}$, the three primary trigonometric ratios are related by $\tan\theta = \frac{\sin\theta}{\cos\theta}$.

Sketch the graphs of $f(\theta) = \sin\theta$ and $g(\theta) = \cos\theta$, for $-2\pi \le \theta \le 2\pi$. Select key points in the domain and use the values of $f(\theta)$ and $g(\theta)$ at those points to sketch the graph of $h(\theta)$, where $h(\theta) = \frac{f(\theta)}{g(\theta)} = \tan\theta$.

Inquire

1. How does the domain of $h(\theta)$ differ from that of $f(\theta)$ and $g(\theta)$? Explain why.

2. What is the period of $h(\theta)$?

3. What is the range of $h(\theta)$?

4. Does $h(\theta)$ have an amplitude? Explain.

5. Predict how the graph of $y = 2\tan\theta$ would compare with $h(\theta)$. Describe the similarities and differences. Use a graphing calculator to check.

6. Predict how the graph of $y = \tan\theta + 1$ would compare with $h(\theta)$. Describe the similarities and differences. Use a graphing calculator to check.

7. Predict how the graph of $y = \tan 2\theta$ would compare with $h(\theta)$. Describe the similarities and differences. Use a graphing calculator to check.

8. How could you use the graph of $f(\theta)$ to sketch a graph of $y = \csc\theta$?

The graphs of $y = \tan \theta$ and the reciprocal trigonometric functions are periodic functions, but they differ from the sinusoidal functions $y = \sin \theta$ and $y = \cos \theta$ in that they have restrictions on their domains.

For example, graphs of $y = \cos x$ and $y = \sec x$ are shown.

Since $\cos x = 0$ for $x = \dfrac{\pi}{2} + n\pi$, where

n is any integer, $y = \dfrac{1}{\cos x} = \sec x$ is undefined for these values of x and so has no amplitude.

The vertical lines $x = \dfrac{\pi}{2} + n\pi$ are asymptotes for the function $y = \sec x$.

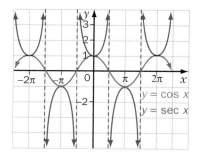
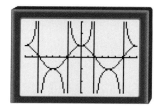

The domain of $y = \sec x$ is all real numbers such that $x \neq \dfrac{\pi}{2} + n\pi$, and the range of $y = \sec x$ is $|y| \geq 1$. The period of $y = \sec x$ is 2π.

The function $y = \sec x$ has no x-intercepts, and has a y-intercept of 1.

Example 1 Graphing a Transformation of $y = \tan x$

Consider the functions $f(x) = \tan x$ and $g(x) = \tan 3x$. Predict how the domain, range, and period of $g(x)$ compare with those of $f(x)$. Graph the functions to check your prediction. State the domain, range, and period of each function.

Solution

First graph $f(x) = \tan x$ for $-2\pi \leq x \leq 2\pi$. The period of $f(x) = \tan x$ is π.

Since $\tan x = \dfrac{\sin x}{\cos x}$, the restriction is $\cos x \neq 0$. So, $f(x)$ is undefined for $x = \dfrac{\pi}{2} + n\pi$, and thus has no amplitude.

The domain of $f(x) = \tan x$ is all real numbers such that $x \neq \dfrac{\pi}{2} + n\pi$.

The range of $f(x) = \tan x$ is any real number.

For $g(x) = \tan 3x$, since x is multiplied by 3, the graph has a horizontal stretch by a factor of $\dfrac{1}{3}$ with respect to $f(x) = \tan x$. So, the period of $g(x)$ is $\dfrac{\pi}{3}$. Similarly, any restrictions in the domain of $f(x)$ are multiplied by a factor of $\dfrac{1}{3}$ to give the restrictions in the domain of $g(x)$.

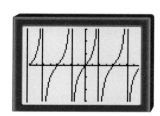

The domain of $g(x)$ is all real numbers such that $x \neq \dfrac{\pi}{6} + \dfrac{n\pi}{3}$.

The range of $g(x)$ is any real number.

The graphing calculator screen shows $f(x) = \tan x$ as Y1 and $g(x) = \tan 3x$ as Y2 using a window setting of $[-\pi/2, \pi/2, \pi/4]$ by $[-3, 3, 1]$.

Example 2   Distinguishing $y = \tan x$ and $y = \cot x$

The functions $f(x) = \tan x$ and $g(x) = \cot x$ were graphed on the same screen. The window used was $[-\pi, \pi, \pi/2]$ by $[-4, 4, 1]$.

Distinguish between the graphs, by comparing their periods, domains, ranges, x-intercepts, and asymptotes.

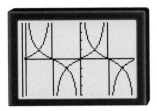

Solution

Both functions have a period of π. Since $\tan x = \dfrac{\sin x}{\cos x}$, $f(x) = 0$ when $\sin x = 0$, and is undefined when $\cos x = 0$. Hence, the x-intercepts of $f(x)$ are $x = n\pi$, and the asymptotes occur at $x = \dfrac{\pi}{2} + n\pi$, where n is any integer.

Because $\cot x = \dfrac{\cos x}{\sin x}$, $g(x) = 0$ when $\cos x = 0$, and is undefined when $\sin x = 0$. The x-intercepts of $g(x)$ are $x = \dfrac{\pi}{2} + n\pi$, and the asymptotes occur at $x = n\pi$, where n is any integer. The features of each function, based on the above reasoning, are as follows.

	$f(x) = \tan x$	$g(x) = \cot x$
Domain	$x \neq \dfrac{\pi}{2} + n\pi,$ where n is any integer	$x \neq n\pi,$ where n is any integer
Range	y is any real number	y is any real number
x-intercepts	$n\pi,$ where n is any integer	$\dfrac{\pi}{2} + n\pi,$ where n is any integer
Asymptotes	$x = \dfrac{\pi}{2} + n\pi,$ where n is any integer	$x = n\pi,$ where n is any integer

Example 3   Transforming a Reciprocal Function

a) Sketch the graph of $y = \sin x$, $-\pi \leq x \leq \pi$, and use this graph to sketch the graph of $y = \csc x$.

b) Predict how the domain, range, and period of $y = 2 \csc x$ compare with the graph of $y = \csc x$. Use a graphing calculator to check.

c) Predict how the domain, range, and period of $y = \csc 2x$ compare with the graph of $y = \csc x$. Use a graphing calculator to check.

Solution

a) The graph of $y = \sin x$ is sketched using selected values in the domain $-\pi \le x \le \pi$.

Since $\csc x = \dfrac{1}{\sin x}$, the graph of $y = \csc x$ is graphed by finding the reciprocals of the selected points. At values of x for which $\sin x = 0$ the reciprocals are undefined, so $y = \csc x$ has asymptotes at $x = n\pi$, where n is any integer. Selected points are shown in the table.

x	sin x	csc x
$-\pi$	0	undefined
$-\dfrac{\pi}{2}$	-1	-1
0	0	undefined
$\dfrac{\pi}{2}$	1	1
π	0	undefined

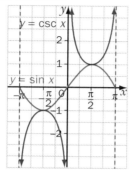

b) The graph of $y = 2 \csc x$ is transformed from the graph of $y = \csc x$ by a vertical stretch of factor 2. Points such as $\left(\dfrac{\pi}{2}, 1 \right)$ are transformed to $\left(\dfrac{\pi}{2}, 2 \right)$, so the range becomes $|y| \ge 2$. The asymptotes are the same, so the domain does not change, nor does the period.

The graphing calculator screen shows $y = \csc x$ as Y1 and $y = 2 \csc x$ as Y2 with a window of $[-\pi, \pi, \pi/2]$ by $[-4, 4, 1]$.

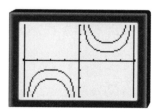

c) The graph of $y = \csc 2x$ is transformed from the graph of $y = \csc x$ by a horizontal stretch of factor $\dfrac{1}{2}$. Some key points are $\left(\dfrac{\pi}{4}, 1 \right)$, $\left(\dfrac{\pi}{2}, \text{undefined} \right)$, $\left(\dfrac{3\pi}{4}, -1 \right)$, $(\pi, \text{undefined})$, and so on. The range remains the same. The asymptotes occur at twice as frequent intervals, at $x = \dfrac{n\pi}{2}$, where n is any integer, so the domain becomes all real numbers such that $x \ne \dfrac{n\pi}{2}$, and the period is π.

The graphing calculator screen shows $y = \csc x$ as Y1 and $y = \csc 2x$ as Y2 with a window of $[-\pi, \pi, \pi/2]$ by $[-4, 4, 1]$.

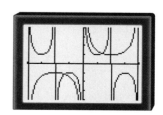

Practice

Each graph is a function of the form y = tan kx.
Determine the value of k for each.

1.

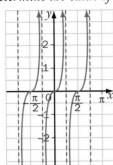

2.

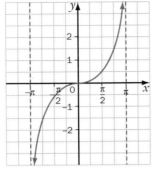

3.

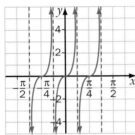

Determine the period and the phase shift with respect to
y = tan x for each function.

4. $y = \tan(3x - \pi)$

5. $y = \tan 2x$

5. $y = \tan\left(x + \dfrac{\pi}{3}\right)$

7. $y = \tan\left(x - \dfrac{\pi}{4}\right)$

8. $y = \tan\left(x - \dfrac{\pi}{2}\right)$

9. $y = \tan(2x - \pi)$

10. $y = \tan\left(\dfrac{x}{2} + \dfrac{\pi}{2}\right)$

11. $y = \tan\left(3x + \dfrac{\pi}{3}\right)$

Predict how the period, domain, and range of the
functions in each pair compare. Graph both functions to
check your predictions.

12. $y = \tan x,\ y = 2\tan x$

13. $y = \sec x,\ y = 3\sec x$

14. $y = \cot x,\ y = \cot 5x$

15. $y = \csc x,\ y = 4\csc x$

Applications and Problem Solving

16. a) Write an equation for a tangent function

with period 2π and phase shift $\dfrac{\pi}{4}$ to the left.

b) Is the equation you gave the only possible
answer? Why or why not?

232   *Chapter 4*

17. A function is given by $y = \tan(2x - 90°)$.
a) What is the smallest positive x value at which an
asymptote occurs?
b) Write a general equation for all possible vertical
asymptotes.

18. Sketch the graph of $y = -3\tan\dfrac{x}{2}$, by hand,
for $-\pi \le x \le \pi$.
a) Describe the process that you used to sketch the
graph.
b) Is the amplitude of this function 3? Explain.
c) What are the equations of the asymptotes?

19. How is the graph of $y = \csc x$ related to the
graph of $y = \sec x$? Describe the similarities and
differences. Is there a single transformation that
would map one onto the other?

20. If $0° \le x \le 360°$, for what value(s) of x does
$\csc x$ reach its smallest positive value, and what is
that value?

21. In the domain $-\pi \le x \le 2\pi$, for what value(s) of
x is each of the following true?
a) $\tan x = \cot x$ **b)** $\cot x = -1$
c) $\cot x = 0$ **d)** $\cot x > \tan x$

22. a) Find the points of intersection of $y = \cos x$
and $y = \sec x$.
b) Find the points of intersection of $y = \sin x$ and
$y = \csc x$.
c) Compare the answers to parts a) and b) and give
reasons for any similarities or differences.

23. Predict the domain, range, and period of
$y = |\tan x|$. Use a graph to check your predictions.

24. Predict how the graph of $y = -\tan x$ compares
with the graph of $y = \cot x$. Use a graph to check.

25. For what values of x is $|\sec x| \ge |\tan x|$?

26. Technology The screen shows the graph of
$y = \sec x$, using a window of $[-\pi/2, \pi/2, \pi/4]$ by
$[0, 3, 1]$ in dot mode. The curve resembles a
parabola. Could it possibly be a parabola? Explain.

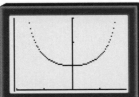

Absolute Value and Trigonometric Functions

In some applications of trigonometric functions, for example in the field of electronics, formulas involving the absolute value of trigonometric functions occur.

1. a) Visualize the graph of $y = \sin x$, $-2\pi \le x \le 2\pi$. Predict how the graph of $y = |\sin x|$ differs from the graph of $y = \sin x$.
b) Sketch a graph to show both functions.
c) Use graphing technology to check your predictions.

2. Sketch the graphs of $y = \cos x$ and $y = |\cos x|$, $-2\pi \le x \le 2\pi$. Describe the similarities and the differences between the two graphs.

3. Compare the graphs of $y = |\sin x|$ and $y = |\cos x|$. Describe their similarities and their differences.

4. For each of the following functions, describe the graph giving the period, the maximum and minimum values, and the x- and y-intercepts. Use graphing technology to check your answers.
a) $y = |4 \sin x|$
b) $y = |\cos x - 1|$
c) $y = |\tan x|$
d) $y = \left| 3 \cos x + \dfrac{1}{2} \right|$
e) $y = |-2 \sin x + 3|$
f) $y = |\sec x|$

5. Sketch the graph of each of the following functions, for $-2\pi \le x \le 2\pi$. Describe their similarities and their differences.
a) $y = \sin x$
b) $y = \csc x$
c) $y = |\csc x|$

6. The voltage, $V(t)$, of an alternating current (AC) generator is given by $V(t) = 170 \cos 120\pi t$, where t is the time, in seconds. A bridge rectifier takes AC as its input and outputs the absolute value of the input waveform. The output voltage of a simple bridge rectifier is given by $V(t) = 170 |\cos 120\pi t|$.
a) Sketch the graphs of both functions.
b) Describe the similarities and the differences between the two graphs.

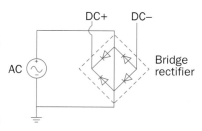

CONNECTING MATH AND ASTRONOMY
Graphing Around the Sun With a Graphing Calculator

Johannes Kepler (1571–1630) showed empirically that the planets follow elliptical orbits.

In 1599, Kepler was appointed assistant to the renowned Danish-Swedish astronomer Tycho Brahe. When Brahe died in 1601, Kepler succeeded him as court astronomer to Kaiser Rudolph II. With this position, Kepler inherited Brahe's immense collection of precise observations on the position of the planets. He sought to find a mathematical expression that would fit this data accurately.

Such was his faith in the exactness of the data that, if he discovered a pattern that fit with even a small error, he threw his work out and started over. Such was his perseverance that he worked for eight years to deduce his first two laws of planetary motion, and a further ten years to discover the third in 1619.

Kepler's laws of planetary motion are:

I. The planets move in elliptical orbits around the sun. The sun occupies one focus of the ellipse.

II. A straight line from the centre of the sun to the planet sweeps out equal areas in equal time intervals. Therefore, the closer the planet is to the sun, the faster it moves.

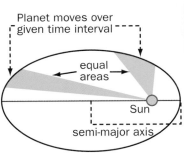

III. The square of the orbital period of any planet is proportional to the cube of its mean distance from the sun.

In the diagram of a planet's orbit around the sun,
r = distance from the sun to the planet,
a = length of the semi-major axis,
b = length of the semi-minor axis.

The distance from the sun, r, is dependent on the angle θ, and is defined by the polar function

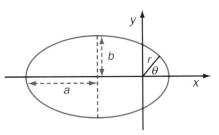

$$r(\theta) = \frac{b^2}{a + \sqrt{a^2 - b^2}\,\cos\theta}\ , \text{ where } \theta \text{ is measured in radians.}$$

In a polar coordinate system, any point in the plane is described by the distance r from the pole and the angle θ formed by the terminal arm and the positive x-axis.

A planet is at its **perihelion**, that is, its closest point to the sun, when $\theta = 0$. A planet is at its **aphelion**, that is, its furthest point from the sun, when $\theta = \pi$.
The perihelion distance is called the **perigee**, and the aphelion distance is called the **apogee**. The length of the semi-major axis is equal to the average of the perigee and the apogee.

The length of the semi-minor axis can be found from the formula

$$b = \sqrt{2ad - d^2}$$

where d is the perigee.

1. Use the data and the given steps to graph the orbit of Earth around the sun.

Perigee: 147 000 000 km
Apogee: 152 000 000 km
Average of these distances: 149 500 000 km
$a = 149\ 500\ 000$
$b = 149\ 480\ 000$

a) Select **MODE Pol** to work with polar coordinates.
b) Enter the equation for $r(\theta)$. Be careful with the use of brackets.
c) Use $\theta\text{min} = 0$, $\theta\text{max} = 2\pi$, and $\theta\text{Step} = 0.1$.
Choose suitable X and Y ranges to accommodate the data.
d) Graph. Go back and change the range values, if necessary.

2. The table contains data for some of the other planets.

Planet	Perigee (km)	Apogee (km)
Mercury	46 000 000	69 800 000
Venus	107 500 000	108 900 000
Mars	206 600 000	249 200 000
Jupiter	740 600 000	816 000 000

a) Graph the orbit of each planet.
b) Look up the perigee and the apogee of the remaining planets. Graph their orbits as well.
c) After 1999, Neptune and Pluto are expected to interchange places relative to their distances from the sun. Graph the orbits of both planets to confirm this.

Review

4.1 *Find the equivalent measure in degrees, to the nearest tenth, for each of the following radian measures.*
1. 1.3 **2.** 0.7 **3.** −2.4
4. $\dfrac{\pi}{12}$ **5.** −3π **6.** $\dfrac{5\pi}{6}$

Find the equivalent measure in radians for each of the following degree measures. Leave answers in terms of π.
7. 45° **8.** 100° **9.** 36°
10. 20° **11.** −150° **12.** −600°

Find one positive and one negative coterminal angle for each given angle.
13. 57° **14.** 95° **15.** −123°
16. $-\dfrac{5\pi}{12}$ **17.** $\dfrac{4\pi}{3}$ **18.** $\dfrac{\pi}{6}$

Determine whether the angles in each pair are coterminal.
19. $\dfrac{7\pi}{12}, \dfrac{43\pi}{12}$ **20.** $\dfrac{\pi}{7}, \dfrac{15\pi}{7}$
21. −30°, 690° **22.** 397°, 38°

4.2 *Find the exact values of all six trigonometric ratios for θ if the terminal arm of ∠θ in standard position contains the given point.*
23. P(−3, −3) **24.** P(4, −7)
25. P(−4, 8) **26.** P(2, 5)

Give the exact value of each.
27. sin 270° **28.** $\tan\dfrac{2\pi}{3}$
29. $\cot\left(-\dfrac{\pi}{6}\right)$ **30.** sec 225°

31. If $\cos\theta = \dfrac{1}{3}$, find all the possible values of sin θ.

4.3 *Determine the amplitude and the period, in radians, of each function.*
32. $y = 4.2\sin 3\theta$ **33.** $y = -2\cos\dfrac{\theta}{3}$
34. $y = 0.7\cos\dfrac{3\theta}{4}$ **35.** $y = 5\sin\dfrac{7\theta}{12}$

36. Determine the equation of the sine graph.

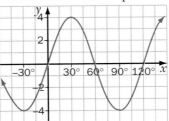

37. Determine the equation of the cosine graph.

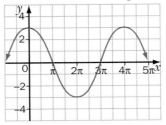

4.4 *Determine the amplitude, period, horizontal phase shift, and vertical displacement for each function with respect to y = sin x or y = cos x. Graph each function.*
38. $y = 2.5\sin x - 1$
39. $y = \cos 6(x - 45°)$
40 $y = -4\cos 2\left(x + \dfrac{\pi}{3}\right) + 8$
41. $y = 2\sin\dfrac{1}{3}(x + 90°) + 4$

📏 *Write an equation for each graph in the form*
y = A sin B(x + C) + D and in the form
y = A cos B(x + C) + D. Explain the process used in obtaining the equations.
42.

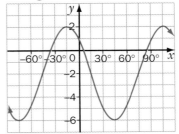

43.

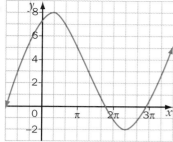

44. Tide The depth of water in a harbour can be approximated by the equation
$$d(t) = -3.5 \cos 0.17\pi t + 12$$
where $d(t)$ is the depth, in metres, and t is the time, in hours, after low tide.

a) Graph the function.

b) What is the period of the tide, from one high tide to the next?

c) An ocean liner needs a minimum of 13 m of water to dock safely. For how many hours per cycle can the ocean liner dock safely?

45. Temperature The average daily maximum temperature in Victoria reaches a high of 23°C on July 27, and a low of 5°C on January 5.

a) Use a cosine model to approximate this variation in temperature.

b) How many days will have an expected maximum of 20°C or higher?

Each graph is a function of the form y = tan kx. Determine the value of k for each.

46.

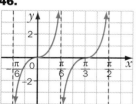

47.

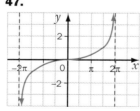

Determine the period and the phase shift with respect to y = tan x for each function.

48. $y = \tan\left(2x - \dfrac{\pi}{2}\right)$
49. $y = \tan\left(4x + \dfrac{\pi}{3}\right)$

Graph each pair of functions. Compare the period, domain, and range of the functions.

50. $y = \cot x, y = \cot 2x$

51. $y = \sec x, y = 4 \sec x$

Exploring Math

Trigonometric Series

Since ancient Greek times, trigonometric ratios have been determined geometrically. However, ideas developed in the eighteenth century by Taylor, Maclaurin, and Euler led to a numerical way of finding the value of trigonometric ratios. The following infinite power series converge to sin x and cos x, where x is measured in radians.

$$\sin x = x - \frac{x^3}{3!} + \frac{x^5}{5!} - \frac{x^7}{7!} + \ldots + (-1)^{n+1}\frac{x^{2n-1}}{(2n-1)!} + \ldots$$

$$\cos x = 1 - \frac{x^2}{2!} + \frac{x^4}{4!} - \frac{x^6}{6!} + \ldots + (-1)^{n+1}\frac{x^{2n-2}}{(2n-2)!} + \ldots$$

1. a) What is the exact value of $\sin\dfrac{\pi}{6}$, based on the geometry of special triangles?

b) Evaluate the sum of the first three terms of the series for sin x, using $x = \dfrac{\pi}{6}$.

c) Evaluate the sum of the first four terms of the series, then the first five terms, and so on. How many terms do you need to add before the sum, to six decimal places, converges to the value of $\sin\dfrac{\pi}{6}$?

2. Repeat the steps of question 1 for each of the following.

a) $\sin\dfrac{\pi}{2}$ **b)** $\cos\dfrac{\pi}{3}$ **c)** $\sin \pi$ **d)** $\cos \pi$

3. a) Using the sine key on a calculator, what is the value of sin 1, to four decimal places?

b) Determine the value of sin 1 using successive partial sums of the series. How many terms do you need to add before the result matches the value in part a)?

4. Use a graphing calculator, or graphing software, to graph $y = \sin x$, $y = x - \dfrac{x^3}{3!} + \dfrac{x^5}{5!}$, $y = x - \dfrac{x^3}{3!} + \dfrac{x^5}{5!} - \dfrac{x^7}{7!}, \ldots$, for $0 \le x \le 2\pi$. Sketch your results and write a paragraph describing your observations. For which values of x does the series give a close approximation for sin x, using the first three terms? the first four terms?

Chapter Check

Find the equivalent measure in degrees, to the nearest tenth, for each of the following radian measures.

1. 3.4   **2.** 1   **3.** −2.7

4. $\dfrac{5\pi}{12}$ **5.** −π   **6.** $\dfrac{4\pi}{3}$

Find the equivalent measure in radians for each of the following degree measures. Leave answers in terms of π.

7. −30°   **8.** 140°   **9.** 80°

10. 420°   **11.** −405°   **12.** 600°

Determine whether the angles in each pair are coterminal.

13. $\dfrac{2\pi}{5}, \dfrac{13\pi}{5}$ **14.** $\dfrac{\pi}{8}, -\dfrac{15\pi}{8}$

15. −10°, 700°   **16.** 385°, 25°

Given ∠θ in standard position with its terminal arm in the stated quadrant, find the exact values of the remaining five trigonometric ratios for θ.

17. $\cos\theta = -\dfrac{1}{3}$, quadrant III

18. $\csc\theta = \dfrac{4}{3}$, quadrant I

19. $\tan\theta = -\dfrac{5}{2}$, quadrant IV

Give the exact value of each.

20. $\cos\left(-\dfrac{\pi}{6}\right)$ **21.** tan 540°   **22.** cot 135°

23. Graph $y = \sin x$ and $y = \cos x$ on the same set of axes.
a) Describe how the period and the amplitude of the two graphs compare.
b) How is the graph of $y = \cos x$ related to the graph of $y = \sin x$?

Write an equation of the cosine function with the given characteristics.
24. amplitude 5, period π
25. amplitude 1.7, period 240°

26. Determine the equation of the sine graph.

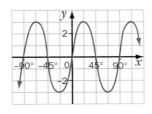

27. Determine the equation of the cosine graph.

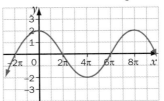

Determine the amplitude, period, horizontal phase shift, and vertical displacement for each function with respect to $y = \sin x$ or $y = \cos x$. Graph each function.

28. $y = 3.7\cos\left(x + \dfrac{\pi}{6}\right)$ **29.** $y = \sin 4(x - 15°)$

30. $y = -2\cos 3\left(x + \dfrac{\pi}{3}\right) - 5$

31. $y = 7\sin(2x + 90°) + 4$

32. Write an equation for the graph in the form $y = A\sin B(x + C) + D$ and in the form $y = A\cos B(x + C) + D$. Explain the process used in obtaining the equations.

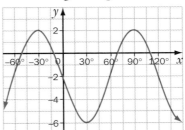

33. Sunrise At Prince Albert, Saskatchewan, the latest sunrise time is 09:17 on December 24. The earliest sunrise time is 04:35 on June 22. Sunrise times on other dates can be predicted from a sinusoidal equation. There is no daylight saving time in Saskatchewan, and the period is 365 days.
a) Write a sinusoidal equation that relates the sunrise time to the day of the year.
b) How many days out of the year does the sun rise before 05:00?

Graph each pair of functions. Compare the periods, domains, and ranges of the functions.
34. $y = \tan x, y = \tan 4x$
35. $y = \csc x, y = 5\csc x$

Using the Strategies

1. How many multiples of 4 are there between 1 and 10 001?

2. Measurement A cube measures 1 cm on each edge. What is the measure of the acute angle formed by a diagonal of the cube and an edge of the cube? In other words, in the diagram, what is the measure of $\angle AGH$?

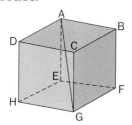

3. Solve the equation $4^{x^2} = 16$.

4. Measurement a) If the radius of each circle is 5 cm, determine the exact area of the shaded part of the diagram.
b) Generalize the solution if each circle has radius r units.

5. What is the arithmetic mean of the first fifty successive positive integers that have first digit 3?

6. Job bids June, Kate, and Lia are bidding on a small job. Together, they can complete the job in x hours. If June works alone, she will need an additional 6 h. Kate working alone will require one additional hour, and Lia working alone will need an extra x hours. How long will the job take if they work together?

7. Watches Two friends, Sean and Nadia, set their watches to the same time at 9:00 on Monday morning. Sean's watch is running 2 min/h too fast, but Nadia's is running 1 min/h too slow. When will Sean's watch be one hour ahead of Nadia's?

8. Use each of the digits 1 through 9 once to replace the Xs and make a true addition statement, so that no two consecutive digits are next to each other.

$$\begin{array}{r} X\ X\ X \\ +\ X\ X\ X \\ \hline X\ X\ X \end{array}$$

9. If $AB = 19$ cm, $BC = 18$ cm, and $AC = 17$ cm, what is the perimeter of $\triangle ADE$?

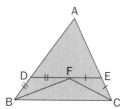

10. Floor tiles A rectangular floor is covered with square tiles all of the same size. There are 81 tiles along one side and 63 along the other. If a straight line is drawn diagonally across the floor, how many tiles will it cross?

11. A regular hexagon and an equilateral triangle have equal perimeters. The area of the triangle is 2 m^2. What is the area of the hexagon?

12. Chess Place eight queens on a chessboard so that no queen is vulnerable to attack from another queen.

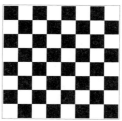

13. Birthdays The birthdays of four friends occur in January, July, September, and December. Carla was not born in the winter. Brian celebrates his birthday close to Canada Day. Ardith's birthday is the month after Don's. In what month was each person born?

14. What is the minimum number of cuts needed in a rectangle 9 m by 16 m to form a square that has the same area as the rectangle?

CHAPTER 5

Trigonometric Equations

Turning movements are common in many forms of dance, particularly ballet, and can be analyzed using trigonometry. A pirouette requires the dancer to turn about a vertical axis on a straight supporting leg while the other leg is raised to the side in some manner. Realistically, during an almost-vertical turn the dancer becomes slightly unbalanced. The turning force, or torque, required for the dancer to regain balance can be determined using the equation

$$T = mgR \sin \theta$$

where T is the torque, in newton metres (N·m), m is the mass of the dancer, in kilograms, g is the gravitational force or acceleration due to gravity (which is constant at 9.8 m/s²), R is the distance from the point of support on the floor to the centre of the dancer's mass, and θ is the angle of lean of the body from the vertical.

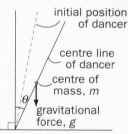

initial position of dancer

centre line of dancer

centre of mass, m

θ

gravitational force, g

1. A ballet dancer is performing an off-balance pirouette. She is turning at the rate of two revolutions per second. The dancer has a mass of 50 kg, and a height of 1.7 m, and her centre of mass is about 1 m from her balancing toe. Determine her torque, to the nearest whole number, at each of the following times.
a) At the beginning of the pirouette, her angle of lean from the vertical is 2°.
b) After 0.5 s, her angle of lean is 4°.
c) After 1 s, her angle of lean is 15°.

2. Why do you think the torque becomes greater as the time of unbalance increases?

3. Determine the angle of lean, to the nearest tenth, for the dancer in question 1 when her torque is as follows:
a) 55 N·m   **b)** 72 N·m

Whose Angle Is It Anyway?

Make three large "trig wheels." Label each wheel to show the special angles for which exact primary trigonometric values are known. The sine wheel is started for you.

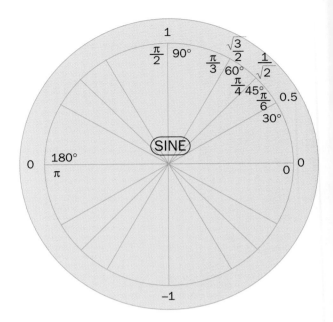

Answer the following questions. Use the trig wheels to help you, if necessary.

1. What is the measure of the smallest principal angle, in degrees, for which each of the following is true?

a) $\sin x = 0.5$ **b)** $\tan x = 1$ **c)** $\cos x = -1$

d) $\sin x = \dfrac{\sqrt{3}}{2}$ **e)** $\tan x = \dfrac{1}{\sqrt{3}}$ **f)** $\cos x = \dfrac{1}{\sqrt{2}}$

g) $\sin x = -1$ **h)** $\tan x = -\sqrt{3}$ **i)** $\cos x = \dfrac{\sqrt{3}}{2}$

2. What is the measure of the smallest principal angle, in radians, for which each of the following is true?

a) $\cos x = -1$ **b)** $\tan x = -1$ **c)** $\sin x = 1$

d) $\cos x = 0$ **e)** $\tan x = -\dfrac{1}{\sqrt{3}}$ **f)** $\sin x = -\dfrac{1}{\sqrt{2}}$

g) $\tan x = 0$ **h)** $\tan x = -\sqrt{3}$ **i)** $\cos x = -0.5$

3. If $0 \le x < 360°$, give all angles, in degree measure, for which each of the following is true.

a) $\sin x = 1$ **b)** $\cos x = 0.5$ **c)** $\tan x = 1$

d) $\sin x = -\dfrac{1}{2}$ **e)** $\cos x = \dfrac{\sqrt{3}}{2}$ **f)** $\sin x = 0$

g) $\cos x = \dfrac{1}{\sqrt{2}}$ **h)** $\tan x = \sqrt{3}$ **i)** $\sin x = -\dfrac{1}{\sqrt{2}}$

4. If $0 \le x < 2\pi$, give all angles, in radian measure, for which each of the following is true.

a) $\tan x = -1$ **b)** $\sin x = 0.5$ **c)** $\tan x = \dfrac{1}{\sqrt{3}}$

d) $\sin x = -\dfrac{1}{\sqrt{2}}$ **e)** $\cos x = -\dfrac{1}{2}$ **f)** $\tan x = 1$

g) $\sin x = \dfrac{\sqrt{3}}{2}$ **h)** $\sin x = -0.5$ **i)** $\cos x = \dfrac{1}{\sqrt{2}}$

5. If x is measured in degrees, give expressions to represent all angles for which each of the following is true.

a) $\sin x = 0$ **b)** $\tan x = -1$ **c)** $\cos x = -\dfrac{\sqrt{3}}{2}$

d) $\sin x = 0.5$ **e)** $\tan x = 0$ **f)** $\cos x = -\dfrac{1}{\sqrt{2}}$

g) $\sin x = -1$ **h)** $\tan x = -\sqrt{3}$ **i)** $\sin x = \dfrac{1}{\sqrt{2}}$

6. If x is measured in radians, give expressions to represent all angles for which each of the following is true.

a) $\cos x = -1$ **b)** $\sin x = -0.5$ **c)** $\tan x = 1$

d) $\cos x = \dfrac{\sqrt{3}}{2}$ **e)** $\sin x = -\dfrac{1}{\sqrt{2}}$ **f)** $\tan x = -\sqrt{3}$

g) $\sin x = \dfrac{1}{2}$ **h)** $\tan x = \dfrac{1}{\sqrt{3}}$ **i)** $\cos x = \dfrac{1}{\sqrt{2}}$

Warm Up

Find the measure of ∠θ, to the nearest tenth of a degree.

1.
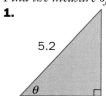
5.2
θ
3.5

2.
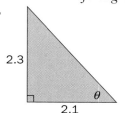
2.3
θ
2.1

3.
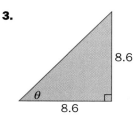
8.6
θ
8.6

4.
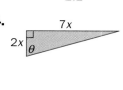
7x
2x
θ

5.
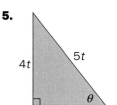
4t
5t
θ

6.
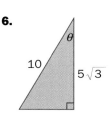
θ
10
$5\sqrt{3}$

Evaluate each expression, to four decimal places.

7. $\cos 25° + \cos 20°$ **8.** $\tan 65° - \tan 20°$

9. $\csc 15° - \csc 35°$ **10.** $\sin 47° + \sin 43°$

11. $\sin 135° - \sin 65°$ **12.** $\sec 190° - \sec 10°$

13. $\cot 27° + \cot 18°$ **14.** $\tan 39° + \tan 21°$

15. $\cos 93° - \cos 3°$ **16.** $\csc 10° + \csc 15°$

Solve each equation.

17. $x^2 + 5x + 6 = 0$ **18.** $x^2 - 1 = 0$

19. $4x^2 - 25 = 0$ **20.** $x^2 - 3x - 4 = 0$

21. $2x^2 + x - 3 = 0$ **22.** $5x^2 - 30x = 0$

23. $1.6x^2 - 2.5 = 0$ **24.** $9x^2 + 24x + 16 = 0$

25. $6x^2 - 16x - 6 = 0$ **26.** $35 + 13x - 12x^2 = 0$

Find the roots of each equation, to the nearest hundredth.

27. $2x^2 + 5x - 2 = 0$ **28.** $x^2 - 3x + 1 = 0$

29. $3x^2 - 4x + 1 = 0$ **30.** $2x^2 + 7x - 5 = 0$

31. $5x^2 + 8x + 3 = 0$ **32.** $1.5x^2 - 6.2x - 2.4 = 0$

33. $4t^2 - 10 = 0$ **34.** $1 - 3y + y^2 = 0$

35. $5k^2 + 3k - 2 = 0$ **36.** $2.5n^2 - 8n + 3 = 0$

Mental Math

Factor each expression.

1. $8x - 12$ **2.** $24x^2 + 9x$

3. $x^2 - 25$ **4.** $4x^2 - 49$

5. $x^2 - 3x + 2$ **6.** $x^2 + 4x + 4$

7. $x^2 + x - 2$ **8.** $x^2 + 7x + 6$

9. $x^2 - x - 12$ **10.** $0.25x^2 - 0.16$

11. $4x^2 + 20x + 25$ **12.** $x^2 - 6xy + 9y^2$

Give the measure of each ∠θ, if angles are in the first quadrant. Give exact answers in radians.

13. $\sin \theta = \dfrac{1}{2}$ **14.** $\tan \theta = 1$

15. $\cos \theta = \dfrac{1}{\sqrt{2}}$ **16.** $\sin \theta = \dfrac{\sqrt{3}}{2}$

17. $\tan \theta = \sqrt{3}$ **18.** $\cos \theta = \dfrac{\sqrt{3}}{2}$

19. $\sin \theta = \dfrac{1}{\sqrt{2}}$ **20.** $\tan \theta = \dfrac{1}{\sqrt{3}}$

Give the exact value of each expression.

21. $\cos 30° + \cos(-90°)$ **22.** $\tan 45° - \tan 180°$

23. $\sin 60° + \sin 270°$ **24.** $\cos 90° - \cos 720°$

25. $\sin 135° - \sin 45°$ **26.** $\tan(-45°) + \tan 225°$

27. $\tan 150° + \tan(-30°)$ **28.** $\cos(-180°) - \cos 540°$

Give the six exact trigonometric ratios for ∠θ in each triangle.

29.
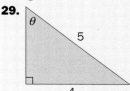
θ
5
4

30.
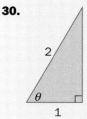
2
θ
1

31.
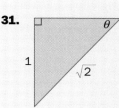
θ
1
$\sqrt{2}$

32.
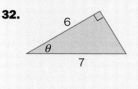
6
θ
7

5.1 Relating Graphs and Solutions

A tsunami is a series of ocean waves that are caused by the sudden displacement of large volumes of water. Typically caused by earthquakes that occur on the ocean floor, this release of energy generates waves of extremely long wavelength and period, in all directions from the source. In the open ocean, a tsunami can reach speeds of 800 km/h with 650 km between successive crests. However, the height of the waves may be only between 30 cm and 60 cm, thus allowing the tsunami to go undetected. When the propagated wave reaches the shallow waters of a coastline, its wavelength decreases, forcing the water into a giant wave with potentially disastrous effects.

Depending on the size of the area affected, a tsunami can be categorized as local, regional, or ocean-wide. Due to the large amount of seismic activity in the Pacific Basin, British Columbia participates in the Pacific Tsunamis Warning System, an international program dedicated to the study of tsunamis and minimizing tsunami effects through timely and effective communication.

Explore: Use a Graph

A graph of $f(x) = 2 \sin x$ is shown.
a) What are the x-intercepts of the function in the domain $0 \le x < 360°$?
b) Interpolate to find the values of x for which $f(x) = 1$, where $0 \le x < 360°$.

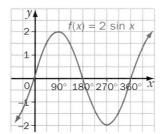

Inquire

1. For what equation do the x-intercepts of the graph provide solutions?

2. What equation have you solved by doing the interpolation?

3. Explain how you could use the graph to solve the equation $2 = 2 \sin x$. What is the solution when $0 \le x < 360°$?

4. At what x-value does the minimum value of $f(x)$ occur, for $0 \le x < 360°$? For what equation does this x-value provide the solution?

5. What does the graph tell you about the solution to the equation $3 = 2 \sin x$? Explain.

6. How could you use the graph to solve $\sin x = -0.5$? Explain.

Example 1　Using a Sketch Graph to Solve a Trigonometric Equation

Sketch the graph of $y = \sin 4x$. Use the graph to find all the solutions of $\sin 4x = 0$, in the interval $0 \le x < 2\pi$.

Solution

The graph of $y = \sin 4x$ is related to the graph of $y = \sin x$ by a horizontal compression of factor $\frac{1}{4}$. In the interval $0 \le x < 2\pi$, $y = \sin x$ has one period; $y = \sin 4x$ has four periods.

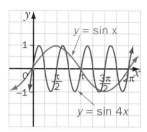

The period of $y = \sin 4x$ is $\frac{2\pi}{4}$ or $\frac{\pi}{2}$.

The solutions to the equation $\sin 4x = 0$ are equivalent to finding the x-intercepts of the graph for the specified interval. From the graph, the x-intercepts of $y = \sin 4x$, occur at 0, $\frac{\pi}{4}$, $\frac{\pi}{2}$, $\frac{3\pi}{4}$, π, $\frac{5\pi}{4}$, $\frac{3\pi}{2}$, and $\frac{7\pi}{4}$.

The solutions of $\sin 4x = 0$, in the interval $0 \le x < 2\pi$, are 0, $\frac{\pi}{4}$, $\frac{\pi}{2}$, $\frac{3\pi}{4}$, π, $\frac{5\pi}{4}$, $\frac{3\pi}{2}$, and $\frac{7\pi}{4}$.

Example 2　Relating Graphs and Equations

a) Graph the functions $y = \cos x$, for $0° \le x < 360°$, and $y = \frac{1}{2}$ on the same axes. Use the graph to solve the equation $\cos x = \frac{1}{2}$, where $0° \le x < 360°$.

b) Determine a general solution to the equation $\cos x = \frac{1}{2}$.

c) Explain how the solution to the equation $2 \cos x - 1 = 0$ is related to the solution found in part b). How can you check your answer using the graph of the function $y = 2 \cos x - 1$?

Solution

a) Graph $y = \cos x$ and $y = 0.5$ using a window $[-360°, 360°, 60°]$ by $[-1, 1, 0.5]$.

The solution to the equation $\cos x = \frac{1}{2}$ is given by the points of intersection of the curve $y = \cos x$ and the line $y = 0.5$. Points of intersection occur at $x = 60°$, $300°$, $-60°$, and $-300°$.

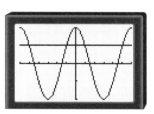

The solutions to the equation $\cos x = \frac{1}{2}$, where $0° \le x < 360°$, are $60°$ and $300°$.

b) All coterminal angles will have the same cosine value and differ by multiples of the period of the function. The period of $y = \cos x$ is $360°$, so the general solutions are $x = 60° + n(360°)$ and $x = 300° + n(360°)$, where n is any integer.

These two general forms may be combined and expressed as $x = (360°)n \pm 60°$.

Increase the viewing window in the x-direction to $[-720°, 720°, 60°]$ by

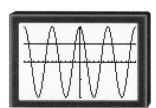

c) The equation $2 \cos x - 1 = 0$ can be rearranged by isolating the term involving $\cos x$ to give the equivalent equation $\cos x = \dfrac{1}{2}$. Therefore, the solutions to the equation $2 \cos x - 1 = 0$ are the same as those found in part b).

The function $y = 2 \cos x - 1$ is related to the graph of $y = \cos x$ by a vertical stretch of factor 2 and a vertical displacement of -1. Select a window to show the maximum value 1 and minimum value -3.
The screen shows the graph of $y = 2 \cos x - 1$ using a window $[-360°, 360°, 60°]$ by $[-3, 1, 0.5]$. The solutions to the equation $2 \cos x - 1 = 0$ are the x-intercepts of this graph.

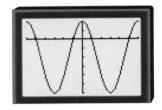

In the domain $-360° \le x < 360°$, the x-intercepts are at $-300°, -60°, 60°$, and $300°$. These values check with the results obtained in part b).

Example 3   Using Technology as an Aid in Finding Exact Solutions
Use graphing technology as an aid in finding all the exact solutions, in radians, for the equation $\cos 3x = \dfrac{1}{2}$.

Solution
Step 1: Use your knowledge of the basic cosine curve and special angles to help select a convenient window. Recall $\cos \dfrac{\pi}{3} = \dfrac{1}{2}$, so use Xscl $= \pi/3$.

Step 2: Graph $y = \cos x$ and $y = 0.5$ using a window $[0, 2\pi, \pi/3]$ by $[-2, 2, 1]$.
The graph shows that $\cos x = \dfrac{1}{2}$ has two solutions in the interval $0 \le x < 2\pi$;

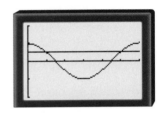

namely, $x = \dfrac{\pi}{3}$ or $x = \dfrac{5\pi}{3}$. In general, $x = \dfrac{\pi}{3} + 2n\pi$ or $x = \dfrac{5\pi}{3} + 2n\pi$, where n is any integer.

Step 3: Since $y = \cos 3x$ is related to $y = \cos x$ by a horizontal compression factor of 3, the equation $\cos 3x = \dfrac{1}{2}$ will have six solutions in the same interval, $0 \le x < 2\pi$. Setting $3x$ equal to the general solutions for $\cos x = \dfrac{1}{2}$ yields

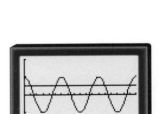

$$3x = \dfrac{\pi}{3} + 2n\pi \qquad \text{or} \qquad 3x = \dfrac{5\pi}{3} + 2n\pi$$
$$x = \dfrac{\pi}{9} + \dfrac{2n\pi}{3} \qquad\qquad\qquad x = \dfrac{5\pi}{9} + \dfrac{2n\pi}{3}$$

These solutions are confirmed with a graph of $y = \cos 3x$ and $y = 0.5$ using a window $[0, 2\pi, \pi/9]$ by $[-2, 2, 1]$.

Since the period of $y = \cos 3x$ is $\dfrac{2\pi}{3}$, additional solutions can be determined by adding or subtracting multiples of $\dfrac{2\pi}{3}$.

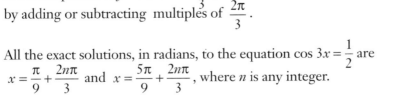

All the exact solutions, in radians, to the equation $\cos 3x = \dfrac{1}{2}$ are
$x = \dfrac{\pi}{9} + \dfrac{2n\pi}{3}$ and $x = \dfrac{5\pi}{9} + \dfrac{2n\pi}{3}$, where n is any integer.

Example 4   Using Technology as an Aid in Finding Exact Solutions

Use graphing technology as an aid in finding all the exact solutions, in radians, of the equation $\sin 2x = \dfrac{1}{\sqrt{2}}$.

Solution

The solutions can be deduced using the graph of the basic sine curve and special angles. Recall $\sin \dfrac{\pi}{4} = \dfrac{1}{\sqrt{2}}$. Graph $y = \sin x$ and $y = \dfrac{1}{\sqrt{2}}$ using a window $[0, 2\pi, \pi/4]$ by $[-2, 2, 1]$.

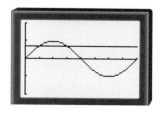

The graph confirms that there are two solutions for $\sin x = \dfrac{1}{\sqrt{2}}$, in the interval $0 \le x < 2\pi$, at $x = \dfrac{\pi}{4}$ or $\dfrac{3\pi}{4}$. In general, $x = \dfrac{\pi}{4} + 2n\pi$ or $x = \dfrac{3\pi}{4} + 2n\pi$, where n is any integer.

Since $y = \sin 2x$ is related to $y = \sin x$ by a horizontal compression factor of 2, four solutions can be expected for $y = \sin 2x$ in the same interval. Setting $2x$ equal to the general solutions for $\sin x = \dfrac{1}{\sqrt{2}}$ yields

$$2x = \frac{\pi}{4} + 2n\pi \qquad \text{or} \qquad 2x = \frac{3\pi}{4} + 2n\pi$$

$$x = \frac{\pi}{8} + n\pi \qquad\qquad x = \frac{3\pi}{8} + n\pi$$

The period of $y = \sin 2x$ is π, so all other solutions are obtained by adding or subtracting multiples of π.

These solutions are confirmed by a graph of $y = \sin 2x$ and $y = \dfrac{1}{\sqrt{2}}$ using a window $[0, 2\pi, \pi/4]$ by $[-2, 2, 1]$.

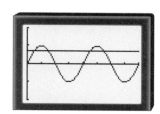

Therefore, the exact solutions, in radian measure, of $\sin 2x = \dfrac{1}{\sqrt{2}}$ are

$x = \dfrac{\pi}{8} + n\pi$ and $x = \dfrac{3\pi}{8} + n\pi$, where n is any integer.

Practice

Use the graph $y = \sin x$ to help find the exact solutions to each of the following.

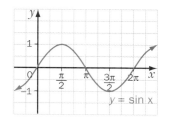

1. the solutions of $\sin x = 0$, in the interval $0 \le x < 2\pi$

2. the solutions of $\sin 2x = 0$, in the interval $0 \le x < 2\pi$

3. all solutions of $\sin 2x = 0$

4. the solutions of $\sin x = 1$, in the interval $0 \le x < 2\pi$

5. the solutions of $\sin 3x = 1$, in the interval $0 \le x < 2\pi$

6. all solutions of $\sin 3x = 1$

7. the solutions of $\sin x = -1$, in the interval $0 \le x < 2\pi$

8. the solutions for the equation $\sin 4x = -1$, in the interval $0 \le x < 2\pi$

9. all solutions of $\sin 4x = -1$

Sketch the graph of $y = \cos x$, for $0 \le x < 360°$. Use the graph to help find the exact solutions to the following.

10. the solutions of $\cos x = 0$, for $0 \le x < 360°$

11. the solutions of $\cos 2x = 0$, in the interval $0 \le x < 360°$

12. all the solutions of $\cos 2x = 0$

13. the solutions of $\cos x = 1$, for $0 \le x < 360°$

14. the solutions of $\cos 4x = 1$, in the interval $0 \le x < 360°$

15. all solutions of $\cos 4x = 1$

The graph shows $y = \tan x$ and $y = 1$ using a window $[0, 360°, 45°]$ by $[-2, 2, 1]$. Use the graph to help answer the following.

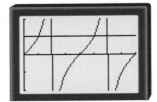

16. Solve $\tan x = 1$, for $0 \le x < 360°$.

17. Determine the general solution to the equation $\tan x = 1$.

18. How is the graph of $y = \tan 3x$ related to the graph of $y = \tan x$?

19. Solve $\tan 3x = 1$, for $0 \le x < 360°$.

20. Determine all the solutions to the equation $\tan 3x = 1$.

Applications and Problem Solving

21. a) By graphing the functions defined by each side of the equation $\sin 3x = \dfrac{1}{2}$, find the solutions in the interval $0 \le x < 2\pi$.

b) Write the general solution to the equation $\sin 3x = \dfrac{1}{2}$.

22. a) By graphing the functions defined by each side of the equation $\tan 4x = 1$, find the solutions in the interval $0 \le x \le 2\pi$.

b) Write the general solution to the equation $\tan 4x = 1$.

23. a) Sketch graphs of $y = \cos x$ and $y = \cos \dfrac{1}{2}x$, on the same axes.

b) Use the graph to solve $\cos \dfrac{1}{2}x = 0$, where $0 \le x < 2\pi$. Explain your reasoning.

24. a) On the same axes, sketch the graph of $y = \tan x$ and $y = \tan \dfrac{1}{2}x$, in the interval $0 \le x < 4\pi$.

b) Use the graph to solve $\tan \dfrac{1}{2}x = 0$, where $0 \le x < 4\pi$.

c) How many solutions are there to the equation $\tan \dfrac{1}{4}x = 0$ in the interval $0 \le x < 4\pi$? Explain.

25. Technology Use graphing technology to help find all the exact solutions, in radians, to each equation. Describe the steps used.

a) $\sin 3x = \dfrac{\sqrt{3}}{2}$

b) $\cos 4x + \dfrac{1}{2} = 0$

26. Explain how to solve the equation $2\sin \theta + 1 = 0$, where $0 \le \theta < 360°$ by graphing two functions. What is the general solution to the equation?

27. Find the exact values of A that satisfy the equation $2\sin 4A - 1 = 0$, $0 \le A \le 2\pi$.

28. Tsunami The height, in metres, of a certain tsunami can be modelled by the equation
$$h(t) = 10\sin\left(\dfrac{\pi}{8} - t\right)$$
where t represents the elapsed time, in minutes, after the occurrence of an earthquake. Approximately how long after the earthquake will the wave reach a height of 10 m?

29. Technology Use graphing technology to help find all the exact solutions, in radians, to each equation. Describe the steps used.

a) $\cos 2x = \cos x$

b) $\sin 2x = 2\cos x$

30. Owls Ecologists have studied a small provincial park and have determined an equation that gives the number of owls as a function of time. The number of owls, $n(t)$, is modelled by the equation
$$n(t) = 10\cos\left(2t - \dfrac{\pi}{4}\right) + 50$$
where t is the time, in years. Determine the years when there are likely to be 55 owls.

5.2 Solving Trigonometric Equations

Determining your position on Earth can be done quite accurately by the global positioning system (GPS). The GPS consists of 24 satellites orbiting Earth in such a precise manner as to repeat an almost identical ground track every day. This satellite navigation system is funded and controlled by the United States Department of Defense but is available to civilian users worldwide with intentionally degraded accuracy. The specially coded satellite signals can be processed by a GPS receiver, which in turn computes position and time. The receiver must lock onto the signal of at least four GPS satellites in order to calculate position dimensions in Earth-Centred Earth-Fixed X, Y, Z coordinates (and time). The GPS receiver then converts these coordinates into latitude, longitude, and altitude using trigonometric equations.

Explore: Use a Graph

Graphs of $f(x) = 2 \cos x$ and $g(x) = \dfrac{1}{2} + \cos x$ are shown.

Estimate the values of x at the points of intersection, for $-180° \le x < 180°$.

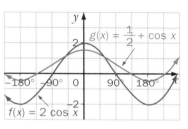

Inquire

1. What equation have you solved with the estimates?

2. Explain how you could use the graph to solve the equation $2 \cos x - 0.5 - \cos x = 0$. What is the solution, for $-180° \le x < 180°$?

3. Will the graph of $y = 2 \cos x - 0.5 - \cos x$ be identical to the graph of $y = \cos x - 0.5$? Verify your answer by graphing the two equations.

4. Is the solution for $\cos x - 1 = 0$ the same as the solution for $2 \cos x - 1 - \cos x = 0$? Explain how this can be true.

5. Will the zeros of $f(x) = \cos^2 x - 1$ and $g(x) = (\cos x + 1)(\cos x - 1)$ be the same? Verify graphically.

Example 1   Solving First Degree Equations
If $1 + \sin x = 4 \sin x$, $0 \le x < 2\pi$, find the possible values of x, both algebraically and graphically. Round answers to four decimal places.

Solution
Solving graphically:
The equation $1 + \sin x = 4 \sin x$ is of the form $f(x) = g(x)$, which can be solved by graphing both functions $f(x)$ and $g(x)$ to determine the x-value at points of intersection. Since solutions are to be in the domain $0 \le x < 2\pi$, choose radian mode and use a window with Xmin = 0, Xmax = 2π, and Xscl = $\pi/2$. Graph $y = 1 + \sin x$ as Y1 and $y = 4 \sin x$ as Y2.

Since the amplitude of $y = 4 \sin x$ is 4, set Ymin $= -4$, Ymax $= 4$, and Yscl $= 1$. The solutions to $1 + \sin x = 4 \sin x$, $0 \le x < 2\pi$, occur where the two functions intersect at $x = 0.3398$ rad and $x = 2.8018$ rad, rounded to four decimal places.

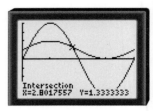

Alternatively, another graphical option would be to transform the equation $1 + \sin x = 4 \sin x$ into $3 \sin x - 1 = 0$, then graph the function $y = 3 \sin x - 1$ and find its zeros.

Solving algebraically:
$$1 + \sin x = 4 \sin x$$
$$1 = 4 \sin x - \sin x$$
$$1 = 3 \sin x$$
$$\sin x = \frac{1}{3}$$
$$\therefore \quad x = \sin^{-1}\left(\frac{1}{3}\right)$$

For $0 \le x < 2\pi$, $\sin x$ is positive in the first or second quadrants.
In the first quadrant, $x \doteq 0.3398$.
In the second quadrant, $x \doteq \pi - 0.3398$
$$\doteq 2.8018$$
The possible values for x, where $0 \le x < 2\pi$, are 0.3398 rad and 2.8018 rad, rounded to four decimal places.

Example 2 Finding Exact Roots of Second Degree Trigonometric Equations
Find the exact solutions for each of the following equations.
a) $\cos^2 x - \cos x = 0$, $0 \le x < 2\pi$ **b)** $2 \sin^2 x - \sin x - 1 = 0$, $-\pi \le x < \pi$

Solution
a) Since $\cos^2 x - \cos x = 0$ is a quadratic equation of the form $x^2 - x = 0$, it can be solved by factoring.
$$\cos^2 x - \cos x = 0$$
$$\cos x(\cos x - 1) = 0$$
$$\therefore \cos x = 0 \quad \text{or} \quad \cos x - 1 = 0$$
$$\cos x = 1$$
Visualize the basic cosine function in the domain $0 \le x < 2\pi$.

$\cos x = 0$ at $x = \dfrac{\pi}{2}$ and $x = \dfrac{3\pi}{2}$, and $\cos x = 1$ at $x = 0$.

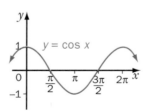

The exact solutions for $\cos^2 x - \cos x = 0$, $0 \le x < 2\pi$, are 0, $\dfrac{\pi}{2}$, and $\dfrac{3\pi}{2}$.

b) Since $2 \sin^2 x - \sin x - 1 = 0$ is a quadratic equation of the form $2x^2 - x - 1$, it can be solved by factoring.
$$2 \sin^2 x - \sin x - 1 = 0$$
$$(2 \sin x + 1)(\sin x - 1) = 0$$
$$\therefore 2 \sin x + 1 = 0 \qquad \text{or} \qquad \sin x - 1 = 0$$
$$\sin x = -\frac{1}{2} \qquad\qquad\qquad \sin x = 1$$

For $\sin x = -\dfrac{1}{2}$, use the facts that $\sin \dfrac{\pi}{6} = \dfrac{1}{2}$ and sine is negative in the third and

fourth quadrants. Therefore, for $-\pi \leq x < \pi$, $\sin x = -\dfrac{1}{2}$ at $x = -\dfrac{\pi}{6}$ and $x = -\dfrac{5\pi}{6}$.

For $\sin x = 1$, visualize a basic sine curve.

In the domain $-\pi \leq x < \pi$, $\sin x = 1$ at $x = \dfrac{\pi}{2}$.

The exact solutions for $2 \sin^2 x - \sin x - 1 = 0$, for $-\pi \leq x < \pi$, are

$-\dfrac{5\pi}{6}$, $-\dfrac{\pi}{6}$, and $\dfrac{\pi}{2}$.

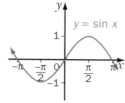

If a quadratic equation cannot be factored, then a way to solve it algebraically is to use the quadratic formula. The same strategy must sometimes be used to solve second degree trigonometric equations.

Example 3 Finding Approximate Roots of Trigonometric Equations
For what values of x is $3 \tan^2 x - \tan x - 1 = 0$, if $0 \leq x < \pi$? Round answers to four decimal places.

Solution 1 Solving Algebraically
The equation $3 \tan^2 x - \tan x - 1 = 0$ is a quadratic equation of the form $3x^2 - x - 1 = 0$. Since this equation does not factor, use the quadratic

formula $x = \dfrac{-b \pm \sqrt{b^2 - 4ac}}{2a}$.

Substitute $a = 3$, $b = -1$, $c = -1$.

$$\tan x = \dfrac{1 \pm \sqrt{1 - 4(3)(-1)}}{2(3)}$$

$$= \dfrac{1 \pm \sqrt{13}}{6}$$

So, $\tan x \doteq -0.4343$ or $\tan x \doteq 0.7676$

In the domain $0 \leq x < \pi$, $\tan x$ is negative when x is in the second quadrant. So, to solve $\tan x \doteq -0.4343$, use $\tan^{-1}(0.4343) \doteq 0.4097$. The related angle in the second quadrant is $\pi - 0.4097$ or approximately 2.7319. For $\tan x \doteq 0.7676$, in the domain $0 \leq x < \pi$, $\tan x$ is positive when x is in the first quadrant, and $\tan^{-1}(0.7676) \doteq 0.6547$.

The solutions to $3 \tan^2 x - \tan x - 1 = 0$, $0 \leq x < \pi$, are 0.6547 rad and 2.7319 rad, rounded to four decimal places.

Solution 2 Solving Graphically
Graph $y = 3 \tan^2 x - \tan x - 1$ and then find the zeros.
The screen shows $y = 3 \tan^2 x - \tan x - 1$ using a window
$[0, \pi, \pi/6]$ by $[-3, 10, 1]$ and one of its zeros.
The solutions to the equation $3 \tan^2 x - \tan x - 1 = 0$, $0 \leq x < \pi$, are 0.6547 rad and 2.731 rad, rounded to four decimal places.

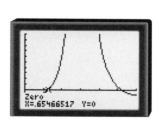

Since trigonometric functions are periodic, general solutions to trigonometric equations can be determined by adding multiples of the period.

Example 4   Determining a General Solution

Find all possible solutions for the following equation.

$\sin x \tan x = \sin x$

Solution

$$\sin x \tan x = \sin x$$
$$\sin x \tan x - \sin x = 0$$
$$\sin x(\tan x - 1) = 0$$
$$\therefore \sin x = 0 \quad \text{or} \quad \tan x - 1 = 0$$
$$\tan x = 1$$

For one period of the basic sine curve, $0 \le x < 2\pi$, $\sin x = 0$ at $x = 0$ and at $x = \pi$. Since the period of $\sin x$ is 2π, add $2n\pi$, where n is any integer, to account for all coterminal angles. Then,

$x = 0 + 2n\pi \quad \text{or} \quad x = \pi + 2n\pi.$

These solutions for $\sin x = 0$ can be combined and expressed as $x = n\pi$.

Recall that the period of $\tan x$ is π. For $0 \le x < \pi$, $\tan x = 1$ at $x = \dfrac{\pi}{4}$ and at $x = \dfrac{5\pi}{4}$. So, the general solutions for $\tan x = 1$ are $x = \dfrac{\pi}{4} + n\pi$ and $x = \dfrac{5\pi}{4} + n\pi$, where n is any integer. These two general forms can be combined and expressed as $x = \dfrac{\pi}{4} + n\pi$, where n is any integer.

Therefore, the general solutions to the equation $\sin x \tan x = \sin x$ are $x = n\pi$ and $x = \dfrac{\pi}{4} + n\pi$, where n is any integer.

Practice

Solve for θ, $0 \le \theta < 2\pi$.

1. $\cos \theta - 0.5 = 0$
2. $\sin \theta + 0.5 = 0$
3. $2 \tan \theta - 2 = 0$
4. $2 \sin \theta - \sqrt{3} = 0$
5. $4 \cos \theta + 2 = 0$
6. $\tan \theta + \sqrt{3} = 0$
7. $\sin \theta = -1$
8. $0.5 \cos \theta - 0.5 = 0$
9. $2 \sin \theta + 1 = 2$
10. $\sec \theta = -2$

Solve for x, $0 \le x < 360°$.

11. $\cos 2x = 0$
12. $\sin 2x = 1$
13. $\tan 2x + 1 = 0$
14. $\sin 2x + 1 = 0$
15. $\cos 2x + 1 = 0$
16. $\cos 2x - 1 = 0$
17. $2 \sin 2x = 1$
18. $2 \cos \dfrac{1}{2}x = 1$
19. $2 \cos 3x = 1$
20. $\tan \dfrac{1}{2}x = 1$

Solve for x, where $0 \le x < 2\pi$. Then give a general solution.

21. $\cos^2 x = 1$
22. $\sin^2 x - 1 = 0$
23. $\sin x(\sin x + 1) = 0$
24. $\cos^2 x - 0.25 = 0$
25. $(\sin x - 1)(\tan x - 1) = 0$
26. $2 \cos^2 x + \cos x - 1 = 0$
27. $2 \sin^2 x + \sin x = 1$
28. $2 \cos^2 x - \cos x - 1 = 0$
29. $\cos^2 2x + \cos 2x = 0$
30. $4 \sin^2 x + 2 \sin x - 2 = 0$
31. $4 \sin^2 x - 3 = 0$

Applications and Problem Solving

32. Determine all the exact roots of each equation.
a) $\cos x - 2 \sin x \cos x = 0$
b) $4 \sin^2 x + 3 = 0$
c) $2 \cos^2 x - 5 \cos x + 2 = 0$

33. Solve each equation for $0 \le x < 2\pi$. Verify your answers by graphing.
a) $3 \tan^2 x + \tan x = 4$
b) $\sin^2 x + \sin x - 2 = 0$
c) $2 \cos^2 x - 3 \cos x + 1 = 0$

34. Solve each equation for $0 \le x < 2\pi$, rounding solutions to the nearest tenth.
a) $4 \cos^2 x = \cos x$
b) $\sec x \sin x = 2 \sin x$
c) $\sin^2 x + \sin x - 1 = 0$

35. Solve each equation for $0 \le x < 2\pi$, rounding solutions to four decimal places.
a) $5 \tan^2 x + 2 \tan x - 7 = 0$
b) $\tan^2 x - 5 \tan x + 6 = 0$
c) $\tan^2 x - 4 \tan x = 0$

36. **Water management** A storm drain has a cross section in the shape of an isosceles trapezoid. The base and each of the sides measure
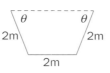
2m 2m
2m
2 m and θ is the measure of the angle between the side and the horizontal.
a) Show that the cross-sectional area, A, of the drain is given by $A = 4 \sin \theta (1 + \cos \theta)$.
b) Find the value of θ if the cross-sectional area is $3\sqrt{3}$ m^2.

37. In right triangle ABC, AC = 4, BD = 1, and AC $\perp$ BD.

a) Show that $\sin A \cos A = \dfrac{1}{4}$.
b) Find the value of A.

38. **Measurement** The area of a rectangle is represented by the function $A(\theta) = |\cos \theta \sin \theta|$.
a) What are the coordinates of the vertices of the rectangle?
b) What is the minimum area of the rectangle? For what values of θ does this occur?
c) What is the maximum area?

39. **Coordinate system** Use the prime meridian as a reference line.
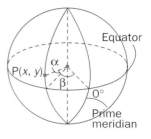
a) Show that a position $P(x, y)$ on Earth near the equator can be approximated by $y = R \sin \alpha$, and $x = R \sin \beta$ where R is the radius of the earth, in metres, and α and β represent the latitude and longitude, respectively.
b) What assumptions must be made regarding the distances from the equator and the curvature of Earth in order for these equations to give "reasonable" answers?
c) How could the equation for x be modified to account for the curvature of Earth as you move away from the equator?

40. **Measurement** A right circular cone is inscribed in a sphere of radius 30 cm. The semi-vertical angle of the cone is $\angle \theta$, as shown.
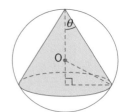
a) Show that the volume, V, of the cone is given by $V = 9000\pi \sin^2 2\theta(1 + \cos 2\theta)$.
b) Find the value of θ when the volume of the cone is 9000π cm^3. *Hint:* Use graphing technology.

NUMBER POWER

In the following multiplication, all of the digits from 1 to 9 have been used once. Complete the product.

5.3 Using Technology to Solve More Complex Equations

Surveying is the measurement of distances, directions, and angles on, above, or beneath Earth's surface, and uses trigonometry to determine missing or inaccessible measurements. Natural features and other structures are surveyed for the purpose of map-making or to determine a property boundary. Construction sites are surveyed as a means of guidance as work progresses.

Several types of surveying exist. Land surveying includes geodetic surveying and plane surveying. Geodetic surveying takes the curvature of Earth into account, and positions are indicated in terms of longitude and latitude. Plane surveying, such as surveying a home construction site, disregards the surface curvature because of the small area in question. Hydrographic surveying deals with bodies of water and coast lines. Information from hydrographic surveying is used for navigational charts and underwater construction.

A person working in this field typically requires a college, technical institute, or university education, or specialized training in accordance with the position of interest, be it surveying technician, surveying technologist, or land surveyor. Success in this field depends on the person's mathematical, computer, and electronic equipment skills. The ability to solve complex trigonometric equations is an important requirement.

Explore: Use a Graph

A graphing calculator was used to graph $y = \cos x$ and $y = x$ using a window $[-2\pi, 2\pi, \pi/4]$ by $[-2, 2, 1]$.

a) Estimate the x-value at the point of intersection of the two functions.

b) Graph both functions, using a graphing calculator, and use the INTERSECT operation to find the x-value, to four decimal places.

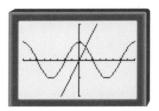

Inquire

1. Explain how the x-value at the point of intersection of the graphs of $y = \cos x$ and $y = x$ is related to the solution of the equation $\cos x - x = 0$.

2. Graph the function $y = \cos x - x$. Use this graph to find the solution(s) to the equation $\cos x - x = 0$, to four decimal places.

3. Do you think you have found all possible solutions to the equation $\cos x - x = 0$? Give reasons for your answer.

4. By visualizing the component functions, determine the solution(s) to the equation $\sin x - x = 0$. How would the solution to the equation $\sin x + x = 0$ compare? Give reasons for your answer.

Equations that involve both trigonometric functions and polynomial functions are difficult to solve by simple algebraic methods. However, especially with the help of a graphing calculator or graphing software, they can be solved graphically.

Example 1   Solving by Graphing

Graph $y = x - 2 \cos x$. Use the graph to solve the equation $2 \cos x = x$, expressing answers, in radians, to three decimal places.

Solution
The trigonometric part of the function has amplitude 2, so try using a window $[-2\pi, 2\pi, \pi/4]$ by $[-3, 3, 1]$.

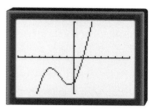

The solution to the equation $2 \cos x = x$ is given by the x-intercept of the graph because the equation can be expressed as $0 = x - 2 \cos x$.

Using the ZERO operation, the x-intercept is at $x = 1.0299$, to four decimal places.

The solution to the equation $2 \cos x = x$ is $x = 1.0299$ rad, to four decimal places.

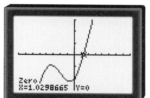

The solution can be verified by substitution.

L.S. $= 2 \cos x$ **R.S.** $= x$
$\quad \doteq 2 \cos 1.0299 \qquad \doteq 1.0299$
$\quad = 1.029\ 809$

Example 2   Using Graphs to Solve Related Equations

The screen shows the graphs of $y = x + \sin x$ and $y = x^3$.
a) Based on the graph, how many solutions do you expect for the equation $x^3 = x + \sin x$?
b) What single function can you graph, and then find the zeros of, to solve the equation $x^3 = x + \sin x$? Graph this function and determine the zeros, to three decimal places.

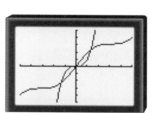

Solution
a) The graphs of the functions $y = \sin x + x$ and $y = x^3$ appear to intersect at three points, so the equation $x^3 = x + \sin x$ probably has three solutions. From the graph, the solutions appear to be $x = 0$ and $x \doteq \pm 1.3$.
b) An equivalent equation is $0 = x + \sin x - x^3$.
If the function $y = x + \sin x - x^3$ is graphed, its x-intercepts will give the solutions to the equation. The screen shows the graph of $y = x + \sin x - x^3$ using a window $[-5, 5, 1]$ by $[-5, 5, 1]$. Its x-intercepts are found using the ZERO operation.

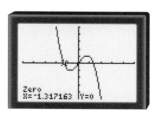

The zeros are at $x = 0$ and $x \doteq \pm 1.317163$.
The solutions to the equation $x^3 = x + \sin x$ are $x = 0$ and $x = \pm 1.317$ rad, to three decimal places.

Example 3   Solving a Problem

The velocity of a particle is related to time by the function

$$v(t) = t \cos t$$

where $v(t)$ is the velocity, in centimetres per second, and t is the time, in seconds. Graph the function for the first 10 s of motion. At what times is the particle at rest?

Solution

Graph $y = x \cos x$ using a window $[0, 10, 1]$ by $[-10, 10, 1]$.
A range of $-10 \le y \le 10$ is chosen, because the maximum amplitude of $v(t)$ in the specified time interval will be 10 when $t = 10$. Another option would be to use anything initially for the range, and then use ZOOM-FIT.

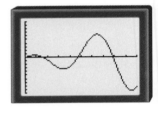

When the particle is at rest, its velocity is zero. The velocity is zero at the x-intercepts of the function. Using the ZERO operation, or by tracing, the x-intercepts are at 0 and approximately 1.571, 4.712, and 7.854.

Therefore, the particle is at rest at 0 s and approximately 1.571 s, 4.712 s, and 7.854 s.

Alternatively, this problem could be solved algebraically as follows.
If $t \cos t = 0$ then either $t = 0$ or $\cos t = 0$.

$$\therefore t = 0 \text{ or } t = \frac{\pi}{2}, \frac{3\pi}{2}, \frac{5\pi}{2}, \dots$$

Within the domain $0 \le t \le 10$, these values give the same results as the values found graphically.

Practice

The graph shows $y = \sin x$ and $y = x - 1$ using a window $[-2\pi, 2\pi, \pi/4]$ by $[-2, 2, 1]$.

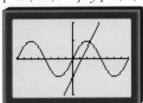

1. To what single equation does the intersection of the graphs provide the solution? Use the graph to give the approximate solution.

2. Explain how you could use a graph of $y = \sin x - x$ to solve the same equation as in the previous question.

3. Describe how the graphs of $y = \sin x + 1$ and $y = x$ would compare with those shown. What would you expect their point of intersection to be, approximately?

4. a) Graph $y = x - 2 \sin x$ using a window $[-\pi, \pi, \pi/4]$ by $[-2, 2, 1]$.
b) Use the graph to solve the equation $2 \sin x = x$, expressing your answers to three decimal places.
c) Explain how you could use the graph to tell how many roots the equation $1 + x - 2 \sin x = 0$ has.
d) Determine the root(s) of the equation $1 + x - 2 \sin x = 0$, to three decimal places.

The graph shows $y = x^3 - \sin x$ using a window $[-\pi, \pi, \pi/4]$ by $[-2, 2, 1]$.

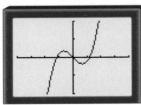

5. What is one exact root of the equation $x^3 - \sin x = 0$? Estimate the other two roots.

6. An alternative approach to solving the equation is to find the points of intersection of two functions. What are the two functions?

7. Would the equation $\sin x - x^3 = 0$ have the same roots? Why or why not?

Applications and Problem Solving

8. a) Graph $y = \sin x$ and $y = 0.5x$, for $-\pi \le x \le \pi$.
b) Use your graph to solve the equation $\sin x = 0.5x$.
c) Do you think you have found all the solutions to the equation? Give reasons for your answer.
d) Would the equation $|\sin x| = 0.5x$ have the same roots as those found in part b)? Explain.

9. Technology Consider solving the equation $\sin x = x^2$ using a graphing calculator.
a) What is the range of the function $f(x) = x^2$? What is the range of the function $g(x) = \sin x$? Explain how these answers help in the choice of the domain and the range for a graph.
b) How many solutions do you expect?
c) Solve the equation by graphing the two functions represented by each side of the equation.
d) Confirm your solution(s) by graphing a single function.

10. Technology a) Use a graphing calculator to solve $\tan x = 2x$, for $-\dfrac{\pi}{2} \le x \le \dfrac{\pi}{2}$, rounding answers to four decimal places.
b) How many solutions are there to the equation $\tan x = 2x$, for $-\dfrac{\pi}{2} \le x \le \dfrac{\pi}{2}$? Do you think these are the only solutions to the equation $\tan x = 2x$? Give reasons for your answer. Explain how you could check your response.

11. Consider the equation $x \sin x - 1 = 0$.
a) Rewrite the equation so that one side of the equation is a trigonometric function and the other side is another type of function. Classify the other function.
b) Based on your knowledge of the behaviour of the two functions, how many solutions do you expect for the original equation? Give reasons for your answer.
c) Select appropriate values for the window and then use your graphing calculator to solve the original equation.

12. Surveying A surveying technologist is working on a clam-shaped patio for a resort hotel. The owner's design uses $f(x) = 10 \sin\left(\dfrac{\pi}{45}x\right)$ (x in radians) for the scalloped edge and $g(x) = 0.004(x - 160)^2 - 100$ for the outer boundary.
a) At what point(s) do the functions intersect? Round answers to the nearest hundredth.
b) Will the patio be symmetrical? Explain.

13. Consider the equation $\sqrt{\sin x} = x$.
a) If you decide to solve this equation by finding the points of intersection of the functions $f(x) = \sqrt{\sin x}$ and $g(x) = x$, what is a suitable domain to choose? Explain. What is a suitable range? Why?
b) Graph the two functions. What are the roots of the equation?
c) Verify the roots by substitution.

14. If the equation $\cos x = x^2 + a$ has only one root, what is the value of a? What is the root?

15. For what value(s) of q does the equation $\cos x = ax^2 + q$, where $a > 0$, have no real roots?

16. How many solutions can there be for an equation of the form $\cos x - kx = 0$, where k is any real number? Illustrate your answer with appropriate sketch diagrams.

LOGIC POWER

A string of real pearls consists of 33 pearls. The middle one is the largest and most valuable. Starting from one end, each pearl is worth $100 more than the one before it, up to and including the middle pearl. From the other end, each pearl is worth $150 more than the one before it, up to and including the middle pearl. The string of pearls is worth $65 000. What is the value of the middle pearl?

5.4 Trigonometric Identities

A conical pendulum is so named
because of the cone-shaped
path that the weight and string
trace. A formula that relates the
length of the pendulum string,
L, and the angle, θ, that the
string makes with the vertical is

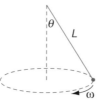

$$L = \frac{g\sec\theta}{\omega^2}$$

where g is the acceleration due to gravity and ω is
the angular speed of the mass about the vertical,
in radians per second.

Explore: Use Inductive Reasoning

a) Copy and complete the table, using exact values.

Measure of ∠A	0°	30°	45°	60°	90°
sin A					
cos A					
$\sin^2 A + \cos^2 A$					

b) Make a conjecture about the value of $\sin^2 A + \cos^2 A$.
c) Use a calculator, in radian mode, to test your
conjecture for at least five other measures of ∠A,
where $0° < A < 90°$. Can you find a counterexample?

Inquire

1. In the table, you used values of A in the first quadrant.
Is the same result obtained for measures of ∠A in the other
three quadrants? Give reasons for your answer.

2. Use the diagram of a unit circle to prove your
conjecture for $0° < A < 90°$.

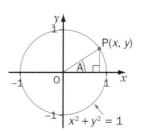

3. Does the proof still hold if ∠A is in one of the other
three quadrants? Justify your answer.

4. Another way of expressing the relationship between the
length of the pendulum and the ∠θ for a conical pendulum
is $L = \dfrac{g\tan\theta}{\omega^2\sin\theta}$. Show that this formula and the one given
in the introduction above are equivalent when $\angle\theta = \dfrac{\pi}{6}$.

5. How could you prove that the two expressions for L are
equivalent for any angle?

A trigonometric equation is an equation that involves at least one trigonometric function of a variable. Such an equation is called a **trigonometric identity** if it is true for all values of the variable for which both sides of the equation are defined.

For example, $\csc x = \dfrac{1}{\sin x}$ is an identity. The equation is true for all values of x for which $\sin x \neq 0$.

If an equation is believed to be an identity, graph both sides of the equation on the same screen. The appearance of only one curve is a strong indication that the equation is an identity but not a proof. One or the other of the curves might have discontinuities that are not visible. A proof must be done algebraically. To prove an identity, it is necessary to show that one side of the equation is equivalent to the other side. Each side of the equation must be treated independently. A typical approach is to transform one side of the equation into the other.

Example 1   Proving an Identity

a) Show that $1 + \tan^2 x = \sec^2 x$, for any real number x such that $\cos x \neq 0$.
b) Explain why the restriction $\cos x \neq 0$ is necessary.

Solution
a) *Step 1:* Check the graphs of the functions defined by each side of the equation. Graph $y = 1 + \tan^2 x$ as Y1 and $y = \sec^2 x$ as Y2.
A window $[-\pi, \pi, \pi/6]$ by $[-1, 5, 1]$ was used.
Since an identical graph appears to be displayed for both functions, $1 + \tan^2 x = \sec^2 x$ is probably an identity.
Step 2: Prove the identity algebraically.

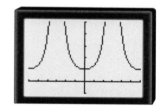

$$\textbf{L.S.} = 1 + \tan^2 x$$

Substitute $\tan^2 x = \dfrac{\sin^2 x}{\cos^2 x}$, $\cos x \neq 0$.
$$= 1 + \dfrac{\sin^2 x}{\cos^2 x}$$

Use a common denominator.
$$= \dfrac{\cos^2 x + \sin^2 x}{\cos^2 x}$$

Substitute $\sin^2 x + \cos^2 x = 1$.
$$= \dfrac{1}{\cos^2 x}$$

Substitute $\dfrac{1}{\cos x} = \sec x$.
$$= \left(\dfrac{1}{\cos x}\right)^2$$

$$= \sec^2 x$$
$$= \textbf{R.S.}$$

Therefore $1 + \tan^2 x = \sec^2 x$ is an identity for any real number x such that $\cos x \neq 0$.

b) Both sides of a trigonometric identity must be defined over the same domain. In this case, since $\tan x = \dfrac{\sin x}{\cos x}$ and $\sec x = \dfrac{1}{\cos x}$ are not defined for $\cos x = 0$, the domain is any real number x such that $\cos x \neq 0$.

Sometimes one identity can be transformed into another identity by expressing parts of one, or both, sides in equivalent forms.

Example 2   Transforming One Identity Into Another

a) Use the identity $\sin^2 x + \cos^2 x = 1$ to show that $1 + \cot^2 x = \csc^2 x$.
b) State, and give reasons for, any restrictions.

Solution

a)

$$\sin^2 x + \cos^2 x = 1$$

Divide both sides by $\sin^2 x$, $\sin x \neq 0$.

$$\frac{\sin^2 x + \cos^2 x}{\sin^2 x} = \frac{1}{\sin^2 x}$$

$$\frac{\sin^2 x}{\sin^2 x} + \frac{\cos^2 x}{\sin^2 x} = \frac{1}{\sin^2 x}$$

$$1 + \left(\frac{\cos x}{\sin x}\right)^2 = \left(\frac{1}{\sin x}\right)^2$$

Substitute $\dfrac{x}{\sin x} = \cot x$ and $\dfrac{1}{\sin x} = \csc x$.

$$1 + \cot^2 x = \csc^2 x$$

b) The second step in the proof involves division by $\sin x$ and so the restriction is $\sin x \neq 0$.

The **basic trigonometric identities**, which hold true for all values of θ except those for which either side of the equation is undefined, are as follows.

$$\frac{\sin\theta}{\cos\theta} = \tan\theta \qquad \sin^2\theta + \cos^2\theta = 1$$

$$\tan^2\theta + 1 = \sec^2\theta$$

$$\frac{\cos\theta}{\sin\theta} = \cot\theta \qquad \cot^2\theta + 1 = \csc^2\theta$$

The basic identities can be proved by considering the definitions of the trigonometric ratios. For example, to show that $\dfrac{\sin\theta}{\cos\theta} = \tan\theta$,

$$\frac{\sin\theta}{\cos\theta} = \frac{y}{r} \div \frac{x}{r}$$

$$= \frac{y}{x}$$

$$= \tan\theta$$

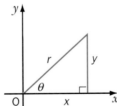

Example 3   Using Exact Values to Verify an Identity

Consider $\dfrac{\cos x}{1 - \sin x} = \dfrac{1 + \sin x}{\cos x}$.

a) Verify that this statement is true for $x = \dfrac{\pi}{6}$.

b) Use a graph to show that the equation is probably an identity.
c) Use an algebraic approach to prove that the identity is true in general. State any restrictions.

Solution

a) Evaluate each side of the equation independently for $x = \dfrac{\pi}{6}$.

$$\text{L.S.} = \frac{\cos x}{1 - \sin x} \qquad\qquad \text{R.S.} = \frac{1 + \sin x}{\cos x}$$

$$= \frac{\cos \dfrac{\pi}{6}}{1 - \sin \dfrac{\pi}{6}} \qquad\qquad = \frac{1 + \sin \dfrac{\pi}{6}}{\cos \dfrac{\pi}{6}}$$

$$= \frac{\dfrac{\sqrt{3}}{2}}{1 - \dfrac{1}{2}} \qquad\qquad = \frac{1 + \dfrac{1}{2}}{\dfrac{\sqrt{3}}{2}}$$

$$= \frac{\sqrt{3}}{2} \div \frac{1}{2} \qquad\qquad = \frac{3}{2} \div \frac{\sqrt{3}}{2}$$

$$= \sqrt{3} \qquad\qquad\qquad = \sqrt{3}$$

$\therefore \text{L.S.} = \text{R.S.}$

So, for $x = \dfrac{\pi}{6}$, $\dfrac{\cos x}{1 - \sin x} = \dfrac{1 + \sin x}{\cos x}$ is a true statement.

b) Graph $y = \dfrac{\cos x}{1 - \sin x}$ as Y1 and $y = \dfrac{1 + \sin x}{\cos x}$ as Y2 using a window $[-2\pi, 2\pi, \pi/2]$ by $[-4, 4, 1]$.

Since the functions defined by each side of the equation appear to have the same graph, the equation is probably an identity.

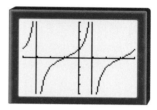

c) $\text{L.S.} = \dfrac{\cos x}{1 - \sin x}$

$\qquad = \dfrac{\cos x}{1 - \sin x} \times \dfrac{1 + \sin x}{1 + \sin x} \qquad$ Multiply the numerator and the denominator by $1 + \sin x$ (the conjugate of $1 - \sin x$), with $\sin x \neq 1$.

$\qquad = \dfrac{\cos x (1 + \sin x)}{1 - \sin^2 x}$

$\qquad = \dfrac{\cos x (1 + \sin x)}{\cos^2 x} \qquad$ Since $\sin^2 x + \cos^2 x = 1$, then $1 - \sin^2 x = \cos^2 x$.

$\qquad = \dfrac{1 + \sin x}{\cos x}$

$\qquad = \text{R.S.}$

Note that the left side has the restriction $1 - \sin x \neq 0$, or $\sin x \neq 1$. So, $x \neq \dfrac{\pi}{2} + 2n\pi$, where n is any integer. Also, the restriction $\sin x \neq 1$ means that $x \neq \dfrac{3\pi}{2} + 2n\pi$, where n is any integer. The right side has the restriction $\cos x \neq 0$, that is, $x \neq \dfrac{\pi}{2} + n\pi$, where n is any integer. Therefore, $\dfrac{\cos x}{1 - \sin x} = \dfrac{1 + \sin x}{\cos x}$ is an identity with the restriction $x \neq \dfrac{\pi}{2} + n\pi$ where n is any integer.

Example 4 Proving That an Equation Is an Identity

Consider the equation $(\tan x - 1)^2 = \sec^2 x - 2 \tan x$.

a) Show that the equation is true for the particular case $x = \dfrac{\pi}{3}$.

b) Use a graph to show that the equation appears to be an identity.

c) Prove that the equation is an identity. State any restrictions.

Solution

a) Evaluate each side of $(\tan x - 1)^2 = \sec^2 x - 2 \tan x$ for $x = \dfrac{\pi}{3}$.

$$\textbf{L.S.} = \left(\tan\frac{\pi}{3} - 1\right)^2 \qquad\qquad \textbf{R.S.} = \sec^2\frac{\pi}{3} - 2\,\tan\frac{\pi}{3}$$

$$= (\sqrt{3} - 1)^2 \qquad\qquad\qquad\qquad = \frac{1}{\left(\dfrac{1}{2}\right)^2} - 2\left(\sqrt{3}\right)$$

$$= 3 - 2\sqrt{3} + 1$$

$$= 4 - 2\sqrt{3} \qquad\qquad\qquad\qquad\qquad = 4 - 2\sqrt{3}$$

Therefore, $(\tan x - 1)^2 = \sec^2 x - 2 \tan x$ for $x = \dfrac{\pi}{3}$.

b) Graph $y = (\tan x - 1)^2$ as Y1 and $y = \sec^2 x - 2 \tan x$ as Y2 using a window $[-2\pi, 2\pi, \pi/4]$ by $[-1, 4, 1]$.
Since the graphs appear to be identical, the equation
$(\tan x - 1)^2 = \sec^2 x - 2 \tan x$ is probably an identity.

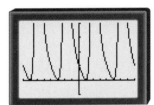

c) $\textbf{L.S.} = (\tan x - 1)^2$

$\qquad = \tan^2 x - 2 \tan x + 1 \qquad$ Expand.

$\qquad = (\tan^2 x + 1) - 2 \tan x \qquad$ Rearrange terms.

$\qquad = \sec^2 x - 2 \tan x \qquad\qquad$ Substitute $\tan^2 x + 1 = \sec^2 x$.

$\qquad = \textbf{R.S.}$

Neither side of the equation is defined for $\cos x = 0$. Therefore,
$(\tan x - 1)^2 = \sec^2 x - 2 \tan x$ is an identity with the restriction $x \neq \dfrac{\pi}{2} + n\pi$,
where n is any integer.

Example 5 Proving an Equation Is an Identity

Consider the equation $\dfrac{\cos^2 \theta}{1 + 2\sin\theta - 3\sin^2 \theta} = \dfrac{1 + \sin\theta}{1 + 3\sin\theta}$.

a) Show that the equation is true for $\theta = 3.2$ rad.

b) Use a graph to show that the equation may be an identity.

c) Prove that the equation is an identity. State any restrictions.

Solution

a) Evaluate each side of $\dfrac{\cos^2 \theta}{1 + 2\sin\theta - 3\sin^2 \theta} = \dfrac{1 + \sin\theta}{1 + 3\sin\theta}$ for $\theta = 3.2$ rad.

$$\textbf{L.S.} = \frac{\cos^2 \theta}{1 + 2\sin\theta - 3\sin^2 \theta} \qquad\qquad \textbf{R. S.} = \frac{1 + \sin\theta}{1 + 3\sin\theta}$$

$$= \frac{(\cos 3.2)^2}{1 + 2\sin 3.2 - 3(\sin 3.2)^2} \qquad\qquad = \frac{1 + \sin 3.2}{1 + 3\sin 3.2}$$

$$\doteq 1.14153 \qquad\qquad\qquad\qquad\qquad\qquad \doteq 1.14153$$

Therefore, $\dfrac{\cos^2\theta}{1+2\sin\theta-3\sin^2\theta}=\dfrac{1+\sin\theta}{1+3\sin\theta}$ for $\theta=3.2$ rad.

b) Graph $y=\dfrac{\cos^2\theta}{1+2\sin\theta-3\sin^2\theta}$ as Y1 and $y=\dfrac{1+\sin\theta}{1+3\sin\theta}$ as Y2

using a window $[-2\pi, 2\pi, \pi/4]$ by $[-3, 3, 0.5]$.

Since the graphs appear the same, the equation is probably an identity.

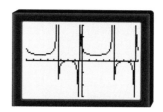

c) $\text{L. S.}=\dfrac{\cos^2\theta}{1+2\sin\theta-3\sin^2\theta}$

$=\dfrac{1-\sin^2\theta}{1+2\sin\theta-3\sin^2\theta}$ Substitute $\cos^2\theta=1-\sin^2\theta$.

$=\dfrac{(1-\sin\theta)(1+\sin\theta)}{(1-\sin\theta)(1+3\sin\theta)}$ Factor the quadratic expressions.

$=\dfrac{1+\sin\theta}{1+3\sin\theta}$ Simplify; $1-\sin\theta\neq0$.

$=\textbf{R. S.}$

$y=\dfrac{\cos^2\theta}{1+2\sin\theta-3\sin^2\theta}$ has restrictions $\sin\theta\neq1$ and $\sin\theta\neq-\dfrac{1}{3}$;

$y=\dfrac{1+\sin\theta}{1+3\sin\theta}$ has the restriction $\sin\theta\neq-\dfrac{1}{3}$.

Note that the second restriction concurs with the graph: asymptotes occur at $\theta=\sin^{-1}\left(-\dfrac{1}{3}\right)+2n\pi$

and $\theta=\pi-\sin^{-1}\left(-\dfrac{1}{3}\right)+2n\pi$, which is approximately $3.4814+2n\pi$ or $5.9433+2n\pi$, where n

is any integer. (The restriction $\sin\theta\neq1$, or $\theta\neq\dfrac{\pi}{2}+2n\pi$, is only visible when plotting Y1 alone.)

The basic trigonometric identities are sometimes used to simplify trigonometric expressions.

Example 6   Using Identities to Simplify a Trigonometric Expression

a) Simplify $\dfrac{1}{1+\cos x}+\dfrac{1}{1-\cos x}$.

b) Verify your result using a graphing calculator.

Solution

a) $\dfrac{1}{1+\cos x}+\dfrac{1}{1-\cos x}=\dfrac{(1-\cos x)+(1+\cos x)}{(1+\cos x)(1-\cos x)}$

$=\dfrac{2}{1-\cos^2 x}$ Use a common denominator.

$=\dfrac{2}{\sin^2 x}$ Substitute $1-\cos^2 x=\sin^2 x$.

$=2\csc^2 x$ Substitute $\dfrac{1}{\sin x}=\csc x$.

b) Graph $y = \dfrac{1}{1+\cos x} + \dfrac{1}{1-\cos x}$ as Y1 and $y = 2\csc^2 x$ as Y2 using a window $[-2\pi, 2\pi, \pi/4]$ by $[-1, 4, 1]$.

Since the graph of both functions appears to be the same, the result is verified.

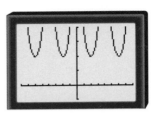

Practice

Verify the possibility of an identity graphically. Then, prove each identity algebraically.

1. $\sin\theta\sec\theta = \tan\theta$
2. $\cos\theta\csc\theta = \cot\theta$
3. $\cot A \sin A = \cos A$
4. $\cos A + \tan A \sin A = \sec A$
5. $\tan\theta + \cot\theta = \sec\theta\csc\theta$
6. $\dfrac{\sin^2\theta}{\cos^2\theta} = \sec^2\theta - 1$
7. $\cot x + \tan x = \sec x \csc x$
8. $\dfrac{\cos x}{\sin x \cot x} = 1$
9. $\dfrac{\sin x + \tan x}{\cos x + 1} = \tan x$
10. $\dfrac{\sec x}{\cot x + \tan x} = \sin x$

For each identity:
a) *show that it is true for $\theta = 30°$, using exact values*
b) *prove the result algebraically*
c) *state any restrictions*
11. $\sin^4\theta - \cos^4\theta = 2\sin^2\theta - 1$
12. $\sin\theta + \cos\theta\cot\theta = \csc\theta$
13. $\cos\theta(\csc\theta - \sec\theta) = \cot\theta - 1$
14. $(\sin\theta - \cos\theta)^2 + (\sin\theta + \cos\theta)^2 = 2$
15. $1 - \sin\theta\cos\theta\tan\theta = \cos^2\theta$
16. $\dfrac{1+\cos\theta}{\sin\theta} = \dfrac{\sin\theta}{1-\cos\theta}$
17. $\dfrac{1+\tan\theta}{1+\cot\theta} = \tan\theta$
18. $\dfrac{\cos\theta}{\sec\theta-1} + \dfrac{\cos\theta}{\sec\theta+1} = 2\cot^2\theta$

19. $\dfrac{\sec\theta}{\sin\theta} - \dfrac{\sin\theta}{\cos\theta} = \cot\theta$
20. $\dfrac{\tan\theta}{1+\tan\theta} = \dfrac{\sin\theta}{\sin\theta+\cos\theta}$

Use a graphing calculator to determine whether each equation might be an identity. Use an algebraic approach to confirm the identities.
21. $\sin^2 x \sec^2 x = \sec^2 x - 1$
22. $\dfrac{1}{\sec x} + \dfrac{1}{\csc x} = 1$
23. $\cot^2 x(\sec^2 x - 1) = 1$
24. $\cot x + \tan x = \csc x \cot x$
25. $\dfrac{\csc^2 x}{\csc x - 1} = \dfrac{1+\sin x}{\sin x}$

Use your knowledge of the fundamental trigonometric identities and algebraic processes to simplify each expression. Use a graphing calculator to verify that the result is equivalent to the original expression.
26. $\tan x \cos^2 x$
27. $\csc^2 x - \cot^2 x$
28. $\dfrac{\sin x}{1+\cos x} + \dfrac{\cos x}{\sin x}$
29. $(1+\sin x)^2 + \cos^2 x$
30. $2(\csc^2 x - \cot^2 x)$
31. $\dfrac{\csc x \sec x}{\cot x}$
32. $\dfrac{\sin^2 x}{\cos^2 x} + \sin x \csc x$
33. $\dfrac{\tan^2 x - \sin^2 x}{\tan^2 x \sin^2 x}$

Applications and Problem Solving

34. Consider the equation
$\sec \theta + \sec \theta \cos \theta = 1 + \sec \theta$.
a) Show that the equation is true for $\theta = 45°$.
b) Prove algebraically that the equation is an identity.
c) Graph $y = \sec \theta + \sec \theta \cos \theta$ and $y = 1 + \sec \theta$. Sketch and describe the results. Explain what has happened.

35. Technology Consider the equation
$$\frac{\csc B + \cot B}{\tan B + \sin B} = \cot B \csc B.$$
a) Use a graphing calculator to show that the identity appears to be true.
b) Prove the identity algebraically.
c) List any restrictions.

36. a) Graph the function
$$f(x) = \frac{\cos x}{1 + \sin x} + \frac{\cos x}{1 - \sin x}.$$
b) Make a conjecture stating which single trigonometric function is probably equivalent to $f(x)$.
c) Prove your conjecture algebraically.
d) State the domain of both functions.

37. Sports When a ball is kicked from ground level, the maximum height that it will reach is given by the formula
$$h = \frac{v_0{}^2 \sin^2 \theta}{2g}$$
where h is the height in metres, v_0 is the initial velocity of the ball, g is the acceleration due to gravity, and θ is the measure of the angle that the ball makes with the ground when kicked.

a) Prove that the formula $h = \dfrac{v_0{}^2 \tan^2 \theta}{2g \sec^2 \theta}$ is
equivalent to the one given above.
b) If a ball is kicked with an initial velocity of 32 m/s at an angle of 50°, what is the maximum height that the ball will reach? The acceleration due to gravity is 9.8 m/s².

38. Connections The sine and cosine functions are **cofunctions** because of a special relationship that occurs for complementary angles:
$\sin A = \cos(90° - A)$ and $\cos A = \sin(90° - A)$.

a) Prove the cofunction identities for sine and cosine geometrically.
b) Name two other pairs of trigonometric cofunctions.

39. Connections In the diagram, DA is a tangent to the unit circle centre O and $\angle AOD = \theta$. Point C is where the terminal arm of $\angle \theta$ intersects the unit circle. The identities $\sin^2 \theta + \cos^2 \theta = 1$, $\tan^2 \theta + 1 = \sec^2 \theta$ and $1 + \cot^2 \theta = \csc^2 \theta$ are sometimes called **Pythagorean identities**. Use the diagram to prove the second and third of these identities geometrically. Why is the name Pythagorean identities appropriate?

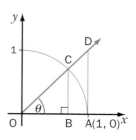

40. Give an example of a trigonometric equation that is true for three different values of the variable but is not an identity. Provide one counterexample to show that the equation is not an identity.

41. Prove the following identity algebraically.
$\csc^4 x - 2 \csc^2 x \cot^2 x + \cot^4 x = 1$

42. Use the substitution $x = 2 \cos t$, $0 \le t \le \pi$, to rewrite the radical expression $\sqrt{(4 - x^2)^3}$ as a trigonometric expression that contains no radical. Explain why the restriction on t is needed.

WORD POWER

Copy and complete the grid, using the letters A, A, A, A, E, E, F, F, L, L, T, and T, to make four-letter words. The word in each column is the same as that in its corresponding row.

INVESTIGATING MATH

Sum and Difference Identities

1 Investigating cos(A – B)

1. Use the substitution $A = \dfrac{\pi}{3}$ and $B = \dfrac{\pi}{6}$ to show that the following conjecture is not true:
$\cos(A - B) = \cos A - \cos B$.

2. Consider the diagram shown, where X is the point $(1, 0)$ and points W, Z, and R lie on the unit circle such that $\angle WOX = A$, $\angle ZOX = B$, and $\angle ROX = A - B$.

a) Explain why the coordinates of Z are $(\cos B, \sin B)$. Write the coordinates for W and for R in a similar form.

b) Explain why chord XR is congruent to chord WZ.

c) The distance between two points (x_1, y_1) and (x_2, y_2) is given by the formula $d = \sqrt{(x_1 - x_2)^2 + (y_1 - y_2)^2}$. Use this formula to write a statement equating the distance XR and the distance WZ.

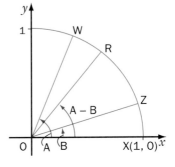

d) Simplify the equation from part c) to show that
$\cos(A - B) = \cos A \cos B + \sin A \sin B$.

e) Verify that the identity in part d) is true when $A = \dfrac{\pi}{3}$ and $B = \dfrac{\pi}{6}$.

3. The difference identity from part 2d) can be used to find an exact value for cos 15°.

a) Use $\cos(60° - 45°)$ as the left side, and then simplify the resulting expression for the right side.

b) Use $\cos(45° - 30°)$ as the left side. Show that this expression simplifies to the same exact measure as found in part a).

2 Deriving an Identity for cos(A + B)

1. Use the identity $\cos(A - B) = \cos A \cos B + \sin A \sin B$ to derive a related identity for $\cos(A + B)$.

a) Express $\cos(A + B)$ as $\cos(A - (-B))$. Rewrite the right side of the identity accordingly, and simplify the right side using the fact that $\cos(-B) = \cos B$ and $\sin(-B) = -\sin B$.

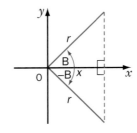

b) Verify the identity for $\cos(A + B)$ is true when $A = \dfrac{\pi}{3}$ and $B = \dfrac{\pi}{6}$.

2. Use the identity for $\cos(A + B)$ to find an exact value for cos 75°.

3 Deriving Identities for sin(A + B), sin(A − B), tan(A + B), and tan(A − B)

1. Use the fact that $\sin\theta = \cos(90° − \theta)$ for all θ and substitute $\theta = A + B$ to obtain an identity for $\sin(A + B)$. Simplify the right side to show that
$\sin(A + B) = \sin A \cos B + \cos A \sin B$.

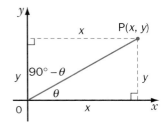

2. Show that $\sin(A − B) = \sin A \cos B − \cos A \sin B$.

3. Use the sum identities for sine and cosine, and the fact that
$\tan\theta = \dfrac{\sin\theta}{\cos\theta}$, to show that $\tan(A + B) = \dfrac{\tan A + \tan B}{1 − \tan A \tan B}$.
Hint: Start with the left side.

4. Derive an identity for $\tan(A − B)$.

4 Double-Angle Identities

1. Use the sum identities to prove each of the following double-angle identities.
a) $\sin 2A = 2 \sin A \cos A$
b) $\cos 2A = \cos^2 A − \sin^2 A$
c) $\cos 2A = 2 \cos^2 A − 1$
d) $\cos 2A = 1 − 2 \sin^2 A$

e) $\tan 2A = \dfrac{2\tan A}{1 − \tan^2 A}$, where $\tan A \neq \pm 1$

2. Verify that each double-angle identity is true when $A = \dfrac{\pi}{6}$.

5.5 Using Sum, Difference, and Double-Angle Identities

Robotic devices can increase the accuracy of certain tasks and can be used in environments that are hazardous to humans. Canadian robotic technology has played an important role in the field of space exploration, first with the Canadarm and then with the development of the larger, more flexible, and much stronger Mobile Servicing System. In order for a robotic device to carry out its specific task, it needs to be able to determine its current position as it moves around in its environment. The mathematics behind the manipulation of these devices involves the use of trigonometric identities.

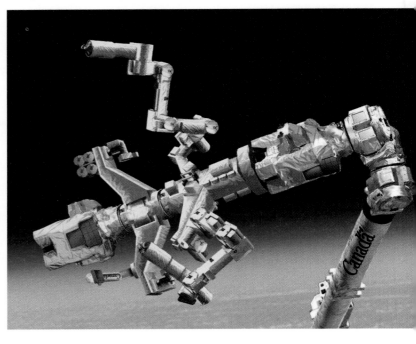

Explore: Use Inductive Reasoning

Copy and complete the table using exact values.

∠A	30°	45°	60°	90°
sin A				
cos A				
2 sin A cos A				
$\cos^2 A - \sin^2 A$				

Make a conjecture stating a single trigonometric function that each expression is equivalent to.
a) $2 \sin 30° \cos 30°$ **b)** $2 \sin 45° \cos 45°$
c) $\cos^2 30° - \sin^2 30°$ **d)** $\cos^2 45° - \sin^2 45°$

Inquire

1. Generalize. Make a conjecture stating what single trigonometric function $2 \sin A \cos A$ is equivalent to.

2. Use a graphing calculator to test your conjecture. Explain your method and state what conclusion can be made.

3. What single trigonometric function do you think $\cos^2 A - \sin^2 A$ is equivalent to?

4. Use a graphing calculator to test your conjecture. Explain your method and state what conclusion can be made.

The conjectures that you explored above, and the sum and difference identities developed in the preceding Investigating Math section, lead to the following identities.

Sum and Difference Identities

$\sin(A + B) = \sin A \cos B + \cos A \sin B$

$\sin(A - B) = \sin A \cos B - \cos A \sin B$

$\cos(A + B) = \cos A \cos B - \sin A \sin B$

$\cos(A - B) = \cos A \cos B + \sin A \sin B$

$\tan(A + B) = \dfrac{\tan A + \tan B}{1 - \tan A \tan B}$, where A, B, A + B $\neq \dfrac{\pi}{2} + n\pi$

$\tan(A - B) = \dfrac{\tan A - \tan B}{1 + \tan A \tan B}$, where A, B, A + B $\neq \dfrac{\pi}{2} + n\pi$

Double-Angle Identities

$\sin 2A = 2 \sin A \cos A$

$\cos 2A = \cos^2 A - \sin^2 A$

$\cos 2A = 2 \cos^2 A - 1$

$\cos 2A = 1 - 2 \sin^2 A$

$\tan 2A = \dfrac{2 \tan A}{1 - \tan^2 A}$, where A $\neq \dfrac{\pi}{4} + \dfrac{n\pi}{2}$, and

$A \neq \dfrac{\pi}{2} + n\pi$

The sum, difference, and double-angle identities can be used to simplify expressions involving trigonometric functions.

Example 1 Simplifying Trigonometric Expressions

Express each as a single trigonometric function.

a) $\sin\dfrac{5\pi}{6}\cos\dfrac{3\pi}{8} - \cos\dfrac{5\pi}{6}\sin\dfrac{3\pi}{8}$
b) $\dfrac{\tan 30° + \tan 45°}{1 - \tan 30° \tan 45°}$

Solution

a) The expression $\sin\dfrac{5\pi}{6}\cos\dfrac{3\pi}{8} - \cos\dfrac{5\pi}{6}\sin\dfrac{3\pi}{8}$ has the same pattern as

the right side of the identity $\sin(A - B) = \sin A \cos B - \cos A \sin B$, with

$A = \dfrac{5\pi}{6}$ and $B = \dfrac{3\pi}{8}$.

$$\sin\dfrac{5\pi}{6}\cos\dfrac{3\pi}{8} - \cos\dfrac{5\pi}{6}\sin\dfrac{3\pi}{8} = \sin\left(\dfrac{5\pi}{6} - \dfrac{3\pi}{8}\right)$$

$$= \sin\left(\dfrac{20\pi}{24} - \dfrac{9\pi}{24}\right)$$

$$= \sin\dfrac{11\pi}{24}$$

b) The expression $\dfrac{\tan 30° + \tan 45°}{1 - \tan 30° \tan 45°}$ has the same pattern as the right side

of the identity $\tan(A - B) = \dfrac{\tan A - \tan B}{1 + \tan A \tan B}$, with A = 30° and B = 45°.

$$\dfrac{\tan 30° + \tan 45°}{1 - \tan 30° \tan 45°} = \tan(30° + 45°)$$

$$= \tan 75°$$

The graph of a more complicated expression involving trigonometric functions sometimes reveals that the expression might be equivalent to a simpler expression. The sum, difference, and double angle identities can then be used to prove the conjecture algebraically.

Example 2   Using a Graph

Graph the function $f(x) = \dfrac{2\tan x}{1 + \tan^2 x}$.

a) Use the graph to make a conjecture about the period and the amplitude of $f(x)$.
b) Make a conjecture stating what single trigonometric function $f(x)$ is equivalent to. Graph this function. Does your conjecture appear to be true?
c) Prove your conjecture algebraically.

Solution

The graph of $y = \dfrac{2\tan x}{1 + \tan^2 x}$ as Y1 using a window $[-2\pi,\ 2\pi,\ \pi/2]$ by $[-2, 2, 1]$ is shown.

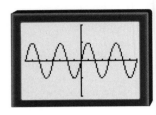

a) Since four complete periods of the function appear in the domain $-2\pi \le x \le 2\pi$, the period of $f(x)$ is π. The amplitude is 1.

b) The graph appears to be sinusoidal. It has no horizontal shift or vertical displacement compared with $y = \sin x$. The function graphed appears to be equivalent to $y = \sin 2x$.

Conjecture: $f(x) = \dfrac{2\tan x}{1 + \tan^2 x}$
$= \sin 2x$

Graphing $y = \sin 2x$ as Y2 using the same window appears to give the same graph as Y1, $y = \dfrac{2\tan x}{1 + \tan^2 x}$.

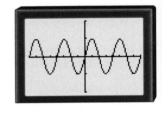

c) $f(x) = \dfrac{2\tan x}{1 + \tan^2 x}$

$= \dfrac{2\tan x}{\sec^2 x}$

$= 2\tan x \cos^2 x$

$= 2 \times \dfrac{\sin x}{\cos x} \times \cos^2 x$

$= 2\sin x \cos x \qquad \cos x \ne 0$

$= \sin 2x$

Therefore, $\dfrac{2\tan x}{1 + \tan^2 x} = \sin 2x$, provided $\cos x \ne 0$, that is,

$x \ne \dfrac{\pi}{2} + n\pi$, where n is any integer.

Example 3   Applying Skills to Solve a Problem

The horizontal distance that a soccer ball will travel, when kicked at an angle θ, is given by $d = \dfrac{2v_0^2}{g}\sin\theta\cos\theta$, where d is the horizontal distance in metres, v_0 is the initial velocity in metres per second, and g is the acceleration due to gravity, which is 9.81 m/s^2.

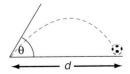

a) To model this function with a graph, what is a practical domain for θ? What are the implications of $\theta = 0$? Of $\theta = \dfrac{\pi}{2}$?

b) Rewrite the expression for d as a sine function.

c) Write the function for a soccer ball that is kicked with an initial velocity of 20 m/s. Use the graph of this function to determine the angle at which the ball should be kicked to give the maximum horizontal distance.

Solution

a) In $d = \dfrac{2v_0^2}{g} \sin\theta\cos\theta$, the domain of θ is any real number. However, to model kicking the soccer ball, only values of θ between 0 and $\dfrac{\pi}{2}$ need be considered.

If $\theta = 0$, then $d = 0$, since $\sin 0 = 0$. This means the ball remains on the ground and travels 0 m.

If $\theta = \dfrac{\pi}{2}$, then again $d = 0$, since $\cos\dfrac{\pi}{2} = 0$. The ball is kicked vertically, straight up and down, and travels no horizontal distance.

A practical domain for the graph that models the function in the context is $0 \le \theta \le \dfrac{\pi}{2}$.

b) Use the identity $\sin 2A = 2 \sin A \cos A$.

$$d = \dfrac{2v_0^2}{g} \sin\theta\cos\theta$$

$$= \dfrac{v_0^2}{g} \sin 2\theta$$

As a sine function, the expression for d is $d = \dfrac{2v_0^2}{g} \sin 2\theta$.

c) Substitute $v_0 = 20$ and $g = 9.81$.

$$d = \dfrac{v_0^2}{g} \sin 2\theta$$

$$= \dfrac{400}{9.81} \sin 2\theta$$

Graph $y = \dfrac{400}{9.81} \sin 2\theta$ using a window $[0, \pi/2, \pi/8]$ by $[-5, 50, 5]$.

From the graph, the maximum distance occurs when the angle is approximately 0.7854 rad.

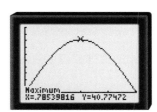

Alternatively, an exact angle can be found, using your knowledge of the sine function. The graph of $\sin\theta$ reaches its maximum when $\theta = \dfrac{\pi}{2}$, so $\sin 2\theta$ will reach a maximum when $2\theta = \dfrac{\pi}{2}$ or $\theta = \dfrac{\pi}{4}$.

Example 4   Applying Skills to an Application

The x-y position of a gripper on the end of a robotic arm can be defined by the following

$$x = L_1 \cos \theta_1 + L_2 \cos \theta_1 \cos \theta_2 - L_2 \sin \theta_1 \sin \theta_2$$
$$y = L_1 \sin \theta_1 + L_2 \sin \theta_1 \cos \theta_2 + L_2 \cos \theta_1 \sin \theta_2$$

where L_1 and L_2 represent the lengths of the links in metres, and θ_1 and θ_2 represent the joint angles as shown in the diagram.

a) Simplify the equations for x and y by using sum identities for cosine and sine, respectively.

b) If $\theta_1 = 30°$, $\theta_2 = 45°$, and the length of each link is 1 m, determine the x- and y-coordinates of the gripper, rounded to four decimal places.

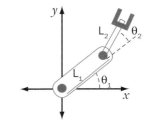

Solution

a) Use the identity $\cos(A + B) = \cos A \cos B - \sin A \sin B$.

$x = L_1 \cos \theta_1 + L_2 \cos \theta_1 \cos \theta_2 - L_2 \sin \theta_1 \sin \theta_2$
$\quad = L_1 \cos \theta_1 + L_2 \cos(\theta_1 + \theta_2)$

Use the identity $\sin(A + B) = \sin A \cos B + \cos A \sin B$.

$y = L_1 \sin \theta_1 + L_2 \sin \theta_1 \cos \theta_2 + L_2 \cos \theta_1 \sin \theta_2$
$\quad = L_1 \sin \theta_1 + L_2 \sin(\theta_1 + \theta_2)$

The simplified equations for x and y are $x = L_1 \cos \theta_1 + L_2 \cos(\theta_1 + \theta_2)$ and $y = L_1 \sin \theta_1 + L_2 \sin(\theta_1 + \theta_2)$.

b) Substitute $\theta_1 = 30°$, $\theta_2 = 45°$, and $L_1 = L_2 = 1$.

$x = L_1 \cos \theta_1 + L_2 \cos(\theta_1 + \theta_2)$
$\quad = (1)\cos 30° + (1)\cos(30° + 45°)$
$\quad \doteq 1.1248$

$y = L_1 \sin \theta_1 + L_2 \sin(\theta_1 + \theta_2)$
$\quad = (1)\sin 30° + (1)\sin(30° + 45°)$
$\quad \doteq 1.4659$

The coordinates of the gripper are $x = 1.1248$ and $y = 1.4659$, to four decimal places.

Practice

Give the exact value of each expression.

1. $\sin 65° \cos 35° - \cos 65° \sin 35°$

2. $\sin 40° \cos 20° + \cos 40° \sin 20°$

3. $\cos 25° \cos 5° - \sin 25° \sin 5°$

4. $\cos 80° \cos 20° + \sin 80° \sin 20°$

5. $\sin \dfrac{\pi}{3} \cos \dfrac{\pi}{6} + \cos \dfrac{\pi}{3} \sin \dfrac{\pi}{6}$

6. $\cos \dfrac{7\pi}{12} \cos \dfrac{\pi}{3} + \sin \dfrac{7\pi}{12} \sin \dfrac{\pi}{3}$

7. $\sin 40° \cos 50° + \cos 40° \sin 50°$

8. $\cos(-10°) \cos 35° + \sin(-10°) \sin 35°$

Find the exact value of each by choosing values for $\angle A$ and $\angle B$ and applying an appropriate sum or difference identity.

9. $\cos \dfrac{2\pi}{3}$

10. $\tan 15°$

11. $\sin 105°$

12. $\cos \dfrac{7\pi}{12}$

13. $\tan 105°$

14. $\sin 345°$

15. $\sin(-105°)$

16. $\cos \dfrac{5\pi}{6}$

Express each as a single trigonometric function.

17. $2 \sin \dfrac{\pi}{6} \cos \dfrac{\pi}{6}$

18. $2 \cos^2 \dfrac{\pi}{4} - 1$

19. $\cos^2 \dfrac{\pi}{3} - \sin^2 \dfrac{\pi}{3}$

20. $1 - 2 \sin^2 15°$

21. $\dfrac{\tan \pi - \tan \dfrac{\pi}{6}}{1 + \tan \pi \tan \dfrac{\pi}{6}}$

22. $\dfrac{\tan \dfrac{\pi}{3} + \tan \dfrac{\pi}{12}}{1 - \tan \dfrac{\pi}{3} \tan \dfrac{\pi}{12}}$

23. $\sin \pi \cos \dfrac{\pi}{4} + \cos \pi \sin \dfrac{\pi}{4}$

24. $\cos \dfrac{\pi}{12} \cos \pi - \sin \dfrac{\pi}{12} \sin \pi$

Use the sum and difference identities to prove each identity.

25. $\sin(90° + A) = \cos A$
26. $\cos(90° + A) = -\sin A$
27. $\cos(90° - A) = \sin A$
28. $\sin(270° - A) = -\cos A$
29. $\sin(\pi + A) = -\sin A$
30. $\cos(2\pi + A) = \cos A$

31. $\sin\left(\dfrac{\pi}{2} - A\right) = \cos A$

32. $\cos\left(\dfrac{3\pi}{2} - A\right) = -\sin A$

Determine whether each equation is true, giving reasons for your conclusion.

33. $\cos 140° = \cos 60° \cos 80° - \sin 60° \sin 80°$
34. $\cos(-24°) = \cos 16° - \cos 40°$

35. $\sin \dfrac{5\pi}{12} = \sin \dfrac{\pi}{6} \cos \dfrac{\pi}{4} + \cos \dfrac{\pi}{6} \sin \dfrac{\pi}{4}$

36. $\tan 75° = \dfrac{\tan 35° - \tan 40°}{1 - \tan 35° \tan 40°}$

Applications and Problem Solving

37. If $\angle A$ and $\angle B$ are both in the first quadrant, and $\sin A = \dfrac{3}{5}$ and $\cos B = \dfrac{5}{13}$, evaluate each of the following.
a) $\cos(A - B)$ **b)** $\sin(A + B)$
c) $\tan(A + B)$

38. Evaluate $\tan(A - B)$, given that $\tan A = \dfrac{4}{3}$ and $\cos B = \dfrac{12}{13}$, and both angles are in the first quadrant.

39. If $\cos A = \dfrac{12}{13}$, and $\angle A$ is in the fourth quadrant, find the exact value of $\sin 2A$.

40. Given that $\angle P$ is in the first quadrant such that $\sin P = \dfrac{3}{5}$, and $\angle Q$ is in the second quadrant such that $\cos Q = -\dfrac{5}{13}$, find each of the following.
a) $\cos P$ **b)** $\sin Q$
c) $\sin(P + Q)$ **d)** $\cos(P + Q)$
e) Which quadrant is $\angle(P + Q)$ in?

41. Graph the function $f(x) = \dfrac{2 \tan x}{1 - \tan^2 x}$.
a) Use the graph to make a conjecture about the period and the amplitude of the function.
b) Make a conjecture stating to what single trigonometric function $f(x)$ is equivalent. Graph this function. Does your conjecture appear to be true?
c) Prove your conjecture algebraically.

42. Graph the function $f(x) = (\cos x - \sin x)(\cos x + \sin x)$.
a) Use the graph to make a conjecture about the period and the amplitude of the function.
b) Make a conjecture stating to what single trigonometric function $f(x)$ is equivalent. Graph this function. Does your conjecture appear to be true?
c) Prove your conjecture algebraically.

43. Prove each of the following algebraically, and then compare the graphs of the functions defined by the expressions on the left side and on the right side of the equation. Record the two functions that you graphed and a sketch of the graph obtained.
a) $\dfrac{1 + \cos 2x}{\sin 2x} = \cot x$ **b)** $\sec^2 x = \dfrac{2}{1 + \cos 2x}$
c) $\cos 3x + 1 = 4 \cos^3 x - 3 \cos x + 1$
d) $1 + \sin 2x = (\sin x + \cos x)^2$
e) $\sin(x + y) \sin(x - y) = \sin^2 x - \cos^2 y$

44. Physical geography On the winter solstice, the maximum amount of light energy, E, that falls on each square metre of a location in the northern hemisphere is given by the expression $E\sin(113.5° + \theta)$, where θ is the latitude of the location.
a) Explain why locations on or above the Arctic Circle, which is at 66.5°N, receive no light energy on the winter solstice.
b) Use the sum of sines identity to find the maximum amount of light energy, in terms of E, that falls on Edmonton on the winter solstice.

45. Coordinate geometry
The slope of a line is equal to the tangent of the angle that the line makes with the x-axis. Lines l_1 and l_2 make angles measuring α and β with the x-axis. The measure of the smaller angle formed by the intersection of the two lines has measure θ. If the slopes of lines l_1 and l_2 are m_1 and m_2, respectively, show that

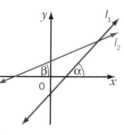

$$\tan\theta = \frac{m_2 - m_1}{1 + m_2 m_1}.$$

46. Interior design A painting, 1.0 m in height, is hung so that its top edge is 0.8 m from the ceiling. A light is to be installed on the ceiling, directly in front of the painting, so that the angle subtended from the light to the painting equals the angle of depression to the top of the painting. How far out from the wall should the light be installed?

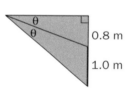

0.8 m

1.0 m

47. Prove that $\tan\theta = \dfrac{1 - \cos 2\theta}{\sin 2\theta}$. State any restrictions.

48. Derive an identity for $\cot(A + B)$ in terms of $\cot A$ and $\cot B$.

49. Derive an identity for $\cot(A - B)$ in terms of $\cot A$ and $\cot B$.

50. Half-angle identities Derive half-angle identities for sine and cosine as follows.
a) Use a double-angle identity for cosine and substitute $A = \dfrac{x}{2}$ to show that $\sin\dfrac{x}{2} = \pm\sqrt{\dfrac{1 - \cos x}{2}}$.
b) Use a double-angle identity for cosine and substitute $A = \dfrac{x}{2}$ to show that $\cos\dfrac{x}{2} = \pm\sqrt{\dfrac{1 + \cos x}{2}}$.

51. Use a graphing calculator to help determine the principal measure for θ, in degrees, that would make each equation true.
a) $\sin(\theta + x) = -\cos x$ **b)** $\tan(\theta + x) = -\cot x$

52. Find the measure of $A + B$, in radians, if $\tan A = x$ and $\tan B = y$ and $(3x + 3)(2y + 2) = 12$.

53. Robotic arm The x- and y-coordinates of the gripper at the end of a robotic arm are as follows.
$x = L_1 \cos\theta_1 + L_2 \cos(\theta_1 + \theta_2)$
$y = L_1 \sin\theta_1 + L_2 \sin(\theta_1 + \theta_2)$
where L_1 and L_2 represent the lengths of the links in metres, while θ_1 and θ_2 represent the joint angles as shown in the diagram.

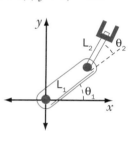

a) Show that the equations for x and y are correct.
b) What is the maximum distance that the gripper can reach if L_1 and L_2 are each 2 m?
c) Given that $\theta_1 = 30°$, and L_1 and L_2 are each 2 m, will the end of the gripper reach an object located at $x = 3.3$ and $y = 2.5$? If so, what is θ_2? If not, explain why not.

NUMBER POWER

Use each of the digits 1 through 9 once to make true equations.

$$\blacksquare \div \blacksquare + \blacksquare = 5$$
$$\blacksquare + \blacksquare - \blacksquare = 5$$
$$\blacksquare \times \blacksquare - \blacksquare = 5$$

Ports Around the World

Use the *Ports* database, from the Computer Data Bank, to complete the following.
a) *Devise a plan to answer each question. Remember to exclude records for which the required data are not available.*
b) *Compare your plan with the plans of your classmates.*
c) *Revise your plan, if necessary, and then carry it out.*

1 Tides

Tides are the periodic variations in sea level that correspond to changes in the relative positions of the moon and the sun.

1. For most places, there are two high tides and two low tides per day. What is the average tide period on Mar. 21? on Sept. 21?

2. The greatest tide ranges occur at new moon, when the moon and the sun are in the same direction, and at full moon, when they are in opposite directions. The smallest tide ranges occur at intermediate phases of the moon. Do Pacific Canada ports and Atlantic Canada ports have greater tide ranges on Mar. 21 or Sept. 21?

3. For the ports from question 2 with greater tide ranges on Mar. 21, graph tide range versus port.

2 Port Accessibility

Key factors in the accessibility of a port are its maximum vessel length and its least depths (channel and anchorage). The **draft** of a vessel is the depth of the vessel in the water, that is, the vertical distance between the water line and the bottom of the keel. The **under-keel clearance** is 15% of the draft of a vessel.
a) *The largest container ship in the world, the Regina Maersk, built in 1996, has a length of 318 m and a draft of 14.0 m.*
b) *The largest cruise ship in the world, the Grand Princess, built in 1998, with a passenger capacity of 3300, has a length of 290 m and a draft of 8.5 m.*

1. What depth is required by each vessel?

2. At any given time, how many ports are accessible to each vessel?

3. At any given time, how many ports, for which the tide range data are available, are accessible to each vessel?

4. How many ports would be accessible to each vessel at high tide on Mar. 21? on Sept. 21? What assumption are you making? What conclusions can you make?

3 Periodic Functions

1. a) Which port has the greatest tide range on Sept. 21?
b) What is its tide range on Sept. 21? its tide period on Sept. 21? its least channel depth? its least anchorage depth?
c) Explain each graph.

i)

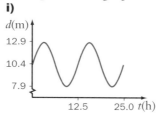

ii)

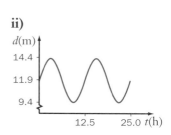

2. Depth as a function of time can be modelled using $d(t) = a \sin b\pi t + k$. For the port in question 1, how would you find
a) a?   **b)** b?   **c)** k for each graph?

3. Write the functions that model channel depth and anchorage depth on Sept. 21 for that port.

4. Prepare the database so that the functions modelling channel depth and anchorage depth on Sept. 21 and on Mar. 21 for all ports with the required data could be written.

CONNECTING MATH AND COMMUNICATIONS
Radio and Television Broadcasting

Electronic communication is commonplace in today's world. Every day people watch television images from around the world, make cellular phone calls, listen to radio broadcasts, and connect to the Internet. These are all examples of electronic communication systems.

1 Radio Stations

Radio stations use a carrier waveform to broadcast the music and voices that we hear when we listen to the radio. A carrier waveform is a waveform that carries another electrical waveform or message. This boost is necessary for a radio signal to be received many kilometres from the radio station. A simple analogy of the relationship between a carrier waveform and message waveform is a message on a piece of paper wrapped around a rock. Together the paper and the rock can reach a greater distance than can the paper alone. A typical carrier waveform has an equation of the form $y = A \sin 2\pi f_c t$, where A is the amplitude, f_c is the frequency of the carrier waveform, and t is time, in seconds.

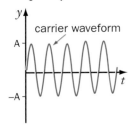

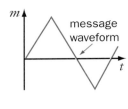

AM radio stations broadcast sounds (messages) through amplitude modulation. The amplitude modulated waveform for the message above would look similar to the illustration shown below.

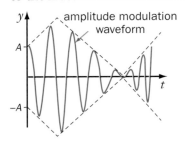

1. The equation of the modulated waveform is given by $y = [A + km(t)] \sin 2\pi f_c t$.
a) What is the amplitude of the modulated waveform?
b) What does the function $m(t)$ represent?

c) Is the frequency of the amplitude modulated waveform constant? What is it?

d) What is the equation of the message waveform?

2. a) What waveform appears to act as the boundary for the amplitude modulated waveform?

b) What transformation has the message waveform undergone?

c) If the message waveform was a square wave, sketch the amplitude modulated waveform.

3. Research what carrier frequencies are used by commercial AM radio stations.

4. a) What quantity is modulated for an FM station?

b) Sketch what you think the graph of an FM waveform might look like using a square wave as the message waveform.

2 Television Stations

Television stations also use carrier waveforms to broadcast their programs. A television transmission is comprised of video and sound signals. The video signal is amplitude modulated, while the sound signal is frequency modulated. One complete television signal covers a bandwidth of 6 MHz.

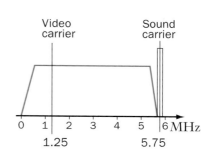

Frequency-division multiplexing enables channels to reside in adjacent frequency bands. The switching of channels on the television set causes the tuner in the TV to extract the correct signal from the transmitted radio waves.

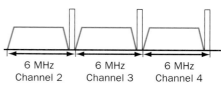

The shifting of a signal in frequency involves a trigonometric identity

$$\cos(f_c t)\cos(ft) = \frac{1}{2}\cos(f_c t + ft) + \frac{1}{2}\cos(f_c t - ft)$$

where f and f_c are the frequencies of the message and carrier waveforms, respectively.

1. a) Use the sum and difference identities for cosine to prove the trigonometric identity $\cos(f_c t)\cos(ft) = \frac{1}{2}\cos(f_c t + ft) + \frac{1}{2}\cos(f_c t - ft)$.

b) If $f = 2$ and $f_c = 10$, graph $y = \cos(f_c t)\cos(ft)$ using graphing technology. Determine the amplitude and the period of the function.

2. Research the actual radio frequencies allocated for television transmission. What channels are represented in these frequency bands?

Review

5.1 *Use a graph of $y = \cos x$, $0 \leq x < 2\pi$, to help find the exact solutions to each of the following.*

1. the solutions of $\cos x = \dfrac{1}{2}$, in the interval $0 \leq x < 2\pi$

2. the solutions of $\cos 3x = \dfrac{1}{2}$, in the interval $0 \leq x < 2\pi$

3. all solutions of $\cos 3x = \dfrac{1}{2}$

4. the solutions of $\cos x = -1$, in the interval $0 \leq x < 2\pi$

5. the solutions of $\cos 4x = -1$, in the interval $0 \leq x < 2\pi$

6. all solutions of $\cos 4x = -1$

7. a) Graph the functions $y = \sin x$ and $y = \dfrac{1}{\sqrt{2}}$ on the same axes.

b) Determine a general solution to the equation $\sin x = \dfrac{1}{\sqrt{2}}$.

c) Explain how the solution to the equation $\sqrt{2} \sin x - 1 = 0$ is related to the solution found in part b). How can you check this using the graph of the function $y = \sqrt{2} \sin x - 1$?

5.2 *Solve for x, $0 \leq x < 360°$.*

8. $3 \sin 2x = 3$ **9.** $\sqrt{3} \tan 2x = 1$

10. $\tan x = \sqrt{3}$ **11.** $\sin 3x + 1 = 1$

12. $2 \cos 2x + 1 = 0$ **13.** $2 \cos x - \sqrt{3} = 0$

14. $\sqrt{2} \cos \dfrac{1}{2}x = 1$ **15.** $2 \sin \dfrac{1}{2}x = \sqrt{3}$

Solve for θ, $0 \leq \theta < 2\pi$, and then give a general solution.

16. $\cos \theta \left(\cos \theta - \dfrac{1}{2} \right) = 0$

17. $\sin^2 \theta - \dfrac{3}{4} = 0$

18. $\left(\sin \theta - \dfrac{1}{2} \right)(\tan \theta + 1) = 0$

19. $\tan^2 \theta - 1 = 0$

20. $\sin^2 2\theta + \sin 2\theta = 0$

21. $4 \cos^2 \theta + 2 \cos \theta - 2 = 0$

22. $\cos^2 3\theta + \cos 3\theta = 0$

23. $\sin \theta \left(\sin \theta - \dfrac{\sqrt{3}}{2} \right) = 0$

24. Solve each equation for $0 \leq x < 2\pi$, rounding solutions to the nearest tenth of a radian when necessary.

a) $4 \sin^2 x - 3 \sin x - 1 = 0$

b) $3 \cos^2 x - \cos x = 0$

c) $2 \tan^2 x - 3 \tan x - 5 = 0$

d) $12 \cos^2 x - \cos x - 6 = 0$

e) $\tan^2 x - 2 \tan x - 15 = 0$

5.3 25. The screen shows the graphs of $y = 3 \sin^2 x$, and $y = x + \cos x$ using a window $[-\pi, 2\pi, \pi/2]$ by $[-3, 5, 1]$.

a) Based on the graph, how many solutions do you expect for the equation $3 \sin^2 x = x + \cos x$?

b) What single function can you graph, and then find the zeros of, to solve the equation $3 \sin^2 x = x + \cos x$? Graph this function and determine the zeros, to three decimal places.

26. a) Graph $y = \dfrac{1}{3}x - \sin x$ using a window $[-2\pi, 2\pi, \pi/4]$ by $[-5, 5, 1]$.

b) Use the graph to solve the equation $\sin x = \dfrac{1}{3}x$, rounding answers to three decimal places.

c) Explain how you could use the graph to tell how many roots the equation $\dfrac{1}{3}x - \sin x - 1 = 0$ has.

d) Determine the root(s) of the equation $\dfrac{1}{3}x - \sin x - 1 = 0$, to three decimal places.

5.4 *Verify the possibility of an identity graphically. Then, prove each identity algebraically.*

27. $\csc^2 x (1 - \cos^2 x) = 1$

28. $\sin x \sec x \cot x = 1$

29. $\dfrac{\sin^2 x + \cos^2 x}{\sec x} = \cos x$

30. $\dfrac{\cot x + \tan x}{\sec x} = \csc x$

31. $\dfrac{\cos x + 1}{\sin x + \tan x} = \cot x$

For each identity,
a) *show that it is true for* $\theta = 30°$, *using exact values*
b) *prove the result algebraically*
c) *state any restrictions*

32. $\sec^4 \theta - \sec^2 \theta = \tan^4 \theta + \tan^2 \theta$

33. $\cos \theta + \cos \theta \tan^2 \theta = \sec \theta$

34. $\cos \theta (\sec \theta - \csc \theta) = 1 - \cot \theta$

35. $\dfrac{\sin \theta + \tan \theta}{\cos \theta + 1} = \tan \theta$

Use your knowledge of the fundamental trigonometric identities and algebraic processes to simplify each expression. Use a graphing calculator to verify that the result is equivalent to the original expression.

36. $\dfrac{\csc x \cos x}{\tan x}$

37. $\sec^2 x - \tan^2 x$

38. $\dfrac{\cos^2 x}{\sin^2 x} + \cos x \sec x$

39. $(1 + \cos x)^2 + \sin^2 x$

Give the exact value of each expression.

40. $\sin \dfrac{\pi}{3} \cos \dfrac{\pi}{4} - \cos \dfrac{\pi}{3} \sin \dfrac{\pi}{4}$

41. $\sin 100° \cos 20° + \cos 20° \sin 100°$

42. $\dfrac{\tan \pi + \tan \dfrac{\pi}{6}}{1 - \tan \pi \tan \dfrac{\pi}{6}}$

43. $\cos \dfrac{\pi}{3} \cos \dfrac{\pi}{6} - \sin \dfrac{\pi}{3} \sin \dfrac{\pi}{6}$

44. $\cos 80° \cos 50° + \sin 80° \sin 50°$

Express each as a single trigonometric function.

45. $\cos^2 \dfrac{\pi}{4} - \sin^2 \dfrac{\pi}{4}$

46. $\dfrac{\tan \dfrac{\pi}{3} + \tan \dfrac{\pi}{12}}{1 - \tan \dfrac{\pi}{3} \tan \dfrac{\pi}{12}}$

47. $2 \sin 75° \cos 75°$

48. $2 \cos^2 \dfrac{\pi}{3} - 1$

49. Prove the following algebraically.
a) $\cos(A + B) \cos(A - B) = \cos^2 A - \sin^2 B$

b) $\dfrac{1 + \cos 2\theta}{\sin 2\theta} = \cot \theta$

Exploring Math

Mach Numbers

The Mach number, M, of an aircraft is the ratio of its speed to the speed of sound. An aircraft breaks the sound barrier when its speed is greater than the speed of sound. In this case, $M > 1$ and the aircraft produces sound waves that form a cone. The angle at the vertex of a cross section of the cone is related to the Mach number as follows.

$$\frac{1}{M} = \sin \frac{\theta}{2}$$

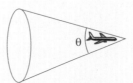

1. Use the half-angle identity,
$\sin \dfrac{\theta}{2} = \pm \sqrt{\dfrac{1 - \cos \theta}{2}}$, to express the Mach number, M, as a function of θ.

2. If an aircraft is flying at twice the speed of sound, its Mach number is 2. Find the measure of $\angle \theta$ in this case.

3. A supersonic jet is flying at a speed that is producing a sound wave in the form of a cone with vertex angle measuring 45°. What is the Mach number in this situation? Express the answer in exact form.

4. A reconnaissance jet has a top speed of 3530 km/h.
a) What is the Mach number of this jet, to the nearest tenth, if the speed of sound is 1226 km/h?
b) What is the measure of the vertex angle of its sound cone, to the nearest degree?

5. As the speed of an aircraft that is flying supersonically increases, does the cone angle θ increase or decrease? Justify your answer.

Chapter Check

1. a) Graph the functions $y = \cos x$ and $y = \dfrac{\sqrt{3}}{2}$ on the same axes.

b) Solve $\cos x = \dfrac{\sqrt{3}}{2}$, for $0 \le x < 2\pi$.

c) Determine a general solution for $\cos x = \dfrac{\sqrt{3}}{2}$.

d) Explain how the solution to the equation $2 \cos x - \sqrt{3} = 0$ is related to the solution found in part c). How can you check this, using the graph of the function $y = 2 \cos x - \sqrt{3}$?

Solve for x, $0 \le x < 360°$.

2. $3 \cos x = -3$

3. $\sin 2x = \dfrac{1}{2}$

4. $\tan x = \dfrac{1}{\sqrt{3}}$

5. $2 \cos 2x + 1 = 0$

Solve for θ, $0 \le \theta < 2\pi$, and then give a general solution.

6. $\sin^2 \theta - \dfrac{1}{4} = 0$

7. $\cos^2 2\theta + \cos 2\theta = 0$

8. The screen shows the graphs of
$y = \dfrac{1}{2}x + \sin x$
and $y = 2 \cos^2 x$ using a window $[-2\pi, 2\pi, \pi/4]$ by $[-3, 5, 1]$.

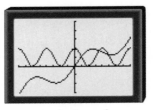

a) Based on the graph, how many solutions do you expect for the equation $2 \cos^2 x = \dfrac{1}{2}x + \sin x$?

b) What single function can you graph, and then find the zeros of, to solve the equation $2 \cos^2 x = \dfrac{1}{2}x + \sin x$? Graph this function and determine the zeros correct to three decimal places.

9. Daylight In a given region, the number of daylight hours varies, depending on the time of year. This variation can be approximated with a sinusoidal function. The model for a certain region is given by the function

$$d(t) = 5 \sin \dfrac{2\pi}{365}(t - 95) + 13$$

where $d(t)$ is in hours and t represents the number of days after January 1. Find two days when the approximate number of daylight hours is 16 h.

For each identity,
a) *verify the possibility of an identity graphically*
b) *show that it is true for $x = 30°$, using exact values*
c) *prove the result algebraically*
d) *state any restrictions*

10. $1 + \cot^2 x = \csc^2 x$

11. $\tan x \cos x \csc x = 1$

12. $\sin x + \cos x \tan x = 2 \sin x$

13. $\dfrac{\tan x}{1 + \tan x} = \dfrac{\sin x}{\sin x + \cos x}$

Simplify the following trigonometric expressions. Verify your result by graphing both the original and the resulting equation on the same set of axes.

14. $\dfrac{\csc^2 x}{\csc x - 1}$

15. $\dfrac{1 + \tan x}{1 + \cot x}$

16. $\dfrac{\sec x}{\sin x} - \dfrac{\sin x}{\cos x}$

17. $(\cot x + 1)^2 - 2 \cot x$

Find the exact value of each by choosing values for $\angle A$ and $\angle B$ and applying the appropriate sum or the appropriate difference identity

18. $\cos 105°$

19. $\tan \dfrac{7\pi}{12}$

20. $\sin (-15°)$

21. $\cos 165°$

Determine whether each equation is true, giving reasons for your conclusion.

22. $\sin 100° = 2 \sin 100° \cos 100°$

23. $\cos \dfrac{\pi}{5} = \cos^2 \dfrac{\pi}{10} + \sin^2 \dfrac{\pi}{10}$

24. $\cos \dfrac{\pi}{7} = 1 - 2\sin^2 \dfrac{\pi}{14}$

25. $\tan 80° = \dfrac{2 \tan 40°}{1 - \tan^2 40°}$

26. $\cos 28° = 1 - 2 \cos^2 14°$

27. Use the sum identity to prove the double-angle identity for the same trigonometric function.
a) sine   **b)** cosine   **c)** tangent

Using the Strategies

1. Tic-tac-toe Imagine that you are playing a game of tic-tac-toe. What is the greatest number of squares that can be left empty when the game is won?

2. Measurement ABCDE is a right square-based pyramid, with AB = 12 cm and EC = 10 cm. What is the angle of inclination of each triangular face from the base?

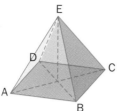

3. Walking Mich and Cheryl are 100 km apart. They set out at the same time walking directly towards each other. Mich ambles along at a constant speed of 6 km/h. Cheryl walks at a speed of 5 km/h for the first hour, 5.5 km/h for the second hour, 6 km/h for the third hour, and so on. To the nearest minute, for how many hours and minutes will they each walk before they meet?

4. Each side of the square measures *a* units, and the radii of the circles are all the same. Find an expression for the shaded area.

5. Lockers At an outdoor pool there are 25 lockers. Suppose all the lockers are open. A child closes every second locker. Then, a second child changes the state of every third locker, that is, she closes the locker if it is open but opens it if it is closed. A third child then changes the state of every fourth locker. Suppose this process continues until the 24th child changes the state of the 25th locker. Which lockers are open?

6. Take-out food At a take-out restaurant, chicken bits are sold in boxes of 6, 9, or 20. By ordering two boxes of 6, you can obtain 12 chicken bits, but it is impossible to order 13. What is the greatest number of chicken bits that it is impossible to order?

7. Each letter represents a different digit. What sum is shown?

$$\begin{array}{r} \text{H A L F} \\ + \ \text{H A L F} \\ \hline \text{W H O L E} \end{array}$$

8. Which two consecutive natural numbers have squares that differ by 75?

9. Find the measure of *x*.

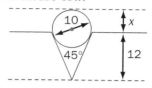

10. The square of an integer is a four-digit number whose digits are all even numbers. Find the greatest such number.

11. Gear wheels Two gear wheels each have 12 teeth and the same diameter. The lower wheel is fixed. The upper wheel turns around the lower one in a clockwise direction. How many times does the upper wheel turn on its own axis in making one complete revolution of the lower wheel?

12. Grazing area A fence in the shape of an equilateral triangle encloses a section of meadow that has an area of 50 m². A goat is tethered to a post in one corner. How long should the tether rope be, to allow the goat to graze half the grass in the enclosure?

13. Geometry The lines through PQ and RS are parallel and ∠PRQ = 90°. If PR = QR and PQ = PS, what is the measure of *x*?

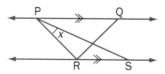

14. What is the value of $\sqrt{11+\sqrt{72}} + \sqrt{11-\sqrt{72}}$?

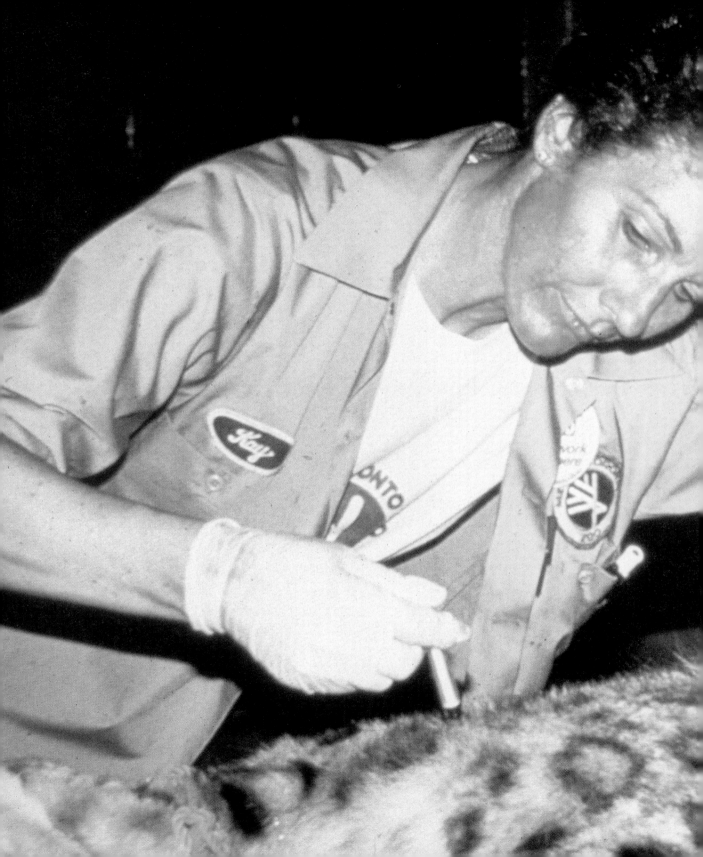

Sequences and Series

A veterinarian prescribes a drug to treat an animal's infection. The dose is 400 mg to be taken three times a day. The animal's body eliminates 50% of the drug out of its system every eight hours. The drug must be present in the body at a level of at least 350 mg to be totally effective against the infection.

Number of Pills Taken	1	2	3	4	5	6
Level of Drug in Blood	400 mg	600 mg	700 mg	750 mg	775 mg	788 mg
Number of Hours Passed	0	8	16	24	32	40 h

1. How long after the first pill will the drug reach a consistently effective level?

2. The drug must be maintained at its effective level for seven days. What is the minimum number of pills the doctor would prescribe?

3. Given this prescription, what is the maximum level the drug could ever reach in the animal's body?

4. The veterinarian recommends that the animal be given two pills right away, and then one pill each eight hours after that. Why?

GETTING STARTED

1 Recognizing Patterns

1 Find the pattern and list the missing elements.

a) toonie, loonie, quarter, ■, ■, ■

b) ■, Edmonton, Fredericton, Halifax, ■, Quebec City, Regina, ■, Toronto, Victoria, Whitehorse, ■, Yellowknife

c) ADH, BEI, ■, DGK, ■, ■, GJN

d) 2, 8, 32, ■, 512, ■

e) −3, 2, 7, ■, 17, 22, ■

f) 3, 5, 7, 11, 13, 17, ■, 23, ■, 31

g) Northwest Territories, ■, British Columbia, Saskatchewan, ■, Nova Scotia, ■, Alberta, Ontario, Nunavut, ■, ■.

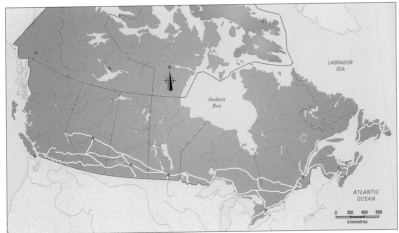

2 Fractals

1. Complete the following steps to draw a fractal.

Step 1: Draw a long vertical line segment to represent 1 unit length.

Step 2: At each end of the line segment, draw a horizontal line of $\frac{1}{2}$ unit length attached at the midpoint.

Step 3: At each end of these two line segments, draw vertical line segments of $\frac{1}{4}$ unit length attached at the midpoints. Continue the pattern.

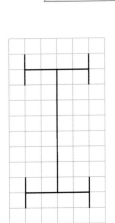

2. Copy and complete the table.

Number of Steps	Total Length of All Line Segments
1	1
2	$1 + \frac{1}{2} + \frac{1}{2} = 2$
3	$1 + \frac{1}{2} + \frac{1}{2} + \frac{1}{4} + \frac{1}{4} + \frac{1}{4} + \frac{1}{4} = ?$
4	
...	...

3. What is the total length of this fractal?

4. Complete the following steps to draw a different fractal.

Step 1: Draw a vertical line segment of 1 unit length.

Step 2: At each end of this line segment, draw a horizontal line segment of $\frac{1}{4}$ unit length attached at the midpoint.

Step 3: At each end of these horizontal line segments, draw vertical line segments of $\frac{1}{16}$ unit length attached at the midpoints.

Step 4: At each end of all of these vertical line segments, draw horizontal line segments of $\frac{1}{64}$ unit length attached at the midpoints. Continue the pattern.

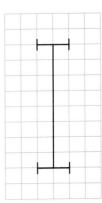

5. Copy and complete the table.

Number of Steps	Total Length of All Line Segments
1	1
2	$1 + \frac{1}{4} + \frac{1}{4} = 1\frac{1}{2}$
3	
4	
...	

6. What is the total length of this fractal?

Warm Up

Evaluate each expression.

1. $\dfrac{1-\left(\dfrac{1}{2}\right)^2}{1-\dfrac{1}{2}}$

2. $\dfrac{1-\left(\dfrac{1}{3}\right)^2}{1-\dfrac{1}{3}}$

3. $\dfrac{1-\left(\dfrac{1}{2}\right)^4}{1-\dfrac{1}{2}}$

4. $\dfrac{1-\left(\dfrac{1}{3}\right)^4}{1-\dfrac{1}{3}}$

Solve for n.

5. $16 = 4(2^{n-1})$

6. $9(3^{n-1}) = 81$

7. $4\left(\dfrac{1}{2}\right)^{n-1} = \dfrac{1}{256}$

8. $0.01 = 10(0.1)^{n-1}$

9. $\dfrac{1}{121} = 11\left(\dfrac{1}{11}\right)^{n-1}$

10. $2(3^{n-1}) = 54$

Solve each system of equations.

11. $16 = a + 3d$
$31 = a + 8d$

12. $37 = a + 5d$
$63 = a + 9d$

13. $18 = a + 5d$
$33 = a + 13d$

14. $91 = a + 4d$
$79 = a + 8d$

Solve each system of equations.

15. $18 = ar^3$
$162 = ar^5$

16. $8 = ar^3$
$64 = ar^6$

17. $100 = ar^2$
$0.01 = ar^6$

18. $135 = ar^3$
$1215 = ar^5$

By guessing and testing, find the value of the variable.

19. $5^x = 3125$

20. $3^x = 729$

21. $y^3 = 3.375$

22. $y^5 = 1024$

By guessing and testing, find the approximate value of the variable, to two significant digits.

23. $5^x = 11.18$

24. $2^x = 2.83$

25. $10^x = 630.96$

26. $y^{1.5} = 22.63$

Write each of the following in the form k log 8.

27. $\log 64$

28. $\log (16\sqrt{2})$

29. $\log 0.015625$

30. $\log 1$

Use logarithms to solve each equation, to three decimal places.

31. $1.78^x = 3.2$

32. $\pi^x = 17$

33. $y^{5.6} = 4$

34. $y^{\sqrt{2}} = 9$

Mental Math

Estimate the value of each power.

1. 39^2 **2.** 2.49^2 **3.** 51^2 **4.** 2.02^3
5. 103^2 **6.** 98.4^3 **7.** 0.21^4 **8.** 0.89^3

Estimate the value of each expression.

9. $79^2 \div 1.9^3$ **10.** $99 \times 23 \div 12$
11. $111 \times 23 \div 7^2$ **12.** $245 \div 5^2 \times 31$
13. $802 \div 9^2 \times 59$ **14.** $634 \div 8^2 \times 9^2$

Estimate each amount.

15. 9% of $212.99   **16.** 18% of $999.09
17. 69% of $23.44   **18.** 7% of $199.99
19. 8% of 109.99   **20.** 15% of $4.99

Give the value of each power.

21. 2^3 **22.** 3^4 **23.** 5^4 **24.** 6^3
25. 4^5 **26.** 2^5 **27.** 0.5^3 **28.** 2.5^2

Use a pattern to find the value of each expression.

29. $1 + 2 + 3 + 4 + \dots + 10$
30. $2 + 4 + 6 + 8 + \dots + 20$
31. $3 + 5 + 7 + 9 + \dots + 21$
32. $-1 - 2 - 3 - 4 - \dots - 10$
33. $-10 - 9 - 8 - \dots - 0 + 1 + 2 + \dots + 10$
34. $9 + 15 + 21 + 27 + \dots + 63$
35. $1 + \dfrac{1}{2} + \dfrac{1}{4} + \dfrac{1}{8} + \dots + \dfrac{1}{512}$

What is the value of each amount?

36. 75 increased by 10%
37. 120 decreased by 2%
38. 1 decreased by 0.1%
39. $500 increased by 11%
40. 64 decreased by 75%
41. k decreased by 1%

What is the value of each factorial?

42. 1!   **43.** 2!   **44.** 3!   **45.** 4!
46. 5!   **47.** 6!   **48.** 0!   **49.** $\dfrac{26!}{24!}$

What are the next two terms in each sequence?

50. 1, 2, 4, 7, 11, 16, ...
51. 1, 21, 213, 4321, 43 215, ...
52. 1, $\dfrac{1}{8}$, $\dfrac{1}{27}$, $\dfrac{1}{64}$, ...
53. 1, 2, 6, 24, 120, ...

6.1 Sequences

Logging is a multi-million dollar industry in Canada. Of all the provinces, British Columbia generates the most revenue from logging, followed by Quebec, and then Ontario. Calculations of quantities of lumber are often based on sequences, that is, on recognizing and using patterns in ordered lists of numbers.

Explore: Use a Pattern

Logs are often stacked in such a way that their ends form a triangular shape.

Use pencils to simulate triangular piles of logs. Find the total number of logs in the pile as the number of logs across the base increases. Copy and complete the table for 3, 4, 5, 6, and 7 logs across the base of the pile.

Number of Logs Across the Base	Total Number of Logs in the Pile
1	1
2	3
3	
4	
5	
6	
7	

Inquire

1. Do the numbers in the second column of the table follow a pattern? How would you describe the pattern?

2. Using the pattern, calculate how many logs are in a pile with 10 logs across the base.

3. A pile of logs with n logs in its base has t_n logs in the pile, and a pile of logs with $n-1$ logs in its base, has t_{n-1} logs in the pile. What is the relationship between t_n and t_{n-1}?

A **sequence** is an ordered list of numbers usually written separated by commas. For example, 5, 7, 10, 14, 19, …

When talking about sequences, we refer to the first term as t_1, the second term as t_2, the third term as t_3, and the nth term as t_n. In this example, $t_1 = 5$, $t_2 = 7$, and $t_3 = 10$.

A formula that relates each term of a sequence to the term before it is called a **recursive formula**. In the example 5, 7, 10, 14, 19, …, the terms of the sequence can be defined by the recursive formula $t_n = t_{n-1} + n$, where $t_1 = 5$. Here, $t_2 = t_1 + 2$, $t_3 = t_2 + 3$, and $t_4 = t_3 + 4$.

Example 1   Finding a Recursive Formula to Generate a Sequence

One way of arranging oranges for display is to stack them in square-based pyramids. Find a recursive formula that describes the sequence of the total number of oranges in square-based pyramids of increasing size.

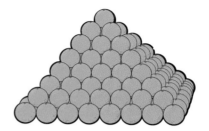

Solution

To observe a pattern, visualize or model stacks of increasing sizes.

Number of Layers in Pyramid	Number of Oranges in Base Layer	Total Number of Oranges in Stack
1	1	1
2	4	$1 + 4 = 5$
3	9	$5 + 9 = 14$
...	...	...
n	n^2	$t_{n-1} + n^2$

Examination of the first few terms in the third column reveals that each term is equal to the square of the number of layers in the pyramid, plus the previous term in the third column. The recursive formula for the sequence is $t_n = t_{n-1} + n^2$, where $t_1 = 1$.

Example 2   Two Different Types of Recursive Formulas

The recursive formula for a sequence is $t_n = t_{n-1} + \dfrac{3}{2}$, where $t_1 = 1$. Write the first seven terms of this sequence. The recursive formula for another sequence is $t_n = \dfrac{3}{2}t_{n-1}$, where $t_1 = 1$. Write the first seven terms of this sequence. Use a graphing calculator to create a table of values for the terms of each sequence and plot the terms of each sequence. Compare and contrast the two sequences. Which sequence grows faster?

Solution

Use the recursive formula $t_n = t_{n-1} + \dfrac{3}{2}$ to find the terms of the first sequence.

$t_1 = 1$

$t_2 = t_1 + \dfrac{3}{2} = 1 + \dfrac{3}{2} = \dfrac{5}{2}$

$t_3 = t_2 + \dfrac{3}{2} = \dfrac{5}{2} + \dfrac{3}{2} = 4$

$t_4 = t_3 + \dfrac{3}{2} = 4 + \dfrac{3}{2} = \dfrac{11}{2}$

$t_5 = t_4 + \dfrac{3}{2} = \dfrac{11}{2} + \dfrac{3}{2} = 7$

$t_6 = t_5 + \dfrac{3}{2} = 7 + \dfrac{3}{2} = \dfrac{17}{2}$

$t_7 = t_6 + \dfrac{3}{2} = \dfrac{17}{2} + \dfrac{3}{2} = 10$

The first seven terms of the first sequence are $1, \dfrac{5}{2}, 4, \dfrac{11}{2}, 7, \dfrac{17}{2}, 10$.

Use the recursive formula $t_n = \frac{3}{2} t_{n-1}$ to find the terms of the second sequence.

$$t_1 = 1$$
$$t_2 = \frac{3}{2} t_1 = \frac{3}{2} \times 1 = \frac{3}{2}$$
$$t_3 = \frac{3}{2} t_2 = \frac{3}{2} \times \frac{3}{2} = \frac{9}{4}$$
$$t_4 = \frac{3}{2} t_3 = \frac{3}{2} \times \frac{9}{4} = \frac{27}{8}$$
$$t_5 = \frac{3}{2} t_4 = \frac{3}{2} \times \frac{27}{8} = \frac{81}{16}$$
$$t_6 = \frac{3}{2} t_5 = \frac{3}{2} \times \frac{81}{16} = \frac{243}{32}$$
$$t_7 = \frac{3}{2} t_6 = \frac{3}{2} \times \frac{243}{32} = \frac{729}{64}$$

The first seven terms of the sequence are $1, \frac{3}{2}, \frac{9}{4}, \frac{27}{8}, \frac{81}{16}, \frac{243}{32}, \frac{729}{64}$.

 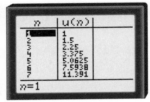 

Each term of the first sequence is three halves plus the previous term. In contrast, each term in the second sequence is three halves times the previous term. The terms of the second sequence grow faster than the terms of the first sequence.

Some sequences have a pattern that can be described mathematically by the number of the term. A formula for the nth term of a sequence as an expression of n is called an **explicit formula**. For example, the sequence 0, 7, 26, 63, 124, 215, ... can be defined by the explicit formula $t_n = n^3 - 1$, starting with $n = 1$.
So $t_1 = 1^3 - 1 = 0$,
$\quad t_2 = 2^3 - 1 = 7$,
$\quad t_3 = 3^3 - 1 = 26$
$\quad ...$

Example 3 Finding an Explicit Formula to Generate a Sequence

Logging trucks often have vertical supports so that the pile of logs when viewed from the back of truck is in the shape of a square. Find an explicit formula that describes the sequence of the total number of logs in a square pile as the number of logs across the base of the pile increases.

Solution

Examine the pattern for square piles of logs.

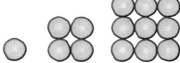

Number of Logs Across the Base	Total Number of Logs in the Pile
1	1
2	4
3	9
4	16

The pattern reveals the explicit formula to be $t_n = n^2$, where n represents the number of logs across the base of the square pile.

Some sequences can be expressed by both a recursive formula and an explicit formula. For example, the sequence 2, 4, 6, 8, 10, … could be described by the recursive formula $t_n = t_{n-1} + 2$, where $t_1 = 2$, or by the explicit formula $t_n = 2n$.

Example 4   Finding the Pattern

Find the next two terms in each sequence. Write a formula for the nth term. Is the formula recursive or explicit?

a) 3, 6, 11, 18, 27, …   **b)** 1, 8, 27, 64, 125, …

Solution

a) *Method 1*
Each term of the sequence is generated from the previous one by adding consecutive odd integers.
$$t_1 = 3$$
$$t_2 = 3 + 3 = 6$$
$$t_3 = 6 + 5 = 11$$
$$t_4 = 11 + 7 = 18$$
$$t_5 = 18 + 9 = 27$$

So, $t_6 = 27 + 11 = 38$ and $t_7 = 38 + 13 = 51$.
The next two terms in the sequence are 38 and 51. The nth term is given by the recursive formula $t_n = t_{n-1} + (2n - 1)$, where $t_1 = 3$.

Method 2
Another way of looking at this sequence is:
$$t_1 = 3 = 1^2 + 2$$
$$t_2 = 6 = 2^2 + 2$$
$$t_3 = 11 = 3^2 + 2$$
$$t_4 = 18 = 4^2 + 2$$
$$t_5 = 27 = 5^2 + 2$$

So, $t_6 = 6^2 + 2 = 38$ and $t_7 = 7^2 + 2 = 51$
The next two terms in the sequence are 38 and 51. The nth term is given by the explicit formula $t_n = n^2 + 2$.

b) *Method 1*
By observation, the terms exhibit the following pattern:
$$t_1 = 1 = 1^3$$
$$t_2 = 8 = 2^3$$
$$t_3 = 27 = 3^3$$
$$t_4 = 64 = 4^3$$
$$t_5 = 125 = 5^3$$

So, $t_6 = 6^3 = 216$ and $t_7 = 7^3 = 343$
The next two terms in the sequence are 216 and 343, and the nth term is given by the explicit formula $t_n = n^3$.

Method 2
There is also a recursive formula for this sequence, but it is more difficult to observe the pattern. It is
$t_n = t_{n-1} + 3n(n-1) + 1$, where $t_1 = 1$.

Practice

Given each recursive formula,
a) *list the first five terms of the sequence*
b) *use a graphing calculator to create a table of values for the sequence and plot it*

1. $t_n = t_{n-1} + 1$, where $t_1 = 1$
2. $t_n = (t_{n-1})^2$, where $t_1 = 2$
3. $t_n = 3t_{n-1} + n$, where $t_1 = 5$
4. $t_n = \dfrac{1}{t_{n-1}}$, where $t_1 = 10$
5. $t_n = t_{n-1} + 3n$, where $t_1 = 4$
6. $t_n = 0.5t_{n-1} + 5$, where $t_1 = -8$

Find the next two terms in each sequence. Then, find a recursive formula for each sequence.

7. 1, 4, 16, 64, …
8. 3, −9, 27, −81, …
9. 100, 10, 1, 0.1, …
10. −1000, 500, −250, 125, …
11. 1, 4, 13, 40, 121, …
12. 256, 64, 16, 4, …

Given each explicit formula,
a) *list the first five terms of the sequence*
b) *use a graphing calculator to create a table of values for the sequence and plot it*

13. $t_n = 2n + 1$
14. $t_n = 2^n - 1$
15. $t_n = (n + 1)^2$
16. $t_n = |n - 4|$
17. $t_n = (1 - n)^2$
18. $t_n = n^3 - 3$

Find the next two terms in each sequence. Then, find an explicit formula for each sequence.

19. 1, 4, 7, 10, …
20. 0.3, 0.09, 0.027, 0.0081, …
21. 2, −4, 8, −16, …
22. 10 000, 1000, 100, 10, …
23. 45, 40, 35, 30, …
24. 2, 8, 32, 128, …

Applications and Problem Solving

25. Different sized cubes can be made by putting unit cubes together.

a) Find a defining statement that describes the sequence of the volumes of the cubes as the side length increases. Use your formula to find the ninth term in the sequence.
b) Determine the defining statement for the sequence of the surface area of the cubes. Use the formula to find the surface area of a cube of side length 6 units.

26. Fibonacci Leonardo of Pisa (1175–1250), also known as Fibonacci, was one of the most skilled European mathematicians of the Middle Ages. In 1202, he published his famous work *Liber abaci*. In this book, he studies the sequence 1, 1, 2, 3, 5, 8, 13, ….
a) Determine the recursive formula for this sequence. Extend the sequence to 10 terms.
b) Fibonacci arrived at his famous sequence by studying the reproductive nature of rabbits. Suppose that it takes two months for a rabbit to mature. Once mature, a pair of rabbits reproduce to give another pair of rabbits every month. Use a diagram to illustrate the lives of a newly born pair of rabbits and their offspring for seven months. Identify how the Fibonacci sequence arises out of this model. Describe any assumptions that you make.

27. Pascal In 1654, the French mathematician Blaise Pascal (1623–1662) suggested a solution to a mathematical problem known as the "Problem of Points." Pascal's solution was based upon a triangular sequence of numbers, now known as Pascal's triangle. The first five rows of Pascal's triangle are shown.

row 1					1				
row 2				1		1			
row 3			1		2		1		
row 4		1		3		3		1	
row 5	1		4		6		4		1

a) Identify the pattern in Pascal's triangle and use it to write the next two rows.
b) The notation $t_{i,j}$ represents the term in the ith row and the jth position, for example, $t_{4,2} = 3$ and $t_{5,4} = 4$. Use the notation $t_{i,j}$ to write the recursive formula used to build Pascal's triangle.

28. Does every sequence have a formula for its terms? Describe a way to make a sequence for which there will not be any formula for the terms.

29. Geometry Find the sequence of the number of diagonals in a convex polygon as the number of sides in the polygon increases. Record your results in a table.

Polygon	Number of Sides	Number of Diagonals
Triangle	3	0
Quadrilateral	4	2
Pentagon	5	
Hexagon		
Heptagon		
...		

a) Determine an explicit formula for the number of diagonals in an n-sided polygon.
b) Use your formula to find the number of diagonals of a one-dollar coin.

30. Tower of Hanoi In 1883, Edouard Lucas, a French mathematician, invented a puzzle called the Tower of Hanoi. The puzzle has three pegs and a pile of disks of increasing diameters. The object of the puzzle is to move the pile of disks from one peg to another peg in the least number of moves. Only one disk may be moved at a time, and a larger disk cannot be placed on top of a smaller disk.

a) Simulate the puzzle using a dime, a nickel, a quarter, a one-dollar coin, and a two-dollar coin for the first five disks in order of increasing size. Then, solve the puzzle for different numbers of disks and tabulate your results.

Number of Disks	Number of Moves
1	1
2	
3	
4	
5	

b) Study the sequence of the number of moves and determine a recursive formula that describes it. Use your formula to find the number of moves necessary to move 10 disks.
c) Determine an explicit formula that relates the number of moves, t_n, to the number of disks, n.
d) The original puzzle was to determine the number of moves necessary to move 64 disks. If you could move 1 disk every second, how long would it take to complete this task, assuming that you work 24 hours each day, 365 days of the year?

31. Two different sequences may have the same first few terms.
a) Write the first three terms of the sequence $t_n = 2t_{n-1}$, where $t_1 = 1$, and the first three terms of the sequence $t_n = \dfrac{n^2}{2} - \dfrac{n}{2} + 1$. Are they different sequences? Now, write out the first five terms of each sequence. Are they different sequences?
b) Find formulas for two different sequences that have 1, 3, 5, ... as the first three terms. Write out the first six terms of each of your sequences to confirm that they are different.
c) What do you think determines a sequence?

LOGIC POWER

The figure has eight congruent triangles made up of 16 toothpicks. Remove four toothpicks to leave just four similar triangles.

6.2 Reviewing Arithmetic Sequences and Series

Althea Shaw had the winning female time in the first Canadian Rocky Mountain Marathon on September 15, 1996. Althea ran the 42-km distance in 3 h 5 min 28 s. The marathon is now an annual event, starting at Canmore, Alberta, and run in somewhat challenging, but very beautiful, mountain conditions.

Explore: Use a Pattern

Melanie has decided to enter the marathon race. She has 17 training weeks. The first week, each of her five training runs is 9 km. Each successive week her five runs are each 3 km longer than the previous week. Write a seven-term sequence to show the distance of a daily run, for the first seven weeks.

Inquire

1. Describe how each term in the sequence of running distances is determined from the previous one. Write a recursive formula for t_n in this sequence.

2. An **arithmetic sequence** is a sequence that has a constant common difference d between successive terms. Is the sequence of running distances an arithmetic sequence? Write an explicit formula for the distance run on the nth day.

3. If Melanie continued her pattern, by which week would she be running the marathon distance, 42 km?

4. What information does the sum of the first ten terms in the sequence give you?

For an **arithmetic sequence**, if the first term t_1 is a and the common difference is d, then
$$t_2 = t_1 + d = a + d$$
$$t_3 = t_2 + d = a + 2d$$
$$t_4 = t_3 + d = a + 3d$$
$$\ldots$$
$$t_n = a + (n-1)d$$

Example 1   Working with Arithmetic Sequences

In an arithmetic sequence, $t_{12} = 52$ and $t_{22} = 102$. Find the first three terms of the sequence and an explicit formula for t_n. Plot the first ten terms of the sequence on your graphing calculator. Graphically, what is the relationship between the terms?

Solution

Method 1

Given $t_{22} = 102$ $102 = a + 21d$ (1)
and $t_{12} = 52$: $\underline{52 = a + 11d}$ (2)
Subtract: $50 = 10d$
                                         $d = 5$

Method 2

$t_{22} = t_{12} + 10d$
$102 = 52 + 10d$
$50 = 10d$
$d = 5$

Substitute $d = 5$ in (2)
$$52 = a + 55$$
$$a = -3$$
The first three terms of the sequence are $-3, 2, 7$.

$$t_n = -3 + (n - 1)5$$
$$= -3 + 5n - 5$$
$$= 5n - 8$$

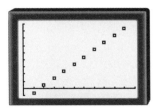

Since all of the terms lie on a straight line, there is a linear relationship between the terms.

When the mathematician Carl Friedrich Gauss (1777–1855) was nine years old, his teacher assigned the class the problem of summing the integers from 1 to 100. Gauss gave the answer quickly using following strategy.

$$
\begin{aligned}
2(1 + 2 + 3 + 4 + 5 + \ldots + 100) = \quad & 1 + \ 2 + \ 3 + \ldots + 98 + 99 + 100 \\
& + 100 + 99 + 98 + \ldots + \ 3 + \ 2 + \ 1 \\
= \ & 100(101) \\
= \ & 10\ 100
\end{aligned}
$$

So, $1 + 2 + 3 + 4 + \ldots + 100 = 5050$.

A formula for finding the sum of the first n terms of an arithmetic sequence can be found by adapting Gauss' method.
$$S_n = t_1 + t_2 + t_3 + \ldots + t_n$$
First, list the sum of the terms of the sequence.
$$S_n = a + (a + d) + (a + 2d) + \ldots + [a + (n - 2)d] + [a + (n - 1)d]$$
Then, list the sum of the terms of the sequence in reverse order.
$$S_n = t_n + (t_n - d) + (t_n - 2d) + \ldots + [t_n - (n - 2)d] + [t_n - (n - 1)d]$$
Add vertically:
$$2S_n = (a + t_n) + (a + t_n) + (a + t_n) + \ldots + (a + t_n) + (a + t_n)$$
$$= n(a + t_n) \qquad \text{There are } n \text{ terms in the sequence.}$$
$$\therefore \ S_n = \frac{n}{2}(a + t_n)$$
Then, substituting $t_n = a + (n - 1)d$,
$$S_n = \frac{n}{2}[a + a + (n - 1)d]$$
$$= \frac{n}{2}[2a + (n - 1)d]$$

Example 2   Using the Sum of an Arithmetic Sequence

A theatre has 24 rows of seats. The front row has 5 seats on each side of the centre aisle. Each successive row has one more seat on each side. How many seats are there altogether?

Solution

The front row has 10 seats, the second row has 12 seats, the third row has 14 seats, and so on. The numbers of seats in the rows form the arithmetic sequence
$10, 12, 14, 16, \ldots$.

So, the total number of seats is the sum of the first 24 terms of the sequence $10 + 12 + 14 + \ldots$.

In $S_n = \dfrac{n}{2}[2a + (n-1)d]$, substitute $n = 24$, $a = 10$, $d = 2$

$$S_{24} = 12[20 + 23(2)]$$
$$= 792$$

The theatre has 792 seats altogether.

A **series** is the sum of the terms of a sequence. If t_n is a sequence, then the sum of the first n terms of the sequence is the series S_n.

So, $S_1 = t_1$

$$S_2 = t_1 + t_2,$$
$$S_3 = t_1 + t_2 + t_3,$$
$$\ldots$$
$$S_n = t_1 + t_2 + t_3 + \ldots + t_n$$

S_n is called the nth partial sum and can be thought of as forming a sequence with the recursive formula $S_n = S_{n-1} + t_n$.

The Greek letter Σ (sigma) corresponds to the English letter S and stands for "sum." **Sigma notation** is often used to abbreviate the writing of a series. For example, the series formed from summing the first five terms of the sequence defined by $t_k = 2k$ is written:

$$\sum_{k=1}^{5} 2k \ .$$

Substituting the values of k from $k = 1$ to $k = 5$ gives the expanded form of the series.

$$\sum_{k=1}^{5} 2k = 2(1) + 2(2) + 2(3) + 2(4) + 2(5)$$
$$= 2 + 4 + 6 + 8 + 10$$

The variable k is called the **index of summation**. The number below the Σ is the **lower limit of summation** and the number above the Σ is the **upper limit of summation**. The number of terms summed equals the upper limit minus the lower limit plus one. For example,

$$\sum_{n=3}^{7} (n^2 + 1) = (3^2 + 1) + (4^2 + 1) + (5^2 + 1) + (6^2 + 1) + (7^2 + 1)$$
$$= 10 + 17 + 26 + 37 + 50$$

Example 3   Working With Sigma Notation

Write each series in expanded form and then find the sum.

a) $\displaystyle\sum_{k=1}^{6} (3k - 2)$ **b)** $\displaystyle\sum_{k=3}^{9} (-k + 5)$

Solution 1 Solving Algebraically

a) $\displaystyle\sum_{k=1}^{6} (3k - 2) = [3(1) - 2] + [3(2) - 2] + [3(3) - 2] + [3(4) - 2] + [3(5) - 2] + [3(6) - 2]$
$$= 1 + 4 + 7 + 10 + 13 + 16$$

In $S_n = \dfrac{n}{2}[2a + (n-1)d]$, substitute $a = 1$, $n = 6$, $d = 3$ for the first sequence.

$$S_n = 3[2 + 5(3)]$$
$$= 51$$

b) $\displaystyle\sum_{k=3}^{9}(-k+5) = (-3 + 5) + (-4 + 5) + (-5 + 5) + (-6 + 5) + (-7 + 5) + (-8 + 5) + (-9 + 5)$
$$= 2 + 1 + 0 - 1 - 2 - 3 - 4$$

In $S_n = \dfrac{n}{2}[2a + (n-1)d]$, substitute $a = 2$, $n = 7$, $d = -1$.

$$S_n = \dfrac{7}{2}[4 + 6(-1)]$$
$$= -7$$

Solution 2 Using a Graphing Calculator

a) Use $t_k = 3k - 2$ to find the terms of the sequence between $k = 1$ and $k = 6$. Then, use the sum sequence feature.

$\therefore \displaystyle\sum_{k=1}^{6}(3k - 2) = 1 + 4 + 7 + 10 + 13 + 16$
$$= 51$$

b) Use $t_k = -k + 5$ to find the terms of the sequence between $k = 3$ and $k = 9$. Then, use the sum sequence feature.

$\therefore \displaystyle\sum_{k=3}^{9}(-k + 5) = 2 + 1 + 0 - 1 - 2 - 3 - 4$
$$= -7$$

Practice

Determine whether each sequence is arithmetic. For those that are, state the values of a and d. Find an explicit formula for the sequences in questions 1, 2, and 3, and use this formula to plot the terms of the sequence on a graphing calculator. Do the terms lie on a straight line?

1. $2, 5, 8, 11, 14, \ldots$ **2.** $20, 16, 12, 8, \ldots$
3. $2, 4, 8, 16, 32, \ldots$ **4.** $1, 1.6, 2.2, 2.8, \ldots$

5. $-2, -5, -8, -11, \ldots$ **6.** $2, 2\dfrac{1}{2}, 2\dfrac{3}{4}, 3\dfrac{1}{4}, \ldots$

7. $x, x + y, x + 2y, x + 3y, \ldots$
8. $x, x^2, x^3, x^4, \ldots$

Use the two given terms to find a, d, and t_n for each arithmetic sequence.

9. $t_5 = 16, t_8 = 25$ **10.** $t_{50} = 140, t_{70} = 180$
11. $t_2 = -12, t_5 = 9$ **12.** $t_7 = 37, t_{10} = 22$
13. $t_{13} = -177, t_{22} = -207$
14. $t_7 = 3 + 5x, t_{11} = 3 + 23x$

Find the number of terms in each arithmetic sequence. What is the sum of the terms of each sequence?

15. $3, 5, 7, \ldots, 129$
16. $-29, -24, -19, \ldots, 126$
17. $4, 4.5, 5, 5.5, \ldots, 57$
18. $61, 55, 49, \ldots, -119$
19. $p, p + 3, p + 6, \ldots, p + 78$
20. $1 + 2k, 2 + 4k, 3 + 6k, \ldots, 19 + 38k$

Write each series in expanded form. Then, find the sum of the series.

21. $\displaystyle\sum_{k=1}^{8}(k - 6)$ **22.** $\displaystyle\sum_{k=1}^{6}(4k - 1)$

23. $\displaystyle\sum_{k=1}^{5}(16 - 7k)$ **24.** $\displaystyle\sum_{k=1}^{6}(2.5k + 200)$

25. $\displaystyle\sum_{k=10}^{15}(100 - 3k)$ **26.** $\displaystyle\sum_{k=3}^{9}(7.8 - 1.2k)$

Determine the explicit formula for the terms in each series. Then, write the series using sigma notation with the specified lower limit.

27. $2 + 6 + 10 + 14 + 18 + 22$, lower limit 1

28. $5 + 10 + 15 + 20 + 25 + 30 + 35 + 40$, lower limit 1

29. $-2 - 5 - 8 - 11 - 14 - 17 - 20$, lower limit 3

30. $1.5 + 3.5 + 5.5 + 7.5 + 9.5 + 11.5$, lower limit 1

31. $4.4 + 2.4 + 0.4 - 1.6 - 3.6 - 5.6 - 7.6$, lower limit 2

32. $120 + 100 + 80 + 60 + 40 + 20$, lower limit -5

Applications and Problem Solving

33. A sequence is defined by the explicit formula $t_n = 5n + 4$. Show that the sequence is arithmetic. Find the values of a and d.

34. a) Show that the sum of an arithmetic sequence is given by $S_n = \dfrac{n}{2}(a + l)$, where l represents the last term of the sequence.
b) An arithmetic sequence has 16 terms such that $t_1 = 11$ and $t_{16} = 386$. Find the sum of the sequence.

35. Salary increases An apprentice is hired at a starting salary of \$1000 per month. Each subsequent month for the first year her salary is increased by \$150.
a) What was her salary for the last month of the year?
b) How much did she earn for the whole year?

36. Multiples a) How many multiples of 6 are there between 65 and 391?
b) How many multiples of 7 are there from -56 to 560 inclusive?

37. Leap years How many leap years were there in the twentieth century?

38. Odd numbers Determine a formula for the sum of the first n odd numbers.

39. What is the value of x if the three terms x, $\dfrac{x}{2} + 7$, and $3x - 1$ form an arithmetic sequence?

40. If every term of an arithmetic sequence is multiplied by a constant, is the new sequence arithmetic? Explain.

41. Two arithmetic sequences both have 100 as their tenth term. For their third term, one of the sequences has 16 and the other has 44.
a) Determine the explicit formula for each sequence.
b) Graph the first twenty terms of each sequence. Describe the similarities and the differences between the graphs.

42. An arithmetic sequence $t_1, t_2, \ldots, t_n$ has $\displaystyle\sum_{k=1}^{8} t_k = 52$ and $\displaystyle\sum_{k=1}^{16} t_k = -88$. Determine the value of the first term and the common difference, d.

43. Find the three numbers that form an arithmetic sequence such that the sum of the first and the third numbers is 10, and the product of the first and second numbers is $\dfrac{15}{2}$.

44. In an arithmetic sequence, if $t_i = j^2$ and $t_j = i^2$, show that the common difference is $-i - j$.

45. Fertilizer Sacks of fertilizer are stored in piles. The bottom layer has 20 sacks along its length and is 4 sacks wide. Each layer above has one less sack lengthwise than the previous layer but the same width. The top layer has 16 sacks. How many sacks are there altogether in the pile?

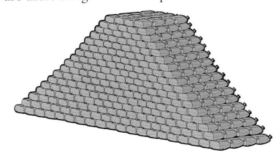

46. The sum of the first three terms of an arithmetic sequence is 15. The sum of their squares is 93. What is the fifth term of the sequence?

47. Solve for k if $\displaystyle\sum_{j=2}^{k} (23 - 2j) = 91$.

48. Find the sum of the first 17 terms of an arithmetic sequence if $t_9 = 24$.

6.3 Geometric Sequences

Japanese samurai swords are made by repeatedly heating, folding, and pounding steel into a multi-layered blade. This process requires great skill and patience on the part of the sword maker. The end result is a sword with unique and desirable characteristics.

Explore: Use Modelling

Repeatedly fold a sheet of paper in half. At each stage, record the number of layers of paper in your folded sheet.

Number of Times Folded	Number of Layers of Paper
0	1
1	2
2	
3	
4	

Inquire

1. What factors affect the number of times you can fold a sheet of paper in half? Test your ideas. Do you think there is a limit to the number of times that you can actually fold *any* sheet of paper? Explain.

2. Consider the number of layers as a sequence. Write an expression for the number of layers after the paper has been folded n times. What expression would represent the $(n + 1)$th term in the sequence?

3. Suppose you start with 3 sheets of paper of the same size. After the first fold, you have 6 layers. Write the numbers of layers that you would have after each of the first four foldings as a sequence. What is the nth term of this sequence? What is the relationship between successive terms of the sequence?

4. Consider the area of the original sheet of paper to be one square unit. Then, write the area that the paper covers after each successive folding as a sequence. What is the multiplying factor between successive terms of this sequence? What expression would represent the nth term, t_n, in the sequence?

Sequences whose terms result from multiplying the previous term by a fixed factor are called **geometric sequences**. If t_n is a geometric sequence with $t_1 = a$, and a common ratio between successive terms, r, then
$t_2 = t_1 r = ar$
$t_3 = t_2 r = ar^2$
and so on.
Each term has the form $t_n = ar^{n-1}$.

Example 1   Representing a Geometric Sequence

Use the geometric sequence 5, 10, 20, 40, 80, ...
a) Write the defining statement of the sequence in the form $t_n = ar^{n-1}$.
b) Determine the value of t_8.
c) Plot the graph of the first ten terms. What is the shape of the curve?

Solution
a) Since $t_1 = 5$, then $a = 5$.
Find the ratio of successive terms.

$$\frac{10}{5} = 2 \qquad \frac{20}{10} = 2 \qquad \frac{40}{20} = 2 \qquad \frac{80}{40} = 2$$

$\therefore r = 2$
So, $t_n = 5(2)^{n-1}$

b) In $t_n = 5(2)^{n-1}$, substitute $n = 8$.

$t_8 = 5(2)^7$
$\quad = 640$

The value of t_8 is 640.

c)

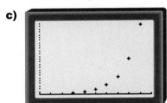

The curve increases exponentially.

Example 2   Using a Geometric Sequence

After each washing, 1% of the dye in blue jeans is washed out.
How much of the original dye remains after 10 washings?

Solution
Let the original amount of dye in the new blue jeans be 1 unit.
After 1 washing,
since 1% of the dye is washed out, there will be 1(0.99) units of dye left.
After 2 washings,
there will be $1(0.99)(0.99) = 1(0.99)^2$ units of dye left.
The amounts of dye left after successive washings form the geometric sequence:
$1, 1(0.99), 1(0.99)^2, 1(0.99)^3, ...$
In the geometric sequence, $a = 1, r = 0.99$

$t_n = ar^{n-1}$
$\quad = 1(0.99)^{n-1}$

Since $n = 1$ corresponds to the jeans in their original state, after 10 washings $n = 11$.

$t_{11} = 1(0.99)^{10}$
$\quad = 0.904\ 382$

After 10 washings, approximately 90% of the dye remains.

Example 3   Geometric Modelling

Population projections are an important aspect of governmental planning. In 1990 the population of Canada was 26.6 million. The population in 2025 is projected to be 38.4 million. If this projection were based on a geometric sequence, what would be the annual growth rate?

Solution

For the geometric sequence, $t_1 = a = 26.6$ million.
Find the term associated with the year 2025.
$2025 - 1990 = 35$
The population in 2025 is the 36th term; $t_{36} = 38.4$ million.

Method 1

$t_n = ar^{n-1}$

$t_{36} = 26.6r^{35}$

$38.4 = 26.6r^{35}$

$r^{35} = \dfrac{38.4}{26.6}$

$r = \sqrt[35]{\dfrac{38.4}{26.6}}$

$\doteq 1.0105$

Method 2

$\log r^{35} = \log \dfrac{38.4}{26.6}$

$35\log r = \log 38.4 - \log 26.6$

$\log r = \dfrac{\log 38.4 - \log 26.6}{35}$

$\doteq 0.004\,55$

$r \doteq 1.0105$

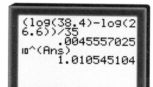

The population growth rate used in the projection was approximately $(101.05 - 100)\%$, or 1.05%.

Example 4   Depreciation

Two years after purchase, the resale value of a car was $10 000. The resale value of the same car three years later was $5000. If the annual depreciation of the car forms a geometric sequence, what was the original price of the car?

Solution

If a represents the original price of the car and r the annual rate of depreciation, then the geometric sequence giving the value of the car each year is
$a, ar, ar^2 = 10\,000, ar^3, ar^4, ar^5 = 5000, \ldots$

So, $ar^2 = 10\,000$ (1)
       $ar^5 = 5000$ (2)
Divide equation (2) by equation (1).

$\dfrac{ar^5}{ar^2} = \dfrac{5000}{10000}$

$r^3 = 0.5$

$r = \sqrt[3]{0.5}$

Substitute $r = \sqrt[3]{0.5}$ into (1) to find a.

$a = \dfrac{10\,000}{(\sqrt[3]{0.5})^2}$

$= 15\,874.01$

The original price of the car was $15 874, to the nearest dollar.

Practice

Extend each geometric sequence to 5 terms. Write a defining statement, in the form $t_n = ar^{n-1}$, for each sequence.

1. $15, 5, \dfrac{5}{3}, \ldots$
2. $0.5, 1, 2, \ldots$
3. $-12, 6, -3, \ldots$
4. $0.11, 0.33, 0.99, \ldots$
5. $100, 25, 6.25, \ldots$
6. $686, 98, 14, \ldots$
7. $4, 16, 64, \ldots$
8. $121, 11, 1, \ldots$
9. $1.28, 0.64, 0.32, \ldots$
10. $-15, 225, -3375, \ldots$

Find the indicated term of each geometric sequence.

11. $8, 16, 32, \ldots$ Find t_6.
12. $7, 35, 175, \ldots$ Find t_{11}.
13. $66, 22, \dfrac{22}{3}, \ldots$ Find t_5.
14. $0.1, 0.5, 2.5, \ldots$ Find t_8.
15. $\dfrac{1}{5}, \dfrac{3}{5}, \dfrac{9}{5}, \ldots$ Find t_9.
16. $-999, -111, -\dfrac{37}{3}, \ldots$ Find t_6.

Use the given two terms of a geometric sequence to find the indicated term.

17. $t_3 = 10, t_6 = 80$ Find t_8.
18. $t_4 = 3, t_8 = 243$ Find t_{11}.
19. $t_2 = -50, t_4 = -2$ Find t_7.
20. $t_5 = 900, t_7 = 0.09$ Find t_3.
21. $t_{13} = 4, t_{16} = 108$ Find t_{10}.
22. $t_3 = 59\,049, t_6 = 81$ Find t_{10}.

Applications and Problem Solving

23. Algebra If each set of four numbers forms a geometric sequence, find the values of x and y.
a) $x, 6, 18, y$ **b)** $6, 18, x, y$
c) $6, x, 18, y$ **d)** $6, x, y, 18$

24. Photography Single lens reflex (SLR) cameras have f-stops that control the aperture of the camera. The aperture allows light onto the film. The f-stops are numbered in a geometric sequence. The third f-stop is 2 and the fifth f-stop is 4. What number is associated with the tenth f-stop?

25. Demographics In 1990 the world population was 5.2953 billion people. It is projected that the world population in 2025 will be 8.4724 billion people.
a) If this projection were based on geometric growth, what would be the annual growth rate of the world population? Use a calculator to make a table of estimates of the world population between 2000 and 2010.
b) Do you think it is reasonable to make population projections based on geometric progressions? What factors do you think affect the population? Look into different ways to model population growth.

26. Music On a piano, the frequencies of the notes in a musical scale form a geometric progression. The note G has a frequency of 392.00 Hz. The next five notes in the progression after G are G#, A, A#, B, and middle C. Middle C has a frequency of 523.25 Hz. Find the frequencies of the four notes between G and middle C.

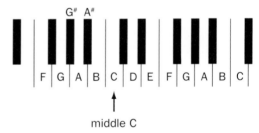

27. Depreciation Revenue Canada allows 30% annual depreciation on computer equipment that is used for business purposes. If a business computer costs $3000 today, what value would Revenue Canada assign the computer four years from now?

28. Rumours Someone starts a rumour by telling two people. Each person who hears the rumour tells it to two more people within five minutes. These people each tell two more people within the next five minutes, and so on. What is the minimum number of people that will have heard the rumour within an hour?

29. Photocopying Many photocopiers have a feature that reduces the image of the original. Usually the maximum reduction capability is 64%. How many reductions, at the maximum setting, would you need to reduce an image to less than 10% of its original size?

30. Geometric means A number m is a geometric mean between terms t_k and t_j if t_k, m, and t_j form a geometric sequence.
a) Find the geometric mean between 256 and 4.
b) Find the five geometric means between 256 and 4.

31. Geometry The first term of a sequence is the length of the hypotenuse of a right triangle with legs each one unit long. The second term is the length of the hypotenuse of the right triangle with legs each h units long.
a) Show that the lengths of the hypotenuses of right triangles constructed by continuing this pattern form a geometric sequence.
b) What is the length of the hypotenuse of the seventh triangle in the pattern?

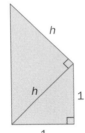

32. Connections How does the graph of the terms of a geometric sequence differ from that of an arithmetic sequence? To what functions do they each seem to be related ? Give reasons for your answer, including specific examples and illustrations. Plot several examples against each other on a graphing calculator.

33. Eureka! In 1614 John Napier recognized an important relationship between arithmetic and geometric sequences, from which he developed the theory of logarithms. Napier noticed that, if n, p, q, r are terms of an arithmetic sequence, then x^n, x^p, x^q, x^r form a geometric sequence.
a) Show that the terms 5, 9, 13, 17, ... form an arithmetic sequence, and that 2^5, 2^9, 2^{13}, 2^{17} are terms of a geometric sequence.
b) If n, p, q, r are terms of an arithmetic sequence, show that x^n, x^p, x^q, x^r form a geometric sequence.

34. Which term of the sequence 2, −6, 18, ... is the number 162?

35. Find the first three terms of the geometric sequence in which $t_1 + t_2 + t_3 = 21$ and $t_4 + t_5 + t_6 = 168$.

36. The geometric sequence 2^{200}, 2^{196}, 2^{192}, ... contains only one odd number. Which term is the odd number? To what value of n does it correspond?

37. Is there a sequence of three different terms that is both arithmetic and geometric? Think about this geometrically.

38. A sequence of inscribed squares is formed by joining the midpoints of the previous square. If each side of the outer square is 8 cm long, find the defining statement for the sequence of the perimeters of the squares. Use your formula to find the perimeter of the tenth square.

6.4 Geometric Sequences and Compound Interest

Your ability to retire comfortably may depend on how wisely you invest some of your income during your working years. Even small amounts of money invested grow substantially over long periods because of the compounding effect of interest. Interest rates are generally quoted as an annual rate with a compounding time period. Examples of interest rates are 6%/a compounded annually, or 10%/a compounded semi-annually.

The formula for compound interest is
$$A = P(1 + i)^n$$
where A is the amount of money after investing a principal, P, at rate of interest, i, per compounding period for n compounding periods. The interest rate per period, i, is found by dividing the annual interest rate by the number of compounding periods per year.

Explore: Use a Spreadsheet

Set up a spreadsheet to show the effect of annual compound interest at 5% on an initial deposit of $1000 over a time period of 20 years. Include columns to show the year number, the amount at the beginning of the year, the interest for the year, and the amount at the end of the year. Complete the entries, using a repeating feature of your graphing calculator if a computer is not available.

Inquire

1. By how much does the initial investment grow over 20 years? After how many years did the original amount double?

2. Why do the amounts at the end of each year form a geometric sequence? What is the common ratio? What would the common ratio be if the interest rate were 7% compounded annually?

3. Write an expression for the general term of the sequence of amounts at the end of each year if the interest rate is i % compounded annually and the initial principal is P dollars.

Example 1 Optimizing Investment Choices

New parents are considering education saving plans for their newborn. The parents have $2000 to invest. Fund A pays 9%/a interest compounded annually. Fund B pays 8.5%/a compounded semi-annually. Which fund will be worth more in 17 years?

Solution

Fund A:

In $A = P(1 + i)^n$, use $P = 2000$, $i = 0.09$, $n = 17$.

$A = 2000(1.09)^{17}$

$\quad = 8655.27$

Fund B:

In $A = P(1 + i)^n$, use $P = 2000$, $i = \dfrac{0.085}{2}$, $n = 34$

$A = 2000(1.0425)^{34}$

$\quad = 8234.10$

Fund A will be worth more in 17 years.

Example 2　Investment Doubling

a) Use a spreadsheet to determine the approximate number of years that it takes for a $100 investment to double with each of the following annual rates of interest: 5%, 6%, 7%, 8%, 9%, 10%, and 12%, all compounded annually.
b) Multiply the interest rate in each case by the number of years it took for the investment to double. Comment.

Solution

a) Prepare a spreadsheet using the formula $A = P(1 + i)^n$ and compute the values of the investment after each year.

	A	B	C	D	E	F	G	H
1					Interest Rates			
2	Year	5%	6%	7%	8%	9%	10%	12%
3	1	105.00	106.00	107.00	108.00	109.00	110.00	112.00
4	2	110.25	112.36	114.49	116.64	118.81	121.00	125.44
5	3	115.76	119.10	122.50	125.97	129.50	133.10	140.49
6	4	121.55	126.25	131.08	136.05	141.16	146.41	157.35
7	5	127.63	133.82	140.26	146.93	153.86	161.05	176.23
8	6	134.01	141.85	150.07	158.69	167.71	177.16	**197.38**
9	7	140.71	150.36	160.58	171.38	182.80	**194.87**	221.07
10	8	147.75	159.38	171.82	185.09	**199.26**	214.36	247.60
11	9	155.13	168.95	183.85	**199.90**	217.19	235.79	277.31
12	10	162.89	179.08	**196.72**	215.89	236.74	259.37	310.58
13	11	171.03	189.83	210.49	233.16	258.04	285.31	347.85
14	12	179.59	**201.22**	225.22	251.82	281.27	313.84	389.60
15	13	188.56	213.29	240.98	271.96	306.58	345.23	436.35
16	14	**197.99**	226.09	257.85	293.72	334.17	379.75	488.71
17	15	207.89	239.66	275.90	317.22	364.25	417.72	547.36

From the spreadsheet, with interest compounding annually, it takes approximately 14 years for $100 to double at 5%, 12 years at 6%, 10 years at 7%, 9 years at 8%, 7 years at 10%, and 6 years at 12%.

b) Organize the length of time for an investment to double and the rates of interest in a table.

Years to Double	14	12	10	9	8	7	6
Interest Rate	5%	6%	7%	8%	9%	10%	12%
Years × Interest Rate	0.70	0.72	0.70	0.72	0.72	0.70	0.72

It appears that the product of the interest rate and approximate number of years that it takes for an investment to double is either 0.70 or 0.72.

Financial planners sometime use the "rule of 72" to obtain a quick estimate of the time it takes for an investment to double. The rule is: number of years to double = 72 ÷ (annual interest rate × 100), rounded to nearest integer.

Practice

What is the interest rate per compounding period for each of the following?

1. 10%/a compounded semi-annually

2. 7%/a compounded annually

3. 10%/a compounded quarterly

4. 6%/a compounded semi-annually

5. 12%/a compounded monthly

6. $4\frac{1}{2}$%/a compounded monthly

7. $3\frac{3}{4}$%/a compounded semi-annually

8. 8%/a compounded daily

9. 5.5%/a compounded semi-annually

10. 6.78%/a compounded semi-annually

What is the number of compounding periods, n, under the following conditions?

11. interest at 10%/a compounded semi-annually for 5 years

12. interest at $5\frac{1}{2}$%/a compounded annually for 10 years

13. interest at 8%/a compounded quarterly for $5\frac{1}{2}$ years

14. interest at 9.76%/a compounded semi-annually for 8 years

15. interest at 4.6%/a compounded monthly for 6 years

16. interest at 11%/a compounded semi-annually for $4\frac{1}{2}$ years

Determine the amount of each investment.

17. $5000 invested at 6%/a compounded annually for 8 years

18. $2000 invested at 8%/a compounded semi-annually for 5 years

19. $12 000 invested at 5.75%/a compounded semi-annually for 10 years

20. $1000 invested at 9%/a compounded quarterly for 3 years

21. $3950 invested at $7\frac{1}{2}$%/a compounded monthly for 18 months

Use the "rule of 72" to estimate, to the nearest year, the number of years it will take each investment to double.

22. $4000 invested at $9\frac{3}{4}$%/a compounded annually

23. $6000 invested at 7.25%/a compounded annually

24. $10 000 invested at 16%/a compounded annually

25. $25 000 invested at 7.5%/a compounded annually

26. $8500 invested at 5.95%/a compounded annually.

Applications and Problem Solving

27. Investment options Owen has won $100 000 in a lottery and is looking at investment options. A trust company offers a 5-year GIC (Guaranteed Investment Certificate) that pays 6%/a interest compounded semi-annually. An investment broker guarantees a return of 7% compounded annually for three years and then a return of 5% compounded annually for the next two years. Which option provides the greater return after five years?

28. Savings plans Planning for a skiing holiday in two years, a family can afford to set aside $1000 per year. At the beginning of the first year, they invest $1000 at 8%/a compounded semi-annually for two years. At the beginning of the next year, they invest $1000 at 9%/a compounded quarterly for one year. How much will the investments provide for their holiday?

29. Investment growth Five years ago, $10 000 was invested at 6%/a compounded semi-annually. Today the interest rates have risen to 7%/a compounded annually. If the original investment and accumulated interest is rolled into the new investment conditions, how much will it be worth in five years?

30. Bonds Farhana invests $500 in a high yield bond at 12%/a interest compounded monthly.
a) How much is her bond worth in 15 months?
b) After how many months is the investment worth $650?

31. RRSP To take advantage of the tax deductions that Registered Retirement Savings Plan contributions can provide, Marla borrows $3000 at 9%/a compounded semi-annually and invests it in an RRSP, which she estimates will give a return of 8%/a compounded annually.
a) How much more interest will be charged on the loan over three years?
b) How much will her RRSP investment be worth in three years?
c) What loss will she take over three years?
d) Explain why this type of financial activity might be to Marla's advantage.

32. Investment doubling a) Set up a spreadsheet, or simulate one with a table, to determine the approximate number of years that it takes for an investment of $100 to double with annual rates of interest 5.5%, 6.5%, 7.5%, 8.5%, 9.5%, 10.5%, and 11.5% compounded annually.
b) Based on these results and those found earlier for whole number rates of interest, which seems more valid, a "rule of 72" or a "rule of 70?"

33. Growth factor When he was 18, Rick inherited $10 000. He invested the money in an RRSP. If his investment earns rates equivalent to an annual rate of 9.5%, by about what factor will his original deposit have increased by the time he retires at age 65?

34. "Rule of 72" This holds approximately true when the interest rate is about 8%/a, but it breaks down for interest rates that are much greater or much less than 8%/a.
a) Does the rule overestimate or underestimate the doubling time for interest rates much less than 8%/a?
b) Does the rule overestimate or underestimate the doubling time for interest rates much greater than 8%/a?

35. Estimating doubling time a) Using logarithms, show that an investment of a principal P at i% compounded annually doubles after
$$\frac{\log 2}{\log(1+i)},$$ rounded to the nearest integer, years
have passed.
b) The "rule of 72" states that the investment doubles after $n = \dfrac{72}{100i}$, rounded to the nearest integer, years have passed. Using a graphing calculator, create a table for both of these estimates for different values of i. Compare and contrast the estimates.

LOGIC POWER

Place the letters A, B, C, D, E, F, G, I, J, K, L, M, N, and P in the squares so that the following are true.
• E is in the same row as K.
• C occupies a corner square.
• M is in a corner square.
• B is in the top row.
• P is not in the top row.
• D is in the right column.
• J is in the right column.
• No row or column contains two consecutive letters.
• No row or column contains two vowels.

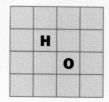

6.5 Geometric Series

If you could invest $1000 each year on your birthday from age 18 on, and earn an average of 12%/a interest compounded annually, how much do you think you would have by your 61st birthday? The answer is over one million dollars! To find the exact amount, find sum of the geometric sequence
$1000(1.12)^{42}$, $1000(1.12)^{41}$, ... , $1000(1.12)$, 1000.
If you could invest $100 each month, and earn 12%/a interest compounded monthly, how much do you think you would have by your 61st birthday? To answer questions such as these efficiently, you need a formula for the sum of the terms of a geometric sequence. In the following exploration, you will develop this formula.

Explore: Build a Formula

Step 1: Write $S_n = a + ar + ar^2 + ar^3 + \ldots + ar^{n-2} + ar^{n-1}$ as equation 1.

Step 2: Multiply both sides of equation 1 by r, to form equation 2.

Step 3: Subtract equation 2 from equation 1, lining up terms to make the difference, $S_n - rS_n$, as simple as possible.

Step 4: Solve the equation resulting from step 3 for S_n.

Inquire

1. How is the equation in step 1 related to a geometric sequence? What does S_n represent?

2. Why was multiplying by r, in step 2, a helpful step in building a simpler formula for S_n?

3. What value of r would make this formula invalid? Why? What is the value of S_n for this value of r?

4. Test that your formula works by finding the result of $1 + 2 + 4 + 8 + 16$ in two ways.

In words, S_n is called the ***n*th partial sum**. For the sequence 1, 3, 9, 27, 81, 243, the third partial sum, S_3, is $1 + 3 + 9$ or 13.

Example 1   Summing a Geometric Series
Find the sum of the first 12 terms, the 12th partial sum, of the geometric series $1 + \dfrac{1}{3} + \dfrac{1}{9} + \dfrac{1}{27} + \ldots$.

Solution

The formula for the sum of a geometric series is $S_n = \dfrac{a(1 - r^n)}{1 - r}$.

Use $a = 1$, $r = \dfrac{1}{3}$, and $n = 12$.

$$S_{12} = \frac{1\left(1 - \left(\dfrac{1}{3}\right)^{12}\right)}{1 - \dfrac{1}{3}}$$

$$= \frac{1 - \dfrac{1}{3^{12}}}{\dfrac{2}{3}}$$

$$\doteq 1.499\ 997$$

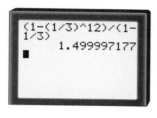

```
(1-(1/3)^12)/(1-
1/3)
        1.499997177
■
```

The sum of the first 12 terms of the geometric series is approximately 1.5.

Example 2　Using the Sum of a Geometric Sequence

The tallest totem pole carved from a single log is 38.28 m high and is in Beacon Hill Park in Victoria, B.C. If a lacrosse ball is dropped from this height and bounces back up 60% of the original height, find the total distance travelled by the ball by the time it hits the ground for the tenth time.

Solution
Draw a sketch of the situation.

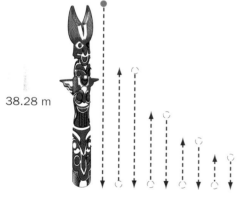

38.28 m

Initially, the ball drops 38.28 m.
Then, it bounces up to 38.28(0.60) m, drops 38.28(0.60) m, bounces up 38.28(0.60)(0.60), or 38.28(0.60)^2 m, drops 38.28(0.60)^2 m, and so on.

The total distance travelled by the ball is the value of the following series.

$38.28 + 2(38.28(0.60)) + 2(38.28(0.60)^2) + 2(38.28(0.60)^3) + \ldots + (38.28(0.60)^9)$

$= 38.28 + 76.56(0.60) + 76.56(0.60)^2 + 76.56(0.60)^3 + \ldots + 76.56(0.60)^9$

$= 38.28 + 76.56(0.60)(1 + (0.60) + (0.60)^2 + \ldots + (0.60)^8)$

To calculate the value of the series $1 + 0.60 + 0.60^2 + \ldots + 0.60^8$,

use $S_n = \dfrac{a(1-r^n)}{1-r}$ and substitute $n = 9$, $a = 1$, $r = 0.60$.

$$S_9 = \dfrac{1(1-0.60^9)}{1-0.60}$$
$$\doteq 2.474\,81$$

Then, the total distance travelled by the ball is
$38.28 + 76.56(0.60)(S_9)$
$\doteq 38.28 + 76.56(0.60)(2.474\,81)$
$\doteq 151.96$
The total distance travelled by the ball is approximately 151.96 m.

Geometric series can also be written using Σ notation.
For example, the series with defining statement $t_n = 3^n$ for $n = 1$ to $n = 4$
is written as follows.

$$\sum_{k=1}^{4} 3^k = 3^1 + 3^2 + 3^3 + 3^4$$

Example 3   Using Sigma Notation
Write the following series using sigma notation. Then, find the sum of the terms.

$$8 + 4 + 2 + \ldots + \dfrac{1}{64}$$

Solution
The common ratio of this geometric series is $\dfrac{1}{2}$.

$$8 + 4 + 2 + \ldots + \dfrac{1}{64}$$
$$= 8\left(1 + \dfrac{1}{2} + \dfrac{1}{4} + \ldots + \dfrac{1}{512}\right)$$
$$= 8\left(\dfrac{1}{2}\right)^0 + 8\left(\dfrac{1}{2}\right)^1 + 8\left(\dfrac{1}{2}\right)^2 + \ldots + 8\left(\dfrac{1}{2}\right)^9$$
$$= \sum_{k=1}^{10} 8\left(\dfrac{1}{2}\right)^{k-1}$$

Find the sum of the series by substituting $a = 8$, $r = \dfrac{1}{2}$ or 0.5, $n = 10$

in $S_n = \dfrac{a(1-r^n)}{1-r}$

$$S_{10} = \dfrac{8(1-0.5^{10})}{1-0.5}$$
$$= 15.984\,375$$

The sum of the terms is 15.984 375.

Practice

Find the indicated partial sum of each geometric series.

1. $10 + 15 + 22.5 + \dots$ Find S_8.

2. $70 + 35 + 17.5 + \dots$ Find S_6.

3. $66 + 22 + \dfrac{22}{3} + \dots$ Find S_5.

4. $1111 + 111.1 + 11.11 + \dots$ Find S_7.

5. $\dfrac{1}{3} + \dfrac{2}{3} + \dfrac{4}{3} + \dots$ Find S_9.

6. $-99 - 11 - \dfrac{11}{9} - \dots$ Find S_{10}.

7. $\dfrac{1}{13} - \dfrac{2}{13} + \dfrac{4}{13} - \dots$ Find S_9.

Write each series in expanded form. Determine the sum of each.

8. $\displaystyle\sum_{k=1}^{3} 4(2)^{k-1}$

9. $\displaystyle\sum_{i=1}^{4} 10(0.1)^i$

10. $\displaystyle\sum_{k=1}^{5} 9^{k-1}$

11. $\displaystyle\sum_{m=3}^{8} 200\left(\dfrac{1}{2}\right)^m$

12. $\displaystyle\sum_{k=1}^{10} 1^{k-1}$

13. $\displaystyle\sum_{k=-1}^{7} 3(5)^{k-1}$

14. $\displaystyle\sum_{k=-2}^{8} (3^2)^{k-1}$

15. $\displaystyle\sum_{k=3}^{10} 0.3(0.15)^{k-1}$

Write each series using sigma notation. Determine the sum of each.

16. $12 + 3 + \dfrac{3}{4} + \dots + \dfrac{3}{64}$

17. $0.5 + 1 + 2 + \dots + 256$

18. $-12 - 6 - 3 - \dots - \dfrac{3}{16}$

19. $0.11 + 0.33 + 0.99 + \dots + 721.71$

20. $100 + 25 + \dfrac{25}{4} + \dots + \dfrac{25}{256}$

21. $1.99 + 19.9 + 199 + \dots + 1\ 990\ 000$

Applications and Problem Solving

22. **Chess** According to an old tale, the inventor of chess, Sissa Dahir, was granted anything he wished by the Indian king, Shirham. Sissa asked for one grain of wheat for the first square on the chess board, two grains for the second square, four grains for the third, eight for the fourth, and so on, for all 64 squares. "Is that all you wish for?" asked the king, unknowingly.

a) How much grain did Sissa ask for?

b) If one grain of wheat has a mass of 65 mg, what fraction of Canada's annual wheat production did Sissa ask for?

23. **Chess tournament** A chess tournament has 64 entries. When a player loses a game, he or she is out. Winners play in the next round. How many games are played before the ultimate winner is determined?

24. **Ecology** Recent estimates, based on data from satellite observations, report 775 million hectares of rain forest remaining. The average annual rate of deforestation in the world is 0.77%. How many million hectares of rain forest will be lost in the next decade?

25. **Trust funds** A generous aunt wants to establish a trust fund for a newborn niece. The aunt decides to put the equivalent of $100 into a trust fund each year on the niece's birthday, until and including, her 21st birthday. To hedge against inflation, the aunt adds an extra 10% of the previous year's gift each year. How much money does the aunt contribute to the fund for her niece?

26. **Lunar gravity** On July 20, 1969, Neil Armstrong and Edwin Aldrin were the first people to land on the moon, via the Apollo 11 space mission. The force of gravity on the moon is approximately one sixth of the force of gravity on Earth. If a bouncing ball on the moon returns to 90% of the height from which it is dropped, what is the total distance that a ball dropped from a height of 3 m would travel by the sixth bounce?

27. **Retirement savings** Ruta wishes to plan for her retirement. She decides to invest $1000 each year starting at age 20 until age 30. Cynthia on the other hand, invests $1000 a year from age 30 until age 65. Assuming that the interest rate is fixed at 8%/a compounded annually, who will have more money at age 65?

28. Automotive design The shock absorbers on a car are designed to dampen the vibrations when the car goes over a bump. If a shock absorber reduces the vibration of the body of the car by 70% each time it passes the equilibrium line of the shock absorber, how far would the piston of the shock absorber travel in 3 bounces after the car hit a pothole 20 cm deep?

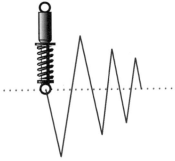

29. Bungie jumping A bungie jumper jumps from a bridge into a canyon. On the first fall, the cord stretches to 100 m. The jumper is recoiled 60 m and then falls again. Each time the jumper goes down, the cord stretches to 90% of the stretch from the previous fall. Similarly, the recoil is 90% of the previous recoil.
a) Write the distance travelled in five falls and five recoils as a geometric series.
b) Determine the total distance travelled by the bungie jumper in the five bounces.

30. Trapeze artist A circus trapeze artist uses a swing with cables 17.4 m long. The half-angle at the suspension point of the swing decreases by 0.5% each time it passes the equilibrium line. If the original half-angle when the swing starts is 45°, determine the total distance that the trapeze artist travels in 10 passes across the equilibrium point.

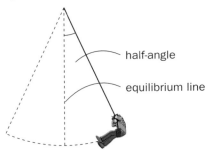

half-angle

equilibrium line

31. Sinking fund A manufacturing company needs to replace a certain machine January 1, 2010. It is estimated that the cost of the machine will be $100 000 in 2010. To save for this purchase, the company decides to establish a type of investment called a sinking fund. Starting January 1, 2000, and including January 1, 2010, the company invests a fixed amount of money in this fund each year at an interest rate of 10%/a compounded annually. If all the fund payments are equal, how much is each individual payment?

32. Show that the following are true.

a) $\displaystyle\sum_{k=1}^{n} ar^{k-1} = \sum_{k=0}^{n-1} ar^{k}$ **b)** $\displaystyle\sum_{k=1}^{n} ar^{k} = \sum_{k=0}^{n-1} ar^{k+1}$

33. A geometric sequence has terms $t_1, t_2, t_3, \ldots$ such that $\displaystyle\sum_{k=1}^{10} t_k = 244 \sum_{k=1}^{5} t_k$. Find the common ratio for the sequence.

34. Find the sum of the divisors of 65 536.

LOGIC POWER

Place a single digit in each box of the second row so that the following are true.
• The digit in the box below 0 indicates the number of 0's in all twenty boxes.
• The digit in the box below 1 indicates the number of 1's is all of the boxes.

Continue this pattern until the box below 9 indicates the number of 9's in all of the boxes. You may use a digit more than once, and you may not need to use every digit.

0	1	2	3	4	5	6	7	8	9

The Concept of a Limit

1 An Algebraic Application

You can solve the equation $x^2 - 2x - 1 = 0$ using the quadratic formula to obtain the exact roots $1 \pm \sqrt{2}$. Consider the following alternative approach to solving this equation.

$$x^2 - 2x - 1 = 0$$
$$x^2 = 2x + 1$$

Divide by x, which is permissible since $x = 0$ is not a solution.

$$x = 2 + \frac{1}{x}$$

To try to eliminate x from the right side, substitute $x = 2 + \dfrac{1}{x}$.

$$x = 2 + \cfrac{1}{2 + \cfrac{1}{x}}$$

Repeated substitution of $x = 2 + \dfrac{1}{x}$ leads to the following **continued fraction**.

$$x = 2 + \cfrac{1}{2 + \cfrac{1}{2 + \cfrac{1}{2 + \dots}}}$$

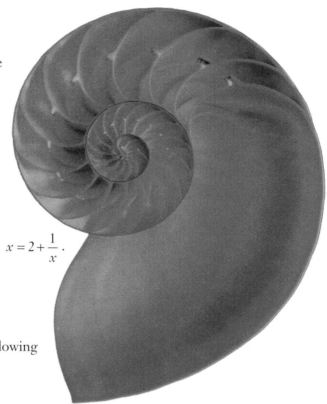

1. a) Find at least ten successive approximations for the value of the continued fraction by evaluating

$$2 + \frac{1}{2}, \ 2 + \cfrac{1}{2 + \cfrac{1}{2}}, \ 2 + \cfrac{1}{2 + \cfrac{1}{2 + \cfrac{1}{2}}}, \ \dots$$

b) Describe how successive approximations can be found efficiently using the reciprocal key on a calculator.

2. What value does the continued fraction seem to approach? How does this value compare with an approximation of the exact root of the equation found using the quadratic formula?

3. Use a similar method to approximate a root of the equation $x^2 - 4x - 1 = 0$ and compare your answer with the roots found by using the quadratic formula.

2 A Function Application

1. Consider the function $f(x) = 1 - \dfrac{1}{2^x}$.

a) Construct a table of values for the function using $x = -3, -2, -1, 0, 1, 2, 3, 4, \ldots$.

b) As x becomes increasingly large, what happens to the value of $\dfrac{1}{2^x}$?

c) What is the domain of this function? the range?

d) How is the line $f(x) = 1$ related to the graph of the function?

3 A Series Application

Consider the series $1 - \dfrac{1}{1} + \dfrac{1}{2!} - \dfrac{1}{3!} + \dfrac{1}{4!} - \cdots$

Recall factorial notation.
4! means $4 \times 3 \times 2 \times 1$

1. Find at least ten successive approximations for the value of this series. Record your results in a table.

Number of Terms	Value
1	1
2	0
3	$\frac{1}{2}$
4	

2. a) Does the series given look familiar in any way? What happens to the value of $\dfrac{1}{n!}$ as n increases?

b) What value does the sum of this series seem to approach?

c) Recall your work in Chapter 2 with the irrational number e. What value does your calculator show for $\dfrac{1}{e}$? Compare this value to the first ten approximations of the series $1 - \dfrac{1}{1} + \dfrac{1}{2!} - \dfrac{1}{3!} + \dfrac{1}{4!} - \ldots$. To how many decimal places does the approximation found by summing the first ten terms of the series agree with the value shown on your calculator for $\dfrac{1}{e}$?

6.6 Infinite Geometric Series

A classic paradox posed by Zeno of Elea was to suggest that Achilles, running to overtake a tortoise, must first reach the place where the tortoise started, but the tortoise has already departed from there. So, Achilles runs on to the new point where the tortoise is, but the tortoise has once again departed, and so on. The conclusion is that Achilles can never catch up with the tortoise!

Explore: Use a Pattern

Imagine that you are standing 100 m from a doorway. You approach the doorway by first moving half the distance to the door, then moving half the remaining distance, continuing to move half the remaining distance for as long as possible. Write the sequence of distances moved in each step.

Inquire

1. What type of sequence is the pattern of steps? Why?

2. How far have you moved toward the doorway after 3 steps? after 5 steps? Will you ever reach the doorway? Explain.

3. What expression could you use to calculate the total distance that you have moved after 100 of these steps? Predict what approximate answer you would expect. If you were able to move an infinite number of steps, what total distance would you have moved?

4. You know that the sum of the geometric series $a + ar + ar^2 + \ldots + ar^n$ is

given by $S_n = \dfrac{a(1-r^n)}{1-r}$. Explain why, if a geometric series does not end at the nth

term but continues indefinitely, then the expression for the sum simplifies to $S_\infty = \dfrac{a}{1-r}$,

for $-1 < r < 1$. What happens if $r \geq 1$ or $r \leq -1$?

The expression for the sum of an infinite geometric sequence can be visualized as follows.
Draw a line segment AC through D where AD is one unit.
Draw a line with slope r through A.
Draw a line with slope 1 through D.
These two lines intersect at B and in $\triangle$BCD, BC = CD.
Draw the vertical line DE. Then, in $\triangle$ADE, the slope

of AE is r. Since slope = $\dfrac{\text{rise}}{\text{run}}$ and AD = 1, DE = r.

Draw a sequence of similar, diminishing right triangles as shown. The rise for each smaller triangle is the next greater power of r.
Let AC = S. Then, BC = $S - 1$.
By summing horizontal sides of $\triangle$ADE, $\triangle$EFG, ... ,
$S = 1 + r + r^2 + r^3 + \ldots$

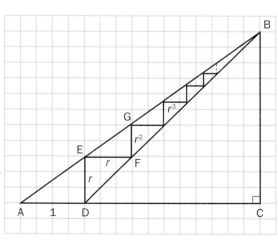

By summing the vertical sides of $\triangle ADE$, $\triangle EFG$, ..., $S - 1 = r + r^2 + r^3 + \ldots$
$\triangle ADE$ is similar to $\triangle ACB$, so

$$\frac{AC}{AD} = \frac{BC}{ED}$$

$$\frac{S}{1} = \frac{S-1}{r}$$

$$Sr = S - 1$$

$$Sr - S = -1$$

$$S(1 - r) = 1$$

$$\therefore S = \frac{1}{1 - r}$$

Therefore, the sum of the infinite geometric sequence $1, r, r^2, \ldots$ is $\dfrac{1}{1-r}$.

Example   Diminishing Resources

Last month a well produced 15 000 m^3 of oil. Its production is known to be dropping by 2.9% each month.

a) How much oil will be produced over the next year, to three significant digits?
b) If the well is worked until it is dry, estimate what its total future production will be.
c) Actually, once the monthly production drops below 5000 m^3, it is not profitable to work the well. When should this well be capped?

Solution

a) Since the quantity of oil is dropping by 2.9% each month, the amount each month will be 97.1% of the previous month's amount.
The amount produced over the next year is given by the geometric series
$15\ 000(0.971) + 15\ 000(0.971)^2 + \ldots + 15\ 000(0.971)^{12}$.
In the series, $a = 15\ 000(0.971)$ or 14 565, $r = 0.971$, $n = 12$

$$S_n = \frac{a(1 - r^n)}{1 - r}$$

$$S_{12} = \frac{14\ 565(1 - (0.971)^{12})}{1 - 0.971}$$

$$= 149\ 429.4591$$

Over the next year, the well will produce 149 000 m^3 of oil, to three significant digits.

b) If the well is worked until it is dry, the total future production is the infinite sum of the series.

$$S_\infty = \frac{a}{1 - r}$$

$$= \frac{14\ 565}{1 - 0.971}$$

$$= 502\ 241.3793$$

If the well is worked until it is dry, the total production would be 502 000 m^3, to three significant digits.

c) The well should be capped when the monthly production falls below 5000 m³. We need to find the value of n when the value of the term $t_n = ar^{n-1}$ falls below 5000 m³.

Method 1: Guessing and testing
Try $n = 30$.
$$t_{30} = 14\ 565(0.971)^{29}$$
$$\doteq 6203.95 \qquad \text{too high}$$

Try $n = 40$.
$$t_{40} = 14\ 565(0.971)^{39}$$
$$\doteq 4622.32 \qquad \text{too low, but closer to 5000 than } t_{30}$$

Try $n = 37$.
$$t_{37} = 14\ 565(0.971)^{36}$$
$$\doteq 5048.97 \qquad \text{still more than 5000}$$

Try $n = 38$.
$$t_{38} = 14\ 565(0.971)^{37}$$
$$\doteq 4902.55 \qquad \text{just a little under 5000}$$
The well should be capped in the 38th month of production.

Method 2: Using functions on a graphing calculator
Graph $y = 14\ 565(0.971)^{x-1}$ as Y1
and $y = 5000$ as Y2,
and find their intersection.
The graphs intersect at $x \doteq 37.331182$.

The well should be capped in the 38th month of production.

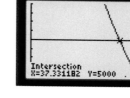

Method 3: Using logarithms
Solve
$$14\ 565(0.971)^{x-1} = 5000$$
$$0.971^{x-1} = 0.343\ 289$$
Take logarithms of both sides.
$$\log 0.971^{x-1} = \log 0.343\ 289$$
$$(x-1)\log 0.971 = \log 0.343\ 289$$
$$x - 1 = \frac{\log 0.343\ 289}{\log 0.971}$$
$$x \doteq 1 + 36.33$$
$$= 37.33$$

The well should be capped in the 38th month of production.

Practice

Find the sum of each infinite geometric series if it exists.

1. $10 + 1 + 0.1 + 0.01 + \dots$

2. $8 + 7 + \dfrac{49}{8} + \dots$

3. $2 + 0.5 + 0.125 + \dots$

4. $625 + 25 + 1 + 0.04 + \dots$

5. $-81 - 27 - 9 - \dots$

6. $1 + x + x^2 + x^3 + \dots$

7. $1 - 1 + 1 - 1 + 1 - \dots$

Write the first four terms in each series, and then find the infinite sum of the series.

8. $\displaystyle\sum_{i=1}^{\infty} \left(\dfrac{1}{3}\right)^i$

9. $\displaystyle\sum_{i=0}^{\infty} 2(0.1)^i$

10. $\displaystyle\sum_{i=0}^{\infty} 2(1 - 0.1)^i$

11. $\displaystyle\sum_{i=-1}^{\infty} 10(0.5)^i$

12. $\displaystyle\sum_{i=1}^{\infty} 1000(0.25)^i$

13. $\displaystyle\sum_{i=5}^{\infty} 8\left(\dfrac{1}{2}\right)^i$

14. $\displaystyle\sum_{i=1}^{\infty} 3\left(\dfrac{7}{6}\right)^i$

15. $\displaystyle\sum_{i=1}^{\infty} 2(1 + 0.1)^i$

Applications and Problem Solving

16. Equivalent numbers Numbers may have different representations. For example, $\sqrt[3]{8}$ and $4^{0.5}$ are both expressions for the number 2. Show that, in each set of three representations, the expressions have the same value.

a) $0.999\ 999\ 999\ \dots, 0.9 + 0.09 + 0.009 + \dots, 1$

b) $99.999\ 999\ \dots, 99 + 0.9 + 0.09 + 0.009 + \dots, 100$

c) $5.499\ 999\ \dots, 5.5,$
$4.5 + 0.99 + 0.0099 + 0.000\ 099 + \dots$

17. Repeating decimals By expressing each repeating decimal as the sum of an infinite geometric series, find the common fraction equivalent to each.

a) $0.111\ 111\ \dots$

b) $7.777\ 777\ \dots$

c) $0.212\ 121\ 212\ \dots$

d) $0.672\ 727\ 272\ \dots$

e) $0.456\ 123\ 123\ 123\ \dots$

f) $3.523\ 523\ 523\ \dots$

18. Measurement Nested squares are drawn inside one another by joining the midpoints of the sides of the previous square. The outer square has sides of length 8 cm.

a) Show that the second square has sides of length $4\sqrt{2}$ cm.

b) Find the sum of the perimeters of the infinite nest of squares.

c) Find the sum of the areas of the infinite nest of squares.

d) Show that the area of the first square is equal to the total area covered by all of the other nested squares.

19. Lead mining Canada is the world's third largest producer of lead. Lead production declined from 242 000 t in 1996 to 224 000 t the next year.

a) If this trend continued, what total mass of lead was produced in the four years 1998 to 2001?

b) If the trend were to continue indefinitely, what is the total mass of lead that would be produced from 1996 on?

20. Forestry The Canadian forest industry is concentrated in British Columbia, Quebec, and Ontario. Assume there is a 5% annual decline in Canadian lumber production.

a) Express this year's lumber production as a percent of the total lumber production over the next three years.

b) What would be the total lumber production over the next ten years as a percent of the total of all future lumber production?

21. Maple sap The first year that a sugar maple tree is tapped, it produces 50 L of sap. As the tree ages, the sap production drops by 4% each year.
a) Find the total volume of sap taken from the tree in the first five years.
b) Estimate the total amount of sap that the tree can produce.

22. Dragonfly Suppose two joggers, each running towards the other at a rate of 8 km/h, are 10 km apart on a straight road. A dragonfly, flying at a steady speed of 45 km/h, passes over the head of one jogger and flies until it reaches the other jogger's position. The dragonfly then turns back and flies towards the first jogger, and continues this pattern until the joggers meet.
a) Write the geometric series that represents the sum of the distances that the dragonfly travels.
b) Find the total distance that the dragonfly covers.
c) Find an alternative solution for the same problem by considering time instead of distance.

23. Measurement The midpoints of the sides of a square are joined to form a new square and the process is repeated. A section of each square is coloured as shown. If the pattern continues indefinitely, what fraction of the original square is coloured?

24. Fractals In the **Getting Started** at the beginning of this chapter, you examined the sum of the lengths of lines in two different fractals. Assume each construction is continued indefinitely.
a) Find the total length of all the lines in the first fractal.
b) Find the total length of all the lines in the second fractal.
c) Compare the answers in a) and b). Do these results surprise you? Discuss.

25. Sierpinski's triangle A fractal, Sierpinski's triangle, can be created from an equilateral triangle by joining the midpoint of each side of the triangle, then joining the midpoint of each side of each upward pointing sub-triangle, and then repeating the process on each upward pointing sub-sub-triangle, and so on.

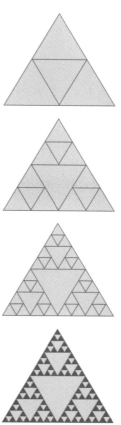

a) If the perimeter of the initial triangle is 3 units, what is the sum of the lengths of all the lines of all the triangles in Sierpinski's triangle?
b) If the area of the original triangle is $\frac{\sqrt{3}}{4}$ square units, what is the sum of all the areas of all the downward pointed triangles in Sierpinski's triangle? What is the sum of all the areas of all the upward pointed triangles in Sierpinski's triangle?

6.7 Exploring Other Infinite Series

The special irrational number π has fascinated people for thousands of years. Using infinite series expressions for π, supercomputers have calculated its decimal approximation to more than 6 billion decimal places. It is suspected that the frequency of each digit 0, 1, 2, 3, 4, 5, 6, 7, 8, 9 in the decimal expansion of π is exactly one tenth. If true, this would provide an interesting method of generating random numbers.

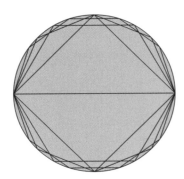

Explore: Use a Code

Decode the following sentence to find an approximate value for π which is correct to 16 decimal places.

Yes. I know I could determine in record speed the right decimal expansion claimed realistic for pi.

Compare this value with the values displayed on various calculators that are available to you.

Inquire

1. The most commonly used approximation for π is $\frac{22}{7}$. This value was used as early as 3000 B.C., by the ancient Egyptians. What is this value to eight decimal places?

2. The Rhind Papyrus, dating from around 2000 B.C., is one of the oldest mathematical documents in existence. It gives an approximate value of π as $\left(\frac{16}{9}\right)^2$. Calculate this value to eight decimal places.

3. Around 240 B.C., Archimedes showed that $3\frac{10}{71} < \pi < 3\frac{1}{7}$. Are the approximations found in the previous two questions within this range?

4. Around A.D. 125, in Greece, Ptolemy gave π as $3 + \frac{8}{60} + \frac{30}{60^2}$. Find this value to 8 decimal places.

5. Around A.D. 480, Chinese engineer Tsu Ch'ung-chih gave π as $\frac{355}{113}$. What is this value, to eight decimal places?

6. Around A.D. 1150, the Indian mathematician Bhaskara gave several values for π, the most accurate being $\frac{3927}{1250}$. What is the decimal equivalent of this fraction?

7. Of the five approximations described above, which is closest to your calculator's approximation for π?

Many of the approximations arrived at prior to the
sixteenth century were based on geometric
arguments. For example, circumscribe and inscribe a
hexagon about a circle of radius one unit. The area
of this circle, π, lies between the area of the interior
hexagon and the area of the exterior hexagon.

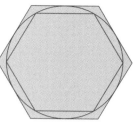

Many of the later approximations for π have been determined using an
increasing number of terms of certain infinite series. These series are derived
using different techniques, some based on calculus, and others based on more
involved function theory.

The following example shows a series proposed in 1674 by Leibnitz, the
famous German mathematician, who, independently but concurrently with
Newton, developed many of the concepts of calculus.

Example 1   Using an Infinite Series to Approximate π

a) Find the first five approximations of π based on the series $\dfrac{\pi}{4} = \displaystyle\sum_{k=1}^{\infty} \dfrac{(-1)^k}{1-2k}$.

b) Comment on how well this series seems to give an approximate value for π.
Estimate how many terms of this series are needed to obtain an approximation
of π accurate to two decimal places.

Solution
a) Expand the sigma notation to give the first five terms.

$$\frac{\pi}{4} = \sum_{k=1}^{\infty} \frac{(-1)^k}{1-2k}$$

$$= \frac{(-1)^1}{1-2(1)} + \frac{(-1)^2}{1-2(2)} + \frac{(-1)^3}{1-2(3)} + \frac{(-1)^4}{1-2(4)} + \frac{(-1)^5}{1-2(5)} +\cdot$$

$$= \frac{-1}{-1} + \frac{1}{-3} + \frac{-1}{-5} + \frac{1}{-7} + \frac{-1}{-9} + \ldots$$

$$= 1 - \frac{1}{3} + \frac{1}{5} - \frac{1}{7} + \frac{1}{9} + \ldots$$

The first approximation is the first term of the series:

$$\frac{\pi}{4} = 1$$
$$\pi = 4$$

The second approximation is the sum of the first two terms, the second partial
sum of the series:

$$\frac{\pi}{4} = 1 - \frac{1}{3}$$
$$\pi = 4\left(\frac{2}{3}\right)$$
$$= 2.\overline{6}$$

The third approximation is the sum of the first three terms, the third partial sum:

$$\frac{\pi}{4} = 1 - \frac{1}{3} + \frac{1}{5}$$

$$\pi = 4\left(\frac{13}{15}\right)$$

$$= 3.4\overline{6}$$

The fourth approximation is the fourth partial sum:

$$\frac{\pi}{4} = 1 - \frac{1}{3} + \frac{1}{5} - \frac{1}{7}$$

$$\pi = 4\left(\frac{76}{105}\right)$$

$$\doteq 2.90$$

The fifth approximation is the fifth partial sum:

$$\frac{\pi}{4} = 1 - \frac{1}{3} + \frac{1}{5} - \frac{1}{7} + \frac{1}{9}$$

$$\pi = 4\left(\frac{789}{945}\right)$$

$$\doteq 3.34$$

Based on this series, the first five approximations for π are
$4,\ 2.\overline{6},\ 3.4\overline{6},\ 2.90,\ 3.34$.

b) The first five partial sums of the series show that this series does not yield a very accurate approximation for π.
Note: Only after summing the first 628 terms does the series provide an approximation accurate to two decimal places. After summing the first 5000 terms, the approximation given by the series is 3.141 392 654, which is accurate only to three decimal places.

Practice

Determine the first five partial sums of each series.

1. $\displaystyle\sum_{n=1}^{\infty} \frac{1}{n}$

2. $\displaystyle\sum_{k=1}^{\infty} k^2$

3. $\displaystyle\sum_{n=1}^{\infty} \frac{n}{n+1}$

4. $\displaystyle\sum_{m=0}^{\infty} \sqrt{m}$

5. $\displaystyle\sum_{m=5}^{\infty} m\sqrt{m}$

6. $\displaystyle\sum_{k=0}^{\infty} \frac{k}{k^2+1}$

Applications and Problem Solving

7. Machin's formula A reasonable approximation for π can be obtained using Machin's Formula:

$$\pi \doteq 16\left(\frac{1}{5} - \frac{1}{3\times5^3} + \frac{1}{5\times5^5} - \frac{1}{7\times5^7} + \dots\right)$$
$$- 4\left(\frac{1}{239} - \frac{1}{3(239)^3} + \frac{1}{5(239)^5} - \frac{1}{7(239)^7} + \dots\right)$$

Find the first five approximations for π using this formula. Compare these approximations to the value given for π on your calculator.

8. Irrational e Another special irrational number, with applications in science, commerce, and advanced mathematics, is e. The value of e is given by the following infinite series.

$$e = 1 + \frac{1}{1} + \frac{1}{1 \times 2} + \frac{1}{1 \times 2 \times 3} + \frac{1}{1 \times 2 \times 3 \times 4} + \ldots$$

a) Approximate the value of e by finding the first five partial sums of the infinite series.

b) Use a scientific calculator to find the value of e, to six decimal places.

9. Golden ratio The golden ratio has been incorporated into many works of art and architecture, both modern and ancient, because of its aesthetic appeal. Ancient Greek architects supposedly used the golden ratio in the construction of the Parthenon to give the building its pleasing proportions. Two line segments of lengths a and b satisfy the golden ratio if $a : b = (a + b) : a$.

a) Let the length b be 1 unit. Solve the proportion above for a, leaving the answer in radical form. This value is called the golden ratio and is denoted ϕ (the Greek letter phi).

b) The value of ϕ can be determined also using either of the following infinite series.

(i) $\phi = 1 + \dfrac{1}{1 + \dfrac{1}{1 + \dfrac{1}{1 + \ldots}}}$

(ii) $\phi = \sqrt{1 + \sqrt{1 + \sqrt{1 + \sqrt{1 + \ldots}}}}$

Find the first five approximations for ϕ using each of the series. To how many decimal places do these approximations, and the decimal approximation of the radical expression found in part a), agree?

c) Part of the beauty of mathematics is the surprising connections obtained between seemingly unrelated areas. In Section 6.1, question 26, you

found a recursive formula for the term, t_n, of the Fibonacci sequence 1, 1, 2, 3, 5, 8, 13, ... Find the ratio of successive terms of the Fibonacci sequence for the first 13 terms, that is, $\dfrac{t_2}{t_1}$, $\dfrac{t_3}{t_2}$, ..., $\dfrac{t_{13}}{t_{12}}$. Do you recognize the decimal expansions of the ratios? What do you think will happen as you continue to take this ratio for further terms of the sequence?

d) Find some examples where the golden ratio appears in art, architecture, and nature. Make a golden rectangle, that is, a rectangle whose length to width ratio is ϕ, and several other rectangles. See if your friends can pick out the golden rectangle. Do you find it to be proportionally appealing?

10. Series and π The value of π can also be determined using the following equation.

$$\frac{\pi^2}{6} = \sum_{n=1}^{\infty} \frac{1}{n^2}$$

a) Approximate the value of π by finding the tenth partial sum of the infinite series.

b) How accurate is this approximation for π?

11. Supercomputer calculation Certain modern techniques for approximating π are also based on series. In 1994, David and Gregory Chudnovsky of Columbia University, New York, used the remarkable series

$$\frac{1}{\pi} = 12 \sum_{k=0}^{\infty} \frac{(-1)^k (6k)!(13591409 + 545140134k)}{(3k)!(k!)^3 640320^{3k+3/2}}$$

together with a home-made supercomputer, to calculate π to four billion decimal places. Each term of this series provides an additional 14 correct digits for π.

a) Find the first approximation for π using the partial sums S_1 of the series.

b) How accurately do you think we need to approximate π? What are the benefits of accurate approximations? Why would someone want to approximate π to four billion decimal places? Discuss.

12. If x and y are both single-digit positive integers, for what value(s) of x and y does the following infinite geometric series have a sum of $\dfrac{1}{3}$?

$$\frac{x}{y} + \frac{x}{y^2} + \frac{x}{y^3} + \ldots$$

TECHNOLOGY

Using a Spreadsheet for Sequences and Series

1 Exploring Radioactive Decay

Canada and other countries with nuclear power plants must ensure the safety of these facilities and the proper disposal of radioactive waste. The world's worst nuclear accident occurred on April 26, 1986, at Chernobyl, Russia. There was an explosion and fire in the graphite core of one of the four reactors there and radioactive material was released into the atmosphere.

Radioactive decay can be modelled using a spreadsheet on a computer.

1. Uranium-232 has a half-life of 70 years. Using an initial amount of 1 000 000 atoms of uranium-232, set up a spreadsheet:
Enter the headings, Year and Number of Atoms of Uranium-232, in cells A1 and B1. Enter 1986 in A2 and 1 000 000 in B2.
In the cell below Year 1986 enter the formula =A2+70.
For the cell below 1 000 000 enter the formula =B2/2.
Highlight the column from A3 to A24 and choose 'fill down'. Repeat this for the column from B3 to B24.

2. a) How many years does it take for the original one million atoms of uranium-232 to decay to one atom?
b) In the year 2336, what fraction of the original number of atoms still remains?

3. If you were setting up a spreadsheet for another radioactive material with a half-life of 120 years, what part of the spreadsheet would you need to change and how would you change it?

2 Using Spreadsheets to Explore Other Sequences

Use a spreadsheet to answer the following questions.

1. The Fibonacci sequence is given by 1, 1, 2, 3, 5, 8, 13, … Which number, 102 334 155 or 102 334 156, is a term of the Fibonacci sequence?

2. What irrational number does the sequence defined by $t_n = \left(1 + \dfrac{1}{n}\right)^n$ approach?

3. The English mathematician John Wallis (1616–1703) used the following infinite product to approximate a value for π.

$$\frac{\pi}{2} = \frac{2}{1} \times \frac{2}{3} \times \frac{4}{3} \times \frac{4}{5} \times \frac{6}{5} \times \frac{6}{7} \times \frac{8}{7} \times \frac{8}{9} \times \dots$$

Evaluate this product to 100 terms.

Sequences and Searching

The Internet and the World Wide Web provide a vast resource of information. In order to search this huge database efficiently, search engines have been developed to sift through the data. The computer algorithms used in programming the search engines are often based on the mathematics of sequences.

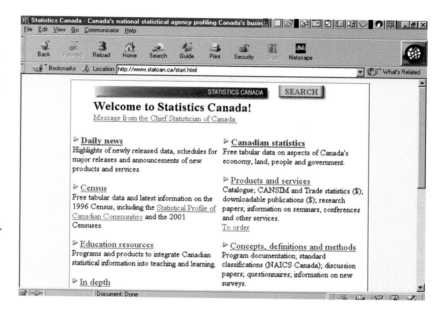

1 The Binary Search

Suppose data has been sorted alphabetically, stored, and numbered from 1 to n in a database. We are interested in locating a certain name. Simulate this search with the following activity that represents a database with 1000 items.

1. Have a friend choose a secret number from 1 to 1000.

2. Your first guess for the secret number is the midpoint 500 of the range 1 to 1000.

3. If your guess is "too high," your next guess will be the midpoint of the range from 1 to 500. Similarly, if your first guess is "too low," make your second guess the midpoint of the upper half of the range.

4. Continue the process until you determine the secret number.

5. Write the sequence formed by the size of the range of possible numbers at each stage of the guessing. What type of sequence is this?

6. How many guesses will it take to find the secret number when n is 1000?

7. Consider a database that contains 1 000 000 files. Using the binary search method, what is the maximum number of trials that the search engine will have to test before it finds the desired file?

Review

6.1 *Find the next two terms in each sequence. Write a recursive formula for each.*

1. $-12, -9, -6, \ldots$

2. $\dfrac{1}{2}, 1, \dfrac{3}{2}, \ldots$

3. $0.21, 0.32, 0.43, \ldots$

4. $1, 2, 4, 8, \ldots$

Use each explicit formula to find the first five terms of each sequence.

5. $t_n = 5 - 2n$

6. $t_n = n^2 + 3$

7. $t_n = 2(n - 1)$

8. $t_n = 5 - 2n + n^2$

9. Write the defining recursive statements for
a) multiples of 7, beginning with 35
b) multiples of 6, beginning with 72
c) powers of k, beginning with k^3

6.2 *Use the two given terms to find a, d, and t_n for each arithmetic sequence.*

10. $t_3 = 17, t_8 = 57$

11. $t_4 = 3, t_9 = 63$

12. $t_2 = -50, t_{11} = 85$

13. $t_3 = 18, t_8 = -27$

Find the indicated sum for each arithmetic sequence.

14. $12 + 17 + 22 + \ldots$ Find S_{11}.

15. $66 + 55 + 44 + \ldots$ Find S_{20}.

16. $1.1 + 6.3 + 11.5 + \ldots$ Find S_8.

17. $\dfrac{1}{3} + 1 + \dfrac{5}{3} + \ldots$ Find S_9.

6.3 *Given each geometric sequence, find the indicated term.*
18. $100, 10, 1, \ldots$ Find t_9.

19. $-2, -8, -32, \ldots$ Find t_6.

20. $600, 300, 150, \ldots$ Find t_8.

21. $499.9, 49.9, 4.99, \ldots$ Find t_7.

22. $1, \dfrac{1}{3}, \dfrac{1}{9}, \ldots$ Find t_6.

Given two terms of the geometric sequence, find the indicated term.
23. $t_5 = 70, t_7 = 0.007$ Find t_3.

24. $t_4 = 5, t_8 = 405$ Find t_2.

25. $t_4 = 10, t_7 = 270$ Find t_{10}.

26. $t_3 = 27, t_7 = 2187$ Find t_{11}.

6.4 **27. CPI** The consumer price index is a measure of the average price of household goods. From 1982 to 1991, the CPI increased each year by a constant amount. In 1982, the CPI was 83.7, and the following year, it was 88.5.
a) Express the CPI as a recursive sequence.
b) Use your defining statement to find the CPI in 1991.

28. **10% solution** Financial advisors make reference to the "10% solution" in order to build financial security. This solution is to take 10% of your earnings each month and invest it. Suppose your 10% amount is $980.67.
a) The first month you invest the $980.67 at 6%/a compounded semi-annually. How much will this first investment be worth after three years?
b) The second month you invest the $980.67 at 5.85%/a compounded monthly. How much will this investment be worth after 35 months?
c) How much are the first two months' investments worth three years from the time that you started the 10% solution?

6.5 *For each geometric series, find the indicated partial sum.*
29. $100 + 300 + 900 + \ldots$ Find S_{11}.

30. $33 + 11 + \dfrac{11}{3} + \ldots$ Find S_5.

31. $700 + 350 + 175 + \ldots$ Find S_6.

32. $-999 - 111 - 12.\overline{3} - \ldots$ Find S_{10}.

33. $\dfrac{11}{30} + \dfrac{22}{30} + \dfrac{44}{30} + \ldots$ Find S_9.

34. $\dfrac{1}{13} - \dfrac{2}{13} + \dfrac{4}{13} - \ldots$ Find S_9.

Find the sum of each series.

35. $\displaystyle\sum_{k=1}^{4} 3(2)^{k-1}$

36. $\displaystyle\sum_{i=1}^{5} 20(0.25)^i$

37. $\displaystyle\sum_{k=1}^{6} 4^{k-1}$

38. $\displaystyle\sum_{m=1}^{7} 300\left(\dfrac{2}{3}\right)^m$

39. $\displaystyle\sum_{k=-2}^{8} (3^2)^{k-1}$

40. $\displaystyle\sum_{k=3}^{10} 0.3(0.15)^{k-1}$

41. Rebounding ball Measuring the height from the bottom of the ball, a dropped basketball returns to 55% of the height from which it is dropped. If one of these balls is dropped from a height of 3 m, find the total distance that it travels by the time it hits the floor for the fourth time.

Find the sum of each infinite geometric series.
42. $1000 + 100 + 10 + \ldots$
43. $-810 + 270 - 90 - \ldots$
44. $4 + 2 + 1 + \ldots$

45. Coal mining Coal production from a mine has declined 11% annually from an initial production of 300 000 t.
a) What mass of coal was mined in the first five years of production?
b) How many years will it take before the production falls below 100 000 t per year?
c) Estimate the mine's total production capacity over the lifetime of the mine.

46. Measurement Nested circles are drawn as shown. At each stage, the diameter of the circles drawn is half the diameter of a circle from the previous stage. The radius of the largest circle is r units.

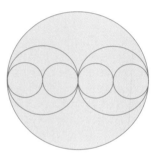

a) Write the total circumferences of the circles at each stage as a geometric sequence.
b) Determine the total length of all the circumferences.
c) Write the areas of the circles at each stage as a geometric sequence.
d) Determine the total area of all the circles.

47. Approximate the value of e by finding the first five sums of the following:

$$e = 2 + \cfrac{1}{1 + \cfrac{1}{2 + \cfrac{2}{3 + \cfrac{3}{4 + \cfrac{4}{\ldots}}}}}$$

Exploring Math

Alignment of the Planets

Astrology depends on the alignment of the planets in the sky. The periods of revolution of the planets around the sun are shown in the table.

Planet	Period
Mercury	88 Earth days
Venus	225 Earth days
Earth	365.25 Earth days
Mars	687 Earth days
Jupiter	11.86 Earth years
Saturn	29.46 Earth years
Uranus	84 Earth years
Neptune	165 Earth years
Pluto	248 Earth years

1. Assume that at one time Mercury, Venus, and Earth were aligned on the same side of the sun in a line l, and that l passed through the sun.
a) Write five terms of the sequence that would represent the subsequent days when Mercury would return to the same position.
b) Write similar sequences that represent Venus and Earth returning to the same position.
c) Use a spreadsheet to generate these three sequences, in columns beside each other.
d) By inspection of the spreadsheet, when will the three planets next align along line l?

2. Consider another set of three planets and determine how frequently they will be aligned.

3. Choose a set of four planets. Determine how often they will be aligned along a given line.

4. How often will all nine planets be aligned along a given line?

Chapter Check

Find the indicated term in each sequence.

1. $8, 24, 72, 216, \ldots$ Find t_{11}.
2. $80, 20, 5, 1.25, \ldots$ Find t_6.
3. $10, 7, 3, 4, -1, \ldots$ Find t_8.

For each series, find the indicated partial sum.

4. $99 + 33 + 11 + \ldots$ Find S_5.
5. $-0.01 - 0.1 - 1 - \ldots$ Find S_7.
6. $2 + 1 + \dfrac{1}{2} + \ldots$ Find S_{10}.

Determine whether each series is arithmetic or geometric. Then, find its sum if it exists.

7. $14 + 20 + 26 + \ldots + 80$
8. $1200 + 300 + 75 + \ldots + 4.6875$
9. $-22 - 19 - 16 - \ldots - 1$
10. $2.22 + 22.2 + 222 + \ldots + 2\,220\,000$
11. $8 + 4 + 2 + \ldots + 0.125$
12. $62\,500 + 2500 + 100 + \ldots$
13. $1996 + 2001 + 2006 + \ldots$

14. In a geometric sequence, $t_4 = 8$ and $t_7 = 216$. Find the value of t_2.

Find the sum of each series.

15. $10 + 20 + 30 + \ldots + 380$
16. $1000 + 500 + 250 + \ldots + 15.625$
17. $\displaystyle\sum_{i=0}^{\infty} 75(0.1)^i$
18. $\displaystyle\sum_{k=1}^{6} 3^{k-1}$

19. **Netherlands** Much of the Netherlands is land that was reclaimed from the sea and is now protected by dikes to prevent flooding. An earthen dike has a trapezoid-shaped cross section with the bottom 50 m across, and the top 15 m across. The width of the dike decreases by one metre for each metre increase in height.

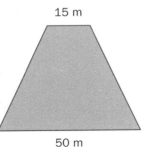

15 m

50 m

a) Write a sequence for the width of the dike as the height increases in one-metre units, starting at the bottom.
b) What is the width of the dike 15 m from the top?
c) What is the height of the dike?

20. **Biology** Mitosis is the stage of cell division when the cell nucleus divides into two; cytokinesis is the stage when the whole cell divides into two.
a) If you start with a single cell and it takes three minutes for cytokinesis to take place, how many cells are present after 30 min?
b) If a cell mass contains 32 768 cells, how long has it being undergoing cytokinesis?

21. What constant must be added to each of the numbers, 60, 135, 285, for them to form a geometric sequence?

22. **Investment** A five-year investment plan has the investor putting $2000 into GICs (Guaranteed Investment Certificates) at the beginning of each year for three years. The first GIC pays 6%/a compounded semi-annually for five years, the second GIC pays 6.2%/a compounded annually for four years and the third GIC pays 6.25%/a compounded monthly for three years. Determine the amount that the investment plan provides at the end of the five years.

23. **Physiology** Exercise therapists have found that repeated tasks produce a predictable muscle fatigue. Suppose that a muscle loses 15% of its strength after each performance of a task. The first time that a particular task is performed a person's muscles produce a 100 N force.
a) Write the sequence of forces that are used during repeated performances of the task.
b) How much force do the muscles exert in the sixth repetition?

24. a) For the infinite series,
$$\frac{1}{6} + \frac{13}{6^2} + \frac{19}{6^3} + \frac{97}{6^4} + \ldots + \frac{3^n + (-2)^n}{6^n} + \ldots$$
determine the first five partial sums of the series.
b) Write the series using sigma notation.
c) Which of the values, 1, $\dfrac{3}{4}$, $\dfrac{5}{6}$, or $\dfrac{1}{2}$, is the likely sum of the infinite series?

Using the Strategies

1. Calendar a) What date was exactly 2000 days before the first day of the year 2000?
b) What date is exactly 2000 days after the first day of the year 2000?

2. Measurement An octagon is formed by trisecting the sides of a square that measures 18 cm by 18 cm. What is the area of the octagon?

3. Measurement The inner circle has radius 3 cm, passes through the centre of the larger circle, and is also tangent to it. Find the area of the shaded region.

4. Unit cube Find the sum of the lengths of the interior diagonals of a unit cube.

5. Which term of the following infinite sequence has the least value?
$$\frac{19.96^0}{1}, \ \frac{19.96^1}{2\times 1}, \ \frac{19.96^2}{3\times 2\times 1}, \ \frac{19.96^3}{4\times 3\times 2\times 1}, \ \ldots$$

6. What is the units digit of the sum of the following series?
$$1 + 9 + 9^2 + 9^3 + 9^4 + 9^5 + \ldots + 9^{1999}$$

7. Measurement The line segment PQ is 50 units long and passes through the centres of six congruent circles that are tangent to each other as shown. P and Q are at the centre the circle at each end. Find the total area of the circles.

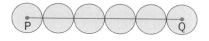

8. Solve for n.
$$\frac{1}{100} + \frac{2}{100} + \frac{3}{100} + \ldots + \frac{n}{100} = 100n$$

9. Four fours can be used to make the following numbers using no operation symbols.
$$4444, \ 444^4, \ 44^{44}, \ 44^{4^4}, 4^{444}, 4^{44^4}, 4^{4^{44}}, 4^{4^{4^4}}$$
Order the numbers from greatest to least.

10. Diagonals How many diagonals does a regular octagon have?

11. How many zeros are there in all the numbers from 1 to 1 000 000?

12. Birds A farmer bought 100 birds for $100. Each rooster cost $10, each hen cost $3, and each chick cost $0.50. If the farmer bought at least one of each type of bird, how many of each did he buy?

13. Magic cube In a magic square the sum of the numbers in any line is the same number. Magic cubes also exist. Consider a cube of order three. The magic property is that any three numbers that form a line have the same magic sum. Each of the six faces of the cube is a magic square, and the three numbers on each of the four diagonals of the cube also have the same magic sum.

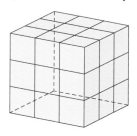

Separate the three layers of the cube as shown. Copy and complete the magic cube, using each of the numbers from 1 to 27 once. *Hint:* The number in the centre of the cube is 14.

Bottom Layer	Middle Layer	Top Layer

14. The difference in the squares of two numbers is 16. One number is exactly three fifths of the other number. What are the two numbers?

CUMULATIVE REVIEW, CHAPTERS 4–6

Find the equivalent measure in degrees, to the nearest tenth, for each of the following radian measures.

1. $\dfrac{7\pi}{8}$ 2. $\dfrac{25\pi}{12}$ 3. $-\dfrac{5\pi}{6}$

Find the equivalent measure in radians for each of the following degree measures. Leave answers in terms of π.

4. $-70°$ 5. $500°$ 6. $230°$

Given $\angle A$ in standard position with its terminal arm in the stated quadrant, find the exact values of the remaining five trigonometric ratios for A. Give the measure of $\angle A$.

7. $\sin A = \dfrac{1}{\sqrt{2}}$, quadrant II

8. $\tan A = 1$, quadrant III

9. $\cos A = \dfrac{\sqrt{3}}{2}$, quadrant IV

Determine the amplitude, period, horizontal phase shift, and vertical displacement for each function as compared with $y = \sin x$ or $y = \cos x$. Graph each function.

10. $y = 3 \sin x + 1$

11. $y = \cos\left(x - \dfrac{\pi}{4}\right)$

12. $y = \cos(3x - 45°) + 7$

13. $y = \cos 5\left(x + \dfrac{\pi}{6}\right) - 2$

14. Write an equation for the graph in the form $y = A \sin B(x + C) + D$ and in the form $y = A \cos B(x + C) + D$. Explain the process used in obtaining the equations.

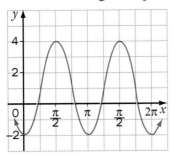

15. **Sales** The value of all sales at an electronics store can be approximated by the function $s(t) = 0.5 \sin(0.24\pi t + 0.76) + 4.5$, where $s(t)$ is the value of sales in millions of dollars, and t is time in months.
a) Graph the function.
b) What is the period of the function?
c) What is the maximum value of sales in any month?

16. Determine the period, phase shift, domain, and range of each function.
a) $y = 5 \sec x$ b) $y = \cot 3x$

c) $y = \csc 2x$ d) $y = \tan\left(x + \dfrac{\pi}{6}\right)$

Solve for A, $0 \le A < 2\pi$, and then give a general solution.

17. $2 \sin A = -2$

18. $\tan^2 A - \dfrac{1}{3} = 0$

19. $2 \sin^2 A + \sin A - 1 = 0$

20. $\cos 3A = \dfrac{\sqrt{3}}{2}$

21. $\sqrt{2} \sin 2A - 1 = 0$

22. **Technology** The screen shows the graphs of $y = 5 \sin^2 x$ and $y = 3x - 11 \cos x$, using a window $[-5, 5, 1]$ by $[-15, 6, 1]$.

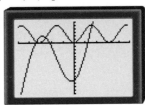

a) From the graph, how many solutions are there for the equation $5 \sin^2 x = 3x - 11 \cos x$?
b) What single function can be graphed to solve the equation $5 \sin^2 x = 3x - 11 \cos x$? Graph this function and determine the zeros, rounded to the nearest thousandth.

For each identity,
a) *verify the possibility of an identity graphically*
b) *show that it is true for x = 60°, using exact values*
c) *prove the result algebraically*
d) *state any restrictions*

23. $\tan x \sin x + \cos x = \sec x$

24. $1 - \cos x = \dfrac{\sin^2 x}{1 + \cos x}$

25. $\dfrac{1}{\tan x + \sec x} = \sec x - \tan x$

26. $\dfrac{\sin x + \tan x}{\cot x + \csc x} = \sin x \tan x$

Simplify.
27. $2 \cos^2 40° - 1$

28. $\cos^2 \dfrac{\pi}{8} - \sin^2 \dfrac{\pi}{8}$

29. $2 \sin \dfrac{5\pi}{12} \cos \dfrac{5\pi}{12}$

30. $\dfrac{2 \tan 125°}{1 - \tan^2 125°}$

31. Find $\sin(A + B)$, $\cos(A + B)$, $\sin(A - B)$, and $\cos(A - B)$ given

a) $\sin A = \dfrac{4}{5}$, $\cos B = \dfrac{5}{13}$, $\angle A$ and $\angle B$ are in quadrant I.

b) $\sin A = \dfrac{1}{\sqrt{2}}$ and $\cos B = -\dfrac{1}{\sqrt{3}}$, $\angle A$ and $\angle B$ are in quadrant II.

32. Find the number of terms in each arithmetic series for the given sum.
a) $15 + 20 + 25 + \ldots = 1250$
b) $3 + 7 + 11 + \ldots = 1830$
c) $10 + 8 + 6 + \ldots = -350$

Given each geometric sequence, find the indicated term.
33. $1000, 200, 40, \ldots$ Find t_6.

34. $1, -\dfrac{1}{3}, \dfrac{1}{9}, \ldots$ Find t_7.

35. $-4, -8, -16, \ldots$ Find t_9.

36. Find t_8 of a geometric sequence in which $t_3 = \dfrac{3}{2}$ and $t_5 = \dfrac{3}{8}$.

37. Saving for a car Colette is saving to buy a car in three years time. At the beginning of the first year, she invests $3000 at 7%/a compounded quarterly for three years. At the beginning of the next year, she invests $2000 at 9%/a compounded semi-annually for two years. At the beginning of the third year, she invests $1000 at 8%/a compounded monthly for one year. How much money will her investments provide toward a down payment on a car at the end of the third year?

Write each series in expanded form. Determine the sum of each.

38. $\displaystyle\sum_{k=1}^{4} 5(3)^{k-1}$

39. $\displaystyle\sum_{i=1}^{5} 10(0.4)^i$

40. $\displaystyle\sum_{k=1}^{7} 2^{k-1}$

41. $\displaystyle\sum_{i=1}^{6} 800\left(\dfrac{1}{2}\right)^i$

42. Salary raise Kristina was promised a 5% raise after each of the first four years that she worked for a company. If her starting salary was $45 000, find the total amount the company will have paid her by the end of the fourth year.

Find the sum of each infinite geometric series.
43. $3 + 0.3 + 0.03 + \ldots$

44. $-8 + 1 - \dfrac{1}{8} + \ldots$

45. $6 + 3 + 1.5 + \ldots$

46. Hot-air balloon In the first minute of flight, a hot-air balloon rises 50 m. In each succeeding minute, the balloon rises only 75% as far as in the previous minute.
a) What altitude will the balloon have reached after 5 min, to the nearest metre?
b) What will be the balloon's maximum altitude if it is allowed to rise indefinitely?
c) In which minute will the balloon reach an altitude of 175 m?

47. Infinite geometric series can be used to determine a rational number equivalent to a repeated decimal expansion. Let $q = 0.13\overline{71}$. Then, $q = 0.1 + 0.03 + 0.0071 + 0.000\ 071 + \ldots$ Find the rational number q whose decimal expansion is $0.13\overline{71}$.

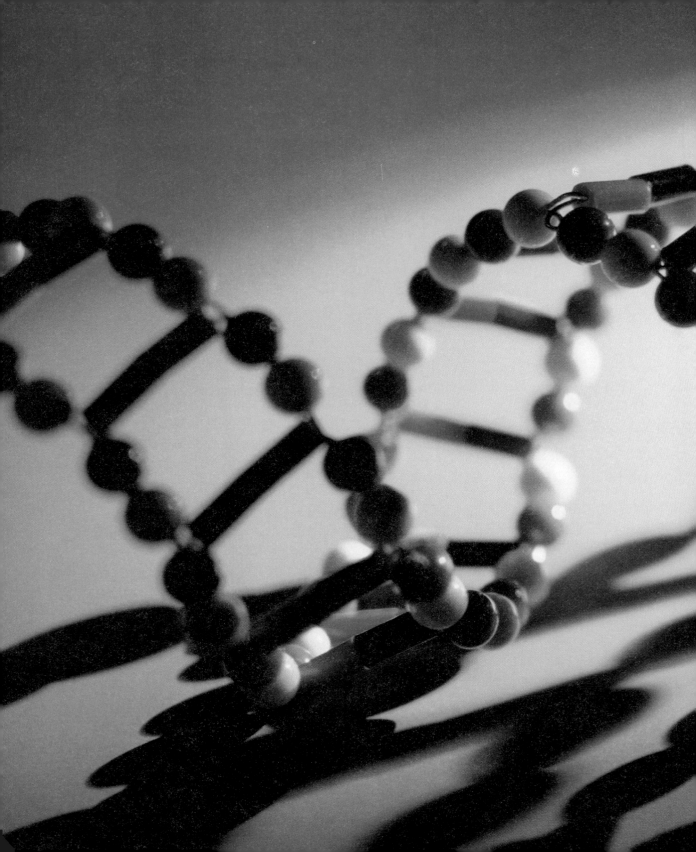

CHAPTER 7

Combinatorics

Every strand of DNA has components containing genetic information (exons) as well as components that supply no relevant genetic information (introns). Introns contain repeated sequences of base pairs called Variable Number Tandem Repeats (VNTRs). Testing for a particular VNTR is what is referred to as taking a DNA "fingerprint." From a DNA fingerprint scientists can determine whether two DNA samples are from the same person, related people, or non-related people.

DNA fingerprinting has become an important part of many legal cases. It can be used to confirm the presence of a suspect at the scene of a crime or to free incarcerated individuals who were wrongfully convicted prior to the availability of such an analysis.

The mathematics behind DNA fingerprinting is related to the number of ways that the bases—adenine, cytosine, guanine, and thymine—can be arranged in a VNTR, the number of VNTRs looked at, and the unlikely possibility that any two DNA fingerprints will be the same.

Counting the number of possible VNTRs is similar to counting the number of faces that can be made from three features, such as eyes, nose, and mouth.

1. How many different faces can be made from two possible pairs of eyes, two possible noses, and two possible mouths?

2. How many different faces could be made if there were three possibilities for each feature?

GETTING STARTED

Number Patterns

1. An employee at a local grocery store has been asked to arrange a display of canned vegetables. The manager wants the display 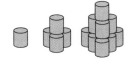 in the shape of a triangular pyramid. In the piles shown, the first contains one can, the second contains four cans, and the third contains ten cans.
a) How many cans high is the tallest complete pyramid that can be made with 100 cans of vegetables?
b) How many cans make up the base level of the pyramid in part a)?
c) How many cans were used for the entire pyramid in part a)?
d) How does the number of cans in each triangular level relate to the natural numbers 1, 2, 3, …?

2. What is the greatest possible number of rectangles that can be drawn on a
a) 1 by 5 grid?   **b)** 2 by 5 grid?   **c)** 3 by 5 grid?

d) Develop a general formula to represent the greatest possible number of rectangles that can be drawn on an *n* by *m* grid.
e) Use your answer from part d) to determine the greatest possible number of rectangles that can be drawn on an 8 by 5 grid.

3. When analyzing the rolling of two dice, it is convenient to visualize all possible rolls by organizing them in a table with each possible roll for one die along one axis, and for the other die on the other axis.
a) Copy and complete the table to show the sum obtained from each pair rolled.
b) Which sum is most frequent?
c) Suppose you were playing with two dodecahedral (12-sided) dice.
What sum would be the most frequent in this case?

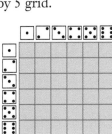

4. Find the greatest number of regions into which a circle can be divided by a given number of chords.

One line segment gives 2 regions.

Two line segments gives 4 regions.

a) Copy and complete the table.

Number of Chords, n	Number of Regions
1	2
2	4
3	
4	
5	
6	

b) Write a general expression to represent the pattern in part a).
c) Use your answer to part b) to find the greatest number of regions into which 15 chords can divide a circle.

5. A hollow square-based pyramid shape is built using cube-shaped blocks of stone. Each layer has one less block on each side than the layer below it. The bottom layer of a five-layer pyramid is shown.

a) How many blocks are used in building a five-layer pyramid?
b) Use patterns to help you determine how many blocks are needed to build a twenty-layer pyramid.

Mental Math

Use the laws of exponents to simplify each expression.

1. $(2x)^3$

2. $(27x^6)^{\frac{1}{3}}$

3. $(3a)^2(4a^2)^3$

4. $\left(\dfrac{2}{x}\right)^3$

5. $(5x)^{-\frac{1}{3}}$

6. $(xy)^3(x^2y)^3$

7. $(3\sqrt{x})^3$

8. $\left(\dfrac{3}{b^2}\right)^{-2}$

9. $(\sqrt[4]{25ab^2})^2$

10. $x\left(\dfrac{1}{x}\right)^{\frac{1}{3}}$

11. $x^a(3x)^{2a-b}$

12. $(6a\sqrt{b})^n(ab)^{4-n}$

Simplify each expression. State the restrictions.

13. $\dfrac{x^3}{y^4} \times \dfrac{y^6}{x^5}$

14. $\dfrac{y+y^2}{x^2} \times \dfrac{x}{y}$

15. $\dfrac{(x+2)(x+3)}{(x-1)(x+2)} \times \dfrac{x-1}{x+4}$

16. $\dfrac{(x-3)(x-2)}{(x-7)(x-3)} \times \dfrac{(x+5)(x-7)}{(x-2)(x+5)}$

Expand and simplify each of the following.

17. $(x+1)^2$　　　**18.** $(3x-2)^2$
19. $(x-3)^2$　　　**20.** $(5x-7)^2$
21. $(x^2-4)^2$　　**22.** $(x^2-6)^2$

Find the sum of each series.

23. $\displaystyle\sum_{k=1}^{5} k$

24. $\displaystyle\sum_{k=0}^{4} (k+3)$

25. $\displaystyle\sum_{k=2}^{5} 2k$

26. $\displaystyle\sum_{k=1}^{4} 1^{k-1}$

27. $\displaystyle\sum_{k=0}^{4} 2^k$

28. $\displaystyle\sum_{k=0}^{3} 2^{3-k}$

7.1 The Fundamental Counting Principle

In Western Canada, vehicle registration started as early as 1905, with owners having to create their own markers to display the assigned registration numbers. The cost of registration was anywhere from $2 to $10. By 1912, legislation had been passed in the provinces of Manitoba, Saskatchewan, Alberta, and British Columbia requiring annual vehicle registration of a province-issued licence plate. The Yukon and Northwest Territories followed suit in 1924 and 1941, respectively.

Licence plates have gone through many changes over the years. Most of the early government-issued licence plates were made of porcelain. Next, steel was used, and finally, aluminum. A variety of slogans and "numbering" systems have appeared on licence plates throughout their history. Most licence plates are rectangular, the exceptions being the licence plates for the Northwest Territories and Nunavut, which are polar-bear shaped. The winning design for a licence plate to mark the Northwest Territories Centennial in 1970 was a polar bear in colours of ice, snow, and sky entered by Klaus Schoene of Sir John Franklin High School in Yellowknife, NWT.

Explore: Draw a Tree Diagram

The licence plate for a non-commercial vehicle in British Columbia has an ABC123 format, that is, three alphabetic characters followed by three numeric characters. Suppose some British Columbians would prefer to have only the letters B and C on their licence plates. To determine how many ways three letters can be arranged using only the letters B and C, copy and complete a tree diagram as started here.

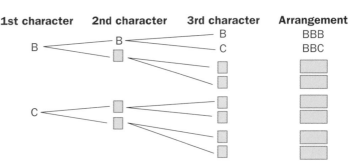

Inquire

1. How many ways are there to arrange the three letters if only Bs and Cs are used?

2. If the licence plate has only the letters A, L, or T, predict how many three-letter combinations can be made. Draw a tree diagram to list all the three-letter arrangements.

3. The province of Ontario had issued all possible licence plates of the ABC123 and 123ABC format by 1997. Ontario has moved to a seven-character licence plate of the format ABCD123, that is, four alphabetic characters followed by three numeric characters.
a) How many ways are there to arrange the four letters if only the letters B and C are used?

b) How many ways are there to arrange the four letters if only the letters A, L, or T are used?

4. How can the number of arrangements be determined without drawing a tree diagram?

The Fundamental Counting Principle

If a task is made up of stages, the total number of possibilities for the task is given by $m \times n \times p \times \ldots$, where m is the number of choices for the first stage, n is the number of choices for the second stage, p is the number of choices for the third stage, and so on.

Example 1   Using the Fundamental Counting Principle

The assembly of a new automobile requires that certain choices be made. For example, what colour, type of transmission, type of interior, and type of stereo are desired? Given the following table of options, in how many different ways can an automobile be assembled?

Colour	Transmission	Interior	Stereo
white	automatic	cloth	cassette
black	standard	leather	CD
red			
silver			

Solution

The task has four stages, namely, choosing the colour, choosing the transmission, choosing the interior, and choosing the stereo. Draw a tree diagram to visualize the choices. Each colour option in the tree diagram will have branches similar to the ones shown.

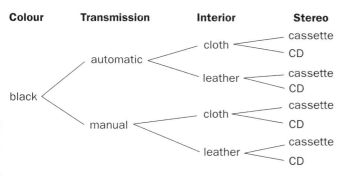

The total number of ways that the automobile can be assembled is the product of the choices available at each stage of the task.

Number of possible automobiles $= 4 \times 2 \times 2 \times 2$
$$= 32$$

For the options given, there are 32 different ways the automobile can be assembled.

Example 2 Counting Licence Plates

How many different licence plates can be made that consist of three digits followed by three letters?

Solution

The task has six stages, one stage for each character on the licence plate.
The first stage, choosing the first number, has 10 choices.
The 2nd and 3rd stages also have 10 possible choices each.
The 4th stage, choosing a letter, has 26 possible choices.
The 5th and 6th stages also have 26 possible choices each.

$$\text{Number of possible licence plates} = 10 \times 10 \times 10 \times 26 \times 26 \times 26$$
$$= 17\ 576\ 000$$

For licence plates that consist of three digits followed by three letters, 17 576 000 different licence plates can be made.

Practice

Draw a tree diagram to list all the possibilities for the tasks in questions 1–4.

1. How many different outfits can be made from two different shirts and three different pairs of pants?

2. How many different sundaes can be made from two choices of ice cream and four different toppings?

3. If you must choose two elective courses, one from three possible science courses and one from four possible humanities courses, how many different course selections are there?

4. A combination-meal menu has four choices for the appetizer, two choices for the entrée, and three choices for dessert. How many different meals can be chosen?

Applications and Problem Solving

5. Licence plates Example 2 showed that there are 17 576 000 different licence plates consisting of three digits followed by three letters. How many more licence plates can be issued in Ontario using a seven-character format, with four letters followed by three digits?

6. Genetic code Molecular biologists have discovered that a gene contains a long molecule that is made up of smaller molecules, called nucleotides. Nucleotides are composed of a sequence of the bases: adenine, cytosine, guanine, and thymine. These bases are often referred to by the letters A, C, G, and T. How many different genetic codes can be made if the sequence is
a) three bases long?
b) four bases long?
c) n bases long?

7. Braille Louis Braille (1809–1852) devised a system of six raised or not-raised dots to signify a letter of the alphabet. For example, the letter N is denoted by the arrangement shown, where a solid dot represents a raised dot.

a) How many different letters or characters may be coded in Braille?
b) If you wanted to code 94 distinct characters, such as those found on a computer keyboard, how many dots would the system need?

8. Postal codes Canadian postal codes have six characters, with the first, third, and fifth characters being letters, and the other characters being digits.
a) How many postal codes are possible?
b) The first two characters locate the regional post office. How many locations can the last four characters pinpoint?

9. Morse code Samuel Morse (1791–1872) developed a character coding system that was used to send messages along telegraph lines and also for light signalling between ships. Morse code is based on a series of dots and dashes (short or long bursts). The most frequently used letter, E, is coded as a single dot. The least frequently used letter, Q, is coded as dash, dash, dot, dash.
a) How many letters can be coded by a single burst? by two bursts? by three bursts? by four?
b) How many characters can be coded, in total, by up to four bursts?

10. Keys Key shapes are designed by dividing a key into separate parts. Each part can have several patterns.

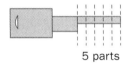

5 parts

a) How many different keys can be cut if the key design has five parts and each part has four possible patterns?
b) Suppose a company wants to ensure that it supplies a unique design to all 10 000 of its keyed safes. If the keys have six parts, how many patterns are needed for each part in order to have 10 000 different keys?
c) If a key had five parts and five patterns for each part, which modification would give more possible different keys: increasing the number of parts by one or increasing the number of patterns by one? Explain why.

11. Vacation planning A family is planning a vacation from Regina to Vancouver and back. They are considering the options: Regina to Calgary by bus, train, car, or airplane; Calgary to Vancouver by bus, train, or motor home; and then Vancouver back to Regina by train or plane.
a) In how many different ways can the family travel from Regina to Vancouver?
b) In how many different ways can the family make the entire journey?

12. Area codes In Canada and the United States, telephone area codes consist of three digits. Suppose the first digit is from 2 through 9 inclusive, the second digit is either 0 or 1, and the third digit is any digit except 0.
a) How many different area codes are possible with these criteria?
b) Suppose the restrictions on the first digit remain, but the restrictions on the second and third digits are removed so that any digit is allowed. How many different codes are now possible?

13. Computers and colour Each pixel of a colour monitor is comprised of three dots: one red, one green, and one blue. By combining these colours and varying their individual intensities, the pixels are able to display many different colours. There are 256 intensity levels for each red, green, and blue dot in a pixel. How many colours are possible?

14. Licence plates The province of New Brunswick uses a six-character licence plate, three letters followed by three digits, with the restriction that the first letter must be a B.
a) How many different licence plates are possible?
b) Compare your answer in part a) with the current population of New Brunswick. Speculate when and how the licence plate might be changed.

LOGIC POWER

Three sportscasters predicted the following teams to win in the weekend games.

Sportscaster A: Halifax, Winnipeg, Edmonton, Vancouver

Sportscaster B: Québec City, Winnipeg, Montréal, Edmonton

Sportscaster C: Edmonton, Montréal, Vancouver, Calgary

None of the sportscasters picked Toronto to win. Which teams played each other in the weekend games?

7.2 Permutations

For a photographer, taking a family photo can require far more time to arrange than to snap the picture. Taller family members might stand behind shorter family members, or the taller people might be asked to stand in the centre with the shorter people on either side. Does the group arrangement fit in the camera's viewing window? Can everyone's smiling face be seen?

Explore: Look for a Pattern

The Baca family is getting ready to have their family portraits taken. The photographer wants to arrange varying numbers of family members in a line. Copy and complete the following table to determine the number of ways of arranging the family members in a line.

Line Positions	Number of Choices
1st	5
1st, 2nd	5×4
1st, 2nd, 3rd	
1st, 2nd, 3rd, 4th	
1st, 2nd, 3rd, 4th, 5th	

Inquire

1. Notice that, in the table, one person is added at a time. Describe the pattern that emerges for the number of choices, depending on the number of persons being considered.

2. Suppose a family consists of eleven people. In how many ways can the first four people be arranged in a line? In how many ways can all eleven people be arranged in a line?

3. Explain how you would determine the number of ways of arranging n people in a line.

4. Explain how you would determine the number of ways of arranging r objects in a line if they are chosen from n objects.

5. Suppose the Baca family includes one set of identical twins and they are dressed the same. An arrangement with twin A in the first position and twin B in the second position will appear to be the same as twin B in the first position and twin A in the second. How is the number of possible arrangements affected?

6. What if the Baca family had identical triplets? In how many ways can the family be arranged in a line?

7. Explain how you would determine the number of ways of arranging n objects in a line if m objects are identical.

The product of consecutive natural numbers, in decreasing order to the number one, can be represented using **factorial notation**. For example:
$$3 \times 2 \times 1 = 3! \qquad \text{Read as "3 factorial."}$$
$$10 \times 9 \times 8 \times 7 \times 6 \times 5 \times 4 \times 3 \times 2 \times 1 = 10!$$
By definition, for a natural number n,
$$n! = n \times (n - 1) \times (n - 2) \times (n - 3) \times \ldots \times 3 \times 2 \times 1, \text{ and } 0! = 1$$

Example 1   Simplifying Factorial Expressions

Express each as a product in reduced form.

a) $4!$ **b)** $\dfrac{7!}{3!}$ **c)** $\dfrac{9!}{5!}$

Solution

a) $4! = 4 \times 3 \times 2 \times 1$

b) $\dfrac{7!}{3!} = \dfrac{7 \times 6 \times 5 \times 4 \times 3 \times 2 \times 1}{3 \times 2 \times 1}$
$= 7 \times 6 \times 5 \times 4$

c) $\dfrac{9!}{6!} = \dfrac{9 \times 8 \times 7 \times 6 \times 5 \times 4 \times 3 \times 2 \times 1}{6 \times 5 \times 4 \times 3 \times 2 \times 1}$
$= 9 \times 8 \times 7$

A **permutation** is an arrangement of objects in a *definite order*.
The number of permutations of n distinct objects is $n!$.

Example 2   Finding the Number of Permutations

a) Determine the number of different ways in which six people can be arranged in a line.
b) Determine the number of permutations of five candidates' names on a ballot.

Solution

a) Order is important. The number of permutations is $n!$
Since there are six people, $n = 6$.
$6! = 6 \times 5 \times 4 \times 3 \times 2 \times 1$
$= 720$
Six people can be arranged in a line in 720 different ways.

b) Since there are five names, $n = 5$.
$5! = 5 \times 4 \times 3 \times 2 \times 1$
$= 120$
The five names on the ballot can be arranged in 120 different orders.

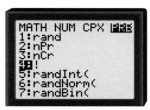

There are situations in which some of the objects that are being arranged are the same. For example, suppose you are lining up three identical green chairs and two identical blue chairs. How many different arrangements of the chairs are possible?
The answer is not 5!, because there are not five distinct objects being arranged.

Let G_1, G_2, G_3, B_1, and B_2 represent the chairs. Then, the following arrangements are considered to be the same.

$G_1\ G_2\ G_3\ B_1\ B_2$
$G_1\ G_3\ G_2\ B_1\ B_2$
$G_2\ G_1\ G_3\ B_1\ B_2$
$G_2\ G_3\ G_1\ B_1\ B_2$
$G_3\ G_1\ G_2\ B_1\ B_2$
$G_3\ G_2\ G_1\ B_1\ B_2$

First, looking at the green chairs, all six arrangements begin with three green chairs. To eliminate these duplications, the number of arrangements becomes $5! \div 6$ or $5! \div 3!$. In addition, to account for the duplications that will occur because of the two blue chairs, $2!$, the number of arrangements becomes $\dfrac{5!}{3!2!}$.

Therefore, the number of different chair arrangements is

$$\frac{5!}{3!2!} = \frac{5 \times 4 \times 3 \times 2 \times 1}{2 \times 1 \times 3 \times 2 \times 1}$$
$$= 10$$

The arrangements are:

green - green - green - blue - blue
green - green - blue - green - blue
green - green - blue - blue - green
green - blue - green - green - blue
green - blue - green - blue - green
green - blue - blue - green - green
blue - blue - green - green - green
blue - green - blue - green - green
blue - green - green - blue - green
blue - green - green - green - blue

Permutations of n Objects When Some Are Alike

The number of permutations of n objects of which a objects are alike, another b objects are alike, another c objects are alike, and so on, is

$$\frac{n!}{a!\,b!\,c!\ldots}$$

Example 3   Finding the Number of Permutations When Some Objects Are Alike

A builder has three models of homes from which customers can choose: A, B, and C. On one side of a street, the builder sold three model A homes, four model B homes, and two model C homes. In how many ways can the homes be arranged along the street?

Solution

Order is important. Some objects are alike.
The total number of homes is nine, so $n = 9$.
There are three model A homes, so $a = 3$.
There are four model B homes, so $b = 4$.
There are two model C homes, so $c = 2$.

Number of arrangements $= \dfrac{n!}{a!\,b!\,c!}$

$$= \dfrac{9!}{3!\,4!\,2!}$$

$$= 1260$$

There are 1260 different ways that the homes can be arranged along the street.

In some situations, not all of the n objects are being considered in the arrangement. For example, nine groups of students are required to prepare oral presentations, four of which are to be presented at the next class. The interest is in the possible arrangements of groups for the first four presentations. In this case, the number of possible arrangements is $9 \times 8 \times 7 \times 6$ or 3024. This product can be expressed in factorial notation as follows.

$$9 \times 8 \times 7 \times 6 = \dfrac{9 \times 8 \times 7 \times 6 \times 5 \times 4 \times 3 \times 2 \times 1}{5 \times 4 \times 3 \times 2 \times 1}$$

$$= \dfrac{9!}{5!}$$

$$= \dfrac{9!}{(9-4)!}$$

Permutations of n Distinct Objects Taken r at a Time

The notation $_nP_r$ is used to abbreviate the number of permutations of n distinct objects taken r at a time.

$$_nP_r = \dfrac{n!}{(n-r)!}$$

Example 4 Permutations of *n* Distinct Objects Taken *r* at a Time

A photographer is taking pictures for a catalogue. There are eight different styles of watch, but the retailer has asked that each arrangement be composed of only three items. How many different arrangements of the watches are possible for the catalogue?

Solution

Order is important. Use $_nP_r$.
There are eight styles of watch, so $n = 8$.
Only three watches at a time are needed, so $r = 3$.

$$_nP_r = {_8}P_3$$

$$= \dfrac{8!}{(8-3)!}$$

$$= \dfrac{8!}{5!}$$

$$= 8 \times 7 \times 6$$

$$= 336$$

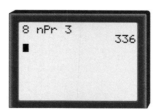

There are 336 possible watch arrangements for the catalogue.

Practice

Express each in factorial notation.

1. $5 \times 4 \times 3 \times 2 \times 1$

2. $3 \times 2 \times 1$

3. $8 \times 7 \times 6 \times 5 \times 4 \times 3 \times 2 \times 1$

4. $6 \times 5 \times 4 \times 3 \times 2 \times 1$

Express each as a product of natural numbers in reduced form.

5. $4!$

6. $7!$

7. $_5P_2$

8. $_6P_4$

9. $_{11}P_3$

10. $_9P_5$

11. $\dfrac{8!}{4!3!}$

12. $\dfrac{14!}{9!3!2!}$

13. $\dfrac{10!}{5!2!}$

Express each in the form $_nP_r$.

14. $5 \times 4 \times 3$

15. $8 \times 7 \times 6$

16. $17 \times 16 \times 15 \times 14 \times 13$

17. $55 \times 54 \times 53 \times 52 \times 51$

18. $8 \times 7 \times 6 \times 5 \times 4$

19. $99 \times 98 \times 97 \times 96$

20. 88×87

Applications and Problem Solving

21. Codes How many three-character codes can be made from the letters F, C, and P if
a) the letters may be repeated?
b) letters cannot be repeated?

22. Clubs A chess club has eight members.
a) In how many ways can the eight members be arranged in a row to have their photo taken?
b) In how many ways can the club choose a president, vice-president, and treasurer?
c) A neighbouring club invites some of the club members to speak at a dinner. Construct a problem in this context for which $_8P_4$ gives the answer.

23. Euchre The game of euchre uses 24 cards out of the regular deck.
a) A shuffle of the cards creates one arrangement. How many different arrangements are possible when you shuffle 24 euchre cards?
b) A euchre hand has five cards in it. In how many different ways can the five cards in a hand be arranged from left to right?
c) If you were to lay out five cards from a euchre deck in a row, how many different permutations could be created?

24. Signalling A ship carries four signal flags, each a different colour. The order in which the flags are hoisted on the flagpole constitutes a signal.
a) How many different signals can be made when all four flags are raised?
b) How many different signals can be made using three flags?
c) How many different signals can be made in total using any number of the four flags?
d) Assuming each flag is a different colour, and only two flags are displayed at a time, how many flags would be needed to code 90 different signals?

25. Pathways Rita lives five blocks east and three blocks north of her friend Marion.

a) Each time Marion walks to visit Rita, she likes to follow a different route. How many different routes are there if she goes only eastward and northward?
b) In how many different ways can you arrange the letters EEEEENNN?
c) How are your answers to parts a) and b) related? Explain.

26. Travel itineraries Over the past week an airline pilot was in Vancouver three days, Calgary two days, Whitehorse one day, and Winnipeg two days.
a) How many different itineraries could the pilot have had?
b) If you knew that the two days in Calgary were consecutive (a layover), how many itineraries could the pilot have had?

27. Team statistics A lacrosse team's record over a season was 15 wins, 4 losses, and 2 ties.
a) In how many orders could this record have occurred?
b) If you know that the team started the season strongly with five straight wins, how many orders are possible for the team's results?

28. Alphabets The language with the most letters in it is Cambodian, which has 72 letters.
a) How many three-letter permutations, with no letters repeating, can be created with this alphabet?
b) How many three-letter permutations can be created if letters may be repeated?
c) How many five-letter permutations, in which the first and last letters are the same but no other letters repeat, can be created?

29. Ice cream toppings An ice cream store offers 20 different topping combinations, each composed of two different items. Determine how many actual toppings there are.

30. Tournaments A soccer league has 26 teams. The top 16 teams play in the season-end tournament, with the first-round tournament match-ups being determined by the order in which the teams finish in the league standings. If a team loses a game in the tournament, it is out.
a) How many different arrangements of the top 16 teams are possible?
b) If the league expands to 30 teams, but still only the top 16 compete in the season-end tournament, how many different arrangements of the top 16 teams are possible?
c) With 30 teams in the league, how many arrangements are possible if the top 24 teams play in an end-of-season tournament?

31. Rock concert A popular rock group has written 30 songs, from which it selects to perform at a concert.
a) How many different opening sequences of three songs can be performed?
b) If the group performs all of its songs during the evening without repeating any of them, in how many orders could the songs be performed?

32. CD-ROM stories A children's CD-ROM has 24 character and object icons that the user can click on to fill in the blanks of a short story.
a) If one complete story has six blanks, how many different stories can be created if the user chooses not to repeat any of the fill-in choices?
b) The next story has seven blanks. If the child chooses to use one particular icon in two of the spaces, a second in two other spaces, but does not repeat any other choices, how many stories are possible?

33. Combination locks A combination lock has 60 numbers on it, from 0 to 59.
a) How many three-number combinations are possible?
b) How many three-number combinations are there that do not repeat any numbers in the combination?
c) Using parts a) and b), determine how many three-number combinations have at least two numbers the same.

34. a) What does $_nP_n$ mean?
b) Use $_nP_n$ to show that $0! = 1$.

35. a) In how many ways can five students be seated at a round table?
b) In how many ways can five students be seated at a round table if two students will not sit next to each other?

36. a) How many ways are there to label the corners of a square with the numbers 1 to 4?
b) If you start with the square labelled as shown, is it possible to move the square in some fashion so that it will be labelled with all the possibilities you demonstrated in part a)? Explain your reasoning.

37. How many different permutations of six beads of different shapes are possible on a circular ring?

INVESTIGATING MATH

Sets and Subsets

The concept of grouping objects is reflected frequently in our language. We talk about a pod of whales, a litter of kittens, a herd of cattle, and so on.

In mathematics, any collection of objects is called a **set**. The objects, or **elements**, in the set are usually listed between brace brackets, { }, and separated by commas. The order of the elements in the set does not matter. For example, the colours of the spectrum may be written as a set as {red, orange, yellow, green, blue, indigo, violet} or {blue, green, indigo, orange, red, violet, yellow}. Both represent the set of the colours of the spectrum.

1 Writing Sets and Subsets

1. Use set notation to list the elements of each.
a) the school subjects that you are taking
b) the prime numbers less than 25

2. A set P is a **subset** of a set Q if all the elements of P are also elements of Q. The empty set, { } or ϕ, and the entire set, Q, are both considered to be subsets of Q. P is a **proper subset** of Q, if P is a subset of Q and P ≠ Q.
a) A = {head, tail}. List the four subsets of A. Which are proper subsets of A?
b) B = {penny, nickel, dime}. List the eight subsets of B. Which are proper subsets of B?
c) C = {ace, king, queen, jack}. How many subsets does C have? How many are proper subsets?
d) What pattern appears to be emerging for the total number of subsets of a set with n elements? Test your prediction on a set with five elements, such as D = {a, b, c, d, e}. Write an explanation of the prediction.

2 Subsets of a Particular Size

1. A restaurant offers a choice of condiments for its hamburgers, as listed in set C.
C = {ketchup, mustard, relish, onions, tomatoes}
How many different two-condiment hamburgers can be made? List all of these as subsets of C.

2. A small pizza company offers four choices of topping: pepperoni, mushrooms, green peppers, and olives. How many different three-topping pizzas can be made?

3. Create a context for a situation that has a set of five elements and the requirement to find the number of subsets that have exactly two elements.

4. The primary colours are red, blue, and yellow. The secondary colours are made by mixing any two of the primary colours. Intermediate, or tertiary, colours are made by mixing a secondary and a primary colour together. How many secondary colours are there? How many intermediate colours are there? List the set(s) and subsets that you need to consider in answering these questions.

7.3 Combinations

Lotteries have become an important source of revenue for provincial governments. The temptation to buy a ticket is always very great when the jackpot is a multimillion-dollar prize.

Lotto 6/49 is a nation-wide lottery game in which the jackpot grows until it is won. The jackpot is never less than $1 000 000. Forty-five percent of sales from each draw is reserved for prizes. Once all $10 prizes (fifth place) have been paid, the remainder of the prize pool is divided up as shown in the circle graph.

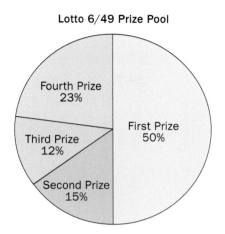

Lotto 6/49 Prize Pool

Explore: Look for a Pattern

Many lotteries are based on selecting a small set of numbers from a larger set of numbers. For example, a 6/49 lottery player must select six numbers from the numbers 1 through 49 inclusive. Consider a simpler game, where two numbers must be chosen from the numbers 1 through 5 inclusive.

Use a tree diagram to show all possible two-number combinations. Group these combinations in an appropriate way to make counting the combinations easier.

Inquire

1. How is the tree diagram that you have drawn different from the ones that you used in the first section of this chapter? Why can the Fundamental Counting Principle not be used here to count the number of combinations? How many different two-number combinations are there for the 2/5 lottery?

2. If you were to permute two numbers chosen from 1 through 5 inclusive, how many permutations would you have? List all the permutations. Compare the list of permutations with the two-number combinations that you found using a tree diagram. How are the two lists related?

3. Consider a 3/5 lottery. List all possible three-number combinations and all three-number permutations. Compare the two lists. Which criterion is essential with permutations, but is unimportant with combinations?

4. Looking at your permutation lists for the 2/5 and 3/5 lotteries, compare the number of ordered permutations with the unordered permutations. Conjecture a formula for the number of combinations possible.

A **combination** is a selection of objects in which *order is not important*. For example, in a 6/49 draw the numbers could be drawn in the order 17 43 8 21 16 25, but the results are printed 8 16 17 21 25 43 for ease of comparison.

Example 1   Comparing Permutations and Combinations

a) How many three-card permutations can be made from the ten, jack, queen, king, and ace of spades?

b) List all of the three-card combinations that can be made from these five cards. How is the number of combinations related to the number of three-card permutations?

Solution

a) Order is important in a permutation. Use $_nP_r$.

There are five cards to choose from, so $n = 5$.

Three cards are being selected at a time, so $r = 3$.

The number of permutations is

$$_5P_3 = \frac{5!}{(5-3)!}$$
$$= \frac{5!}{2!}$$
$$= 5 \times 4 \times 3$$
$$= 60$$

There are 60 three-card permutations that can be made from these five cards.

b) Since the order is not important in a combination, the easiest way to find all combinations is to write them in an ordered fashion. Use a tree diagram to list the combinations.

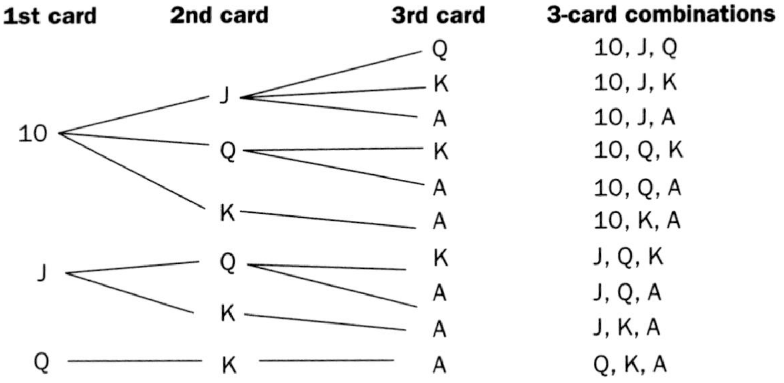

1st card	2nd card	3rd card	3-card combinations
		Q	10, J, Q
	J	K	10, J, K
		A	10, J, A
10	Q	K	10, Q, K
		A	10, Q, A
	K	A	10, K, A
	Q	K	J, Q, K
J		A	J, Q, A
	K	A	J, K, A
Q	K	A	Q, K, A

There are ten different three-card combinations.

The tree diagram for the permutations would contain 3! or 6 arrangements for each of the three-card combinations listed. Thus, in order to find the number of combinations from the number of permutations, these additional arrangements must be eliminated.

$$\frac{60}{6} = 10$$

In other words,

$$\text{number of combinations} = \frac{\text{number of permutations}}{\text{number of permutations in the three cards selected}}$$
$$= \frac{_5P_3}{3!}$$

Combinations of r Objects Taken From n Distinct Objects

The notation $_nC_r$ is used for the number of combinations of r objects taken from n distinct objects.

$$_nC_r = \frac{_nP_r}{r!}$$

$$= \frac{\dfrac{n!}{(n-r)!}}{r!}$$

$$= \frac{n!}{(n-r)!\,r!}$$

Example 2   Combinations of r Objects Taken from n Distinct Objects

Determine the number of possible lottery tickets that can be created in a 6/49 lottery where each ticket has six different numbers, in no particular order, chosen from the numbers 1 through 49 inclusive.

Solution

Order is not important, so the answer is the number of combinations.
Use $_nC_r$, with $n = 49$ and $r = 6$.

$$_{49}C_6 = \frac{49!}{(49-6)!\,6!}$$

$$= \frac{49!}{43!\,6!}$$

$$= \frac{49 \times 48 \times 47 \times 46 \times 45 \times 44}{6 \times 5 \times 4 \times 3 \times 2 \times 1}$$

$$= 13\ 983\ 816$$

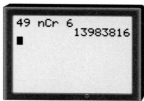

The number of possible lottery tickets that can be created is 13 983 816.

Example 3   Solving a Problem Involving Combinations

A group of five students is to be selected from a class of 35 students.
a) How many different groups can be selected?
b) Lisa, Gwen, and Al are students in this class. How many of the possible groups include all three of these students?
c) How many groups do not include all three of these students?

Solution

a) The order in which the group members are chosen is not important.
Use $_nC_r$ with $n = 35$ and $r = 5$.

$$_{35}C_5 = \frac{35!}{(35-5)!\,5!}$$

$$= \frac{35!}{30!\,5!}$$

$$= \frac{35 \times 34 \times 33 \times 32 \times 31}{5 \times 4 \times 3 \times 2 \times 1}$$

$$= 324\ 632$$

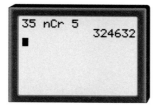

The number of different groups of five students is 324 632.

b) If Lisa, Gwen, and Al must be in the group of five, then there are only two more students to be chosen from the remaining 32 students. Order is not important, so use $_nC_r$ with $n = 32$ and $r = 2$.

$$\begin{aligned}
_{32}C_2 &= \frac{32!}{(32-2)!\,2!} \\
&= \frac{32!}{30!\,2!} \\
&= \frac{32 \times 31}{2} \\
&= 496
\end{aligned}$$

The number of groups of five that include Lisa, Gwen, and Al is 496.

c) Number of groups excluding Lisa, Gwen, and Al
= total number of groups – number of groups including Lisa, Gwen, and Al
= 324 632 – 496
= 324 136

The number of groups of five that do not include all three students, Lisa, Gwen, and Al, is 324 136.
Note that these groups will include any one or any two of the three members, Lisa, Gwen, and Al, but not all three.

Practice

Express each as a product in reduced form.
1. 4!
2. $_5C_2$
3. $_6C_4$
4. $_6P_4$
5. $_{22}P_3$
6. $_{29}C_5$

Express each either in factorial notation, in the form $_nP_r$, or in the form $_nC_r$.
7. $8 \times 7 \times 6$
8. $7 \times 6 \times 5 \times 4 \times 3 \times 2 \times 1$
9. $\dfrac{7 \times 6 \times 5}{3 \times 2 \times 1}$
10. $17 \times 16 \times 15 \times 14 \times 13$
11. $\dfrac{17 \times 16 \times 15 \times 14 \times 13}{5 \times 4 \times 3 \times 2 \times 1}$
12. $\dfrac{27 \times 26 \times 25}{3 \times 2 \times 1}$
13. $99 \times 98 \times 97 \times 96$
14. $\dfrac{74 \times 73 \times 72 \times 71}{4 \times 3 \times 2 \times 1}$

Applications and Problem Solving

Where necessary, express answers in scientific notation.

15. Flags The flags of most countries are designed in some combination of the colours: red, white, blue, green, yellow, and black.
a) How many two-colour combinations of these colours are possible?
b) How many three-colour combinations are possible?
c) Name at least three countries that have flags that use a two-colour combination and three that have flags that use a three-colour combination.

16. Bridge The game of bridge derives its name from the Russian word *biritch*, a now obsolete word that means "declarer." Each hand in bridge has 13 cards dealt from a regular deck of 52 cards.
a) How many different bridge hands are possible?
b) How many different bridge hands have all four aces in them?
c) How many different bridge hands have no aces in them?

17. Family reunions According to the *Guinness Book of Records*, Adam Borntrager's family is the largest in the world. Mr. Borntrager and his wife have 11 children, 115 grandchildren, 529 great-grandchildren, and 20 great-great-grandchildren.
a) If each table at a family reunion were to seat 20 people, how many different combinations of family members could be at the head table?

b) How many of the possible head-table combinations do not include any great-grandchildren?
c) How many of the possible head-table combinations include at least one great-grandchild?
d) How many handshakes would take place if every family member at the reunion shook every other family member's hand?

18. Pizza The largest pizza ever was baked in Norwood, South Africa, and had a diameter of 37.39 m. A pizza company advertises that it has 15 toppings from which to choose.
a) How many different two-topping pizzas can the company make?
b) How many different deluxe (five-topping) pizzas can be made?
c) One of the toppings available is anchovies. How many three-topping pizzas do not include anchovies?
d) There are six vegetable toppings: onions, green peppers, red peppers, zucchini, tomatoes, and green onions. How many different three-topping pizzas have no vegetables?
e) How many different three-topping pizzas have at least one vegetable?

19. Algebra Solve for n.
a) $_nC_1 = 15$
b) $_nC_2 = 6$
c) $4(_nC_2) = 2(_nC_1)$
d) $_nC_2 = 10$
e) $_nC_3 = 3(_nP_2)$
f) $_nP_3 = 2(_nC_4)$

20. Patterns a) Evaluate and compare each pair of combinations.
$_{10}C_1$ and $_{10}C_9$ $_{10}C_2$ and $_{10}C_8$
$_{10}C_3$ and $_{10}C_7$ $_{10}C_4$ and $_{10}C_6$
Describe the pattern that is revealed. Write an equivalent expression for $_{10}C_r$.
b) Make a general statement about $_nC_r$ based on this pattern.
c) Test your result with $_{50}C_7$.

21. Committee work To study the unity of Canada, a seven-person committee is to be selected from five public figures from Western Canada, five public figures from Central Canada, and five public figures from Eastern Canada.
a) How many possible committees can be formed?

b) How many of the possible committees would have no representation from Eastern Canada?
c) How many committees would have at least one representative from each region of Canada?

22. Polygons a) Draw three non-collinear points. How many lines are needed to join all possible pairs of points? Draw them.
b) Draw four points, no three of which are collinear. How many lines are needed to join all possible pairs of points? Draw them.
c) Draw five points, no three of which are collinear. How many lines are needed to join all possible pairs of points? Draw them.
d) How many lines are needed to join all possible pairs of eight points, no three of which are collinear? How many interior diagonals are there in a regular octagon?
e) How many interior diagonals are there in an n-gon?

23. Cards Use a regular deck of 52 cards.
a) How many different five-card hands are there?
b) How many different five-card hands containing only red cards are there?
c) How many different five-card hands containing all cards of the same suit are there?

24. Write a formula for each product.
a) $20 \times 18 \times \ldots \times 2$
b) $19 \times 17 \times 15 \times \ldots \times 1$
c) $n \times (n-2) \times \ldots \times 2$, where n is even
d) $n \times (n-2) \times \ldots \times 1$, where n is odd
e) $27 \times 24 \times 21 \times \ldots \times 3$

NUMBER POWER

In how many ways can these nine cards be arranged, in three rows of three cards, so that no card has a number smaller than its own number below it or to the right of it?

7.4 Pathways and Pascal's Triangle

The destiny of Ottawa changed forever when Queen Victoria chose it as the capital of the province of Canada in 1857. Construction of the Parliament Buildings began in 1860 and was completed approximately six years later, just in time to be reaffirmed as the national capital at Confederation in 1867.

Prior to European settlement, various aboriginal groups occupied the region, including the Ottawa nation from which the city took its name. With the arrival of the French in the 1600s, and later the British, the fur trade became the mainstay of the economy in the Ottawa River valley. Despite this fact, Europeans did not settle the Ottawa area until 1800.

Not long after the timber trade began, and with the completion of the Rideau Canal in 1832 by Lieutenant-Colonel John By of the Royal Engineers, a community called Bytown was firmly established as a service centre for the timber trade. This thriving town was incorporated as the city of Ottawa in 1855.

Explore: Look for a Pattern

The simplified street map shows a portion of downtown Ottawa, close to the Parliament Buildings. If you start at the corner of Bank and Laurier, and travel only eastward or northward, there are two routes you could take to walk to corner B. How many routes are possible to walk from the corner of Bank and Laurier to the corner of Rideau and Elgin? To help count routes, record the number of available paths to each intersection.

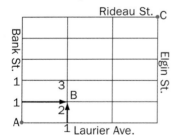

Draw your own copy of the map, recording the number of routes to each intersection.

Inquire

1. How many different routes are there from A to C?

2. Study the pattern of the numbers that you have used to determine the number of routes from A to C. What relationship do you observe among the "triangles" of numbers?

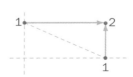

3. Continue the following pattern.

$n = 0$ $_0C_0 = 1$

$n = 1$ $_1C_0 = 1$ $_1C_1 = 1$

$n = 2$ $_2C_0 = 1$ $_2C_1 = 2$ $_2C_2 = 1$

$n = 3$ $_3C_0 = 1$ $_3C_1 = 3$ $_3C_2 = 3$ $_3C_3 = 1$

Calculate $_nC_r$ for $n = 4$ and $r = 0$ to 4. Repeat for $n = 5$ and $r = 0$ to 5.

4. Use the pattern established in the previous questions to write the next two rows.

Example 1   Pathways

In a television game show, a network of paths into which a ball falls is used to determine which prize a winner receives. Determine the number of paths that lead into each lettered slot.

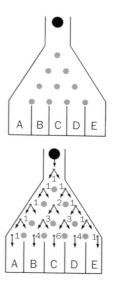

Solution

Locate the points where the ball has a choice of paths and mark each one with a dot. Starting at the top, record the number of possible paths to each marked point below. Record the results on a diagram.

There is only one pathway to each of slots A and E, four pathways to each of slots B and D, and six pathways to slot C.

The triangular array of numbers shown in the pathway network of Example 1 is known as **Pascal's triangle.** It is named after Blaise Pascal (1623–1662), the highly talented French mathematician who developed many ideas associated with these numbers. The first seven rows are as follows.

Example 2   Relating Combinations and Pascal's Triangle

Marion has invited six friends to a barbecue at her home. She did not ask for a response to her invitation, so she is not sure how many people are coming.
a) How many combinations of guests could actually occur?
b) How does the answer to part a) relate to Pascal's triangle?

Solution

a) Since the order in which the guests accept is not important, use $_nC_r$ to find the number of combinations in each case. There are six possible guests, so $n = 6$.

Case 1: No friends come over. Use $r = 0$.

$_6C_0 = 1$.

There is one way that this can occur.

Case 2: One friend comes over. Use $r = 1$.

$_6C_1 = 6$

There are six possible ways that this can occur.

Case 3: Two friends come over. Use $r = 2$.

$_6C_2 = 15$

There are 15 possible ways that this can occur.

Case 4: Three friends come over. Use $r = 3$.

$_6C_3 = 20$

There are 20 possible ways that this can occur.

Case 5: Four friends come over. Use $r = 4$.

$_6C_4 = 15$

There are 15 possible ways that this can occur.

Case 6: Five friends come over. Use $r = 5$.

$_6C_5 = 6$

There are six possible ways that this can occur.

Case 7: All six friends come over. Use $r = 6$.

$_6C_6 = 1$

There is one way that this can occur.

The total number of possible guest combinations is the sum of all these cases.

$1 + 6 + 15 + 20 + 15 + 6 + 1 = 64$

The number of possible guest combinations that might occur is 64.

b) Each of the entries in the seventh row of Pascal's triangle is equivalent to one of the possible cases for guest combinations.

```
                1
             1     1
          1     2     1
       1     3     3     1
     1     4     6     4     1
   1     5    10    10     5     1
 1     6    15    20    15     6     1
```

The sum of the entries in the seventh row of Pascal's triangle is also 64.

Practice

Determine the number of pathways from A to B in the following street arrangements.

1.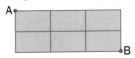

2.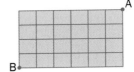

3.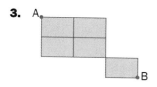

4.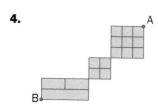

Applications and Problem Solving

5. Pascal's triangle Write the first 10 rows of Pascal's triangle.
a) Find the sum of the numbers in each row and complete a table to show the results.

Row, n	Sum of the Numbers in the Row
0	1
1	$1 + 1 = 2$

b) Predict the sum of the numbers in the 11th row (when $n = 10$). Check your prediction.
c) Predict the sum of the numbers in the $(n + 1)$st row of Pascal's triangle.

6. Checkers The game of checkers has been played since the twelfth century. A checkerboard is an 8 by 8 game board, and the pieces can travel only diagonally on the dark squares, one square at a time.

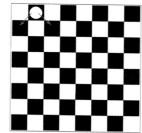

a) If a checker is placed as shown, how many possible paths are there for that checker to reach the opposite side of the game board?
b) Analyze the top row of the checkerboard to determine the total number of pathways to the opposite side from each of the other three starting locations.

c) When a checker reaches the opposite side, it becomes a "king." If the starting squares are labelled 1 to 4, from left to right, from which starting square does a checker have the most chances to become a king?

7. Pascal's Theorem Write the first six rows of Pascal's triangle.
a) Beside the triangle, write the equivalent numbers using $_nC_r$ notation.
b) What is the third entry in the fifth row in terms of $_nC_r$?
c) Write the relationship between the answer to b) and the second and third entries from the fourth row in terms of $_nC_r$.
d) Generalize this result to complete the equation: $_nC_r + _nC_{r+1} = \blacksquare$, which is known as Pascal's Theorem.
e) Apply Pascal's Theorem to complete each of the following equations.
$$_3C_2 + _3C_3 = \blacksquare$$
$$_5C_3 + _5C_4 = \blacksquare$$
$$_{10}C_6 + _{10}C_7 = \blacksquare$$

8. For the triangular letter arrangement given, start at the top and work diagonally left or right toward the bottom. How many different paths will spell PASCAL?

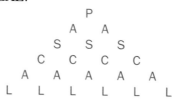

9. Neighbourhoods Use a street map of the vicinity around your school.
a) How many routes are there from the school to the nearest store?
b) How many routes are there from the school to the nearest public library?
c) How many routes are there from the school to your home?

10. Show that $_8C_0 + _8C_2 + _8C_4 + _8C_6 + _8C_8$ is equal to $_8C_1 + _8C_3 + _8C_5 + _8C_7$.

7.5 The Binomial Theorem

Blaise Pascal was a French mathematician, physicist, and philosopher. His accomplishments include: studies on atmospheric pressure, and the invention and construction of the first calculating machine. He also helped lay the foundation for the theory of probability.

The previous section of this chapter introduced Pascal's triangle. This triangular array of numbers contains many interesting patterns and relationships. For example, the summation of diagonal sequences in Pascal's triangle is related to the Fibonnaci sequence. Sierpinski's triangle can be constructed from Pascal's triangle. Some interesting and unexpected applications arise as well. A useful one occurs in algebra with the expansion of powers of binomials.

Explore: Look for a Pattern

Expand and simplify each of the following powers of the binomial $a + b$.

$(a + b)^0$

$(a + b)^1$

$(a + b)^2$

$(a + b)^3$

$(a + b)^4$

Inquire

1. Look at the numerical coefficients in the expansions. What pattern is revealed?

2. Predict the numerical coefficients of successive terms in the expansion of $(a + b)^5$.

3. Each term in the expansion is made up of a numerical coefficient, a power of a, and a power of b. What pattern do you see in the powers of a? What pattern do you see in the powers of b? What is the relationship between the power of the binomial and the numerical coefficient of the second term in the expansion? Predict the terms, made up of a numerical coefficient, a power of a, and a power of b, in the expansion of $(a + b)^5$.

4. Expand and simplify $(a + b)^5$ to verify your predictions.

5. Conjecture a formula involving $_nC_r$ for a general term in the expansion of $(a + b)^n$.

Example 1 Binomial Expansion

Expand.

a) $(a + b)^6$ **b)** $(2x + 3)^4$

Solution

a) The numerical coefficients in the expansion can be found from Pascal's triangle. The row whose second entry matches the exponent 6 is the correct row.

```
                    1
                1       1
            1       2       1
        1       3       3       1
      1     4       6       4       1
    1     5    10      10      5       1
  1     6    15      20      15      6       1
```

The expansion is of the form:

$(a + b)^6 = 1(\ )(\ ) + 6(\ )(\ ) + 15(\ )(\ ) + 20(\ )(\ ) + 15(\ )(\ ) + 6(\ )(\ ) + 1(\ )(\ )$

The terms are made up of decreasing powers of a from 6 to 0, and increasing powers of b from 0 to 6. Insert these powers into the expansion and simplify.

$(a + b)^6 = 1(a^6)(b^0) + 6(a^5)(b^1) + 15(a^4)(b^2) + 20(a^3)(b^3) + 15(a^2)(b^4) + 6(a^1)(b^5) + 1(a^0)(b^6)$

$\quad = a^6 + 6a^5b + 15a^4b^2 + 20a^3b^3 + 15a^2b^4 + 6ab^5 + b^6$

b) The numerical coefficients for $(2x + 3)^4$ occur in row 5 of Pascal's triangle.

```
                1
            1       1
        1       2       1
      1     3       3       1
    1     4       6       4       1
```

Therefore, so far,

$(2x + 3)^4 = 1(\ )(\ ) + 4(\ )(\ ) + 6(\ )(\ ) + 4(\ )(\ ) + 1(\ )(\ )$

With $a = 2x$ and $b = 3$, insert decreasing powers of a, increasing powers of b, and simplify.

$(2x + 3)^4 = 1(2x)^4(3)^0 + 4(2x)^3(3)^1 + 6(2x)^2(3)^2 + 4(2x)^1(3)^3 + 1(2x)^0(3)^4$

$\quad = 16x^4 + 96x^3 + 216x^2 + 216x + 81$

Recall that each entry in Pascal's triangle can be written in the form $_nC_r$. This means that the numerical coefficients of a binomial expansion can be written using $_nC_r$ notation. For example, the previous expansion could have been expressed as

$(2x + 3)^4 = {_4C_0}(\ )(\ ) + {_4C_1}(\ )(\ ) + {_4C_2}(\ )(\ ) + {_4C_3}(\ )(\ ) + {_4C_4}(\ )(\ ).$

This fact and the pattern of the powers in successive terms lead to the following theorem.

The Binomial Theorem

The expansion of $(a + b)^n$, where n is a natural number, is given by
$$(a + b)^n = {}_nC_0a^nb^0 + {}_nC_1a^{n-1}b^1 + {}_nC_2a^{n-2}b^2 + {}_nC_3a^{n-3}b^3 + \ldots + {}_nC_na^0b^n.$$

The general term is of the form $t_{r+1} = {}_nC_ra^{n-r}b^r$, where $r = 0$ gives the first term, $r = 1$ gives the second term, $r = 2$ gives the third term, and so on. Therefore,

$$(a + b)^n = \sum_{r=0}^{n} {}_nC_ra^{n-r}b^r$$

The Binomial Theorem can be proved by induction. This proof is typically reserved for more advanced mathematical courses.

Example 2   Applying the Binomial Theorem

a) Use the Binomial Theorem to expand $(x + 3)^5$.
b) Determine the general term and the fifth term in the expansion of $(2x + 5)^7$.

Solution

a) Use the Binomial Theorem with $a = x$, $b = 3$, and $n = 5$.

$$(a + b)^n = \sum_{r=0}^{n} {}_nC_ra^{n-r}b^r$$

$$(x + 3)^5 = \sum_{r=0}^{5} {}_5C_rx^{5-r}3^r$$

$$= {}_5C_0x^{5-0}(3)^0 + {}_5C_1x^{5-1}(3)^1 + {}_5C_2x^{5-2}(3)^2 + {}_5C_3x^{5-3}(3)^3 + {}_5C_4x^{5-4}(3)^4 + {}_5C_5x^{5-5}(3)^5$$
$$= 1x^5(1) + 5x^4(3) + 10x^3(9) + 10x^2(27) + 5x^1(81) + 1x^0(243)$$
$$= x^5 + 15x^4 + 90x^3 + 270x^2 + 405x + 243$$

b) For the general term, use $a = 2x$, $b = 5$, and $n = 7$.
$$t_{r+1} = {}_nC_ra^{n-r}b^r$$
$$t_{r+1} = {}_7C_r(2x)^{7-r}(5)^r$$
The general term in the expansion of $(2x + 5)^7$ is given by the expression
$$t_{r+1} = {}_7C_r(2x)^{7-r}(5)^r.$$

For the fifth term, r is one less, so use $r = 4$.
$$t_{r+1} = {}_7C_r(2x)^{7-r}(5)^r$$
$$t_{4+1} = {}_7C_4(2x)^{7-4}(5)^4$$
$$t_5 = 35(2^3)x^3(625)$$
$$= 175\ 000x^3$$

Practice

Use Pascal's triangle and the pattern of decreasing powers of a and increasing powers of b to expand.
1. $(x + 1)^5$
2. $(x - 2)^4$
3. $(2x + 1)^6$
4. $(3x - 2)^3$
5. $(4x + 1)^4$
6. $(1 + x)^3$
7. $(2 - x)^5$
8. $(x + y)^6$
9. $(2x + 3y)^4$
10. $(4a - 3b)^3$

Use the Binomial Theorem to expand.
11. $(x + 3)^4$
12. $(2x + 1)^3$
13. $(x - 3)^5$
14. $(3x - 5)^6$
15. $(2 + x)^3$
16. $(4x + y)^5$
17. $(4 - x)^3$
18. $(2x - 3y)^7$
19. $(7x + 2y)^3$
20. $(11 - 9x)^5$

Use the general term of the Binomial Theorem to determine the indicated term.

21. the third term of $(x + 7)^7$

22. the fifth term of $(x - 2)^6$

23. the fourth term of $\left(2x + \dfrac{1}{3}\right)^8$

24. the second term of $\left(3x + \dfrac{1}{2}\right)^7$

25. the second term of $(5 + x)^6$

26. the sixth term of $(4 - 3x)^9$

27. the fourth term of $(x + 2y)^6$

28. the third term of $(2x + 3y)^7$

29. the fourth term of $(3x - 7y)^5$

30. the eleventh term of $(2x + y)^{13}$

Applications and Problem Solving

31. What is the greatest numerical coefficient in the expansion of $(3x + 1)^8$?

32. Expand $(a + b + c)^3$ by writing it as $(a + [b + c])^3$ and using the Binomial Theorem.

33. **Work backward** Factor each in the form $(a + b)^n$.
a) $k^3 + 3k^2m + 3km^2 + m^3$
b) $x^5 + 5x^4y + 10x^3y^2 + 10x^2y^3 + 5xy^4 + y^5$
c) $x^3 + 6x^2 + 12x + 8$

34. **Rolling a die** An analysis of the probability of obtaining a 6 when rolling a die repeatedly three times can lead to the binomial expression $\left(\dfrac{1}{6} + \dfrac{5}{6}\right)^3$.

a) Expand $\left(\dfrac{1}{6} + \dfrac{5}{6}\right)^3$ into its four terms.

b) Add the four terms. Comment on this sum.
c) The first term in the expansion is the probability of rolling a 6 three times in a row. What is this probability? What do you think the last term represents?
d) What situations do you think the second and third terms of the expansion represent?
e) Predict what binomial expression could be considered if you were interested in the number of even numbers occurring in the repeated rolling of a die five times.

35. In the expansion of $(mx + n)^5$, the numerical coefficient of the second term is -48 and of the third term is 28.8. Find the values of m and n.

36. Determine if the expansion $\left(x^2 - \dfrac{1}{x}\right)^2$ contains an x^3 term.

37. a) In the expansion of $(1 + x)^n$, the first two terms are $1 + 5x$. Determine the value of n.
b) The first three terms in the expansion of $(1 + a)^n$ are $1 - 18 + 144$. Determine the values of a and n.
c) When $(1 - ax)^n$ is expanded, the first three terms are $1 - 12x + 63x^2$. What are the values of a and n?

38. Find the values of r and n if, in the expansion of $(1 + x)^n$, the numerical coefficient of the $(r + 1)$th term is twice that of the rth term and the coefficient of the $(r + 10)$th term is twice that of the $(r + 11)$th term.

39. Find the term involving x^7 of $\left(x + \dfrac{1}{2x}\right)^9$ and simplify.

40. Find the numerical coefficient of x^5 in
a) $(2 + x)^7$
b) $(1 + 3x)^5$
c) $(x^5 + 1)^3$
d) $(x^4 + 1)(x + 1)^2$
e) $(x^3 + 1)^7$

41. Expand $\left(x^2 - \dfrac{2}{x}\right)^4$ and compare it with the expansion of $\dfrac{1}{x^4}(x^3 - 2)^4$.

42. **Sierpinski's triangle** Explain how Pascal's triangle can be used to generate Sierpinski's triangle.

43. Prove the Binomial Theorem.

CONNECTING MATH AND COMPUTERS

Cryptography

Cryptography is the study of encryption or translating messages into ciphers or codes. Originally developed to provide secrecy for written messages, cryptography is used today to secure data flow between computers and between communications satellites and ground stations.

1 Classification by Key Type

Cryptographic systems can be classified by the type of key used in sending and receiving a message. A symmetric cryptosystem uses the same secret (private) key to encrypt and decrypt a message, while an asymmetric cryptosystem uses one key for encryption and a different key for decryption. These keys are known as public and private keys, respectively.

An example of a hybrid asymmetric cryptosystem is PGP (Pretty Good Privacy). It is the most widely used software program to encrypt and decrypt e-mail and files on the Internet. Typical e-mail sent over the Internet is like a postcard; anyone who sees it along the way between the sender and the receiver can read it. PGP acts as a secure "envelope" that keeps your e-mail private while it is in transit.

PGP makes use of two different encryption algorithms, RSA (asymmetric) and IDEA (symmetric). The message is first encrypted using the IDEA algorithm with a 128-bit randomly generated key. Then, this key is encrypted using the RSA algorithm with 512, 768, 1024, or 2048-bit keys. The mathematics behind the RSA keys is as follows:
- Choose two very large primes, p and q.
- Find $n = pq$.
- Choose e such that $e < n$ and relatively prime to $(p - 1)(q - 1)$.
- Compute d such that $(de - 1)$ is divisible by $(p - 1)(q - 1)$.
- The public key is (n, e) and the private key is (n, d). The public key can be given out to anyone with whom you wish to correspond. That person in turn uses your public key to encrypt a message that only you can read with your private key.

1. Chances are that, if you are a computer user, you have used passwords to sign on to a system, access your e-mail, or open a password-protected document.
a) How many possibilities exist for a four-character password if only the digits 0 to 9 can be used for each character?
b) How many possibilities exist for a four-character password if only letters can be used for each character?
c) How many possibilities exist for a four-character password if each character can be a digit or a letter?
d) Why is it typically recommended that a password be composed of both letters and digits?

2. Each bit can be either a 1 or a 0. How many possibilities exist for the 128-bit key of the IDEA algorithm?

3. In order to decipher a message that is PGP encrypted, the RSA public key must be factored. Research whether this has ever occurred. If so, how long did it take and what was the size of the key that was factored?

2 Classification by Mathematical Operations

Cryptographic systems can also be classified by the mathematical operations that are performed on the message, namely, transposition or substitution ciphers. A transposition cipher rearranges the order of the characters in the message, but does not change the characters themselves. A substitution cipher, on the other hand, replaces the characters being used in the message but does not change the order in which the characters appear.

1. A double transposition cipher involves the use of a keyword in determining the order in which the enciphered message is written. An example, using the keyword MATH, is shown.
Message: I HAVE A SECRET
Enciphered message: HARVETIECASE

keyword:	M	A	T	H
	3	1	4	2
	I	H	A	V
	E	A	S	E
	C	R	E	T

a) Explain how the double transposition cipher works, using the given example.
b) What information would the receiver of this message need in order to decipher the message?

2. The best-known polyalphabetic substitution ciphers are the Vigenère ciphers, named after Blaise de Vigenère (1523–1596). In the simplest Vigenère cipher, the key word or phrase is repeated as many times as is required. For example, using the keyword MATH and the message I HAVE A SECRET, first the keyword letters are written above the message letters. Then, the keyword letter is correlated with the message letter on the Vigenère tableau. The enciphered letter is found at the intersection of the column headed by the message letter and the row indexed by the keyword letter.

Keyword letters: M   ATHM   A   THMATH
Message letters: I   HAVE   A   SECRET
Enciphered letters: U   HTC

a) Finish the enciphering of the message in the example.
b) Use the keyword given to decipher the message given below.
Keyword: KEYWORD
Message: MSSHR PRE HCYWGKOV RDWJ POWQWUV ZSXFKIK WRI IAMNRBH
c) Use the Internet to locate a website for encrypting a Vigenère cipher, and to research a method for breaking a Vigenère cipher that uses a repeated key.

Vigenère Tableau

		Message Letter		

Message Letter: A B C D E F G H I J K L M N O P Q R S T U V W X Y Z

Key Letter:

A	A B C D E F G H I J K L M N O P Q R S T U V W X Y Z
B	B C D E F G H I J K L M N O P Q R S T U V W X Y Z A
C	C D E F G H I J K L M N O P Q R S T U V W X Y Z A B
D	D E F G H I J K L M N O P Q R S T U V W X Y Z A B C
E	E F G H I J K L M N O P Q R S T U V W X Y Z A B C D
F	F G H I J K L M N O P Q R S T U V W X Y Z A B C D E
G	G H I J K L M N O P Q R S T U V W X Y Z A B C D E F
H	H I J K L M N O P Q R S T U V W X Y Z A B C D E F G
I	I J K L M N O P Q R S T U V W X Y Z A B C D E F G H
J	J K L M N O P Q R S T U V W X Y Z A B C D E F G H I
K	K L M N O P Q R S T U V W X Y Z A B C D E F G H I J
L	L M N O P Q R S T U V W X Y Z A B C D E F G H I J K
M	M N O P Q R S T U V W X Y Z A B C D E F G H I J K L
N	N O P Q R S T U V W X Y Z A B C D E F G H I J K L M
O	O P Q R S T U V W X Y Z A B C D E F G H I J K L M N
P	P Q R S T U V W X Y Z A B C D E F G H I J K L M N O
Q	Q R S T U V W X Y Z A B C D E F G H I J K L M N O P
R	R S T U V W X Y Z A B C D E F G H I J K L M N O P Q
S	S T U V W X Y Z A B C D E F G H I J K L M N O P Q R
T	T U V W X Y Z A B C D E F G H I J K L M N O P Q R S
U	U V W X Y Z A B C D E F G H I J K L M N O P Q R S T
V	V W X Y Z A B C D E F G H I J K L M N O P Q R S T U
W	W X Y Z A B C D E F G H I J K L M N O P Q R S T U V
X	X Y Z A B C D E F G H I J K L M N O P Q R S T U V W
Y	Y Z A B C D E F G H I J K L M N O P Q R S T U V W X
Z	Z A B C D E F G H I J K L M N O P Q R S T U V W X Y

3. The Data Encryption Standard (DES) is the most widely adopted and used cipher in the history of cryptography. Research and write a report on the DES. When was this encryption system introduced? How does it work?

Review

7.1 *Draw a tree diagram to list all possibilities for each of the tasks in questions 1 and 2.*

1. Menus How many daily menus can be made from three choices for breakfast: cereal, bagel, or eggs; three choices for lunch: sandwich, salad, or soup; and four choices for dinner: pasta, steak, chicken, or casserole?

2. Portraits Four portraits, each of a different child in a family, are to be hung in a hallway.
a) The portraits are to be hung in the order of the children's ages.
b) There are no restrictions as to the order of the portraits.

7.2 **3. Logic game** A popular logic game uses eight different coloured pegs to create a secret code that is five pegs long. The order of the colours is an important part of the code.
a) If no two pegs of the same colour are in the secret code, how many different codes are possible?
b) If colours may be repeated, how many different secret codes are possible?
c) If a code is allowed to have blanks in any of the five locations as well as being able to repeat colours, how many codes are possible?

4. SCRABBLE® In the game of SCRABBLE®, you try to create words from a group of seven lettered tiles on your rack. How many different orders of the tiles must you consider for each of the following?
a) You are trying to make a three-letter word from the tiles G S U T Y R A.
b) You are trying to make a four-letter word from the tiles F I B W O D L.
c) You are trying to use all the tiles S S A N T T E.

5. School photograph A student council of seven people is to have its photograph taken for the school yearbook. In how many ways can the seven students be arranged if
a) they all line up in a row?
b) they line up in two rows with three students in the front and four in the back?

7.3 **6. Volunteers** A teacher requires some help to prepare a bulletin board for the class. There are 28 students in the class.
a) How many different volunteer groups of four students are possible?
b) How many of the groups include Miye, one of the students in the class?

7. Halloween A trick-or-treater is given the choice of five treats at one of the houses that she visits.
a) If the home-owner allows her to choose three treats, in how many different ways can she select them?
b) If she decides to take only two treats, how many combinations of treats can she select?

8. Fitness Two friends play squash together regularly.
a) If they decide to play three times a week, in how many ways can they select the days on which to play?
b) In preparation for an upcoming tournament, they decide to increase the number of times that they play per week to four. In how many ways can they choose the days?

7.4 **9. Marbles** A marble game has a board as shown. A marble is dropped at the top. You win if the marble exits from the middle hole; otherwise you lose.

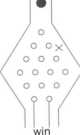

a) How many pathways lead to a win?
b) How many pathways lead to a loss?
c) Suppose you started a marble at position X. How many pathways lead to a win?

10. Walking tour The simplified street map shows of a portion of downtown Calgary. How many routes are there from

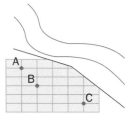

a) point A to point B?
b) point B to point C?
c) point A to point C?
d) Is the answer to part c) equal to the sum of the answers from parts a) and b)? Explain.

11. Bus schedules A bus line connects the seven cities with scheduled routes as shown in the diagram.

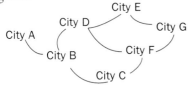

a) Determine the number of possible routes from city A to city G (without backtracking).
b) How many possible routes are there from city A to city G and back to city A?
c) How many of the return routes travel through city D?

12. Use the Binomial Theorem to expand and simplify each of the following.
a) $(5 + x)^3$ **b)** $(3x - 1)^6$
c) $(2x - y)^5$ **d)** $(x - 3y)^4$

13. Write the general term and the indicated term for each expansion .
a) the third term in $(x + 1)^5$
b) the second term in $(3 + x)^4$
c) the fifth term in $(7 - 2x)^9$
d) the fourth term in $(x + y)^7$

Exploring Math

Chebyshev Polynomials

Pafnuti Lvovich Chebyshev (1821–1894) was a Russian mathematician who did research in probability theory. A group of polynomials whose coefficients are taken from the diagonals of Pascal's triangle are called Chebyshev polynomials. Rewrite the first nine rows of Pascal's triangle flush to the left side.

```
1
1   1
1   2   1
1   3   3   1
1   4   6   4   1
1   5   10  10  5   1
1   6   15  20  15  6   1
1   7   21  35  35  21  7   1
1   8   28  56  70  56  28  8   1
```

Then, using the ninth diagonal of Pascal's triangle, a Chebyshev polynomial with these coefficients is $x^4 + 7x^3 + 15x^2 + 10x + 1 = 0$. This polynomial has four zeros, given by

$$x = -4\cos^2 \frac{k\pi}{9}, \text{ where } k = 1, 2, 3, 4.$$

1. a) Use the fifth diagonal of Pascal's triangle to write a Chebyshev polynomial.
b) Find the zeros of this polynomial using

$$x = -4\cos^2 \frac{k\pi}{5}, \text{ where } k = 1, 2.$$

c) Find the zeros of the same polynomial using the quadratic formula. How do they compare with your answers from part b)?

2. a) Use the seventh diagonal of Pascal's triangle to write a Chebyshev polynomial.
b) Find the zeros of this polynomial using

$$x = -4\cos^2 \frac{k\pi}{7}, \text{ where } k = 1, 2, 3.$$

c) Find the zeros of the same polynomial using a graphing calculator. How do they compare with your answers from part b)?

3. Write a general formula for the zeros of a polynomial that corresponds to the nth diagonal.

Chapter Check

1. a) Evaluate $4! + {}_4C_2 - {}_5P_2$.

b) Solve ${}_nP_2 = 210$ for n.

2. Expand each binomial, making use of Pascal's triangle.

a) $(2 - y)^4$

b) $(3x + 5)^7$

3. Use the Binomial Theorem to expand and simplify each of the following.

a) $(2x - 5)^5$

b) $(x - 3y)^6$

4. Find the general term and the term indicated.

a) the second term in the expansion of $(x - 5)^8$

b) the fifth term in the expansion of $(3 - 2y)^7$

c) the middle term in the expansion of $(2x + 5y)^8$

5. Quality control An electronics store receives a shipment of 12 CD players of 12 different models. Three of the players are selected to be displayed in the store window.

a) How many selections can be made?

b) If two of the CD players are found to be defective, how many of the selections in a) will contain no defective CD players?

6. Food service A delicatessen offers sandwiches with the following options: four types of bread, five choices of filling, and either lettuce or alfalfa sprouts. Assume that one item is chosen from each category.

a) How many different sandwiches are possible?

b) By adding one more option to each category, how many more choices of sandwiches would the delicatessen have to offer?

7. Baseball Suppose that the Montreal Expos and the Toronto Blue Jays play each other in the World Series.

a) How many ways can the Blue Jays win the series in seven games?

b) How many ways can the Expos win the series in six games?

c) How many possible ways can the series be decided?

8. Spider webs A spider weaves a web using non-sticky threads to allow it to cross its own web, and sticky threads in order to capture its prey. The circular threads are the sticky ones.

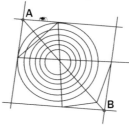

a) How many ways are there for the spider to get from point A to the centre of the web without backtracking to the perimeter?

b) In how many ways can the spider get from point A, through the centre, to point B on the other side?

9. Word games For each of the following jumbled words, determine the number of possible sequences in which the letters could be arranged. What English word has been jumbled for each?

a) R Y U O

b) B I M O E L

c) F F I I C L A O

d) S A C M I T T H E A M

10. Travel routes There are three possible routes from city A to city B: rural roads, a four-lane highway, and a two-lane highway.

a) How many different trips, from city A to city B and back to city A, are possible?

b) If it is too dark to return to city A via the rural roads, how many return trips are possible?

11. Choosing music A disc jockey is preparing a tape for a party. She has room for fifteen songs on the tape.

a) If she has chosen 20 possible songs to include, in how many different sequences can she record 15 of them on the tape?

b) She knows that the first three songs are very important as they set the tone for the party. In how many ways can she select the first three songs?

Using the Strategies

1. Fuel tank A fuel tank is $\frac{1}{4}$ full. If 5 L of fuel are added, then it is $\frac{1}{2}$ full. What is the volume of the tank?

2. The centres, R, S, and T, of three identical circles are collinear. The circles are inscribed in a rectangle. If $RT = 8x$, determine an expression, in terms of x, for the area of the shaded region.

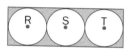

3. Given that $f(1) = 2$ and $f(n+1) = \dfrac{2f(n)+1}{2}$, what is the value of $f(235)$?

4. Escalator Jackie and Marla are walking down an escalator that has n steps visible at all times. The escalator is descending at a constant speed, but Jackie negotiates twice as many steps per minute as Marla. Jackie reaches the bottom after taking 27 steps, but Marla reaches the bottom after taking 18 steps. How many steps are in the escalator?

5. Futons One dozen futon mattresses are placed in a single pile in a warehouse. Each mattress was originally 20 cm thick, but each mattress is compressed by 1 cm for each mattress that is placed above it in the pile.
a) What is the height of the pile of mattresses?
b) Write an algebraic expression for the height of a pile of n mattresses. What is the greatest number of mattresses to which you could reasonably apply this mathematical model?

6. a) What two-digit number is three times the sum of its digits?
b) What two-digit number is the square of its units digit?

7. The sum of the first n terms of a sequence is given by $S_n = 2n^2 + 3n$. What is the sum of the next n terms?

8. Find two pairs of rational numbers, such that $a \neq b$ and $a^b = b^a$.

9. Highway driving A transport truck leaves Winnipeg at 09:30 travelling at an average speed of 80 km/h toward Edmonton. At 11:30 a car leaves the same place in Winnipeg and passes the truck 10 hours later. What is the average speed of the car?

10. Four positive integers have a sum of 125. If you increase one of these integers by 4, decrease another by 4, multiply another by 4, and divide the other by 4, you obtain four equal numbers. What are the four integers?

11. In the figure, $PR = PQ$ and $\angle RPS = 30°$. If $PS = PT$, what is the measure of $\angle QST$?

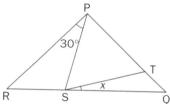

12. When riding on a train, a passenger often listens to the clicks as the train passes over the joins in the rails. If each rail is 10 m long, for how many seconds must a passenger count clicks for the number of clicks to be exactly the same as the speed of the train in kilometres per hour?

13. If a, b, and c are unequal real numbers whose sum is zero and whose product is two, what is the value of $a^3 + b^3 + c^3$?

14. Pens An office received a shipment of 80 pens. The invoice showed a total price of $80. The pens were of three different types priced at $10, $2, and 50¢. How many of each type of pen were there?

15. What is the missing number in the sequence 2, 8, 31, 88, ■, 384, …?

16. Measurement Find the area of a rhombus that has side length 10 cm, and diagonals that differ by 4 cm.

17. Prove that the sum of three consecutive integers is divisible by 3, the sum of five consecutive integers is divisible by 5, but the sum of four consecutive integers is not divisible by 4.

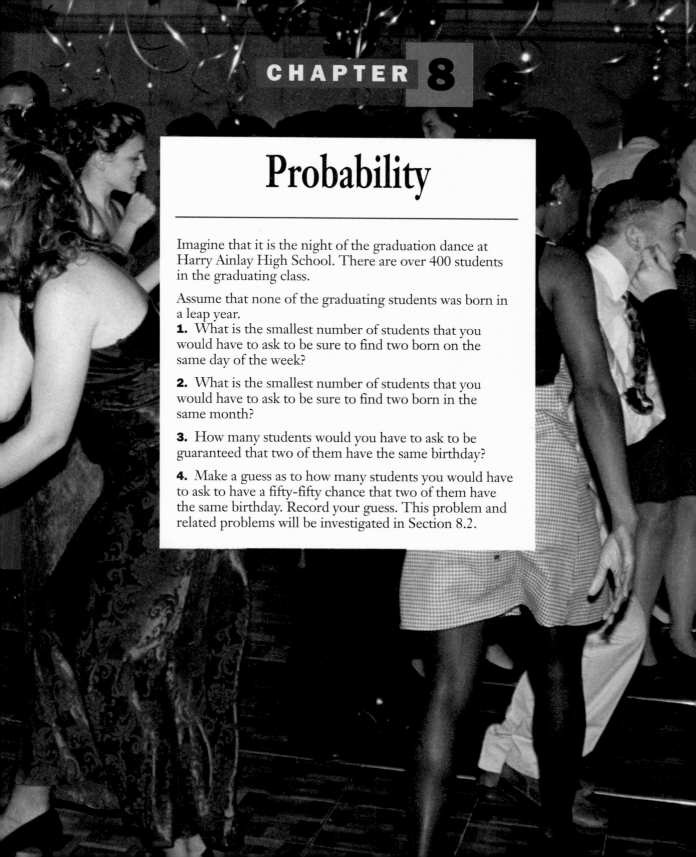

CHAPTER 8

Probability

Imagine that it is the night of the graduation dance at Harry Ainlay High School. There are over 400 students in the graduating class.

Assume that none of the graduating students was born in a leap year.

1. What is the smallest number of students that you would have to ask to be sure to find two born on the same day of the week?

2. What is the smallest number of students that you would have to ask to be sure to find two born in the same month?

3. How many students would you have to ask to be guaranteed that two of them have the same birthday?

4. Make a guess as to how many students you would have to ask to have a fifty-fifty chance that two of them have the same birthday. Record your guess. This problem and related problems will be investigated in Section 8.2.

Modelling Using Diagrams

1 Tree Diagrams

Use tree diagrams to answer the following.

1. An outdoor club near Parksville, British Columbia, offers a three-stage trip. The first stage can be completed by mountain bike or on foot, the second by canoe, kayak, or sailboat, and the third on horseback or motorbike. List all possible options for the trip.

2. A store in Brandon, Manitoba, stocks T-shirts in small, medium, large, and extra-large sizes. Each size is available in lime green, blue, or khaki. List all the possible choices for a T-shirt.

3. As a company benefit, Stella has a choice of health plans from three different insurance companies—Somestate, Green Circle, and Geneva Life. Each insurance company offers either standard coverage or extended coverage. For extended coverage, Stella must pay supplementary premiums. Determine all of Stella's health-plan options.

4. In Edmonton, Alberta, there are four daily newspapers—*The Edmonton Journal*, *The Edmonton Sun*, *The National Post*, and *The Globe and Mail*. Each paper can be delivered daily or only on weekends. List the possible options for delivery and choice of newspaper.

2 Venn Diagrams

Venn diagrams can be used to visualize statements by using circles inside a rectangle to model the given information. The Venn diagram shows all factors of 24 and all factors of 30. The interior of the rectangle represents whole numbers, and the overlapping region of the two circles shows the factors that are common to both 24 and 30.

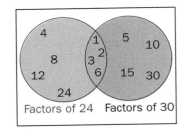

1. Draw a Venn diagram to visualize the whole number solutions to each of the following statements.

a) All values of x such that x is a factor of 12, and x is an even number.

b) All values of x such that x is a factor of 30, and x is an odd number.

c) All values of x such that x is a prime number, and x is less than 25.

d) All values of x such that x is a factor of 32, x is a factor of 24, and x is an even number less than 7.

2. A recent survey of a group of students found that each student participated in at least one of three sports activities: volleyball, soccer, or baseball. The Venn diagram shows the results of the survey.

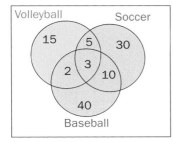

a) How many students participated in the survey?
b) How many students play soccer and baseball?
c) How many students play volleyball?
d) How many students do not play baseball?

3 Probability

Try this experiment with a classmate.

1. Shuffle a standard deck of 52 cards. What is the probability that the top card is the queen of diamonds? the king of clubs?

2. Sort through the deck until you find the queen of diamonds. Place the queen of diamonds face down on top of the deck. What is the probability that the top card is the queen of diamonds? What is the probability that the top card is the king of clubs?

3. Reshuffle the deck. Pick a card randomly out of the deck. Look at it, but do not show it to anyone. Place it on top of the deck. From your classmate's point of view, what is the probability the top card is the queen of diamonds? From your point of view, what is the probability the top card is the queen of diamonds? Discuss.

Mental Math

Each figure is drawn on a square with sides measuring 12 cm. Estimate the area of the dark part of each shaded figure, in square centimetres.

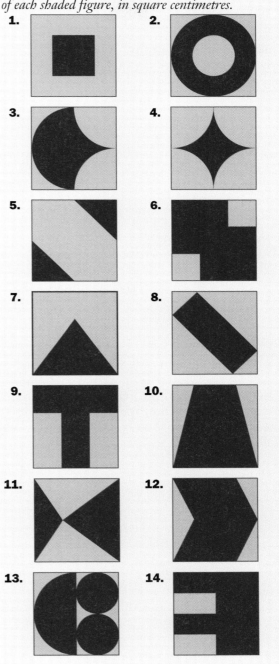

8.1 Probability and Sample Space

What are the chances of getting a job? of meeting an old friend? of snow tomorrow? We talk loosely about chance all the time. For many endeavours—winning a contest, being elected to a position, planning the distribution of health-care resources—it is useful to calculate or to estimate a numerical value for the chance that something will occur.

Explore: Use a Diagram

1. Draw a tree diagram to show all the possible outcomes of tossing four coins.

2. Draw a tree diagram to show all the possible outcomes of rolling two regular six-sided dice.

Inquire

1. a) What is the total number of possible outcomes when tossing four coins?
b) How many outcomes have at least three heads?
c) What is the probability of at least three heads? Express your answer as a fraction, a decimal, or a percent.

2. a) What is the total number of possible outcomes when rolling two six-sided dice?
b) How many outcomes have double numbers?
c) What is the probability of rolling two different numbers?

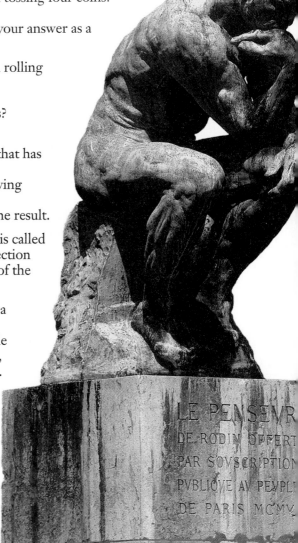

In the language of probability, an **experiment** is an action that has measurable or quantifiable results. For example:
Experiment 1: Roll a die and record the number that is showing on the top face.
Experiment 2: Measure the height of a student and record the result.

The set of all possible outcomes of a particular experiment is called the **sample space** for the experiment. An **event** is any collection of possible **outcomes** of an experiment, that is, any subset of the sample space.

The distinction between an *event* and an *outcome* may seem a little subtle.
In the experiment of rolling a six-sided die, the only possible outcomes are: rolling a 1, rolling a 2, rolling a 3, rolling a 4, rolling a 5, or rolling a 6. These comprise the sample space. One possible event in this sample space is *rolling a 4 or rolling a 5*. This event covers two outcomes. Another possible event is *not rolling a 3*. This event consists of five outcomes: rolling a 1, rolling a 2, rolling a 4, rolling a 5, or rolling a 6. A third possible event is *rolling a 1*. This last event is made up of only one outcome.

In an experiment with outcomes that are equally likely, the probability that a particular event will occur is given by:

$$P(\text{event}) = \frac{\text{number of outcomes favourable to the event}}{\text{total number of outcomes in the sample space}}$$

Example 1   Listing the Sample Space of an Experiment
a) List the sample space of an experiment in which one coin is tossed and one six-sided die is rolled at the same time.
b) Determine the probability of the event of tossing a head and rolling a 5.
c) Determine the probability of the event of tossing a head and rolling either a 4 or a 2.

Solution
a) Use a tree diagram to show the sample space.

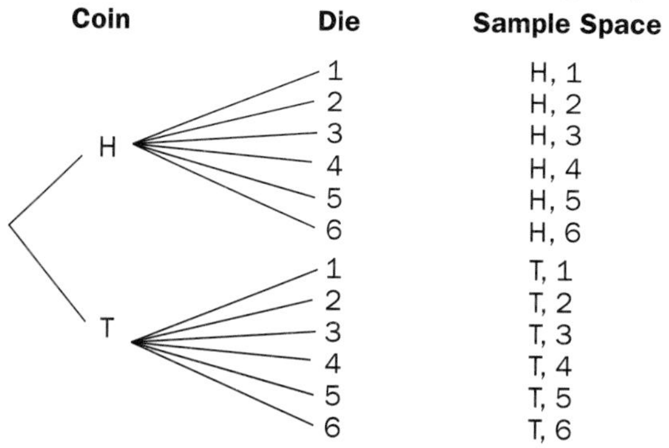

Coin	Die	Sample Space
H	1	H, 1
	2	H, 2
	3	H, 3
	4	H, 4
	5	H, 5
	6	H, 6
T	1	T, 1
	2	T, 2
	3	T, 3
	4	T, 4
	5	T, 5
	6	T, 6

b) $P(H,5) = \dfrac{\text{number of outcomes in the event of H,5}}{\text{total number of outcomes in the sample space}}$

$= \dfrac{1}{12}$

c) $P(H,4 \text{ or } H,2) = \dfrac{\text{number of outcomes in the event of H,4 or H,2}}{\text{total number of outcomes in the sample space}}$

$= \dfrac{1+1}{12}$

$= \dfrac{1}{6}$

Notice, in Example 1, that the probability of tossing a head is $\dfrac{1}{2}$, the probability of rolling a 5 is $\dfrac{1}{6}$, the probability of rolling a 4 is $\dfrac{1}{6}$, and the probability of rolling a 2 is $\dfrac{1}{6}$. A probability tree diagram can be drawn as shown with the probability of each outcome labelled directly on the diagram.

Tossing a coin and rolling a die are independent events. The rolling of the die is not in any way affected by the tossing of the coin. When the coin comes up heads $\frac{1}{2}$ of the time, a 5 is rolled $\frac{1}{6}$ of this time.

$$P(H,5) = P(H) \times P(5)$$
$$= \frac{1}{2} \times \frac{1}{6}$$
$$= \frac{1}{12}$$

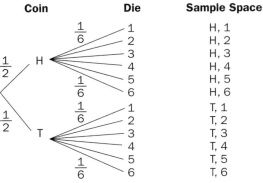

Since either a head on the coin and a four on the die or a head on the coin and a 2 on the die can occur, but not both simultaneously,

$$P(\text{H,4 or H,2}) = P(\text{H,4}) + P(\text{H,2})$$
$$= \frac{1}{12} + \frac{1}{12}$$
$$= \frac{1}{6}$$

Example 2   Using a Probability Tree

According to blood records, 4% of Canadians have type AB blood. Based on surveys, it is thought that 10% of the population is left-handed. Assume that there is no relationship between handedness and blood type.

a) Estimate the probability that a randomly selected Canadian is left-handed and has type AB blood.

b) In a group of three randomly selected Canadians, what is the estimated probability that at least two of them have type AB blood?

Solution

a) List the sample space, using a probability tree.

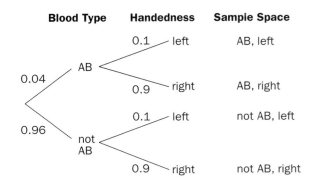

$$P(\text{AB,left}) = P(\text{AB}) \times P(\text{left})$$
$$= 0.04 \times 0.1$$
$$= 0.004$$

The probability that a person has type AB blood and is left-handed is 0.004, or 0.4%.

b) List the sample space, using a probability tree.

Identify the branches that give outcomes of at least two people with type AB blood. There are eight outcomes in the sample space. The outcomes with at least two people with type AB are indicated with a check mark. The probability that at least two people have type AB blood is the sum of the probabilities of each of these outcomes.

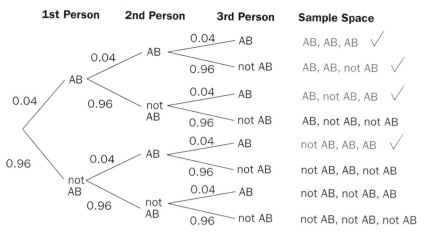

	1st Person	2nd Person	3rd Person	Sample Space

$P(\text{at least 2 type AB}) = P(3 \text{ type AB}) + P(2 \text{ type AB})$

$= P(\text{AB, AB, AB}) + P(\text{AB, AB, not AB}) + P(\text{AB, not AB, AB}) + P(\text{not AB, AB, AB})$

$= (0.04 \times 0.04 \times 0.04) + (0.04 \times 0.04 \times 0.96) + (0.04 \times 0.96 \times 0.04) + (0.96 \times 0.04 \times 0.04)$

$= 0.004\ 672$

The probability that at least two out of three randomly selected Canadians have type AB blood is 0.004 672.

Practice

In questions 1-7, use a probability tree to list the sample space of the experiments and determine the probability of the required event.

1. When tossing a coin and cutting a deck of cards, what is the probability of obtaining a head and a spade card?

2. When rolling a six-sided die and cutting a deck of cards, what is the probability of obtaining a two and an ace?

3. When cutting a deck of cards and randomly choosing a direction (north, south, east, or west), what is the probability of obtaining a face card and north?

4. In the random selection of a movie (comedy, drama, adventure, or science fiction) and a snack (chips, chocolate, or popcorn), what is the probability of choosing a comedy with chips?

5. Randomly selecting a time (17:00, 18:00, or 19:00) and a physical activity (jogging, rollerblading, cycling, or swimming), what is the probability of choosing swimming at 17:00?

6. Randomly picking a day of the week and then a month, what is the probability that Friday and April will be chosen?

7. What is the probability of being chosen as one of the three class representatives from a class of 28 students, if three names were selected at random from the class list?

Applications and Problem Solving

8. Prime numbers Two numbers are **relatively prime** if they have no common prime factors.
a) List the sample space in the experiment of rolling two dice.
b) Identify the outcomes that are relatively prime.
c) Determine the probability of rolling two numbers that are relatively prime.

9. Sociology Approximately 77% of the Canadian population is urban. About 12% of Canadian adults have a university degree. Assuming that there is no relationship between urban dwelling and level of education, what is the estimated probability that a Canadian adult, randomly selected, is
a) an urban dweller with a university degree?
b) a rural dweller with a university degree?
c) an urban dweller without a university degree?

10. Trade The U.S.A. is Canada's largest trading partner. Canada exports 76% of its goods to the U.S.A. and 65% of Canada's imports come from the U.S.A. If a Canadian import and export are randomly selected, what is the probability that
a) both trades are with the U.S.A.?
b) neither is with the U.S.A.?
c) the export is to the U.S.A. but the import is not from the U.S.A.?

11. Odds The **odds** of an event are defined as the ratio of favourable outcomes to unfavourable outcomes for an event. For example, when rolling a six-sided die, the odds of a six occurring are 1:5; the odds of a 1 or a 3 are 2:4. Find the odds for each of the following events.
a) Two six-sided dice sum to 7.
b) Two six-sided dice sum to 12.
c) Three six-sided dice sum to 3.
d) Three six-sided dice sum to 17.

12. Spares Mrs. Jafari asks her grade 12 mathematics class of 32 students each to record a number between 1 and 100 inclusive. She is willing to wager spares against extra classes that there will be at least two numbers that are the same. If Mrs. Jafari offers odds of 5:3, should the class accept the wager? Explain your reasoning.

13. Meeting plans Paul and Maya arrange to meet at 17:00. Paul expects to arrive at any minute between 17:00 and 17:05 inclusive. Maya foresees that she will reach the meeting place between 17:03 and 17:10 inclusive. Use minute time intervals, that is, 5:00—5:01 and so on.
a) List the sample space in a probability tree.
b) What is the probability that they both arrive in the same minute time interval?
c) What is the probability that Paul arrives before Maya?
d) An alternative way to list the sample space is with the times as ordered pairs. For example, arrival times of 17:02 for Paul and 17:07 for Maya is written as (2, 7). Graph the sample space with Paul's arrival time on the horizontal axis and Maya's on the vertical axis.
e) What is the probability of each point in the sample space?

f) Use the points on your graph to find the probability that Maya arrives before Paul. Explain your method.
g) If the time intervals were in seconds instead of minutes, how would your answers to parts b) and c) change?

14. Hockey At a certain hockey tournament, a tie is decided by a sudden death shootout. In each round of the shootout, each team nominates one player who has not previously shot. If all the players on a team have had a shot, the coaches proceed through the list as before. In any round, if one team scores and the other does not, the scoring team wins. From previous records, the shooters on the Orcas team have a probability of 0.35 of scoring and the shooters on the Bisons team have a probability of 0.4 of scoring. What is the probability that
a) no one scores in a round?
b) both teams score in a round?
c) another round is necessary?
d) the Orcas win on the second round?
e) the Bisons win on the third round?
f) the Orcas win the tournament? (*Hint*: You will have to sum an infinite geometric series.)
g) that the Bisons win the tournament?

15. Raffle A community bike network holds a fund-raising raffle. The three prizes are a bike, a bike trailer, and a bike pump. There are 9000 tickets sold.
a) What is the probability of winning the grand prize with one ticket?
b) What is the probability of winning any of the prizes with one ticket?
c) What is the probability of winning the bike pump if one buys nine tickets?
d) What is the probability of winning the bike and the bike trailer but not the bike pump, if one buys 15 tickets?

Probability and Reasonable Assumptions

In estimating the probability of an outcome in an experiment, we are usually modelling a real-life situation. To create a feasible model, assumptions are made. It is important to be aware of these assumptions, which are sometimes subtle, and their implications. **Statistical sampling** is used to design accurate and representative experiments to estimate empirically the probability of the occurrence of an event.

1 Tossing a Coin

1. A **fair** coin comes up heads half the time and tails half the time. Is there such a thing as a fair coin? Does a coin have an edge? Could it land on its edge when flipped on a table? Discuss.

2. Instead of taking a theoretical approach to tossing a coin, an experimental one could be taken. Take a toonie, toss it ten times, and record the results, heads or tails. Divide the number of tails by ten.
a) Do you think this represents the probability of tossing a tail?
b) If you tossed the coin 11 times, recorded the results, and divided the number of tails by 11, would the result represent the probability of tossing a tail?
c) How many times would you have to toss the coin to get a good estimate for tossing a tail on this toonie? Discuss.

3. a) Would the probability of tossing a tail on another toonie be exactly the same as tossing a tail on the toonie used in question 2? Discuss.
b) Design a method to get a good estimate of the probability of tossing a tail on any toonie.

2 Birthdays

a) What is the probability that a stranger has exactly the same birthday as you? List any assumptions that you need to make.
b) Records indicate that babies are not born uniformly over the year. Births in the months of April through August are more popular. If you took this information into account, how would this affect your answer to part a)?

Births in Canada for One Year — Most Popular Months	
May	33 119
July	32 460
April	31 802
June	31 316
August	31 296
Total births for one year	366 200

INVESTIGATING MATH

Visualizing Events

Tree diagrams are used to represent the sample space of outcomes in an easy-to-read form. To see the interaction of different events, Venn diagrams can be used.

Consider the experiment of tossing two coins. The collection of outcomes, the sample space, is: *two heads*, *a head and a tail*, *a tail and a head*, and *two tails*. A Venn diagram represents this sample space with a rectangle.

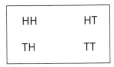

Events are depicted as regions of the rectangle. Let A be the event of having at least one tail. Let B be the event of having at least one head. Let C be the event of having both coins exactly the same. These events can be shown using Venn diagrams.

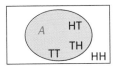 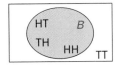 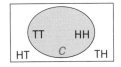

For two events, the overlapping region in the rectangle represents the outcomes common to both events. **Mutually exclusive events** do not have any outcomes in common, so they occupy separate regions of the rectangle. Events E and F are mutually exclusive, while G and H are not.

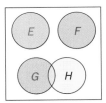

1. Consider the experiment of picking a random number between 5 and 20 inclusive from a hat.
a) Represent the sample space using a Venn diagram.
b) Organize the outcomes to represent three events: the event A of picking a prime number, the event B of picking a number divisible by 3, and the event C of picking a number greater than 9.
c) What outcomes are common to A and B? What outcomes are common to all of A, B, and C? Are A and B mutually exclusive? A and C? B and C?

2. Draw a Venn diagram to represent the event of choosing a number less than or equal to 11. On the same Venn diagram, represent the event of choosing a number greater than 11. Together, what do these two events comprise? Are the two events mutually exclusive?

3. Four different events—A, B, C, and D—are represented in this Venn diagram by red, green, blue, and yellow regions, respectively.

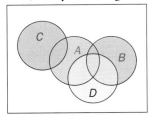

a) Are A and B mutually exclusive events?
b) Which events are mutually exclusive with D?
c) What region represents the outcomes common to all of A, B, and D?
d) How many outcomes are common to all of A, B, and C?
e) Are the outcomes common to A and B mutually exclusive with those common to C and D?

8.2 Classifying Events

Playing cards similar to our present day decks were introduced into Western Europe in the fourteenth century. A deck of cards painted in 1393 for the king of France is stored in the Bibliothèque Nationale in Paris.

Explore: Conduct a Sequence of Experiments

1. From a full deck of cards, remove the ten, jack, queen, king, and ace of hearts and of spades. Shuffle these ten cards together. Deal out two cards from this ten-card deck. Keep a tally of whether or not the two cards are of the same suit. Repeat this experiment 50 times.

2. Reshuffle the ten-card deck from the previous question; deal one card and remember its suit. Replace the card in the deck; reshuffle and deal one card. Keep a tally of whether the two cards are of the same suit or not. Repeat this experiment 50 times.

3. Compare your results with those of your classmates.

Inquire

1. Did you expect the outcomes of the two sequences of experiments to be different? Theoretically, is the probability of dealing two cards of the same suit identical in both sequences of experiments? What conditions make the two sequences of experiments different?

2. Draw a probability tree for each experiment. How does the first card dealt affect the probabilities that you have assigned to the branches of the tree associated with the second card dealt?

In an experiment, two events are **independent** if the probability that each event will occur is not affected by the occurrence of the other event. If events are *not* independent, they are called **dependent**.

Example 1   Independence versus Dependence

Classify the following events as either *independent* or *dependent*.

a) The experiment is rolling a die and flipping a coin. The first event is rolling a six and the second event is obtaining tails.

b) The experiment is rolling a pair of dice. The first event is rolling an odd number on one die and the second event is rolling an even number on the other die.

c) The experiment is to sample two members of a family, a mother and her child. The first event is that the mother has blonde hair, and the second event is that the child has blonde hair.

d) The experiment is dealing five cards from a standard deck. The first event is that the first card dealt is a spade, the second event is that the second card is a spade, the third event is that the third card is a spade, and so on.

Solution
a) The rolling of a die has no effect on the toss of a coin. The events are independent of each other.
b) The roll of one die has no effect on the roll of the other die. The events are independent.
c) Personal traits like hair colour are hereditary: a child's hair colour is related to the hair colour genes of its parents. The events are dependent.
d) The probability that the second card dealt is a spade is changed, depending on the outcome of the first card dealt. Similarly, the probability changes as the subsequent cards are dealt. The events are dependent.

Sometimes an event that seems intuitively improbable turns out to have quite a high probability of occurring.

Example 2   Finding the Probability of the Same Birthday
a) In a group of six people, what is the probability that at least two have their birthdays in the same month?
b) In a class of 35 students, what is the probability that at least two have the same birthday?
c) How many students would you have to ask to have a fifty-fifty chance that two of them have the same birthday?

Solution
a) Assume that each person's birthday is independent of each other person's.

It is easier to find the probability of the complementary event, that is, the probability that *no two* of the people have their birthdays in the same month. Draw a portion of the probability tree.

Month of 2nd Person's Birthday	Month of 3rd Person's Birthday	Month of 4th Person's Birthday

Multiply the probabilities along the branches for birthdays in different months.

$$P(6\text{ birthdays in different months}) = \frac{11}{12} \times \frac{10}{12} \times \frac{9}{12} \times \frac{8}{12} \times \frac{7}{12}$$
$$\doteq 0.2228$$

Then,
$$P(\text{at least two birthdays in the same month}) = 1 - P(6\text{ birthdays in different months})$$
$$\doteq 1 - 0.2228$$
$$\doteq 0.7772$$

In a group of six people, there is a probability of approximately 0.7772, or almost 78%, that at least two people will have their birthdays in the same month.

b) Assume that the students' birthdays are independent, and that every year has 365 days. Find the probability of the complementary event: that no two have their birthday on the same day. Draw a portion of the probability tree.

2nd Person's Birthday	3rd Person's Birthday	4th Person's Birthday

$\dfrac{364}{365}$ different from 1st person

$\dfrac{363}{365}$ different from 1st and 2nd person

$\dfrac{362}{365}$ different from 1st, 2nd, and 3rd person

$\dfrac{1}{365}$ same as 1st person

$\dfrac{2}{365}$ same as 1st or 2nd person

$\dfrac{3}{365}$ same as 1st, 2nd, or 3rd person

$P(\text{no 2 of the 35 students have the same birthday}) = \underbrace{\dfrac{364}{365} \times \dfrac{363}{365} \times \dfrac{362}{365} \times \ldots \times \dfrac{331}{365}}_{34 \text{ factors}}$

$$= \dfrac{_{364}P_{34}}{365^{34}}$$
$$\doteq 0.1856$$

Then,

$P(\text{at least two of the 35 students have the same birthday}) \doteq 1 - 0.1856$
$$= 0.8144$$

In a class of 35 students, the probability that at least two have the same birthday is approximately 0.8144, or just over 81%.

c) Assume that the students' birthdays are independent. Find the probability of the complementary event: that there is a 50% chance that no two have their birthdays on the same day. Using the probability tree from part b),

$P(\text{2 students do not have the same birthday}) = \dfrac{364}{365}$
$$\doteq 0.997$$

$P(\text{3 students do not have the same birthday}) = \dfrac{364}{365} \times \dfrac{363}{365}$
$$\doteq 0.992$$

$P(\text{4 students do not have the same birthday}) = \dfrac{364}{365} \times \dfrac{363}{365} \times \dfrac{362}{365}$
$$\doteq 0.983$$

$P(\text{5 students do not have the same birthday}) = \dfrac{364}{365} \times \dfrac{363}{365} \times \dfrac{362}{365} \times \dfrac{361}{365}$
$$\doteq 0.973$$

$\vdots$

$P(\text{21 students do not have the same birthday}) = \underbrace{\dfrac{364}{365} \times \dfrac{363}{365} \times \ldots \times \dfrac{345}{365}}_{20 \text{ factors}}$
$$\doteq 0.556$$

$$P(22 \text{ students do not have the same birthday}) = \underbrace{\frac{364}{365} \times \frac{363}{365} \times \ldots \times \frac{344}{365}}_{21 \text{ factors}}$$

$$\doteq 0.524$$

$$P(23 \text{ students do not have the same birthday}) = \underbrace{\frac{364}{365} \times \frac{363}{365} \times \ldots \times \frac{343}{365}}_{22 \text{ factors}}$$

$$\doteq 0.492$$

You would have to ask a group of 23 randomly selected students in order to have at least a 50% chance that two of them have the same birthday.

In a single experiment, two events that share no common outcomes are called **mutually exclusive**.

Example 3   Classifying Exclusivity

Classify the events in each experiment as either *mutually exclusive* or *not mutually exclusive*.

a) The experiment is rolling a die. The first event is rolling an even number and the second event is rolling a prime number.

b) The experiment is playing a game of hockey. The first event is that your team scores a goal and the second event is that your team wins the game.

c) The experiment is selecting a gift. The first event is that the gift is edible and the second event is that the gift is a CD.

d) The experiment is cutting a deck of cards. The first event is that the card is a spade and the second event is that the card is a face card.

Solution

a) The first event, an even number, occurs when the outcome is 2, 4, or 6. The second event, a prime number, occurs when the outcome is 2, 3, or 5. The outcome 2 is common to both events, so the events are not mutually exclusive.

b) In a hockey game it is necessary to score a goal to win the game, so the events are not mutually exclusive.

c) The events are mutually exclusive.

d) Since the jack, queen, and king of spades are common to both events, the events are not mutually exclusive.

For two mutually exclusive events, the probability that either of them will occur is equal to the sum of the probabilities that each of them will occur. For example, if a letter or vowel is picked at random,

$P(\text{selecting a vowel or a consonant}) = P(\text{selecting a vowel}) + P(\text{selecting a consonant})$

This is not true for two non-exclusive events, as there are outcomes that are common to both.

Example 4   Probability and Exclusivity

The results of a survey on reading habits include the following:

  85% read at least one newspaper in the past week
  35% read at least one book in the past week
  25% read both

What is the probability that an individual, chosen at random from the same population,

a) reads books but not newspapers?
b) reads either books or newspapers?

Solution

a) Since 25% of the population read both, reading newspapers and books are not mutually exclusive.
Draw the probability tree. There are four possibilities:

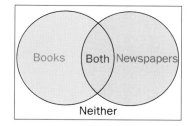

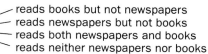

Label the branches with their probabilities. Start with the 25% that read both. Since the 85% that read a newspaper must include those that read both, then 85% − 25%, or 60%, must read newspapers only. Similarly, of the 35% that read books, 10% must read books but not newspapers.
Since the sum of all the probabilities must be 1, the probability of the event reads neither books nor newspapers is

P(neither newspapers nor books) = 1 − (0.6 + 0.1 + 0.25)
                    = 0.05

The probability tree can be completed:

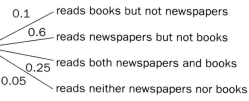

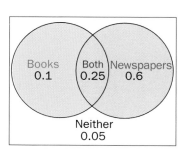

The probability that an individual, chosen at random from the population, reads books but not newspapers is 0.1.

b) P(either newspapers or books) = P(newspapers only) + P(books only) + P(newspapers and books)
                    = 0.6 + 0.1 + 0.25
                    = 0.95

The probability that the individual reads either newspapers or books is 0.95.

Practice

Classify the events in questions 1–6 as either independent or dependent.

1. The experiment is to check the eyesight and the hearing of a patient. The first event is that the patient has poor eyesight and the second event is that the patient has good hearing.

2. The experiment is to check the training of employees and the productivity of a company. The first event is that the employee is well trained and the second event is that the company meets its production quota.

3. The experiment is to observe the sky and the season of the year. The first event is that the sky is cloudy and the second event is that the season is winter.

4. The experiment is to cut a deck of cards and to roll two dice. The first event is that a club is chosen and the second event is that a pair is rolled.

5. The experiment is to check the handedness of a student and to check the hair colour. The first event is that the student is left-handed and the second event is that the student has blonde hair.

6. The experiment is to study the athletic activities of a person. The first event is that the person plays squash and the second event is that the person plays tennis.

Classify the events in questions 7–13 as either mutually exclusive or not mutually exclusive.

7. The experiment is rolling a die. The first event is that the number is greater than 3 and the second event is that the number is even.

8. The experiment is choosing a single activity for Saturday evening. The first event is to watch a video at home and the second event is to go dancing.

9. The experiment is answering a multiple-choice question. The first event is that the correct answer is chosen and the second event is that answer A is chosen.

10. The experiment is choosing a tie from a rack of ties. The first event is that the tie is a solid colour and the second event is that the tie is blue with red dots.

11. The experiment is selecting a chocolate bar. The first event is that the chocolate bar has nuts in it and the second event is that it contains caramel.

12. The experiment is choosing one student representative from your class. The first event is that the student is female and the second event is that the student wears glasses.

13. The experiment is cutting a deck of cards. The first event is that the card is a face card and the second event is that the card is less than 7.

Applications and Problem Solving

14. Driver training Sixty percent of young drivers take professional driver training. In their first year of driving, 25% of young drivers have an accident.
a) Assume that the events, taking driver training and having an accident, are independent. Draw the probability tree.
b) Based on part a), what is the probability that someone who has taken driver training will have an accident in the first year of driving?
c) Studies show that 10% of those who do take driver training have an accident in their first year. Is your result from part b) supported by the studies?
d) What does this tell you about the assumption made in part a)? What advice would you give to someone who has just got a learner's permit?

15. Prime ministers' birthdays Sir John A. Macdonald, Canada's first prime minister, and Jean Chrétien, Canada's twentieth prime minister, were both born on January 11.
a) What is the probability that at least two of the next ten Canadian prime ministers will be born in the same month?
b) What is the probability that at least two of the next ten Canadian prime ministers will have the same birthday?
c) What is the probability that at least two of the next twenty Canadian prime ministers will have the same birthday?

16. Blood types The distribution of blood types in North America is:

type O: 44% type A: 42%
type B: 10% type AB: 4%

a) Are the blood types mutually exclusive? Defend your decision using the data given.
b) What is the probability that a couple both have type O blood?
c) What is the probability that neither person in a couple has type AB blood?
d) When would you not consider blood types of two people independent?

17. Marketing A small town has a network of 115 residential streets, each containing approximately the same number of residents. A canvasser randomly selects twenty names from the phone book.
a) What is the probability that at least two of the people selected live on the same street?
b) Why is the information "approximately the same number of residents" relevant?
c) How many people must the canvasser sample to have at least a 75% chance of having at least two on the same street?

18. Magazine circulation Three of the top Canadian paid-circulation magazines are *Reader's Digest (Canadian Edition)*, *Chatelaine*, and *Maclean's*. A market survey has estimated that the probability of a household's subscribing to these magazines is:

Subscription	Probability
Reader's Digest	0.6
Chatelaine	0.5
Maclean's	0.4
Reader's Digest and Chatelaine	0.2
Reader's Digest and Maclean's	0.25
Chatelaine and Maclean's	0.15
All three	0.05

a) What is the probability that a household chosen at random subscribes to only *Reader's Digest*?
b) What is the probability that a household chosen at random subscribes to neither *Chatelaine* nor *Maclean's*?
c) What is the probability that a household chosen at random subscribes to one magazine only?

19. Movie madness If a five-minute segment is chosen at random from a certain full-length movie, the probability that it contains a violent scene is 0.4. The probability that it contains a humorous scene is 0.3, and the probability that it contains both a humorous scene and a violent scene is 0.1.
a) Are the events, violent scene and humorous scene, mutually exclusive? Explain.
b) Draw the probability tree for the random selection of a five-minute segment from the movie.
c) Assuming that violent scene and humorous scene are mutually exclusive, what is the probability that a five-minute segment chosen at random contains neither a violent nor a humorous scene?

20. Traffic lights There are three traffic lights along the route that Kia takes from home to school. The first traffic light is red 50% of the time. The second light is red 40% of the time, and the third light is red 60% of the time. The lights operate on separate timers. What is the probability that all three lights will be red as Kia reaches them on her way to school?

21. Each person in a group of people was asked to choose a letter from the alphabet, record it on a piece of paper, and place the paper face down on the table. How many people would have to be asked to turn over their papers in order for the probability that two people will choose the same letter is greater than $\frac{1}{2}$?

NUMBER POWER

Fifteen balls, numbered 1 through 15, are placed in a triangular arrangement as shown. The three balls in the centre have a sum of 39, and so do the five balls on each side of the triangle. Copy the diagram and number each ball.

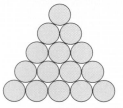

8.3 Probability and Combinatorics

The marathon, a race of about 40 km, commemorates the endurance of the Greek soldier Pheidippides. In 490 B.C., he ran from the battlefield near Marathon, Greece, to bring news to Athens of a Greek victory over the Persians. More recently, the Canadian runner Thian K. Mah (1926–1988) ran an astounding 524 marathons in his lifetime.

Explore: Draw a Tree Diagram

Among the competitors in a marathon race are seven premier runners who are expected to lead the pack. They are all capable of winning on a given day. Label the premier runners 1 through 7, and draw a tree diagram to represent the possible first and second place finishers among the premier runners.

Inquire

1. How many branches are in the tree diagram?

2. If the tree diagram were to include the first, second, and third place finishers from the seven premier runners, how many branches would you need? If the tree diagram were to include the top ten finishers, how many branches would you need? Express your answer in factorial notation.

3. If all the competitors in the marathon were included, what expression would represent the number of different possible finishes of the n runners? What expression would represent the number of possible top ten finishers?

When a tree diagram is too complicated to represent a situation, counting techniques (combinatorics) can be used to determine the size of the sample space and the size of the event set.

Example 1   Using Permutations in Determining Probability

The Queen's Plate is a prestigious horse race that occurs each summer in Toronto. Suppose nine horses are entered in the race, and all are equally likely to win. What is the probability that one horse, Western Dancer, will finish in the top three?

Solution

$$P(\text{Western Dancer is in top 3}) = \frac{\text{number of races in which Western Dancer is in the top 3}}{\text{total number of possible race finishes}}$$

Since the order of the horses at the finish line needs to be determined, the total number of possible race finishes is a permutation of all nine horses. Total number of possible race finishes is 9!

There are three cases in which Western Dancer is in the top three:
Case 1: Western Dancer comes first.
The remaining eight horses can be permuted 8! ways.
Case 2: Western Dancer comes second.
The remaining eight horses can be permuted in the positions 1st,
3rd, 4th, . . . , 9th, in 8! ways.
Case 3: Western Dancer comes third.
The remaining eight horses can be permuted in the positions 1st,
2nd, 4th, . . . , 9th, in 8! ways.
So the total number of ways in which Western Dancer can be in
the top three is 8! + 8! + 8!, or 3(8!).
Then,

Finishes

Western Dancer is in the top 3

1st

2nd   3rd

$$P(\text{Western Dancer is in top three}) = \frac{3(8!)}{9!}$$
$$= \frac{3(8!)}{9 \times 8!}$$
$$= \frac{1}{3}$$

The probability that Western Dancer finishes in the top three is $\frac{1}{3}$,
or approximately 33%.

Example 2   Using Combinations in Determining Probabilities

Sir John Suckling invented the card game cribbage in
the seventeenth century. This card game is played with a
regular 52-card deck. An advantageous hand in cribbage
contains many cards that total to 15 in different ways. A
hand that contains 5s is desirable.

a) What is the probability of being dealt four 5s in a
cribbage hand of six cards?

b) What is the probability of being dealt at least one 5
in a cribbage hand of six cards?

Solution

a) $P(\text{four 5s}) = \dfrac{\text{number of hands with four 5s}}{\text{total number of possible hands}}$

The order of cards in the hand is not important.
If a six-card hand contains the four 5s from the deck,
the other two cards in the hand are selected from the
remaining 48 cards. This can be done in $_{48}C_2$ ways.
Since there is only one way to choose four 5s ($_4C_4 = 1$),
the number of cribbage hands with four 5s is $_{48}C_2$.

A six-card hand can be dealt from the 52 cards in
the deck in $_{52}C_6$ ways. So the total number of possible
cribbage hands is $_{52}C_6$.

Then,

$$P(\text{four 5s}) = \frac{\text{number of hands with four 5s}}{\text{total number of possible hands}}$$

$$= \frac{{}_{48}C_2}{{}_{52}C_6}$$

$$= \frac{\dfrac{48!}{46!2!}}{\dfrac{52!}{46!6!}}$$

$$= \frac{48!6!}{52!2!}$$

$$= \frac{6 \times 5 \times 4 \times 3}{52 \times 51 \times 50 \times 49}$$

$$\doteq 0.000\ 055$$

The probability of being dealt a hand of six cards containing four 5s is approximately 0.000 055, or 0.0055%.

b) Consider the complementary event.
The six cards for a hand with no 5s can be chosen from the remaining 48 cards in the deck that are not 5s. This can be done in ${}_{48}C_6$ ways.

$$P(\text{at least one 5}) = 1 - P(\text{no 5s})$$

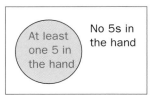

$$= 1 - \frac{\text{number of hands with no 5s}}{\text{total number of possible hands}}$$

$$= 1 - \frac{{}_{48}C_6}{{}_{52}C_6}$$

$$= 1 - \frac{\dfrac{48!}{42!6!}}{\dfrac{52!}{46!6!}}$$

$$= 1 - \frac{48!46!}{52!42!}$$

$$= 1 - \frac{46 \times 45 \times 44 \times 43}{52 \times 51 \times 50 \times 49}$$

$$\doteq 0.397\ 23$$

The probability of being dealt at least one 5 in a cribbage hand is approximately 0.397 23, or almost 40%.

Example 3   Using Permutations in Determining Probability
A lock on a briefcase has three wheels, each labelled from 0 to 9.
What is the probability of a person's guessing the correct entry code, if
a) there are no repeated digits in the code?
b) the code may have repeated digits?

Solution

a) There is only one correct entry code.
For the total number of possible codes, order is important. Digits may not be repeated, so this is a permutation with $n = 10$ and $r = 3$. There are $_{10}P_3$ possible lock entry codes.

$$P(\text{correct lock combination}) = \frac{\text{number of correct codes}}{\text{total number of possible codes}}$$

$$= \frac{1}{_{10}P_3}$$

$$= \frac{1}{\frac{10!}{7!}}$$

$$= \frac{1}{10 \times 9 \times 8}$$

$$\doteq 0.001\ 389$$

The probability of guessing the correct code if no digits are repeated is approximately 0.001 389, or 0.14%.

b) Since digits may be repeated, use the fundamental counting principle. The total number of possible three-digit lock entry codes is $10 \times 10 \times 10$.

$$P(\text{correct lock combination}) = \frac{\text{number of entry codes}}{\text{total number of entry codes}}$$

$$= \frac{1}{10 \times 10 \times 10}$$

$$= 0.001$$

The probability of guessing the correct lock entry code if digits may be repeated is 0.001, or 0.1%.

Practice

A committee of five people is selected from ten females and eight males.

1. What is the probability that there are exactly three females on the committee?
2. What is the probability that there are exactly three males on the committee?
3. What is the probability that there are exactly two females on the committee?

Three people line up to buy a ticket at the movie theatre.
4. What is the probability that they line up in descending order of age?
5. What is the probability that they line up in ascending order of age?

At a school party, ten students sit randomly around a circular table that seats ten people.
6. What is the probability that Janna is sitting next to Roberto?
7. What is the probability that Janna and Roberto are sitting opposite each other?
8. What is the probability that Janna and Roberto are not sitting opposite or beside each other?

Applications and Problem Solving

9. Card tricks A card trick involves the drawing of aces from a well-shuffled deck of 54 cards, including jokers.
a) What is the probability of cutting an ace from a full deck of cards?
b) What is the probability of drawing out four aces?

10. Lottery A lottery has a player choose six different numbers from 1 through 49 inclusive. This sequence is then matched against the lottery's random selection of six numbers.
a) What is the total number of possible six-number sequences that can be chosen?
b) Prizes are awarded to tickets that have the first two numbers of their six-number sequence the same as the lottery's. What is the probability of winning this prize?
c) The grand prize is won by the ticket that has exactly the same six-number sequence as the lottery's. What is the probability of winning this prize?

11. Hockey Two sisters, Zana and Kari, are among 15 girls trying out for forward positions on a hockey team. On the first day of practice, the coach randomly sets up five forward lines of three players each. If the coach differentiates between the positions of right wing, left wing, and centre,
a) how many ways can the coach choose the first line? the second line?
b) how many ways can the coach set up the five lines?
c) what is the probability that Zana and Kari are on the same line?
d) What are the answers to parts a), b), and c) if the coach does not differentiate between the three positions on the line?

12. Bridge In the game of bridge, four players are dealt 13 cards each from a well-shuffled deck of 52 playing cards.
a) What is the probability that one of the players is dealt all the spades?
b) What is the probability that one of the players holds a hand that is made up of only one suit?
c) What is the probability that each of the four players receives a complete suit in his or her hand?
d) What is the probability that a player holds all the aces?
e) What is the probability that a player does not have a face card, or an ace, in his or her hand?

13. Touch typing Matching the world typing record of 176 words/min would be difficult even if one started early in life. If an infant types three keyboard strokes and all the characters are letters of the alphabet, what is the probability that
a) the first letter typed is a vowel?
b) all three characters typed are vowels?
c) the three letters typed are in alphabetical order?

14. Yahtzee® The dice game of Yahtzee® uses five regular dice. A yahtzee occurs when you roll the same number on each of the dice. What is the probability that a single roll of all of the dice yields
a) a yahtzee of sixes?   **b)** any yahtzee?
c) not even one pair of dice with the same number?

15. Family size The percent of Canadian families with five children decreased from 3.9% in 1961 to 0.4% in 1991. Suppose a family is planning to have five children. If a male child and female child are equally likely, what is the probability that the children are
a) two boys, one girl, two boys, in that order?
b) all boys?
c) one girl, three boys, one girl, in that order?
d) Is it a reasonable assumption that a newborn is equally likely to be a male or female? Is the gender of a child independent of that of a previous child? Research and discuss.

16. Bridge hand A bridge hand, of 13 cards, is called a 'Yarborough' when it contains no tens and no face cards.
a) Is the dealing of a bridge hand a sequence of independent or dependent events?
b) What is the probability of being dealt a Yarborough?
c) What is the probability of not being dealt a Yarborough?
d) How many hands would you expect to be dealt before being dealt a Yarborough?

LOGIC POWER

A bag contains only two different colours of marbles, green and white. If two marbles are removed without replacements, the probability that they are both green is $\frac{2}{15}$. If three are removed, the probability that they are all green is $\frac{1}{30}$. How many of each colour are in the bag?

Canadian First Ministers

Use the *First Ministers* database, from the Computer Data Bank, to complete the following:

a) *Devise a plan to answer each question. Remember to exclude records for which the required data are not available.*
b) *Compare your plan with the plans of your classmates.*
c) *Revise your plan, if necessary, and then carry it out.*

1 Names

1. If a record is randomly selected from the database, what is the probability that the given name is
a) Robert?   **b)** Rita ?   **c)** William?
d) John?   **e)** Arthur?   **f)** George?
g) that of the current prime minister?
h) that of the current premier of your province?
i) your given name?

2. a) If two records are selected with replacement, what is the probability that the given name in each record is Andrew?
b) If two records are selected without replacement, what is the probability that the given name in each record is James?
c) If one record is selected, what is the probability that the given name is either Pierre or Frank?
d) If one record is selected, what is the probability that the given name is John and the surname is Macdonald?
e) If one record is selected, what is the probability that the given name is John or the surname is Macdonald?

2 Birthdays

1. If one record is selected from the database, what is the probability that the birthday is the same as
a) yours?   **b)** Gordon Conant's?

3 Age of Taking Office

1. What is the average age of taking office, rounded to the nearest year?

2. Three records are selected at random without replacement. What is the probability that the age of taking office in one of the records is above average, in another record is below average, and in the remaining record is equal to the average? Give your answer rounded to 3 decimal places.

4 Political Parties of Prime Ministers

1. What is the average number of months served, rounded to the nearest month, by Liberal prime ministers? by Progressive Conservative prime ministers?

2. The first full month served by Jean Chretien in his initial term was November in 1993.
a) Has Chretien served more months or fewer months than the average for his political party?
b) Including Chretien, what would the average be for his political party?

5 Native Language of Prime Ministers

1. If five records of prime ministers are randomly selected, what is the probability, rounded to 3 decimal places, of at least three native English speakers?

6 Chronological Lists

It is not possible to create a precise chronological list of prime ministers since Confederation from this database. However, it is possible to create a slightly less-than-perfect chronological list.
1. Prepare such a list of prime ministers, including only the name fields and the field(s) created to help determine the order.

2. Who were the first and second prime ministers?

3. Explain why the list is not precise.

4. Repeat questions 1 and 2 for the premiers of your province.

5. Use your research skills and make any changes necessary to your lists.

8.4 Conditional Probability

Information is key to probability. Whatever information you have about the outcomes of an experiment can change your perspective on the probability of an event's occurring. Consider the following scenario. A stranger on the bus bets you $20 he can guess the birth month of the lady sitting across from you. You take the bet, thinking that he has only a 1 in 12 shot of getting it right. He guesses April and wins the bet. Was he lucky or was that lady his mother?

If you randomly select someone, what is the probability that that person was born on the first of the month? If the person tells you his/her date of birth is June 4, 1983, what is the probability now that the person was born on the first of the month, given that you know the person's birth date? The day of the month on which the person was born has not changed—only the information you had about it.

Explore: Use an Experiment

Roll a six-sided die. Do not look at it.
a) Draw a probability tree for rolling the die.
b) If someone else looks and tells you that the value on the die is an even number, draw a restricted probability tree, given this information.
c) If you reroll the die and your friend tells you now that the value is a power of 2, draw a restricted probability tree, given this information.

Inquire

1. What is the probability of getting a 2 when rolling a die?

2. If you were told that the value on the die is an even number, what is the probability that the value on the die is 2, given this information?

3. If you were told that the value on the die is a power of 2, what is the probability that the value on the die is 2, given this information?

If A and B are events from an experiment, the **conditional probability of B given A** is the probability that the event B will occur, given that the event A has already occurred. This conditional probability is equal to the probability that A and B will occur divided by the probability that A will occur. In symbols:

$$P(B|A) = \frac{P(A \text{ and } B)}{P(A)} \text{ , where } P(A) \neq 0$$

For example, the probability that the value on a die is 2, given that an even number is rolled, can be written as $P(2\,|\,\text{even number})$.

Reliable testing is important for an accurate medical diagnosis and hence early and effective treatment. Conditional probability is central to the careful analysis of medical testing.

If a medical test for an illness is 95% accurate,
  95% of randomly selected patients *with the illness* will test positive for the illness
  and
  95% of randomly selected people *without the illness* will test negative for the illness.

Example 1   Finding Conditional Probability

A test for Type 2 diabetes (non-insulin dependent) measures the blood glucose level after eight hours of fasting. Consider a blood glucose level above normal to be a positive result and anything else to be a negative result. This test is 85% accurate, and 2% of the world's population actually has diabetes. Determine

a) $P(\text{diabetic} \mid \text{tests positive})$ **b)** $P(\text{not diabetic} \mid \text{tests negative})$
c) $P(\text{tests positive} \mid \text{diabetic})$ **d)** Do you think this is an effective test?

Solution

a) Draw the probability tree.

Individual	Test Result	Probability

diabetic
0.85 — test positive $P(\text{diabetic and tests positive}) = 0.02 \times 0.85$
     $= 0.017$

0.02
0.15 — test negative $P(\text{diabetic and tests negative}) = 0.02 \times 0.15$
     $= 0.003$

0.98
0.15 — test positive $P(\text{not diabetic and tests positive}) = 0.98 \times 0.15$
     $= 0.147$

not diabetic
0.85 — test negative $P(\text{not diabetic and tests negative}) = 0.98 \times 0.85$
     $= 0.833$

There are two branches leading to a positive test.
$P(\text{tests positive}) = P(\text{diabetic and tests positive}) + P(\text{not diabetic and tests positive})$
     $= 0.017 + 0.147$
     $= 0.164$

Then, for the individuals that actually are diabetic, given that they test positive,

$$P(\text{diabetic} \mid \text{tests positive}) = \frac{P(\text{diabetic and tests positive})}{P(\text{tests positive})}$$

$$= \frac{0.017}{0.164}$$
$$\doteq 0.1037$$

There is a probability of approximately 0.1037, or just over 10.3%, that an individual is diabetic, if the test is positive.

b) From the probability tree,
$P(\text{not diabetic and tests negative}) = 0.833$
There are two branches leading to a negative test.
$P(\text{tests negative}) = P(\text{diabetic and tests negative}) + P(\text{not diabetic and tests negative})$
     $= 0.003 + 0.833$
     $= 0.836$

Therefore,

$$P(\text{not diabetic} \mid \text{tests negative}) = \frac{P(\text{not diabetic and tests negative})}{P(\text{tests negative})}$$

$$= \frac{0.833}{0.836}$$

$$\doteq 0.9964$$

The probability that an individual who tests negative does not have diabetes is approximately 0.9964, or just over 99%.

c) $P(\text{tests positive} \mid \text{steroid}) = \dfrac{P(\text{tests positive and diabetic})}{P(\text{diabetic})}$

$$= \frac{0.017}{0.02}$$

$$= 85\%$$

The probability that an individual who has diabetes tests positive is 85%.

d) There is only a 10% chance that an individual has diabetes, given a high blood glucose level. The test may seem ineffective. However, 85% of the time individuals test positive given they are diabetic and, moreover, the test rarely gives false negatives. With over 99% certainty, an individual does not have diabetes given a normal blood glucose level. Since this test is simple and inexpensive, it is the standard initial diagnostic test for diabetes. It rarely gives false negatives, and those who test positive can be tested further with more elaborate and accurate techniques.

Example 2   Applying Conditional Probability

A recent health survey asked Canadians aged 18 and older what physical activities they had participated in during the year. The survey estimates the participation rate of Canadians in skating at 30%. In a random sample of three Canadians, at least one person is known to participate in skating. Estimate the probability that exactly two in the sample participate in skating.

Solution

Draw the probability tree.

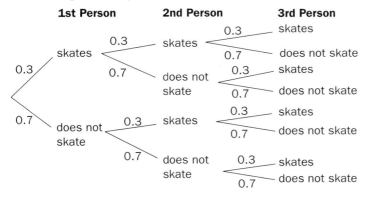

There are three branches that have exactly two who skate and at least one who skates.

Note that the event of *exactly* two who skate is subsumed in the event of at least one skates.

So,

P(exactly 2 skate and at least 1 skates) = P(exactly 2 skate)

                       = P(skates, skates, does not skate)

                         + P(skates, does not skate, skates)

                         + P(does not skate, skates, skates)

                         = $0.3 \times 0.3 \times 0.7 + 0.3 \times 0.7 \times 0.3 + 0.7 \times 0.3 \times 0.3$

                         = 0.189

Since there are seven branches that have at least one skates, the complementary event, none skate, is easier to calculate. Thus,

P(at least 1 skates) = $1 - P$(none skate)

                    = $1 - 0.7 \times 0.7 \times 0.7$

                    = 0.657

Therefore,

$$P(\text{exactly 2 skate} \mid \text{at least 1 skates}) = \frac{P(\text{exactly 2 skate and at least 1 skates})}{P(\text{at least 1 skates})}$$

$$= \frac{0.189}{0.657}$$

$$\doteq 0.2877$$

In a random group of three Canadians, the probability that there are exactly two people who skate, given that at least one skates, is approximately 29%.

Practice

Determine the conditional probability in questions 1–5 each case. Round answers to three decimal places where necessary.

1. Given: $P(A \text{ and } B) = 0.5$
           $P(B) = 0.75$
    Find $P(A \mid B)$.

2. Given: $P(\text{even and divisible by 5}) = 0.1$
           $P(\text{even}) = 0.4$
    Find $P(\text{even and divisible by 5} \mid \text{even})$.

3. Given: P(blonde and blue eyes) = 0.2
           $P(\text{blue eyes}) = 0.25$
    Find P(blonde and blue eyes $\mid$ blue eyes).

4. Given: $P(\text{over 40 and overweight}) = 0.5$
           $P(\text{overweight}) = 0.6$
    Find P(over 40 and overweight $\mid$ overweight).

5. Given: $P(\text{red and size medium}) = 0.3$
           $P(\text{size medium}) = 0.4$
    Find P(red and size medium $\mid$ size medium).

Applications and Problem Solving

6. Find the probability of having two boys, given that the first child is a boy. Assume that the gender of a child is independent of its sibling's gender.

7. Find the probability of drawing two cards from a deck of 52 cards and obtaining heart cards both times, given that a heart is drawn the first time.

8. Family size The results of a recent census on the number of children in families in Canada are:

no children	40%
1 child	25%
2 children	18%
3 or more	17%

If a Canadian family is selected at random, what is the estimated probability that
a) there are more than two children?
b) there are more than two children, given that the family has at least one child?

9. Passing courses At a certain university, 75% of the first-year engineering students passed mathematics, 85% passed chemistry, and 90% passed mathematics or chemistry. A first-year engineering student is selected at random.
a) Determine the estimated probability that the student passed mathematics, given that the student passed chemistry.
b) Determine the estimated probability that the student passed chemistry, given that the student passed mathematics.

10. Lie detection Polygraph or lie detector tests are generally not very accurate. Suppose a polygraph is 70% accurate: that is, if you lie the polygraph indicates so 70% of the time, and if you tell the truth the polygraph indicates so 70% of the time.
a) Assume that the average person is truthful 90% of the time. Determine the probability that a person is telling the truth, given that the polygraph test indicates truth.
b) Assume that criminals are truthful 15% of the time. What is the probability that a criminal is lying, given that the polygraph test indicates truth?

11. Life expectancy Life expectancy in Canada is among the highest in the world. Newborn females can expect to live for almost 80 years, while newborn males can expect to live for 74 years. It is possible that aging itself may increase the risk for glucose intolerance and diabetes. Use the test for diabetes from Example 1, which is 85% accurate, and the fact that diabetes occurs in 20% of the population over 85. Different applications of the test are independent events.
a) What is the probability that a person over 85 does not have diabetes, given that the person tested positive?
b) When a person tests positive, the doctor usually orders the test again. What is the probability that a person over 85 does not have diabetes, given that the person tests positive twice? What if the person tests positive three times in a row?
c) How many times should the test be repeated for the doctor to be 95% certain that the person over 85 has diabetes, given that the test is positive each time?

12. Independence, exclusivity, and conditional probability a) If A and B are mutually exclusive events, what is $P(A|B)$?
b) If C and D are independent events, what is $P(C|D)$?

13. Breathalyzer test Suppose that a breathalyzer test is 95% accurate. Also assume that the drivers the police ask to take the test have drunk too much alcohol 80% of the time.
a) Determine the estimated probability that a driver is falsely charged with impaired driving, that is, the driver is not impaired given that the breathalyzer tests over the limit.
b) What is the estimated probability that a driver is charged with impaired driving? That is, the driver has drunk too much, given that the test is positive?
c) After a driver tests positive on a breathalyzer, the police generally administer a blood test. Why?

14. Coins Two coins are tossed.
a) What is the probability that both coins are heads?
b) What is the probability that both coins are heads, given that at least one of them is a head?
c) What is the probability that one is a tail and one is a head, given that at least one of them is a head?
d) What is the sum of the answers to parts b) and c)? How are the events in parts b) and c) related?

LOGIC POWER

Design a pair of dice that satisfy the following conditions.
• The dice are regular six-sided dice.
• When the two dice are rolled the possible sums are 1, 2, 3, 4, 5, 6, 7, 8, 9, 10, 11, and 12.
• Each of the above sums has the same probability of being rolled.
What numbers are on the faces of each die?

Biostatistics

Doctors rely heavily on the predictive value of many tests—blood, urine, X-ray, ultrasound, MRI—to name but a few. Biostatisticians are partly responsible for determining the accuracy and effectiveness of these tests.

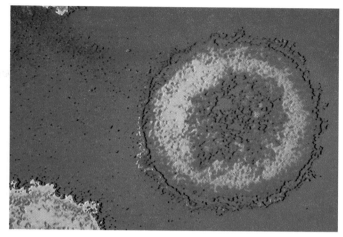

The sensitivity and the specificity are two statistical values associated with a medical test.

The **sensitivity** is the estimated percent of infected patients who will test positive. If the sensitivity of a test is 95%, it is expected that, out of 1000 infected patients tested, approximately 950 will test positive and 50 will test negative. Such negatives are called *false negatives*.

The **specificity** is the estimated percent of people without the disease who will test negative. If the specificity of a test is 99%, it is expected that, out of 1000 uninfected people, 990 will test negative and 10 will test positive. Such positives are called *false positives*.

Two or more tests are often used to confirm the diagnosis of a disease. The first test is typically inexpensive and rarely gives false negatives; the second is definitive but much more expensive. This sort of procedure is very cost effective for health-care systems.

The Mantoux test is the standard test used to detect mycobacterium tuberculosis. A small amount of tuberculin is injected just under the skin on the lower part of the arm. A small bump or induration may occur within 48 to 72 h. The diameter of the induration, together with the patient's risk of disease, help determine the cut off value for a positive test. Administered and read properly, the sensitivity and specificity of the Mantoux test can be as high as 95%, but accuracy varies with the prevalence of tuberculosis in the population being tested.

Even though the Mantoux test results in a low number of false positives, a subsequent test, sputum microscopy and culture, can be used to confirm the presence of mycobacterium tuberculosis. Expensive equipment, technical aptitude, and substantial experience are necessary to analyze the results of the sputum microscopy and culture.

1. Ruby is concerned that she may have been exposed to tuberculosis. The local medical clinic recommends that she be tested with the Mantoux test, and, if the results are negative, that she be retested in three months. If the sensitivity of the Mantoux test is 95%, what is the probability that both tests are negative, even though Ruby is infected? Assume that the tests are independent events.

2. Suppose the specificity of the Mantoux test is 95%. Suppose, in relative terms, the Mantoux test costs $5, and the sputum microscopy and culture costs $100. What is the approximate cost of testing 1000 healthy people with the sputum microscopy and culture? How much money would be saved if each of the 1000 healthy people were first tested with the Mantoux test and then, if necessary, with the sputum microscopy and culture?

CONNECTING MATH AND ASTROPHYSICS

Search for Extraterrestrial Intelligence

In 1959, two scientists, Giuseppe Cocconi and Philip Morrison, laid the groundwork for Project SETI (**S**earch for **E**xtra**t**errestrial **I**ntelligence). SETI entails searching the heavens for alien signals with radio and optical telescopes.

Radio waves can travel vast distances and can be generated efficiently. All of our radio, television, and other electromagnetic signals are dispersing throughout the galaxy. Has anyone out there heard them?

In 1961, Frank Drake, in preparation for the first SETI conference, derived an equation to estimate the probability of finding intelligent extraterrestrial life:

$$N = N^* f_p n_e f_l f_i f_c f_L$$

N = the number of civilizations that can communicate in the Galaxy

N^* = the number of stars in the Milky Way Galaxy

f_p = the fraction of stars with planets around them

n_e = the number of planets per star that are capable of sustaining life

f_l = the fraction of the n_e planets where life evolves

f_i = the fraction of f_l where intelligent life evolves

f_c = the fraction of the f_i planets that have civilizations that can broadcast and receive signals

f_L = the fraction of a planet's existence during which a communicating civilization survives

Current estimates for these values are as follows.
There are 100 billion stars in the galaxy.
20% to 50% of these stars have planets.
Each such star has one to five planets that could sustain some form of life.
The probability of life's evolving, as well as of life's being intelligent, is debated to be anywhere from near 0% to near 100%.
Estimates for f_c range from 10% to 20%.
The value of f_L is also difficult to estimate. For example, Earth is expected to have a lifespan of 10 billion years. Humans have been communicating via electromagnetic signals for roughly 100 years. If humans destroy themselves shortly $f_L = \dfrac{1}{100\,000\,000}$. If humans persist for 100 000 years, then, $f_L = \dfrac{1}{100\,000}$.

1. **a)** Using your calculator, obtain three different estimates for *N*. Pick values for each variable in the ranges given above. Try using the least value for each variable, the greatest value for each variable, and some value in the middle of the described range. By how much do your values of *N* vary?

b) How reasonable are the assumptions in Drake's equation? Investigate and discuss.

2. SETI is widely supported by many educational institutes. Investigate and summarize the history of SETI and explore current SETI projects.

3. If extraterrestrial life were discovered, what language would humans use to communicate with the life form? Investigate the different types of message that have been sent by radio telescopes. How are these messages encoded? What do we suspect is, and use as, a universal language?

Review

8.1 **1.** Use a probability tree to show the sample space and to determine the probability of the required event.

a) In the random selection of a condiment (mustard, ketchup, or relish) and a bun (plain or sesame seed), what is the probability that a hamburger has mustard on a sesame seed bun?

b) In the random selection of a category of movie (comedy, thriller, drama, or action) and a snack (licorice, carrot sticks, or popcorn), what is the probability of watching a thriller while eating popcorn?

2. **Schedules** The train from Jasper to Calgary arrives between 16:20 and 16:25. The bus from Jasper to Calgary arrives between 16:15 and 16:30.

a) Draw a probability tree to show the sample space of the arrival times of the bus and the train using minute intervals.

b) What is the probability that the train and the bus arrive in the same minute time interval?

c) What is the probability that the train arrives before the bus?

d) Consider the arrival times as ordered pairs (train time, bus time). For example, (22, 16) would represent the train arriving at 16:22 and the bus at 16:16. Graph the data from the sample space.

e) Use your graph to determine the probability that the bus arrives before the train.

3. **Marks** Olivia always seems to get between 75% and 85% on her English essays, while Andrew gets between 70% and 78%. Assume the essay marks are whole numbers.

a) List the sample space that shows their possible marks on the next essay.

b) What is the probability that Andrew will receive a higher mark than Olivia?

c) What is the probability that they both receive the same mark?

8.2 **4.** **University** The probability that Chi will go to the University of British Columbia is estimated to be 0.2. The probability that she will go to some other university is 0.35. The probability that Farhana will go to U.B.C. is 0.25. Calculate the probability that

a) Chi and Farhana will both go to U.B.C.

b) Chi will not go to a university

c) either Chi or Farhana, but not both, will go to U.B.C.

5. **Team spirit** The coach of a hockey team tries to boost team spirit by celebrating players' birthdays. The team is made up of 12 forwards, 6 defence players, and 2 goalies.

a) What is the probability that at least two of the defence players will have their birthdays in the same month?

b) What is the probability that at least two players will have their birthdays on the same day?

6. **Magazines** The two leading magazines published in Canada are *Chatelaine* and *Flare*. The probability that a woman reads *Chatelaine* is 0.5, the probability that she reads *Flare* is 0.35, and the probability that she reads both is 0.25.

a) Are the events, reading *Chatelaine* and reading *Flare*, mutually exclusive?

b) What is the probability that a woman, chosen at random, reads neither *Chatelaine* nor *Flare*?

c) What is the probability that a woman reads either *Flare* only or *Flare* and *Chatelaine*?

8.3 **7.** **Homework** A committee is to be formed to investigate whether students have too much homework. The committee is to have five members, chosen randomly from four interested teachers and four interested students.

a) What is the probability that there is only one teacher on the committee?

b) What is the probability that students outnumber teachers on the committee?

8. **Horse race** Five horses of equal ability are in a race. What is the probability that

a) the finish will be in the same order as the starting gates in which the horses were placed?

b) that one of the horses, named Salmon Run, will finish in the top three?

9. **Medical research** Five research centres, out of eight suitable ones, are to be selected for a study on heart disease. The choice is to be made by a random draw.

a) Three of the possible research centres are in Western Canada. What is the probability that all three western centres will be chosen?

b) What is the probability that one of the two

research centres that are located in Atlantic Canada will be chosen?

c) What is the probability that none of the research centres located in Central Canada will be chosen?

10. Field trip Twenty-five boys and 20 girls are going on a field trip in a 36-passenger bus and a minivan. The students are distributed at random between the vehicles, filling the bus first. Find the probability that

a) there are no girls in the van

b) there are no boys in the van

c) there are equal numbers of boys and girls in the bus

d) there are both equal numbers of boys and girls in the bus and equal numbers of boys and girls in the van

11. Determine the conditional probability in each.

a) Given: P(tall and dark) = 0.5, P(dark) = 0.75 Find P(tall|dark).

b) Given: P(broken and old) = 0.21, P(broken) = 0.63 Find P(old|broken).

12. Glaucoma tests A test for glaucoma measures the intraocular fluid pressure. This test is 60% accurate. Consider an above normal pressure inside the eye to be a positive result, and anything else to be a negative result. If only 1% of the population has glaucoma, what is the probability that a person

a) who has glaucoma, tests positive?

b) who tests negative, does not have glaucoma?

c) Doctors have found that only 75% of all glaucoma patients have elevated pressure within their eyes. What is the probability that a person with glaucoma actually tests positive?

13. Police work A new lie-detector test has been devised and must be tested before it is put into use. One hundred people are selected at random and each person draws a card from a box of 100. Half the cards instruct the person to lie and the other half instruct the person to tell the truth. The new lie-detector test indicates lying in 80% of those who did lie and in 5% of those who told the truth.

a) What is the probability that a randomly chosen person has really lied, given that the test indicates lying?

b) What is the probability that the person actually told the truth, if the test indicates lying?

Exploring Math

The Pigeonhole Principle

The pigeonhole principle is also known as the Dirichlet pigeonhole principle, after the German mathematician Peter Gustav Lejeune Dirichlet (1805–1859).

The pigeonhole principle states:
If n objects are put into p boxes ($1 \leq p < n$), then some box contains at least two of the objects.

A common application occurs when $p = n - 1$. For example, let the birthdays of eight people correspond to the objects ($n = 8$) and the days of the week correspond to the boxes ($p = 7$). By the pigeonhole principle, at least two birthdays will fall on the same day of the week.

In general, if there are more than k times as many objects as boxes, then some boxes must contain at least $k + 1$ objects. For example, assume that the population of Edmonton, Alberta, exceeds 1 000 000 and that a person has no more than 250 000 hairs on his or her head. Applying the pigeonhole principle with $p = 250\ 000$, there are more than 4 ($k = 4$) times as many people as boxes (1 000 000 = 4 × 250 000), so there must be at least $k + 1$ or 5 people with the same number of hairs on their heads.

1. Show that in a group of 37 people there are at least four people who were born in the same month of the year.

2. A drawer contains 10 different pairs of socks. How many socks must be taken out, in the dark, to guarantee at least one correctly matched pair?

3. A high school basketball team has 11 weeks to prepare for a tournament. They wish to play at least one game every day, but no more than 12 games in any seven day period. Show that there exists a succession of days during which they play exactly 21 games.

Chapter Check

1. Demographics Approximately 69% of Canada's population is in the 15 to 64 age range. Suppose 62% of the total population are urban dwellers. Use a probability tree to show the sample space. What is the probability that a Canadian, selected at random, is
a) in the 15 to 64 age range and also lives in a city?
b) not in the 15 to 64 age range and lives in the country?

2. Learning In an experiment to test learning ability, a rat is placed at the base of a T-shaped corridor and some food is placed at the end of the right arm of the T. The probability that the rat turns left on the first trial is 0.5. Every time the rat turns left, the probability that it turns left on the next trial is decreased by 10%. Each time it turns right, the probability that it turns right on the next trial is increased by 15%.
a) Draw the probability tree for the first three trials.
b) Find the probability that the rat turns left on the second trial.
c) Find the probability that the rat gets to the food at least once in the three trials.

3. Music marketing Market researchers are finding that country and western music has a wider audience now than before. A survey reveals that the probabilities that a teenager listens to particular types of music are as follows.

Type of Music	Probability
rock music	0.8
country and western	0.15
both	0.1

a) Are the events listening to rock music and listening to country and western music mutually exclusive?
b) Draw the probability tree for the teenage taste in music.
c) What is the probability that a teenager chosen at random does not listen to either rock or country and western music?

4. Tuberculosis (TB) screening TB used to account for 20% of the world's deaths. Fortunately, in 1944 Selman Waksman discovered the drug streptomycin, which not merely prevents the disease but also cures it. A test for TB was given to 1000 people, 8% of whom were known to have TB. The test results were positive for 90% of the people who had TB, and negative for the other 10%. For the people who did not have TB, the test results were positive for 5% and negative for the other 95%.
a) Determine the probability that a randomly selected person in the sample has TB, given that the person tests positive.
b) Determine the probability that a randomly selected person in the sample does not have TB, given that the person tests negative.

5. Lottery luck The 6/49 lottery requires the player to choose six different numbers from the numbers 1 through 49 inclusive. Prizes are awarded according to the quantity of numbers in the player's chosen set that match the six numbers that are randomly chosen by the lottery company. What is the probability that a player
a) has all six numbers match?
b) has three numbers that match?
c) has at least one number that matches?

6. Passwords Computer systems are protected by passwords. A person trying to log on usually has only three tries to enter the correct password. Suppose a password has four characters which are all letters of the alphabet, with no repetition of letters.
a) What is the probability that a hacker will guess the correct password on the first attempt?
b) What is the probability that a hacker will guess the password within three attempts?
c) In practice, passwords may include any of the 68 keyboard characters, and often are eight characters long with no restriction on repeated characters. What is the probability that a hacker will break into a computer with this type of password on the first attempt?

Using the Strategies

1. The following pattern lists all the digits from 0 through 9. Discover the pattern to complete the sequence.

8, 5, 4, 9, 1, ■, ■, ■, ■, ■

2. Progressions The non-zero numbers a, b, and c are in arithmetical progression. Increasing a by 1 or increasing c by 2 will result in a geometrical progression instead. What are the values of a, b, and c?

3. The whole numbers from 1 to 1000 are written in order around a large circle. Starting at 1, every fifteenth number is crossed out (1, 16, 31, 46, ...) This is continued until a number is reached that has already been crossed out. How many numbers are left?

4. Measurement The area of square PQRS is n square units. Each vertex of the square is joined to the midpoint of the opposite side. What figure is formed in the centre of the figure and what is its area?

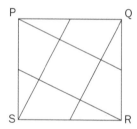

5. In the following addition, each different letter represents a different digit. What is the sum?

$$\begin{array}{r} T\,W\,O \\ S\,E\,V\,E\,N \\ +\,E\,L\,E\,V\,E\,N \\ \hline T\,W\,E\,N\,T\,Y \end{array}$$

6. What is the numerical coefficient of $x^{-\frac{1}{2}}$ in the expansion of $\left(x - \dfrac{1}{\sqrt{x}} \right)^{7}$?

7. The first four terms of a sequence are 35, 1225, 42 875, and 1 500 625. What is the next term?

8. Unit circles Three circles of radius one unit intersect at the origin as shown. What is the area of the shaded region?

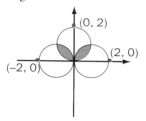

9. Astronauts Two astronauts, Roberta and Darrin, are orbiting Earth in separate rockets. Both are travelling in the same direction, in circles of different radii, above the equator. Roberta orbits Earth once every 3 h, but Darrin takes 7.5 h to complete each orbit. At noon Pacific Standard Time, Darrin sees Roberta's rocket directly below. What is the next time when this situation will happen?

10. Bases If 352 and 747 are two numbers in base 8, what is their sum in base 8?

11. If one side of a square is a diagonal of a second square, what is the ratio of the area of the smaller square to that of the larger square?

12. Visible-factor number A visible-factor number is a natural number that is divisible by each of its non-zero digits. For example, 624, 315, and 105 are all visible-factor numbers. How many visible-factor numbers are there between 10 and 100?

13. Given $f(x) = \sqrt{1 - \sqrt{1 - x^2}}$, what are the domain and the range of f?

14. Mean A set of 50 numbers has a mean of 35. If two of the numbers, which have a sum of 100, are removed from the set, what is the mean of the remaining set of numbers?

15. Each root of the equation $x^2 - kx + 6 = 0$ is 5 greater than the corresponding root of the equation $x^2 + kx + 6 = 0$. What is the value of k?

16. How many digits are there in the standard form of the number $(2^{1999})(5^{2005})$?

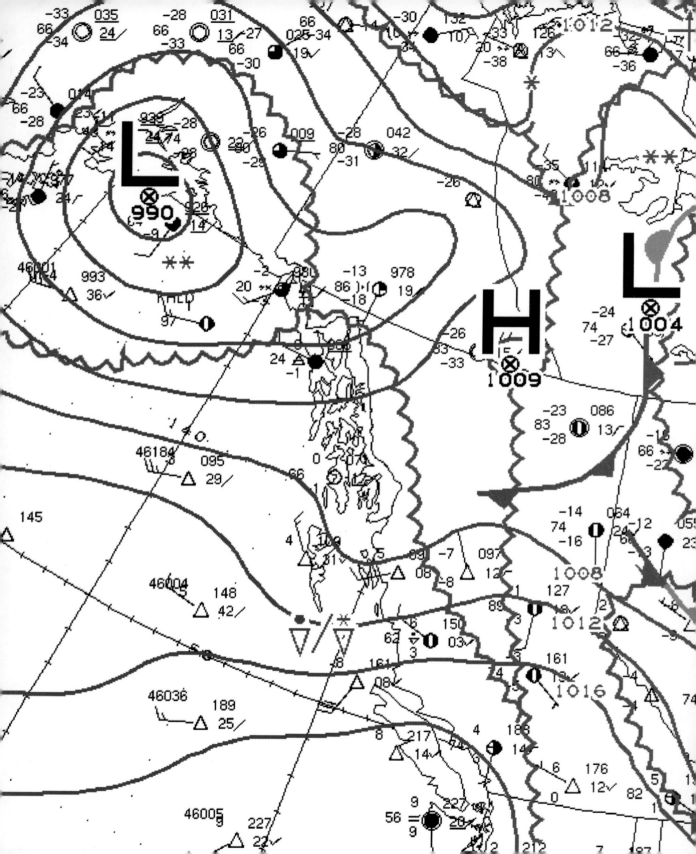

CHAPTER 9

Probability Distributions

Meteorologists study and interpret huge sets of data in order to predict the weather. This large volume of information is condensed into just a few figures and presented in the daily weather report.

"Today's high will be 19 with possible showers. Clearing overnight with a low near 12."

Should we be surprised when such meager information fails to predict accurately a complex phenomenon such as weather?

1. One day in October, Marie-Claude sent e-mail to her parents in Manitoba from her dorm room at the University of Alberta. "The average temperature here this week was 13°C. That might sound fine for fall in Calgary but I've been really cold this week." How could this be possible?

2. Calculate the mean temperature for each improbable weather week.

	S	S	M	T	W	Th	F
a)	34	2	0	2	–2	0	1
b)	26	10	–2	–1	0	1	3
c)	–3	0	–2	11	12	11	10
d)	4	3	4	14	4	4	3
e)	2	3	4	5	6	7	8

Does the mean accurately reflect the weather for the week? Explain.

3. How would you summarize the weather data for each week in a more meaningful way?

GETTING STARTED

Comparing Sets of Data

Each student in a class was asked to estimate the total area of the windows in the classroom. Some students used a metre stick to make measurements, while the other students estimated without any aids.

The following data were collected.

Without Measuring Aids		With a Metre Stick	
Area (m²)	Number of Students	Area (m²)	Number of Students
10	I	10	
11		11	
12	II	12	
13	I	13	
14		14	II
15	III	15	⊞I
16	IIII	16	⊞ II
17	III	17	
18		18	I
19		19	
20		20	
21	I	21	
22	I	22	

1. How many students were in the class?

2. Determine the mean area for each set of data. What do you conclude?

3. Graph the data in a double bar graph, with the estimated area on the horizontal axis and the number of students on the vertical axis. What is the noticeable difference between the two sets of data? What is the same?

4. One way to determine the variability of a set of data is to find the **range**, that is, the difference between the greatest and the least data item recorded. What is the range for each set of area estimates?

5. Another method for determining the variability of a set of data is to calculate the **mean deviation** of the data from the mean. For example, the data set {3, 10, 12, 12, 13} has a mean of 10. Since $|3 - 10| = 7$, the first data point has deviation 7. Thus, the set of deviations from the mean is {7, 0, 2, 2, 3}. The mean of these deviations is 2.4. Determine the mean deviation of each set of data collected from the students.

6. Which measure of variability, the range or the mean deviation, best describes the variability of data concerning the window area? Why?

Warm Up

Find the mean, median, and mode for each set of data.
1. 4, 6, 12, 5, 8, 9, 7
2. 9, 9, 8, 9, 8, 9, 11
3. 7, 19, 9, 4, 7, 2, 3, 5
4. 300, 34, 40, 50, 60
5. 25, 25, 25, 15, 15, 15
6. 10, 3, 17, 1, 8, 6, 12, 15

7. A high school basketball team decided to raise money for new uniforms by having a free-throw contest. Each member of the team canvassed the community asking for pledges per successful free throw. The histogram shows the results of the team's contest.

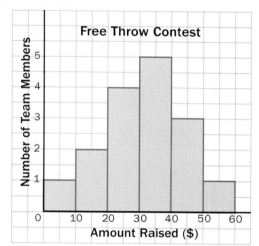

a) How many team members participated in the free-throw contest?
b) How many team members raised more than $30? less than $30?
c) In what interval does the median amount raised fall?
d) What percent of the team members raised above the interval containing the median? below it?
e) Using the histogram, what is the maximum possible amount the team could have raised? the minimum amount?

Mental Math

Evaluate.
1. 0.1^4
2. 3^5
3. 4^4
4. $\left(\dfrac{2}{3}\right)^3$
5. $\left(\dfrac{1}{2}\right)^4$
6. 11^3
7. 2^6
8. 0.6^3
9. $8^{\frac{1}{3}}$
10. $81^{\frac{1}{4}}$
11. $\left(\dfrac{3}{2}\right)^3$
12. 20^4

Determine the percent discount implied by each of the following promotions.
13. Buy one, get one free.
14. Buy three tires and get the fourth one free.
15. Buy two for the price of one.
16. Buy one, get the second at half price.
17. Rent five videos and the sixth is free.

Using only mental estimation, order the numbers in each group from least to greatest. Check your answers using a calculator.
18. $3^2, 2^3, 2^2 \times 3^2, 2^{-1} \times 3^3$
19. $\log 27, \log 9, \log \pi^3, \log 3^\pi$
20. $625, 5^5, 10^3, 2^{10}$
21. $\dfrac{1}{2}, \left(\dfrac{2}{3}\right)^3, \left(\dfrac{1}{3}\right)^2, \left(\dfrac{8}{27}\right)^{\frac{1}{3}}$
22. $\dfrac{1}{\sqrt{3}}, \dfrac{1}{\sqrt[3]{10}}, \sqrt{\dfrac{4}{7}}, \sqrt[3]{0.125}$

Simplify.
23. $\dfrac{3}{\sqrt{3}}$
24. $\dfrac{5}{\sqrt{2}}$
25. $\sqrt{7} \times 5\sqrt{11}$
26. $3\sqrt{6} \times 5\sqrt{6}$
27. $\sqrt{150}$
28. $\sqrt{54}$
29. $\dfrac{\sqrt{55}}{\sqrt{5}}$
30. $\dfrac{18}{\sqrt{15}} \div 6\sqrt{3}$
31. $\dfrac{1}{\sqrt{7}} \div \dfrac{6}{\sqrt{7}}$
32. $\dfrac{8}{\sqrt{2}} \div \dfrac{2\sqrt{2}}{7}$

9.1 The Binomial Distribution

Many actions have only two possible outcomes: a tossed coin comes up heads or tails, a foul shot in basketball is in or out, and a light switch is on or off. Such *identical* and *independent* repeated events lead to the binomial distribution.

Explore: Look for a Pattern

Kaia is an excellent archer. Under good conditions at her local archery range, she can hit the bull's-eye 75% of the time.

a) Kaia shoots four arrows at the target. Draw a probability tree diagram to show her chances of hitting the bull's-eye.

b) Use your probability tree to help complete this table.

Arrow Outcomes	Hits	Probability
hit, hit, hit, hit	4	$0.75 \times 0.75 \times 0.75 \times 0.75 = (0.75)^4$
hit, hit, hit, miss	3	$0.75 \times 0.75 \times 0.75 \times 0.25 = (0.75)^3(0.25)$
hit, hit, miss, hit	3	$0.75 \times 0.75 \times 0.25 \times 0.75 = (0.75)^3(0.25)$
⋮		

c) Complete the summary of the hits (successes) begun in the table.

Hits in 4 Throws	Ways	Probability of Each	Total Probability
4	1	$(0.75)^4$	$(0.75)^4$
3	4	$(0.75)^3(0.25)$	$4(0.75)^3(0.25)$
⋮			

d) Make a histogram with the number of hits in four shots on the x-axis and the corresponding probability on the y-axis. Each bar in your graph should have a width of 1 and height corresponding to the probability of that number of hits.

Inquire

1. What pattern emerges with the exponents in the calculation of the probability of the number of successes (hits)?

2. What pattern emerges with the factors that make up the probabilities?

3. Expand $(H + M)^4$. Substitute $H = 0.75$ and $M = 0.25$ in each term but do not simplify. Compare the terms with the values found in Explore part c). Explain how this polynomial includes all the probabilities of possible outcomes for Kaia.

4. What polynomial should you consider if Kaia shoots three arrows instead of four?

5. Describe the shape of your histogram. What is the total area of all the bars? Why?

Not all outcomes for an event have an equal probability. A list of possible outcomes and the associated probabilities is called a **distribution**. A probability distribution is a graph, table, or formula that specifies the probability associated with each possible outcome in an experiment. From the distribution of probabilities, we can better understand an event.

Binomial Distribution

The **binomial distribution** is the pattern of probabilities for the outcomes of repeated independent and identical trials. If p is the probability of success and q is the probability of failure ($q = 1 - p$), then the probability of x successes in n trials is

$$P(x \text{ successes}) = \frac{n!}{x!(n-x)!} p^x q^{n-x}$$
$$= {}_nC_x p^x q^{n-x}$$

In the above definition, the term success refers to the outcome whose probability is to be determined. Any other outcome is called a failure. Note that the terms success and failure imply nothing about the desirability of the outcomes. The binomial distribution is so named because its probabilities correspond to the terms of the binomial expansion of $(p + q)^n$, that is, ${}_nC_r p^{n-r} q^r$, as seen in Chapter 7.

Note that in n trials, $P(x \text{ successes}) = P(n - x \text{ failures})$

Example 1   Determining Probabilities in Basketball

Vince Carter's foul-shooting success rate is 85%. In a game in which Carter shoots 15 foul shots, what is the probability that
a) he sinks exactly 13 of the foul shots?
b) he sinks at least 13 of the foul shots?
c) he sinks at least one foul shot?

Solution

a) Assume that these are independent identical foul shots. The probabilities are modelled by the binomial distribution.
$n = 15$ (number of trials)
$x = 13$ (number of successes)
$p = 0.85$ (probability of success on each trial)
$q = 0.15$ (probability of failure on each trial)

$$P(13 \text{ successes}) = {}_nC_x p^x q^{n-x}$$
$$= {}_{15}C_{13}(0.85)^{13}(0.15)^{15-13}$$
$$= \frac{15!}{13!2!}(0.85)^{13}(0.15)^2$$
$$\doteq 105(0.120\ 905)(0.0225)$$
$$\doteq 0.285\ 639$$

```
binompdf(15,0.85
,13)
          .2856392285
■
```

Use a graphing calculator to solve the problem.

The probability that Carter will sink exactly 13 foul shots in 15 attempts is approximately 29%.

b) "At least 13" means that Carter sinks either 13, or 14, or 15 foul shots.

$n = 15$

$x = 13, 14, 15$

$p = 0.85$

$q = 0.15$

$P(\text{at least 13 successes}) = P(13 \text{ successes}) + P(14 \text{ successes}) + P(15 \text{ successes})$

$$= {}_{15}C_{13}(0.85)^{13}(0.15)^2 + {}_{15}C_{14}(0.85)^{14}(0.15)^1$$
$$+ {}_{15}C_{15}(0.85)^{15}(0.15)^0$$
$$\doteq 0.285\ 639 + 0.231\ 232 + 0.087\ 354$$
$$\doteq 0.604\ 225$$

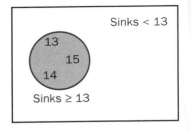

A graphing calculator can calculate several binomial probabilities at once. Then, you can add them.

The probability that Carter will sink at least 13 foul shots is approximately 60%.

c) Sinking "at least one" foul shot means sinking either 1, 2, 3, ..., or all 15 shots. The only event not being considered is the case when $x = 0$, that is, there are no successful shots. Although a calculator can do all 15 successful calculations, since the sum of all the probabilities must equal one, it is even easier to calculate the probability of the unsuccessful outcome and subtract.

$P(1, 2, 3, ..., 15 \text{ successes}) = 1 - P(0 \text{ successes})$

$$= 1 - {}_{15}C_0(0.85)^0(0.15)^{15-0}$$
$$\doteq 1 - 0.000\ 000\ 000\ 000\ 437\ 894$$
$$\doteq 1$$

It is almost certain that Carter will sink at least one foul shot.

Example 2 Using Probability in Quality Control

A manufacturer of a gas generator estimates that 0.1% of their generators are defective. If a customer places an order for 25 generators, what is the probability that at least two of them are defective?

Solution

In this context, consider a "success" to be a defective generator.

$n = 25$ (number of trials, or generators being made)

$x = 2, 3, 4, ..., 25$ (number of defective products)

$p = 0.001$ (probability of success, or a defective product, on each trial)

$q = 0.999$ (probability of failure on each trial)

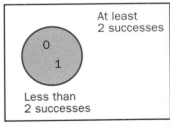

Calculate the required probability indirectly.

$P(\text{at least 2 successes}) = P(2 \text{ successes}) + P(3 \text{ successes}) + ... + P(25 \text{ successes})$

$P(\text{at least 2 successes}) = 1 - P(0 \text{ successes}) - P(1 \text{ success})$

$$= 1 - {}_{25}C_0(0.001)^0(0.999)^{25-0} - {}_{25}C_1(0.001)^1(0.999)^{25-1}$$
$$\doteq 1 - 0.975\ 298 - 0.024\ 407$$
$$\doteq 0.000\ 295$$

The probability that at least two generators will be defective in an order of 25 is very small, about 0.03%.

Example 3 Finding the Binomial Distribution for Coin Tosses

Find the binomial distribution for the number of heads when tossing a coin four times. Use a histogram to illustrate the data.

Solution

Find all possible outcomes and their probabilities.
$n = 4$ (the number of tosses)
$x = 0, 1, 2, 3,$ or 4 (the possible numbers of heads)
$p = \dfrac{1}{2}$ (the chance of success, or flipping a head)

$q = \dfrac{1}{2}$ (the chance of failure, or flipping a tail)

Number of Heads	Probability	
0	${}_4C_0\left(\dfrac{1}{2}\right)^0\left(\dfrac{1}{2}\right)^{4-0}$	$= \dfrac{1}{16}$
1	${}_4C_1\left(\dfrac{1}{2}\right)^1\left(\dfrac{1}{2}\right)^{4-1}$	$= \dfrac{1}{4}$
2	${}_4C_2\left(\dfrac{1}{2}\right)^2\left(\dfrac{1}{2}\right)^{4-2}$	$= \dfrac{3}{8}$
3	${}_4C_3\left(\dfrac{1}{2}\right)^3\left(\dfrac{1}{2}\right)^{4-3}$	$= \dfrac{1}{4}$
4	${}_4C_4\left(\dfrac{1}{2}\right)^4\left(\dfrac{1}{2}\right)^{4-4}$	$= \dfrac{1}{16}$

Distributions can also be found using a graphing calculator.

Practice

Using the binomial distribution, where n represents the number of trials, p, the probability of success, and q, the probability of failure, find the indicated probability.

1. $n = 12, p = 0.2$, find $P(2 \text{ successes})$
2. $n = 10, p = 0.4$, find $P(1 \text{ success})$
3. $n = 20, p = 0.5$, find $P(10 \text{ successes})$
4. $n = 15, p = 0.9$, find $P(11 \text{ successes})$
5. $n = 7, p = \dfrac{1}{3}$, find $P(4 \text{ successes})$
6. $n = 11, p = 0.05$, find $P(3 \text{ failures})$
7. $n = 15, p = 0.99$, find $P(1 \text{ failure})$
8. $n = 6, p = 0.35$, find $P(\text{at least 3 successes})$
9. $n = 100, p = 0.01$, find
   $P(\text{no more than 3 successes})$

Find the binomial distribution for each event. Illustrate with a histogram.

10. the number of times a slugger strikes out in four at-bats if the chance of a strikeout is 30%
11. the number of sixes rolled in six rolls of a die
12. the number of goals in five penalty shots if the probability of the goalkeeper stopping a shot is 60%
13. the number of triple twenties hit in seven darts thrown, if the chance of any dart hitting the triple twenty is only 10%

Applications and Problem Solving

14. **Quiz results** In history class, Colin and Diana both write a multiple-choice quiz. There are ten questions. Each question has five possible answers. What is the probability that
   a) Colin will pass the test if he guesses an answer to each question?
   b) Diana will pass the test if she studies so that she has a 75% chance of answering each question correctly?

15. Manufacturing The manufacturing sector contributes 17% of Canada's gross domestic product. A customer orders 50 components from a factory that has a 99% quality production rate (99% of the products are defect-free). Find the probability that
a) none of the components in the order are defective
b) there is at least one defective product in the order
c) there are at least two defective products in the order

16. Eggs Approximately 3% of the eggs in a supermarket are cracked. If you buy two dozen eggs, what is the probability that
a) none of your eggs are cracked?
b) at least one egg is cracked?
c) exactly two eggs are cracked?

17. Rolling dice A pair of dice is rolled 20 times. What is the probability that double sixes are rolled
a) exactly twice?
b) more than once, but no more than three times?

18. Pan American Games At the 1999 Pan American Games, Kim Eagles won gold for Canada in the women's air pistol event. Max averages a 60% hit rate when shooting pop cans with his air rifle. He lines up ten pop cans against the wall.
a) Estimate the probability that he will hit eight cans.
b) Estimate the probability that he will hit at least five cans.
c) Estimate the probability that he will hit at least eight cans.
d) Draw a Venn diagram showing the events of parts b) and c).
e) Estimate the probability that he will hit at least five, but no more than seven, cans.

19. Commuting time On Alan's journey to work, he has to pass through 12 intersections with traffic lights that operate independently. The chance that any set is green when he reaches it is 0.5. If he is stopped at fewer than three sets of lights, he has time for a coffee before work. But if he is stopped at more than 8 sets of lights, he is late. If Alan is late more than twice in a five-day work week, he has to see his manager. What is the probability that
a) Alan has time for coffee on any given day?
b) Alan has to see the manager in any given week?

20. Chain strength If a chain link is stressed over its recommended maximum limit, the probability that the link will break is 0.7. What is the probability that a chain will break if it is overloaded and is
a) five links long?   **b)** ten links long?

21. Unfair coin The binomial distribution for tossing an unfair coin six times is summarized in this histogram.

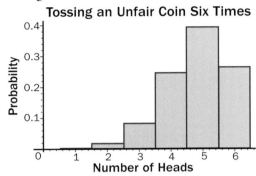

Tossing an Unfair Coin Six Times

If heads are a success and tails are a failure, use the diagram to estimate
a) the probability of seeing six heads
b) the probability of seeing at least four heads
c) the probability of getting a head on a single toss of the unfair coin

22. Basketball Lina was told that Vince Carter makes 85% of his free-throw attempts. Since $15 \times 0.85 = 12.75$, Lina expects that in 15 attempts Carter will make 13 baskets. Is Lina's reasoning correct? Which is more likely, that Carter makes exactly 13 baskets or that Carter does not make exactly 13 baskets? Explain.

23. Coin experiment As an experiment, toss four coins at once and record the number of heads in a table. Repeat this experiment ten times.
a) How many times does each result—0, 1, 2, 3, 4 —occur? Combine your results with those of three classmates and record all the results in the table.

Number of Heads	Tally	Tally ÷ 10
0		
1		
⋮		

b) How does this combined data compare with the distribution in Example 3? Explain your conclusions.

9.2 The Mean and the Standard Deviation

"The mean daily temperature in Calgary in January is –9.6°C." This simple weather fact does not indicate the variety of conditions that Calgarians face each January. A single number, like the mean, is often inadequate to describe accurately a large set of data. What is also needed is to know how data differ (or deviate) from the mean. One measure of this difference is called the **standard deviation**.

Explore: The Spread of Data

Boxes of crocus bulbs claim to contain an average of 50 bulbs. Five cartons of bulbs were opened and the bulbs in the boxes in each carton were counted. Find the mean and the range for each carton.

Carton A: 49, 51, 49, 51, 49, 51, 49, 51, 49, 51
Carton B: 48, 52, 48, 52, 48, 52, 48, 52, 48, 52
Carton C: 48, 51, 49, 52, 47, 52, 46, 51, 53, 51
Carton D: 54, 49, 46, 49, 51, 53, 50, 50, 49, 49
Carton E: 60, 36, 31, 50, 48, 50, 54, 56, 52, 63

Inquire

1. In what way(s) are the data for all cartons the same? In what way(s) are they different?

2. Which carton has the widest range of data? Which has the least range of data?

3. Rank the cartons, from least to greatest, according to their maximum deviation, that is, the largest difference from the mean.

4. Create a list for an imaginary carton G whose mean is 50 and whose range is approximately 20.

The Greek letter μ (pronounced "mu") is often used to represent the mean of a set of data $x_1, x_2, ..., x_n$.

$$\text{mean} = \frac{\text{sum of data}}{\text{number of data}}$$

$$\mu = \frac{x_1 + x_2 + ... + x_n}{n}$$

$$= \frac{1}{n}\sum_{i=1}^{n} x_i$$

In statistics, the symbol $\bar{x}$ is sometimes used to represent the mean. Your graphing calculator may use the symbol $\bar{x}$; with this text, read it as μ.

The range and the mean are measurements that describe a set of data. Individually, or even together, they may not be adequate to describe a data set. Another way to describe data is by the **standard deviation** σ. The standard deviation is an important statistical measure of the spread of data around the mean μ.

$$\text{standard deviation} = \sqrt{\frac{\text{sum of the squares of the deviations from the mean}}{\text{number of data}}}$$

$$\sigma = \sqrt{\frac{(x_1 - \mu)^2 + (x_2 - \mu)^2 + \ldots + (x_n - \mu)^2}{n}}$$

$$= \sqrt{\frac{\sum_{i=1}^{n}(x_i - \mu)^2}{n}}$$

The calculation of the mean and the standard deviation can be done using a scientific calculator, a graphing calculator, or a spreadsheet. The following example demonstrates this.

Example 1   Determining the Mean and the Standard Deviation

Determine the mean and the standard deviation for each set of sports data.
a) golf scores: 72, 74, 73, 76, 74, 71, 75, 76, 72, 77
b) 100-m dash, in seconds: 10.8, 10.6, 10.8, 9.9, 10.2, 10.3, 10.4, 10.5

Solution

a) $\text{mean} = \dfrac{\text{sum of data}}{\text{number of data}}$

$$\mu = \frac{72 + 74 + 73 + 76 + 74 + 71 + 75 + 76 + 72 + 77}{10}$$

$$\mu = 74$$

```
1-Var Stats
x̄=74
Σx=740
Σx²=54796
Sx=2
σx=1.897366596
↓n=10
■
```

$$\text{standard deviation} = \sqrt{\frac{\text{sum of the squares of the deviations from the mean}}{\text{number of data}}}$$

$$\sigma = \sqrt{\frac{(72-74)^2 + (74-74)^2 + \ldots + (77-74)^2}{10}}$$

$$\sigma \doteq 1.897$$

The mean of the golf scores is 74, and the standard deviation is approximately 1.897.

b) A spreadsheet is a useful tool for organizing data and making statistical calculations.

	A	B
	Time	**Deviation from Mean**
1		
2	10.8	0.3625
3	10.6	0.1625
4	10.8	0.3625
5	9.9	−0.5375
6	10.2	−0.2375
7	10.3	−0.1375
8	10.4	−0.0375
9	10.5	0.0625
10		
11	**Mean of Times**	**Standard Deviation**
12	10.4375	0.286956
13		

The mean of the 100-m dash data is 10.4375 s, and the standard deviation is approximately 0.287 s.

Example 2   Using the Standard Deviation to Analyze Data

The marks on a math test had a mean of 74 and a standard deviation of 4. The marks on the second math test had a mean of 72 and a standard deviation of 9.
a) Which set of marks is more widely dispersed?
b) Aleem had a mark of 80 on both tests. Determine the number of standard deviations that Aleem's mark is from the mean on each test. Which result appears to be the better mark?

Solution

a) The second test marks have a greater standard deviation, which indicates that those marks are more widely dispersed than the first test marks.

b) For Aleem's mark on the first test:

$$\text{Number of standard deviations from the mean for first test} = \frac{80-74}{4}$$
$$= 1.5$$

For Aleem's mark on the second test:

$$\text{Number of standard deviations from the mean for second test} = \frac{80-72}{9}$$
$$\doteq 0.8889$$

Since Aleem's first test mark is a greater number of standard deviations above the mean, it may be considered the better mark.

The number of multiples of the standard deviation σ that a data item x is from the mean μ is called its **z-score**. The z-score is negative when x is less than μ and positive when x is greater than μ.

$$z\text{-score} = \frac{\text{difference from the mean}}{\text{standard deviation}}$$

$$z_x = \frac{x - \mu}{\sigma}$$

You will see that for many sets of data, approximately 68.3% of the data are within one standard deviation of the mean, and 95.4% are within two standard deviations.

Example 3   Using the z-Score to Solve a Problem
February's average daily maximum temperature is $-0.5°C$ in Calgary and $-4.2°C$ in Montréal. Assume the standard deviations are $3°C$ and $6°C$, respectively. During a nationwide cold snap Calgary has a high of $-15°C$, while Montréal has a high of $-20°C$. Relative to their normal temperature, which city is having the colder snap?

Solution
For Calgary, $\mu = -0.5$, $\sigma = 3$, and $x = -15$.

$$z_{-15} = \frac{-15 - (-0.5)}{3}$$
$$\doteq -4.83$$

So, the high of $-15°C$ in Calgary is about 4.83 standard deviations below the mean.

For Montréal, $\mu = -4.2$, $\sigma = 6$, and $x = -20$.

$$z_{-20} = \frac{-20 - (-4.2)}{6}$$
$$\doteq -2.63$$

So, the high of $-20°C$ in Montréal is about 2.63 standard deviations below the mean.

Since $4.83 > 2.63$, the cold snap is worse in Calgary. The weather in Calgary is further from the average than is the weather in Montréal.

Practice

1. Each data set has a mean of 50.
set A: 0, 20, 40, 50, 60, 80, 100
set B: 0, 48, 49, 50, 51, 52, 100
set C: 0, 1, 2, 50, 98, 99, 100
a) By inspection, predict which set of data has the greatest standard deviation, and which has the least.
b) Calculate the standard deviation for each set and check whether your prediction is correct.

2. Each set of data has a mean of 100.
set P: 97, 99, 100, 101, 103
set Q: 96, 98, 100, 102, 104
set R: 96, 99, 100, 101, 104
a) By inspection, predict which set of data has the

greatest standard deviation, and which has the least.
b) Calculate the standard deviation for each set and check whether your prediction is correct.

3. For each pair of data sets, calculate the means and the standard deviations. How is set B related to set A in each case?
a) set A: 1, 3, 4, 5, 7
set B: 6, 8, 9, 10, 12
b) set A: 1, 3, 4, 5, 7
set B: 3, 9, 12, 15, 21
c) set A: 5, −4, 3, −1, 7
set B: −5, 4, −3, 1, −7

4. Soft drink cans Soft drink cans have a mean capacity of 355 mL and a standard deviation of 1.5 mL.
a) A sample of four cans found that they actually contained 354 mL, 357 mL, 358 mL, and 352 mL. Determine the z-score of each of the cans in the sample.
b) Two cans had z-scores of 3 and -3. What amount did each contain?

Applications and Problem Solving

5. Choose 10 numbers so that the standard deviation is as large as possible provided that the given condition occurs.
a) Each number is a one or a nine. For example, 1, 9, 1, 1, 1, 1, 9, 9, 9, 1.
b) Each number is a one, a five, or a nine.

6. Repeat question 5, but make the standard deviation as small as possible.

7. Height requirements For entry into the Canadian armed forces, the height requirement used to be 158 cm to 194 cm for males and 152 cm to 194 cm for females.
a) If the mean height for males was 176 cm with standard deviation 8 cm, what was the z-score range for the allowable heights?
b) An applicant's height had a z-score of -1.5. What was his height?
c) If the mean height for females was 163 cm with standard deviation 7 cm, what was the z-score range for female heights?
d) An applicant was 176 cm tall. What was her z-score?
e) Based on the two z-score ranges, which height requirement was more restrictive?

8. Marks Two students have the same mean percent mark for the six courses that they are studying.
a) If one student has a better mark in all the courses except one, what is one possible list of marks for each student?
b) If one student's marks have a small standard deviation and the other student's marks have a large standard deviation, write a possible list of marks for each student.

9. Given numbers x, y, and z, such that $x < y < z$, find expressions for the mean and the standard deviation of the three numbers.

10. Human proportions One of Leonardo da Vinci's well-known illustrations shows the proportions of a human figure by enclosing it in a circle. It appears that the arm span is equal to the height.
a) Measure the arm span and height of ten students in your class. Calculate the mean and the standard deviation of each of the two sets of data.
b) Do the means fall within one standard deviation of each other? Comment.
c) Another approach to this question would be to calculate the difference between each person's height and arm span. From your data what would you expect the mean and the standard deviation of the ten differences to be? Calculate these two statistics to check your prediction.

11. a) Can the standard deviation ever be negative? Can the standard deviation ever be zero? Explain.
b) For a data set of positive numbers, can the standard deviation ever be larger than the mean? Explain.
c) If 5 were added to each number in a set of data, what effect would it have on the mean? on the standard deviation? What if each element in the data set were multiplied by -3?

12. If possible, create an example with ten or more data points so that
a) the standard deviation is twice the mean
b) the mean is twice the standard deviation
c) more than 80% of the data are positive, but the mean is negative
d) more than 80% of the data have the same value, but the standard deviation is greater than 100
e) the mean is positive, but there are negative values in the data set
f) all values except one are less than the mean
g) the standard deviation is 1, but there is a data point greater than 100

INVESTIGATING MATH

The Standard Normal Curve

One way of analyzing data is to graph the frequency distribution as a histogram. In many situations, the spread of data is such that the histogram is shaped like the one shown. The shape can be approximated by a **normal curve**, or bell curve, due to the fact that the data are concentrated around the centre portion of the distribution.

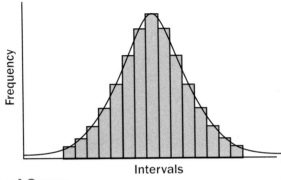

1 Relating a Normal Curve to the Standard Normal Curve

For a set of data with mean μ and standard deviation σ, the normal curve is denoted by $N(\mu, \sigma^2)$. There are an infinite number of normal curves. The z-score provides a standard measure for comparing two different normal curves, by transferring each to the **standard normal curve $N(0, 1)$**. The z-score represents the number of standard deviations that a data item is from the mean.

$$z\text{-score} = \frac{\text{difference from the mean}}{\text{standard deviation}}$$

$$z_x = \frac{x - \mu}{\sigma}$$

In general, the distribution of the z-scores of a set of data is often approximated well by the standard normal curve $N(0, 1)$.

1. Given the following data set: 10   11   14   16   19
a) Calculate the mean and standard deviation for the data set.
b) Calculate the z-score for each item in the set.
c) Calculate the mean and standard deviation of the z-scores from part b).

2. A set of data, x_1, x_2, x_3, x_4, has mean μ and standard deviation σ. Show that the mean and standard deviation of the z-scores for the set are 0 and 1, respectively.

2 The Area Under the Standard Normal Curve

The area under the normal curve relates to the probability that an event will occur, with the total area equalling 1. A table of previously calculated values is found on pages 416–417. These values correspond to the area under the standard normal curve $N(0, 1)$ to the left of a given z-score. The table is organized into two parts, one for positive z-scores and one for negative z-scores.

To determine the area under the curve associated with a positive z-score of 0.32, first locate 0.3 in the left column, and then move across that row until the column headed 0.02 is reached.

	0.00	0.01	0.02
0.0	0.5000	0.5040	0.5080
0.1	0.5398	0.5438	0.5478
0.2	0.5793	0.5832	0.5871
0.3	0.6179	0.6217	0.6255

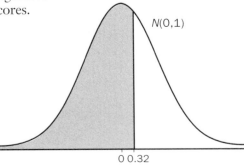

The area under the curve to the left of a z-score of 0.32 is 0.6255, or approximately 63% of the total area.

The table for negative z-scores is used in the same manner. For a negative z-score of −2.41, first locate −2.4 in the left column, and then move across that row to the column headed 0.01.

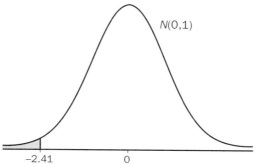

N(0,1)

	0.00	0.01	0.02
−2.9	0.0019	0.0018	0.0018
−2.8	0.0026	0.0025	0.0024
−2.7	0.0035	0.0034	0.0033
−2.6	0.0047	0.0045	0.0044
−2.5	0.0062	0.0060	0.0059
−2.4	0.0082 → 0.0080		0.0078

−2.41   0

The area under the curve to the left of a z-score of −2.41 is 0.0080, or approximately 1% of the total area.

Use the table of areas under the standard normal curve N(0,1) to answer the following questions.

1. Find the area under the standard normal curve to the left of each z-score.
a) 1.13   **b)** −2.16   **c)** 1.90
d) 0.31   **e)** −0.89   **f)** −1.55

2. Given the value of the area under the standard normal curve, find the corresponding z-score.
a) 0.0089   **b)** 0.3409   **c)** 0.1230
d) 0.9911   **e)** 0.7580   **f)** 0.8888

3. The area between two z-scores z_a and z_b, where $z_a > z_b$, is given by the difference between the corresponding table values of z_a and z_b. Determine the area between the z-scores in each pair for a normal distribution.
a) 1.12 and 1.98
b) −2.12 and −1.0
c) 0.42 and 1.07
d) 1.11 and 2.22
e) 1.09 and 0.09
f) −1 and 1

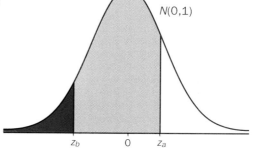

N(0,1)

z_b 0 z_a

4. a) How are the areas to the left of the z-scores of −2.00 and 2.00 related?
b) Without using the table, what is the area to the left of a z-score of 0?
c) Given that the area to the left of a z-score of −0.32 is 0.3745, how could you determine the area to the right of z-score 0.32?

Areas Under the Standard Normal Curve, to the Left of z

	0.00	0.01	0.02	0.03	0.04	0.05	0.06	0.07	0.08	0.09
−2.9	0.0019	0.0018	0.0018	0.0017	0.0016	0.0016	0.0015	0.0015	0.0014	0.0014
−2.8	0.0026	0.0025	0.0024	0.0023	0.0023	0.0022	0.0021	0.0021	0.0020	0.0019
−2.7	0.0035	0.0034	0.0033	0.0032	0.0031	0.0030	0.0029	0.0028	0.0027	0.0026
−2.6	0.0047	0.0045	0.0044	0.0043	0.0041	0.0040	0.0039	0.0038	0.0037	0.0036
−2.5	0.0062	0.0060	0.0059	0.0057	0.0055	0.0054	0.0052	0.0051	0.0049	0.0048
−2.4	0.0082	0.0080	0.0078	0.0075	0.0073	0.0071	0.0069	0.0068	0.0066	0.0064
−2.3	0.0107	0.0104	0.0102	0.0099	0.0096	0.0094	0.0091	0.0089	0.0087	0.0084
−2.2	0.0139	0.0136	0.0132	0.0129	0.0125	0.0122	0.0119	0.0116	0.0113	0.0110
−2.1	0.0179	0.0174	0.0170	0.0166	0.0162	0.0158	0.0154	0.0150	0.0146	0.0143
−2.0	0.0228	0.0222	0.0217	0.0212	0.0207	0.0202	0.0197	0.0192	0.0188	0.0183
−1.9	0.0287	0.0281	0.0274	0.0268	0.0262	0.0256	0.0250	0.0244	0.0239	0.0233
−1.8	0.0359	0.0351	0.0344	0.0336	0.0329	0.0322	0.0314	0.0307	0.0301	0.0294
−1.7	0.0446	0.0436	0.0427	0.0418	0.0409	0.0401	0.0392	0.0384	0.0375	0.0367
−1.6	0.0548	0.0537	0.0526	0.0516	0.0505	0.0495	0.0485	0.0475	0.0465	0.0455
−1.5	0.0668	0.0655	0.0643	0.0630	0.0618	0.0606	0.0594	0.0582	0.0571	0.0559
−1.4	0.0808	0.0793	0.0778	0.0764	0.0749	0.0735	0.0721	0.0708	0.0694	0.0681
−1.3	0.0968	0.0951	0.0934	0.0918	0.0901	0.0885	0.0869	0.0853	0.0838	0.0823
−1.2	0.1151	0.1131	0.1112	0.1093	0.1075	0.1056	0.1038	0.1020	0.1003	0.0985
−1.1	0.1357	0.1335	0.1314	0.1292	0.1271	0.1251	0.1230	0.1210	0.1190	0.1170
−1.0	0.1587	0.1562	0.1539	0.1515	0.1492	0.1469	0.1446	0.1423	0.1401	0.1379
−0.9	0.1841	0.1814	0.1788	0.1762	0.1736	0.1711	0.1685	0.1660	0.1635	0.1611
−0.8	0.2119	0.2090	0.2061	0.2033	0.2005	0.1977	0.1949	0.1921	0.1894	0.1867
−0.7	0.2420	0.2389	0.2358	0.2327	0.2296	0.2266	0.2236	0.2206	0.2177	0.2148
−0.6	0.2743	0.2709	0.2676	0.2643	0.2611	0.2578	0.2546	0.2514	0.2483	0.2451
−0.5	0.3085	0.3050	0.3015	0.2981	0.2946	0.2912	0.2877	0.2843	0.2810	0.2776
−0.4	0.3446	0.3409	0.3372	0.3336	0.3300	0.3264	0.3228	0.3192	0.3156	0.3121
−0.3	0.3821	0.3783	0.3745	0.3707	0.3669	0.3632	0.3594	0.3557	0.3520	0.3483
−0.2	0.4207	0.4168	0.4129	0.4090	0.4052	0.4013	0.3974	0.3936	0.3897	0.3859
−0.1	0.4602	0.4562	0.4522	0.4483	0.4443	0.4404	0.4364	0.4325	0.4286	0.4247
−0.0	0.5000	0.4960	0.4920	0.4880	0.4840	0.4801	0.4761	0.4721	0.4681	0.4641

Areas Under the Standard Normal Curve, to the Left of z

	0.00	0.01	0.02	0.03	0.04	0.05	0.06	0.07	0.08	0.09
0.0	0.5000	0.5040	0.5080	0.5120	0.5160	0.5199	0.5239	0.5279	0.5319	0.5359
0.1	0.5398	0.5438	0.5478	0.5517	0.5557	0.5596	0.5636	0.5675	0.5714	0.5753
0.2	0.5793	0.5832	0.5871	0.5910	0.5948	0.5987	0.6026	0.6064	0.6103	0.6141
0.3	0.6179	0.6217	0.6255	0.6293	0.6331	0.6368	0.6406	0.6443	0.6480	0.6517
0.4	0.6554	0.6591	0.6628	0.6664	0.6700	0.6736	0.6772	0.6808	0.6844	0.6879
0.5	0.6915	0.6950	0.6985	0.7019	0.7054	0.7088	0.7123	0.7157	0.7190	0.7224
0.6	0.7257	0.7291	0.7324	0.7357	0.7389	0.7422	0.7454	0.7486	0.7517	0.7549
0.7	0.7580	0.7611	0.7642	0.7673	0.7704	0.7734	0.7764	0.7794	0.7823	0.7852
0.8	0.7881	0.7910	0.7939	0.7967	0.7995	0.8023	0.8051	0.8079	0.8106	0.8133
0.9	0.8159	0.8186	0.8212	0.8238	0.8264	0.8289	0.8315	0.8340	0.8365	0.8389
1.0	0.8413	0.8438	0.8461	0.8485	0.8508	0.8531	0.8554	0.8577	0.8599	0.8621
1.1	0.8643	0.8665	0.8686	0.8708	0.8729	0.8749	0.8770	0.8790	0.8810	0.8830
1.2	0.8849	0.8869	0.8888	0.8907	0.8925	0.8944	0.8962	0.8980	0.8997	0.9015
1.3	0.9032	0.9049	0.9066	0.9082	0.9099	0.9115	0.9131	0.9147	0.9162	0.9177
1.4	0.9192	0.9207	0.9222	0.9236	0.9251	0.9265	0.9279	0.9292	0.9306	0.9319
1.5	0.9332	0.9345	0.9357	0.9370	0.9382	0.9394	0.9406	0.9418	0.9429	0.9441
1.6	0.9452	0.9463	0.9474	0.9484	0.9495	0.9505	0.9515	0.9525	0.9535	0.9545
1.7	0.9554	0.9564	0.9573	0.9582	0.9591	0.9599	0.9608	0.9616	0.9625	0.9633
1.8	0.9641	0.9649	0.9656	0.9664	0.9671	0.9678	0.9686	0.9693	0.9699	0.9706
1.9	0.9713	0.9719	0.9726	0.9732	0.9738	0.9744	0.9750	0.9756	0.9761	0.9767
2.0	0.9772	0.9778	0.9783	0.9788	0.9793	0.9798	0.9803	0.9808	0.9812	0.9817
2.1	0.9821	0.9826	0.9830	0.9834	0.9838	0.9842	0.9846	0.9850	0.9854	0.9857
2.2	0.9861	0.9864	0.9868	0.9871	0.9875	0.9878	0.9881	0.9884	0.9887	0.9890
2.3	0.9893	0.9896	0.9898	0.9901	0.9904	0.9906	0.9909	0.9911	0.9913	0.9916
2.4	0.9918	0.9920	0.9922	0.9925	0.9927	0.9929	0.9931	0.9932	0.9934	0.9936
2.5	0.9938	0.9940	0.9941	0.9943	0.9945	0.9946	0.9948	0.9949	0.9951	0.9952
2.6	0.9953	0.9955	0.9956	0.9957	0.9959	0.9960	0.9961	0.9962	0.9963	0.9964
2.7	0.9965	0.9966	0.9967	0.9968	0.9969	0.9970	0.9971	0.9972	0.9973	0.9974
2.8	0.9974	0.9975	0.9976	0.9977	0.9977	0.9978	0.9979	0.9979	0.9980	0.9981
2.9	0.9981	0.9982	0.9982	0.9983	0.9984	0.9984	0.9985	0.9985	0.9986	0.9986

9.3 The Normal Distribution

Manufacturers sample and measure their products to ensure that they meet company standards. It is normal to have small variations in quality or quantity at each stage of production. These many small errors combine to produce items with a range of possible measurements. The distribution of the measurements for the final product is similar across many industries and is called the normal distribution.

Explore: Draw a Graph

A certain cereal is packaged in boxes that are labelled 200 g. The actual amount of cereal in fifty packages from the production line was accurately measured. The results are listed in grams.

193	193	207	190	186	224	207	177	205	210
195	186	195	195	199	194	198	219	199	220
181	221	209	220	186	172	190	172	226	179
187	197	176	191	202	227	191	165	171	188
228	229	208	211	199	211	210	209	209	207

a) Complete the table to summarize the data. Then, use the table to draw a histogram.

Range (in grams)	Tally
163 – 167	|
168 – 172	|||
173 – 177	||
⋮	

b) If you were the production manager, would you accept this day's packaging? Explain.

Inquire

1. Use the histogram to estimate μ, the mean of the data. Then, calculate the actual mean.

2. Which phrase best describes the distribution of the data?
A: There are more data above the mean than below it.
B: There are more data below the mean than above it.
C: The data are symmetrically distributed about the mean.

3. For this data, as the mass moves further away from the mean, what happens to the probability of obtaining a package with that mass?

4. The standard deviation for this data set is 16.2. How many boxes in the sample have a mass between $\mu - 16.2$ and $\mu + 16.2$? What percent of the boxes have a mass within one standard deviation of the mean? within two standard deviations of the mean?

5. What is the probability that a box has more than 225 g of cereal? less than 170 g?

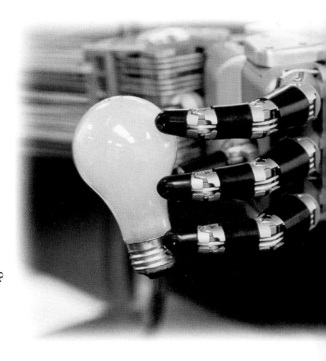

Normal Distribution

Data that are distributed in this bell shape are said to be *normally distributed*. The **normal curve** is defined as

$$f(x) = \frac{1}{\sigma\sqrt{2\pi}} e^{\frac{-(x-\mu)^2}{2\sigma^2}}$$

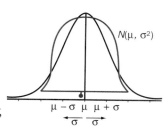

and represents the distribution of data with mean μ and standard deviation σ, denoted $N(\mu, \sigma^2)$. The properties of the normal curve include:
- It is symmetric about the mean.
- The total area under the curve is 1.
- The area under the curve between $x = a$ and $x = b$ is the probability that a data value will fall between a and b.
- Approximately 68.3% of the data occur within one standard deviation of the mean, approximately 95.4% occur within two standard deviations of the mean, and approximately 99.7% are within three standard deviations of the mean.

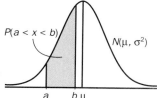

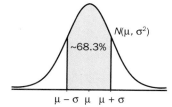

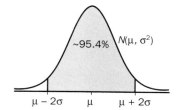

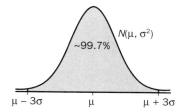

Example 1   Using the Normal Distribution

The Bright Light Company tested a new line of light bulbs and found their lifetimes to be normally distributed with a mean lifetime of 98 h and a standard deviation of 13 h.
a) What percent of these light bulbs last between 72 h and 124 h?
b) What is the probability that a light bulb selected at random will last more than 111 h?
c) In a shipment of 1200 of these light bulbs, how many would you expect to have a lifetime in the range from 80 h to 120 h? μ

Solution
a) $\sigma = 13$ (standard deviation) $a = 72$ (lower bound)
$\mu = 98$ (mean) $b = 124$ (upper bound)
Sketch the distribution. The probability that a light bulb will last between 72 h and 124 h is the area under the normal curve $N(98, 13^2)$ between 72 and 124. Use a graphing calculator to find the area.

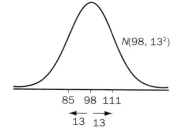

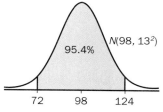

95.4% of the light bulbs are expected to last between 72 h and 124 h. Notice that, since $98 - (2 \times 13) = 72$ and $98 + (2 \times 13) = 124$, 95.4% of the light bulbs will have a lifetime within two standard deviations of the mean.

b) $a = 111$ (lower bound)

The probability that a light bulb lasts more than 111 h is the area under the normal curve $N(98, 13^2)$ after 111.

Use a graphing calculator to find this area:

The probability that a light bulb lasts more than 111 h is approximately 0.1587.

c) $a = 80$ (lower bound)
$b = 120$ (upper bound)

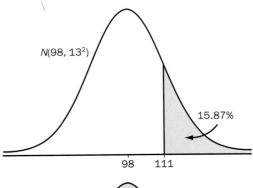

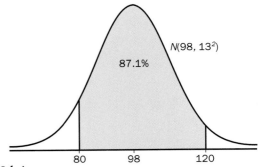

The probability that a light bulb will last between 80 h and 120 h is approximately 87.1%. Expect that, in a shipment of 1200 bulbs, about 1046 have a lifetime between 80 h and 120 h.

To find areas under a normal curve without a calculator, use previously-calculated tables of values. Rather than using a different table for each normal curve $N(\mu, \sigma^2)$, use z-scores to re-scale the curve to the normal curve $N(0, 1)$. Then, use the table on pages 416–417 for the curve $N(0, 1)$.

The area under the normal curve $N(\mu, \sigma^2)$ between a and b is equal to the area under the normal curve $N(0, 1)$ between z_a and z_b.

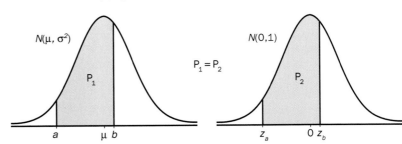

Solution to Example 1   Using z-Scores
a) $\sigma = 13$ (standard deviation)
$\mu = 98$ (mean)
$a = 72$ (lower bound)
$b = 124$ (upper bound)
Calculate the z-scores for a and b.

$$z_{72} = \frac{72 - 98}{13} \quad \text{and} \quad z_{124} = \frac{124 - 98}{13}$$
$$= -2.00 \qquad\qquad\qquad = 2.00$$

From the table on pages 416–417, the area to the left of z_{72} is 0.0228.

The area to the left of z_{124} is 0.9772.

The area between z_{72} and z_{124} is $0.9772 - 0.0228 = 0.9544$.

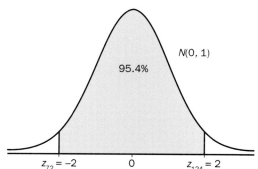

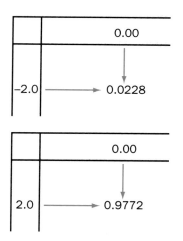

Thus, 95.4% of the bulbs last between 72 h and 124 h.

b) Find the z-score of 111.

$$z_{111} = \frac{111 - 98}{13}$$
$$= 1.00$$

From the table on pages 416–417, the area under the curve to the left of z_{111} is 0.8413. The area to the right of z_{111} is $1 - 0.8413$, or 0.1587.

Therefore, 15.87% of the light bulbs last more than 111 h. The probability of randomly selecting one of these bulbs is 0.1587.

c) Find the z-scores of 80 and 120.

$$z_{80} = \frac{80 - 98}{13} \quad \text{and} \quad z_{120} = \frac{120 - 98}{13}$$
$$\doteq -1.38 \qquad\qquad\qquad \doteq 1.69$$

From the table on pages 416–417, the area to the left of z_{80} is 0.0838 and to the left of z_{120} is 0.9545.
The required area can be found by subtracting.
$0.9545 - 0.0838 = 0.8707$

Approximately 87.07% of the light bulbs have a lifetime of between 80 h and 120 h. In a shipment of 1200 bulbs, 87.07% of 1200, or about 1045 light bulbs, have a lifetime between 80 h and 120 h.

Example 2   Determining an Expected Range
The mass of the cherries grown on a farm in the Okanagan Valley is normally distributed with a mean of 7.0 g and a standard deviation of 1.1 g. Determine the range in which you would expect the mass of 90% of the cherries to be.

Solution
Sketch the distribution.
A symmetric 90% interval about the mean leaves 5% at each end of the distribution. From the table on pages 416–417, the z-score that has 5% of the area to its left is approximately −1.64.

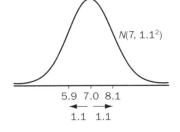

$N(7, 1.1^2)$

5.9 7.0 8.1
1.1 1.1

Use $z_x = \dfrac{x - \mu}{\sigma}$, where $z_x = -1.64$, $\mu = 7.0$, and $\sigma = 1.1$. Solve for x.

$$z_x = \frac{x - \mu}{\sigma}$$
$$-1.64 = \frac{x - 7.0}{1.1}$$
$$1.1(-1.64) = x - 7.0$$
$$x = 5.196$$

The left end of the interval is approximately 5.196 g.
By the symmetry of normal distribution, the right end will be the same distance from the mean. So the right end of the interval will be $7.0 + 1.804$, or 8.804 g.

This interval can also be found using a graphing calculator.

Note that the slight discrepancy between the calculator result and the table solution is due to rounding error in the table answer. However, both answers agree to within 0.01 g.

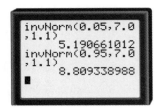

```
invNorm(0.05,7.0
,1.1)
         5.190661012
invNorm(0.95,7.0
,1.1)
         8.809338988
■
```

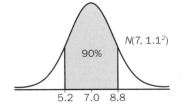

$N(7, 1.1^2)$

90%

5.2 7.0 8.8

Therefore, 90% of the cherries will have a mass in the range 5.2 g to 8.8 g.

Practice

For a normal distribution, determine the percent of the data that satisfies the given criteria.
1. less than 21 g, if the mean is 20 g and the standard deviation is 4 g
2. greater than 5 min, if the mean is 3 min and the standard deviation is 2 min
3. less than 201 mL, if the mean is 210 mL and the standard deviation is 18 mL
4. less than 33.15 m, if the mean is 30.0 m and the standard deviation is 1.575 m
5. greater than $1.11, if the mean is $1.20 and the standard deviation is $0.05
6. greater than −5.4, if the mean is −5 and the standard deviation is 0.25

For a normal distribution, determine the percent of the data that lies in the given intervals.
7. between 10 cm and 11 cm, when the mean is 9 cm and the standard deviation is 2 cm
8. between 555 kg and 595 kg, when the mean is 570 kg and the standard deviation is 15 kg
9. between −24°C and −21°C, when the mean is −20°C and the standard deviation is 5°C

For data that is normally distributed, find the measurement that satisfies the given facts.
10. 10% of the data is to the left of it; the mean is 25 h and the standard deviation is 6 h
11. 5% of the data is to the right of it; the mean is 110 V and the standard deviation is 10 V
12. 60% of the data is to the left of it; the mean is 72% and the standard deviation is 12%
13. 70% of the data is to the right of it; the mean is −12°C and the standard deviation is 3°C

Find the range of measurements that is symmetric about the mean of normally distributed data and satisfies the following facts.

14. It contains 50% of the data; the mean is 43 years and the standard deviation is 5 years.

15. It contains 80% of the data; the mean is 567 km and the standard deviation is 25 km.

16. It contains 90% of the data; the mean is $12.12 and the standard deviation is $4.32.

17. It contains 10% of the data; the mean is 80 L and the standard deviation is 10 L.

Applications and Problem Solving

18. Manufacturing Nylon strands are manufactured to a mean tensile strength of 1.5 N, with a standard deviation of 0.04 N. If the tensile strength of strands is normally distributed,
a) what percent of the strands would have a strength of less than 1.4 N, and will be recycled?
b) what range of strengths, symmetrical about the mean, would you expect 90% of the strands to have?

19. Pitching machine The accuracy of an automatic pitching machine for batting practice is based on the off-line distance that a pitch is from a target line that is 30 m away. The off-line distance is normally distributed with a mean of 0.3 m and a standard deviation of 0.05 m. What percent of the pitches fall within 0.2 m of the target line?

20. Preventative maintenance Major manufacturing companies operate on the principle of preventative maintenance to avoid a complete shutdown of the assembly line if a component fails. The lifetime of one component is normally distributed with a mean of 321 h and a standard deviation of 23 h. How frequently should the component be replaced so that the probability of its failing during operation is less than 0.001?

21. Highway speeds The Trans-Canada highway stretches from St. John's to Victoria. On one section of the highway it has been found that motorists drive at speeds that are normally distributed with a mean of 110 km/h and a standard deviation of 16 km/h.
a) What percent of motorists are driving less than or at the posted speed limit of 100 km/h on this section?
b) Below what speed do 90% of the motorists drive?

22. Marks Students' marks on a test were normally distributed with a mean of 70 and a standard deviation of 8.
a) What percent of the students obtained a mark above 80?
b) What percent of the students obtained a C grade (60 to 70)?
c) Determine the mark under which 75% of the students' marks occur. (This is referred to as the 75th percentile.)

23. Manufacturing Ball bearings manufactured on Earth have a mean diameter of 2 mm with a standard deviation of 0.01 mm. Using the same manufacturing process in space, in the absence of gravity, the ball bearings have the same mean diameter but a standard deviation of 0.0001 mm. Ball bearings are rejected if their diameter is less than 1.98 mm or greater than 2.02 mm.
a) What percent are rejected in each environment?
b) Determine the upper and lower bound of the interval symmetrical about the mean and containing 99% of the ball bearings in each environment.

24. Baseball In the 1940's, major league baseball batting averages were normally distributed with a mean of 0.260 and a standard deviation of 0.07. Recently the batting average has been found to be the same, but the standard deviation is 0.05.
a) What percent of players would bat over 400 (an average of greater than 0.400) in each era?
b) Determine the batting average below which you would find 90% of the players in each era.
c) Explain why you think this change in the standard deviation has occurred, while the mean has remained constant.

25. Technology Using a graphing calculator and the formula for normal distribution, graph the pairs of distributions on the same axes. What do you observe? Explain.
a) $N(0, 1)$ and $N(5, 1)$ **b)** $N(0, 10)$ and $N(5, 10)$
c) $N(0, 1)$ and $N(0, 10)$

26. Random numbers Anna's computer can generate random numbers that are normally distributed with mean 17 and standard deviation 4. As each number is generated, Anna subtracts 17, divides by 4, and then shows the result to Ghita. How are the numbers that Ghita sees distributed? Explain.

9.4 The Normal Distribution Approximation of the Binomial Distribution

The binomial distribution arises in situations that have independent and identical repeated trials with success or failure outcomes. Consider taking a multiple-choice test consisting of 100 questions, each with four possible answers. If you guess the answer to every question, what is the probability of passing the test? To answer this using the binomial distribution, it is necessary to calculate $P(\text{passing}) = P(50 \text{ correct}) + P(51 \text{ correct}) + \ldots + P(100 \text{ correct})$. The computations involved could be quite difficult and tedious, especially without a calculator or a computer, but the answer can be approximated easily using a normal distribution.

Explore: Use the Binomial Distribution Formula

A quiz has 16 questions to which the answer is either true or false. Use the binomial distribution formula
$$P(x \text{ successes}) = {}_nC_x \, p^x q^{n-x}$$
where p is the probability of success, q is the probability of failure $(q = 1 - p)$, and n is the number of trials.
Let $n = 16$, $p = 0.5$, and $q = 0.5$ to find the probability of guessing each number of answers correctly.
Complete a table like the one started here. Then, draw a graph to show the results.

x successes	P(x successes)
0	${}_{16}C_0(0.5)^0(0.5)^{16} = 0.0000$
1	${}_{16}C_1(0.5)^1(0.5)^{15} = 0.0002$
⋮	

Inquire

1. In the binomial distribution formula, explain why the values $n = 16$, $p = 0.5$, and $q = 0.5$ were used.

2. Describe the shape of the graph of the probabilities. Do you think this is a normal distribution? Give reasons for your answer.

3. a) Use the graph to estimate the mean score that you would expect if the quiz results were binomially distributed. Estimate the expected standard deviation.
b) Find the product $n \times p$. How is this related to the mean score?
c) Calculate np and nq. Are both larger than 5?
d) For binomially distributed data, it can be shown that $\sigma = \sqrt{npq}$. Use this formula to find σ for the quiz situation and compare it with your estimate from part a).

4. If the pass mark on this quiz is 10, find the probability of obtaining a pass mark by guessing
a) using your graph   **b)** using your table of probabilities
c) using normal distribution with mean np and standard deviation $\sqrt{npq}$

5. Do all three methods give approximately the same answer?

If a binomial distribution has a probability of success of p, a probability of failure of q, and there are n trials, then the mean is $\mu = np$ and the standard deviation is $\sigma = \sqrt{npq}$.

Furthermore, when both $np \geq 5$ and $nq \geq 5$, the binomial distribution is usually well approximated by a normal distribution with the same mean and standard deviation.

Example 1   Using the Normal Distribution Approximation

A balloon manufacturer acknowledges that 3% of the balloons made are defective. In a shipment of 4000 balloons, what is the probability that fewer than 100 are defective?

Solution

Each balloon manufactured can be considered an independent trial, with success being a defective balloon. This is a binomial distribution problem with
$n = 4000$ (number of trials)
$p = 0.03$ (probability of a defect on each trial)
$q = 0.97$ (probability of no defect on each trial)
$x = 0, 1, 2, 3, …, 99$ (number of defective balloons)
To find $P(0, 1, 2, …, 99) = P(0) + P(1) + … + P(99)$ using the binomial distribution is a formidable task.
Check to see whether a normal approximation is reasonable.

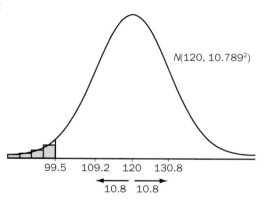

N(120, 10.789²)

$np = 4000 \times 0.03 \qquad nq = 4000 \times 0.97$
$\quad\; = 120 \qquad\qquad\quad\;\; = 3880$
Since both np and nq are greater than 5, approximate the binomial distribution using a normal distribution.

mean $= np \qquad$ standard deviation $= \sqrt{npq}$
$\quad\; = 120 \qquad\qquad\qquad\qquad = \sqrt{4000 \times 0.03 \times 0.97}$
$\qquad\qquad\qquad\qquad\qquad\qquad\;\; \doteq 10.789$

Sketch the distribution.

Find the z-score of 99.5.
$$z_{99.5} = \frac{99.5 - 120}{10.789}$$
$$\doteq -1.90$$

From the table on pages 416–417, the area to the left of $z_{99.5}$ is 0.0287.
Confirm this, using a graphing calculator.

```
normalcdf(-1E99,
99.5,120,10.789)
      .0287110197
■
```

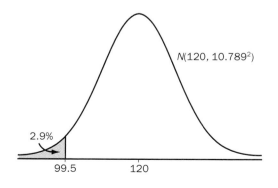

N(120, 10.789²)

2.9%

The probability that a shipment of 4000 balloons contains fewer than 100 defective balloons is approximately 2.9%.

Example 2   Applying the Normal Distribution Approximation to Polling

It is estimated that 15% of the Canadian population, given a choice of musical events, would choose a pop/rock concert. If a poll of 700 Canadians were conducted, what is the probability that more than 100 of them would choose a pop/rock concert?

Solution

Polling can be considered to be independent repeated trials, with a success being a pop/rock concert choice.
This is a binomial distribution problem with
$n = 700$ (number of trials)
$p = 0.15$ (probability of success on each trial)
$q = 0.85$ (probability of failure on each trial)
$x = 101, 102, \ldots, 700$ (number of successes)
Check to see whether a normal approximation is reasonable.

$np = 700 \times 0.15 \qquad nq = 700 \times 0.85$
$\quad = 105 \qquad\qquad\quad = 595$

Since $np \geq 5$ and $nq \geq 5$, a normal distribution model can be used.

mean $= np$ standard deviation $= \sqrt{npq}$
$\quad = 105 \qquad\qquad\qquad = \sqrt{700 \times 0.15 \times 0.85}$
$\qquad\qquad\qquad\qquad\qquad \doteq 9.447$

Sketch the distribution.
Find the z-score of 100.5.

$z_{100.5} = \dfrac{100.5 - 105}{9.447}$
$\qquad \doteq -0.48$

From the table on pages 416–417, the area to the left of $z_{100.5}$ is 0.3156. The probability of more than 100 people choosing a pop/rock concert is the area to the right of $z_{100.5}$, which is $1 - 0.3156$, or 0.6844.
Confirm this, using a graphing calculator.

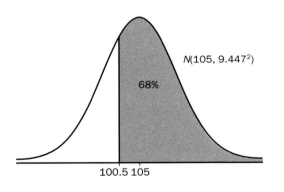

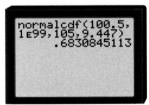

In a poll of 700 Canadians, the probability that more than 100 would choose a pop/rock concert is approximately 68%.

Practice

Decide whether each binomial distribution situation can be reasonably approximated by a normal distribution. For those that can, find the mean and the standard deviation of the normal distribution.

1. 10 trials, probability of success on each trial is 0.4
2. 1000 trials, probability of success on each trial is 0.05

3. 21 trials, probability of success on each trial is 0.21
4. 5 trials, probability of success on each trial is 0.5
5. 1000 trials, probability of success on each trial is 0.001
6. 500 trials, probability of success on each trial is 0.1
7. 25 trials, probability of success on each trial is 0.3

Applications and Problem Solving

8. Test answers A multiple-choice test consists of 50 questions, and each question has four answers from which to choose. If a student guesses every answer, what is the probability that the student
a) will get exactly 10 questions correct?
b) will get more than 10 questions correct?
c) will pass (get 25 or more correct)?

9. Border customs It is estimated that 10% of the vehicles crossing the border between Canada and the USA contain undeclared goods. If the customs officers search 400 vehicles at random, what is the probability that
a) more than 50 vehicles contain undeclared goods?
b) fewer than 25 vehicles contain undeclared goods?

10. Mining In a mining region, it is found that 15% of the ore is copper. In a sample of 50 plugs of ore, what is the probability that
a) exactly 10 of the plugs contain copper?
b) at least 10 of the plugs contain copper?
c) between 10 and 20, inclusive, of the plugs contain copper?

11. Computer simulation A computer is used to simulate the rolling of a die 10 000 times. What is the probability that in this simulation
a) more than 2000 ones will be rolled?
b) more than 3000 prime numbers will be rolled?

12. Oil wells Canada's oil industry produces 1.6 million barrels of oil per day. Suppose that during exploration 70% of the wells drilled are productive. What is the probability that
a) more than 80 of the next 100 wells drilled will be productive?
b) fewer than 65 of the next 100 wells drilled will be productive?

13. Seasickness The captain of a ferry estimates that 40% of the passengers will get seasick in rough weather. If, on a trip with 70 passengers, the ferry sails into rough weather, what is the probability that
a) more than half of the passengers get seasick?
b) fewer than 25 of the passengers get seasick?
c) exactly 30 of the passengers get seasick?

14. Pollution It is estimated that in some metropolitan areas 60% of the vehicles are operating below peak performance and hence are polluting excessively. If Transport Canada conducts a random survey of 50 vehicles, what is the probability that
a) exactly half of the vehicles are creating unnecessary pollution?
b) more than half of the vehicles are polluting too much?
c) fewer than 25 of the vehicles are operating below peak performance?

15. Technology Using a calculator, calculate the exact answer to Example 1 on page 425. Use the binomcdf function on the DISTR menu. How does this answer compare with the approximate answer in Example 1?

16. Since p and q play similar roles, why is the mean np and not nq? What does nq represent?

17. Statisticians do not usually use normal approximations to approximate binomial distributions if $np < 5$ or $nq < 5$.
a) Why do you think this is so?
b) Use some values of n, p, and q so that $np < 5$ or $nq < 5$. Calculate the binomial distribution and graph it. Does it appear normally distributed? Explain.
c) For each example from part b), calculate the expected mean (np) and the standard deviation ($\sqrt{npq}$). Draw the normal curve with the same mean and standard deviation, preferably on the same graph as the distribution. What can you conclude?

18. a) Find values of n, p, and q so that both np and nq are less than 5. Graph the corresponding binomial distribution. Does the graph appear normally distributed? Explain.
b) Can you find a binomial distribution where np and nq are both greater than 5 but the distribution does not appear to be normal?
c) Can you find a binomial distribution that appears to be normal but where np or nq is less than 5?

COMPUTER DATA BANK

Canadian Fitness Test Results

Use the *Fitness* database, from the Computer Data Bank, to complete the following.
Apply the standard deviation summary provided in the database software you are using, when applicable.

a) *Devise a plan to answer each question. Remember to exclude records for which the required data are not available.*
b) *Compare your plan with the plans of your classmates.*
c) *Revise your plan, if necessary, and then carry it out.*

1 Maximum Oxygen Intake

The most common method of expressing aerobic or cardiovascular fitness is maximum oxygen intake, or VO_2 max. It is a measure of the volume of oxygen consumed during strenuous exercise. Indirect measurement is possible because of the linear relation given by this regression equation,
VO_2 max $= 42.5 + 16.6x - 0.12m - 0.12f - 0.24a$,
where x is the average oxygen cost of the final aerobic stage in litres per minute, m is the mass of the participant in kilograms, f is the final aerobic heart rate of the participant in beats per minute, and a is the age of the participant in years. The greater the VO_2 max, the more aerobically fit the participant is.

Final Aerobic Stage	x for M	x for F
1	1.1391	0.9390
2	1.3466	1.0484
3	1.6250	1.3213
4	1.8255	1.4935
5	2.0066	1.6267
6	2.3453	1.7867
7	2.7657	—

For a final aerobic stage and gender of your choice, complete the following.
1. What is the VO_2 max, to 2 decimal places, for each participant?
2. What is the mean VO_2 max, to 2 decimal places?
3. What is the standard deviation, to 2 decimal places?
4. Compare your results with the results of classmates who used a different final aerobic stage and gender combination.
5. Why is it desirable to be aerobically fit?

2 Flexibility

Females are generally more flexible than males. The greater the trunk flexion, the more flexible the participant is.
1. What is the mean trunk flexion, to 2 decimal places, for each gender?
2. What is the standard deviation, to 2 decimal places, for each gender? Which gender has more dispersed data?
3. Determine the z-score, to 2 decimal places, for each participant for each gender. In a normal distribution, approximately 68.3% of the data occur within one standard deviation of the mean, and approximately 95.4% occur within two standard deviations of the mean. Which gender has a distribution that more closely resembles this feature of a normal distribution?
4. Why is it desirable to be flexible?

3 Body Mass Index

1. Review BMI by reading Exploration 2 on page 41 in Chapter 1, and determine the BMI of the participants, to 1 decimal place.
2. Predict whether a greater percent of participants aged 35 and older or a greater percent of participants aged less than 35 have BMIs in the healthy range. Then, check your prediction.
3. What is the mean BMI, to 1 decimal place?
4. How many standard deviations, to 1 decimal place, is a BMI of 18 from the mean? a BMI of 25?

4 Waist Girth to Hip Girth Ratio (WHR)

WHR is also an indicator of health risks. WHRs of 0.90 or greater for males and 0.80 or greater for females are associated with health risks.
1. What is the WHR, to 2 decimal places, for each participant?
2. Repeat questions 1 to 3 from Exploration 2 for WHR instead of trunk flexion.

9.5 Confidence Intervals

Literacy is the key to having an educated and successful society. According to statistics from UNESCO (United Nations Educational, Scientific and Cultural Organization), the world adult literacy rate is 75%. This rate represents the percent of persons aged 15 and over who can read and write a simple message in their own language. If you pick a group of 100 people at random, do you expect that 75 will be able to read and write? How much confidence can you place in that expectation?

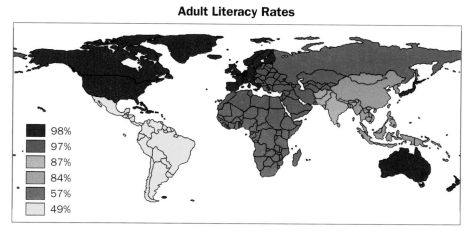

Adult Literacy Rates

■	98%
■	97%
■	87%
■	84%
■	57%
□	49%

Explore: Take a Poll

In a general survey, Statistics Canada asked people, "Have you read a book in the last week?" The results indicated that approximately 43.9% of those surveyed had read a book in the previous week.
a) How many people in a group of 30 chosen at random, would you expect to have read a book in the last week? Why?
b) Conduct a poll among people in your area. Ask 30 people at random in your school or town if they have read a book in the last week. Record the number of successes, that is, the positive responses. Express this as a percent.
c) Did the results agree with your expectations?

Inquire

1. Explain why this kind of polling is a binomial distribution question and why the normal approximation of the binomial distribution applies here.

2. If you were to repeat the poll many times, what would you expect the mean for the number of successes to be? the standard deviation to be?

3. What is the probability that the number of successes will fall within one standard deviation of the mean? Find a range of values, symmetric about the mean, within which the number of successes in the poll should fall approximately 95% of the time. This is called a **95% confidence interval**.

4. In what percent range will your poll results fall 95% of the time?

5. Calculate $\sqrt{\dfrac{pq}{n}}$. This is called the **standard error**. How many multiples of the standard error on either side of the expected percent p will give you the same result as question 4?

If your data is known to have a normal distribution with mean μ and standard deviation σ, then a $(1 - \alpha)\%$ **confidence interval** is an interval symmetric about the mean so that the probability of a data value falling in that interval is $(1 - \alpha)$.

$$P(\mu - a < x < \mu + a) = 1 - \alpha$$

The probability of falling outside that interval is just α.

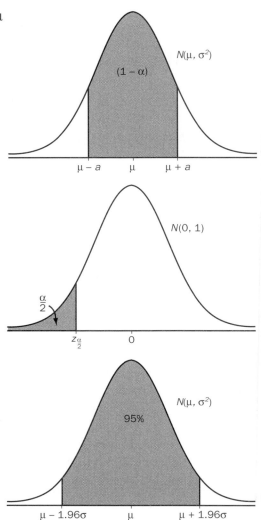

Let $z_{\frac{\alpha}{2}}$ be the z-score that has an area of $\dfrac{\alpha}{2}$ to the left of it under the standard normal curve $N(0, 1)$ as determined by the table on pages 416–417.

Then, the $(1 - \alpha)\%$ confidence interval is given by

$$\bar{x} + z_{\frac{\alpha}{2}}\sigma < x < \bar{x} - z_{\frac{\alpha}{2}}\sigma$$

For a 95% confidence interval, $\alpha = 0.05$. Thus, locating $\dfrac{\alpha}{2} = 0.025$ in the table on pages 416–417 gives $z_{\frac{\alpha}{2}} = -1.96$.

This means that the probability that a data value will fall within 1.96 standard deviations of the mean is 95%.

For a 99% confidence interval, $\alpha = 0.01$. Thus, from the table $z_{\frac{\alpha}{2}}$ is approximately -2.575. This means that the probability that a data value will fall within 2.575 standard deviations of the mean is 99%.

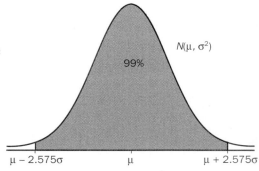

Example 1   Constructing a Confidence Interval

A non-stop Vancouver to Tokyo flight has a total of 237 people on board, counting all the passengers and the flight crew. A planner for the airline has ordered 300 individually wrapped hard candies to be distributed at takeoff to help deal with the change in air pressure.

a) If 3% of the wrappers are likely not to contain a candy, construct a 95% confidence interval for the number of candies in the order. Will there be enough for everyone on board?

b) If only 250 candies are sent on the flight, can you have 95% confidence that there will be enough for everyone on board?

Solution

a) This is a binomial distribution situation with $n = 300$, $p = 0.97$, and $q = 0.03$. Here a success is that a wrapper contains a candy.

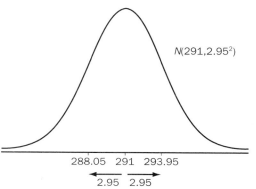

$$\text{mean} = np \qquad\qquad \text{standard deviation} = \sqrt{npq}$$
$$\begin{aligned} &= 300(0.97) &&= \sqrt{300(0.97)(0.03)} \\ &= 291 &&\doteq 2.95 \end{aligned}$$

So, the number of actual candies is approximately normally distributed with mean 291 and standard deviation 2.95.

For a 95% confidence interval, $z_{\frac{\alpha}{2}}$ is -1.96. The interval is $\bar{x} + z_{\frac{\alpha}{2}}\sigma < x < \bar{x} - z_{\frac{\alpha}{2}}\sigma$

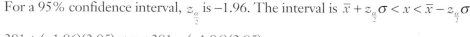

$$291 + (-1.96)(2.95) < x < 291 - (-1.96)(2.95)$$
$$285.218 < x < 296.782$$

The integral values of x covered by this interval are 286, 287, ..., 296.

With 95% confidence, there will be between 286 and 296 actual candies in the order. If each person on board gets one candy, there are more than enough candies for this flight.

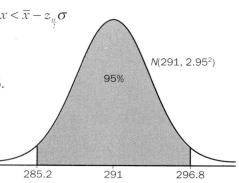

b) Now $n = 250$, while p and q are still 0.97 and 0.03, respectively.

$$\text{mean} = np \qquad\qquad \text{standard deviation} = \sqrt{npq}$$
$$\begin{aligned} &= 250(0.97) &&= \sqrt{250(0.97)(0.03)} \\ &= 242.5 &&\doteq 2.70 \end{aligned}$$

For a 95% confidence interval, the data must lie within 1.96 standard deviations of the mean, that is, within $(1.96)(2.70) \doteq 5.29$ of the mean 242.5. So, the 95% confidence interval is between $242.5 - 5.29 \doteq 237.2$ and $242.5 + 5.29 \doteq 247.8$.

The integral values of x covered by this interval are 238, 239, ..., 247.

With 95% confidence, the number of actual candies on the flight will be between 238 and 247. At the lower end of the interval there is still enough for one candy per person.

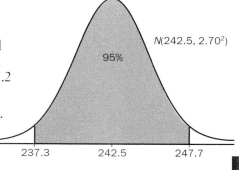

Statisticians have developed a formula for a measure of the **standard error** that can be expected in drawing conclusions about a sample based on a population.

$$\text{standard error} = \sqrt{\frac{pq}{n}}$$

where p is the probability of a successful outcome in the population, $q = 1 - p$ is the probability of a failure, and n is the size of the sample. The percent of successes in a sample is normally distributed with mean p and standard deviation $\sqrt{\frac{pq}{n}}$. That is why it is called the standard error.

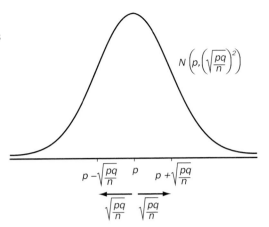

A $(1 - \alpha)\%$ confidence interval for x, the percent of successes in a sample, is given by

$$p + z_{\frac{\alpha}{2}}\sqrt{\frac{pq}{n}} < x < p - z_{\frac{\alpha}{2}}\sqrt{\frac{pq}{n}}$$

where $z_{\frac{\alpha}{2}}$ is the z-score that has area of $\frac{\alpha}{2}$ to the left of it under the standard normal curve $N(0, 1)$.

Thus, $(1 - \alpha)\%$ of the time the percent of successes in the sample is within $z_{\frac{\alpha}{2}}\sqrt{\frac{pq}{n}}$ of the expected percent p.

The value $\pm z_{\frac{\alpha}{2}}\sqrt{\frac{pq}{n}}$ is often called the **error range** or the **margin of error**.

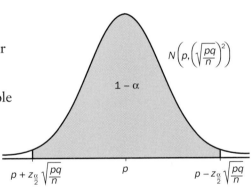

Example 2 Applying Confidence Intervals

The president of a large union knows that 55% of the membership is in favour of the new contract, but only 500 members will attend the meeting to vote on the contract.

a) Construct a 90% confidence interval for the percent of votes at the meeting in favour of the contract.

b) The president wants this contract to pass. Should he be worried? What is the probability that the contract will not be approved?

c) The president would like to have 99% confidence that the result of the vote will be 55% in favour, with a ±5% margin of error. How many members must attend for him to be this confident?

Solution

a) Here $n = 500$, $p = 0.55$, and $q = 1 - 0.55 = 0.45$.

expected percent of votes $= p$
$\qquad = 0.55$

standard error $= \sqrt{\dfrac{pq}{n}}$
$\qquad\qquad\quad = \sqrt{\dfrac{(0.55)(0.45)}{500}}$
$\qquad\qquad\quad \doteq 0.022$

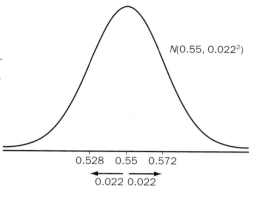

$N(0.55, 0.022^2)$

0.528　0.55　0.572

0.022　0.022

Sketch the distribution.

For a 90% confidence interval, $\alpha = 0.10$. So, the area under the normal curve $N(0, 1)$ to the left of $z_{\frac{\alpha}{2}}$ must be 0.05. This means that $z_{\frac{\alpha}{2}}$ is approximately -1.64, from the table on pages 416–417.

You can also find $z_{\frac{\alpha}{2}}$ using a graphing calculator.

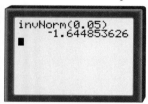

```
invNorm(0.05)
        -1.644853626
■
```

For a 90% confidence interval, the vote must fall within 1.64 standard errors of the expected percent 0.55. Since $1.64(0.022) \doteq 0.036$, the interval will be from $0.55 - 0.036$ or 0.514 to $0.55 + 0.036$, or 0.586. Thus, with 90% confidence the percent of votes cast for the contract will be between 51.4% and 58.6%.

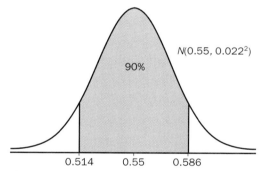

$N(0.55, 0.022^2)$

90%

0.514　0.55　0.586

b) There is a 10% probability that the percent of votes cast for the contract will be outside the range of 51.4% to 58.6%. There could be more than 58.6% or less than 51.4%.

Since the outcome of the votes is normally distributed with mean 0.55 and standard deviation 0.022, the z-score for a 50% vote is

$z_{50} = \dfrac{0.50 - 0.55}{0.022}$
$\qquad \doteq -2.27$

The probability of less than 50% in the vote is the area under the standard normal curve $N(0, 1)$ to the left of -2.27, which is 0.0116 from the table on pages 416–417.

In other words, there is about a 1.2% chance that the vote will not pass. This should be only a small worry to the president of the union.

c) A 99% confidence interval means that $z_{\frac{\alpha}{2}}$ is -2.575, as determined earlier in this section.

$$\text{standard error} = \sqrt{\frac{pq}{n}}$$
$$= \sqrt{\frac{(0.55)(0.45)}{n}}$$
$$\doteq \frac{0.497}{\sqrt{n}}$$

For an error range of $\pm 5\%$, $2.575\left(\dfrac{0.497}{\sqrt{n}}\right) = 0.05$.

Solve for n.

$$\sqrt{n} = \frac{(2.575)(0.497)}{0.05}$$
$$n = \left(\frac{(2.575)(0.497)}{0.05}\right)^2$$
$$\doteq 655.13$$

Thus, if $n = 655$, there would be 99% confidence that the vote will be in the range $55 \pm 5\%$, that is, between 50% and 60%. If 655 members show up at the meeting, the president could feel more secure that the new contract will be approved.

Practice

Calculate $z_{\frac{\alpha}{2}}$ for each confidence interval.

1. 95% **2.** 99%
3. 90% **4.** 99.5%

Calculate a 95% confidence interval for the number of successes in each binomial distribution situation, where n represents the number of trials and p, the probability of a success.

5. $n = 100$, $p = 0.6$ **6.** $n = 350$, $p = 0.2$
7. $n = 750$, $p = 0.25$ **8.** $n = 60$, $p = 0.61$

Calculate a 95% confidence interval for the percent of successes in each polling situation, where n represents the number of individuals polled and p, the expected percent of successes.

9. $n = 50$, $p = 0.7$ **10.** $n = 150$, $p = 0.2$
11. $n = 500$, $p = 0.25$ **12.** $n = 300$, $p = 0.61$

What sample size is needed to obtain an error range of 3% in each situation, given the confidence interval and the expected percent of successes, p?

13. 95% confidence interval, $p = 0.75$
14. 90% confidence interval, $p = 0.33$
15. 99% confidence interval, $p = 0.6$
16. 99.5% confidence interval, $p = 0.2$

Applications and Problem Solving

17. Car sales A successful salesperson estimates that she can sell a car to 15% of the potential customers who enter her dealership.
a) Estimate the number of sales that she would make in a month in which 250 potential customers enter the dealership.
b) Construct a 90% confidence interval for her monthly sales.

18. Reading Statistics Canada reported that 74.8% of females in Canada had read a book in the last 12 months. Amy decided to poll the 375 females in her school to see if they read more or less often than the national average.
a) Construct a 95% confidence interval for the number who had read a book in the last 12 months.
b) Amy found 304 readers in her poll. Does this fall in the 95% confidence interval? Would it fall in the 99% confidence interval?
c) What factors might explain why the poll result was so much higher than expected?

19. Drug testing A new drug was found to improve the recovery rate from a certain disease in 40% of patients who use it. A group of patients agreed to test the drug for Health Canada.
a) Construct a 95% confidence interval for the recovery rate of the new drug.
b) What must the group size be in order to reduce the standard error of the success rate to 2%? Using this group size, what is the 95% confidence interval?

20. Recycling A random survey of Canadian households found that 49.5% of them were actively recycling as much of the paper, glass, and metal waste as possible. Consider a small community of 400 homes.
a) Construct a 99% confidence interval for the percent of active recyclers in the community.
b) What level of confidence provides a confidence interval of 0.495 ± 0.024?

21. Debate It is known that 73% of voters in a city support the current mayor in a bid for re-election. An important pre-election debate will be judged by audience applause.
a) Construct a 95% confidence interval for the percent support the mayor can expect from the audience if there are 200 voters in attendance.
b) Construct a 95% confidence interval for the percent support the mayor can expect from the audience if there are 400 voters in attendance.
c) How large must the audience be before the margin of error is ±1%?

22. Election campaign A popular politician knows she is favoured by 73% of the voters in her riding. In the past, very few voters in her riding have actually bothered to vote. Rather than debate issues with the other candidates, she and her campaign workers have spent their time encouraging people to vote.
a) If only 3300 voters turn out, construct a 99% confidence interval for the share of the vote she will receive. Is she in any danger of losing?
b) If her support dropped to 63% from 73%, would she be in any danger of losing?
c) How low would her support have to drop before she should change her strategy and actually debate the issues?

23. Jury selection During jury selection, jurors are chosen from a pool of candidates. For a celebrity trial involving a famous pop singer, the judge wants to be certain there are no jurors who are fans. It is estimated that 67% of the population have heard this singer's music.
a) Construct a 99% confidence interval for the percent of jurors who will know the singer.
b) How many jurors should there be in the pool if the judge wants to have more than 99% confidence of having at least 20 non-fans in the jury pool?

24. Candies What quantity of wrapped candies should be sent on the plane in Example 1 to have more than 99% confidence that there will be enough for everyone?

25. Population According to Statistics Canada, 8.89% of Canada's population was between 35 and 39 years old in 1998.
a) In a random sample of 1000 people, how many would you expect to be in this age range?
b) What is the probability that between 80 and 100 people in the sample would be in the age range 35–39?
c) How much confidence could you put in the expectation that between 80 and 100 people would be in the age range 35–39?
d) Why are the answers to parts b) and c) the same? Explain.

INVESTIGATING MATH

Polling

Marketing companies
and political parties
employ opinion polls
to gage the popularity
of new products,
candidates, and
emerging policy. The
results of these surveys
pervade newscasts and
newspapers, especially
during provincial and
federal elections.

The Illusory Herald

48% FAVOUR CURRENT MP

In a recent survey, 48% of eligible voters in Canada indicated they would re-elect their current MP. These results are considered accurate, plus or minus 3%, 19 times out of twenty.

The statement in the newspaper clipping is interpreted
through confidence intervals: "19 times out of 20" means a 95% confidence
interval; "plus or minus 3%" is the range of the interval. So, the statement
indicates that the 95% confidence interval is from 45% to 51% for the
percent of eligible voters who would favour their current Member of
Parliament (MP) for re-election.

Section 9.5 presented methods for predicting the responses of a small
sample to a question based on the responses of a larger population.
Reversing this process to predict how the larger population will respond
based on the answers of only a small group is a more sophisticated problem.

Surprisingly accurate information about the opinions of all Canadians can
be forecast from the opinions of a few thousand people. Political parties
employ pollsters, who are experts in statistical methods, to predict the
election outcomes throughout each campaign. Despite the accuracy of polls,
there have been several notorious cases where election outcomes have varied
significantly from the polls. The only truly definitive poll is the one cast on
election day.

1 Interpreting Poll Results

1. a) Interpret the following headline using confidence intervals.
"In a recent survey, 15% of Canadians disliked the quantity of soft rock
played on radio stations. This result is considered accurate, plus or minus
2%, nineteen times out of twenty."
b) What does this poll suggest about the future of soft rock played on radio
stations?

2. a) Interpret the following headline using confidence intervals.
"5 out of every 14 Canadians think that the government should subsidize
professional sport teams in Canada. These results are considered accurate,
plus or minus 4%, nine out of ten times."
b) What does this poll suggest about the future of professional sport teams
in Canada?

2 Using Opinion Polls

1. As an MP, if 48% of eligible voters say they would vote for you, would you run for office again? If 52% of voters are likely to vote against you, will you lose in the election? Explain.

2. Politicians often spend the last few days of a campaign "getting out the vote." They encourage people to vote regardless of their opinion. Is this a good strategy? If polls indicate that a candidate is likely to win 60% of the vote, should the candidate stop campaigning?

3. If "getting out the vote" is a good strategy for a leading candidate, is it also a good strategy for the trailing candidate? Explain.

4. Find three statistics from your local news sources. Interpret each through confidence intervals and explain your results to your classmates.

5. One polling company, Gallup, has become a household name. Explore their website: www.gallup.com, and investigate their techniques for creating and executing a public opinion poll.

6. Investigate and explore the Statistics Canada website at www.statscan.ca. Choose two examples of surveys from this website. Explain to your classmates what is being surveyed and why it would be useful to survey this.

CONNECTING MATH AND SUCCESS

Probability and Chain of Events

The probability of obtaining a head or a tail, when tossing a fair coin, is 0.5. If the process of tossing the coin is repeated a second time, the probability of obtaining a head or a tail is still 0.5. These are independent trials because the outcome of the first trial does not affect the outcome of the second, and so on. However, in many real-life situations the result of a trial can be affected by the outcome of past trials.

A process in which the outcome of a trial is affected by the outcome of the immediately preceding trial is known as a **Markov chain,** after a Russian mathematician Andrey Andreyevich Markov (1856–1922).

1 Success in Sports

Suppose an athlete wins a race. That success might positively affect the outcome of the next race in which the athlete participates. On the other hand, not winning a race might have a different effect on the confidence of the athlete.

Kelly and Mimi meet every week to play a game of one-on-one basketball. The initial probability that either Kelly or Mimi will win is 0.5, but a pattern relating to confidence emerges over time. If Kelly wins one week, a boost in confidence increases her probability of winning the next week to 0.7. However, if she loses, her lack of confidence drops her probability of winning the next week to 0.4.

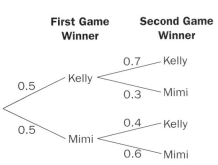

Notice in the probability tree that the second set of branches show conditional probabilities based on the outcome of the first game.

What is the probability, for each person, of winning the second game? There are two branches that lead to Kelly's winning the second game and two that lead to Mimi's winning the second game.

P(Kelly wins 2nd game) = P(Kelly wins 1st) $\times$ P(Kelly wins 2nd | Kelly wins 1st)
$\qquad\qquad$ + P(Mimi wins 1st) $\times$ P(Kelly wins 2nd | Mimi wins 1st)
$\qquad$ = 0.5(0.7) + 0.5(0.4)
$\qquad$ = 0.55

P(Mimi wins 2nd game) = P(Kelly wins 1st) $\times$ P(Mimi wins 2nd | Kelly wins 1st)
$\qquad\qquad$ + P(Mimi wins 1st) $\times$ P(Mimi wins 2nd | Mimi wins 1st)
$\qquad$ = 0.5(0.3) + 0.5(0.6)
$\qquad$ = 0.45

So, the probability that Kelly will win the second game is 0.55, and the probability that Mimi will win the second game is 0.45.

1. a) For the example given, draw the probability tree, including branches for a third and fourth game.
b) What is the probability that Kelly will win the third game?
c) What is the probability that Mimi will win the fourth game?

2. Mohammed is the goalkeeper for his school's soccer team. Every time he prevents a goal, his confidence increases, so that there is a 70% chance that he will save the next shot on goal. However, if the other team scores a goal on him, he becomes nervous, so there is only a 40% chance that he saves the next shot on goal. Initially, going into any game, Mohammed has a 65% chance of preventing a goal.
a) Draw the probability tree for a soccer game showing the first three attempts on goal.
b) What is the probability that Mohammed saves all three attempts?
c) What is the probability that the opposing team scores one goal in the first three attempts?

2 Success in Marketing

People are bombarded with advertising every day. The marketing intent, in most cases, is to entice consumers to buy the particular product, shop at the advertised store, or choose the promoted services. All age groups are susceptible to such marketing strategies. For example, a child who sees a memorable cereal commercial on TV is more likely to ask for that item when seeing it in the store.

1. There are two brands of an over-the-counter cold remedy available at a local pharmacy. If a consumer buys Brand A, there is a 50% chance the consumer will buy Brand A the next time. If a consumer buys Brand B, there is a 60% chance the consumer will buy Brand B the next time. The Brand A Company is trying a new marketing strategy. They have changed the design of their packaging to make it more eye-catching. The company predicts that initially there is a 75% chance a person will buy their product.
a) Find the probability that a consumer will buy Brand A the second time; Brand B the second time.
b) Prior to the packaging change, there was only a 40% chance that a consumer would buy Brand A. What was the probability that a consumer will buy Brand A the second time?

2. In a community there are two courier services, Roadrunner and Reliable. If a person tries Roadrunner, there is a 60% chance the person will use their services the next time. If a person tries Reliable, there is a 70% chance the person will use their services the next time. Because a Roadrunner advertising campaign is aired on a local radio station, initially there is an 80% chance that a person will try Roadrunner's services.
a) What is the probability of a person using Roadrunner's services the second time?
b) What is the probability that a person will use Reliable's services the third time?
c) Prior to the airing of radio advertisement, there was a 50% chance that a person would try either service. What affect did the advertising campaign have on the probability that a person would use Roadrunner's services the second time? the third time?

Review

9.1 *Using the binomial distribution, where n represents the number of trials, p represents the probability of success, and q represents the probability of failure, find the indicated probability.*

1. $n = 8$, $p = 0.3$, find $P(3\ successes)$
2. $n = 11$, $p = 0.1$, find $P(1\ success)$
3. $n = 5$, $p = 0.5$, find $P(at\ least\ 1\ success)$
4. $n = 15$, $p = 0.8$, find $P(13\ or\ more\ successes)$

5. Driver education A driver education instructor estimates that 80% of beginning students are unable to engage the clutch of a training automobile satisfactorily on the first attempt. What is the probability that, of the eight students taking training per day,
a) exactly six will not engage the clutch satisfactorily on the first try?
b) none of them will engage the clutch satisfactorily?
c) at least one of them will engage the clutch properly on the first try?

6. Seeds Fifteen hills of green beans are planted. Both the seed producer and the local seed store guarantee an 80% fertility rate based on years of past experience with the particular brand of seed. What is the probability that
a) more than 12 hills come up?
b) fewer than 10 hills are fertile?
c) exactly 11 hills are fertile?

9.2 **7.** Calculate the mean and the standard deviation for each set of data. How is set A related to set B?
a) set A: 8, 12, 15, 17, 18
set B: 12, 13, 14, 15, 16
b) set A: 21, 23, 25, 29, 32
set B: 45, 47, 49, 53, 56

8. Milk cartons A carton of milk contains a mean volume of 1 L, with a standard deviation of 10 mL.
a) A sample of cartons was found to contain volumes of 998 mL, 1007 mL, 995 mL, 1015 mL, and 1012 mL. Determine the z-score of each carton in the sample.
b) Two cartons had z-scores of 2.1 and −1.5. How many millilitres of milk did each contain?

9. Given the data set: 22, 33, 44, 55, 66.
a) Determine the mean and the standard deviation of the data set.
b) Determine the z-score of each entry in the data set.
c) Determine the mean and the standard deviation of the five z-scores. Comment on your results.

9.3 **10. IQ** The intelligence quotients (IQs) of the students in a high school are normally distributed with mean 105 and standard deviation 12. What percent of the IQs
a) are less than 100?
b) are greater than 110?
c) are in the interval from 100 to 120?
d) What IQ is the 95th percentile? (That is, 95% of the IQs are less than this value.)

11. Manufacturing The quality of CDs is measured by the amount of "noise" on the disk. A process for manufacturing CDs has the noise measured by an index number that is normally distributed with a mean of 3 and a standard deviation of 0.2. Quality control insists that the acceptable allowance be within the range 2.6 to 3.4.
a) What percent of the CDs produced are within the acceptable range?
b) In what range, symmetric about the mean, would you find 99% of the CDs?

12. Unemployment rate In a certain region of Canada, the unemployment rate is normally distributed with a mean of 12% and a standard deviation of 2%. Economists classify an area as being in recession when the unemployment rate reaches 15%. If an interval of time is chosen at random,
a) what is the probability that this region is in recession?
b) what is the probability that this region is below the national unemployment rate of 9%?

9.4 **13.** Check that a normal distribution approximation is reasonable for the following binomial distribution situations. Then, determine the indicated probability.
a) $n = 50$, $p = 0.4$, find $P(more\ than\ 20\ successes)$
b) $n = 75$, $p = 0.1$, find $P(less\ than\ 10\ successes)$
c) $n = 1000$, $p = 0.03$, find $P(between\ 25\ and\ 30,\ inclusive,\ successes)$

14. Education In Canada, 75% of secondary school students go on to some form of higher education—the highest proportion in the world. What is the probability that, in a random poll of 50 secondary school students,
a) more than 40 intend to take some form of higher education?
b) fewer than 30 intend to take higher education?
c) over 80% will take some form of higher education?

15. Immigration Toronto is the destination of 50% of the immigrants to Canada. What is the probability that, in a random survey of 100 new immigrants,
a) at least 60 settled in Toronto?
b) fewer than 45 settled in Toronto?
c) between 40 and 60, inclusive, settled in Toronto?

16. Government spending An opinion poll concludes that 73% of Canadians favour greater government spending on conservation and the environment. The poll was based on a sample of 120 interviews.
a) Construct a 95% confidence interval for this attitude.
b) What must the sample size be in order to reduce the standard error to 2%? Using this sample size, what is the 95% confidence interval?

17. Anemia In an examination of 400 patients at a screening clinic, 64 were found to exhibit symptoms of anemia.
a) Calculate the standard error of the percent of patients with anemia.
b) Construct a 99% confidence interval for the true percent.

18. Medicine A medical research team feels confident that a serum they have developed will cure about 75% of the patients suffering from a disease.
a) Construct a 95% confidence interval for the percent of cured patients the team can expect from a study group of 200 patients suffering from the disease; 400 patients suffering from the disease.
b) How large must the sample group be before the margin of error is ±1%?

Exploring Math

The Waiting Period

The **geometric distribution** is a probability model that allows the determination of how long it will take until a success occurs in repeated independent and identical trials. The number of trials prior to the first success is called the **waiting period.**

If p is the probability of success and q is the probability of failure ($q = 1 - p$), then the probability of x waiting period is given by $P(x) = q^x p$.

Consider the experiment of rolling a pair of dice. What is the probability that the first occurrence of doubles will happen on the third roll? If the first occurrence of doubles is to happen on the third roll, then $x = 2$. The probability of success is $p = \dfrac{6}{36}$ or $\dfrac{1}{6}$, and the probability of failure is $q = 1 - \dfrac{1}{6}$ or $\dfrac{5}{6}$.

$$P(2) = \left(\frac{5}{6}\right)^2\left(\frac{1}{6}\right)$$
$$\doteq 0.1157$$

The probability that the first occurrence of doubles will happen on the third roll is approximately 11.6%.

1. In the repeated rolling of a die, what is the probability of rolling
a) a two for the first time on the third roll?
b) a three or a four for the first time on the fourth roll?

2. In the repeated rolling of a pair of dice, what is the probability of rolling
a) a sum of eight in three rolls?
b) a sum of eight in fewer than three rolls?
c) Explain how the answers to parts a) and b) relate to the sum of a geometric series.

3. a) In the repeated cutting of a regular deck of 52 cards, what is the probability of cutting an ace in at most five cuts? a face card in at most five cuts? an ace or a face card in at most five cuts?
b) Explain why the probability of an ace or a face card in exactly five cuts is less than the probability of a face card in exactly five cuts.

Chapter Check

1. If data are binomially distributed, with the number of trials $n = 20$ and the probability of success $p = 0.4$, determine the value of the following probabilities.
a) $P(0 \text{ successes})$
b) $P(\text{at least 1 success})$
c) $P(8 \text{ or } 9 \text{ successes})$

2. Strawberry crop Blight has struck 10% of a strawberry crop. If you pick 12 strawberries at random, what is the probability that
a) none of them have the blight?
b) only one of them has the blight?

3. Given the data set: 96, 99, 100, 102, 103. Find
a) the mean and standard deviation
b) the z-score of 103

4. Height requirements A child's amusement park slide requires a minimum height of 102 cm, a maximum height of 120 cm, and the child's age to be at least three years.
a) If the mean height of the children going down the slide is 111 cm, with standard deviation 4 cm, what is the z-score range for the allowable heights?
b) One child's height has a z-score of -1.5. How tall is the child?

5. Mass The masses of seventeen-year-old males in a school are normally distributed with a mean of 70 kg and a standard deviation of 6 kg.
a) If you randomly choose one of these students, what is the probability that he has a mass of more than 80 kg? less than 55 kg? between 70 kg and 75 kg?
b) Below what mass are 90% of these male students?
c) Find the range of measurements that is symmetrical about the mean and contains 50% of these students.

6. Fishing The tonnage of fish caught annually in Canada is normally distributed with a mean of 1 339 505 t and a standard deviation of 201 245 t. It is considered a banner year when the tonnage exceeds 1 600 000 t. How many banner years can be expected in the next two decades?

Determine whether each binomial distribution situation can be reasonably approximated by a normal distribution. If so, find the mean and the standard deviation of the normal distribution approximation.
7. 20 trials, probability of success on each trial is 0.65
8. 75 trials, probability of success on each trial is 0.07
9. 100 trials, probability of success on each trial is 0.04

10. Manufacturing A production process has been shown to have an accuracy rating of 99.9%, that is, the product is made within allowable limits 99.9% of the time. If 2000 of the products are made each day, what is the probability that
a) no defective products are made in one day?
b) at least one defective product is made in a day?
c) at least two defective products are made in a day?

11. Honey A company that produces flavoured honeys ran a local taste test for two possible new flavours. The company found that 45 of 75 people preferred mesquite to red chili. To confirm the preferred flavour, a larger taste test involving 1000 people was arranged.
a) Estimate the number of people that are expected to choose mesquite over red chili.
b) Construct a 90% confidence interval for the population proportion favouring mesquite-flavoured honey.

12. Cookies A group of students decides to investigate what percent of cookie packages contain broken cookies. In a sample of 40 packages, it was found that 2 of the packages contained broken cookies.
a) Construct a 95% confidence interval for the true portion of packages containing broken cookies.
b) Construct a 75% confidence interval.
c) What sample size would reduce the standard error to 2%?
d) If you buy five packages, what is the probability that none of them contain broken cookies?

Using the Strategies

1. Measurement A regular hexagon and an equilateral triangle have equal perimeters. If the area of the triangle is 2 m^2, what is the area of the hexagon?

2. If $\dfrac{A}{x+2} + \dfrac{B}{x-3} = \dfrac{x-18}{x^2-x-6}$, determine the values of A and B.

3. Measurement Each of the squares PQRS and TUVW has sides of length 10 cm. T is placed at the intersection of the diagonals of PQRS, and PX is 4 cm. What is the area of quadrilateral TKSX?

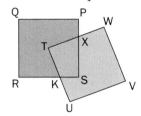

4. Series The sum of the first n terms of a series is given by $S_n = 2n + 3n^2$. What is the nth term of this series, in terms of n?

5. The expression $2^2 - 2 + \dfrac{22}{2}$ uses six 2s to give a value of 13. Using eight 8s, write an expression that has a value of 1000.

6. Draw three intersecting circles as shown. Place each of the numbers 1 through 7, one in each part of the diagram, so that the sums of the four numbers in each circle are the same. The number 3 has been placed for you.

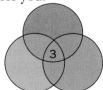

7. Language What is the only word in the English language that contains the letter sequence GNT?

8. The sum of the digits in a three-digit number is 7. The tens digit is twice the units digit, and the units digit is twice the hundreds digit. What is the number?

9. The point P is anywhere inside the rectangle ABCD. Show that $a^2 + c^2 = b^2 + d^2$.

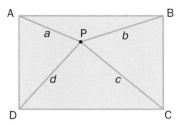

10. Tennis Three men, Ken, Leo, and Matt, and their wives, Alice, Cora, and Freya, were playing tennis. In a doubles match, Ken partnered Leo's wife and Cora's husband partnered Alice. Matt sat out with his sister. Who is married to whom?

11. Cryptogram Each letter represents a different digit. Solve the cryptogram.

$$\begin{array}{r} S\,L\,E\,D \\ +\,S\,N\,O\,W \\ \hline R\,I\,D\,E \end{array}$$

12. Twenty-dollar bills About how many twenty-dollar bills would it take to tile the floor of the gymnasium in your school?

13. Measurement The square formed by joining the centres of the circles has side length 4. Find the area of the shaded region.

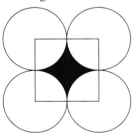

14. What is the next letter in the sequence F, S, T, F, F, S, S, …?

15. The product of a distinct set of positive integers is 48. What is the least possible sum of these integers?

1. Dessert choices A buffet-style restaurant offers five types of pie, three types of ice cream, two types of cookies, and three types of cake in its dessert bar.
a) Draw a tree diagram to list all possibilities for a plate containing one of each type of dessert.
b) Determine how many different plates are possible, choosing one item from each dessert type.

2. Parking cars a) Determine the number of different ways that eight cars of the same make and model, but of different colours, can be parked in a row.
b) If three of the cars are blue, two of the cars are red, and three of the cars are black, then in how many different ways can the cars be parked in a row?
c) A car dealership sells eight different models of cars and three are needed for display in the showroom. How many different arrangements of cars are possible?

3. a) What is the essential difference between a permutation and a combination?
b) Write one situation for a permutation and one for a combination.

4. Committee selection A club has 24 members with 14 females and 10 males.
a) In how many ways can a four-person committee be selected from the club members?
b) Sharon and Jennifer are two of the club members. In how many ways can a four-person committee be selected if Sharon and Jennifer must be on the committee?
c) How many four-person committees do not include both Sharon and Jennifer?

5. Pathways Determine the number of pathways from A to B, proceeding always in a northerly or easterly direction.

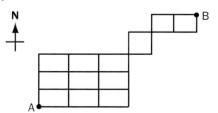

6. Motel sign Seven different letters are in the name on a motel sign.
a) How many combinations of seven different letters are possible?
b) How does the answer to part part a) relate to Pascal's triangle?

Expand each binomial, making use of Pascal's triangle.
7. $(4 - x)^4$
8. $(2x + 7)^5$

Use the Binomial Theorem to expand each of the following.
9. $(x + 2)^4$
10. $(3x - 1)^6$

Write the general term for each expansion and the term indicated.
11. the third term in $(x + 5)^7$
12. the fourth term in $(2x - 3)^6$

Use a probability tree to determine the sample space of the experiments and the probability of the required event in questions 13 and 14.
13. Randomly select a textbook (literature, physics, or chemistry) and a colour (red, green, blue, or yellow.) What is the probability of choosing the physics textbook and blue?
14. Randomly select a meal (breakfast, lunch, or dinner) and a national park (Jasper, Banff, Yoho, or Wood Buffalo). What is the probability of choosing lunch and Yoho National Park?

15. Eye colour and gender The enrolment at a certain high school is 60% male. At the same school, 70% of the students have brown eyes. Assume that there is no relationship between gender and eye colour.
a) Find the probability that a student chosen at random from this high school is a female with brown eyes.
b) Find the probability that a student chosen at random from this high school is a male with an eye colour other than brown.
c) In a group of three randomly selected students from this high school, what is the probability that at least two of them are males?

Classify the events in questions 16 and 17 as either independent or dependent.

16. The experiment is playing soccer and shoe size. The first event is that the person plays soccer and the second event is that the person wears size 11 shoes.

17. The experiment is dealing three cards from a deck. The first event is that the first card dealt is a diamond, the second event is that the second card is a diamond, and the third event is that the third card is a diamond.

Classify the events in questions 18 and 19 as either mutually exclusive or not mutually exclusive.

18. The experiment is choosing a number between 1 and 100. The first event is that the number is even and the second event is that the number is odd.

19. The experiment is cutting a deck of cards. The first event is that the card is not a face card and the second event is that the card is greater than five.

20. **Track meet** Six high school track athletes of equal ability are in an 800-m race. What is the probability that
a) the athletes finish in the same order as their starting lane numbers?
b) the athlete in lane three finishes in the top three?

21. **CDs** A CD collection consists of eight rock CDs, four alternative CDs, and five pop/r&b CDs. If three CDs are chosen at random, find the probability that
a) all three are rock
b) one is alternative
c) none are pop/r&b

22. **Rolling dice** Two dice are thrown. What is the probability that
a) both are 3s?
b) both are 3s, given that at least one die rolled is a 3?
c) a sum greater than seven occurs, given that one die rolled is a 3?

Using the binomial distribution, where n represents the number of trials, p represents the probability of success, and q the probability of failure, find the indicated

probability.
23. $n = 10$, $p = 0.5$, find P(1 success)
24. $n = 15$, $p = 0.4$, find P(2 successes)
25. $n = 20$, $p = 0.5$, find P(15 successes)

26. Given the data set: 34, 35, 36, 39, 42. Find the following quantities.
a) the mean and standard deviation
b) the z-score of the datum 39

27. **Manufacturing** The length of the bolts in a manufacturing process are normally distributed with a mean of 55 mm and a standard deviation of 2 mm.
a) What percent of these bolts will be between 52 mm and 58 mm?
b) What is the probability that a bolt, selected at random, will be longer than 57 mm?

Given the following binomial distribution situations, find the mean and the standard deviation for those that can be approximated by a normal distribution.
28. 100 trials, probability of success on each trial is 0.4
29. 15 trials, probability of success on each trial is 0.35

30. **Poll** State whether a normal distribution approximation is reasonable for the following binomial distribution situation. Then, determine the indicated probability.
It is estimated that 71% of the Canadian population age 20–44 are non-smokers. If a poll of 500 Canadians in this age group is conducted, what is the probability that more than 350 of them are non-smokers?

31. **School election** Glenda is one of two candidates running for senior class president at her high school. She believes that 60% of the ballots cast will be in her favour; however, typically only 175 seniors actually vote.
a) Construct a 90% confidence interval for the percent of ballots to be cast in Glenda's favour.
b) What is the probability of her losing?
c) Glenda would like to have 95% confidence that the result of the vote will be 60% in her favour with a ±5% margin of error. How many seniors must vote for her to be this confident?

Use transformations to sketch the graphs of the following pairs of functions.

1. $y = x$
   $y = x - 2$

2. $y = |x|$
   $y = |x + 3|$

3. $y = \sqrt{x}$
   $y = \sqrt{x + 1}$

4. $y = x^2$
   $y = (x - 5)^2 - 6$

5. a) Given $f(x) = x^3 - 4$, write the equations for $-f(x), f(-x),$ and $f^{-1}(x)$.
b) Sketch the four graphs on the same set of axes.
c) Determine any points that are invariant for each reflection.

For each set of three functions
a) *sketch them on the same grid or graph them in the same viewing window of a graphing calculator*
b) *describe how the graphs of the second and third functions are related to the graph of the first function*

6. $y = x^2, y = \dfrac{1}{2}x^2,$ and $y = \dfrac{1}{2}(x - 1)^2 - 3$

7. $y = |x|, y = -\dfrac{1}{4}|x|,$ and $y = -\dfrac{1}{4}|x + 3| + 5$

8. $y = x^3, y = (2x)^3,$ and $y = -(2x)^3 + 1$

9. $y = \sqrt{x}, y = \sqrt{3x},$ and $y = 2\sqrt{3(x - 1)} - 1$

Sketch the graphs of $y = f(x)$ and $y = \dfrac{1}{f(x)}$ on the same set of axes.

10. $f(x) = 4x - 3$

11. $f(x) = x(x - 3)$

Sketch the graphs of $y = f(x)$ and $y = |f(x)|$ on the same set of axes.

12. $f(x) = -x + 7$

13. $f(x) = x^2 - 25$

14. Bacteria growth A certain culture of bacteria doubles every 15 h. The initial count of a sample shows 5000 bacteria present.
a) Write an exponential function that models the given conditions.
b) How many bacteria will there be in five days?
c) Approximately how many bacteria were there two days prior to the initial count?

15. Radioactive decay A radioactive substance decays according to the equation $A(t) = A_0 \left(\dfrac{1}{2}\right)^{\frac{t}{25}}$, where t is the time in days and A_0 is the original amount of the substance.
a) What is the half-life of this substance?
b) Approximately what percent of the original amount will be left after five days?
c) How long will it take until there is only 25% of the original amount left?

Use the laws of logarithms to express each as a single logarithm. Then, evaluate.

16. $\log_{10} 12.5 + \log_{10} 8$

17. $2 \log_4 36 - 2 \log_4 9$

18. $\log_2 32^4$

19. $\log_6 \sqrt[3]{216}$

20. $\dfrac{1}{2}\log_5 102 - \log_5 \sqrt{17} + \log_5 \dfrac{125}{\sqrt{6}}$

21. Find the value of x, to the nearest hundredth.
a) $6^x = 100$
b) $7^{4x - 5} = 95$
c) $3^{8x + 1} = 84^{2x + 3}$

22. Solve for x.
a) $\log_3 27 = x$
b) $\log_x 125 = 3$
c) $\log_2(x^2 - 5x + 10) = 4$
d) $\left(\log_5 x^2\right)^2 = \log_5 x^4$
e) $\log(2x - 7) - \log(x + 4) = \log 3x$

23. Investing Greta invests $5000 in savings certificates that are paying interest at 5.25%/a compounded semi-annually. After what time period will this investment amount to more than $6000?

24. Write the equation of each circle in standard form and general form.
a) centre $(2, 7)$, radius $\sqrt{6}$
b) centre $(5, 3)$, passing through $(8, 8)$

25. Determine whether the point P$(4, 6)$ lies inside, outside, or on the circle given by $x^2 + y^2 - 2x + 4y - 20 = 0$.

26. Find the centre and radius of each circle.
a) $x^2 - 12x + y^2 + 6y - 5 = 0$
b) $x^2 + 4x + y^2 - 10y + 22 = 0$

27. Write the equation of each ellipse in standard form and general form.
a) centre $(2, 5)$, passing through $(-4, 5)$, $(8, 5)$, $(2, 3)$, and $(2, 7)$
b) centre $(-3, -8)$, passing through $(-6, -8)$, $(0, -8)$, $(-3, -15)$, and $(-3, -1)$

28. Find the coordinates of the centre, the lengths of the major and minor axes, and the coordinates of the foci of each ellipse.

a) $\dfrac{(x-4)^2}{9}+\dfrac{(y+7)^2}{16}=1$

b) $7x^2+10y^2+70x-120y+465=0$

29. Find the coordinates of the centre, the coordinates of the vertices, and the equations of the asymptotes. Then, sketch the graph of each hyperbola.

a) $\dfrac{(x+2)^2}{4}-\dfrac{(y-3)^2}{16}=1$

b) $-49x^2+9y^2+294x-162y-153=0$

30. For each equation of a parabola, state the equation of the axis of symmetry, the coordinates of the focus, the equation of the directrix, and the direction of opening.

a) $(x-h)^2=4p(y-k)$ **b)** $(y-k)^2=4p(x-h)$

31. Describe how to find the equivalent measure in degrees for an angle measure given in radians.

32. Find one positive and one negative coterminal angle for each given angle.

a) $\dfrac{5\pi}{6}$ **b)** $-50°$ **c)** $\dfrac{12\pi}{7}$

33. Find the exact values of the three primary trigonometric ratios for θ, if the terminal arm of $\angle\theta$ in standard position contains the given point.
a) P$(-4, 4)$ **b)** P$(5, -2)$ **c)** P$(-3, -7)$

34. Determine the amplitude and the period, in radians, of each function. Then, sketch the graph.

a) $y=4\sin\dfrac{2\theta}{3}$ **b)** $y=0.3\cos\dfrac{5\theta}{7}$

c) $y=2.5\cos 6\theta$ **d)** $y=-5\sin 2\theta$

35. Determine the vertical displacement and the horizontal phase shift of each function with respect to $y=\sin x$. Sketch the graph of each function.

a) $y=\sin(x-30°)+4$ **b)** $y=\sin\left(x+\dfrac{5\pi}{12}\right)-3$

36. Determine the vertical displacement and the horizontal phase shift of each function with respect to $y=\cos x$. Sketch the graph of each function.

a) $y=\cos(x+50°)-2$ **b)** $y=\cos\left(x-\dfrac{3\pi}{4}\right)+1$

37. Modelling temperature The table shows the average monthly temperature, in degrees Celsius, for Saskatoon.

Month	1	2	3	4	5	6
Temperature	-18	-14	-7	4	12	16
Month	7	8	9	10	11	12
Temperature	19	17	11	5	-6	-15

a) Graph the data.
b) Determine the amplitude, period, phase shift, and vertical displacement with respect to $y=\cos x$.
c) Model the data using an equation of the form $t=A\cos B(m+C)+D$, where t represents the temperature and m the month.
d) Use the model to predict the average monthly temperature for April. How does this value compare with the actual value?

Sketch the graph of each function, for $-\pi\le x\le\pi$. Then, determine the amplitude, period, phase shift, domain, and range.

38. $y=\tan\left(x+\dfrac{\pi}{3}\right)$ **39.** $y=2\csc 3x$

40. Determine the exact solutions for $0\le x\le 2\pi$. Then, give the general solution(s).
a) $3\tan^2 2x-1=0$

b) $\left(\cos x+\dfrac{1}{2}\right)(\tan x-\sqrt{3})=0$

41. Technology The screen shows the graphs of $y=2\tan 0.4x$ and $y=x+3\sin x$ using a window $[-4, 4, 1]$ by $[-5, 5, 1]$.
a) From the graph, how many solutions are expected for the equation $x+3\sin x=2\tan 0.4x$?
b) Do you think these are the only solutions to the equation $x+3\sin x=2\tan 0.4x$? Explain.
c) Graph the function $y=x+3\sin x-2\tan 0.4x$, and determine the zeros for $-4\le x\le 4$, to two decimal places.

For each identity,
a) *show that it is true for x = 45°, using exact values*
b) *prove the result algebraically*
c) *state any restrictions*

42. $\csc^2 x(1 - \cos^2 x) = 1$

43. $\cot x + 3\sec x = \dfrac{\cos^2 x + 3\sin x}{\sin x \cos x}$

44. $\csc x - \cot x = \dfrac{\sin x}{1 + \cos x}$

45. $\dfrac{\tan x \cos^2 x - \cos x}{\cos^3 x} = \sec^2 x(\sin x - 1)$

Express as a single trigonometric function. Then, find the exact value.

46. $\cos^2 \dfrac{\pi}{12} - \sin^2 \dfrac{\pi}{12}$ **47.** $2\sin \dfrac{\pi}{8} \cos \dfrac{\pi}{8}$

48. $\sin 175° \cos 130° - \cos 175° \sin 130°$

49. $\dfrac{\tan 140° - \tan 80°}{1 + \tan 140° \tan 80°}$

50. $\cos \dfrac{\pi}{5} \cos \dfrac{13\pi}{10} - \sin \dfrac{\pi}{5} \sin \dfrac{13\pi}{10}$

Write an explicit formula for t_n in each sequence. Then, determine each indicated term.

51. $-5, 2, 9, \dots$ Find t_{15}.   **52.** $18, 6, 2, \dots$ Find t_8.

53. $7, 21, 63, \dots$ Find t_{10}.

54. $\dfrac{9}{10}, \dfrac{2}{5}, -\dfrac{1}{10}, \dots$ Find t_{20}.

55. Write each series in expanded form. Then, find the sum of the series.

a) $\displaystyle\sum_{k=1}^{5}(3k - 4)$ **b)** $\displaystyle\sum_{k=5}^{12}(5k + 6)$

c) $\displaystyle\sum_{k=4}^{11}3(2)^{k-1}$ **d)** $\displaystyle\sum_{k=1}^{8}10\left(\dfrac{1}{5}\right)^{k-1}$

56. Savings plan An investment company offers a savings plan to their employees. An employee must make an initial contribution of at least $1000. The company pays interest at 8%/a compounded quarterly. After the employee has been with the company for five years, the company contributes $1000 to the employee's savings plan. What is the value of an employee's savings plan at the beginning of the sixth year, if the initial deposit was $1500?

57. Rolling ball A ball rolls down an incline and gains speed. The ball travels a distance of 3 cm in the first second, 6 cm in the next second, 9 cm in the third second, and so on. Find the distance that the ball travels in 15 s.

58. Find the indicated sum of each geometric series.
a) $1 - 3 + 9 - 27 + \dots$ Find S_6.
b) $512 + 256 + 128 + 64 + \dots$ Find S_5.

59. Mining Canada's copper production declined from 688 400 t in 1996 to 657 400 t in the next year.
a) If this trend continued, what total mass of copper was produced in the next three years?
b) If this trend continues indefinitely, what is the total mass of copper that would be produced from 1996 on?

60. Lunch menu On its lunch menu, a restaurant offers a choice of two soups, five entrees, and three desserts. The lunch special consists of one choice of soup, one entree, and one dessert.
a) Draw a tree diagram to list all the possibilities for one selection for each part of a lunch.
b) Determine the number of different meal combinations that could be chosen.

61. Jewellery display A display case in a jewellery store contains twelve distinct class rings.
a) Determine the number of different ways in which the rings can be arranged in a row.
b) Three of the rings contain onyx and three others contain tiger's eye. If only one of each stone variety is to be on display, how many different ways can the rings be arranged in a row?
c) During the months when sales of class rings are slow, the jeweller displays any three rings. How many different arrangements of class rings are possible?

62. Flower arrangements A florist shop has 20 varieties of flowers to choose from.
a) How many different three-flower arrangements can be made?
b) One of the choices is roses. How many four-flower arrangements include roses?
c) How many four-flower arrangements do not include roses?

63. In the arrangement of letters given, start at the top and work towards the bottom. How many different paths spell PATHWAYS?

64. Expand, using the Binomial Theorem.
a) $(x - 4)^5$ **b)** $(2x + 3)^6$

65. Write the general term for each expansion, and the term indicated.
a) the third term in $(x + 4)^8$
b) the fourth term in $(3x - 5)^7$

66. A set of cards is numbered 1 to 100 inclusive. From this set, a single card is selected at random. What is the probability that the number on the card is divisible by 5 or by 7?

67. Traffic lights On the way to Sherwood Park from Edmonton, there are seven traffic lights. The lights change randomly, and the probability of arriving at a light when it is green is 0.3.
a) Draw the probability tree for this situation.
b) What is the probability of arriving at all seven lights when they are green?
c) What is the probability of arriving at five of the seven lights when they are green?

68. a) When are two events in an experiment considered independent? Give an example.
b) When are two events in an experiment considered mutually exclusive? Give an example.

69. Languages Of the 60 members in the Foreign Language Club, 30 are studying Japanese, 25 are studying Spanish, and 10 are studying both Japanese and Spanish. What is the probability that a club member, chosen at random, is studying Japanese only?

70. Cards Three cards are chosen from a regular deck of 52 cards. What is the probability that exactly two are face cards, given that at least one card is a face card?

71. Keyless entry lock The keyless entry lock keypad on a sports utility vehicle has five buttons, labelled 1 to 5. Find the probability of guessing the correct three-digit entry code if
a) there are no repeated digits in the code?
b) the code can have repeated digits?

72. If data are binomially distributed, with the number of trials $n = 25$ and the probability of success $p = 0.3$, determine the value of each of the following probabilities.
a) $P(20$ successes$)$ **b)** $P($at least 20 successes$)$
c) $P($at least 2 successes$)$

73. Temperatures February's average daily maximum temperature is $-11.5°C$ in Grand Rapids, Manitoba, and $-3.9°C$ in Red Deer, Alberta. Assume their standard deviations are $4°C$ and $6°C$, respectively. During a warm spell, Grand Rapids has highs of $9°C$, while Red Deer's high is $18°C$. Relative to their normal temperature, which place is having the warmer spell?

74. Apples The mass of an apple grown on a farm is normally distributed with a mean of 180 g and a standard deviation of 27 g.
a) What percent of the apples have a mass between 160 g and 200 g?
b) What is the probability that an apple, selected at random, has a mass greater than 200 g?

75. Health care Canada's national health service is available to the whole population. However, about 25% of the population also use private medical facilities. A random survey of 1000 Canadians is conducted.
a) Verify that a normal distribution approximation is reasonable for this data.
b) What is the probability that fewer than 250 Canadians also use private health facilities?
c) What is the probability that between 250 and 275 Canadians also use private health facilities?

76. Flu virus In one day the doctors at a walk-in medical clinic examined 250 patients, of whom 75 were found to exhibit symptoms of the flu.
a) Calculate the standard error of the proportion.
b) Construct a 99% confidence interval for the percent of patients that have the flu.

ANSWERS

Math Standards

Number and Operation p. xvi
1 Coin Collecting
1. $4680 **2.** $9413.15 **3. a)** 0.749 **b)** $5.65
2 Palindromic Numbers and Bank Notes
1. The serial number reads the same forward and backward. **2. a)** The sum is a palindrome. **3. a)** yes **b)** no **c)** 11, 13, 17, 31, 37, 71, 73, 79, 97
4. $\dfrac{1}{1000}$, 0.1%

Geometry and Spatial Sense p. xviii
1 Euler's Formula **1.** Number of Vertices: 4, 8, 6, 12, 20; Number of Faces: 4, 6, 8, 20, 12; Number of Edges: 6, 12, 12, 30, 30 **2.** $V + F = E + 2$, where V is the number of vertices, F is the number of faces, and E is the number of edges. **3.** square-based pyramid: $V = 5$, $F = 5$, $E = 8$; triangular prism: $V = 6$, $F = 5$, $E = 9$
2 Fractal Geometry **2.** 3^n **3.** Answers may vary. nesting boxes, concentric circles at centre ice in hockey

Measurement p. xix
2 Maximizing Area **1. a)** 37.5 m² **b)** No. The area is quartered (9.375 m²). **2.** A semicircle gives an area per pig of about 47.75 m².

Data Analysis, Statistics, and Probability p. xx
1 Human Demographics **1. a)** 20% **b)** This population decreased by about 50%. This could be because fewer people are having babies. **c)** This population has increased as the large bulge of young people in 1951 has aged.
2 A Fair Game? **1. a)** no **b)** It is not fair. **c)** Make the amount you win equal to the amount you lose.

Problem Solving p. xxi
1 Solving Problems **1.** Answers may vary. 16 moves: 7-2, 1-6, 9-4, 6-7, 2-9, 3-8, 4-3, 8-1, 1-6, 3-8, 7-2, 8-1, 6-7, 9-4, 2-9, 4-3 **2.** Yes. In a non-leap-year: if January 1 is a Sunday, January 13 is a Friday. If January 1 is a Monday, April 13 is a Friday. If January 1 is a Tuesday, September 13 is a Friday. If January 1 is a Wednesday, June 13 is a Friday. If January 1 is a Thursday, February 13 is a Friday. If January 1 is a Friday, August 13 is a Friday. If January 1 is a Saturday, May 13 is a Friday. In a leap-year: if January 1 is a Sunday, January 13 is a Friday. If January 1 is a Monday, September 13 is a Friday. If January 1 is a Tuesday, June 13 is a Friday. If January 1 is a Wednesday, March 13 is a Friday. If January 1 is a Thursday, February 13 is a Friday. If January 1 is a Friday, May 13 is a Friday. If January 1 is a Saturday, September 13 is a Friday. **3. a)** 8 **b)** 12 **4. a)** 5 150 000 km **b)** 59.6 days, assuming it takes 1 s to write each number. **5.** One possible answer is $108.24. **6.** Saskatoon, Edmonton, Prince George, Prince Rupert, Vancouver, Edmonton, Saskatoon (or the reverse).

Reasoning and Proof p. xxii
1 Stay or Switch? That is the Question! **1.** There is a $\dfrac{1}{3}$ chance that the car is in 1 and a $\dfrac{2}{3}$ chance it is in 2 or 3. After the host opens 3, there is still a $\dfrac{2}{3}$ chance it is in 2 and a $\dfrac{1}{3}$ chance it is in 1. Thus, there is twice the chance the car is in 1, so you should switch.
2 Using Logic **1.** apple Petra, banana Pat, peach Anna, pear Bonnie **2.** Neither. They both give the same price.
3 True or False **1. a)** True. If $xy > 0$, then $x > 0$ and $y > 0$: false. **b)** True. If $n + 2$ is an odd integer, then n is an odd integer: true.

Communication p. xxiii
2 Interpreting Graphs **1.** Answers may vary. **a)** As time passes, the population increases. First it increases slowly, then very quickly, then slowly again. **b)** As time passes, the water temperature cools very quickly, then levels off at a constant temperature equal to the surrounding temperature. **c)** As the mass of mail increases, so does the cost of sending the mail. The cost is about 35¢ for masses up to 30 g, then about 60¢ for masses over 30 g up to 50 g, then $1 for masses over 50 g up to 100g, then about $1.60 for masses over 100 g up to 200 g.

Connections p. xxiv
1 Cryptography **1.** with the letter X
2. $\begin{bmatrix} 15 & 4 \\ 23 & 45 \end{bmatrix} \begin{bmatrix} 6 & 0 \\ 28 & 54 \end{bmatrix}$ **3.** IT'S COLD

Representation p. xxv
1 Königsberg Bridge Problem **1.** No. All the vertices have odd degree. **2. a)** Answers may vary. Remove bridge 1, 2, 3, or 4, giving exactly two odd degree vertices. **3. a)** All the vertices have even degree. **c)** If the edges are adjacent, removing them would result

in exactly 2 vertices with odd degree, which makes tracing possible. If the edges are not adjacent, removing them would result in all vertices having odd degree, which makes tracing impossible.

Chapter 1

Transformations p. 1
1. a) 1 and 3; 2 and 4 **b)** 1 and 2; 1 and 4; 3 and 2; 3 and 4 **c)** same as part b **2.** parallel **3.** reflection followed by a translation, or a translation followed by a reflection, where the reflection line and the direction of the translation are parallel
4. a) A detailed horseman and a shadowed horseman are each translated horizontally and vertically.
b) The detailed and shadowed horsemen are related by a glide-reflection. **c)** They are vertical and pass through the points where the reins cross the back of each horse's neck.

Getting Started pp. 2–3
Human Pysiology
1 The Heart 1. b) First quadrant. The quantities represented by x and y can have only positive values. **2. b)** The y-coordinates are 6 times as great. **c)** $(0, 0)$ is the only common point. **3. b)** It represents the time required (in minutes) to pump a given volume (in litres) of blood. **4. b)** The two graphs are the same. A reflection in the line $y = x$ interchanges the x- and y-coordinates.
2 Breathing 1. a) $b = 12t$, which is graphed as $y = 12x$ **2.** Equation is $t = \frac{1}{12}b$ or $y = \frac{1}{12}x$
Warm Up 1. a) 3 **b)** 1 **c)** 5 **d)** 2 **e)** 4 **f)** 0 **g)** 11 **h)** 2.5
2. a) 1 **b)** 2 **c)** 3 **d)** 0 **e)** 1.1 **f)** 1.5 **g)** 0.5 **h)** does not exist **3. a)** 1 **b)** 2 **c)** –6 **d)** 29 **e)** –25 **f)** 1.875 **g)** 2.125 **h)** 1.999 **4. a)** translation, upward 2 units
b) translation, downward 5 units **c)** translation, right 1 unit **d)** translation, left 3 units **e)** translation, left 2 units and downward 1 unit **f)** translation, right 3 units and upward 4 units **5. a)** $y = x + 1$ **b)** $y = x + 1$
c) same **d)** $y = x^2 + 1$ **e)** $y = (x + 1)^2$ **f)** not the same
g) There is an operation (squaring) in $y = x^2$; it makes a difference whether you add 1 before or after the operation.
6. 2; 1 **7.** 4; –3 **8.** 1; –1 **9.** $-\frac{3}{2}$; 3 **10.** 1; 1 **11.** –1 and
2; –2 **12. a)** Yes; for every x-value in the domain there is only one corresponding y-value. **b)** domain: all real numbers; range: $y \geq 0$ **13. a)** No; for every positive x-values there are two y-values. **b)** domain: $x \geq 0$; range:

real numbers **14.** domain: all real numbers; range: $y \geq -1$ **15.** domain: all real numbers; range: $y \geq 0$
16. domain: $x \neq 2$; range: $y \neq 0$ **17.** domain: $x \geq -4$; range: $y \geq 0$

Mental Math
1. $(-2, 8)$ **2.** $(-2, -1)$ **3.** $(-5, 5)$ **4.** $(2, 5)$ **5.** $(-1, 3)$
6. $(-7, 7)$ **7.** right 2 units **8.** downward 4 units **9.** left 6 units **10.** upward 5 units **11.** right 4 units and upward 1 unit **12.** left 3 units and downward 2 units
13. 10 **14.** 100 **15.** 2 **16.** – 4 **17.** 0.2 **18.** 0.4 **19.** 2.5
20. –0.05 **21. a)** 5 **b)** –10 **22. a)** 3 **b)** 2 **23. a)** 5 **b)** 10
24. a) 5 **b)** –30 **25. a)** 4 **b)** 1 **26. a)** $\frac{1}{5}$ **b)** $\frac{1}{10}$ **27.** 1
28. $-\frac{1}{2}$ **29.** 0 and –1 **30.** 1 and –1 **31.** –2 **32.** 12
33. 2 **34.** –6 **35.** $-\frac{9}{2}$ **36.** 2 **37.** –3 **38.** $\frac{5}{2}$

Technology pp. 4–6
1 Linear Functions 2. parts a, b, c have same slope, but different y-intercepts; parts d, e, f, have same slope, but different y-intercepts; parts a, d have same y-intercept; parts b, e have same y-intercept; parts c, f have same y-intercept; all have same steepness
3. a) slope **b)** A positive slope means the line goes up to the right; negative slope means the line goes up to the left (or down to the right).
4. a) 0; 0 **b)** $-\frac{5}{2}$; 5 **c)** 3; –6 **d)** 0; 0 **e)** $\frac{5}{2}$; 5
f) –3; 6 **5. a)** $y = -\frac{2}{3}x + 2$ **b)** $y = -\frac{1}{5}x + 3$
c) $y = 3x - 14$ **d)** $y = 3x + \frac{9}{2}$ **6. a)** slope: $-\frac{2}{3}$;
y-intercept: 2 **b)** slope: $-\frac{1}{5}$; y-intercept: 3 **c)** slope: 3;
y-intercept: –14 **d)** slope: 3; y-intercept: $\frac{9}{2}$

2 Absolute Value Functions 2. The part above the x-axis is the same. In each case, the part below the x-axis in the first graph is reflected above the x-axis in the second. **3.** The operation turns a negative value into the corresponding positive value. **5. a)** open up: parts a, b, f; open down: parts c, d, e **b)** the sign outside the absolute value **6. a)** a) $(0, 0)$; b) $(0, 0)$; c) $(0, 0)$; d) $(-1, 0)$; e) $(2, 0)$; f) $(2, 0)$ **b)** domains: a) all real numbers b) all real numbers c) all real numbers; d) all real numbers; e) all real numbers; f) all real numbers; ranges: a) $y \geq 0$; b) $y \geq 0$; c) $y \leq 0$; d) $y \leq 0$; e) $y \leq 0$; f) $y \geq 0$ **c)** a) $x = 0$; b) $x = 0$; c) $x = 0$ **d)** $x = -1$; e) $x = 2$; f) $x = 2$
3 Quadratic Functions 2. a) The graph opens up if the coefficient of x^2 is positive, and down if it is

negative. **b)** The graph is steeper, that is the two arms are closer together, if the coefficient is larger in size (unless scale is changed). **3.** a) (0, 4); b) (0,9);

c) (0, –9); d) (0, 8); e) (–2, –9); f) $\left(-\dfrac{3}{4}, 10\dfrac{1}{8}\right)$

4. a) none; b) 3, –3; c) $3\sqrt{2}$, $-3\sqrt{2}$ or approximately

4.243, – 4.243; d) $\sqrt{\dfrac{8}{3}}$, $-\sqrt{\dfrac{8}{3}}$ or approximately

1.633, –1.633; e) –5, 1; f) –3, $\dfrac{3}{2}$ **5.** a) 4; b) 9; c) –9;

d) 8; e) –5; f) 9

4 Cubic Functions 2. a) All have domain and range all real numbers. **b)** a) –1.4, 0, 1.4; b) –2.2; c) 1.3; d) –1.4; **e)** –0.8, 0.4, 2.9; f) –3, –1, 2 **c)** a) 0; b) 4; c) 2; d) –3; e) 2; f) –6 **d)** a) max(–0.8, 1.1), min(0.8, –1.1); b) max(–1, 6), min(1, 2); c) none; d) max(0.7, –1.2), min(–0.7, –4.8); e) max(–0.3, 2.4), min(1.9, –8.0); f) max(–2.1, 4.1), min(0.8, –8.2) **3.** 2; one relative maximum point and one relative minimum point.

5 Rational Functions 2. a) a) $x = -3$, $y = 0$; b) $x = 3$, $y = 1$; c) $x = -1$, $y = -2$; d) $x = -1$, $x = 1$, $y = 0$; e) $x = 2$, $y = x + 1$; f) No asymptote. The graph is itself a line, with one point missing. **b)** a) domain: $x \neq -3$; range: $y \neq 0$; b) domain: $x \neq 3$; range: $y \neq 1$; c) $x \neq -1$; range: $y \neq -2$; d) domain: $x \neq \pm 1$; range: $y > 0$ or $y \leq -3$; e) domain: $x \neq 2$; range: all real numbers; f) domain: $x \neq 1$; range: $y \neq -2$

6 Radical Functions 2. a) domain: $x \geq -2$; range:

$y \geq 0$ **b)** domain: $x \geq 3$; range: $y \leq 0$ **c)** domain: $x \geq \dfrac{2}{3}$;

range: $y \geq 0$ **d)** domain: $x \leq \dfrac{4}{3}$; range: $y \geq 0$ **e)** domain:

$x \geq -2$; range: $y \geq 0$ **f)** domain: $x \leq -4$; range: $y \leq 0$
3. If the sign in front of the radical sign is positive, the graph is the upper half of a parabola. If the sign is negative, the graph is the lower half of a parabola.
4. The sign of the coefficient of x tells whether the parabola opens left or right.

Section 1.1 pp. 10–13
Practice   1. upward 5 units **2.** downward 6 units
3. right 4 units **4.** left 8 units **5.** upward 3 units
6. downward 7 units **7.** left 3 units, downward 5 units
8. right 6 units, upward 2 units **9.** right 5 units,
downward 7 units **10.** left 2 units, upward 9 units
11. $h = 0$, $k = 6$ **12.** $h = 0$, $k = -8$ **13.** $h = 3$, $k = 0$
14. $h = -5$, $k = 0$ **15.** $h = -2$, $k = -4$ **16.** $h = 7$, $k = 7$

21. $y = |x| + 3$ **22.** $y = \sqrt{x} - 5$ **23.** $y = \dfrac{1}{x} - 2$

24. $y = \sqrt{9 - x^2} - 3$ **25.** $y = \sqrt{x + 4}$

26. $y = |x - 3| + 2$ **27.** $y = \sqrt{x + 2} + 4$

28. $y = (x + 4)^2 - 4$ **29.** $y = (x - 2)^3 - 3$

30. $y = \dfrac{1}{x - 3} + 3$

Applications and Problem Solving

37. a) $f(\text{P–C1}) = 210 - 5t^2$, $f(\text{PP}) = 137 - 5t^2$,
$f(\text{CP}) = 125 - 5t^2$ **c)** downward 73 units **d)** upward
12 units **e)** downward 85 units **38. a)** $C = 45 + 35t$
b) $C = 40 + 35t$ **c)** The second graph is 5 units below
the first. **39.** It is the same line. The slope of the
transformation is equal to the slope of the line.
40. a) Each integer starts a line segment on the left.
The right endpoint is not included because it is the
next integer, so we use an open circle.   **41. b)** $5, $6,
$6, $8 **42.** downward 2 units; $y = \sqrt{x} - 2$ **43.** You
can move a point on the line $y = x$ to any point on the
line $y = x + 3$. Each one gives a different translation.

44. a) $C(x) = \dfrac{20}{50 + x} \times 100\%$ **c)** $33\dfrac{1}{3}\%$

d) $C_1(x) = \dfrac{20}{40 + x}$ **f)** 10 units left; $C(x) = C_1(x + 10)$.

The points in part e, for $0 \leq x < 10$, do not exist in
part b) because $x \geq 0$. **45. a)** If $x \geq 0$, $y = |x| + x$
becomes $y = 2x$. If $x < 0$, $y = |x| + x$ becomes $y = -x + x$
or $y = 0$. **b)** graph in part a translated upward 2 units
46. a) If $x \geq 0$, then $y = x - x$ or $y = 0$. If $x < 0$, then
$y = x - (-x)$ or $y = 2x$. **b)** same graph translated
upward 2 units **47.** If $x \geq 0$, then $y = x - x$ or $y = 0$. If
$x < 0$, then $y = -x - x$ or $y = -2x$.

Section 1.2 p. 15
Applications and Problem Solving   1. The distance,
d, will vary, but only slightly, depending on the
height h of the viewer's eyes above the ground. If
$h = 1.6$ m, $d = 64.5$ m. As h increases, d decreases by
about the same amount. **2.** 500 m **3.** 3:2 **5.** Cut so
that a cut AB, on the top face, and a cut DE, on the
bottom face, are on opposite sides of the
corresponding diagonals. **6.** Juan and Sue cross in
2 min; Sue returns in 2 min; Alicia and Larry cross in
8 min; Juan returns in 1 min; Juan and Sue cross in
2 min. The total time to cross is 15 min. *Hint:* Alicia
and Larry must cross together, and someone must be
on the opposite side to return the flashlight.
7. a) 4 **b)** 98 **c)** 792 **8.** Answers will vary.

Section 1.3 pp. 25–28
Practice   7. $y = -x - 3$ **8.** $y = \sqrt{2 - x}$

9. $y = |-x + 4|$ or $y = |x - 4|$ **10.** $y = 2^{-x}$ or $y = \dfrac{1}{2^x}$

11. $y = -\sqrt{x + 3}$ **12.** $y = 3 - x^2$ **13.** $y = -|x - 4|$

14. $y = -\dfrac{4}{x^2 + 1}$ **15.** $x = 2y + 3$ or $y = \dfrac{x - 3}{2}$

16. $x = y^2 + 2$ or $y = \pm\sqrt{x - 2}$ **17.** $x = y^3$ or $y = \sqrt[3]{x}$

18. $x = \sqrt{y - 4}$ or $y = x^2 + 4, x \geq 0$ **19.** yes **20.** yes
21. no **22.** yes **23.** yes **24.** yes **25.** no
26. a) $f(x) = 2x - 4, -f(x) = -2x + 4, f(-x) = -2x - 4,$

$f^{-1}(x) = \dfrac{x + 4}{2}$ **c)** $-f(x)$: $(2, 0), f(-x)$: $(0, -4), f^{-1}(x)$:

$(4, 4)$ **27. a)** $f(x) = -3x + 2, -f(x) = 3x - 2,$

$f(-x) = 3x + 2, \ f^{-1}(x) = \dfrac{2 - x}{3}$ **c)** $-f(x)$: $\left(\dfrac{2}{3}, 0\right),$

$f(-x)$: $(0, 2), f^{-1}(x)$: $\left(\dfrac{1}{2}, \dfrac{1}{2}\right)$ **28. a)** $f(x) = x^3 - 3,$

$-f(x) = 3 - x^3, f(-x) = -x^3 - 3, \ f^{-1}(x) = \sqrt[3]{x + 3}$

29. a) $f(x) = \sqrt{x + 3}, -f(x) = -\sqrt{x + 3},$

$f(-x) = \sqrt{3 - x}, f^{-1}(x) = x^2 - 3, x \geq 0$

30. a) $f(x) = x^2 - 2, -f(x) = 2 - x^2, f(-x) = x^2 - 2,$

$f^{-1}(x) = \pm\sqrt{x + 2}$ **31. a)** $f(x) = \dfrac{6}{x^2 + 2},$

$-f(x) = -\dfrac{6}{x^2 + 2}, \ f(-x) = \dfrac{6}{x^2 + 2}, \ f^{-1}(x) = \pm\sqrt{\dfrac{6}{x} - 2}$

c) Descriptions will vary. Asymptotes: x-axis for $f(x)$, $-f(x)$, and $f(-x)$; y-axis for $f^{-1}(x)$.
Applications and Problem Solving
32. $y = -1.27x + 146$. This is $f(-x)$, because one is a reflection of the other in the y-axis. **33.** $y = 2$
34. They are mirror images in the x-axis. If one is

$f(x)$, the other is $-f(x)$. **35. a)** $-f(x) = -\sqrt{25 - x^2}$,

$f(-x) = \sqrt{25 - x^2}, \ x = \sqrt{25 - y^2}$ **c)** All but $x = f(y)$

represent functions. **d)** $-f(x)$: $(5, 0), (-5, 0); f(-x)$:

$(0, 5); x = f(y)$: $\left(\dfrac{5}{\sqrt{2}}, \dfrac{5}{\sqrt{2}}\right)$ **36. a)** $(0, -6), (-2, 0), (3,0)$

37. a) $y = 40 + 0.15x$ **c)** $y = \dfrac{x - 40}{0.15}$ **d)** This gives
you the distance you can drive for a given sum,
x dollars. **38. b)** Put an open circle on the end of the

line. **c)** $r = \dfrac{C}{2\pi}$; gives the radius for a known

circumference **e)** They are inverses; the x- and
y-coordinates have been interchanged.

39. b) $r = \sqrt{\dfrac{A}{\pi}}$; gives the radius for a known area.

d) They are inverses. **40. b)** $l = \sqrt[3]{V}$; gives the side
length for a known volume **d)** They are inverses.

e) They are numerically equal. **41. b)** $s = \sqrt{\dfrac{4A}{\sqrt{3}}}$;

gives the side length for a known area.
d) They are inverses. **e)** They are numerically equal.
43. a) $y = -x - 2$ **b)** $y = -x^2 + 2$ **44. c)** reflection line:
$y = -x$ **45.** one: $(0, -3)$. Other points are mapped onto
points in the original function, but not onto
themselves. For example, $(1, -2)$ is mapped onto
$(-1, -2)$ and vice versa. **46. a)** opposite **b)** opposite
c) reciprocal **47.** Answers will vary. If (a, b) is a point
on $y = f(x)$, then (b, a) is a point on $y = f^{-1}(x)$. So,
$f(f^{-1}(a)) = f(a) = b$ for any $b; f^{-1}(f(a)) = f^{-1}(b) = a$ for

any a. **48.** $f^{-1}(x) = \dfrac{b - dx}{cx - a}$

Investigating Math p. 29
1 Classifying Functions   1. odd **2.** even **3.** odd
4. neither **5.** even **6.** even **7.** neither **8.** odd **9.** even
10. even
2 Exploring Symmetry   1. a) y-axis; because
$f(-x) = f(x)$, reflection in the y-axis gives the same
graph **b)** no **c)** yes; a rotation of $180°$ about $(0, 0)$ **d)** A
reflection in the x-axis, and a reflection in the y-axis,
in either order. **2. a)** odd **b)** even **c)** neither **d)** odd
3. a) odd **b)** even **c)** even **d)** odd **4.** If n is even, the
function is even. The symmetry is in the y-axis. If n is
odd, the function is odd. The symmetry is a $180°$
rotation about the origin.

Section 1.4 pp. 38–40
Practice   13. b) The second graph is twice as steep;
the third is half as steep. **c)** $(0, 0)$ **14. b)** The second
graph is 3 times as high; third is half as high and
inverted. **c)** $(0, 0)$ **15. b)** The second graph is twice as

high and inverted; the third is $\dfrac{2}{3}$ as high. **c)** $(1, 0)$

16. b) The second graph is 3 times as high and inverted; the third is $1\frac{1}{2}$ times as high and inverted. **c)** $(-4, 0)$ **17. b)** The second graph is half as wide; third is twice as wide. **c)** $(0, 0)$ **18. b)** The second graph is twice as wide and reversed left-to-right; the third is half as wide. **c)** $(0, 0)$ **19.** vertical expansion by a factor of 3 **20.** vertical compression by a factor of $\frac{1}{2}$ **21.** vertical expansion by a factor of 2 and a reflection in the x-axis **22.** vertical compression by a factor of $\frac{1}{3}$ and a reflection in the x-axis **23.** horizontal compression by a factor of $\frac{1}{2}$ **24.** horizontal expansion by a factor of 2 **25.** horizontal compression by a factor of $\frac{1}{4}$ and a reflection in the y-axis **26.** horizontal expansion by a factor of 2 and a reflection in the y-axis **27.** vertical expansion by a factor of 3, and horizontal compression by a factor of $\frac{1}{2}$ **28.** vertical compression by a factor of $\frac{1}{2}$, and horizontal expansion by a factor of 3 **29.** vertical expansion by a factor of 4, and horizontal expansion by a factor of 2 **30.** vertical and horizontal compressions, both by a factor of $\frac{1}{3}$ **31.** vertical expansion by a factor of 2, reflection in the x-axis, and horizontal compression by a factor of $\frac{1}{4}$ **32.** vertical expansion by a factor of 5, horizontal expansion by a factor of 2, and reflection in the y-axis **33.** $y = 2|x|$ **34.** $y = \frac{1}{2}x^2$ **35.** $y = 2(x + 1)$ **36.** $y = -2|x|$ **37.** $y = \sqrt{-3x}$ **38.** $y = \frac{8}{x^2 + 1}$ **39.** $y = \frac{1}{2}x^3$ **40.** $y = -\frac{1}{2}|x|$ **41. a)** $-4, 2$ **b)** $-8, 4$ **c)** $4, -2$ **d)** $-4, 2$ **e)** $-2, 1$ **f)** $8, -4$ **42. a)** $0, -1, 2$ **b)** $0, 3, -6$ **c)** $0, -3, 6$ **d)** $0, -6, 12$ **e)** $0, 3, -6$ **f)** $0, \frac{3}{2}, -3$

Applications and Problem Solving **43. a)** 38.4 m, 57.6 m, 256 m **b)** domain: $0 \le s \le 120$; ranges: $0 \le d \le 86.4$; $0 \le d \le 129.6$; $0 \le d \le 576$ **d)** All are half-parabolas with vertex $(0, 0)$. The three functions can be obtained from $y = x^2$ by vertical compressions and/or horizontal expansions. **44.** $a = 4, k = 1$

45. $a = -3, k = 1$ **46.** $a = 1, k = 3$ **47.** $a = 1, k = -\frac{1}{2}$ **48.** $a = \frac{1}{2}, k = \frac{1}{3}$ **49.** $a = 2, k = 4$ **52.** $f(x) = (x + 2)(x - 2)(x - 4)$; $h(x) = 2(x + 2)(x - 2)(x - 4)$ **53. b)** Answers will vary. **54. b)** Answers will vary. **56. a)** compression by a factor of $\frac{1}{4}$ **b)** expansion by a factor of 2 **c)** $y = \sqrt{4x}$ and $y = 2\sqrt{x}$ have the same graph. **d)** The transformations are equivalent because the results are the same. **e)** These are different, mainly because the transformations do not have the same invariant point.

Computer Data Bank p. 41
1 Canadian Political Leaders **1. a)** Nova Scotia **b)** New Brunswick, Northwest Territories, Prince Edward Island **c)** Northwest Territories, Prince Edward Island, British Columbia **d)** Newfoundland, Prince Edward Island **2.** Québec **3.** Answers will vary.
2 BMI of Canadians **1.** 41.3%
3 Ports Around the World **1. a)** coastal natural **b)** river natural **c)** coastal natural **d)** coastal breakwater **2.** coastal natural **3.** Atlantic **4.** >150 m: 12.3 m; ≤ 150 m: 12.4 m; the least channel depth is the least channel depth on March 21
4 Satellites Orbiting Earth
1. a) communications **b)** surveillance **c)** early warning, earth observation, surveillance, technology

Section 1.5 p. 43
Applications and Problem Solving **1.** Two. Turn over the red card and the card with the circle on it. **2.** Answers may vary. Three possible solutions are: 1) Row 1: 1, 2, 3, 4; Row 2: 3, 4, 1, 2; Row 3: 4, 3, 2, 1; Row 4: 2, 1, 4, 3 2) Row 1: 1, 2, 3, 4; Row 2: 4, 3, 1, 2; Row 3: 3, 4, 2, 1; Row 4: 2, 1, 4, 3 3) Row 1: 1, 2, 3, 4; Row 2: 2, 4, 1, 3; Row 3: 4, 3, 2, 1; Row 4: 3, 1, 4, 2 **3.** November = 4, December = 5 *Hint:* Count the number of letters with closed interiors. **4.** Lions 1, Tigers 0; Tigers 0, Bears 0; Tigers 1, Rams 0; Bears 2, Rams 2; Lions 1, Rams 0; Lions 5, Bears 0 **5.** No. To do so, the car must complete two laps in two minutes. It has already taken two minutes for the first lap. **6.** $\frac{1}{5}$. There are 5 pairs with one or both white. **7.** 3 females, 4 males **8.** $(9, 6)$ and $(3, 10)$ **9.** the odd numbers from 1 to 99 **10.** 8 of each **11.** 26 **12. a)** 125 **b)** 69 375 **13.** Answers will vary.

Section 1.6 pp. 47–49
Practice **1.** vertical expansion by a factor of 2,

translation upward 3 units **2.** vertical compression by a factor of $\frac{1}{2}$, translation downward 2 units

3. translation left 4 units and upward 1 unit
4. vertical expansion by a factor of 3, translation right 5 units **5.** horizontal expansion by a factor of 2, translation downward 6 units **6.** horizontal compression by a factor of $\frac{1}{2}$, translation right 4 units
7. vertical expansion by a factor of 4, translation right 6 and upward 2 units **8.** vertical expansion by a factor of 2, reflection in the x-axis, translation downward 3 units **9.** reflection in the y-axis, translation left 1 unit and downward 1 unit **10.** reflection in the x-axis, translation right 3 units and upward 1 unit
11. vertical expansion by a factor of 3, horizontal compression by a factor of $\frac{1}{2}$, translation downward 6 units **12.** horizontal compression by a factor of $\frac{1}{3}$, translation left 4 units and upward 5 units
13. vertical compression by a factor of $\frac{1}{2}$, horizontal expansion by a factor of 2, translation downward 4 units **14.** vertical expansion by a factor of 2, reflection in the x-axis, horizontal compression by a factor of $\frac{1}{4}$, translation right 2 units
15. reflection in the y-axis, translation right 2 units
16. horizontal compression by a factor of $\frac{1}{2}$, translation left 4 units and downward 4 units
17. reflection in the y-axis, translation right 4 units and upward 5 units **18.** horizontal compression by a factor of $\frac{1}{3}$, translation right 2 units and upward 8 units **44.** $y = -(x-2)^2 - 3$ **45.** $k(x) = 3(x-4)^2 - 2$
46. $h(x) = |3(x+5)| + 1$ **47.** $g(x) = -\frac{1}{3}(x-4)^3 - 5$

48. $g(x) = \sqrt{\dfrac{6-x}{2}}$ or $g(x) = \sqrt{-\dfrac{1}{2}(x-6)}$

Applications and Problem Solving 49. b) sides 6, 5.8, 5.8; height 5 **c)** $\frac{5}{3}$ **d)** vertical expansion by a factor of $\frac{5}{3}$, reflection in the x-axis, translation right 3 units and upward 5 units **50. a)** vertical expansion by a factor of 5, reflection in the x-axis, translation right 4 units and upward 80 units **b)** The vertex $(0, 0)$ of $y = x^2$ is moved to $(4, -80)$. The maximum height is

80 m, after 4 s. **52. a)** $y = -\dfrac{x+3}{(x+3)^2 + 1}$

b) $y = \dfrac{x-4}{2\big((x-4)^2 + 1\big)} - 7$ **c)** $y = \dfrac{\frac{1}{2}(x-5)}{\left(\frac{1}{2}(x-5)\right)^2 + 1} + 2$

53. a) $y = 2^{-x} - 6$ **b)** $y = 2^{2(x-4)} + 5$ **54. a)** $a = 3$, $k = -1$, $h = 0$, $q = 0$ **b)** $a = \frac{1}{3}$, $k = \frac{1}{2}$, $h = 6$, $q = -1$ **c)** $a = -2$, $k = -2$, $h = -7$, $q = 4$ **55. b)** The common point is $(0, 20)$. In both cases, the object starts at a height of 20 m. **c)** horizontal expansion by a factor of $\frac{5}{2}$ **d)** The common point is $(5, 0)$. Both objects take 5 s to reach the ground. **e)** The common point is $(3, 0)$. See part d). **f)** vertical expansion by a factor of 16 **56.** reflection in the line $y = x$, translation left 1 unit and downward 2 units **57.** reflection in $y = x$, reflection in x-axis, translation left 2 units and downward 3 units **58. a)** $y = 2(x + 3) - 5$ simplifies to $y = 2x + 1$ **b)** No; the operation of squaring prevents the same simplification.

Section 1.7 p. 57
Applications and Problem Solving
42. $y = \dfrac{1}{5(x+4)}$ **43.** $y = \left|\dfrac{1}{2}(x-5)\right|$

44. $y = \dfrac{1}{[2(x-4)]^2 - 3}$ **45.** $y = \left|2(x+3)^2 - 5\right|$

54. $\dfrac{1}{f(x)} = \dfrac{1}{2(x+2)}$ which is a reciprocal function, whereas $f^{-1}(x) = \frac{1}{2}x - 2$, the inverse of $f(x)$, is a linear function.

Section 1.8 p.59
Applications and Problem Solving
1.–16. Answers will vary.

Career Connection p. 60
1 Ages of Cats and Dogs   1. 47 **2.** 11 **3. b)** A vertical translation of 5 units upward moves the graph for cats onto the graph for small dogs. **4.** The cat's equivalent age is 5 human years less. **5.** Yes; the rate is 4 human years per year. **6.** No; their equivalent ages are different.
2 Locating Information   1.–5. Answers will vary.

Connecting Math and Design pp. 61–63

1 Using Transformations **1.** 3 translations, 7 units right each time **2.** 3 reflections in a line, $\frac{1}{2}$ unit right of the right edge **3.** reflections in a line $\frac{1}{2}$ unit below the bottom of the diagram, then 3 translations of both images, 7 units right each time **4.** reflection in a horizontal line through the centre of the diagram and translation right 7 units, done 3 times

2 Transforming Triangles **1.** $\sqrt{3}$ units **2. a)** $\sqrt{3}$ **b)** $y = \sqrt{3}x$ **3. a)** $y = -\sqrt{3}x$ **b)** $y = -\sqrt{3}(x-2)$ **c)** $y = \sqrt{3}(x+2)$ **4.** Answers will vary.

3 Creating a Design **1.–3.** Answers will vary.
4 Locating Information **1.–2.** Answers will vary.

Review pp. 64–65

1. translation downward 3 units **2.** translation left 6 units **3.** translation right 4 units and downward 5 units **4.** translation downward 5 units **5.** $y = (x+3)^2 - 2$ **6.** $y = \sqrt{x-1} + 2$ **13.** function **14.** function **15.** function **16.** not a function
17. a) $-f(x) = -x^3 - 3; f(-x) = -x^3 + 3; \ f^{-1}(x) = \sqrt[3]{x-3}$
27. a) $-\frac{1}{2}, \frac{1}{2}, 1$ **b)** $1, -1, -2$ **c)** $-1, 1, 2$ **28.** horizontal compression factor $\frac{1}{2}$, translation left 1 unit
29. vertical expansion by a factor of 3, translation left 2 and downward 4 units **30.** vertical expansion by a factor of 3, reflection in the x-axis, translation upward 5 units **31.** horizontal compression by a factor of $\frac{1}{2}$, translation right 3 units and downward 1 unit
32. vertical compression by a factor of $\frac{1}{2}$, horizontal compression by a factor of $\frac{1}{4}$, translation upward 2 units **33.** horizontal compression by a factor of $\frac{1}{2}$, translation right 2 units and upward 3 units
34. $g(x) = 2(-(x+3))^3 - 4$ or $g(x) = -2(x+3)^3 - 4$
45. $y = \left| \left(\frac{1}{2}(x+3) \right)^2 - 4 \right|$

Exploring Math p. 65

6. a) Winning strategies may vary. **b)** Essentially, one would like to write a number whose multiples and divisors have already been crossed out. If you are able to write a prime number whose multiples have already been crossed out, then this will force your opponent to write 1, if it has not already been crossed out. Then, writing a prime number larger than 50, or any prime whose multiples have already been crossed out, will win the game. **c)** If it is not required that the first number be even, then the player going first may always win as follows: Player 1 writes 97, for example. Player 2 is forced to write 1, the only divisor. Player 1 then wins by writing 89, for example.

Chapter Check p. 66

1. translation upward 4 units **2.** translation right 2 units and upward 3 units **3.** vertical expansion by a factor of 2, reflection in the x-axis, horizontal translation right 1 unit **4.** vertical compression by a factor of $\frac{1}{3}$, horizontal compression by a factor of $\frac{1}{3}$, reflection in the y-axis, translation upward 5 units
9. $y = \sqrt{x+2} - 3$ **10.** $x = 2y$ or $y = \frac{x}{2}$
11. $y = 2|x+1|$ **19.** function **20.** function **21.** not a function **22.** $h(x) = 2(x+3)^2 + 4$
23. $g(x) = -\sqrt{2(x+4)}$ **24.** $y = \frac{3}{4 - (x-3)^2}$
25. $y = |3(x-5) - 3|$ **26.** $y = \frac{1}{4(x+2)^2 + 1}$
27. a) $0, \frac{2}{3}, -1$ **b)** $0, -1, \frac{3}{2}$ **c)** $0, 2, -3$ **d)** $0, 2, -3$

Problem Solving p. 67

1. $\frac{9}{2}$ and $\frac{3}{2}$, or $-\frac{9}{2}$ and $-\frac{3}{2}$ **2.** 45 **3.** One solution: Fill the 5-L and 11-L containers from the 24-L container, leaving 8 L. Pour the contents of the 5-L container into the 13-L container. Fill the 13-L container from the 11-L container, leaving 3 L. Fill the 5-L container from the 13-L container, leaving 8 L. Pour the contents of the 5-L container into the 11-L container, making 8 L. **4. a)** 17 **b)** The equation is $8(x-8) = 9(x-9)$.
5. Answers will vary. **6.** $\frac{x^2}{18}$ **7.** Spartans 0, Eagles 0; Ravens 1, Eagles 0; Penguins 3, Eagles 0; Spartans 3, Penguins 2; Spartans 2, Ravens 0; Penguins 1, Ravens 0 **8.** 119 (y can be any odd number from 1 to

237) **9.** 6 399 999 999 840 000 000 001 **10.** Use the cosine law and the fact that adjacent angles are supplementary. Alternatively, draw in a height; there are 3 right-angled triangles: $h^2 + a^2 = x^2$; $h^2 + (y + a)^2 = t^2$; $h^2 + (y - a)^2 = s^2$. Eliminate h and a to get the result. **11.** $\dfrac{1}{9}$ **12.** $\{a, b, c\} = \{2, 3, 4\}$ **13.** If digit is x, then $\dfrac{1111x}{4x} = \dfrac{1111}{4}$ or 277.75. **14.** 648

15. $h = \dfrac{P}{2} - \dfrac{2A}{P}$ **16.** $\dfrac{99}{100}$: $f_0(x) = f_3(x) = \ldots = f_{99}(x)$;

therefore, $f_{100}(x) = f_1(x) = f_0(f_0(x)) = \dfrac{x-1}{x}$

Chapter 2

Exponents and Logarithms p. 69
1. lowest level people can hear: 1×10^{-12} W/m²; a soft whisper from 5 m: 1×10^{-9} W/m²; light traffic from 15 m: 5×10^{-7} W/m²; jackhammer from 15 m: 5×10^{-4} W/m²; heavy traffic from 15 m: 1×10^{-3} W/m²; vacuum cleaner: 1.2×10^{-3} W/m²; a jet aircraft from 600 m: 1×10^{-2} W/m²; loud discotheque: 0.7 W/m²; jet aircraft takeoff from 30 m: 100 W/m² **2.** 1000 times **3.** 1000 times **4.** No. At 30 m, there would be damage, but 600 m away, the intensity is much less (10 000 times less).

Getting Started pp. 70–71
Depreciation
2. 1.94 years **3.** 6.46 years; In practice, dealers do not want such a car, so any trade-in is given as a discount. In most cases the dealer junks the car.
4. a) $V(t) = 8000 \times (0.7)^t$ **b)** If the car is now n years old, $t \geq -n$. **c)** Yes. The rule does not apply to older cars. They do not lose value as quickly, if they still work. Thus, t should not be more than 8 or 10 years.
5. Yes. It gives the present value of the car. **6.** The value 2 years from now is about $\dfrac{1}{4}$ the value 2 years ago. **7.** $23 300

Warm Up 1. 0.06 **2.** 0.03 **3.** 0.005 **4.** 0.015 **5.** 36
6. 20 **7.** 20 **8.** 18 **9.** 5 **10.** 1 **11.** 5
12. 0.0275, 12 **13.** 0.0325, 4 **14.** 0.0275, 7
15. 0.014, 4 **16.** 0.013, 12 **17.** $6605.33
18. $6041.73 **19.** $5756.17 **20.** $5762.53
21. $2779.53 **22.** $2174.94 **23.** $2462.00
24. $2107.23 **25.** $2220.21
Mental Math
1. a^8 **2.** k^8 **3.** m^4 **4.** t^5 **5.** h^3 **6.** n^9 **7.** p^9 **8.** x^2 **9.** y^{-13}

10. d^{-2} **11.** k^{10} **12.** n **13.** 32 **14.** 27 **15.** 1 **16.** $\dfrac{1}{7}$
17. 2 **18.** −2 **19.** $\dfrac{1}{3}$ **20.** 4 **21.** 1 **22.** 25 **23.** 9 **24.** $\dfrac{1}{2}$
25. 1 **26.** 2 **27.** 5 **28.** 2^{3x} **29.** 2^{5x} **30.** 2^{-x} **31.** 2^{6x}
32. 2^{-2x} **33.** 2^{12x} **34.** $2^{4(x+1)}$ **35.** 2^{-2x} **36.** 2^{2x} **37.** 10^{3x}
38. 10^{-2x} **39.** 10^{-5x} **40.** 10^{-2x} **41.** 10^{4x-2} **42.** $10^{\frac{3x}{2}}$

43. 3^{-2}; $\left(\dfrac{1}{2}\right)^{-2}$ **44.** $32^{\frac{1}{5}}$; $64^{\frac{2}{3}}$ **45.** $\dfrac{4}{8^{\frac{2}{3}}}$; $0.5(121)^{\frac{1}{2}}$

Investigating Math pp. 72–73
1 Exploring Numbers in Other Bases 1. a) 175 **b)** 5336
c) 1793 **d)** 33 300 **e)** 15 **f)** 187
2. $1b^4 + 4b^3 + 8b^2 + 2b + 3$ **3.** 8 **4.** $b \geq 10$ **5.** decimal: 0, 1, 2, 3, 4, 5, 6, 7, 8, 9, 10, 11, 12, 13, 14, 15, 16; binary: 0, 1, 10, 11, 100, 101, 110, 111, 1000, 1001, 1010, 1011, 1100, 1101, 1110, 1111, 10000; number of digits in binary number: 1, 1, 2, 2, 3, 3, 3, 3, 4, 4, 4, 4, 4, 4, 4, 4, 5
2 Converting From Base 10 to Another Base 1. a) 703
b) 100 011 101 **2. a)** 12 digits; 111 110 101 101 **b)** 12 digits; 110 110 000 000 **3. a)** 9ED **b)** D80 **c)** 8C1F
4. decimal: 0, 1, 2, 3, 4, 5, 6, 7, 8, 9, 10, 11, 12, 13, 14, 15, 16; binary: 0, 1, 10, 11, 100, 101, 110, 111, 1000, 1001, 1010, 1011, 1100, 1101, 1110, 1111, 10000; octal: 0, 1, 2, 3, 4, 5, 6, 7, 10, 11, 12, 13, 14, 15, 16, 17, 20; hexadecimal: 0, 1, 2, 3, 4, 5, 6, 7, 8, 9, A, B, C, D, E, F, 10 **5. a)** full intensity green **b)** 256 **6. a)** 4 or 5 **b)** 8 or 9; 16 to 31 inclusive **c)** 9; 256 to 511 inclusive

Section 2.1 p. 75
Applications and Problem Solving 1. Jupiter, Saturn **2. a)** Newfoundland **b)** Prince Edward Island **3.** (Information from the web site of the Canadian Museum of Nature: http://www.nature.ca/english/eladback.htm) **a)** extinct: a species that no longer exists; extirpated: a species no longer existing in the wild, but existing elsewhere; endangered: a species facing imminent extirpation or extinction; threatened: a species likely to become endangered if limiting factors are not reversed; vulnerable: a species of special concern because of characteristics that make it particularly sensitive to human activities or natural events **b)** all living things, including plants and animals **4.** 70 **5. a)** Answers may vary, depending on route taken; 4415 km **b)** About 4.5 days. **8. a)** Hand geometry takes a three-dimensional image of the hand and measures the shape and length of fingers and knuckles. (Information from the web site http://homepages.go.com/~nuts4pi/edt6030/biometrics.htm) This information

is entered into a computer, which can then identify the person when his or her hand is scanned by a security device. **b)** Answers may vary: airports, high-security workplaces, government offices.

Investigating Math p. 76
Exploring Exponential Functions **1. b)** domain: all real numbers, range: $y > 0$, y-intercept: 1, x-intercept: none, asymptote: $y = 0$ **c)** yes **2. a)** Same curve, translated down 1 unit **b)** domain: all real numbers, range: $y > -1$, y-intercept: 0, x-intercept: 0, asymptote: $y = -1$ **c)** Same curve, translated up 1 unit **3. a)** vertical expansion by a factor of 3 **b)** vertical expansion by a factor of 4 **c)** vertical expansion by a factor of $|A|$ if $|A| > 1$, vertical compression by a factor of $|A|$ if $|A| < 1$; reflected in the x-axis if $A < 0$ **4. a)** graphs are similar in shape; both pass through $(0, 1)$: graph of $y = 3^x$ increases faster on the right and decreases faster on the left than the graph of $y = 2^x$ **b)** the graph will be above the other two on the right and below them on the left **c)** domain: all real numbers, range: $y > 0$, y-intercept: 1, x-intercept: none, asymptote: $y = 0$ **d)** $(0, 1)$ **5. a)** reflection in the y-axis **b)** reflection in the y-axis **c)** reflection in the y-axis **d)** $(-4, 2401)$ **6. a)** horizontal line $y = 1$ **b)** same as graph of $y = 2^{-x}$ **c)** same as graph of $y = 3^{-x}$ **7.** Answers may vary. Facts should include: all graphs pass through $(0, 1)$; all graphs go up on one side (right if $b > 1$, left if $0 < b < 1$); domain is the real numbers; range is the positive real numbers (if $b = 1$, the function is not considered to be exponential) **8.** $m = n$ **9. a)** horizontal line $y = 0$, no values for $x < 0$ **b)** no values for $x = \frac{1}{b}$ if b is even

Section 2.2 pp. 81–83
Practice **1.** 5.2 **2.** 1.7 **3.** 0.8 **4.** 1.5 **5.** 1.8 **6.** no value **7.** 0.8 **8.** 3.9 **9.** 2.3 **10.** 0.6 **11.** –1.3 **12.** –1.6 **13.** 40 **14.** 5 **15.** 7 **16.** 1200 **17.** 2400 **18.** 19 200 **19.** 9000 **20.** 240 min **21.** 8 h **22.** 576 000 **23.** 9810
Applications and Problem Solving
24. approximately 7.25 years **25. a)** $P(t) = 5000(2)^{\frac{t}{45}}$ **b)** 20 000; 40 000; 80 000 **c)** 3536 **d)** 51 606 366 **e)** 313 **f)** 150 min **26. a)** $P(t) = 30(1.03)^t$ **b)** 46.7 million **c)** 23 years **27. a)** $P(t) = 18\ 000(0.87)^t$ **b)** 10 300 **c)** 5 years **28. a)** $A(t) = 1700(1.05)^t$ **b)** \$2278.16 **c)** \$1541.95 **d)** 14 years **e)** no **29. a)** $I(d) = (0.95)^d$ **b)** 69.8% **c)** 45 m **30. a)** $L(t) = 1200(1.0625)^t$; $M(t) = 2000(1.0475)^t$ **c)** 11.4 years **d)** 14.9 years **e)** 36 years; \$10 595.30 **31. a)** P_0: initial population; b: rate of growth, $b > 0$; t: time **b)** If $b > 1$, then the population is increasing. If $0 < b < 1$, the population is decreasing.

32. a) 7.95 billion **b)** 35 years **c)** 2.95 billion, assuming that the growth rate was the same before 1970. **33. a)** 30 billion **b)** 2077

34. a) $C(t) = 2700(10)^{\frac{t}{7}}$ **b)** 1.4 billion **c)** 7.2×10^{11}

Section 2.3 p. 85
Applications and Problem Solving **1.** 10 A, 20 B, 30 C, 40 D **2.** any arrangement of the numbers 1, 2, 3, 4 **3.** 12 **4.** Answers may vary: top to bottom, left to right: 1, 6, 2, 4, 8 **5.** 2660 cm³ **6.** A = 8, B =7, C = 4 **7.** 981 **8.** 1, 2; 1, 7 **9.** 271 and 41 **10.** 2 and 4 **11.** 10 **12.** Answers may vary. $1^2 + 4^2 + 8^2 = 9^2$ **13.** 5 packages of 15 and 2 packages of 25 **14.** 8

Section 2.4 pp. 89–90
Practice **1.** 2 **2.** 2 **3.** 2 **4.** –7 **5.** 5 **6.** $\frac{16}{15}$ **7.** $-\frac{5}{2}$ **8.** $-\frac{1}{4}$ **9.** $\frac{1}{2}$ **10.** 0 **11.** –1 **12.** 1 **13.** $\frac{3}{5}$ **14.** 7 **15.** $\frac{7}{4}$ **16.** $-\frac{9}{4}$ **17.** 50 years **18.** 75 years **19.** 125 years **20.** 5 h **21.** 20.4 years **22.** 16 days **23.** 30 s

Applications and Problem Solving **24. a)** 9 **b)** $\frac{5}{4}$ **c)** $\frac{27}{46}$ **d)** 2 or –1 **e)** no solution **f)** 2 **25.** 15 min **26. a)** 4.3 g **b)** 59.6 h **27. a)** $\frac{1}{4}$ **b)** 15.9 years **28. a)** $A(t) = A_0(4)^{\frac{t}{7}}$ **b)** 64 times **c)** 3.5 days **d)** 7 days ago **e)** 252 days **29.** Answers may vary. 3 **32.** $x = -17$, $y = 2$ **33. a)** $x = 2$ **b)** The unknown is not an exponent. **34. a)** $\frac{1}{2}$ **b)** 2, –1 **35. a)** 2, 4, approximately –0.77 **b)** $-0.77 < x < 2$, $x > 4$ **36. a)** approximately 1.37 and 9.94 **b)** $1.37 < x < 9.94$

Technology pp. 91–92
1 Are University Tuition Fees Rising Exponentially?
4. $y = 1225(1.10)^x$, where $x = 0$ represents the year 1988–89. **6.** yes **7.** \$9293
2 Using Exponential Regression to Compare Growth Rates **1.** $y = 1340(1.13)^x$; $y = 1186(1.11)^x$ **2.** The fees for medicine appear to be increasing fastest because the graph is steepest. **3.** The base of the power is greatest for medicines, so it is increasing fastest. **4.** $A = 0.855$, $b = 2.778$

Investigating Math p. 93
1 Exploring the Inverse of $y = 2^x$ **2. b)** reflect in the line $y = x$ **d)** domain: $x > 0$, range: all real numbers, x-intercept: 1, y-intercept: none, asymptote: $x = 0$; yes

3. a) $x = 2^y$ **b)** y is the exponent for base 2 that gives the result x.
2 Exploring the Inverse of $y = 10^x$ **1.** reflect in the line $y = x$; domain: $x > 0$, range: all real numbers, x-intercept: 1, y-intercept: none, asymptote: $x = 0$; it is a function; $x = 10^y$; y is the exponent for base 10 that gives the result x. **2. d)** LOG(X) is the exponent for base 10 that gives the result X. **e)** $10^3 = 1000$ **f)** $x > 0$

Section 2.5 pp. 98–100
Practice **1.** $\log_3 9 = 2$ **2.** $\log_6 216 = 3$
3. $\log_4 1024 = 5$ **4.** $\log_8 1 = 0$ **5.** $\log_{49} 7 = \dfrac{1}{2}$
6. $\log_5 \dfrac{1}{25} = -2$ **7.** $\log_8 4 = \dfrac{2}{3}$ **8.** $\log_9 \dfrac{1}{9} = -1$
9. $\log_{10} 10\,000 = 4$ **10.** $\log_a c = b$ **11.** $5^1 = 5$
12. $7^2 = 49$ **13.** $3^6 = 729$ **14.** $2^{-4} = \dfrac{1}{16}$ **15.** $10^0 = 1$
16. $16^{0.5} = 4$ **17.** $8^{\frac{2}{3}} = 4$ **18.** $2^{12} = 4096$ **19.** $10^{-1} = \dfrac{1}{10}$
20. $3^{0.5} = \sqrt{3}$ **21.** 5 **22.** 3 **23.** 3 **24.** 1 **25.** 0 **26.** 4
27. 9 **28.** –2 **29.** –2 **30.** –4 **31.** $\dfrac{1}{2}$ **32.** $\dfrac{7}{2}$ **33.** 4
34. 25 **35.** 4 **36.** 7 **37.** –3 **38.** 2 **39.** 8 **40.** $\dfrac{3}{4}$

Applications and Problem Solving **42.** $0 < x < 16$
43. If $x = \log_3 100$, $3^x = 100$. $3^4 = 81$ and $3^5 = 243$, so x must be between 4 and 5. **45. a)** $y = \log x$: domain: $x > 0$, range: all real numbers; $y = |\log x|$: domain: $x > 0$, range: $y \geq 0$; they have in common all points for which $x \geq 1$. **46. a)** 2.5 times **b)** 25 times
c) 10 times **d)** 7.2 **47. a)** 631 times **b)** 5012 times
48. a) 0.0052% **b)** 0.037% **49.** 2683 times
50. a) 3.44×10^{11} kWh **b)** 5.56×10^9 kWh
c) 8.69×10^{10} kWh **51. c)** 108.7 million kilometres
d) 4347 days **e)** $T = D^m \times 10^b$ **52. a)** $\dfrac{a}{2}$
b) $2a$ **55.** $x < 0$, $x > 1$

Technology p. 101
1 Logarithmic Functions of the Form $f(x) = \log(x + k)$
1. a) $x > 0$ **b)** all real numbers
c) 1 **d)** none **e)** $x = 0$ **2. a)** translation to the left of 1 unit **3. a)** translation to the right of 1 unit
4. horizontal translation of $-k$ units
2 Logarithmic Functions of the Form $f(x) = \log(ax)$
3. horizontal expansion or compression by a factor of
$\dfrac{1}{|a|}$; reflection in the y-axis if $a < 0$

3 Logarithmic Functions of the Form $f(x) = \log(ax + k)$

1. a) $x > -\dfrac{1}{2}$ **b)** all real numbers **c)** 0 **d)** 0 **e)** $x = -\dfrac{1}{2}$

2. a) horizontal translation of $-k$ units, then a horizontal expansion or compression
by a factor of $\dfrac{1}{|a|}$, and a reflection in the y-axis if
$a < 0$ **b)** domain: $x > -\dfrac{k}{a}$, range: all real numbers,
x-intercept: $\dfrac{1-k}{a}$, y-intercept: $\log k$ (if it exists),
asymptote: $x = -\dfrac{k}{a}$ **3. a)** domain: $x > 0$, range: all
real numbers, x-intercept: 10^{-3}, y-intercept: none, asymptote: $x = 0$ **b)** domain: $x > 0$, range: all real numbers, x-intercept: 0.5, y-intercept: none, asymptote: $x = 0$ **c)** domain: $x > 0$, range: all real numbers, x-intercept: 1, y-intercept: none,
asymptote: $x = 0$ **d)** domain: $x > -\dfrac{1}{3}$, range: all real
numbers, x-intercept: 0, y-intercept: 0, asymptote:
$x = -\dfrac{1}{3}$ **e)** domain: $x < 0$, range: all real numbers,
x-intercept: –1, y-intercept: none, asymptote: $x = 0$
5. period: $\dfrac{\pi}{2}$ **6.** period: π **7.** period: π **9.** period: $\dfrac{\pi}{2}$
10. period: 2π

Section 2.6 pp. 106-107
Practice **1.** 1 **2.** 3 **3.** 3 **4.** 4 **5.** 2 **6.** 3 **7.** –1 **8.** 2
9. $\dfrac{2}{3}$ **10.** 1 **11.** 40 **12.** 75 **13.** $-\dfrac{1}{2}$ **14.** $\dfrac{2}{3}$ **15.** $\dfrac{3}{2}$ **16.** 5
17. $\dfrac{1}{2}$ **18.** 20 **19.** $k + 1$ **20.** $k + 3$ **21.** $k - 1$ **22.** $\dfrac{k}{2}$
23. $10k$ **24.** $k - 3$ **25.** $3x$ **26.** $\dfrac{x}{2}$ **27.** $2x + 2$
28. $\dfrac{7x}{5}$ **29.** 10 **30.** 16 **31.** 29 **32.** –7 **33.** 2
34. 2 **35.** 9 **36.** 3 **37.** 3 **38.** 1 **39.** $\log_2 \dfrac{ab}{c}$
40. $\log \dfrac{x^2}{y^5}$ **41.** $\log \dfrac{A\sqrt{B}}{C^3}$ **42.** $\log \dfrac{\sqrt[3]{x}}{y}$

Applications and Problem Solving **44. a)** $y = 3x$,
$x > 0$ **b)** $y = x^3$, $x > 0$ **c)** $y = \sqrt{5x}$, $x > 0$ **d)** $y = \dfrac{x^2}{4}$,
$x > 0$ **47. a)** 4.2 **b)** 10^{-5} mol/L **c)** $10^{-7.8}$ mol/L
48. a) $\text{pH} = 6.1 + \log_{10} B - \log_{10} C$ **b)** 7.2

49. 0.42 kcal/g **50.** $T = \sqrt{kr^3}$ **51. a)** The first line is wrong: $\log_3 0.1 > 2 \log_3 0.1$. **b)** The last line is wrong. Dividing by $\log \frac{1}{2}$, a negative number, changes the sign > to <. **52.** $y = \log x^2$ has a domain of all real numbers except $x = 0$. $y = 2 \log x$ has a domain of $x > 0$. **53. a)** 35 **b)** $\frac{7}{5}$ **c)** 343 **d)** 3 **54.** $\log 2 = \frac{z}{8}$,

$\log 3 = \frac{y}{2} - 1 + \frac{z}{8}$, $\log 4 = \frac{z}{4}$, $\log 5 = 1 - \frac{z}{8}$,

$\log 6 = \frac{z}{4} + \frac{y}{2} - 1$, $\log 7 = \frac{z}{2} - \frac{z}{8}$, $\log 8 = \frac{3z}{8}$,

$\log 9 = y - 2 + \frac{z}{4}$

Section 2.7 pp. 113–115
Practice 1. 4.39 **2.** 4.85 **3.** 0.98 **4.** – 0.06 **5.** – 0.68 **6.** –2.58 **7.** – 4.32 **8.** ±1.82 **9.** 0.972 **10.** 1.684 **11.** 5.060 **12.** 0.502 **13.** 5.637 **14.** 3.538 **Estimates may vary for 15.–20. 15.** 4; 4.08 **16.** 3.1; 3.25 **17.** 4.25; 4.30 **18.** 3.1; 3.08 **19.** 2.25; 2.19 **20.** 3.1; 3.05 **21.** 15 **22.** 3 **23.** $\frac{2}{3}$ **24.** 20 **25.** 5 **26.** 6.1 years **27.** 5.8 years **28.** 9.7 years **29.** 9.2 years **30.** $V(t) = 12\ 500(0.85)^t$ **31.** 4.3 years **32.** 13.0 years **Applications and Problem Solving 40. a)** 3 **b)** 4 **c)** 8 **d)** 6 **e)** 2, 4 **f)** $\frac{21}{8}$ **g)** 5 **h)** $\frac{1}{3}$, 27 **41.** The value of y at $x = 4$ should be 1. Test $x = 1$. **42.** 57 months **43.** 2 days **44. a)** 0.81 **b)** 0.65 h **c)** 0.41 h ago **45. a)** $H(t) = 140(10)^{-0.034t}$ **b)** 95 h **46. a)** 8.1 days **b)** 14.3 days **c)** 2.8 h **d)** 14.8 h **47. a)** $P(t) = 0.5^{\frac{t}{28.8}}$

b) 95.7 years **c)** 88.7% **d)** 57.6 years **54. a)** 8.2 years **b)** 35 years **d)** 22.3 years **56.** $y = 10^b x^m$ **57.** $b = a^{-2}$ or $b = 1$ **60.** 512 **61.** $x = \log_7(t \pm \sqrt{t^2 - 1})$ **62. a)** $\frac{1}{25}$

b) 1, 2 **c)** $2 + \sqrt{3}$ **63.** $\frac{-1 + \sqrt{65}}{2}$

Section 2.8 pp. 119–120
Practice 1. 0.693 **2.** –0.223 **3.** –1.204 **4.** 4.007 **5.** 2.526 **6.** 1.145 **7.** 1.822 **8.** 2.226 **9.** 1.057 **10.** 0.607 **11.** 0.980 **12.** 1.284 **13.** 126.751 **14.** 0.139 **15.** 0.596 **16.** 50.755 **17.** 37.675 **18.** 15.889 **19.** 202.733 **20.** 2.575 **21.** (0, 1) **22.** (0, 1) **23.** no point of intersection **24.** no point of

intersection **25.** (1, 0)
Applications and Problem Solving 26. a) 871 436 **b)** 2004 **27. a)** 95°C **b)** 58°C **28. a)** decreasing **b)** 82 kPa **c)** 5.7 km **29. a)** 3.47 cm **b)** The exponential part of the intensity is squared.

30. a) 14 years **b)** 14.2 years **c)** $t = \frac{100}{r} \ln \frac{A(t)}{A_0}$

31. 67% **32. a)** $a = 22$, $k = 0.002\ 23$ **b)** 11:58 p.m.

c) $t = -\frac{1}{k} \ln \frac{T - T_0}{a}$ **33. a)** 33.52 W **b)** 402.4 days

34. $0 < x < 1$ **35. b)** domain: all real numbers, range: $y \geq 1$, x-intercept: none, y-intercept: 1, axis of

symmetry: $x = 0$; asymptote: none **36.** $\frac{\ln 5}{\ln 10}$ **37.** 0

Career Connection p. 121
1 Carbon-14 to Carbon-12 Ratio 1. 33 846 years **2.** 15 236 years **3.** 51 374 years **4.** 8270 **2 Percent of Carbon-14 1.** 4223 years **2.** false

Section 2.9 p. 123
Applications and Problem Solving 1. $\frac{91}{30}$ **2.** $v = 2$, $w = 1$, $x = -1$, $y = -2$, $z = 3$ **3.** 39 km **4.** 25 005 000 **5.** 0 **6.** 1027 **7.** 12.9 m **8.** 122 **9.** 202 **10.** 728 **11. a)** 632 cm **b)** approximately 260 000 cm^3 **12.** 3 times **13.** 35

Connecting Math and Physics pp. 124–125
1 Comparing the Intensity of Sounds 2. 10^4 times as loud **3.** $\sqrt{10}$ times as loud **4.** $10^{0.1} I_0$ **2 The Effect of Changing Sounds 1.** 113 dB **2.** 90 dB **3.** 87 dB **4.** 120 dB

Review pp. 126–127
1. domain: all real numbers, range: $y > 0$, x-intercept: none, y-intercept: 1, asymptote: $y = 0$ **2.** domain: all real numbers, range: $y > -2$, x-intercept: $\frac{1}{2}$, y-intercept: –1, asymptote: $y = -2$ **3.** domain: all real numbers, range: $y > 0$, x-intercept: none, y-intercept: 1, asymptote: $y = 0$ **4.** domain: all real numbers, range: $y > 3$, x-intercept: none, y-intercept: 4, asymptote: $y = 3$ **5. a)** $P(t) = 200(2)^{\frac{t}{3}}$ **b)** 80 000 **c)** 1250 **6. a)** $P(t) = 1250(1.05)^t$ **b)** domain: $x \geq 0$, range: $y \geq 1250$, x-intercept: none, y-intercept: 1250, asymptote: $y = 0$ **c)** $1675.12 **d)** 22.5 years **7. a)** 50% **b)** 25% **c)** 4.2% **d)** It is 4 times the population 7 years in the future. **8.** $-\frac{3}{2}$ **9.** 2 **10.** $\frac{1}{13}$ **11.** 2 **12.** 2.5 h

13. 5 days **14.** 24 days **15. a)** 160 h **b)** 26.3°C **16.** 5
17. –1 **18.** 5 **19.** –2 **20.** $-\dfrac{1}{2}$ **21.** 64 **22.** 3 **23.** $10^{0.01}$
24. $3 < x < 19$ **25. a)** 2.80×10^9 kWh
b) 8.12×10^6 kWh **26.** $\log \dfrac{x^2}{y^6}$ **27.** $\log 2A^{\frac{5}{2}}B^3$

28. $\log \sqrt{a-b}$ **29. a)** $-2x$ **b)** $10x$ **30. a)** 8 **b)** 60 **c)** 20

31. a) 7.2 **b)** 2.5×10^{-2} mol/L **32. a)** $y = \dfrac{x^{\frac{1}{3}}}{3}$, $x > 0$

b) $y = \dfrac{x^3}{x-2} - 3$, $x > 2$ **33.** 3.41 **34.** 2.27 **35.** –26.36

36. 4.58 **37.** 5.83 **38.** 4.18 **39.** –1, 4 **40.** 1 **41.** $\dfrac{67}{15}$

42. 27.8 days **45.** $x = \dfrac{2b}{b-1}$ **46.** $t = \dfrac{1}{k}\ln\dfrac{A(t)}{A_0}$

47. a) $20\ 960.74 **b)** 9.9 years

Chapter Check p. 128
1. a) $142.31 **b)** $2.70 **c)** 1993 **2. a)** $P(t) = 200(2)^{\frac{t}{5}}$

b) 1056 **c)** 132 **3. a)** $P(t) = 140\ 000(0.88)^t$ **b)** domain:
$t \geq 0$, range: $0 < P \leq 140\ 000$, t-intercept: none,

P-intercept: 140 000, asymptote: $P = 0$ **c)** $57 215

d) 5.4 years **4. a)** $\dfrac{1}{2}$ **b)** no solution **5. a)** 43.2%

b) 13.7 years **6. a)** $-3x$ **b)** $\dfrac{x}{2}$ **7. a)** 9 **b)** 70 **c)** $-\dfrac{9}{4}$

8. a) $y = 1 - 3x, x < \dfrac{1}{3}$ **b)** $y = \dfrac{x^2}{x+3} - 3$, $x \neq 0, x > -3$

c) $y = 32x - 125, x > 4$ **9. a)** 4.42 **b)** 1.43 **c)** 1.82

d) 2.50 **e)** 3.54 **f)** –0.91 **10. a)** $\dfrac{8}{7}$ **b)** 57 **c)** $\dfrac{3}{2}$ **d)** 2

e) 1, 100 **12. a)** 66.3 m **b)** 125 lumens

c) $I(d) = 125(10)^{-\frac{d}{166.67}}$ **13. a)** 367.9 lumens **b)** 23.0 m

Using the Strategies p. 129
1. 768 **2.** Stan is 28, Paula is 21. **3.** $\dfrac{1}{2}$ **4.** 370, 371;

407 **5.** 6 **6.** 2 h 3 min **7.** 2099 **8.** Answers may vary.
$123 - 45 - 67 + 89 = 100$ **9.** $3 + \pi$ or 6.14 m
10. midnight **11.** 60 m from X **12.** 21 978
13. Answers may vary.

Chapter 3

Conics
Getting Started p. 132-3
Recognizing Conics Around Us
1. bridge: parabola; satellite dish: parabola; sunflower:
circle; stadium: ellipse; roof: hyperbola **2.** Answers
will vary.
Warm-Up
1. b) 2, –2 **2. b)** –1 **3. b)** 0 **4. b)** None.
5. b) 3, –3 **6. b)** 2 **7. b)** $5 + \sqrt{13}, 5 - \sqrt{13}$

8. b) $\dfrac{7+3\sqrt{5}}{2}, \dfrac{7-3\sqrt{5}}{2}$ **9. b)** None.

10. b) $\dfrac{9+4\sqrt{6}}{3}, \dfrac{9-4\sqrt{6}}{3}$ **11. b)** 2, $-\dfrac{2}{5}$

12. a) $(-4, -17)$ **b)** minimum **13. a)** $\left(\dfrac{3}{2}, -\dfrac{3}{2}\right)$

b) minimum **14. a)** $(1, -4.5)$ **b)** minimum

15. a) $\left(\dfrac{3}{2}, 7\right)$ **b)** maximum **16. a)** $(-1, -3)$

b) maximum **17.** 13 **18.** 5 **19.** 17 **20.** $\sqrt{53}$ **21.** $3\sqrt{10}$

22. $\sqrt{61}$ **23.** (6, 5) **24.** $\left(\dfrac{1}{2}, 6\right)$ **25.** $\left(0, \dfrac{13}{2}\right)$

26. $\left(5, -\dfrac{3}{2}\right)$ **27.** $\left(-4, \dfrac{7}{2}\right)$ **28.** $\left(-\dfrac{5}{2}, -6\right)$

Mental Math
1. 12 **2.** 4 **3.** 15 **4.** 5 **5.** 21 **6.** 6 **7.** 17 **8.** 8 **9.** 20
10. 9 **11.** 18 **12.** 13 **13.** $x^2 + 6x + 9$
14. $4x^2 - 20x + 25$ **15.** $9x^2 + 6xy + y^2$
16. $x^2 - 12xy + 36y^2$ **17.** $16x^2 - 56xy + 49y^2$
18. $25x^2 + 30xy + 9y^2$ **19.** $16x^2 + 24xy + 9y^2$

20. $121x^2 - 44xy + 4y^2$ **21.** 36 **22.** 16 **23.** $\dfrac{9}{4}$

24. 9 **25.** $\dfrac{25}{4}$ **26.** 64 **27.** $\dfrac{1}{4}$ **28.** 1 **29.** 4 **30.** 1 **31.** 4

32. 1 **33.** $\dfrac{b^2}{4}$ **34.** $\dfrac{b^2}{4a}$, where a is a perfect square

35. a) $(0, -8)$ **b)** up **c)** $x = 0$ **d)** -8, minimum
36. a) $(3, 0)$ **b)** up **c)** $x = 3$ **d)** 0, minimum
37. a) $(5, 2)$ **b)** up **c)** $x = 5$ **d)** 2, minimum
38. a) $(0, 0)$ **b)** down **c)** $x = 0$ **d)** 0, maximum
39. a) $(-4, 5)$ **b)** up **c)** $x = -4$ **d)** 5, minimum
40. a) $(1, -6)$ **b)** up **c)** $x = 1$ **d)** -6, minimum
41. a) $(-3, -2)$ **b)** down **c)** $x = -3$ **d)** -2, maximum

42. $y = \dfrac{4}{5}x^2$ **43.** $y = 0.5(x - 3)^2 - 2$ **44.** $y = (x + 4)^2$

45. $y = -(x - 2)^2 + 4$

Section 3.1 p. 135
Practice 1.–3. Answers will vary.
Applications and Problem Solving 4. Answers will vary. **5.** circle: base; parabola: generator; hyperbola: central axis; ellipse: none **6.** parabola: symmetric about a line through its vertex, exactly halfway between corresponding points on the two branches; ellipse and hyperbola: symmetric about a line through the vertices, and about a line perpendicular to the first line, halfway between the vertices. **7.** closed: ellipse, circle; open: parabola, hyperbola **8.** Answers will vary. **9. a)** circle **b)** parabola or half-hyperbola **c)** ellipse **10.** Slices through the vertex yield degenerate conic sections. A degenerate ellipse or circle is a point. A degenerate parabola is a line. A degenerate hyperbola is a pair of intersecting lines.
11. a) This gives a linear equation. **b) i)** parabola **ii)** circle **iii)** hyperbola **iv)** ellipse

Section 3.2 p. 137
Applications and Problem Solving 1. 10 946
2. 65 536 **3.** 5 882 895 **4.** 7 **5.** 2475 **6.** 3 **7.** 4010
8. Answers will vary.

Section 3.3 pp. 141–142
Practice 1. $x^2 + y^2 = 81$ **2.** $x^2 + y^2 = 16$
3. $x^2 + y^2 = 25$ **4.** $x^2 + y^2 = 64$ **5.** $x^2 + y^2 = 2.25$
6. $x^2 + y^2 = 36$ **7.** $x^2 + y^2 = 5$ **8.** $x^2 + y^2 = 8$
9. $(x + 2)^2 + (y - 5)^2 = 9$ **10.** $(x + 5)^2 + (y + 1)^2 = 49$
11. $(x - 2)^2 + (y - 8)^2 = 100$
12. $(x + 3)^2 + (y - 3)^2 = 144$
13. $(x + 4)^2 + (y + 5)^2 = 25$
14. $(x - 3)^2 + (y + 4)^2 = 1.21$ **15.** $(x - 5)^2 + (y + 4)^2 = 6$
16. $(x + 6)^2 + (y - 7)^2 = 45$ **17.** (0, 0); 11
18. (0, 0); 12 **19.** (0, 0); 3 **20.** (0, 0); 2 **21.** (0, 0); $\dfrac{5}{2}$
22. (5, 9); 4 **23.** (−3, 1); 9 **24.** (−7, −2); 8
25. (6, −4); 3.1 **26.** (−1, 3); $\dfrac{3}{2}$
27. $(x - 8)^2 + (y - 2)^2 = 13$; $x^2 + y^2 - 16x - 4y + 55 = 0$
28. $(x - 4)^2 + (y + 6)^2 = 193$;
$x^2 + y^2 - 8x + 12y - 141 = 0$
29. $(x - 2)^2 + (y - 3)^2 = 26$; $x^2 + y^2 - 4x - 6y - 13 = 0$
30. $(x + 4)^2 + (y - 5)^2 = 25$; $x^2 + y^2 + 8x - 10y + 16 = 0$
31. $(x + 6)^2 + (y + 5)^2 = 36$; $x^2 + y^2 + 12x + 10y + 25 = 0$
32. $(x - 3)^2 + (y + 2)^2 = 16$
33. $(x + 1)^2 + (y + 1)^2 = 29$ **34.** $(x - 1)^2 + (y - 3)^2 = 17$
35. $(x + 2)^2 + (y - 4)^2 = 61$ **36.** (3, 4); 8
37. $\left(\dfrac{7}{2}, -\dfrac{7}{2}\right)$; $\dfrac{13}{2}$ **38.** (−4, −2); $4\sqrt{2}$ **39.** (0, 4); $2\sqrt{2}$

Applications and Problem Solving 46. c) Answers will vary. **47.** $x^2 + (y - 5)^2 = 1.96$;
$(x - 3.5)^2 + (y - 3.5)^2 = 1.755\ 625$;
$(x + 3.5)^2 + (y - 3.5)^2 = 1.840\ 092\ 25$;
$(x - 1.5)^2 + (y + 4.5)^2 = 1.425\ 636$;
$(x - 3.5)^2 + (y + 3)^2 = 0.812\ 702\ 25$;
$(x + 1.5)^2 + (y + 4.5)^2 = 1.1236$;
$(x + 3.5)^2 + (y + 3)^2 = 0.907\ 256\ 25$
48. $x^2 + (y - 5)^2 = 0.7225$ **49.** There is no Bxy term because any line through the centre is an axis of symmetry. $A = C = 1$ because the line at a 45° angle to the x- and y-axes is an axis of symmetry.
50. $(x, y) \to (x + h, y + k)$ **51.** $(x - 4)^2 + (y - 2)^2 = 9$
52. $(x + 5)^2 + (y + 7)^2 = 9$ **53.** $(x + 3)^2 + (y - 8)^2 = 9$
54. $(x - 1)^2 + (y + 6)^2 = 9$
55. $(m - 3, n + 4)$; $(a + 3, b - 4)$
56. $x^2 + y^2 = 16(\sqrt{2} - 1)^2$ **57.** $(x - 1)^2 + (y + 2)^2 = 4$
58. Yes, at two points. **59.** right 2, upward 1
60. $(x + a)^2 + y^2 = \dfrac{1}{4}$ and $x^2 + (y + a)^2 = \dfrac{1}{4}$, for $a = 3$, 1, −1, −3. **61.** $\left(x - \dfrac{\sqrt{2}}{2}\right)^2 + \left(y - \dfrac{\sqrt{2}}{2}\right)^2 = 1$;
$(x - \sqrt{2})^2 + (y - \sqrt{2})^2 = 4$; $(x - 2\sqrt{2})^2 + (y - 2\sqrt{2})^2 = 16$;
$(x - 4\sqrt{2})^2 + (y - 4\sqrt{2})^2 = 64$
62. $(x + 1)^2 + (y - 3)^2 = \dfrac{81}{4}$
63. all combinations of $\left(\pm\dfrac{1}{2}, \pm\dfrac{\sqrt{3}}{2}\right)$ and $\left(\pm\dfrac{\sqrt{3}}{2}, \pm\dfrac{1}{2}\right)$

Section 3.4 pp. 150–152
Practice 1. a) (4, 2) **b)** 6, 2 **c)** $(4 + 2\sqrt{2}, 2)$, $(4 - 2\sqrt{2}, 2)$ **2. a)** (−3, 2) **b)** 6, 4 **c)** $(-3, 2 + \sqrt{5})$, $(-3, 2 - \sqrt{5})$ **3. a)** (2, −4) **b)** 4, 3
c) $\left(2, -4 + \dfrac{\sqrt{7}}{2}\right)$, $\left(2, -4 - \dfrac{\sqrt{7}}{2}\right)$
4. a) (−6, −4) **b)** 7, 5 **c)** $(-6 + \sqrt{6}, -4)$, $(-6 - \sqrt{6}, -4)$
5. a) (0, 0) **b)** 16, 12 **c)** $(2\sqrt{7}, 0)$, $(-2\sqrt{7}, 0)$ **6. a)** (0, 0)
b) 14, 8 **c)** $(0, \sqrt{33})$, $(0, -\sqrt{33})$ **7. a)** (3, 8) **b)** 20, 6
c) $(3, 8 + \sqrt{91})$, $(3, 8 - \sqrt{91})$ **8. a)** (−7, 5) **b)** 10, 4
c) $(-7, 5 + \sqrt{21})$, $(-7, 5 - \sqrt{21})$ **9. a)** (0, 0) **b)** 8, 6
c) $(\sqrt{7}, 0)$, $(-\sqrt{7}, 0)$ **10. a)** (−12, 1) **b)** $2\sqrt{7}$, 2
c) $(-12, 1 + \sqrt{6})$, $(-12, 1 - \sqrt{6})$
21. $\dfrac{(x - 3)^2}{49} + \dfrac{(y + 2)^2}{9} = 1$;
$9x^2 + 49y^2 - 54x + 196y - 164 = 0$

22. $\dfrac{(x+1)^2}{16}+\dfrac{(y+2)^2}{36}=1$;

$9x^2+4y^2+18x+16y-119=0$

23. $\dfrac{x^2}{9}+\dfrac{(y-4)^2}{25}=1$; $25x^2+9y^2-72y-81=0$

24. $\dfrac{(x-4)^2}{169}+\dfrac{(y+1)^2}{144}=1$;

$144x^2+169y^2-1152x+338y-21\,863=0$

25. a) $(-1, 4)$ **b)** $2\sqrt{30},\ 2\sqrt{10}$

c) $(-1,\ 4+2\sqrt{5}),\ (-1,\ 4-2\sqrt{5})$ **26. a)** $(0, 3)$ **b)** $22, 2$

c) $(2\sqrt{30},\ 3),\ (-2\sqrt{30},\ 3)$ **27. a)** $\left(\dfrac{1}{2},\ 1\right)$ **b)** $10, 6$

c) $\left(\dfrac{9}{2},\ 1\right),\ \left(-\dfrac{7}{2},\ 1\right)$

Applications and Problem Solving
28. Answers will vary.
30. $b^2x^2+a^2y^2-2b^2hx-2a^2ky+(b^2h^2+a^2k^2-a^2b^2)=0$
31. Answers will vary.
32. b) x-intercepts: $4, -4$; y-intercepts: $1, -1$
c) horizontal expansion by a factor of 4 **d)** $(4x, y)$
e) x-intercepts: $1, -1$; y-intercepts: $3, -3$; vertical expansion by a factor of 3; $(x, 3y)$
f) x-intercepts: $3, -3$; y-intercepts: $2, -2$; horizontal expansion by a factor of 3 and vertical expansion by a factor of 2; $(3x, 2y)$ **g)** $(x, y) \rightarrow (ax, by)$
33. horizontal expansion by a factor of 2; vertical

expansion by a factor of 5; $\dfrac{x^2}{4}+\dfrac{y^2}{25}=1$

34. translation right 5 and upward 7; horizontal

expansion by a factor of 2; $\dfrac{(x-5)^2}{4}+(y-7)^2=1$

35. translation left 4; vertical expansion by a factor

of 2; $(x+4)^2+\dfrac{y^2}{4}=1$

36. translation left 3 and upward 6; horizontal
expansion by a factor of 2; vertical expansion by a

factor of 3; $\dfrac{(x+3)^2}{4}+\dfrac{(y-6)^2}{9}=1$

37. translation right 6 and upward 2; horizontal

expansion by a factor of $\dfrac{5}{2}$; vertical expansion by a

factor of 2; $\dfrac{(x-6)^2}{\dfrac{25}{4}}+\dfrac{(y-2)^2}{4}=1$

38. translation right 5 and downward 6; horizontal

expansion by a factor of 4; vertical expansion by a

factor of $\dfrac{3}{2}$; $\dfrac{(x-5)^2}{16}+\dfrac{(y+6)^2}{\dfrac{9}{4}}=1$ **39.** 3.73 m; 2.76 m

40. a) $\dfrac{x^2}{115^2}+\dfrac{y^2}{95^2}=1$ **b)** $\dfrac{x^2}{95^2}+\dfrac{y^2}{60^2}=1$; $y\geq 0$

c) 84.4 m **41.** $\dfrac{x^2}{16}+\dfrac{y^2}{25}=1$; $\dfrac{x^2}{16}+\dfrac{y^2}{9}=1$; $\dfrac{x^2}{4}+\dfrac{y^2}{9}=1$;

$\dfrac{x^2}{4}+\dfrac{y^2}{2}=1$ **42.** yes **43. a)** Angles should be equal.

44. 30 **45.** The corners of the square are on $y = x$ or

$y = -x$. In either case, $x^2=\dfrac{a^2b^2}{a^2+b^2}$, and area is $4x^2$.

Computer Data Bank p. 153
1 Communication Satellites   2. Italsat F2
2 Weather Satellites   2. DMSP 36, 37, and 38,
NOAA-14 and -15, Meteor 3-6; GOES-8, -9,
and -10
3 Elliptical Orbits   1. a) Molniya 1T-2 **b)** 39 199 km,
1156 km **c)** 45 536 is the sum of the apogee and the
radius of Earth, 7493 is the sum of the perigee and
the radius of Earth **d)** $a = (45\,536 + 7493)/2$,
or (apogee + perigee + 2 × radius)/2;
$c = (45\,536 - 7493)/2$, or simply (apogee – perigee)/2
e) $a = 26\,514.5$ km; $c = 19\,021.5$ km
f) $b^2 = 341\,201\,248$

g) $\dfrac{x^2}{703\,018\,710.25}+\dfrac{y^2}{341\,201\,248}=1$

Section 3.5 pp.159–163
Practice   1. a) $(0, 0)$ **b)** transverse axis: horizontal
4 units; conjugate axis: vertical 2 units

c) $(2, 0),\ (-2, 0)$ **d)** $\pm\dfrac{1}{2}$ **2. a)** $(0, 0)$

b) transverse axis: vertical 2 units;

conjugate axis: horizontal 4 units **c)** $(0, 1),\ (0, -1)$

d) $\pm\dfrac{1}{2}$ **3. a)** $(-3, 3)$ **b)** transverse axis: vertical 8 units;

conjugate axis: horizontal 2 units **c)** $(-3, 7),\ (-3, -1)$
d) ± 4 **4. a)** $(6, -8)$ **b)** transverse axis: horizontal
4 units; conjugate axis: vertical 4 units
c) $(8, -8),\ (4, -8)$ **d)** ± 1 **5. a)** $(12, 2)$ **b)** transverse axis:
horizontal 12 units; conjugate axis: vertical 8 units

c) $(18, 2),\ (6, 2)$ **d)** $\pm\dfrac{2}{3}$ **6. a)** $(0, 0)$ **b)** transverse axis:

horizontal 22 units; conjugate axis: vertical 30 units

c) $(11, 0)$, $(-11, 0)$ **d)** $\pm\dfrac{15}{11}$ **7. a)** $(1, 0)$ **b)** transverse axis: horizontal 24 units; conjugate axis: vertical 16 units **c)** $(13, 0)$, $(-11, 0)$ **d)** $\pm\dfrac{2}{3}$ **8. a)** $(-3, 5)$ **b)** transverse axis: horizontal 18 units; conjugate axis: vertical 8 units **c)** $(6, 5)$, $(-12, 5)$ **d)** $\pm\dfrac{4}{9}$ **9. a)** $(0, -4)$ **b)** transverse axis: vertical 14 units; conjugate axis: horizontal 20 units **c)** $(0, 3)$, $(0, -11)$ **d)** $\pm\dfrac{7}{10}$

10. a) $(2, 8)$ **b)** transverse axis: vertical 3 units; conjugate axis: horizontal 26 units **c)** $\left(2, \dfrac{19}{2}\right)$, $\left(2, \dfrac{13}{2}\right)$ **d)** $\pm\dfrac{3}{26}$ **11. a)** $(3, 0)$ **b)** transverse axis: vertical 28 units; conjugate axis: horizontal 16 units **c)** $(3, 14)$, $(3, -14)$ **d)** $\pm\dfrac{7}{4}$

12. a) $(-10, -4)$ **b)** transverse axis: horizontal 12 units; conjugate axis: vertical 10 units **c)** $(-16, -4)$, $(-4, -4)$ **d)** $\pm\dfrac{5}{6}$ **13. a)** $(-2, -6)$ **b)** transverse axis: vertical 6 units; conjugate axis: horizontal 32 units **c)** $(-2, -3)$, $(-2, -9)$ **d)** $\pm\dfrac{3}{16}$

14. $\dfrac{y^2}{36} - \dfrac{x^2}{16} = 1$; $9x^2 - 4y^2 + 144 = 0$

15. $\dfrac{(x-2)^2}{4} - \dfrac{(y-3)^2}{9} = 1$; $9x^2 - 4y^2 - 36x + 24y - 36 = 0$

16. $\dfrac{(x+5)^2}{9} - \dfrac{(y-1)^2}{4} = 1$; $4x^2 - 9y^2 + 40x + 18y + 55 = 0$

17. $\dfrac{(y-2)^2}{4} - \dfrac{(x-2)^2}{4} = 1$; $x^2 - y^2 - 4x + 4y + 4 = 0$

18. $\dfrac{(y+1)^2}{4} - \dfrac{(x+2)^2}{\frac{1}{4}} = 1$; $16x^2 - y^2 + 64x - 2y + 67 = 0$

19. $\dfrac{(x-4)^2}{4} - \dfrac{y^2}{9} = 1$; $9x^2 - 4y^2 - 72x + 108 = 0$

20. $\dfrac{x^2}{16} - \dfrac{(y-5)^2}{9} = 1$; $9x^2 - 16y^2 + 160y - 544 = 0$

21. $\dfrac{(y-2)^2}{4} - \dfrac{(x-1)^2}{165} = 1$; $4x^2 - 165y^2 - 8x + 660y + 4 = 0$

22. $\dfrac{(y-3)^2}{9} - \dfrac{(x+1)^2}{16} = 1$; $9x^2 - 16y^2 + 18x + 96y + 9 = 0$

23. $\dfrac{(y+8)^2}{144} - \dfrac{(x-6)^2}{16} = 1$; $9x^2 - y^2 - 108x - 16y + 404 = 0$ **33. a)** $(3, -1)$ **b)** $(7, -1)$ and $(-1, -1)$ **c)** $x - 2y - 5 = 0$ and $x + 2y - 1 = 0$ **34. a)** $(-5, 1)$ **b)** $(-5, 4)$ and $(-5, -2)$ **c)** $6x + y + 29 = 0$ and $6x - y + 31 = 0$ **35. a)** $(5, 3)$ **b)** $(11, 3)$ and $(-1, 3)$ **c)** $x - 6y + 13 = 0$ and $x + 6y - 23 = 0$ **36. a)** $(-2, 3)$ **b)** $(0, 3)$ and $(-4, 3)$ **c)** $5x - 2y + 16 = 0$ and $5x + 2y + 4 = 0$

Applications and Problem Solving
38. $b^2x^2 - a^2y^2 - 2b^2hx + 2a^2ky + (b^2h^2 - a^2k^2 - a^2b^2) = 0$
39. a) The x^2 and y^2 terms are equal but opposite. **c)** The asymptotes are perpendicular.
40. b) y-intercepts: ± 1 **c)** horizontal expansion by a factor of 3 **d)** $(3x, y)$ **e)** y-intercepts: ± 4; vertical expansion by a factor 4; $(x, 4y)$ **f)** y-intercepts: ± 3; vertical expansion by a factor of 3; horizontal expansion by a factor of 2; $(2x, 3y)$ **g)** $(x, y) \rightarrow (bx, ay)$ **h)** $(x, y) \rightarrow (by, ax)$
41. b) $x = 0$ and $y = 0$ **c)** rectangular
42. $\dfrac{(y-2)^2}{9} - \dfrac{(x-2)^2}{16} = 1$ **43.** Use $y^2 - x^2 = 1$; translation left 4 and upward 3; vertical expansion by a factor of 4; $\dfrac{(y-3)^2}{16} - (x+4)^2 = 1$.

44. Use $y^2 - x^2 = 1$; translation right 4 and upward 6; horizontal expansion by a factor of 2; $(y-6)^2 - \dfrac{(x-4)}{4} = 1$. **45.** Use $x^2 - y^2 = 1$; translation right 4 and downward 6; $(x-4)^2 - (y+6)^2 = 1$. **46.** Answers will vary.
47. b) 125 km/h **48. b)** 21.375 L **49.** Answers will vary. **50.** transverse 6, conjugate 10 **51.** Answers will vary. **52.** Answers will vary.
53. a) $xy = 2$; transverse and conjugate axes are both

2; vertices are $\left(\dfrac{1}{\sqrt{2}}, \dfrac{1}{\sqrt{2}}\right), \left(-\dfrac{1}{\sqrt{2}}, -\dfrac{1}{\sqrt{2}}\right)$; B = 1

b) $y^2 - x^2 = 1$; transverse and conjugate axes are both 2; vertices are (0, 1), (0, –1); B = 0
c) Image is the same circle. **d)** rotation of 45° counterclockwise **e)** $2xy + 1 = 0$; $x^2 - y^2 = 1$

Section 3.6 pp.167–169
Practice **1.** $x^2 = 12(y + 1)$ **2.** $x^2 = -10\left(y + \dfrac{1}{2}\right)$

3. $y^2 = 6\left(x - \dfrac{5}{2}\right)$ **4.** $y^2 = -8(x + 1)$

5. $(x - 2)^2 = 6\left(y - \dfrac{1}{2}\right)$

6. $(y + 2)^2 = -4(x + 2)$ **7.** $(y + 1)^2 = -20x$

8. $(x + 4)^2 = -2\left(y - \dfrac{9}{2}\right)$ **9.** $(y - 2)^2 = -12(x - 4)$;

$y^2 + 12x - 4y - 44 = 0$ **10.** $(x + 3)^2 = -8(y + 1)$;

$x^2 + 6x + 8y + 17 = 0$ **11.** $y^2 = -12x$; $y^2 + 12x = 0$

12. $(y + 5)^2 = \dfrac{16}{9}(x + 7)$; $y^2 - \dfrac{16}{9}x + 10y + \dfrac{113}{9} = 0$

13. $(x - 2)^2 = -8(y + 4)$; $x^2 - 4x + 8y + 36 = 0$

14. $(x - 3)^2 = 8(y + 2)$; $x^2 - 6x - 8y - 7 = 0$ **15.** focus: (3, 0); vertex: (0, 0); directrix: $x = -3$; axis of symmetry:

$y = 0$; opens right. **16.** focus: $\left(3, \dfrac{9}{4}\right)$; vertex: (3, 3);

directrix: $y = \dfrac{15}{4}$; axis of symmetry: $x = 3$;

opens down. **17.** focus: $\left(-2, -\dfrac{7}{2}\right)$; vertex: (–2, –3);

directrix: $y = -\dfrac{5}{2}$; axis of symmetry: $x = -2$;

opens down. **18.** focus: (–8, 4); vertex: (–6, 4); directrix: $x = -4$; axis of symmetry: $y = 4$; opens left.
19. ellipse **20.** circle **21.** hyperbola **22.** parabola
23. parabola **24.** circle
25. $(y + 2)^2 = 12(x + 1)$; $y^2 - 12x + 4y - 8 = 0$

26. $\dfrac{(x - 3)^2}{9} + \dfrac{(y - 4)^2}{\dfrac{49}{4}} = 1$;

$49x^2 + 36y^2 - 294x - 288y + 576 = 0$

27. $\dfrac{(y + 4)^2}{4} - (x - 2)^2 = 1$; $4x^2 - y^2 - 16x - 8y + 4 = 0$

28. $\dfrac{(x + 4)^2}{25} + \dfrac{(y - 3)^2}{4} = 1$;

$4x^2 + 25y^2 + 32x - 150y + 189 = 0$

29. $(x + 3)^2 = -2\left(y + \dfrac{3}{2}\right)$; $x^2 + 6x + 2y + 12 = 0$

30. $(x + 3)^2 + (y + 2)^2 = 9$; $x^2 + y^2 + 6x + 4y + 4 = 0$

31. $\dfrac{(x + 4)^2}{9} - \dfrac{\left(y + \dfrac{3}{2}\right)^2}{\dfrac{1}{4}} = 1$;

$x^2 - 36y^2 + 8x - 108y - 90 = 0$

32. $(x + 4)^2 + (y - 3)^2 = 25$ **33.** $x^2 + (y + 5)^2 = 16$

34. $\dfrac{x^2}{25} - \dfrac{y^2}{16} = 1$ **35.** $\dfrac{y^2}{\dfrac{1}{16}} - \dfrac{x^2}{\dfrac{1}{9}} = 1$

36. $(x - 2)^2 = 2(y + 5)$ **37.** $(y - 4)^2 = 2(x - 3)$

38. $\dfrac{(x + 3)^2}{16} - \dfrac{(y + 1)^2}{4} = 1$ **39.** $(x + 4)^2 = -\dfrac{2}{3}(y + 3)$

40. $\dfrac{(y - 2)^2}{16} - \dfrac{(x - 1)^2}{9} = 1$ **41.** $\dfrac{(x - 3)^2}{25} + \dfrac{(y - 4)^2}{4} = 1$

42. $\dfrac{(x - 2)^2}{9} + \dfrac{(y + 1)^2}{4} = 1$ **43.** $\dfrac{(x - 3)^2}{\dfrac{9}{4}} - \dfrac{(y - 2)^2}{16} = 1$

Applications and Problem Solving
45. $x^2 - 2hx - 4py + (h^2 + 4pk) = 0$ **46. b)** yes **c)** no
47. a) yes **b)** no **48. a)** $x^2 = 1004y$ **b)** 0.90 m
c) Answers will vary. **49. a)** Answers will vary.
b) Answers will vary. **c)** 6.1 m **d)** 11.1 m
e) Answers will vary.

Technology pp. 170–171
1 The Parabola 2. Answers will vary.
2 The Ellipse 2. Answers will vary.
3 The Hyperbola 1. Step b); point C should not be between A and B

Section 3.7 p. 173
Applications and Problem Solving 1. $324.99
2. Loser of first game started with $39. Loser of second game started with $21. Loser of third game

started with $12. **3.** 606 **4.** $37\dfrac{37}{44}$ **5.** 2401 **6.** $\dfrac{17}{450}$

7. none **8. a)** 5 **b)** 4 **9.** 6-step solution: FLOUR, FLOOR, FLOOD, BLOOD, BROOD, BROAD,

BREAD. **10.** 512 and 1 953 125
11. Answers will vary.

Connecting Math and History pp. 174–175
1 Quadrature of a Rectangle **9.** $DG^2 = FG^2 - FD^2$
$= (FG + FD)(FG - FD) = (AF + FD)(FE - ED)$
$= (AD)(ED) = (AD)(DC)$
2 Quadrature of a Triangle
6. $\frac{1}{2}(AC)(BD) = (AC)(\frac{1}{2}BD) = (AC)(ED) = (AC)(AF)$

Review pp. 176–177
2. a) hyperbola **b)** circle **c)** ellipse
3. $(x - 2)^2 + (y + 6)^2 = 16$ **4.** $(x + 1)^2 + (y + 3)^2 = 7$
5. $(x - 5)^2 + (y + 2)^2 = 13$; $x^2 + y^2 - 10x + 4y + 16 = 0$
6. $(x + 5)^2 + (y - 6)^2 = 25$; $x^2 + y^2 + 10x - 12y + 36 = 0$
7. $(x - 2)^2 + (y - 2)^2 = 9$; $x^2 + y^2 - 4x - 4y - 1 = 0$
8. $(x + 1)^2 + (y - 6)^2 = 45$; $x^2 + y^2 + 2x - 12y - 8 = 0$

9. $\left(-\frac{9}{2}, 4\right)$; $\frac{\sqrt{129}}{2}$ **10.** $(-2, 0)$; $2\sqrt{3}$

13. $(x + 1)^2 + (y - 3)^2 = 16$ **14.** $(x - 4)^2 + (y + 6)^2 = 16$
15. $(x + 2)^2 + (y - 5)^2 = 14\ 400$ **16.** Answers will vary.
17. $(6, -2)$; 10, 6; $(10, -2)$, $(2, -2)$
18. $(-2, -4)$; 12, 10; $(-2, -4 + \sqrt{11})$, $(-2, -4 - \sqrt{11})$
19. $(2, -7)$; 8, 2; $(2, -7 + \sqrt{15})$, $(2, -7 - \sqrt{15})$
20. $(0, 0)$; 6, 4; $(\sqrt{5}, 0)$, $(-\sqrt{5}, 0)$
21. $\frac{x^2}{169} + \frac{y^2}{25} = 1$; $25x^2 + 169y^2 - 4225 = 0$

22. $(x - 1)^2 + \frac{(y + 3)^2}{4} = 1$; $4x^2 + y^2 - 8x + 6y + 9 = 0$

23. $(-2, 0)$; major axis: 8, minor axis: 4; $(-2, 2\sqrt{3})$,

$(-2, -2\sqrt{3})$ **24.** $(-1, -2)$; major axis: 8, minor axis:

$\frac{8}{\sqrt{3}}$; $\left(-1, -2 + \frac{4\sqrt{2}}{\sqrt{3}}\right)$, $\left(-1, -2 - \frac{4\sqrt{2}}{\sqrt{3}}\right)$

25. $(x + 3)^2 + 4y^2 = 9$ **26.** $(x - 6)^2 + 4y^2 = 9$
27. $x^2 + 100y^2 = 225$ **28.** $\frac{x^2}{348\ 100} + \frac{y^2}{218\ 500} = 1$

29. Answers will vary. **30. a)** $(0, 0)$ **b)** transverse axis:
vertical, 26; conjugate axis: horizontal, 22 **c)** $(0, \pm 13)$

d) $\pm\frac{13}{11}$ **31. a)** $(-5, -3)$ **b)** transverse axis: horizontal,

10; conjugate axis: vertical, 8 **c)** $(0, -3)$, $(-10, -3)$ **d)** $\pm\frac{4}{5}$

32. $\frac{(x - 3)^2}{4} - \frac{(y - 1)^2}{\frac{16}{9}} = 1$; $4x^2 - 9y^2 - 24x + 18y + 11 = 0$

33. $\frac{(x + 1)^2}{4} - \frac{(y - 5)^2}{5} = 1$;
$5x^2 - 4y^2 + 10x + 40y - 115 = 0$

36. $(0, 0)$; $(\pm\sqrt{6}, 0)$; $x \pm y = 0$
37. $(-4, 2)$; $(-4, 5)$, $(-4, -1)$; $3x - 5y + 22 = 0$,
$3x + 5y + 2 = 0$ **38.** $(y - 3)^2 = 8(x + 4)$;
$y^2 - 8x - 6y - 23 = 0$
39. $(x - 5)^2 = 8(y + 3)$; $x^2 - 10x - 8y + 1 = 0$
40. $(x - 4)^2 = -(y - 3)$; $x^2 - 8x + y + 13 = 0$
41. focus: $(0, 4)$; vertex: $(0, 1)$; directrix $y = -2$;
axis: $x = 0$; opens up. **42.** focus: $(7, 6)$; vertex: $(5, 1)$;
directrix $x = 3$; axis: $y = 1$; opens right.
43. a) Ellipse. Major axis is vertical. **b)** Ellipse. Major
axis is horizontal. **c)** Pair of parallel lines $y = 12$,
$y = -12$. **d)** Hyperbola. Transverse axis is vertical.

44. in metres: $x^2 = \frac{27}{8} y$; $\left(0, \frac{27}{32}\right)$

in centimetres: $x^2 = \frac{675}{2} y$; $\left(0, \frac{675}{8}\right)$

Chapter Check p.178
1. Face the flashlight parallel to the plane surface to
get a circle. Tilt the flashlight a little to get an ellipse.
Tilt it more to get a parabola. Tilt it even more to get
one branch of a hyperbola. **2.** circle;

$(x - 3)^2 + (y + 2)^2 = 16$ **3.** hyperbola; $\frac{x^2}{36} - \frac{y^2}{64} = 1$

4. parabola; $(x - 5)^2 = \frac{1}{2}(y + 3)$

5. ellipse; $\frac{(x + 3)^2}{25} + (y + 8)^2 = 1$

6. ellipse; $\frac{x^2}{25} + \frac{y^2}{9} = 1$ **7.** ellipse; $\frac{(x - 2)^2}{9} + \frac{y^2}{\frac{1}{25}} = 1$

8. circle; $(x + 3)^2 + (y - 4)^2 = 36$

9. hyperbola; $\frac{(y + 7)^2}{9} - \frac{(x - 10)^2}{4} = 1$

10. hyperbola; $\frac{(y + 8)^2}{144} - \frac{(x + 2)^2}{4} = 1$

11. $y^2 = x + 7$; $y^2 - x - 7 = 0$

12. $xy = 5$; $xy - 5 = 0$ **13.** $\dfrac{\left(x+\dfrac{1}{2}\right)^2}{9} + \dfrac{\left(y-\dfrac{1}{2}\right)^2}{25} = 1$;

$50x^2\ 18y^2 + 50x - 18y - 433 = 0$
14. $(x + 2)^2 + (y + 2)^2 = 4$; $x^2 + y^2 + 4x + 4y + 4 = 0$

15. $\dfrac{\left(x-\dfrac{9}{2}\right)^2}{\dfrac{49}{4}} - \dfrac{(y+1)^2}{4} = 1$;

$16x^2 - 49y^2 - 144x - 98y + 79 = 0$
16. $(x + 6)^2 = -16(y + 2)$; $x^2 + 12x + 16y + 68 = 0$

17. $\dfrac{(x+2)^2}{5} + \dfrac{y^2}{45} = 1$; centre: $(-2, 0)$

18. $(x - 1)^2 + (y + 2)^2 = 10$; centre: $(1, -2)$

19. $\dfrac{(y+1)^2}{9} - \dfrac{x^2}{4} = 1$; centre: $(0, -1)$

20. $(x + 2)^2 = \dfrac{4}{3}(y + 6)$; vertex: $(-2, -6)$

21. $4x^2 + y^2 + 16x - 2y - 19 = 0$; $A = 4$, $C = 1$
22. $9x^2 + 36x + 4y - 12 = 0$; $A = 9$, $C = 0$
23. $16x^2 - 9y^2 - 64x - 72y + 64 = 0$; $A = 16$, $C = -9$

24. $x^2 + y^2 + 10y + 9 = 0$; $A = 1$, $C = 1$ **25.** $x^2 = -\dfrac{45}{2}y$
26. 35.7 m

Problem Solving p. 179
1. $(3, \sqrt{3})$, $(3, -\sqrt{3})$ **2.** 999 **3.** 511 purchased exactly
1 item, 112 purchased exactly 2 items, and 32
purchased exactly 3 items. **4.** 1.06 m **5.** Make a
tetrahedron using one triangle as the base and the
three other toothpicks as edges of the 3-dimensional
object.
6. $(x - (\sqrt{2} - 1)r)^2 + (y - (\sqrt{2} - 1)r)^2 = (3 - 2\sqrt{2})r^2$
7. all the points on the circle $(x - 1)^2 + (y - 1)^2 = 2$
8. 387 420 489 **9.** 300 **10.** 128π cm^3 **11.** $n^5 = 5^{5x+5}$
12. $3\sqrt{3}{:}2$ **13.** 3 **14.** 4 **15.** 12
16. $A = 1$, $B = 4$, $C = 8$

Cumulative Review, Chapters 1–3 pp. 180–181
1. a) upward 2 units **b)** right 3 units **c)** left 1 unit,
downward 4 units **d)** right 2 units, upward 5 units
2. a) $y = 0$ **b)** $x = 0$ **c)** $y = x$ **3. a)** yes **b)** no **c)** yes
5. a) vertical expansion by a factor of 5, a reflection in
the x-axis, and a translation upward 3 units
b) horizontal expansion by a factor of 2, a vertical
expansion by a factor of 4, and a translation upward
2 units **c)** vertical expansion by a factor of 2, and a

translation left 3 units and downward 4 units.

d) horizontal compression by a factor of $\dfrac{1}{7}$, and a
translation right 5 units and upward 1 unit

e) horizontal compression by a factor of $\dfrac{1}{8}$, and a
translation left 7 units **f)** vertical compression by a
factor of $\dfrac{1}{3}$, a horizontal compression by a factor of $\dfrac{1}{2}$,
and a translation right 3 units and downward 9 units
8. a) $A = 1500(1.055)^t$ **b)** \$1960.44 **c)** 13 years
9. a) $P(t) = 12\ 000(0.93)^t$ **b)** 9700 **c)** 10 years **10.** $-\dfrac{1}{4}$

11. -1 **12.** $\dfrac{2}{3}$ **13.** 0 **14.** 8 h **15.** 3 h **16.** 5 **17.** 0.01

18. -3 **19.** 3 **20.** $\log_5 \dfrac{1}{x^4 z^3}$ **21.** $\log_6 \dfrac{b}{ac^2}$

22. $\log 5b^3 \sqrt[6]{a}$ **23.** $\log_2 \sqrt[4]{x + y}$, $x > 3y$, $x > 0$, $y > 0$

24. $2a + 2b$ **25.** 3.91 **26.** 1.63 **27.** 0.32 **28.** 2.44

29. $-3\dfrac{2}{3}$ **30.** 6 **31.** 8 **32.** 1, 5 **33. a)** 1.2629

b) 220 970 **34. a)** circle, ellipse, parabola, hyperbola
35. $(x - 6)^2 + (y + 2)^2 = 49$ **36.** $(x + 4)^2 + (y + 5)^2 = 8$
37. $(x - 2)^2 + (y + 5)^2 = 34$; $x^2 + y^2 - 4x + 10y - 5 = 0$
38. $(x - 3)^2 + (y - 2)^2 = 17$; $x^2 + y^2 - 6x - 4y - 4 = 0$
39. $(-5, 9)$; 4 **40.** $(0, -5)$; 6 **43. a)** $(0, 0)$ **b)** transverse:

horizontal, 4; conjugate: vertical, 6 **c)** $(\pm 2, 0)$ **d)** $\pm\dfrac{3}{2}$

e) $\dfrac{x^2}{4} - \dfrac{y^2}{9} = 1$; $9x^2 - 4y^2 = 36$ **44. a)** $(2, 1)$

b) transverse: vertical, 4; conjugate: horizontal, 8

c) $(2, 3)$, $(2, -1)$ **d)** $\pm\dfrac{1}{2}$ **e)** $\dfrac{(y-1)^2}{4} - \dfrac{(x-2)^2}{16} = 1$;

$x^2 - 4y^2 - 4x + 8y + 16 = 0$

Chapter 4

Trigonometric Functions p. 183
1. a) There appears to be a peak every 10–12 years,
but the peaks are all different sizes. **b)** 9 **c)** 11 **d)** Yes.
The average length of time between peaks is the same
as the average length of time between low numbers.
2. no **3. a)** 140 **b)** Answers may vary. 90

Getting Started pp. 184–185
Building a Trig Rule
1. Estimates may vary. Exact answers are rounded to

3 decimal places. **a)** 0.559 **b)** 0.423 **c)** 0.087 **d)** 0.191
e) 0.999 **f)** 0.174 **2.** Estimates may vary. Exact
answers are rounded to 1 decimal place where
necessary. **a)** 11.5° **b)** 60° **c)** 64.2° **d)** 72.5° **e)** 44.4°
f) 23.6° **3.** Since the hypotenuse has length 1 unit,
the sine of the angle is equal to the length of the side
opposite the angle, and the cosine of the angle is
equal to the length of the side adjacent to the angle.
4. a) Yes. Make a semicircle for template 1 and label
it in degrees from 0° to 180°. Label the horizontal
diameter from −1 to 1. **b)** Yes. Make a full circle for
template 1 and label it in degrees from 0° to 360°.
Label the horizontal diameter from −1 to 1. For
angles greater than 180°, the sine of the angle must
be negative. **c)** Yes. Use the model in part b, after
converting the negative angle to a coterminal positive
angle.
Mental Math   1. 8 cm **2.** 13 cm **3.** 3 cm **4.** 2 m
5. 40° **6.** 45° **7.** 30° **8.** 45° **9.** $\cos \theta = \dfrac{3}{5}$, $\tan \theta = \dfrac{4}{3}$

10. $\sin \theta = \dfrac{12}{13}$, $\tan \theta = \dfrac{12}{5}$ **11.** $\sin \theta = \dfrac{\sqrt{3}}{2}$, $\cos \theta = \dfrac{1}{2}$

Estimates may vary for 12. and 13.   12. 30 cm²
13. 19 cm²

Section 4.1 pp. 189–191

Practice   1. 0, $\dfrac{\pi}{6}, \dfrac{\pi}{4}, \dfrac{\pi}{3}, \dfrac{\pi}{2}, \dfrac{2\pi}{3}, \dfrac{3\pi}{4}, \dfrac{5\pi}{6}$, π

2. 210°, 225°, 240°, 270°, 300°, 315°, 330° **3.** 57.3°
4. 22.9° **5.** −160.4° **6.** 243.5° **7.** −206.3° **8.** 36.1°
9. −74.5° **10.** 179.9° **11.** 444.0° **12.** 0.70 **13.** 1.10
14. 2.53 **15.** 0.33 **16.** −1.75 **17.** 0.57 **18.** 3.59
19. 0.48 **20.** −1.96 **21.** 1.4 **22.** 1.4 **23.** 1.9 **24.** 2.3
25. 3.7 **26.** 5.5 **27.** 16.8 **28.** 12.2 **29.** 400°, −320°
30. 630°, −90° **31.** 300°, −420° **32.** 515°, −205°
33. 160°, −560° **34.** 672°, −48° **35.** $\dfrac{11\pi}{4}, -\dfrac{5\pi}{4}$

36. $\dfrac{3\pi}{2}, -\dfrac{5\pi}{2}$ **37.** $\dfrac{7\pi}{3}, -\dfrac{5\pi}{3}$ **38.** $\dfrac{9\pi}{8}, -\dfrac{23\pi}{8}$

39. $\dfrac{23\pi}{6}, -\dfrac{\pi}{6}$ **40.** $\dfrac{4\pi}{5}, -\dfrac{16\pi}{5}$ **41.** no **42.** yes
43. no **44.** yes **45.** no **46.** no **47.** 40° **48.** 155°

49. 120° **50.** 220° **51.** 265° **52.** 230° **53.** π **54.** $\dfrac{5\pi}{3}$

55. $\dfrac{3\pi}{2}$ **56.** $\dfrac{5\pi}{3}$ **57.** $\dfrac{15\pi}{8}$ **58.** $\dfrac{11\pi}{6}$ **59.** −55°
60. −242° **61.** −60° **62.** −230° **63.** −148° **64.** −20°

65. $-\dfrac{4\pi}{3}$ **66.** $-\dfrac{5\pi}{6}$ **67.** $-\dfrac{3\pi}{8}$ **68.** $-\dfrac{\pi}{3}$ **69.** $-\dfrac{\pi}{4}$

70. $-\dfrac{3\pi}{2}$

Applications and Problem Solving   71. a) 0.21 rad/s
b) 1590 m **72.** 0.10 rad/s **73.** 89.01 rad/s
74. 251.33 rad/s **75. a)** 3700 rpm **b)** 7400π rad/min
76. 1.0 **77.** 14π **78.** 0.03° **79. a)** $\dfrac{\pi}{8}$ **b)** $\dfrac{\pi}{12}$ **c)** $\dfrac{2\pi}{n}$

80. a) 38.6 rad/s **b)** 368.4 rad **81.** Any number of
complete rotations of 360° brings the terminal arm
back to its original position.

82. a) 1, 0, undefined **b)** 90°, $\dfrac{\pi}{2}$ rad **c)** $\dfrac{200}{\pi}$ gradians

83. a) 30° + 360°n, where n is an integer. **b)** $\dfrac{\pi}{6} + 2\pi n$,
where n is an integer

Technology pp. 192–193

1 Finding the Index of Refraction of Water   1. They
had the spreadsheet in radian mode instead of degree
mode. **2. a)** Index of Refraction: 1.42, 1.52, 1.54,
1.52, 1.53, 1.51, 1.53, 1.53 **b)** 1.51; Yes, differences
may be due to rounding. **3.** Yes; as angle of incidence
approaches 0, so does angle of refraction. **4.** 0.66; the
reciprocal of the index for air to water
**2 Determining the Index of Refraction of Other
Substances   1. a)** 1.52, 1.54, 1.58, 1.58, 1.55, 1.56
b) 1.55 **2.** Crystals A and C

Section 4.2 pp. 199–201

Practice   1. $\sin \theta = \dfrac{12}{13}$, $\cos \theta = \dfrac{5}{13}$, $\tan \theta = \dfrac{12}{5}$,
$\csc \theta = \dfrac{13}{12}$, $\sec \theta = \dfrac{13}{5}$, $\cot \theta = \dfrac{5}{12}$ **2.** $\sin \theta = -\dfrac{\sqrt{3}}{2}$,
$\cos \theta = -\dfrac{1}{2}$, $\tan \theta = \sqrt{3}$, $\csc \theta = -\dfrac{2}{\sqrt{3}}$, $\sec \theta = -2$,
$\cot \theta = \dfrac{1}{\sqrt{3}}$ **3.** $\sin \theta = \dfrac{1}{\sqrt{2}}$, $\cos \theta = -\dfrac{1}{\sqrt{2}}$,
$\tan \theta = -1$, $\csc \theta = \sqrt{2}$, $\sec \theta = -\sqrt{2}$, $\cot \theta = -1$
4. $\sin \theta = -\dfrac{4}{5}$, $\cos \theta = \dfrac{3}{5}$, $\tan \theta = -\dfrac{4}{3}$, $\csc \theta = -\dfrac{5}{4}$,
$\sec \theta = \dfrac{5}{3}$, $\cot \theta = -\dfrac{3}{4}$ **5.** $\sin \theta = \dfrac{15}{17}$, $\cos \theta = -\dfrac{8}{17}$,
$\tan \theta = -\dfrac{15}{8}$ **6.** $\sin \theta = -\dfrac{3}{\sqrt{34}}$, $\cos \theta = \dfrac{5}{\sqrt{34}}$,
$\tan \theta = -\dfrac{3}{5}$ **7.** $\sin \theta = -\dfrac{8}{\sqrt{65}}$, $\cos \theta = -\dfrac{1}{\sqrt{65}}$,

$\tan \theta = 8$ **8.** $\sin \theta = \dfrac{1}{\sqrt{2}}$, $\cos \theta = \dfrac{1}{\sqrt{2}}$, $\tan \theta = 1$

9. $\sin \theta = -\dfrac{3}{5}$, $\cos \theta = \dfrac{4}{5}$, $\tan \theta = -\dfrac{3}{4}$ **10.** $\sin \theta = \dfrac{5}{\sqrt{29}}$,

$\cos \theta = -\dfrac{2}{\sqrt{29}}$, $\tan \theta = -\dfrac{5}{2}$ **11.** $\sin \theta = -\dfrac{1}{\sqrt{5}}$,

$\cos \theta = -\dfrac{2}{\sqrt{5}}$, $\tan \theta = \dfrac{1}{2}$ **12.** $\sin \theta = \dfrac{1}{\sqrt{5}}$, $\cos \theta = \dfrac{2}{\sqrt{5}}$,

$\tan \theta = \dfrac{1}{2}$ **13.** positive **14.** negative **15.** positive

16. positive **17.** positive **18.** positive **19.** positive

20. positive **21.** $\sin \theta = \dfrac{\sqrt{5}}{3}$, $\tan \theta = -\dfrac{\sqrt{5}}{2}$,

$\csc \theta = \dfrac{3}{\sqrt{5}}$, $\sec \theta = -\dfrac{3}{2}$, $\cot \theta = -\dfrac{2}{\sqrt{5}}$

22. $\cos \theta = \dfrac{2\sqrt{2}}{3}$, $\tan \theta = -\dfrac{1}{2\sqrt{2}}$, $\csc \theta = -3$,

$\sec \theta = \dfrac{3}{2\sqrt{2}}$, $\cot \theta = -2\sqrt{2}$ **23.** $\sin \theta = -\dfrac{3}{\sqrt{34}}$,

$\cos \theta = -\dfrac{5}{\sqrt{34}}$, $\csc \theta = -\dfrac{\sqrt{34}}{3}$, $\sec \theta = -\dfrac{\sqrt{34}}{5}$,

$\cot \theta = \dfrac{5}{3}$ **24.** $\sin \theta = -\dfrac{\sqrt{39}}{8}$, $\cos \theta = -\dfrac{5}{8}$, $\tan \theta = \dfrac{\sqrt{39}}{5}$,

$\csc \theta = -\dfrac{8}{\sqrt{39}}$, $\cot \theta = \dfrac{5}{\sqrt{39}}$ **25.** $\sin \theta = \dfrac{4}{5}$, $\cos \theta = \dfrac{3}{5}$,

$\tan \theta = \dfrac{4}{3}$, $\csc \theta = \dfrac{5}{4}$, $\sec \theta = \dfrac{5}{3}$ **26.** $\sin \theta = \dfrac{5}{12}$,

$\cos \theta = -\dfrac{\sqrt{119}}{12}$, $\tan \theta = -\dfrac{5}{\sqrt{119}}$, $\sec \theta = -\dfrac{12}{\sqrt{119}}$,

$\cot \theta = -\dfrac{\sqrt{119}}{5}$ **27.** $\dfrac{1}{\sqrt{2}}$ **28.** $-\sqrt{3}$ **29.** $-\dfrac{\sqrt{3}}{2}$ **30.** $\sqrt{3}$

31. 2 **32.** $\dfrac{1}{\sqrt{2}}$ **33.** -2 **34.** $\sqrt{3}$ **35.** 1.7321

36. -0.7071 **37.** 2 **38.** 1 **39.** -0.5 **40.** -0.8660

41. -0.7071 **42.** -1.4142

Applications and Problem Solving   43. b) $\pm\dfrac{12}{13}$

44. a) 0, 1, 0, -1; 1, 0, -1, 0; 0, undefined, 0, undefined; undefined, 1, undefined, -1; 1 undefined,

-1, undefined; undefined, 0, undefined, 0 **b)** because $\cos 90° = 0$, and $\dfrac{1}{0}$ is undefined **45. a)** $\left(-\dfrac{1}{\sqrt{2}}, -\dfrac{1}{\sqrt{2}}\right)$

or $(-1, -1)$ **b)** $\sin \theta = -\dfrac{1}{\sqrt{2}}$, $\cos \theta = -\dfrac{1}{\sqrt{2}}$, $\csc \theta = -\sqrt{2}$,

$\sec \theta = -\sqrt{2}$, $\cot \theta = 1$ **46.** $\cos \theta = \pm \dfrac{\sqrt{5}}{3}$

47. $\cos \theta = -\dfrac{1}{3}$, $\tan \theta = \pm 2\sqrt{2}$ **48.** Quadrant I or III

49. a) minimum: $\dfrac{a}{2}$, maximum: $\dfrac{a}{\sqrt{2}}$

b) minimum: $\dfrac{a}{\sqrt{2}}$, maximum: $\dfrac{\sqrt{3}a}{2}$

50. $\sin (-\theta) = \sin \theta$ for 0, π, 2π; $\sin (-\theta) = -\sin \theta$ for all values of θ; $\cos (-\theta) = \cos \theta$ for all values of θ;

$\cos (-\theta) = -\cos \theta$ for $\theta = \dfrac{\pi}{2}, \dfrac{3\pi}{2}$; $\tan (-\theta) = \tan \theta$ for

$\theta = 0, \pi, 2\pi$; $\tan (-\theta) = -\tan \theta$ for all values of θ

51. No, since $\dfrac{1}{\sqrt{2}} + \dfrac{1}{\sqrt{2}} \neq 1$. **52. b)** $\tan \theta$ is undefined

at these angles **c)** $\dfrac{\cos \theta}{\sin \theta} = \cot \theta$, $\theta \neq k\pi$,

k any integer **c)** $\dfrac{\csc \theta}{\sec \theta} = \cot \theta$, $\theta \neq \dfrac{k\pi}{2}$, k any integer

53. a) $-\dfrac{1}{2}$ **b)** 0 **54. a)** $y = mx$ **b)** $m = \tan \theta$

Investigating Math p. 202
1. a) period: 6, amplitude: 4 **b)** period: 4, amplitude: 1 **c)** period: 2, amplitude: 1.5 **d)** period: 8, amplitude: 6

Technology p. 203
1 The Nature of a Sine Curve   1. a) 0; 360°; 45° or 0; 2π; $\dfrac{\pi}{4}$ **b)** 1; -1; 1 **c)** x-intercepts: 0, 180°, 360° or 0, π, 2π; y-intercept: 0; minimum occurs at 270° or $\dfrac{3\pi}{2}$, maximum occurs at 90° or $\dfrac{\pi}{2}$; positive: $0 < x < 180°$ or $0 < x < \pi$; negative: $180° < x < 360°$ or $\pi < x < 2\pi$; it is positive in Quadrants I and II and negative in Quadrants III and IV, as it should be by the ASTC rule. **2. a)** The graph will extend periodically to the left, introducing additional x-intercepts at $-180°$ and $-360°$ or $-\pi$ and -2π. The maximum and minimum

values will occur at $-270°$ or $-\dfrac{3\pi}{2}$ and $-90°$ or $-\dfrac{\pi}{2}$, respectively. The maximum and minimum values of 1 and -1 will remain the same. The amplitude is 1 and the period is 2π.

2 The Nature of a Cosine Curve **1. a)** 0; 2π; $\dfrac{\pi}{4}$ or 0; $360°$; $45°$ **b)** 1; -1; 1 **c)** x-intercepts $\dfrac{\pi}{2}, \dfrac{3\pi}{2}$ or $90°$, $270°$; y-intercept: 1; maximum occurs at 0 and 2π or $360°$; minimum occurs at π or $180°$;

positive: $0 \le x < \dfrac{\pi}{2}, \dfrac{3\pi}{2} < x \le 2\pi$ or $0 < x \le 90°$,

$270° < x \le 360°$; negative: $\dfrac{\pi}{2} < x < \dfrac{3\pi}{2}$ or $90° < x < 270°$; it is positive in Quadrants I and IV and negative in Quadrants II and III, as it should be by the ASTC rule. **2. a)** The graph will extend periodically to the left, introducing additional x-intercepts at $-\dfrac{\pi}{2}$ or $-90°$ and $-\dfrac{3\pi}{2}$ or $-270°$. The maximum and minimum values will occur at -2π or $-360°$ and $-\pi$ or $-180°$. The maximum and minimum values of 1 and -1 will remain the same. The amplitude is 1 and the period is 2π.

3 Comparing Sine and Cosine Curves **1. a)** Both graphs are periodic with period 2π, and each graph has amplitude 1. The x- and y-intercepts are different. **2.** The cosine curve translated to the right $\dfrac{\pi}{2}$ units equals the sine curve: $\cos\left(x - \dfrac{\pi}{2}\right) = \sin x$.

Section 4.3 pp. 209–211

Practice **1.** 5 **2.** 3 **3.** $\dfrac{1}{2}$ **4.** 3.5 **5.** 1 **6.** $\dfrac{2}{3}$ **7.** 12 **8.** 6 **9.** 0.4 **10.** 120 **11.** 180° **12.** 120° **13.** 480° **14.** 720° **15.** 60° **16.** 144° **17.** 1080° **18.** 360° **19.** 90° **20.** 1200° **21.** amplitude: 4, period: 2π **22.** amplitude: 3, period: π **23.** amplitude: 0.5, period: $\dfrac{10\pi}{3}$ **24.** amplitude: 2, period: 4π **25.** amplitude: 3, period: 3π **26.** amplitude: 8, period: $\dfrac{5\pi}{2}$ **27.** amplitude: 2.5, period: 12π **28.** amplitude: 75, period: $\dfrac{\pi}{6}$ **29.** amplitude: 6.8, period: $\dfrac{5\pi}{18}$ **30.** amplitude: 1.4, period: $\dfrac{10\pi}{7}$

31. $y = \dfrac{1}{3}\cos 2\theta$ **32.** $y = 3\cos\theta$ **33.** $y = 7\cos\dfrac{12}{5}\theta$ **34.** $y = 0.5\cos\dfrac{\theta}{2}$ **35.** $y = 2.8\cos 4\theta$ **36.** $y = 6\sin 2\theta$ **37.** $y = 0.4\sin 8\theta$ **38.** $y = 3.5\sin\dfrac{\theta}{5}$ **39.** $y = 15\sin 6\theta$ **40.** $y = 2.8\sin 6\theta$ **41.** $y = 4\sin x$ **42.** $y = 2\sin\dfrac{1}{2}x$ **43.** $y = 3\cos\dfrac{x}{4}$ **44.** $y = 3\cos\dfrac{3}{5}x$ **45.** amplitude: 4, period: 2π **46.** amplitude: $\dfrac{1}{3}$, period: $\dfrac{\pi}{2}$ **47.** amplitude: 3, period: $\dfrac{\pi}{3}$ **48.** amplitude: $\dfrac{1}{4}$, period: 4π **49.** amplitude: 110, period: $\dfrac{2\pi}{3}$ **50.** amplitude: 4.5, period: 8π

Applications and Problem Solving
51. a) reflections in the y-axis **b)** reflections in the y-axis **c)** reflections in the y-axis; reflections in the y-axis; no **52. a)** $45° < x < 225°$ **b)** $0 \le x < 45°$, $225° < x \le 360°$ **c)** $45°$, $225°$ **d)** $135°$, $315°$ **53.** $A = -B$ **54.** $y = 10\sin 880\pi x$ **55. a)** $\dfrac{1}{2\pi}; \dfrac{1}{2\pi}$ **b)** $\dfrac{1}{\pi}; \dfrac{1}{4\pi}$ **56. a)** $S(t) = 20\sin 524\pi t$ **57. a)** amplitude: 170, period: $\dfrac{1}{60}$ **b)** 120 V **c)** 60 cycles/s **d)** 0 **59.** 10^7 cycles/s **60. a)** $y = \sin\dfrac{2\pi}{23}t$; $y = \sin\dfrac{\pi}{14}t$; $y = \sin\dfrac{2\pi}{33}t$ **c)** 0.136; 0.223; 0.372 **61. a)** 0.1 **b)** The maximum size would not change. The period would increase as l increased, and decrease as l decreased. **62. a)** odd; $-\sin x = \sin(-x)$ for all values of x; $y = \sin x$ is not symmetric in the y-axis; yes **b)** even; $\cos x = \cos(-x)$ for all values of x; $y = \cos x$ is symmetric in the y-axis; yes

Section 4.4 pp. 218–219
Practice **1.** vertical displacement: 3, phase shift: 0 **2.** vertical displacement: -1, phase shift: 0 **3.** vertical displacement: 0, phase shift: 45° right **4.** vertical displacement: 0, phase shift: $\dfrac{3\pi}{4}$ right **5.** vertical displacement: 1, phase shift: 60° right **6.** vertical displacement: 4, phase shift: $\dfrac{\pi}{3}$ left

7. vertical displacement: −0.5, phase shift: $\frac{3\pi}{8}$ left **8.** vertical displacement: −4.5, phase shift: 15° right **9.** vertical displacement: 6, phase shift: 0 **10.** vertical displacement: −3, phase shift: 0 **11.** vertical displacement: 0, phase shift: $\frac{\pi}{2}$ left **12.** vertical displacement: 0, phase shift: 72° left **13.** vertical displacement: −2, phase shift: 30° right **14.** vertical displacement: 1.5, phase shift: $\frac{\pi}{6}$ left

15. vertical displacement: 25, phase shift: 110° left

16. vertical displacement: −3.8, phase shift: $\frac{5\pi}{12}$ right

17. amplitude: 2, period: 2π, phase shift: 0, vertical displacement: −3 **18.** amplitude: 1, period: 2π, phase shift: 0, vertical displacement: 3 **19.** amplitude: 1, period: 120°, phase shift: 90° right, vertical displacement: 0 **20.** amplitude: 0.5, period π, phase shift: 0, vertical displacement: −1

21. amplitude: 3, period: $\frac{\pi}{2}$, phase shift: $\frac{\pi}{4}$ right, vertical displacement: 5 **22.** amplitude: 6, period: 120°, phase shift: 20° right, vertical displacement: 0 **23.** amplitude: 5, period: π, phase shift: $\frac{\pi}{6}$ right, vertical displacement: 1

24. amplitude: 0.8, period: 3π, phase shift: $\frac{\pi}{3}$ right, vertical displacement: −7
25. $y = 4\sin x$ **26.** $y = 2\cos 2x + 1$
27. $y = \sin(x - 60°) + 3$ **28.** $y = 5\sin\frac{1}{2}(x + 120°)$

29. $y = 0.5\cos\left(x + \frac{3\pi}{4}\right) - 2$

30. $y = 1.5\cos\frac{2}{3}\left(x - \frac{\pi}{12}\right) + 4$

31. $A = 2$, $B = 3$, $C = -\frac{\pi}{3}$, $D = -1$ **32.** $A = 5$, $B = \frac{1}{2}$, $C = -\pi$, $D = 2$
Applications and Problem Solving 33. The graph of $f(\theta)$ is a vertical expansion by a factor of 3 and a phase shift of $\frac{5\pi}{12}$ right of the graph of $y = \sin\theta$.

34. a) amplitude: 6, period: π, phase shift: $\frac{\pi}{8}$ left, vertical displacement: 3, x-intercepts: 1.44, 2.49, y-intercept: 7.24 **b)** amplitude: 4, period: $\frac{2\pi}{3}$,

phase shift: $\frac{\pi}{2}$ right, vertical displacement: −2, x-intercepts: 1.22, 1.92, y-intercept: −2
c) amplitude: $\frac{1}{2}$, period: 180°, phase shift: 45° right, vertical displacement: 1, x-intercepts: none, y-intercept: 1 **d)** amplitude: 2, period: 720°, phase shift: 45° left, vertical displacement: 0, x-intercepts: 315°, 675°, y-intercept: 0.77 **35. b)** 4.8 m **37.** no; no; yes: maximum $= |A| + D$, minimum $= D - |A|$
38. $A = E$, $D = H$, $B = \pm F$, $G = C - (90° + 360°n)$ or $G = C - \left(\frac{\pi}{2} + 2\pi n\right)$; or, $B = \pm F$, $D = H$, $A = -E$, and $G = C + 90° - 360°n$ or $G = C + \frac{\pi}{2} - 2\pi n$ for n any integer

39. a) $|B| < 1$, $B < 0$ **b)** $|A| < 1$ **c)** $D = 0$, $C = n\pi$
d) $\sin BC = \frac{A - D}{A}$ **e)** $|D| > |A|$

Section 4.5 pp. 225–227
Practice 1. $y = 4\sin\pi t$, $y = 4\cos\pi\left(t - \frac{1}{2}\right)$

2. $y = 170\sin 120\pi\left(t + \frac{1}{240}\right)$, $y = 170\cos 120\pi t$

3. $y = 4\sin\frac{\pi}{4}(t - 1) + 2$, $y = 4\cos\frac{\pi}{4}(t - 3) + 2$

4. $y = 12\sin\frac{\pi}{2}(t + 1) - 3$, $y = 12\cos\frac{\pi}{2}t - 3$

5. $y = 40\sin\pi\left(t - \frac{1}{2}\right) + 10$, $y = 40\cos\pi(t - 1) + 10$

6. 13 m **7.** 6.5 **8.** 12 h **9.** $\frac{\pi}{6}$ **10.** $C = 0$, $D = 0$; the graph passes through the origin **11.** $y = 6.5\sin\frac{\pi}{6}t$

12. 21.5°C, 18.5°C **13.** 18.7°C **14.** 24 min; at 21.5°C the air conditioner turns on, and at 18.5°C the air conditioner turns off **15.** 8.8 min, 15.2 min
Applications and Problem Solving 16. a) 2.9 m **b)** $t = 0$ and $t = 12.4$ h **c)** 0 m **d)** 12.4 h **e)** 2.22 m
17. a) 1500; 900 **b)** 4 years **c)** 1200

18. b) $h(t) = 20\cos\frac{\pi}{15}(t - 15) + 21$

19. b) $h(t) = 1.8 + 2\sin\frac{\pi}{6}(t - 3.86)$, t in seconds

20. a) $y = 6\sin\frac{\pi}{6}(t - 3) + 16$ **21. a)** Let January be 1.

$$T = 18.65 \sin \frac{\pi}{6}(t-4) + 7.65 \text{ or}$$

$$T = 18.65 \cos \frac{\pi}{6}(t-7) + 7.65$$ **b)** 28% **c)** Yes. The model approximates the data quite well. **22. a)** 3.4; 3400 people are employed in the town in July **b)** January **c)** ski resort; the maximum employment is in the winter **d)** The shape would be the same, but the minimum and maximum would increase. **23. a)** Represent the time as minutes from midnight: 03:12 is 192. 09:12 is 552. Represent the date by a number. June 21 is 172. Dec. 21 is 355.

$$T = 180 \cos \frac{2\pi}{365}(t-10) + 372$$ **b)** 08:07 **c)** 06:12

Section 4.6 p. 232
Practice 1. $k = 2$ **2.** $k = \frac{1}{2}$ **3.** $k = 4$ **4.** period: $\frac{\pi}{3}$, phase shift: $\frac{\pi}{3}$ right **5.** period: $\frac{\pi}{2}$, phase shift: 0 **6.** period: π, phase shift: $\frac{\pi}{3}$ left **7.** period: π, phase shift: $\frac{\pi}{4}$ right **8.** period: π, phase shift: $\frac{\pi}{2}$ right **9.** period: $\frac{\pi}{2}$, phase shift: $\frac{\pi}{2}$ right **10.** period: π, phase shift: π left **11.** period: $\frac{\pi}{3}$, phase shift: $\frac{\pi}{9}$ left **12.** periods: equal; domains: equal; ranges: equal **13.** periods: equal; domains: equal: ranges: $|y| \geq 1$, $|y| \geq 3$ **14.** periods: π, $\frac{\pi}{5}$; domains: $x \neq 0$, $n\pi$, $x \neq 0$, $\frac{n}{5}\pi$, n any integer; ranges: equal **15.** periods: equal; domains: equal; range: $|y| \geq 1$, $|y| \geq 4$

Applications and Problem Solving
16. a) $y = \tan \frac{1}{2}\left(x + \frac{\pi}{4}\right)$ **b)** No. $y = a \tan \frac{1}{2}\left(x + \frac{\pi}{4}\right) + b$, where a and b are any numbers. **17. a)** 90° **b)** $x = 90°n$ **18. b)** No. Tangent functions do not have amplitudes. **c)** $x = (2n+1)\frac{\pi}{2}$ **19.** $y = \csc x$ is a translation of $\frac{\pi}{2}$ units right of $y = \sec x$. **20.** $x = 90°$; $\csc 90° = 1$

21. a) $-\frac{3\pi}{4}$, $-\frac{\pi}{4}$, $\frac{\pi}{4}$, $\frac{3\pi}{4}$, $\frac{5\pi}{4}$, $\frac{7\pi}{4}$

b) $-\frac{\pi}{4}, \frac{3\pi}{4}, \frac{7\pi}{4}$ **c)** $-\frac{\pi}{2}, \frac{\pi}{2}, \frac{3\pi}{2}$ **d)** $-\pi < x < -\frac{3\pi}{4}$,

$-\frac{\pi}{2} < x < -\frac{\pi}{4}$, $0 < x < \frac{\pi}{4}$, $\frac{\pi}{2} < x < \frac{3\pi}{4}$, $\pi < x < \frac{5\pi}{4}$, $\frac{3\pi}{2} < x < \frac{7\pi}{4}$ **22. a)** $(2n\pi, 1)$, $((2n+1)\pi, -1)$, n any integer **b)** $(2n\pi + \frac{\pi}{2}, 1)$, $(\left(2n + \frac{3}{2}\right)\pi, -1)$, n any integer **c)** There is a phase shift of $\frac{\pi}{2}$. **23.** domain: $x \neq \frac{\pi}{2} + n\pi$, n any integer, range: $y \geq 0$, period: π **24.** $y = -\tan x$ is a translation of $\frac{\pi}{2}$ units left or right of $y = \cot x$. **25.** all values except $x \neq \frac{\pi}{2} + n\pi$, n any integer **26.** No. The graph of a parabola has only one U-shaped curve. The graph of $y = \sec x$ has infinitely many. A parabola is defined for all values of x. The graph of $y = \sec x$ is not defined for $x \neq \frac{\pi}{2} + n\pi$, n any integer.

Investigating Math p. 233
1. a) All negative parts of the graph will be reflected in the x-axis. **2.** When $\cos x \geq 0$, the graphs are the same. When $\cos x < 0$, the graph of $y = |\cos x|$ is a reflection in the x-axis of the graph of $y = \cos x$. **3.** The graph of $y = |\cos x|$ is the graph of $y = |\sin x|$ translated $\frac{\pi}{2}$ units right. **4. a)** period: π, maximum: 4, minimum: 0, x-intercepts: $n\pi$, n any integer, y-intercept: 0 **b)** period: 2π, maximum: 2, minimum: 0, x-intercepts: $2n\pi$, n any integer, y-intercept: 0 **c)** period: π, maximum: none, minimum: 0, x-intercepts: $n\pi$, n any integer, y-intercept: 0 **d)** period: 2π, maximum: 3.5, minimum: 0, x-intercepts: $\pm 1.74 + 2n\pi$, n any integer, y-intercept: 3.5 **e)** period: 2π, maximum: 5, minimum: 1, x-intercepts: none, y-intercept: 3 **f)** period: π, maximum: none, minimum: 1, x-intercepts: none, y-intercept: 1 **5.** $y = \csc x$ is the reciprocal of $y = \sin x$. When $\sin x$ has large values, $\csc x$ has small values, and vice versa. The graphs of $y = \csc x$ and $y = |\csc x|$ are the same when $\csc x \geq 0$, and reflections of each other in the x-axis when $\csc x < 0$. **6. b)** When $\cos 120\pi t \geq 0$, the graphs are the same. When $\cos 120\pi t < 0$, the graphs are reflections of each other in the x-axis.

Review pp. 236–237
1. 74.5° **2.** 40.1° **3.** −137.5° **4.** 15° **5.** −540° **6.** 150° **7.** $\frac{\pi}{4}$ **8.** $\frac{5\pi}{9}$ **9.** $\frac{\pi}{5}$ **10.** $\frac{\pi}{9}$ **11.** $-\frac{5\pi}{6}$ **12.** $-\frac{10\pi}{3}$ **13.** 417°; −303° **14.** 455°; −265°

15. $237°$; $-483°$ **16.** $\dfrac{19\pi}{12}$; $-\dfrac{29\pi}{12}$ **17.** $\dfrac{10\pi}{3}$; $-\dfrac{2\pi}{3}$

18. $\dfrac{13\pi}{6}$; $-\dfrac{11\pi}{6}$ **19.** no **20.** yes

21. yes **22.** no **23.** $\sin\theta = -\dfrac{1}{\sqrt{2}}$, $\cos\theta = -\dfrac{1}{\sqrt{2}}$,

$\tan\theta = 1$, $\csc\theta = -\sqrt{2}$, $\sec\theta = -\sqrt{2}$, $\cot\theta = 1$

24. $\sin\theta = -\dfrac{7}{\sqrt{65}}$, $\cos\theta = \dfrac{4}{\sqrt{65}}$, $\tan\theta = -\dfrac{7}{4}$,

$\csc\theta = -\dfrac{\sqrt{65}}{7}$, $\sec\theta = \dfrac{\sqrt{65}}{4}$, $\cot\theta = -\dfrac{4}{7}$

25. $\sin\theta = \dfrac{2}{\sqrt{5}}$, $\cos\theta = -\dfrac{1}{\sqrt{5}}$, $\tan\theta = -2$,

$\csc\theta = \dfrac{\sqrt{5}}{2}$, $\sec\theta = -\sqrt{5}$, $\cot\theta = -\dfrac{1}{2}$

26. $\sin\theta = \dfrac{5}{\sqrt{29}}$, $\cos\theta = \dfrac{2}{\sqrt{29}}$, $\tan\theta = \dfrac{5}{2}$,

$\csc\theta = \dfrac{\sqrt{29}}{5}$, $\sec\theta = \dfrac{\sqrt{29}}{2}$, $\cot\theta = \dfrac{2}{5}$ **27.** -1

28. $-\sqrt{3}$ **29.** $-\sqrt{3}$ **30.** $-\sqrt{2}$ **31.** $\pm\dfrac{2\sqrt{2}}{3}$

32. amplitude: 4.2, period: $\dfrac{2\pi}{3}$ **33.** amplitude: 2,

period: 6π **34.** amplitude: 0.7, period: $\dfrac{8\pi}{3}$

35. amplitude: 5, period: $\dfrac{24\pi}{7}$ **36.** $y = 4\sin 3x$

37. $3\cos\dfrac{x}{2}$ **38.** amplitude: 2.5, period: 2π,

phase shift: 0, vertical displacement: -1
39. amplitude: 1, period: $60°$, phase shift: $45°$ right,
vertical displacement: 0 **40.** amplitude: 4,
period: π, phase shift: $\dfrac{\pi}{3}$ left, vertical displacement: 8
41. amplitude: 2, period: $1080°$, phase shift: $90°$ left,
vertical displacement: 4
42. $y = 4\sin 3(x + 45°) - 2$, $y = 4\cos 3(x + 15°) - 2$

43. $y = 5\sin\dfrac{1}{2}\left(x + \dfrac{2\pi}{3}\right) + 3$, $y = 5\cos\dfrac{1}{2}\left(x - \dfrac{\pi}{3}\right) + 3$

44. b) 11.8 h **c)** 4.8 h

45. a) $T = 9\cos\dfrac{2\pi}{365}(d - 208) + 14$ **b)** 99 days **46.** 3

47. $\dfrac{1}{4}$ **48.** period: $\dfrac{\pi}{2}$; phase shift: $\dfrac{\pi}{4}$ right

49. period: $\dfrac{\pi}{4}$; phase shift: $\dfrac{\pi}{12}$ left **50.** periods: π,

$\dfrac{\pi}{2}$, domains: $x \neq n\pi$, $x \neq \dfrac{n\pi}{2}$, n any integer,

ranges: same **51.** periods: same; domains: same;
ranges: $|y| \geq 1$, $|y| \geq 4$

Exploring Math p.237 **1. a)** $\dfrac{1}{2}$ **b)** 0.5000

c) 4 terms **2. a)** 1; 1.0045; 6 terms

b) $\dfrac{1}{2}$; 0.5018; 5 terms **c)** 0; 0.5240; 9 terms

d) -1; 0.1239; 10 terms **3. a)** 0.8415 **b)** 4 terms

Chapter Check p. 238
1. $194.8°$ **2.** $57.3°$ **3.** $-154.7°$ **4.** $75°$ **5.** $-180°$

6. $240°$ **7.** $-\dfrac{\pi}{6}$ **8.** $\dfrac{7\pi}{9}$ **9.** $\dfrac{4\pi}{9}$ **10.** $\dfrac{7\pi}{3}$ **11.** $-\dfrac{9\pi}{4}$

12. $\dfrac{10\pi}{3}$ **13.** no **14.** yes **15.** no **16.** yes

17. $\sin\theta = -\dfrac{2\sqrt{2}}{3}$, $\tan\theta = 2\sqrt{2}$, $\csc\theta = -\dfrac{3}{2\sqrt{2}}$,

$\sec\theta = -3$, $\cot\theta = \dfrac{1}{2\sqrt{2}}$ **18.** $\sin\theta = \dfrac{3}{4}$, $\cos\theta = \dfrac{\sqrt{7}}{4}$,

$\tan\theta = \dfrac{3}{\sqrt{7}}$, $\sec\theta = \dfrac{4}{\sqrt{7}}$, $\cot\theta = \dfrac{\sqrt{7}}{3}$

19. $\sin\theta = -\dfrac{5}{\sqrt{29}}$, $\cos\theta = \dfrac{2}{\sqrt{29}}$, $\csc\theta = -\dfrac{\sqrt{29}}{5}$,

$\sec\theta = \dfrac{\sqrt{29}}{2}$, $\cot\theta = -\dfrac{2}{5}$ **20.** $\dfrac{\sqrt{3}}{2}$ **21.** 0 **22.** -1

23. a) Periods and amplitudes are equal.
b) The graph of $y = \cos x$ is a translation of $\dfrac{\pi}{2}$ units
left of the graph of $y = \sin x$. **24.** $y = 5\cos 2x$

25. $y = 1.7\cos\dfrac{3}{2}x$ **26.** $y = 3\sin 4x$ **27.** $y = 2\cos\dfrac{x}{4}$

28. amplitude: 3.7, period: 2π, phase shift:
$\dfrac{\pi}{6}$ left, vertical displacement: 0 **29.** amplitude: 1,
period: $90°$, phase shift: $15°$ right, vertical
displacement: 0 **30.** amplitude: 2, period: $\dfrac{2\pi}{3}$,

phase shift: $\dfrac{\pi}{3}$ left, vertical displacement: -5

31. amplitude: 7, period: 180°, phase shift: 45° left, vertical displacement: 4
32. $y = 4 \sin 3(x - 60°) - 2$, $y = 4 \cos 3(x + 30°) - 2$

33. a) $S = 141 \cos \dfrac{2\pi}{365}(d - 7) + 416$ **b)** 71 days

34. periods: π, $\dfrac{\pi}{4}$; domains: $x \neq \dfrac{\pi}{2} + n\pi$, $x \neq \dfrac{\pi}{8} + n\pi$, n any integer; ranges: same **35.** periods: same; domains: same; ranges: $|y| \geq 1$, $|y| \geq 5$

Using the Strategies p. 239
1. 2500 **2.** 54.7° **3.** $x = \pm\sqrt{2}$ **4. a)** $100(4 - \pi)$ cm²
b) $4r^2(4 - \pi)$ **5.** 255.78 **6.** 40 min **7.** 5:00 Tuesday morning **8.** Solutions include $397 + 251 = 648$
9. 36 cm **10.** 135 **11.** 3 m² **13.** Ardith: January, Brian: July, Carla: September, Don: December **14.** 3

Chapter 5

Trigonometric Equations p. 241
1. a) 17 N·m **b)** 34 N·m **c)** 127 N·m **2.** The more she becomes unbalanced, the more difficult it becomes for her to straighten herself. **3. a)** 6.4°
b) 8.4°

Getting Started pp. 242–243
Whose Angle Is It Anyway?
1. a) 30° **b)** 45° **c)** 180° **d)** 60° **e)** 30° **f)** 45° **g)** 270°

h) 120° **i)** 30° **2. a)** π **b)** $\dfrac{3\pi}{4}$ **c)** $\dfrac{\pi}{2}$ **d)** $\dfrac{\pi}{2}$ **e)** $\dfrac{5\pi}{6}$

f) $\dfrac{5\pi}{4}$ **g)** 0 **h)** $\dfrac{2\pi}{3}$ **i)** $\dfrac{2\pi}{3}$ **3. a)** 90° **b)** 60°, 300°
c) 45°, 225° **d)** 210°, 330° **e)** 30°, 330° **f)** 0°, 180°

g) 45°, 315° **h)** 60°, 240° **i)** 225°, 315° **4. a)** $\dfrac{3\pi}{4}, \dfrac{7\pi}{4}$

b) $\dfrac{\pi}{6}, \dfrac{5\pi}{6}$ **c)** $\dfrac{\pi}{6}, \dfrac{7\pi}{6}$ **d)** $\dfrac{5\pi}{4}, \dfrac{7\pi}{4}$ **e)** $\dfrac{2\pi}{3}, \dfrac{4\pi}{3}$ **f)** $\dfrac{\pi}{4}, \dfrac{5\pi}{4}$

g) $\dfrac{\pi}{3}, \dfrac{2\pi}{3}$ **h)** $\dfrac{7\pi}{6}, \dfrac{11\pi}{6}$ **i)** $\dfrac{\pi}{4}, \dfrac{7\pi}{4}$ **5. a)** $x = 180°n$,
n any integer **b)** $x = 135° + 180°n$, n any integer
c) $x = 150° + 360°n$, $x = 210° + 360°n$, n any integer
d) $x = 30° + 360°n$, $x = 150° + 360°n$, n any integer
e) $x = 180°n$, n any integer **f)** $x = 135° + 360°n$,
$x = 225° + 360°n$, n any integer **g)** $x = 270° + 360°n$,

n any integer **h)** $x = 120° + 180°n$, n any integer
i) $x = 45° + 360°n$, $x = 135° + 360°n$, n any integer

6. a) $x = (2n + 1)\pi$, n any integer **b)** $x = \dfrac{7\pi}{6} + 2n\pi$,

$x = \dfrac{11\pi}{6} + 2n\pi$, n any integer **c)** $x = \dfrac{\pi}{4} + n\pi$, n any

integer **d)** $x = \dfrac{\pi}{6} + 2n\pi$, $x = \dfrac{11\pi}{6} + 2n\pi$, n any integer

e) $x = \dfrac{5\pi}{4} + 2n\pi$, $x = \dfrac{7\pi}{4} + 2n\pi$, n any integer

f) $x = \dfrac{2\pi}{3} + n\pi$, n any integer

g) $x = \dfrac{\pi}{6} + 2n\pi$, $x = \dfrac{5\pi}{6} + 2n\pi$, n any integer

h) $x = \dfrac{\pi}{6} + n\pi$, n any integer **i)** $x = \dfrac{\pi}{4} + 2n\pi$,

$x = \dfrac{7\pi}{4} + 2n\pi$, n any integer

Warm Up 1. 47.7° **2.** 47.6° **3.** 45° **4.** 74.1° **5.** 53.1°
6. 30° **7.** 1.8460 **8.** 1.7805 **9.** 2.1203 **10.** 1.4134
11. -0.1992 **12.** -2.0309 **13.** 5.0403 **14.** 1.1936
15. -1.0510 **16.** 9.6225 **17.** $-2, -3$ **18.** ± 1 **19.** $\pm\dfrac{5}{2}$
20. $4, -1$ **21.** $-\dfrac{3}{2}, 1$ **22.** $0, 6$ **23.** $\pm\dfrac{5}{4}$ **24.** $-\dfrac{4}{3}$
25. $-\dfrac{1}{3}, 3$ **26.** $-\dfrac{5}{4}, \dfrac{7}{3}$ **27.** $0.35, -2.85$ **28.** $2.62, 0.38$
29. $1, 0.33$ **30.** $0.61, -4.11$ **31.** $-0.6, -1$
32. $4.49, -0.36$ **33.** ± 1.58 **34.** $2.62, 0.38$ **35.** $0.4, -1$
36. $2.77, 0.43$
Mental Math
1. $4(2x - 3)$ **2.** $3x(8x + 3)$ **3.** $(x - 5)(x + 5)$
4. $(2x - 7)(2x + 7)$ **5.** $(x - 2)(x - 1)$ **6.** $(x + 2)^2$
7. $(x + 2)(x - 1)$ **8.** $(x + 6)(x + 1)$
9. $(x - 4)(x + 3)$ **10.** $(0.5x - 0.4)(0.5x + 0.4)$
11. $(2x + 5)^2$ **12.** $(x - 3y)^2$ **13.** $\dfrac{\pi}{6}$ **14.** $\dfrac{\pi}{4}$
15. $\dfrac{\pi}{4}$ **16.** $\dfrac{\pi}{3}$ **17.** $\dfrac{\pi}{3}$ **18.** $\dfrac{\pi}{6}$ **19.** $\dfrac{\pi}{4}$ **20.** $\dfrac{\pi}{6}$
21. $\dfrac{\sqrt{3}}{2}$ **22.** 1 **23.** $\dfrac{\sqrt{3}}{2} - 1$ **24.** -1 **25.** 0 **26.** 0
27. $-\dfrac{2}{\sqrt{3}}$ **28.** 0 **29.** $\sin \theta = \dfrac{4}{5}$, $\cos \theta = \dfrac{3}{5}$, $\tan \theta = \dfrac{4}{3}$,
$\csc \theta = \dfrac{5}{4}$, $\sec \theta = \dfrac{5}{3}$, $\cot \theta = \dfrac{3}{4}$ **30.** $\sin \theta = \dfrac{\sqrt{3}}{2}$,

$\cos \theta = \dfrac{1}{2}$, $\tan \theta = \sqrt{3}$, $\csc \theta = \dfrac{2}{\sqrt{3}}$, $\sec \theta = 2$,

$\cot \theta = \dfrac{1}{\sqrt{3}}$ **31.** $\sin \theta = \dfrac{1}{\sqrt{2}}$, $\cos \theta = \dfrac{1}{\sqrt{2}}$, $\tan \theta = 1$,

$\csc \theta = \sqrt{2}$, $\sec \theta = \sqrt{2}$, $\cot \theta = 1$ **32.** $\sin \theta = \dfrac{\sqrt{13}}{7}$,

$\cos \theta = \dfrac{6}{7}$, $\tan \theta = \dfrac{\sqrt{13}}{6}$, $\csc \theta = \dfrac{7}{\sqrt{13}}$, $\sec \theta = \dfrac{7}{6}$,

$\cot \theta = \dfrac{6}{\sqrt{13}}$

Section 5.1 pp. 247–248

Practice 1. $0, \pi$ **2.** $0, \dfrac{\pi}{2}, \pi, \dfrac{3\pi}{2}$ **3.** $\dfrac{n\pi}{2}$, n any

integer **4.** $\dfrac{\pi}{2}$ **5.** $\dfrac{\pi}{6}, \dfrac{5\pi}{6}, \dfrac{3\pi}{2}$ **6.** $\dfrac{\pi}{6} + \dfrac{2n\pi}{3}$, n any

integer **7.** $\dfrac{3\pi}{2}$ **8.** $\dfrac{3\pi}{8}, \dfrac{7\pi}{8}, \dfrac{11\pi}{8}, \dfrac{15\pi}{8}$ **9.** $\dfrac{3\pi}{8} + \dfrac{n\pi}{2}$,

n any integer **10.** $90°, 270°$ **11.** $45°, 135°, 225°, 315°$
12. $45° + 90°n$, n any integer **13.** $0°$ **14.** $0°, 90°,$
$180°, 270°$ **15.** $90°n$, n any integer **16.** $45°, 225°$
17. $45° + 180°n$, n any integer **18.** The graph of
$y = \tan 3x$ is a horizontal compression by a factor of $\dfrac{1}{3}$
of the graph of $y = \tan x$. **19.** $15°, 75°, 135°, 195°,$
$255°, 315°$ **20.** $15° + 60°n$, n any integer

Applications and Problem Solving 21. a) $\dfrac{\pi}{18}, \dfrac{5\pi}{18},$

$\dfrac{13\pi}{18}, \dfrac{17\pi}{18}, \dfrac{25\pi}{18}, \dfrac{29\pi}{18}$ **b)** $\dfrac{\pi}{18} + \dfrac{2n\pi}{3}, \dfrac{5\pi}{18} + \dfrac{2n\pi}{3},$

n any integer **22. a)** $\dfrac{\pi}{16}, \dfrac{5\pi}{16}, \dfrac{9\pi}{16}, \dfrac{13\pi}{16}, \dfrac{17\pi}{16},$

$\dfrac{21\pi}{16}, \dfrac{25\pi}{16}, \dfrac{29\pi}{16}$ **b)** $\dfrac{\pi}{16}$, n any integer **23. b)** π

24. b) $0, 2\pi$ **c)** 1 **25. a)** $\dfrac{\pi}{9} + \dfrac{2n\pi}{3}, \dfrac{2\pi}{9} + \dfrac{2n\pi}{3}$, n any

integer **b)** $\dfrac{\pi}{6} + \dfrac{n\pi}{2}, \dfrac{\pi}{3} + \dfrac{n\pi}{2}$, n any integer

26. Graph $y = \sin \theta$ and $y = -\dfrac{1}{2}$, and find the points of

intersection; $\theta = 210° + 360°n$, $\theta = 330° + 360°n$, n

any integer **27.** A $= \dfrac{\pi}{24}, \dfrac{5\pi}{24}, \dfrac{13\pi}{24}, \dfrac{17\pi}{24}, \dfrac{25\pi}{24},$

$\dfrac{29\pi}{24}, \dfrac{37\pi}{24}, \dfrac{41\pi}{24}$ **28.** 5.1 min **29. a)** $2n\pi,$

$\dfrac{2\pi}{3} + 2n\pi, \dfrac{4\pi}{3} + 2n\pi$, n any integer **b)** $(2n+1)\dfrac{\pi}{2}$,

n any integer **30.** $\dfrac{7\pi}{24} + n\pi$, $\dfrac{23\pi}{24} + n\pi$, n any

non-negative integer

Section 5.2 pp. 252–253

Practice 1. $\dfrac{\pi}{3}, \dfrac{5\pi}{3}$ **2.** $\dfrac{7\pi}{6}, \dfrac{11\pi}{6}$ **3.** $\dfrac{\pi}{4}, \dfrac{5\pi}{4}$

4. $\dfrac{\pi}{3}, \dfrac{2\pi}{3}$ **5.** $\dfrac{2\pi}{3}, \dfrac{4\pi}{3}$ **6.** $\dfrac{2\pi}{3}, \dfrac{5\pi}{3}$ **7.** $\dfrac{3\pi}{2}$

8. 0 **9.** $\dfrac{\pi}{6}, \dfrac{5\pi}{6}$ **10.** $\dfrac{2\pi}{3}, \dfrac{4\pi}{3}$ **11.** $45°, 135°, 225°, 315°$

12. $45°, 225°$ **13.** $67.5°, 157.5°, 247.5°, 337.5°$
14. $135°, 315°$ **15.** $90°, 270°$ **16.** $0, 180°$ **17.** $15°,$
$75°, 195°, 255°$ **18.** $120°$ **19.** $20°, 100°, 140°, 220°,$
$260°, 340°$ **20.** $90°$ **21.** $0, \pi; n\pi$, n any integer

22. $\dfrac{\pi}{2}, \dfrac{3\pi}{2}$; $(2n+1)\dfrac{\pi}{2}$, n any integer **23.** $0, \pi, \dfrac{3\pi}{2}$;

$n\pi, \dfrac{3\pi}{2} + 2n\pi$, n any integer **24.** $\dfrac{\pi}{3}, \dfrac{2\pi}{3}, \dfrac{4\pi}{3},$

$\dfrac{5\pi}{3}$; $\dfrac{\pi}{3} + n\pi$, $\dfrac{2\pi}{3} + n\pi$, n any integer **25.** $\dfrac{\pi}{2}, \dfrac{\pi}{4},$

$\dfrac{5\pi}{4}$; $\dfrac{\pi}{2} + 2n\pi, \dfrac{\pi}{4} + n\pi$, n any integer **26.** $\dfrac{\pi}{3}, \pi,$

$\dfrac{5\pi}{3}$; $\dfrac{\pi}{3} + 2n\pi, (2n+1)\pi, \dfrac{5\pi}{3} + 2n\pi$, n any integer

27. $\dfrac{\pi}{6}, \dfrac{5\pi}{6}, \dfrac{3\pi}{2}$; $\dfrac{\pi}{6} + 2n\pi, \dfrac{5\pi}{6} + 2n\pi, \dfrac{3\pi}{2} + 2n\pi,$

n any integer **28.** $0, \dfrac{2\pi}{3}, \dfrac{4\pi}{3}$; $2n\pi, \dfrac{2\pi}{3} + 2n\pi,$

$\dfrac{4\pi}{3} + 2n\pi$, n any integer **29.** $\dfrac{\pi}{4}, \dfrac{\pi}{2}, \dfrac{3\pi}{4}, \dfrac{5\pi}{4}, \dfrac{3\pi}{2},$

$\dfrac{7\pi}{4}$; $\dfrac{\pi}{4} + n\pi, (2n+1)\dfrac{\pi}{2}, \dfrac{3\pi}{4} + n\pi$, n any integer

30. $\dfrac{\pi}{6}, \dfrac{5\pi}{6}, \dfrac{3\pi}{2}$; $\dfrac{\pi}{6} + 2n\pi, \dfrac{5\pi}{6} + 2n\pi, \dfrac{3\pi}{2} + 2n\pi,$

n any integer

31. $\dfrac{\pi}{3}$, $\dfrac{2\pi}{3}$, $\dfrac{4\pi}{3}$, $\dfrac{5\pi}{3}$; $\dfrac{\pi}{3}+n\pi$, $\dfrac{2\pi}{3}+n\pi$, n any integer

Applications and Problem Solving 32. a) $\dfrac{\pi}{6}+2n\pi$, $(2n+1)\dfrac{\pi}{2}$, $\dfrac{5\pi}{6}+2n\pi$, n any integer **b)** no solution

c) $\dfrac{\pi}{3}+2n\pi$, $\dfrac{5\pi}{3}+2n\pi$, n any integer **33. a)** $\dfrac{\pi}{4}$, 2.2143, $\dfrac{5\pi}{4}$, 5.3559 **b)** $\dfrac{\pi}{2}$ **c)** $0, \dfrac{\pi}{3}, \dfrac{5\pi}{3}$ **34. a)** 1.3, 1.6, 4.7, 5.0 **b)** 0, 1.0, 3.1, 5.2 **c)** 0.7, 2.5

35. a) 0.7854, 2.1910, 3.9270, 5.3326 **b)** 1.1071, 1.2490, 4.2487, 4.3906 **c)** 0, 1.3258, 3.1416, 4.4674

36. b) 60° **37. b)** 15° or 75° **38. a)** (0, 0), (0, sin x), (cos x, 0), (cos x, sin x) **b)** 0; $\dfrac{n\pi}{2}$, n any integer **c)** $\dfrac{1}{2}$

39. b) $P(x, y)$ must be close to both the equator and the prime meridian, and the curvature of Earth must be negligible. **40. b)** 25.9°, 45°

Section 5.3 pp. 256–257

Practice 1. $\sin x = x - 1$; 1.9 **2.** Find the value of x where $\sin x - x = -1$. **3.** They would be translations of 1 unit up of the graphs shown. Their intersection point would have the same x-value, and the y-value would be 1 greater: (1.9, 1.9). **4. b)** 0, ±1.895 **c)** Visualize the line $y = 1$ crossing the graph at only one point. **d)** −2.380 **5.** 0; ±0.929 **6.** $y = x^3$ and $y = \sin x$ **7.** Yes. The equations are equivalent.

Applications and Problem Solving 8. b) 0, ±1.895 **c)** yes **d)** No. It wouldn't have the negative root. **9. a)** $y \geq 0$; $-1 \leq g(x) \leq 1$; choose a domain where the range of $f(x)$ is restricted to $-1 \leq y \leq 1$, which gives a domain of $-1 \leq x \leq 1$. **b)** 2 **c)** 0, 0.877 **10. a)** 0, ±1.1656 **b)** 3; no, there is an infinite number of solutions; graph the functions for a greater domain and range. **11. a)** $\sin x = \dfrac{1}{x}$; rational function **b)** infinite number; $\dfrac{1}{x}$ approximates the x-axis for large x **c)** for $-2\pi < x < 2\pi$: ±1.1142, ±2.7726 **12. a)** (1.22, 0.85), (317.00, −1.40) **b)** not quite, because the end points are slightly above and slightly below the x-axis **13. a)** $0 \leq x \leq \pi$; $0 \leq y \leq 1$; the domain values must give a positive value for sin x **b)** 0, 0.8767 **14.** $a = 1$, $x = 0$ **15.** $q \geq 1$ if $a > 0$ **16.** $k = 0$: infinitely many solutions; $k \neq 0$: any positive number of solutions (more as $|k|$ decreases)

Section 5.4 pp. 264–265

Practice 11. a) both sides equal $-\dfrac{1}{2}$ **c)** no restrictions **12. a)** both sides equal 2 **c)** $\theta \neq n\pi$, n any integer **13. a)** both sides equal $\sqrt{3} - 1$ **c)** $\theta \neq \dfrac{n\pi}{2}$, n any integer **14. a)** both sides equal 2 **c)** no restrictions **15. a)** both sides equal $\dfrac{3}{4}$ **c)** $\theta \neq (2n+1)\dfrac{\pi}{2}$, n any integer **16. a)** both sides equal $2 + \sqrt{3}$ **c)** $\theta \neq n\pi$, n any integer **17. a)** both sides equal $\dfrac{1}{\sqrt{3}}$ **c)** $\theta \neq \dfrac{n\pi}{2}$, $\theta = \dfrac{3\pi}{4} + n\pi$, n any integer **18. a)** both sides equal 6 **c)** $\theta \neq n\pi$, n any integer **19. a)** both sides equal $\sqrt{3}$ **c)** $\theta \neq \dfrac{n\pi}{2}$, n any integer **20. a)** both sides equal $\dfrac{1}{1+\sqrt{3}}$ **c)** $\theta \neq \dfrac{3\pi}{4} + n\pi$, $(2n+1)\dfrac{\pi}{2}$, n any integer

21. identity **22.** not an identity **23.** identity **24.** not an identity **25.** not an identity **26.** sin x cos x **27.** 1 **28.** csc x **29.** 2(1 + sin x) **30.** 2 **31.** sec^2 x **32.** sec^2 x **33.** 1

Applications and Problem Solving 34. c) The graphs are the same. Their values are the same for all θ.

35. c) $B \neq \dfrac{n\pi}{2}$, n any integer **36. b)** 2 sec x **d)** $x \neq (2n+1)\dfrac{\pi}{2}$ **37. b)** 30.7 m **38. b)** tangent and cotangent; secant and cosecant **39.** The identities use the Pythagorean theorem. **40.** Answers may vary. $\sin x = \cos x$ for $x = \dfrac{\pi}{4}, \dfrac{5\pi}{4}, \dfrac{9\pi}{4}$ but not $x = 0$.

42. 2 sin^3 t; the restriction on t ensures that for each value of x there is only one value of t

Investigating Math pp. 266–267

1 Investigating cos(A – B) 1. $\cos\left(\dfrac{\pi}{3} - \dfrac{\pi}{6}\right) = \dfrac{\sqrt{3}}{2}$, $\cos\dfrac{\pi}{3} - \cos\dfrac{\pi}{6} = \dfrac{1-\sqrt{3}}{2}$

2. a) Z is on a unit circle with centre the origin. Its coordinates are the cosine and sine of the angle for which OZ is the terminal arm; W: (cos A, sin A); R: (cos(A – B), sin(A – B)) **b)** The chords subtend the same angle at the centre of the circle.

c) $(\cos(A - B) - 1)^2 + \sin^2(A - B)$
$= (\cos B - \cos A)^2 + (\sin B - \sin A)^2$

3. a) $\dfrac{1 + \sqrt{3}}{2\sqrt{2}}$ **b)** $\dfrac{1 + \sqrt{3}}{2\sqrt{2}}$

2 Deriving an Identity for cos(A + B)
1. a) $\cos(A + B) = \cos A \cos B - \sin A \sin B$

2. $\dfrac{\sqrt{3} - 1}{2\sqrt{2}}$

**3 Deriving Identities for sin(A + B), sin(A − B),
tan(A + B), and tan(A − B)**

4. $\tan(A - B) = \dfrac{\tan A - \tan B}{1 + \tan A \tan B}$

Section 5.5 pp. 272–274

Practice 1. $\dfrac{1}{2}$ **2.** $\dfrac{\sqrt{3}}{2}$ **3.** $\dfrac{\sqrt{3}}{2}$ **4.** $\dfrac{1}{2}$ **5.** 1 **6.** $\dfrac{1}{\sqrt{2}}$ **7.** 1

8. $\dfrac{1}{\sqrt{2}}$ **9.** $-\dfrac{1}{2}$ **10.** $2 - \sqrt{3}$ **11.** $\dfrac{\sqrt{3} + 1}{2\sqrt{2}}$ **12.** $\dfrac{1 - \sqrt{3}}{2\sqrt{2}}$

13. $-2 - \sqrt{3}$ **14.** $\dfrac{1 - \sqrt{3}}{2\sqrt{2}}$ **15.** $-\dfrac{\sqrt{3} + 1}{2\sqrt{2}}$ **16.** $-\dfrac{\sqrt{3}}{2}$

17. $\sin\dfrac{\pi}{3}$ **18.** $\cos\dfrac{\pi}{2}$ **19.** $\cos\dfrac{2\pi}{3}$ **20.** $\cos 30°$

21. $\tan\dfrac{5\pi}{6}$ **22.** $\tan\dfrac{5\pi}{12}$ **23.** $\sin\dfrac{5\pi}{4}$ **24.** $\cos\dfrac{13\pi}{12}$

33. true **34.** false **35.** true **36.** false

Applications and Problem Solving 37. a) $\dfrac{56}{65}$ **b)** $\dfrac{63}{65}$

c) $-\dfrac{63}{16}$ **38.** $\dfrac{33}{56}$ **39.** $-\dfrac{120}{169}$ **40. a)** $\dfrac{4}{5}$ **b)** $\dfrac{12}{13}$ **c)** $\dfrac{33}{65}$ **d)** $-\dfrac{56}{65}$

e) Quadrant II **41. a)** no amplitude; period: $\dfrac{\pi}{2}$

b) $y = \tan 2x$ **42. a)** period: π; amplitude: 1

b) $y = \cos 2x$ **44. a)** For $\theta \geq 66.5°$, the light energy
is 0. **b)** $0.228E$

46. 2.4 m **47.** $\theta \neq \dfrac{n\pi}{2}$, n any integer

48. $\cot(A + B) = \dfrac{\cot A \cot B - 1}{\cot A + \cot B}$

49. $\cot(A - B) = \dfrac{\cot A \cot B + 1}{\cot B - \cot A}$

51. a) $270°$ **b)** $90°$ **52.** $\dfrac{\pi}{4} + n\pi$, n any integer
53. b) 4 m **c)** No; to reach $x = 3.3$, $\theta_2 \doteq 8°$, but to
reach $y = 2.5$, $\theta \doteq 18°$. Also, the distance is greater

than the maximum: $\sqrt{3.3^2 + 2.5^2} \doteq 4.14$.

Computer Data Bank p. 275
1 Tides 1. Mar. 21, 12.64 h; Sept. 21, 13.01 h
2. Pacific, Sept. 21; Atlantic, Mar. 21
2 Port Accessibility 1. a) 16.1 m **b)** 9.775 m **2. a)** 21
b) 111 **3. a)** 1 **b)** 25 **4. a)** Mar. 21, 2; Sept. 21, 1
b) Mar. 21, 67; Sept. 21, 53; the least channel depth is
the least channel depth on Mar. 21 and on Sept. 21;
many more ports are accessible to the cruise ship at
high tide than at low tide, while high tide made little
or no difference in accessibility for the container ship,
which had the greater depth requirement
3 Periodic Functions 1. a) Saint John **b)** 5.00 m,
12.50 h, 7.9 m, 9.4 m **c)** Both are graphs of sinusoidal
functions with periods of 12.5 h and amplitudes of
2.5 m. **i)** shows a vertical displacement 10.4 m upward
relative to the function $y = \sin x$, and is the change in
the channel depth at Saint John on Sept. 21 **ii)** shows
a vertical displacement 11.9 m upward relative to the
function $y = \sin x$, and is the change in the anchorage
depth at Saint John on Sept. 21 **2. a)** a is half the tide
range on Sept. 21. **b)** b is 2 divided by the tide period
on Sept. 21. **c) i)** k is the least channel depth plus a.
ii) k is the least anchorage depth plus a.
3. i) $d(t) = 2.5 \sin 0.16\pi t + 10.4$
ii) $d(t) = 2.5 \sin 0.16\pi t + 11.9$

Connecting Math and Communications
pp. 276–277
1 Radio Stations 1. a) $A + km(t)$ **b)** modulation
c) yes; f_c **d)** $y = 1 + \dfrac{k}{Am(t)}$ **2. a)** $1 + \dfrac{k}{Am(t)}$
b) reflection in the x-axis **4. a)** frequency
2 Television Stations 1. b) amplitude = 1,
period = $\dfrac{\pi}{2}$

Review pp. 278–279
1. $\dfrac{\pi}{3}, \dfrac{5\pi}{3}$ **2.** $\dfrac{\pi}{9}, \dfrac{5\pi}{9}, \dfrac{7\pi}{9}, \dfrac{11\pi}{9}, \dfrac{13\pi}{9}, \dfrac{17\pi}{9}$

3. $\dfrac{\pi}{9} + \dfrac{2n\pi}{3}, \dfrac{5\pi}{9} + \dfrac{2n\pi}{3}$, n any integer **4.** π **5.** $\dfrac{\pi}{4},$

$\dfrac{3\pi}{4}, \dfrac{5\pi}{4}, \dfrac{7\pi}{4}$ **6.** $\dfrac{\pi}{4}$, n any integer **7. b)** $\dfrac{\pi}{4} + 2n\pi,$

$\dfrac{3\pi}{4} + 2n\pi$, n any integer **c)** The solution is the same.

Find the zeros of the function. **8.** $45°, 225°$ **9.** $15°,$
$105°, 195°, 285°$ **10.** $60°, 240°$ **11.** $0°, 60°, 120°,$

180°, 240°, 300° **12.** 60°, 120°, 240°, 300° **13.** 30°, 330° **14.** 90° **15.** 120°, 240°

16. $\frac{\pi}{3}, \frac{\pi}{2}, \frac{3\pi}{2}, \frac{5\pi}{3}; \frac{\pi}{3} + 2n\pi, (2n+1)\frac{\pi}{2},$

$\frac{5\pi}{3} + 2n\pi, n$ any integer **17.** $\frac{\pi}{3}, \frac{2\pi}{3}, \frac{4\pi}{3}, \frac{5\pi}{3};$

$\frac{\pi}{3} + n\pi, \frac{2\pi}{3} + n\pi, n$ any integer **18.** $\frac{\pi}{6}, \frac{3\pi}{4}, \frac{5\pi}{6},$

$\frac{7\pi}{4}; \frac{\pi}{6} + 2n\pi, \frac{3\pi}{4} + n\pi, \frac{5\pi}{6} + 2n\pi, n$ any integer

19. $\frac{\pi}{4}, \frac{3\pi}{4}, \frac{5\pi}{4}, \frac{7\pi}{4}; (2n+1)\frac{\pi}{4}, n$ any integer

20. $0, \frac{\pi}{2}, \frac{3\pi}{4}, \pi, \frac{3\pi}{2}, \frac{7\pi}{4}; \frac{n\pi}{2}, \frac{3\pi}{4} + n\pi, n$ any

integer **21.** $\frac{\pi}{3}, \pi, \frac{5\pi}{3}; \frac{\pi}{3} + 2n\pi, (2n+1)\pi,$

$\frac{5\pi}{3} + 2n\pi, n$ any integer **22.** $\frac{\pi}{6}, \frac{\pi}{3}, \frac{\pi}{2}, \frac{5\pi}{6}, \pi,$

$\frac{7\pi}{6}, \frac{3\pi}{2}, \frac{5\pi}{3}, \frac{11\pi}{6}; \frac{\pi}{6} + n\pi, (2n+1)\frac{\pi}{3},$

$(2n+1)\frac{\pi}{3}, \frac{5\pi}{6} + n\pi, n$ any integer **23.** $0, \pi, \frac{\pi}{3},$

$\frac{2\pi}{3}; n\pi, \frac{\pi}{3} + 2n\pi, \frac{2\pi}{3} + 2n\pi, n$ any integer

24. a) $\frac{\pi}{2}, 3.4, 6.0$ **b)** $1.2, \frac{\pi}{2}, \frac{3\pi}{2}, 5.1$ **c)** $1.2, \frac{3\pi}{4}, 4.3,$

$\frac{7\pi}{4}$ **d)** $0.7, 2.3, 4.0, 5.6$ **e)** $1.4, 1.9, 4.5, 5.0$

25. a) 3 **b)** $f(x) = 3\sin^2 x - x - \cos x; -0.418, 0.783,$
2.311 **26. b)** $\pm 2.279, 0$ **c)** If the window is expanded
to $[-4\pi, 4\pi]$, it is evident that these are the only
solutions. **d)** 3.106 **32. a)** both sides equal $\frac{4}{9}$

c) $\theta \neq (2n+1)\frac{\pi}{2}, n$ any integer **33. a)** both sides

equal $\frac{\sqrt{2}}{3}$ **c)** $\theta \neq (2n+1)\frac{\pi}{2}, n$ any integer

34. a) both sides equal $1 - \sqrt{3}$ **c)** $\theta \neq \frac{n\pi}{2}, n$ any

integer **35. a)** both sides equal $\frac{1}{\sqrt{3}}$

c) $\theta \neq (2n+1)\frac{\pi}{2}, (2n+1)\pi, n$ any integer **36.** $\cot^2 x$

37. 1 **38.** $\csc^2 x$ **39.** $2 + 2\cos x$ **40.** $\frac{\sqrt{3}-1}{2\sqrt{2}}$ **41.** $\frac{\sqrt{3}}{2}$

42. $\frac{1}{\sqrt{3}}$ **43.** 0 **44.** $\frac{\sqrt{3}}{2}$ **45.** $\cos\frac{\pi}{2}$ **46.** $\tan\frac{5\pi}{12}$

47. $\sin 150°$ **48.** $\cos\frac{2\pi}{3}$

Exploring Math p. 279

1. $M = \sqrt{\frac{2}{1-\cos\theta}}$ **2.** $\theta = 60°$ **3.** $\sqrt{2\sqrt{2}+4}$ **4. a)** 2.9

b) 41° **5.** It decreases.

Chapter Check p. 280

1. b) $\frac{\pi}{6}, \frac{11\pi}{6}$ **c)** $\frac{\pi}{6} + 2n\pi, \frac{11\pi}{6} + 2n\pi, n$ any integer

d) The solution is the same. Find the zeros of the
function. **2.** 180° **3.** 15°, 75°, 195°, 255° **4.** 30°,
210° **5.** 60°, 120°, 240°, 300° **6.** $\frac{\pi}{6}, \frac{5\pi}{6}, \frac{7\pi}{6},$

$\frac{11\pi}{6}; \frac{\pi}{6} + n\pi, \frac{5\pi}{6} + n\pi, n$ any integer

7. $\frac{\pi}{4}, \frac{\pi}{2}, \frac{3\pi}{4}, \frac{5\pi}{4}, \frac{3\pi}{2}, \frac{7\pi}{4};$

$(2n+1)\frac{\pi}{4}, (2n+1)\frac{\pi}{2}, n$ any integer **8. a)** 3

b) $f(x) = 2\cos^2 x - \frac{1}{2}x - \sin x; 0.754, 2.777, 3.777$

9. May 13, August 29 **10. a)** both sides equal 4
d) $x \neq n\pi, n$ any integer **11. a)** both sides equal 1

d) $x \neq \frac{n\pi}{2}, n$ any integer **12. a)** both sides equal 1

d) $x \neq (2n+1)\frac{\pi}{2}, n$ any integer **13. a)** both sides

equal $\frac{\sqrt{3}-1}{2}$ **d)** $x \neq (2n+1)\frac{\pi}{2}, x \neq \frac{3\pi}{4} + n\pi, n$ any

integer **14.** $\frac{1}{\sin x(1-\sin x)}$ **15.** $\tan x$ **16.** $\cot x$

17. $\csc^2 x$ **18.** $\frac{1-\sqrt{3}}{2\sqrt{2}}$ **19.** $-2 - \sqrt{3}$ **20.** $\frac{1-\sqrt{3}}{2\sqrt{2}}$

21. $\dfrac{1-\sqrt{3}}{2\sqrt{2}}$ **22.** false **23.** false **24.** true **25.** true
26. false

Using the Strategies p. 281
1. 4 **2.** 41.4° **3.** 7 h 52 min **4.** $a^2(1 - \dfrac{\pi}{4})$
5. 1, 4, 9, 16, 25 **6.** 43 **7.** 9703 + 9703 = 19 406 or
9604 + 9604 = 19 208 or 9802 + 9802 = 19 604 **8.** 37
and 38 **9.** 5.54 **10.** $98^2 = 9604$ **11.** twice **12.** 6.9 m
13. 15° **14.** 6

Chapter 6

Sequences and Series p. 283
1. after the third pill at 16 h **2.** 23 **3.** 800 mg **4.** So
that the effective level is established right away.

Getting Started p. 284–285
Patterns
1 Recognizing Patterns 1. a) dime, nickel, penny
b) Charlottetown, Inuvik, St. John's, Winnipeg
c) CFJ, EHL, FIM **d)** 128, 2048 **e)** 12, 27 **f)** 19, 29
g) Prince Edward Island, New Brunswick, Manitoba,
Quebec, Yukon
2 Fractals 2. Step 3 total is 3. Step 4:
$$1 + \frac{1}{2} + \frac{1}{2} + \frac{1}{4} + \frac{1}{4} + \frac{1}{4} + \frac{1}{4} + \frac{1}{8} + \frac{1}{8} + \frac{1}{8} + \frac{1}{8} + \frac{1}{8} + \frac{1}{8} = 4$$
3. There is no final answer. The total length after n
steps is n. **5.** Step 3: $1 + \dfrac{1}{4} + \dfrac{1}{4} + \dfrac{1}{16} + \dfrac{1}{16} + \dfrac{1}{16} + \dfrac{1}{16}$
$= 1\dfrac{3}{4}$. Step 4: $1 + \dfrac{1}{4} + \dfrac{1}{4} + \dfrac{1}{16} + \dfrac{1}{16} + \dfrac{1}{16} + \dfrac{1}{16} + \dfrac{1}{64} + \dfrac{1}{64}$
$+ \dfrac{1}{64} + \dfrac{1}{64} + \dfrac{1}{64} + \dfrac{1}{64} + \dfrac{1}{64} + \dfrac{1}{64} = 1\dfrac{7}{8}$ **6.** The total

length after step n is $2 - \dfrac{1}{2^{n-1}}$. So, the total length of

this fractal is 2.

Warm Up 1. $\dfrac{3}{2}$ **2.** $\dfrac{4}{3}$ **3.** $\dfrac{15}{8}$ **4.** $\dfrac{40}{27}$ **5.** 3 **6.** 3 **7.** 11
8. 4 **9.** 4 **10.** 4 **11.** $a = 7, d = 3$ **12.** $a = \dfrac{9}{2}, d = \dfrac{13}{2}$
13. $a = \dfrac{69}{8}, d = \dfrac{15}{8}$ **14.** $a = 103, d = -3$
15. $a = \dfrac{2}{3}, r = 3$, or $a = -\dfrac{2}{3}, r = -3$ **16.** $a = 1, r = 2$
17. $a = 10\ 000, r = \dfrac{1}{10}$, or $a = 10\ 000, r = -\dfrac{1}{10}$

18. $a = 5, r = 3$, or $a = -5, r = -3$ **19.** 5 **20.** 6 **21.** 1.5
22. 4 **23.** 1.5 **24.** 1.5 **25.** 2.8 **26.** 8.0 **27.** 2 log 8
28. 1.5 log 8 **29.** −2 log 8 **30.** 0 log 8 **31.** 2.017
32. 2.475 **33.** 1.281 **34.** 4.729

Mental Math
1.–14. Estimates will vary. Exact answers or
approximations to 4 digits are given. **1.** 1521
2. 6.2001 **3.** 2601 **4.** 8.242 408 **5.** 10 609
6. 952 763.904 **7.** 0.001 944 81 **8.** 0. 704 969
9. 909.9 **10.** 189.75 **11.** 52.10 **12.** 303.8 **13.** 584.2
14. 802.4 **15.** $19.17 **16.** $179.84 **17.** $16.17
18. $14.00 **19.** $8.80 **20.** $0.75 **21.** 8 **22.** 81
23. 625 **24.** 216 **25.** 1024 **26.** 32 **27.** 0.125 **28.** 6.25
29. 55 **30.** 110 **31.** 120 **32.** −55 **33.** 0 **34.** 360
35. $\dfrac{1023}{512}$ **36.** 82.5 **37.** 117.6 **38.** 0.999 **39.** $555
40. 16 **41.** $0.99k$ **42.** 1 **43.** 2 **44.** 6 **45.** 24 **46.** 120
47. 720 **48.** 1 **49.** 650 **50.** 22, 29 **51.** 654 321,
6 543 217 **52.** $\dfrac{1}{125}, \dfrac{1}{216}$ **53.** 720, 5040

Section 6.1 pp. 290–291
Practice 1. a) 1, 2, 3, 4, 5 **2. a)** 2, 4, 16, 256, 65 536
3. a) 5, 17, 54, 166, 503 **4. a)** 10, $\dfrac{1}{10}$, 10, $\dfrac{1}{10}$, 10
5. a) 4, 10, 19, 31, 46 **6. a)** −8, 1, 5.5, 7.75, 8.875
7. 256, 1024; $t_n = 4\ t_{n-1}, t_1 = 1$
8. 243, −729; $t_n = -3\ t_{n-1}, t_1 = 3$
9. 0.01, 0.001; $t_n = 0.1\ t_{n-1}, t_1 = 100$
10. −62.5, 31.25; $t_n = -\dfrac{1}{2}t_{n-1}, t_1 = -1000$
11. 364, 1093; $t_n = 3t_{n-1} + 1, t_1 = 1$
12. 1, $\dfrac{1}{4}$; $t_n = \dfrac{1}{4}t_{n-1}, t_1 = 256$
13. a) 3, 5, 7, 9, 11 **14. a)** 1, 3, 7, 15, 31
15. a) 4, 9, 16, 25, 36 **16. a)** 3, 2, 1, 0, 1
17. a) 0, 1, 4, 9, 16 **18. a)** −2, 5, 24, 61, 122
19. 13, 16; $t_n = 3n - 2$
20. 0.002 43, 0.000 729; $t_n = 0.3^n$
21. 32, −64; $t_n = (-1)^{n-1}2^n$
22. 01, 0.1; $t_n = 10\ 000(0.1)^{n-1}$
23. 25, 20; $t_n = 50 - 5n$ **24.** 512, 2048; $t_n = 2^{2n-1}$
Applications and Problem Solving 25. a) $V_n = n^3$;
729 **b)** $S_n = 6n^2$; 216 **26. a)** $t_n = t_{n-1} + t_{n-2}, t_1 = 1$,
$t_2 = 1$; 1, 1, 2, 3, 5, 8, 13, 21, 34, 55 **b)** Each month,
you have the rabbits you had last month (t_{n-1}), and
the rabbits you had two months ago (t_{n-2}) are all
reproducing. The assumptions are those given in the
problem, and you assume no rabbits die. **27. a)** Each

number is the sum of the two numbers diagonally above it to the left and right. 1, 5, 10, 10, 5, 1; 1, 6, 15, 20, 15, 6, 1 **b)** $t_{i,j} = t_{i-1,j-1} + t_{i-1,j}$ **28.** No. Answers will vary. **29.** sides: 6, 7; diagonals: 5, 9, 14

a) $d_n = \dfrac{n(n-3)}{2}$ **b)** 44 **30. a)** 3, 7, 15, 31

b) $t_n = 2t_{n-1} + 1$; 1023 **c)** $t_n = 2^n - 1$
d) 5.85×10^{11} years **31. a)** First sequence: 1, 2, 4, 8, 16; second sequence: 1, 2, 4, 7, 11. **b)** Answers will vary. **c)** Answers will vary.

Section 6.2 pp. 295–296
Practice
1. $a = 2$, $d = 3$; $t_n = 3n - 1$; yes.
2. $a = 20$, $d = -4$; $t_n = 24 - 4n$; yes.
3. not arithmetic; $t_n = 2^n$; no **4.** $a = 1$, $d = 0.6$
5. $a = -2$, $d = -3$ **6.** not arithmetic **7.** $a = x$, $d = y$
8. not arithmetic **9.** $a = 4$, $d = 3$; $t_n = 3n + 1$
10. $a = 42$, $d = 2$; $t_n = 2n + 40$
11. $a = -19$, $d = 7$; $t_n = 7n - 26$
12. $a = 67$, $d = -5$; $t_n = 72 - 5n$

13. $a = -137$, $d = -\dfrac{10}{3}$; $t_n = \dfrac{-10n - 401}{3}$

14. $a = 3 - 22x$, $d = \dfrac{9}{2}x$; $t_n = 3 + \left(\dfrac{9}{2}n - \dfrac{53}{2}\right)x$

15. 64; 4224 **16.** 32; 1552 **17.** 107; 3263.5
18. 31; −899 **19.** 27; $27p + 1053$ **20.** 19; $190 + 380k$
21. $(-5) + (-4) + (-3) + (-2) + (-1) + 0 + 1 + 2 = -12$
22. $3 + 7 + 11 + 15 + 19 + 23 = 78$
23. $9 + 2 + (-5) + (-12) + (-19) = -25$
24. $202.5 + 205 + 207.5 + 210 + 212.5 + 215 = 1252.5$
25. $70 + 67 + 64 + 61 + 58 + 55 = 375$
26. $4.2 + 3 + 1.8 + 0.6 + (-0.6) + (-1.8) + (-3) = 4.2$

27. $t_n = 4n - 2$; $\displaystyle\sum_{k=1}^{6}(4k - 2)$ **28.** $t_n = 5n$; $\displaystyle\sum_{k=1}^{8}5k$

29. $t_n = 7 - 3n$; $\displaystyle\sum_{k=3}^{9}(7 - 3k)$

30. $t_n = 2n - 0.5$; $\displaystyle\sum_{k=1}^{6}(2k - 0.5)$

31. $t_n = 8.4 - 2n$; $\displaystyle\sum_{k=2}^{8}(8.4 - 2k)$

32. $t_n = 20 - 20n$; $\displaystyle\sum_{k=-5}^{0}(20 - 20k)$

Applications and Problem Solving
33. $t_n - t_{n-1} = 5n + 4 - (5(n - 1) + 4) = 5$; $a = 9$, $d = 5$
34. a) $a + l = a + (a + (n - 1)d) = 2a + (n - 1)d$. The rest of the formula is the same. **b)** 3176 **35. a)** $2650
b) $21 900 **36. a)** 55 **b)** 89 **37.** 25 **38.** $S_n = n^2$ **39.** 5
40. Yes. The new value of d is the old value multiplied by the constant. **41. a)** first sequence: $t_n = 12n - 20$; second sequence: $t_n = 8n + 20$
b) Both graphs are straight lines that have positive slopes. The first sequence has a greater slope and the second sequence has a term with a negative value.

42. $a = 17$, $d = -3$ **43.** $\dfrac{3}{2}$, 5, $\dfrac{17}{2}$ **44.** $d = \dfrac{i^2 - j^2}{j - i}$

45. 816 **46.** 14 or −4 **47.** $k = 8$ or 14 **48.** 408

Section 6.3 pp. 300–301
Practice 1. 15, 5, $\dfrac{5}{3}$, $\dfrac{5}{9}$, $\dfrac{5}{27}$; $t_n = 15\left(\dfrac{1}{3}\right)^{n-1}$

2. 0.5, 1, 2, 4, 8; $t_n = 0.5(2)^{n-1}$

3. −12, 6, −3, $\dfrac{3}{2}$, $\dfrac{3}{4}$; $t_n = -12\left(-\dfrac{1}{2}\right)^{n-1}$

4. 0.11, 0.33, 0.99, 2.97, 8.91; $t_n = 0.11(3)^{n-1}$

5. 100, 25, 6.25, 1.5625, 0.390 625; $t_n = 100\left(\dfrac{1}{4}\right)^{n-1}$

6. 686, 98, 14, 2, $\dfrac{2}{7}$; $t_n = 686\left(\dfrac{1}{7}\right)^{n-1}$

7. 4, 16, 64, 256, 1024; $t_n = 4(4)^{n-1}$

8. 121, 11, 1, $\dfrac{1}{11}$, $\dfrac{1}{121}$; $t_n = 121\left(\dfrac{1}{11}\right)^{n-1}$

9. 1.28, 0.64, 0.32, 0.16, 0.08; $t_n = 1.28\left(\dfrac{1}{2}\right)^{n-1}$

10. −15, 225, −3375, 50 625, −759 375; $t_n = -15(-15)^{n-1}$ **11.** 256 **12.** 68 359 375 **13.** $\dfrac{22}{27}$

14. 7812.5 **15.** $\dfrac{6561}{5}$ **16.** $-\dfrac{37}{2187}$ **17.** 320 **18.** 6561

or −6561 **19.** $-\dfrac{2}{125}$ or $\dfrac{2}{125}$ **20.** 9 000 000 **21.** $\dfrac{4}{27}$

22. $\dfrac{1}{81}$

Applications and Problem Solving 23. a) $x = 2$, $y = 54$
b) $x = 54$, $y = 162$ **c)** $x = 6\sqrt{3}$, $y = 18\sqrt{3}$ or
$x = -6\sqrt{3}$, $y = -18\sqrt{3}$ **d)** $x = 6\sqrt[3]{3}$, $y = 6\sqrt[3]{9}$ **24.** 22.6

25. a) 1.35%; Estimates for the world's population annually from 2000 to 2010, in billions, are 6.0563, 6.1382, 6.2212, 6.3053, 6.3905, 6.4769, 6.5645, 6.6532, 6.7432, 6.8343, 6.9267. **b)** Answers will vary. **26.** to 2 decimal places: G#: 415.31 Hz; A: 440.00 Hz; A#: 466.17 Hz; B: 493.88 Hz. **27.** $720.30 **28.** 8192 **29.** 6 **30. a)** 32 or −32 **b)** 128, 64, 32, 16, 8 or −128, 64, −32, 16, −8 **31. a)** For each triangle, $h = \sqrt{2}$. So, $r = \sqrt{2}$ **b)** $8\sqrt{2}$ units **32.** Answers will vary. **33. a)** For the first sequence, $d = 4$. For the second sequence, $r = 2^4$. **b)** The common difference equals $p - n = q - p = r - q$ and the ratio equals $x^{p-n} = x^{q-p} = x^{r-q}$. Thus, the ratio equals $x^{difference}$, making the sequence geometric. **34.** fifth **35.** 3, 6, 12 **36.** 1; $n = 51$ **37.** only if the terms are the same ($d = 0$, $r = 1$)

38. $t_n = 32\left(\dfrac{1}{\sqrt{2}}\right)^{n-1}$; $\sqrt{2}$

Section 6.4 pp. 304–305

Practice **1.** 5% **2.** 7% **3.** $2\frac{1}{2}$% **4.** 3% **5.** 1% **6.** $\frac{3}{8}$%

7. $1\frac{7}{8}$% **8.** 0.021 92% **9.** 2.75% **10.** 3.39% **11.** 10

12. 10 **13.** 22 **14.** 16 **15.** 72 **16.** 9 **17.** $7969.24 **18.** $2960.49 **19.** $21 153.30 **20.** $1306.05 **21.** $4418.79 **22.** 7 years **23.** 10 years **24.** 5 years **25.** 10 years **26.** 12 years

Applications and Problem Solving
27. the second option **28.** $2262.94 **29.** $18 849.12 **30. a)** $580.48 **b)** 26.4 **31. a)** $906.78 **b)** $3779.14 **c)** $127.64 **d)** The tax reduction could exceed the cost. **32. b)** Answers will vary.
33. a factor of 71.197 313 **34. a)** overestimates **b)** underestimates **35. a)** In $A = P(1 + i)^n$, use $A = 2P$. Then, $2P = P(1 + i)^n$ or $2 = (1 + i)^n$. Applying the logarithmic function to both sides gives

$\log 2 = n \log (1 + i)$. Thus, $n = \dfrac{\log 2}{\log (1+i)}$.

b) Answers will vary depending on the rates used.

Section 6.5 pp. 309–310

Practice **1.** $\dfrac{31\,525}{64}$ **2.** $\dfrac{2205}{16}$ **3.** $\dfrac{2662}{27}$

4. 1234.444 321 **5.** $\dfrac{511}{3}$ **6.** −111.375 **7.** $\dfrac{171}{13}$

8. $4 + 8 + 16 = 28$ **9.** $1 + 0.1 + 0.01 + 0.001 = 1.111$
10. $1 + 9 + 81 + 729 + 6561 = 7381$

11. $25 + \dfrac{25}{2} + \dfrac{25}{4} + \dfrac{25}{8} + \dfrac{25}{16} + \dfrac{25}{32} = \dfrac{1575}{32}$

12. $1 + 1 + 1 + 1 + 1 + 1 + 1 + 1 + 1 + 1 = 10$

13. $\dfrac{3}{25} + \dfrac{3}{5} + 3 + 15 + 75 + 375 + 1875 + 9375$

$+\, 46\,875 = 58\,593\dfrac{18}{25}$

14. $\dfrac{1}{792} + \dfrac{1}{81} + \dfrac{1}{9} + 1 + 9 + 81 + 729 + 6561 + 59\,049$

$+\, 531\,441 + 4\,782\,969 = 5\,380\,840\dfrac{91}{729}$

15. $0.006\,75 + 0.001\,012\,5 + 0.000\,151\,875$
$+\, 0.000\,022\,781\,25 + 0.000\,003\,417\,187\,5$
$+\, 0.000\,000\,512\,578\,125 + 0.000\,000\,076\,886\,718\,75$
$+\, 0.000\,000\,011\,533\,007\,8 \doteq 0.007\,941\,17$

16. $\displaystyle\sum_{k=1}^{5} 12\left(\dfrac{1}{4}\right)^{k-1} = 15\dfrac{63}{64}$ **17.** $\displaystyle\sum_{k=1}^{10} 0.5(2)^{k-1} = 511.5$

18. $\displaystyle\sum_{k=1}^{7} -12\left(\dfrac{1}{2}\right)^{k-1} = -23\dfrac{13}{16}$

19. $\displaystyle\sum_{k=1}^{9} 0.11(3)^{k-1} = 1082.51$

20. $\displaystyle\sum_{k=1}^{6} 100\left(\dfrac{1}{4}\right)^{k-1} = 133\dfrac{77}{256}$

21. $\displaystyle\sum_{k=1}^{7} 1.99(10)^{k-1} = 2.211\,110\,89$

Applications and Problem Solving
22. a) 1.845×10^{19} grains **b)** Answers will vary depending on the year of production. He asked for 1.2 trillion tonnes. **23.** 63 **24.** 57.65 million ha **25.** $7140.27 **26.** 25.113 54 m **27.** Ruta **28.** 118 cm **29. a)** falls: $100 + 90 + 81 + 72.9 + 65.61$; recoils: $60 + 54 + 48.6 + 43.74 + 39.366$ **b)** 655 m **30.** 440 m **31.** $5396.31 **32. a)** Each series in expanded form is $ar^0 + ar^1 + \ldots + ar^{n-1}$. **b)** Each series in expanded form is $ar^l + ar^{l+1} + \ldots + ar^n$. **33.** 3 **34.** 131 071

Investigating Math pp. 311–312

1 An Algebraic Application **1. a)** 2.5, 2.4, 2.41$\overline{6}$, 2.4138, 2.4143, 2.4142, 2,414 216, 2.414 213 2, 2.414 213 6, 2.414 213 55
b) To get the next approximation, use the reciprocal key followed by + 2 and the equals key.
2. $1 + \sqrt{2}$; It is the exact root of the equation.

3. Use $x = 4 + \cfrac{1}{4 + \cfrac{1}{4 + \ldots}}$. This will approach the

value of the exact root of the equation
$2 + \sqrt{5} \doteq 4.236\ 068$.

2 A Function Application   1. a) $f(x)$: $-7, -3, -1, 0, 0.5,$
$0.75, 0.875, 0.9375, \ldots$ **b)** It decreases to approach 0.
c) domain: real numbers; range: $y < 1$.
d) It is a horizontal asymptote.

3 A Series Application   1. Values: $1, 0, \dfrac{1}{2}, \dfrac{1}{3}, \dfrac{3}{8}, \dfrac{11}{30},$

$\dfrac{53}{144}, 0.367\ 857, 0.367\ 882, 0.367\ 879\ 2$

2. a) Answers will vary. As n increases, $\dfrac{1}{n!}$ decreases

to approach 0. **b)** $0.367\ 879\ldots$
c) $0.367\ 879\ 441\ 2$; six places

Section 6.6 pp. 316–317

Practice   1. $\dfrac{100}{9}$ **2.** 64 **3.** $\dfrac{8}{3}$ **4.** $\dfrac{15\ 625}{24}$ **5.** $-\dfrac{243}{2}$

6. $\dfrac{1}{1-x}$ if $|x| < 1$ **7.** no sum

8. $\dfrac{1}{3} + \dfrac{1}{9} + \dfrac{1}{27} + \dfrac{1}{81} + \ldots = \dfrac{1}{2}$

9. $2 + 0.2 + 0.02 + 0.002 + \ldots = \dfrac{20}{9}$

10. $2 + 1.8 + 1.62 + 1.458 + \ldots = 20$

11. $20 + 10 + 5 + 2.5 + \ldots = 40$

12. $250 + 62.5 + 15.625 + 3.90625 + \ldots = \dfrac{1000}{3}$

13. $\dfrac{1}{4} + \dfrac{1}{8} + \dfrac{1}{16} + \dfrac{1}{32} + \ldots = \dfrac{1}{2}$

14. $\dfrac{7}{2} + \dfrac{49}{12} + \dfrac{343}{72} + \dfrac{2401}{432} + \ldots$; no sum: $|r| > 1$

15. $2.2 + 2.42 + 2.662 + 2.9282 + \ldots$; no sum: $|r| > 1$
Applications and Problem Solving
16. a) $0.999\ 999\ 999\ldots = 0.9 + 0.09 + 0.009 + \ldots,$

which is the geometric series $\displaystyle\sum_{i=0}^{\infty} 0.9(0.1)^i$. This

equals 1.

b) $99.999\ 999\ldots = 99 + 0.9 + 0.09 + 0.009 + \ldots,$

which is $99 + \displaystyle\sum_{i=0}^{\infty} 0.9(0.1)^i$. This equals $99 + 1$ or 100.

c) $5.499\ 999\ldots = 5.4 + 0.09 + 0.009 + 0.0009 + \ldots,$

which is $5.4 + \displaystyle\sum_{i=0}^{\infty} 0.09(0.1)^i$. This equals $5.4 + 0.1$ or

5.5. **17. a)** $\dfrac{1}{9}$ **b)** $\dfrac{79}{0}$ **c)** $\dfrac{7}{33}$ **d)** $\dfrac{37}{55}$ **e)** $\dfrac{151\ 889}{333\ 000}$ **f)** $\dfrac{3520}{999}$

18. a) The corner triangles have 4-cm sides. Thus,
the hypotenuse, which is the side of the second
square, is $4\sqrt{2}$ cm.

b) $32 + 16\sqrt{2} + 16 + \ldots = \dfrac{32}{1 - \dfrac{1}{\sqrt{2}}}$ or $32\sqrt{2}(\sqrt{2} + 1)$ cm

c) $64 + 32 + 16 + \ldots = 128$ (cm²) **d)** $64 = \dfrac{1}{2}(128)$

19. a) 741 327 t **b)** 3 253 556 t **20. a)** 36.9%
b) 40.1% **21. a)** 230.8 L **b)** 1250 L

22. a) $45\left(\dfrac{10}{53}\right) + 45\left(\dfrac{10}{53}\right)\left(\dfrac{37}{53}\right) + 45\left(\dfrac{10}{53}\right)\left(\dfrac{37}{53}\right)^2 + \ldots$

b) 28.125 km **c)** The dragonfly is flying while the

joggers cover the 10 km in $\dfrac{5}{8}$ h. Therefore, the

dragonfly covers $45\left(\dfrac{5}{8}\right)$ or 28.125 km. **23.** $\dfrac{1}{4}$

24. a) no total **b)** 2 units **c)** Answers will vary.

25. a) no total **b)** $\dfrac{\sqrt{3}}{4}, 0$

Section 6.7 p. 320–321

Practice   1. $1, \dfrac{3}{2}, \dfrac{11}{6}, \dfrac{25}{12}, \dfrac{137}{60}$ **2.** 1, 5, 14, 30, 55

3. $\dfrac{1}{2}, \dfrac{7}{6}, \dfrac{23}{12}, \dfrac{163}{60}, \dfrac{71}{20}$

4. $0, 1, 1 + \sqrt{2}, 1 + \sqrt{2} + \sqrt{3}, 3 + \sqrt{2} + \sqrt{3}$

5. $-1, -\dfrac{1}{2}, -\dfrac{5}{6}, -\dfrac{7}{12}, -\dfrac{47}{60}$ **6.** $0, \dfrac{1}{2}, \dfrac{9}{10}, \dfrac{6}{5}, \dfrac{122}{85}$

Applications and Problem Solving   7. 3.1833, 3.1406,
3.141 62, 3.141 591 8, 3.141 592 68
8. a) 1, 2, 2.5, 2.667, 2.708 333 **b)** 2.718 281

9. a) $a = \dfrac{1 + \sqrt{5}}{2}$ **b) (i)** $1, 2, 1.5, 1.\overline{6}, 1.6, 1.625;$

(ii) 1, 1.414, 1.554, 1.598, 1.612, 1.616; $\phi \doteq 1.618034$.
So, both approximations agree to 1 decimal place.
c) $1, 2, 1.5, 1.\overline{6}, 1.6, 1.625, 1.6154, 1.6190, 1.617\ 65,$
$1.6\overline{18}, 1.617\ 98, 1.618\ 06$; the sequence is
approaching ϕ. Yes, this will continue.
d) Answers will vary. **10. a)** 3.049 36
b) Not very accurate. The series converges rather

slowly. **11. a)** 3.141 592 653 62 **b)** Answers will vary.
12. $(x, y) = (1, 4)$ or $(2, 7)$

Technology p. 322
1 Exploring Radioactive Decay **2. a)** 1400 years. **b)** $\dfrac{1}{32}$
3. Change "= A3 + 70" to "= A3 + 120".
2 Using Spreadsheets to Explore Other Sequences
1. 102 334 155 **2.** e **3.** 1.563 039 45

Connecting Math and Computer Programming p. 323
1 The Binary Search
5. 500, 250, 125, 63, 32, 16, 8, 4, 2, 1; geometric
6. 10 **7.** 20

Review pp. 324–325
1. $-3, 0; t_n = t_{n-1} + 3$ **2.** $2, \dfrac{5}{2}; t_n = t_{n-1} + \dfrac{1}{2}$

3. $0.54, 0.65; t_n = t_{n-1} + 0.11$ **4.** $16, 32; t_n = 2\,t_{n-1}$
5. $3, 1, -1, -3, -5$ **6.** 4, 7, 12, 19, 28 **7.** 0, 2, 4, 6, 8
8. 4, 5, 8, 13, 20 **9. a)** $t_n = t_{n-1} + 7, t_1 = 35$
b) $t_n = t_{n-1} + 6, t_1 = 72$ **c)** $t_n = k\,t_{n-1}, t_1 = k^3$
10. $a = 1, d = 8, t_n = 8n - 7$
11. $a = -33, d = 12, t_n = 12n - 45$
12. $a = -65, d = 15, t_n = 15n - 80$
13. $a = 36, d = -9, t_n = 45 - 9n$
14. 407 **15.** -770 **16.** 154.4 **17.** 27 **18.** $\dfrac{1}{1\,000\,000}$

19. -2048 **20.** $\dfrac{75}{16}$ **21.** 0.000 499 9 **22.** $\dfrac{1}{243}$

23. 700 000 **24.** $\dfrac{5}{9}$ **25.** 7290 **26.** 177 147

27. a) $t_n = t_{n-1} + 4.8, t_1 = 83.7$ **b)** 126.9

28. a) $1170.97 **b)** $1162.64 **c)** $2333.61

29. 8 857 300 **30.** $\dfrac{1331}{27}$ **31.** $\dfrac{11\,025}{8}$ **32.** -1123.875

33. $\dfrac{5621}{30}$ **34.** $\dfrac{171}{13}$ **35.** 45 **36.** $\dfrac{1705}{256}$ **37.** 1365

38. $\dfrac{411\,800}{729}$ **39.** $\dfrac{3\,922\,632\,451}{729}$

40. 0.007 941 174 4 **41.** 9.113 25 m **42.** $\dfrac{10\,000}{9}$

43. $-\dfrac{1215}{2}$ **44.** 8 **45. a)** 1 204 347 t

b) in the 11th year **c)** 2 727 273 t **46. a)** $(2\pi r)n$

b) no infinite sum **c)** $\pi r^2, \dfrac{1}{4}\pi r^2, \dfrac{1}{16}\pi r^2, \dots$ **d)** $\dfrac{4}{3}\pi r^2$

47. $2, 3, 2.\overline{6}, 2.\overline{72}, 2.716\,98$

Exploring Math p. 325
1. a) 88, 176, 264, 352, 440 **b)** Venus: 225, 450, 675, 900, 1125; Earth: 365.25, 730.5, 1095.75, 1461, 1826.25 **d)** in 7 231 950 days **2.** Answers will vary.
3. Answers will vary. **4.** 1.26×10^{14} days

Chapter Check p. 326
1. 472 392 **2.** $\dfrac{5}{64}$ **3.** 11 **4.** $\dfrac{1331}{9}$ **5.** $-11\,111.11$

6. $\dfrac{1023}{256}$ **7.** arithmetic; 564

8. geometric; 1598.4375 **9.** arithmetic; -92
10. geometric; 2 466 666.42 **11.** geometric; 15.875

12. geometric; $\dfrac{390\,625}{6}$ **13.** arithmetic; no sum

14. $\dfrac{8}{9}$ **15.** 7410 **16.** 1984.375 **17.** $\dfrac{250}{3}$ **18.** 364

19. a) 50, 49, 48, … 15 **b)** 30 m **c)** 35 m **20. a)** 1024
b) 45 min **21.** 15 **22.** $7643.18
23. a) 100, 85, 72.25, 61.4125, … **b)** 44.37 N

24. a) $\dfrac{1}{6}, \dfrac{19}{36}, \dfrac{133}{216}, \dfrac{895}{1296}, \dfrac{5581}{7776}$ **b)** $\displaystyle\sum_{k=1}^{\infty} \dfrac{3^k + (-2)^k}{6^k}$ **c)** $\dfrac{3}{4}$

Using the Strategies p. 327
1. a) July 11, 1994 **b)** June 23, 2005 **2.** 252 cm^2
3. 27π cm^2 **4.** $4\sqrt{3}$ units **5.** no least value (values eventually start decreasing) **6.** 0
7. 150π square units **8.** 19 999
9. $4^{4^{4^4}}$, $4^{4^{44}}$, 4^{44^4}, 44^{4^4}, 4^{444}, 44^{44}, 444^4, 4444
10. 20 **11.** 488 895 **12.** 5 roosters, 1 hen, 94 chicks

13. Bottom   Middle   Top

4	12	26	20	7	15	18	23	1
11	25	6	9	14	19	22	3	17
27	5	10	13	21	8	2	16	24

14. 3 and 5, or -3 and -5

Cumulative Review, Chapters 4–6 pp. 328–329

1. 157.5° **2.** 375° **3.** -150° **4.** $-\dfrac{7\pi}{18}$ **5.** $\dfrac{25\pi}{9}$

6. $\dfrac{23\pi}{18}$ **7.** $\cos A = -\dfrac{1}{\sqrt{2}}$, $\tan A = -1$, $\csc A = \sqrt{2}$,

$\sec A = -\sqrt{2}$, $\cot A = -1$; $A = 135$° **8.** $\sin A = -\dfrac{1}{\sqrt{2}}$,

$\cos A = -\dfrac{1}{\sqrt{2}}$, $\csc A = -\sqrt{2}$, $\sec A = -\sqrt{2}$, $\cot A = 1$;

$A = 225°$ **9.** $\sin A = -\dfrac{1}{2}$, $\tan A = -\dfrac{1}{\sqrt{3}}$,

$\csc A = -2$, $\sec A = \dfrac{2}{\sqrt{3}}$, $\cot A = -\sqrt{3}$; $A = 330°$

10. amplitude 3, period 2π, phase shift 0, vertical displacement 1 **11.** amplitude 1, period 2π, phase shift $\dfrac{\pi}{4}$, vertical displacement 0 **12.** amplitude 1, period 120°, phase shift 15°, vertical displacement 7

13. amplitude 1, period $\dfrac{2\pi}{5}$, phase shift $-\dfrac{\pi}{6}$, vertical displacement -2 **14.** $y = 3\sin 2\left(x - \dfrac{\pi}{4}\right) + 1$;

$y = 3\cos 2\left(x - \dfrac{\pi}{2}\right) + 1$ **15. b)** $8\dfrac{1}{3}$ months **c)** \$5 million

16. a) period 2π; no phase shift; domain: $x \neq \dfrac{\pi}{2} + k\pi$, where k is any integer; range: $y \geq 5$ or $y \leq -5$
b) period $\dfrac{\pi}{3}$; no phase shift; domain: $x \neq k\pi$, where k is any integer; range: all real numbers **c)** period π; no phase shift; domain: $x \neq k\pi$, where k is any integer; range: $y \geq 1$ or $y \leq -1$ **d)** period π; phase shift $-\dfrac{\pi}{6}$; domain $x \neq \dfrac{\pi}{3} + k\pi$, where k is any integer; range all real numbers

17. $\dfrac{3\pi}{2}$; $\dfrac{3\pi}{2} + 2k\pi$, where k is any integer

18. $\dfrac{\pi}{6}, \dfrac{5\pi}{6}, \dfrac{7\pi}{6}, \dfrac{11\pi}{6}$; $k\pi \pm \dfrac{\pi}{6}$, where k is any integer

19. $\dfrac{\pi}{6}, \dfrac{5\pi}{6}, \dfrac{3\pi}{2}$; $\dfrac{\pi}{6} + 2k\pi$, $\dfrac{5\pi}{6} + 2k\pi$, $\dfrac{3\pi}{2} + 2k\pi$, where k is any integer

20. $\dfrac{\pi}{18}, \dfrac{11\pi}{18}, \dfrac{13\pi}{18}, \dfrac{23\pi}{18}, \dfrac{25\pi}{18}, \dfrac{35\pi}{18}$; $\dfrac{1}{3}\left(2k\pi \pm \dfrac{\pi}{6}\right)$

21. $\dfrac{\pi}{8}, \dfrac{3\pi}{8}, \dfrac{9\pi}{8}, \dfrac{11\pi}{8}$; $k\pi + \dfrac{\pi}{4} \pm \dfrac{\pi}{8}$, where k is any

integer **22. a)** 3 **b)** $y = 5\sin^2 x + 11\cos x - 3x$; $x = -3.413, -2.560, 1.591$

23. d) $x \neq \dfrac{\pi}{2} + k\pi$, where k is any integer

24. d) $x \neq (2k + 1)\pi$, where k is any integer

25. d) $x \neq \dfrac{\pi}{2} + k\pi$, where k is any integer

26. d) $x \neq \dfrac{k\pi}{2}$, where k is any integer

27. $\cos 80°$ **28.** $\cos \dfrac{\pi}{4}$ **29.** $\sin \dfrac{5\pi}{6}$

30. $\tan 250°$

31. a) $\sin(A + B) = \dfrac{56}{65}$, $\cos(A + B) = -\dfrac{33}{65}$,

$\sin(A - B) = -\dfrac{16}{65}$, $\cos(A - B) = \dfrac{63}{65}$

b) $\sin(A + B) = \dfrac{-1 - \sqrt{2}}{\sqrt{6}}$, $\cos(A + B) = \dfrac{1 - \sqrt{2}}{\sqrt{6}}$,

$\sin(A - B) = \dfrac{-1 + \sqrt{2}}{\sqrt{6}}$, $\cos(A - B) = \dfrac{1 + \sqrt{2}}{\sqrt{6}}$

32. a) 20 **b)** 30 **c)** 25 **33.** $\dfrac{8}{25}$ **34.** $\dfrac{1}{729}$

35. -1024 **36.** $\dfrac{3}{64}$ or $-\dfrac{3}{64}$ **37.** \$7162.36

38. $5 + 15 + 45 + 135 = 200$
39. $4 + 1.6 + 0.64 + 0.256 + 0.1024 = 6.5984$
40. $1 + 2 + 4 + 8 + 16 + 32 + 64 = 127$
41. $400 + 200 + 100 + 50 + 25 + 12.5 = 787.5$
42. \$193 955.63 **43.** $\dfrac{10}{3}$ **44.** $-\dfrac{64}{9}$ **45.** 12

46. a) 153 m **b)** 200 m **c)** the eighth **47.** $\dfrac{679}{4950}$

Chapter 7

Combinatorics p. 331
1. 8 **2.** 27

Getting Started pp. 332–333

Number Patterns
1. a) 7 **b)** 28 **c)** 84 **d)** $\dfrac{n(n+1)}{2}$,

where n is the height of the pyramid in cans **2. a)** 15

b) 45 **c)** 90 **d)** $\dfrac{nm(n+1)(m+1)}{4}$ **e)** 540 **3. a)** 2, 3, 4,

5, 6, 7; 3, 4, 5, 6, 7, 8; 4, 5, 6, 7, 8, 9; 5, 6, 7, 8, 9, 10;
6, 7, 8, 9, 10, 11; 7, 8, 9, 10, 11, 12 **b)** 7 **c)** 13

4. a) 7, 11, 16, 22 **b)** $\dfrac{n^2+n+2}{2}$ **c)** 121 **5. a)** 60

b) 840

Mental Math
1. $8x^3$ **2.** $3x^2$ **3.** $576a^8$ **4.** $\dfrac{n^2+n+2}{2}$

5. $\dfrac{1}{5x^{\frac{1}{3}}}$ **6.** x^9y^6 **7.** $27x^{\frac{3}{2}}$ **8.** $\dfrac{b^4}{9}$ **9.** $5a^{\frac{1}{2}}b$

10. $x^{\frac{2}{3}}$ **11.** $3^{2a-b}x^{3a-b}$ **12.** $6^n a^4 b^{4-\frac{n}{2}}$

13. $\dfrac{y^2}{x^2}$, $x \neq 0, y \neq 0$ **14.** $\dfrac{1+y}{x}$, $x \neq 0, y \neq 0$

15. $\dfrac{x+3}{x+4}$, $x \neq 1, -2, -4$ **16.** 1, $x \neq -5, 2, 3, 7$

17. $x^2 + 2x + 1$ **18.** $9x^2 - 12x + 4$ **19.** $x^2 - 6x + 9$
20. $25x^2 - 70x + 49$ **21.** $x^4 - 8x^2 + 16$
22. $x^4 - 12x^2 + 36$ **23.** 15 **24.** 25 **25.** 28 **26.** 4
27. 31 **28.** 15

Section 7.1 pp. 336–338
Practice 1. 6 **2.** 8 **3.** 12 **4.** 24
Applications and Problem Solving 5. 439 400 000
6. a) 64 **b)** 256 **c)** 4^n **7. a)** 64 **b)** 7 **8. a)** 17 576 000
b) 67 600 **9. a)** 2; 4; 8; 16 **b)** 30 **10. a)** 1024 **b)** 5
c) increasing the number of parts by one, since
$5^6 = 15\ 625$ is greater than $6^5 = 7776$ **11. a)** 12 **b)** 24
12. a) 144 **b)** 800 **13.** 16 777 216 **14. a)** 676 000

Section 7.2 pp. 342–343
Practice 1. 5! **2.** 3! **3.** 8! **4.** 6! **5.** $4 \times 3 \times 2 \times 1$
6. $7 \times 6 \times 5 \times 4 \times 3 \times 2 \times 1$ **7.** 5×4 **8.** $6 \times 5 \times 4 \times 3$
9. $11 \times 10 \times 9$ **10.** $9 \times 8 \times 7 \times 6 \times 5$

Answers may vary for 11.–13. 11. $8 \times 7 \times 5$
12. $14 \times 13 \times 11 \times 10$ **13.** $10 \times 9 \times 8 \times 7 \times 3$ **14.** $_5\text{P}_3$
15. $_8\text{P}_3$ **16.** $_{17}\text{P}_5$ **17.** $_{55}\text{P}_5$ **18.** $_8\text{P}_5$ **19.** $_{99}\text{P}_4$ **20.** $_{88}\text{P}_2$
Applications and Problem Solving 21. a) 27 **b)** 6
22. a) 40 320 **b)** 336 **23. a)** 24! **b)** 120 **c)** 5 100 480
24. a) 24 **b)** 24 **c)** 64 **d)** 10 **25. a)** 56 **b)** 56 **c)** equal;
Marion must go 5 blocks east (E) and 3 blocks north
(N), or EEEEENNN, to get to Rita's. **26. a)** 1680
b) 420 **27. a)** 813 960 **b)** 120 120 **28. a)** 357 840
b) 373 248 **c)** 24 690 960 **29.** 5 **30. a)** 1.1×10^{20}
b) 3.0×10^{21} **c)** 3.7×10^{29} **31. a)** 24 360 **b)** 2.65×10^{32}
32. a) 96 909 120 **b)** 1 071 100 800 **33. a)** 216 000
b) 205 320 **c)** 10 680 **34. a)** the number of
permutations of n objects selected from n objects
35. a) 24 **b)** 6 **36. a)** 24 **b)** No. **37.** 60

Investigating Math p. 344
1 Writing Sets and Subsets
1. b) {2, 3, 5, 7, 11, 13, 17, 19, 23}
2. a) Ø, {head}, {tail}, {head, tail}; Ø, {head}, {tail}
b) Ø, {penny}, {nickel}, {dime}, {penny, nickel},
{penny, dime}, {nickel, dime}, {penny, nickel, dime};
Ø, {penny}, {nickel}, {dime}, {penny, nickel},
{penny, dime}, {nickel, dime} **c)** 16; 15 **d)** 2^n; Each
item is either in the set or not, so there are 2 choices
for each item.
2 Subsets of a Particular Size 1. 10;
{ketchup, mustard}, {ketchup, relish},
{ketchup, onions}, {ketchup, tomatoes},
{mustard, relish}, {mustard, onions}, {mustard,
tomatoes}, {relish, onions}, {relish, tomatoes},
{onions, tomatoes} **2.** 4 **4.** 3; 9; {red, blue},
{red, yellow}, {blue, yellow}, {red}, {blue}, {yellow},
{{red, blue}, red}, {{red, blue}, blue},
{{red, blue,} yellow}, {{red, yellow}, red},
{{red, yellow}, blue}, {{red, yellow}, yellow},
{{blue, yellow}, red}, {{blue, yellow}, blue},
{{blue, yellow}, yellow}

Section 7.3 pp. 348–349
Practice 1. $4 \times 3 \times 2 \times 1$ **2.** 5×2 **3.** 3×5 **4.** 6×5
$\times 4 \times 3$ **5.** $22 \times 21 \times 20$ **6.** $29 \times 7 \times 9 \times 13 \times 5$ **7.** $_8\text{P}_3$
8. 7! **9.** $_7\text{C}_3$ **10.** $_{17}\text{P}_5$ **11.** $_{17}\text{C}_5$ **12.** $_{27}\text{C}_3$ **13.** $_{99}\text{P}_4$
14. $_{74}\text{C}_4$
Applications and Problem Solving 15. a) 15 **b)** 20
c) Answers may vary. Canada, Japan, China; USA,
Italy, France **16. a)** 6.35×10^{11} **b)** 1 677 106 640
c) 1.93×10^{11} **17. a)** 1.27×10^{38} **b)** 2.72×10^{24}
c) 1.27×10^{38} **d)** 228 826 **18. a)** 105 **b)** 3003 **c)** 364
d) 84 **e)** 371 **19. a)** 15 **b)** 4 **c)** 2 **d)** 5 **e)** 20 **f)** 15
20. a) 10, 10; 45, 45; 120, 120; 210, 210;
$_{10}\text{C}_r = {}_{10}\text{C}_{10-r}$ **b)** $_n\text{C}_r = {}_n\text{C}_{n-r}$ **21. a)** 6435 **b)** 120

c) 6075 **22. a)** 3 **b)** 6 **c)** 10 **d)** 28; 20 **e)** $\dfrac{n^2 - 3n}{2}$

23. a) 2 598 960 **b)** 65 780 **c)** 5148 **24. a)** $2^{10}(10!)$

b) $\dfrac{20!}{2^{10}(10!)}$ **c)** $2^{\frac{n}{2}}\left(\dfrac{n}{2}\right)!$ **d)** $\dfrac{(n+1)!}{2^{\frac{n+1}{2}}\left(\dfrac{n+1}{2}\right)!}$ **e)** $3^9(9!)$

Section 7.4 pp. 352–353
Practice 1. 10 **2.** 210 **3.** 12 **4.** 480
Applications and Problem Solving 5. a) sum of the numbers in the row: 1, 2, 4, 8, 16, 32, 64, 128, 256, 512 **b)** 1024 **c)** 2^n **6. a)** 69 **b)** 103, 89, 35 **c)** 2
7. b) $_4C_2$ **c)** $_3C_1 + {}_3C_2 = {}_4C_2$ **d)** $_nC_r + {}_nC_{r+1} = {}_{n+1}C_{r+1}$
e) $_4C_3;\ {}_6C_4;\ {}_{11}C_7$ **8.** 32

Section 7.5 pp. 356–357
Practice 1. $x^5 + 5x^4 + 10x^3 + 10x^2 + 5x + 1$
2. $x^4 - 8x^3 + 24x^2 - 32x + 16$
3. $64x^6 + 192x^5 + 240x^4 + 160x^3 + 60x^2 + 12x + 1$
4. $27x^3 - 54x^2 + 36x - 8$
5. $256x^4 + 256x^3 + 96x^2 + 16x + 1$ **6.** $1 + 3x + 3x^2 + x^3$
7. $32 - 80x + 80x^2 - 40x^3 + 10x^4 - x^5$
8. $x^6 + 6x^5y + 15x^4y^2 + 20x^3y^3 + 15x^2y^4 + 6xy^5 + y^6$
9. $16x^4 + 96x^3y + 216x^2y^2 + 216xy^3 + 81y^4$
10. $64a^3 - 144a^2b + 108ab^2 - 27b^3$
11. $x^4 + 12x^3 + 54x^2 + 108x + 81$
12. $8x^3 + 12x^2 + 6x + 1$
13. $x^5 - 15x^4 + 90x^3 - 270x^2 + 405x - 243$
14. $729x^6 - 7290x^5 + 30\ 375x^4 - 67\ 500x^3 + 84\ 375x^2 - 56\ 250x + 15\ 625$ **15.** $8 + 12x + 6x^2 + x^3$
16. $1024x^5 + 1280x^4y + 640x^3y^2 + 160x^2y^3 + 20xy^4 + y^5$
17. $64 - 48x + 12x^2 - x^3$
18. $128x^7 - 1344x^6y + 6048x^5y^2 - 15\ 120x^4y^3 + 22\ 680x^3y^4 - 20\ 412x^2y^5 + 10\ 206xy^6 - 2187y^7$
19. $343x^3 + 294x^2y + 84xy^2 + 8y^3$
20. $161\ 051 - 658\ 845x + 1\ 078\ 110x^2 - 882\ 090x^3 + 360\ 855x^4 - 59\ 049x^5$ **21.** $1029x^5$ **22.** $240x^2$
23. $\dfrac{1792}{27}x^5$ **24.** $\dfrac{5103}{2}x^6$ **25.** $18\ 750x$
26. $-7\ 838\ 208x^5$ **27.** $160x^3y^3$ **28.** $6048x^5y^2$
29. $-30\ 870x^2y^3$ **30.** $2288x^3y^{10}$
Applications and Problem Solving 31. 20 412
32. $a^3 + b^3 + c^3 + 3a^2b + 3a^2c + 3ab^2 + 3b^2c + 3ac^2 + 3bc^2 + 6abc$ **33. a)** $(k + m)^3$ **b)** $(x + y)^5$ **c)** $(x + 2)^3$
34. a) $\dfrac{1}{216} + \dfrac{5}{72} + \dfrac{25}{72} + \dfrac{125}{216}$
b) 1; the sum of all the probabilities is 1
c) $\dfrac{1}{216}$; the probability of 0 sixes in 3 rolls

d) rolling exactly 2 sixes; rolling exactly 1 six
e) $\left(\dfrac{1}{2} + \dfrac{1}{2}\right)^5$ **35.** $2, -\dfrac{3}{5}$ **36.** no **37. a)** 5
b) $n = 9, a = -2$ **c)** $n = 8, a = 1.5$ **38.** $r = 10, n = 29$
39. $\dfrac{9}{2}x^7$ **40. a)** 84 **b)** 243 **c)** 3 **d)** 2 **e)** 0
41. The expansion of both polynomials is
$x^8 + 8x^5 + 24x^2 + \dfrac{32}{x} + \dfrac{16}{x^4}$.

42. Write the first 8 rows of Pascal's triangle. Replace all the even numbers with 0s and all the odd numbers with 1s. Draw a triangle around each group of three 1s. Shade in the resulting triangles around the 0s. This gives the 3rd level of Sierpinski's triangle.

Connecting Math and Computers
pp. 358–359
1 Classification by Key Type 1. a) 10 000 **b)** 456 976
c) 1 679 616 **d)** There are more possibilities.
2. 3.40×10^{38}
2 Classification by Mathematical Operations
1. a) The relative position in the alphabet of each letter of the keyword is written below the letter. The message is then written below the keyword as shown. The coded message is read vertically, starting with column 1, then 2 , then 3, then 4. **b)** the keyword
2. a) U HTCQ A LLORXA **b)** Could you decipher this message without the keyword?

Review pp. 360–361
1. 36 **2. a)** 2 **b)** 24 **3. a)** 6720 **b)** 32 768 **c)** 59 049
4. a) 210 **b)** 840 **c)** 1260 **5. a)** 5040 **b)** 5040
6. a) 20 475 **b)** 2925 **7. a)** 10 **b)** 10 **8. a)** 35 **b)** 35
9. a) 20 **b)** 30 **c)** 4 **10. a)** 3 **b)** 10 **c)** 69 **d)** No, because there are paths from A to C that do not pass through B. **11. a)** 3 **b)** 9 **c)** 2
12. a) $125 + 75x + 15x^2 + x^3$ **b)** $729x^6 - 1458x^5 + 1215x^4 - 540x^3 + 135x^2 - 18x + 1$
c) $32x^5 - 80x^4y + 80x^3y^2 - 40x^2y^3 + 10xy^4 - y^5$
d) $x^4 - 12x^3y + 54x^2y^2 - 108xy^3 + 81y^4$
13. a) $_5C_r\ x^{5-r};\ 10x^3$ **b)** $_4C_r\ 3^{4-r}x^r;\ 108x$
c) $_9C_r\ 7^{9-r}(-2x)^r;\ 33\ 882\ 912x^4$ **d)** $_7C_r\ x^{7-r}y^r;\ 35x^4y^3$

Exploring Math p. 361
1. a) $x^2 + 3x + 1$ **b)** $-2.618, -0.382$
c) $-2.618, -0.382$; equal **2. a)** $x^3 + 5x^2 + 6x + 1$
b) $-3.247, -1.555, -0.890$ **c)** $-3.247, -1.555, -0.890$;
equal **3.** $x = -4\cos^2 \dfrac{k\pi}{n}$, $k = 1, 2, \ldots , \dfrac{n-2}{2}$ if n is

even, $k = 1, 2, \ldots, \dfrac{n-1}{2}$ if n is odd

Chapter Check p. 362
1. a) 10 **b)** 15 **2. a)** $16 - 32y + 24y^2 - 8y^3 + y^4$
b) $2187x^7 + 25\,515x^6 + 127\,575x^5 + 354\,375x^4$
$+ 590\,625x^3 + 590\,625x^2 + 328\,125x + 78\,125$
3. a) $32x^5 - 400x^4 + 2000x^3 - 5000x^2 + 6250x - 3125$
b) $x^6 - 18x^5y + 135x^4y^2 - 540x^3y^3 + 1215x^2y^4 - 1458xy^5$
$+ 729y^6$ **4. a)** $_8C_r\,x^{8-r}(-5)^r;\ -40x^7$
b) $_7C_r\,3^{7-r}(-2y)^r;\ 15\,120y^4$
c) $_8C_r\,(2x)^{8-r}(5y)^r;\ 700\,000x^4y^4$ **5. a)** 220 **b)** 120
6. a) 40 **b)** 50 **7. a)** 20 **b)** 10 **c)** 70 **8. a)** 20 **b)** 7
9. a) 24; YOUR **b)** 720: MOBILE **c)** 10 080;
OFFICIAL **d)** 4 989 600; MATHEMATICS
10. a) 9 **b)** 6 **11. a)** 2.03×10^{16} **b)** 1140

Using the Strategies p. 363
1. 20 L **2.** $(4 - \pi)12x^2$ **3.** 119 **4.** 54 **5. a)** 174 cm
b) $\dfrac{n(41-n)}{2}$; 20 **6. a)** 27 **b)** 25, 36 **7.** $6n^2 + 3n$

8. 2 and 4; −2 and −4 **9.** 96 km/h **10.** 5, 16, 24, 80
11. 15° **12.** 36 s **13.** 6 **14.** two \$10 pens, fourteen \$2
pens, sixty-four 50¢ pens **15.** 199 **16.** 96 cm²

Chapter 8

Probability p. 365
1. 8 **2.** 13 **3.** 366

Getting Started pp. 366–367
Using Diagrams
1 Tree Diagrams 1. {bike, canoe, horseback},
{bike, canoe, motorbike}, {bike, kayak, horseback},
{bike, kayak, motorbike}, {bike, sailboat, horseback},
{bike, sailboat, motorbike},
{on foot, canoe, horseback},
{on foot, canoe, motorbike},
{on foot, kayak, horseback},
{on foot, kayak, motorbike},
{on foot, sailboat, horseback},
{on foot, sailboat, motorbike} **2.** {small, lime green},
{small, blue}, {small, khaki}, {medium, lime green},
{medium, blue}, {medium, khaki}, {large, lime green},
{large, blue}, {large, khaki}, {extra-large, lime green},
{extra-large, blue}, {extra-large, khaki}
3. {Somestate, standard}, {Somestate, extended},
{Green Circle, standard}, {Green Circle, extended},
{Geneva Life, standard}, {Geneva Life, extended}
4. {*The Edmonton Journal*, daily}, {*The Edmonton*

Journal, weekend}, {*The Edmonton Sun*, daily},
{*The Edmonton Sun*, weekend},
{*The National Post*, daily}, {*The National Post*, weekend},
{*The Globe and Mail*, daily},
{*The Globe and Mail*, weekend}
2 Venn Diagrams 1. a) 2, 4, 6, 12 **b)** 1, 3, 5, 15 **c)** 2,
3, 5, 7, 11, 13, 17, 19, 23 **d)** 2, 4 **2. a)** 105 **b)** 13 **c)** 25
d) 50
3 Probability 1. $\dfrac{1}{52}; \dfrac{1}{52}$ **2.** 1; 0 **3.** $\dfrac{1}{52}$; 0 or 1

Mental Math
Estimates may vary. 1. 36 cm²
2. 85 cm² **3.** 72 cm² **4.** 31 cm² **5.** 36 cm² **6.** 112 cm²
7. 48 cm² **8.** 54 cm² **9.** 80 cm² **10.** 108 cm²
11. 72 cm² **12.** 108 cm² **13.** 113 cm² **14.** 108 cm²

Section 8.1 pp. 371–372
Practice 1. $\dfrac{1}{8}$ **2.** $\dfrac{1}{78}$ **3.** $\dfrac{3}{52}$ **4.** $\dfrac{1}{12}$ **5.** $\dfrac{1}{12}$ **6.** $\dfrac{1}{84}$ **7.** $\dfrac{3}{28}$
Applications and Problem Solving 8. a) {1, 1},
{1, 2}, {1, 3}, {1, 4}, {1, 5}, {1, 6}, {2, 1}, {2, 2}, {2, 3},
{2, 4}, {2, 5}, {2, 6}, {3, 1}, {3, 2}, {3, 3}, {3, 4}, {3, 5},
{3, 6}, {4, 1}, {4, 2}, {4, 3}, {4, 4}, {4, 5}, {4, 6}, {5, 1},
{5, 2}, {5, 3}, {5, 4}, {5, 5}, {5, 6}, {6, 1}, {6, 2}, {6, 3},
{6, 4}, {6, 5}, {6, 6} **b)** {1, 1}, {1, 2}, {1, 3}, {1, 4}, {1, 5},
{1, 6}, {2, 1}, {2, 3}, {2, 5}, {3, 1}, {3, 2}, {3, 4}, {3, 5},
{4, 1}, {4, 3}, {4, 5}, {5, 1}, {5, 2}, {5, 3}, {5, 4}, {5, 6},
{6, 1}, {6, 5} **c)** $\dfrac{23}{36}$ **9. a)** 9.24% **b)** 2.76% **c)** 67.76%
10. a) 49.4% **b)** 8.4% **c)** 26.6% **11. a)** 1:5 **b)** 1:35
c) 1:215 **d)** 1:71 **12.** No. There is approximately a
99.6% probability that 2 students write the same
number. **13. b)** $\dfrac{1}{16}$ **c)** $\dfrac{7}{8}$ **e)** $\dfrac{1}{48}$ **f)** $\dfrac{1}{16}$ **g)** The probability
of their arriving at the same time decreases to
approximately 10^{-3}. The probability of Paul's arriving
first increases to approximately 0.906. **14. a)** 0.39
b) 0.14 **c)** 0.53 **d)** 0.1113 **e)** 0.073 034 **f)** 0.237
g) 0.293
15. a) $\dfrac{1}{9000}$ **b)** $\dfrac{1}{3000}$ **c)** $\dfrac{1}{1000}$ **d)** 2.59×10^{-6}

Investigating Math p. 373
1 Tossing a Coin 1. no; yes; yes (unlikely, but
possible) **2. a)** probably not; there may be chance
variation **b)** not for a fair coin, since it is impossible
to obtain a result of $\dfrac{1}{2}$

2 Birthdays a) $\dfrac{1}{365}$ **b)** If your birthday fell on a day in
the months April through August, you might be

inclined to increase the probability; otherwise, you might be inclined to decrease the probability.

Investigating Math p. 374
1. c) none; none; yes; no; no **2.** the entire number line; yes **3. a)** no **b)** C **d)** 0 **e)** yes

Section 8.2 pp. 380–381
Practice 1. answers may vary **2.** dependent
3. dependent **4.** independent **5.** independent
6. dependent
7. not mutually exclusive **8.** mutually exclusive
9. not mutually exclusive **10.** mutually exclusive
11. not mutually exclusive **12.** mutually exclusive
13. mutually exclusive
Applications and Problem Solving 14. b) 15%
c) no **d)** The events are not independent. Take driver training. **15. a)** 99.6% **b)** 11.7% **c)** 41.1%
16. a) Yes. The percents add to 100. **b)** 19.36%
c) 92.16% **d)** when they are genetically related
17. a) 82.7% **b)** So that the probability of living on each street is the same. **c)** 18 **18. a)** 0.2 **b)** 0.25
c) 0.45 **19. a)** No. A scene can be both violent and humorous at the same time (in some people's opinion) **c)** 0.4 **20.** 12% **21.** 7

Section 8.3 pp. 385–386
Practice 1. 0.392 **2.** 0.294 **3.** 0.294 **4.** $\frac{1}{6}$ **5.** $\frac{1}{6}$ **6.** $\frac{2}{9}$
7. $\frac{1}{9}$ **8.** $\frac{2}{3}$

Applications and Problem Solving

9. a) $\frac{2}{27}$ **b)** $\frac{1}{316\ 251}$

10. a) 10 068 347 520 **b)** 0.000 43 **c)** 9.93×10^{-11}

11. a) 2730; 1320 **b)** 1.31×10^{11} **c)** $\frac{1}{7}$ **d)** 455; 220;

168 168 000; $\frac{1}{7}$ **12. a)** $\frac{4}{{}_{52}C_{13}}$ **b)** $\dfrac{\dfrac{4^2(39!)}{(13!)^3 3!} - \dfrac{6^2(26!)}{(13!)^2 2!} + 24}{\dfrac{52!}{(13!)^4 4!}}$

c) $\dfrac{4!(13!)^4}{52!}$ **d)** $\dfrac{4 \times 13 \times 12 \times 11 \times 10}{52 \times 51 \times 50 \times 49}$

e) $\dfrac{4 \times 36 \times 35 \times \ldots \times 24}{52 \times 51 \times \ldots \times 40}$ **13. a)** $\frac{5}{26}$ **b)** $\frac{125}{17\ 576}$ **c)** $\frac{25}{169}$

14. a) $\frac{1}{7776}$ **b)** $\frac{1}{1296}$ **c)** $\frac{5}{54}$ **15. a)** $\frac{1}{32}$ **b)** $\frac{1}{32}$ **c)** $\frac{1}{32}$

16. a) dependent **b)** 5.47×10^{-4} **c)** 0.9964 **d)** about 275

Computer Data Bank p. 387
1 Names 1. a) $\frac{7}{245}$ or $\frac{1}{35}$ **b)** $\frac{1}{245}$ **c)** $\frac{16}{245}$ **d)** $\frac{28}{245}$ **e)** $\frac{4}{245}$
f) $\frac{10}{245}$ or $\frac{2}{49}$ **g)** Answers will vary.
h) Answers will vary. **i)** Answers will vary.

2. a) $\frac{9}{60\ 025}$ **b)** $\frac{110}{59\ 750}$ or $\frac{11}{5975}$ **c)** $\frac{6}{245}$ **d)** $\frac{2}{245}$
e) $\frac{30}{245}$ or $\frac{6}{49}$
2 Birthdays 1. a) Answers will vary. **b)** $\frac{4}{245}$

3 Age of Taking Office 1. 49 **2.** 0.066
4 Political Parties of Prime Ministers 1. Liberal: 121 months; Progressive Conservative: 55 months
2. Answers will vary.
5 Native Language of Prime Ministers 1. 0.968
6 Chronological Lists 2. John Macdonald and Alexander Mackenzie **3.** When two prime ministers have the same year of taking office, it is impossible to tell who actually came first. As well, when a prime minister served non-consecutive terms, his name appears only in the position of his first term.
4. Answers will vary.

Section 8.4 pp. 391–392
Practice 1. 0.667 **2.** 0.25 **3.** 0.8 **4.** 0.833 **5.** 0.75

Applications and Problem Solving 6. $\frac{1}{2}$ **7.** $\frac{4}{17}$

8. a) 17% **b)** $\frac{17}{60}$ **9. a)** $\frac{14}{17}$ **b)** $\frac{14}{15}$ **10. a)** $\frac{21}{22}$ **b)** $\frac{17}{24}$

11. a) 41.4% **b)** 17.1%; 7.1% **c)** 4 times **12. a)** 0
b) $P(C)$ **13. a)** 1.30% **b)** 17.39% **c)** As a backup test in case the breathalyzer gives a false positive. **14. a)** $\frac{1}{4}$
b) $\frac{1}{3}$ **c)** $\frac{2}{3}$ **d)** 1; complementary

Career Connection p. 393
1. 0.25% **2.** $100 000; $94 000

Review pp. 396–397
1. a) {mustard, plain}, {mustard, sesame seed}, {ketchup, plain}, {ketchup, sesame seed}, {relish, plain}, {relish, sesame seed}; $\frac{1}{6}$
b) {comedy, licorice}, {comedy, carrot sticks}, {comedy, popcorn}, {thriller, licorice}, {thriller, carrot sticks}, {thriller, popcorn},

{drama, licorice}, {drama, carrot sticks}, {drama, popcorn}, {action, licorice}, {action, carrot sticks}, {action, popcorn};

$\dfrac{1}{12}$ **2. b)** $\dfrac{1}{16}$ **c)** $\dfrac{15}{32}$ **e)** $\dfrac{15}{32}$ **3. b)** $\dfrac{2}{33}$

c) $\dfrac{4}{99}$ **4. a)** 0.05 **b)** 0.45 **c)** 0.4 **5. a)** 77.72%

b) 41.14% **6. a)** No. **b)** 0.4 **c)** 0.35 **7. a)** $\dfrac{1}{14}$ **b)** $\dfrac{1}{2}$

8. a) $\dfrac{1}{120}$ **b)** $\dfrac{3}{5}$ **9. a)** $\dfrac{5}{28}$ **b)** $\dfrac{15}{28}$ **c)** $\dfrac{1}{56}$ **10. a)** 0.0023

b) 1.895×10^{-4} **c)** 0.1031 **d)** 0 **11. a)** $\dfrac{2}{3}$ **b)** $\dfrac{1}{3}$

12. a) 60% **b)** 99% **c)** 45% **13. a)** 94.12% **b)** 5.88%

Exploring Math p. 397
1. Apply the pigeonhole principle with $p = 12$, $k = 3$, and $n = 37$. **2.** 11

Chapter Check p. 398
1. a) 42.78% **b)** 11.78% **2. b)** 0.4375 **c)** 0.908 875

3. a) no **c)** 0.15 **4. a)** 0.6102 **b)** 0.9909 **5. a)** $\dfrac{1}{_{49}C_6}$

b) $\dfrac{8815}{499\ 422}$ **c)** $\dfrac{563\ 383}{998\ 844}$ **6. a)** $\dfrac{1}{358\ 800}$

b) $\dfrac{1}{119\ 600}$ **c)** $\dfrac{1}{68^8}$

Using the Strategies p. 399
1. alphabetical order of name of number; 7, 6, 3, 2, 0

2. 8, 12, 16 **3.** 803 **4.** square; $\dfrac{n}{5}$

5. $923 + 58\ 784 + 868\ 784 = 928\ 491$ or $923 + 68\ 784 + 858\ 784 = 928\ 491$ **6.** -21
7. 52 521 875 **8.** $\pi - 2$ **9.** 17:00

10. 1321 **11.** $\dfrac{1}{2}$ **12.** 24 including 10 and 100

13. $-1 \le x \le 1$, $0 \le y \le 1$ **14.** 34.375 **15.** $k = 5$ **16.** 2004

Chapter 9

Probability Distributions p. 401
1. There may have been some low temperatures and high temperatures that had an average of 13°C.
2. a) 5.29°C **b)** 5.29°C **c)** 5.57°C **d)** 5.14°C
e) 5.0°C; no

Getting Started pp. 402–403
Comparing Sets of Data
1. 32 **2.** 15.625 m²; 15.5 m²; The area of the windows is between 15 m² and 16 m². **3.** The data are more spread out for the measurements without aids. Both sets of data have the same mode and median.
4. 12 m²; 4 m² **5.** 2.17 m²; 0.75 m² **6.** The mean variation; It shows how spread out the data are about the mean.

Warm Up
1. 7.29; 7; no mode **2.** 9; 9; 9 **3.** 7; 6; 7
4. 96.8; 50; no mode **5.** 20; 20; 15 and 25
6. 9; 9; no mode **7. a)** 16 **b)** 9; 7 **c)** $30 to $40
d) 25%; 43.75% **e)** $580; $420

Mental Math
1. 0.0001 **2.** 243 **3.** 256 **4.** $\dfrac{8}{27}$ **5.** $\dfrac{1}{16}$

6. 1331 **7.** 64 **8.** 0.216 **9.** 2 **10.** 3 **11.** $\dfrac{27}{8}$

12. 160 000 **13.** 50% **14.** 25% **15.** 50% **16.** 25%

17. $16\dfrac{2}{3}\%$ **18.** 2^3, 3^2, $2^{-1} \times 3^3$, $2^2 \times 3^2$

19. $\log 9$, $\log 27$, $\log \pi^3$, $\log 3^\pi$ **20.** 625, 10^3, 2^{10}, 5^5

21. $\left(\dfrac{1}{3}\right)^2$, $\left(\dfrac{2}{3}\right)^3$, $\dfrac{1}{2}$, $\left(\dfrac{8}{27}\right)^{\frac{1}{3}}$ **22.** $\dfrac{1}{\sqrt[3]{10}}$, $\sqrt[3]{0.125}$, $\dfrac{1}{\sqrt{3}}$, $\sqrt{\dfrac{4}{7}}$

23. $\sqrt{3}$ **24.** $\dfrac{5\sqrt{2}}{2}$ **25.** $5\sqrt{77}$ **26.** 90 **27.** $5\sqrt{6}$ **28.** $3\sqrt{6}$

29. $\sqrt{11}$ **30.** $\dfrac{\sqrt{5}}{5}$ **31.** $\dfrac{1}{6}$ **32.** 14

Section 9.1 pp. 407–408
Practice 1. 0.283 **2.** 0.040 **3.** 0.176 **4.** 0.043
5. 0.128 **6.** 5.526×10^{-9} **7.** 0.130 **8.** 0.353 **9.** 0.982
10. ordered pairs are (number of strikeouts, probability): (0, 0.240), (1, 0.412), (2, 0.265), (3, 0.076), (4, 0.008) **11.** ordered pairs are (number of sixes, probability): (0, 0.335), (1, 0.402), (2, 0.054), (3, 0.008), (4, 2.14×10^{-5}), (5, 6.43×10^{-4}), (6, 2.14×10^{-5}) **12.** ordered pairs are (number of goals, probability): (0, 0.078), (1, 0.259), (2, 0.201), (3, 0.346), (4, 0.230), (5, 0.010) **13.** ordered pairs are (number of triple twenties, probability): (0, 0.478), (1, 0.372), (2, 0.124), (3, 0.023), (4, 0.003), (5, 1.701×10^{-4}), (6, 6.3×10^{-6}), (7, 1×10^{-7})
Applications and Problem Solving 14. a) 0.033
b) 0.980 **15. a)** 0.605 **b)** 0.395 **c)** 0.089 **16. a)** 0.481
b) 0.519 **c)** 0.127 **17. a)** 0.088 **b)** 0.103 **18. a)** 0.121
b) 0.834 **c)** 0.167 **e)** 0.666 **19. a)** 0.019 **b)** 0.003

20. a) 0.998 **b)** $\doteq 1$ **21. a)** 0.26 **b)** 0.9 **c)** 0.8 **22.** The probability that Carter will make exactly 13 baskets is approximately 29%. The probability of him not making exactly 13 baskets is approximately 71%. It is more likely that he will not make exactly 13 baskets.

Section 9.2 pp. 412–413
Practice **1. a)** C; B **b)** A: 31.62; B: 26.75; C: 45.37
2. a) Q; P **b)** P: 2; Q: 2.83, R: 2.61 **3. a)** A: 4, 2;
B: 9, 2; Each element in B is 5 more than the corresponding element in A. **b)** A: 4, 2; B: 12, 6; Each element in B is 3 times the corresponding element in A. **c)** A: 2, 4; B: −2, 4; Each element in B is the negative of the corresponding element in A.
4. a) $-\dfrac{2}{3}$; $\dfrac{4}{3}$; 2; −2 **b)** 359.5 mL, 350.5 mL

Applications and Problem Solving **5. a)** 1, 1, 1, 1, 1, 9, 9, 9, 9, 9 **b)** 1, 1, 1, 1, 1, 5, 9, 9, 9, 9 or 1, 1, 1, 1, 5, 9, 9, 9, 9, 9 **6. a)** 1, 9, 9, 9, 9, 9, 9, 9, 9, 9 or 1, 1, 1, 1, 1, 1, 1, 1, 1, 9 **b)** 1, 5, 5, 5, 5, 5, 5, 5, 5, 9
7. a) −2.25 to 2.25 **b)** 164 cm **c)** −1.57 to 4.43 **d)** 1.86
e) Answers may vary. **8.** Answers may vary.
a) 80, 80, 80, 80, 80, 70; 78, 78, 78, 78, 78, 80
b) 75, 75, 75, 75, 75, 75; 60, 60, 60, 90, 90, 90

9. mean: $\dfrac{x+y+z}{3}$;

standard deviation: $\dfrac{1}{3}\sqrt{2((x-y)^2+(x-z)(y-2)^2)}$

11. a) No. Its definition gives a non-negative number; Yes, if all the numbers are the same. **b)** Yes, if the range of numbers is large enough. **c)** The mean would increase by 5 and the standard deviation would stay the same; The mean would be multiplied by −3 and the standard deviation would be multiplied by 3.
12. Answers may vary. **a)** 0, 0, 0, 0, 0, 0, 0, 0, 25, 25
b) −1, 9, 9, 9, 9, 11, 11, 11, 11, 21
c) −10, 1, 1, 1, 1, 1, 1, 1, 1, 1
d) 0, 0, 0, 0, 0, 0, 0, 0, 0, 334
e) −1, −1, −1, −1, 1, 1, 1, 1, 1, 1
f) 0, 0, 0, 0, 0, 0, 0, 0, 0, 1
g) 99, 99, 99, 99, 99, 101, 101, 101, 101, 101

Investigating Math pp. 414–415
1 Relating a Normal Curve to the Standard Normal Curve **1. a)** 14; 3.286
b) −1.217, −0.913, 0, 0609, 1.521 **c)** 0, 1
2 The Area Under the Standard Normal Curve
1. a) 0.8708 **b)** 0.0154 **c)** 0.9713 **d)** 0.6217 **e)** 0.1867
f) 0.0606 **2. a)** −2.37 **b)** −0.41 **c)** −1.16 **d)** 2.37
e) 0.70 **f)** 1.22 **3. a)** 0.1075 **b)** 0.1417 **c)** 0.1949

d) 0.1203 **e)** 0.3262 **f)** 0.6826 **4. a)** Their sum is 1.

b) $\dfrac{1}{2}$ **c)** 0.3745

Section 9.3 pp. 422–423
Practice **1.** 59.87% **2.** 15.87% **3.** 30.85%
4. 97.72% **5.** 96.41% **6.** 94.52% **7.** 14.99%
8. 79.36% **9.** 20.89% **10.** 17.31 h **11.** 126.45 V
12. 75.04% **13.** −13.57°C
14. 39.63 years to 46.37 years
15. 534.96 km to 599.04 km **16.** $5.01 to $19.23
17. 78.74 L to 81.26 L
Applications and Problem Solving **18. a)** 0.62%
b) 1.43 N to 1.57 N **19.** 2.28% **20.** approximately every 250 h **21. a)** 26.60% **b)** 130.50 km/h
22. a) 10.56% **b)** 39.44% **c)** 76% **23. a)** Earth: 4.6%; Space: 0% **b)** Earth: 1.97 mm to 2.03 mm; Space: 1.9997 mm to 2.0003 mm **24. a)** 2.28%; 0.26%
b) 0.350; 0.324 **25. a)** $N(5, 1)$ is a translation of 5 units right of $N(0, 1)$. **b)** $N(5, 10^2)$ is a translation of 5 units right of $N(0, 10^2)$.
c) $N(0, 10^2)$ is a vertical compression by a factor of $\dfrac{1}{10}$

and a horizontal expansion by a factor of 10 of $N(0, 1)$.
26. They are distributed under the normal curve

$N(0, 1)$, since $z_x = \dfrac{x-\mu}{\sigma} = \dfrac{x-17}{4}$.

Section 9.4 pp. 426–427
Practice **1.** no **2.** Yes. $\mu = 50$, $\sigma \doteq 6.89$ **3.** no **4.** no
5. no **6.** Yes. $\mu = 50$, $\sigma \doteq 6.71$
7. Yes. $\mu = 7.5$, $\sigma \doteq 2.29$
Applications and Problem Solving **8. a)** 9.85%
b) 74.32% **c)** 0.00% **9. a)** 4.01% **b)** 0.49%
10. a) 8.90% **b)** 21.41% **c)** 21.41% **11. a)** 0 **b)** 1
12. a) 1.91% **b)** 16.31% **13. a)** 3.4% **b)** 19.7%
c) 8.6% **14. a)** 4.05% **b)** 90.30% **c)** 5.62%
15. 0.026 088 298 3 **16.** the expected number of failures **17. a)** The graph does not appear normally distributed (not symmetric); Either n is too small, so the binomial distribution is not well approximated by a smooth curve, or p and/or q are so small that the distribution is asymmetrical.

Computer Data Bank p. 428
1 Maximum Oxygen Intake **1.** Answers will vary.
2. Answers will vary. **3.** Answers will vary.
2 Flexibility **1.** female 29.97 cm; male 25.05 cm
2. female 8.28; male 8.79 **3.** male
3 Body Mass Index **2.** less than 35 **3.** 23.2
4. 18, −1.2; 25, 0.4
4 Waist Girth to Hip Girth Ratio **2.** means: female 0.76 and male 0.87; standard deviations: female 0.06 and male 0.10; female

Section 9.5 pp. 434–435

Practice **1.** -1.96 **2.** -2.58 **3.** -1.64 **4.** -2.81 **5.** 50.4 to 69.6 **6.** 55.3 to 84.7 **7.** 164.3 to 210.7 **8.** 29.2 to 44.0 **9.** 57.30% to 82.70% **10.** 13.6% to 26.4% **11.** 21.2% to 28.8% **12.** 55.5% to 66.5% **13.** 800 **14.** 661 **15.** 1768 **16.** 1404

Applications and Problem Solving **17. a)** 38 **b)** 28 to 47 **18. a)** 264 to 297 **b)** no **c)** Students probably read more than the average Canadian. **19. a)** between 30% and 50% **b)** 600; between 36.1% and 43.9% **20. a)** $43.05\% < x < 55.95\%$ **b)** 66.3% **21. a)** $66.8\% < x < 79.1\%$ **b)** $68.6\% < x < 77.4\%$ **c)** 7572 **22. a)** $71.0\% < x < 75.0\%$ **b)** No. **c)** At a voter support level of 52.24%, the lower end of a 99% confidence interval is less than 50%. **23. a)** between 54.9% and 79.1% **b)** 97 **24.** 250 **25. a)** 89 **b)** 73% **c)** 73% **d)** This is a 73% confidence interval.

Investigating Math pp. 436–437

1 Interpreting Poll Results **1. a)** The 95% confidence level for the percent of Canadians that dislike the quantity of soft rock played on radio stations is 13% to 17%. **2. a)** The 90% confidence level for the percent of Canadians who think that the government should subsidize professional sports teams in Canada is 31.7% to 39.7%.

2 Using Opinion Polls **1.** The results depend on voter turnout. **2.** The results depend on voter turnout.

Connecting Math and Success pp. 438–439

1 Success in Sports **1. b)** 0.565 **c)** 0.4305 **2. b)** 0.3185 **c)** 0.243

2 Success in Marketing **1. a)** Brand A: 0.475; Brand B: 0.525 **b)** 0.44 **2. a)** 0.54 **b)** 0.538 **c)** The advertising campaign increased the probability that a person would use Roadrunner's services the second time from 45% to 54%, and the third time from 43.5% to 46.2%.

Review pp. 440–441

1. 0.254 **2.** 0.384 **3.** 0.969 **4.** 0.398 **5. a)** 0.294 **b)** 0.168 **c)** 0.832 **6. a)** 0.398 **b)** 0.061 **c)** 0.188 **7. a)** A: 14, 3.633; B: 14, 1.414; Both sets have the same mean. **b)** A: 26, 4; B: 50, 4; Both sets have the same standard deviation. **8. a)** -0.2, 0.7, -0.5, 1.5, 1.2 **b)** 1021 mL; 985 mL **9. a)** 44; 15.556 **b)** -1.414, -0.707, 0, 0.707, 1.414 **c)** 0, 1; The z-scores are transformed so as to have mean 0 and standard deviation 1. **10. a)** 33.85% **b)** 33.85% **c)** 55.59% **d)** 125 **11. a)** 95.45% **b)** 2.48 to 3.52 **12. a)** 6.67% **b)** 6.67% **13. a)** 38.70% **b)** 71.62% **c)** 32.30% **14. a)** 12.65% **b)** 0.28% **c)** 12.65%

15. a) 2.28% **b)** 11.5% **c)** 95.45% **16. a)** $65.1\% < x < 80.8\%$ **b)** 493; between 69.1% and 76.9% **17. a)** 1.83% **b)** $11.28\% < p < 20.72\%$ **18. a)** $69.00\% < p < 81.00\%$; $70.76\% < p < 79.24\%$ **b)** 7203

Exploring Math p. 441

1. a) 11.57% **b)** 9.88% **2. a)** 36.15% **b)** 25.85% **c)** It is a geometric series with $a = \dfrac{5}{36}$, $r = \dfrac{31}{36}$, and $n = 2$. **3. a)** 32.98%; 73.07%; 84.10% **b)** It is more likely to get an ace or a face card in fewer than 5 cuts than to get a face card in fewer than 5 cuts.

Chapter Check p. 442

1. a) 0.004% **b)** 99.996% **c)** 33.94% **2. a)** 28.24% **b)** 37.66% **3. a)** 100; 2.449 **b)** 1.225 **4. a)** $-2.25 < z < 2.25$ **b)** 105 cm **5. a)** 4.78%; 0.62%; 29.77% **b)** 77.7 kg **c)** $66.0 \text{ kg} < m < 74.0 \text{ kg}$ **6.** 2 **7.** Yes; 13. 2.133 **8.** Yes; 5.25, 2.210 **9.** no **10. a)** 13.52% **b)** 86.48% **c)** 59.41% **11. a)** 600 **b)** $575 < x < 625$ **12. a)** 0% to 11.8% **b)** 1.03% to 8.97% **c)** 119 **d)** 77.38%

Using the Strategies p. 443

1. 3 m² **2.** $A = 4$, $B = -3$ **3.** 25 cm² **4.** $6n - 1$ **5.** Answers may vary. $\left(8 + \dfrac{8+8}{8}\right)^{\frac{8+8+8}{8}}$ **6.** The missing numbers from left to right and top to bottom are 7, 1, 4, 5, 6, 2. **7.** sovereignty **8.** 142 **10.** Ken and Freya, Leo and Cora, Matt and Alice **11.** Two possible answers are $1856 + 1409 = 3265$ and $4096 + 4173 = 8269$. **13.** $16 - 4\pi$ **14.** E **15.** 12

Cumulative Review, Chapters 7–9 pp. 444–445

1. b) 90 **2. a)** 40 320 **b)** 560 **c)** 336 **3. a)** The order of arrangement is important in a permutation, but not in a combination. **b)** Answers may vary. Permutation: In how many ways can 6 students line up at a drinking fountain? Combination: In how many ways can a committee of 3 students be chosen from 6 students? **4. a)** 10 626 **b)** 231 **c)** 10 395 **5.** 120 **6.** 128; sum of the 8th row of Pascal's triangle **7.** $256 - 256x + 96x^2 - 16x^3 + x^4$ **8.** $32x^5 + 560x^4 + 3920x^3 + 13\ 720x^2 + 24\ 010x + 16\ 807$ **9.** $x^4 + 8x^3 + 24x^2 + 32x + 16$ **10.** $792x^6 - 1458x^5 + 1215x^4 - 540x^3 + 135x^2 - 18x + 1$ **11.** $_7C_r x^{7-r} 5^r$; $525x^5$ **12.** $_6C_r(2x)^{6-r}(-3)^r$; $-4320x^3$

13. $\dfrac{1}{12}$ **14.** $\dfrac{1}{12}$ **15. a)** 0.28 **b)** 0.18 **c)** 0.648

16. independent **17.** dependent **18.** mutually exclusive **19.** not mutually exclusive **20. a)** $\dfrac{1}{720}$ **b)** $\dfrac{1}{2}$

21. a) 0.082 **b)** 0.459 **c)** 0.324 **22. a)** $\dfrac{1}{36}$ **b)** $\dfrac{1}{11}$ **c)** $\dfrac{4}{11}$

23. 0.010 **24.** 0.022 **25.** 0.015 **26. a)** 37.2; 2.926 **b)** 0.62 **27. a)** 86.64% **b)** 6.68% **28.** 40; 4.899 **29.** 5.25; 1.847 **30.** 65.33%

31. a) $55.93\% < x < 65.92\%$ **b)** 0.0027 **c)** 369

Cumulative Review, Chapters 1–9
pp. 446–449

5. a) $-f(x) = 4 - x^3$, $f(-x) = -x^3 - 4$, $f^{-1}(x) = \sqrt[3]{x+4}$

c) $-f(x)$: $\left(\sqrt[3]{4} , 0 \right)$; $f(-x)$: $(0, -4)$; $f^{-1}(x)$: 1.796, 1.796)

6. b) The graph of $y = \dfrac{1}{2}x^2$ is a vertical compression by a factor of $\dfrac{1}{2}$ of the graph of $y = x^2$. The graph of $y = \dfrac{1}{2}(x-1)^2 - 3$ is a translation of 1 unit right, a vertical compression by a factor of $\dfrac{1}{2}$, and a translation of 3 units down of the graph of $y = x^2$.

7. b) The graph of $y = -\dfrac{1}{4}|x|$ is a vertical compression by a factor of $\dfrac{1}{4}$ and a reflection in the x-axis of the graph of $y = |x|$.

The graph of $y = -\dfrac{1}{4}|x+3| + 5$ is a translation of 3 units left, a vertical compression by a factor of $\dfrac{1}{4}$, a reflection in the x-axis, and a translation of 5 units up of the graph of $y = |x|$. **8. b)** The graph of $y = (2x)^3$ is a horizontal compression by a factor of $\dfrac{1}{2}$ of the graph of $y = x^3$. The graph of $y = -(2x)^3 + 1$ is a horizontal compression by a factor of $\dfrac{1}{2}$, a reflection in the x-axis, and a translation of 1 unit up of the graph of $y = x^3$. **9. b)** The graph of $y = \sqrt{3x}$ is a horizontal compression by a factor of $\dfrac{1}{3}$ of the graph of $y = \sqrt{x}$.

The graph of $y = 2\sqrt{3(x-1)} - 1$ is a translation of 1 unit right, a horizontal compression by a factor

of $\dfrac{1}{3}$, a vertical expansion by a factor of 2, and a translation of 1 unit down of the graph of $y = \sqrt{x}$.

14. a) $A(t) = 5000 \times 2^{\frac{t}{15}}$ **b)** 1 280 000 **c)** 544

15. a) 25 days **b)** 87% **c)** 50 days **16.** $\log_{10} 100 = 2$
17. $\log_4 16 = 2$ **18.** $\log_2 2^{20} = 20$ **19.** $\log_6 6 = 1$
20. $\log_5 125 = 3$ **21. a)** 2.57 **b)** 1.84 **c)** −167.65

22. a) 3 **b)** 5 **c)** −1, 6 **d)** 1 **e)** $\dfrac{1 + \sqrt{57}}{2}$ **23.** 3.5 years

24. a) $(x-2)^2 + (y-7)^2 = 6$; $x^2 + y^2 - 4x - 14y + 47 = 0$
b) $(x-5)^2 + (y-3)^2 = 34$; $x^2 + y^2 - 10x - 6y = 0$
25. outside **26. a)** $(6, -3)$; $5\sqrt{2}$ **b)** $(-2, 5)$; $\sqrt{7}$

27. a) $\dfrac{(x-2)^2}{36} + \dfrac{(y-5)^2}{4} = 1$;

$x^2 + 9y^2 - 4x - 90y + 193 = 0$ **b)** $\dfrac{(x+3)^2}{9} + \dfrac{(y+8)^2}{49} = 1$;

$49x^2 + 9y^2 + 294x + 144y + 576 = 0$ **28. a)** $(4, -7)$, 8, 6, $(4, -7 \pm \sqrt{7})$ **b)** $(-5, 6)$, $2\sqrt{10}$, $2\sqrt{7}$, $(-5 \pm \sqrt{3}, 6)$
29. a) $(-2, 3)$, $(0, 3)$, $(-4, 3)$, $y = 2x + 7$, $y = -2x - 1$

b) $(3, 9)$, $(3, 16)$, $(3, 2)$, $y = \dfrac{7}{3}x + 2$, $y = -\dfrac{7}{3}x + 16$

30. a) $x = h$, $(h, k + p)$,
$y + k + p = 0$, up if $p > 0$, down if $p < 0$
b) $y = k$, $(h + p, k)$, $x + h + p = 0$, left if $p < 0$,
right if $p > 0$
31. Divide the angle by π and multiply it by 180°.

32. a) $-\dfrac{7\pi}{6}$, $\dfrac{17\pi}{6}$ **b)** 310°, −410° **c)** $-\dfrac{2\pi}{7}$, $\dfrac{26\pi}{7}$

33. a) $\sin \theta = \dfrac{1}{\sqrt{2}}$, $\cos \theta = -\dfrac{1}{\sqrt{2}}$, $\tan \theta = -1$

b) $\sin \theta = -\dfrac{2}{\sqrt{29}}$, $\cos \theta = \dfrac{5}{\sqrt{29}}$, $\tan \theta = \dfrac{2}{5}$

c) $\sin \theta = -\dfrac{7}{\sqrt{58}}$, $\cos \theta = -\dfrac{3}{\sqrt{58}}$, $\tan \theta = \dfrac{7}{3}$

34. a) 4, 3π **b)** 0.3, $\dfrac{14\pi}{5}$ **c)** 2.5, $\dfrac{\pi}{3}$ **d)** 5, π

35. a) 4, 30° **b)** −3, $-\dfrac{5\pi}{12}$ **36. a)** −2, −50° **b)** 1, $\dfrac{3\pi}{4}$

37. b) 18.5, 12, −7, $\dfrac{1}{2}$

c) $t = 18.5 \cos \dfrac{\pi}{6}(m - 7) + 0.5$ **d)** 0.5

38. no amplitude, π, $\dfrac{\pi}{3}$ left, $x \neq \dfrac{\pi}{6} + n\pi$,

range: all real numbers

39. no amplitude, $\dfrac{2\pi}{3}$, 0, $x \neq \dfrac{n\pi}{3}$, $|y| \geq 2$

40. a) $\dfrac{\pi}{12}, \dfrac{5\pi}{12}, \dfrac{7\pi}{12}, \dfrac{11\pi}{12}, \dfrac{13\pi}{12}, \dfrac{17\pi}{12}, \dfrac{19\pi}{12}, \dfrac{23\pi}{12}$;

$\dfrac{\pi}{12} + \dfrac{n\pi}{2}, \dfrac{5\pi}{12} + \dfrac{n\pi}{2}$

b) $\dfrac{\pi}{3}, \dfrac{2\pi}{3}, \dfrac{4\pi}{3}$; $\dfrac{2\pi}{3} + 2n\pi$, $\dfrac{4\pi}{3} + 2n\pi$, $\dfrac{\pi}{3} + n\pi$

41. a) 3 **b)** No. If the window is expanded, it is evident that there are an infinite number of solutions.
c) ± 2.74, 0 **42. c)** $x \neq n\pi$, n any integer

43. c) $x \neq \dfrac{n\pi}{2}$, n any integer

44. c) $x \neq n\pi$, n any integer

45. c) $x \neq (2n+1)\dfrac{\pi}{2}$, n any integer

46. $\cos \dfrac{\pi}{6} = \dfrac{\sqrt{3}}{2}$ **47.** $\sin \dfrac{\pi}{4} = \dfrac{1}{\sqrt{2}}$ **48.** $\sin 45° = \dfrac{1}{\sqrt{2}}$

49. $\tan 60° = \sqrt{3}$ **50.** $\cos \dfrac{3\pi}{2} = 0$

51. $t_n = -12 + 7n$, $t_{15} = 93$ **52.** $t_n = \dfrac{18}{3^{n-1}}$, $t_8 = \dfrac{2}{243}$

53. $t_n = 7(3)^{n-1}$, $t_{10} = 137\ 781$

54. $t_n = \dfrac{7}{5} - \dfrac{n}{2}$, $t_{20} = -\dfrac{43}{5}$

55. a) $-1 + 2 + 5 + 8 + 11 = 25$
b) $31 + 36 + 41 + 46 + 51 + 56 + 61 + 66 = 388$
c) $24 + 48 + 96 + 192 + 384 + 768 + 1536 + 3072$

$= 6120$ **d)** $10 + 2 + \dfrac{2}{5} + \dfrac{2}{25} + \dfrac{2}{125} + \dfrac{2}{625}$

$+ \dfrac{2}{3125} + \dfrac{2}{15\ 625} = 12.499\ 968$ **56.** $3228.92

57. 360 cm **58. a)** -182 **b)** 992 **59. a)** 1 799 848 t
b) 15 286 921 t **60. b)** 30 **61. a)** 479 001 600 **b)** 362
880 **c)** 1320 **62. a)** 1140 **b)** 969 **c)** 3876 **63.** 112
64. a) $x^5 - 20x^4 + 160x^3 - 640x^2 + 1280x - 1024$
b) $64x^6 + 576x^5 + 2160x^4 + 4320x^3 + 4860x^2 + 2916x$
$+ 729$ **65. a)** $_8C_r x^{8-r} 4^r$; $448x^6$ **b)** $_7C_r (3x)^{7-r}(-5)^r$;
$-354\ 375x^4$ **66.** 32% **67. b)** 0.02% **c)** 2.5%
68. a) When one event does not influence the other: rolling a die and then rolling it again. **b)** When it is impossible for both events to happen at the same

time: a number is even and a number is odd. **69.** $\dfrac{1}{3}$

70. 0.216 **71. a)** $\dfrac{1}{60}$ **b)** $\dfrac{1}{125}$ **72. a)** 3.11×10^{-7}

b) 3.46×10^{-7} **c)** 99.84% **73.** Grand Rapids

74. a) 54.11% **b)** 22.94% **75. b)** 47.09% **c)** 46.61%
76. a) 0.0290 **b)** $22.52\% < p < 37.48\%$

GLOSSARY

A

absolute value   The distance of a number from zero on a real number line.

absolute value equation   An equation with a variable within the absolute value symbol.

$|x + 3| + 1 = x$ is an absolute value equation.

absolute value function   A function with a variable within the absolute value symbol.

$f(x) = |x| + 1$ is an absolute value function.

acute angle   An angle whose measure is between $0°$ and $90°$.

acute triangle   A triangle with three acute angles.

algebraic expression   A mathematical phrase made up of numbers and variables, connected by operators.

altitude of a triangle   The perpendicular distance from one vertex to the opposite side.

amplitude   Half the difference between the maximum and minimum values of a periodic function.

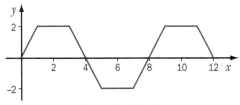

The amplitude is 2.

angular speed   The rate at which the central angle is changing, often measured in radians per second.

apogee of a satellite   The greatest distance that the orbit of the satellite takes the satellite from Earth.

arc   A part of the circumference of a circle.

area   The number of square units contained in a region.

arithmetic sequence   A sequence where the difference between consecutive terms is a constant, called the common difference.

1, 4, 7, 10, 13, 16, 19, 22, ... is an arithmetic sequence.

arithmetic series   The sum of the terms of an arithmetic sequence.

asymptote   A line that a curve approaches more and more closely.

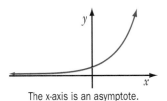

The x-axis is an asymptote.

axes   The intersecting number lines used for reference in locating points on a coordinate plane.

axis of symmetry   A line that is invariant under a reflection.

B

balanced number   A number that has exactly one digit that is the sum of all the other digits.

374 is balanced because $3 + 4 = 7$.

base of a cone   The face opposite the vertex of the cone.

base of a power   The number used as a factor for repeated multiplication.

In 6^3, 6 is the base.

bar graph   A graph using bars to represent data.

binary system   The number system using base 2.

binomial   A polynomial consisting of two terms.

$x^2 - 4$ is a binomial.

binomial distribution   The pattern of probabilities for the outcomes of repeated independent and identical trials. If p is the probability of success and q is the probability of failure where $p + q = 1$, then the probability of x successes in n trials is

$$P(x \text{ successes}) = \frac{n!}{x!(n-x)!} p^x q^{n-x}$$
$$= {}_nC_x p^x q^{n-x}$$

Binomial Theorem   The expansion of $(a + b)^n$, where n is a natural number, given by

$$(a + b)^n = \sum_{r=0}^{n} {}_nC_r a^{n-r} b^r \, .$$

bisect   Divide into two equal parts.

C

capacity   The largest amount that a container can hold.

central angle   An angle formed by two radii of a circle.

central axis of a right circular cone   The perpendicular line segment from the vertex of the cone to the circular base.

Chebyshev polynomial   A polynomial whose coefficients are taken from the diagonals of Pascal's triangle.

chord of a circle   A line segment with its endpoints on a circle.

circle   The set of all points in the plane that are equidistant from a fixed point called the centre.

circle graph   A graph using sectors of a circle to represent data.

circumference   The perimeter of a circle, or the length of this perimeter.

coefficient   A number or symbol immediately preceding a variable in a term.

  In $3x^2$, the coefficient of x^2 is 3.

combination   A selection of objects in which order is not important. The number of combinations of n distinct objects taken r objects at a time, denoted ${}_nC_r$, is $\dfrac{n!}{(n-r)!r!}$

combinatorics   The investigation of different possibilities for the arrangement of objects.

common difference   The difference between two consecutive terms of an arithmetic sequence.

  The common difference of 1, 4, 7, 10 , … is 3.

common factor   A term that is a factor of two or more terms. The common factor of $4x$ and $6x$ is $2x$.

common logarithm   A logarithm in base 10.

common ratio   The ratio of consecutive terms of a geometric sequence.

  The common ratio of 2, 6, 18, 54, 162, … is 3.

complementary angles   Two angles whose sum is $90°$.

complementary events   Two events the sum of whose probabilities is 1.

  In an experiment of rolling a standard die, rolling a 1 and not rolling a 1 are complementary events.

composite number   A whole number that is greater than 1 and is not prime.

  $6 = 1 \times 2 \times 3$, so 6 is a composite number.

compound interest   Interest that is calculated at regular intervals and is added to the principal for the next interest period.

compression   A stretch by a factor less than 1.

conditional probability   The probability of an event under the condition that some preceding event has occurred. The conditional probability of B given A, that is, the probability that event B will occur, given that event A has already occurred, denoted $P(B|A)$, is $\dfrac{P(A \text{ and } B)}{P(A)}$.

conditional statement A compound statement that is written in the form "*If...then...*"

cone A three-dimensional figure generated when a line is rotated about a point.

confidence interval An interval which is believed, with a specified degree of confidence $(1 - \alpha)\%$, to include a particular value of data being estimated. A $(1 - \alpha)\%$ confidence interval for normally distributed data with mean μ and standard deviation σ is symmetrical about the mean with probability $P(\mu - a < x < \mu + a) = 1 - \alpha$.

congruent figures Figures with the same shape and size.

conic section A figure that can be formed by slicing a double-napped cone.

conjecture A generalization, or educated guess, made using inductive reasoning.

conjugate axis The axis of symmetry of a hyperbola that is perpendicular to the transverse axis.

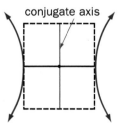

conjugate axis

conjugate hyperbolas Hyperbolas that share the same asymptotes. The transverse axis of one is the conjugate axis of the other.

coordinate plane A one-to-one pairing of all ordered pairs of real numbers with all points of a plane. Also called the Cartesian coordinate plane.

coordinates An ordered pair, (x, y), that locates a point on a coordinate plane.

cosecant ratio The reciprocal of the sine ratio.

cosine ratio For an acute angle in a right triangle, the ratio of the length of the adjacent side to the length of the hypotenuse.

cotangent ratio The reciprocal of the tangent ratio.

coterminal angles Angles that have the same terminal arm.

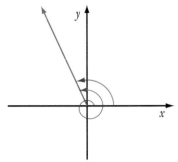

cubic equation A polynomial equation of degree 3.

cubic function A polynomial function of degree 3.

D

decagon A polygon with 10 sides.

deductive reasoning The process of demonstrating that, if certain statements are true, then other statements can be shown to follow from the original statements.

degenerate conic section A figure formed by a slice of a double-napped cone that is not a circle, ellipse, hyperbola, or parabola. A line segment or a point.

degree of a function The greatest exponent of the variable in any one term of the function.

The degree of $f(x) = 5x^4 + 4x^2 + 2x$ is 4.

dependent events Events for which the probability that one will occur is affected by the occurrence of the others.

dependent variable In a relation, a variable whose value is determined by the independent variable.

deviation   The difference between a data item in a set and the mean of the set.

For item x, the deviation is $x - \mu$.

diagonal   A line segment with endpoints on two non-adjacent vertices of a polygon.

diameter   A chord that passes through the centre of a circle.

difference triangle   A triangular arrangement of numbers where the absolute value of the difference between successive digits appears below them.

748
34   is a difference triangle.
1

directrix   The line from which each point of a parabola is the same distance as it is from the focus.

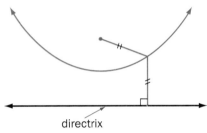

directrix

distortion   A transformation in which a figure is expanded, compressed, or turned so that the image is not congruent to the original.

distribution   A list of possible outcomes and the associated probabilities.

domain of a function   The set of numbers for which a function is defined. The set of all first coordinates of the ordered pairs in a function.

double-napped cone   A three-dimensional figure generated when a line is rotated about a point on the line.

E

element   An object in a set. Elements are usually listed between brace brackets, { }, and are separated by commas.

ellipse   The locus of all points in a plane such that the sum of the distances from two given points in the plane, the foci, is constant.

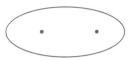

empty set   The set containing no elements, denoted { } or ϕ. The empty set is a subset of every set.

equation   A sentence formed by two expressions related by an equal sign.

$34 + 46 = 80$ and $2x - 7 = 3(4x + 1)$ are equations.

equilateral triangle   A triangle with all sides equal.

equivalent numbers   Different representations for the same number.

5^2 and $\dfrac{50}{2}$ are equivalent numbers for 25.

error range   The value $\pm z_{\frac{\alpha}{2}}\sqrt{\dfrac{pq}{n}}$ where $(1 - \alpha)\%$ of the time the percent of successes in a sample is within $z_{\frac{\alpha}{2}}\sqrt{\dfrac{pq}{n}}$ of the expected probability of success, where p is the probability of success, q is the probability of failure, and n is the size of the sample.

Euler's Formula   The formula that relates the number of vertices and faces to the number of edges of any polyhedron. The number of vertices and faces is two greater than the number of edges.

even function   A function that is invariant under reflection in the y-axis; that is, $f(-x) = f(x)$.

$f(x) = x^4 + 2x^2 + 1$ is an even function.

event   Any collection of possible outcomes of an experiment, that is, a subset of the sample space.

In an experiment of drawing a card from a standard deck of playing cards, drawing a heart is an event.

expansion   A stretch by a factor greater than 1.

experiment   In probability, an action which has measurable or quantifiable results.

explicit formula   A formula for the nth term of a sequence as an expression of n.

$$t_n = n^3 - 1 \text{ is an explicit formula.}$$

exponent   The number of times the base is a factor in a power.

In $3x^4$, the exponent is 4.

exponential equation   An equation that has a variable in an exponent.

$3^{2x} = 81$ is a exponential equation.

exponential function   A function of the form $f(x) = ab^x$ where $a \neq 0$ and $b > 0$.

$f(x) = 1000(2^x)$ is an exponential function.

exponential regression   A method of determining the exponential equation of a curve that fits the distribution of points on a scatter plot.

F

factor   A number or polynomial that is multiplied by another number or polynomial to give a product.

factorial   For a positive integer n, the product of all the positive integers less than or equal to n, denoted $n!$ For $n = 0$, $0! = 1$ by definition.

$$5! = 5 \times 4 \times 3 \times 2 \times 1$$

factoring   Finding the factors of a number or expression.

Fibonacci sequence   The number sequence $\{1, 1, 2, 3, 5, 8, \ldots\}$ in which each term, except the first two, is the sum of the two preceding terms.

focal radii   The line segments joining point P on an ellipse or hyperbola to the foci.

foci of a hyperbola   The two points in the plane, F_1 and F_2, such that $|PF_1 - PF_2|$ is constant for all points P on a hyperbola.

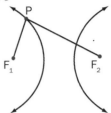

foci of an ellipse   The two points in the plane, F_1 and F_2, such that $PF_1 + PF_2$ is constant for all points P on an ellipse.

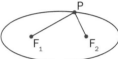

focus of a parabola   The point from which each point of a parabola is the same distance as it is from the directrix.

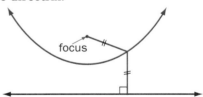

fractal   A geometric figure that has self-similarity, is created using a recursive process, and is infinite in structure.

frieze pattern   A pattern that repeats in one direction.

EEEEE is a frieze pattern.

function   A rule that assigns to each element in the domain a single element in the range.

Fundamental Counting Principle The total number of possibilities for a task, made up of stages, given by $m \times n \times p \times \ldots$, where m is the number of possible choices for the first stage, n is the number of possible choices for the second stage, p is the number of possible choices for the third stage, and so on.

G

general form of a circle When the equation of the circle is written as $x^2 + y^2 + Dx + Ey + F = 0$.

general form of a conic section When the equation of the conic section is written as $Ax^2 + Bxy + Cy^2 + Dx + Ey + F = 0$, where A, B, and C are not all 0.

general form of a hyperbola (with its axes parallel to the x- and y-axes) When the equation of the hyperbola is written as $Ax^2 + Cy^2 + Dx + Ey + F = 0$, where A and C have the opposite sign.

general form of an ellipse (with its axes parallel to the x- and y-axes) When the equation of the ellipse is written as $Ax^2 + Cy^2 + Dx + Ey + F = 0$, where A and C have the same sign and $A \neq C$.

general form of a parabola (with its axes parallel to the x- or y-axes) When the equation of the parabola is written as $Ax^2 + Cy^2 + Dx + Ey + F = 0$, where $A = 0$ or $C = 0$.

general form of a quadratic equation A quadratic equation written in the form $ax^2 + bx + c = 0$, where $a \neq 0$.

generator of a cone The line that is rotated about a point and creates a cone.

geometric means The terms between two given terms of a geometric sequence.

    The two geometric means between 5 and 40 are 10 and 20.

geometric sequence A sequence in which the ratio of every pair of successive terms is a constant, called the common ratio.

    2, 6, 18, 54, 162, … is a geometric sequence.

geometric series The sum of the terms of a geometric sequence.

glide-reflection The combination of a translation and a line reflection.

golden rectangle A rectangle that is pleasing to the eye. The ratio of the length to the width is approximately 1.6:1.

greatest integer function The function $[x]$ = the greatest integer less than or equal to x.

$$[-10.5] = -11$$

H

half-plane The region of a plane on one side of a given boundary line.

happy number A positive integer where the sum of the squares of its digits is 1, or, if, when the process is continued until the sum is one digit, the result is 1.

heptagon A polygon with seven sides.

hexadecimal system The number system using base 16.

hexagon A polygon with six sides.

histogram A bar graph used to display a set of data grouped in consecutive classes.

horizontal stretch A transformation where (x, y) on the graph of $y = f(x)$ is transformed into $\left(\dfrac{x}{k}, y\right)$ on the graph of $y = f(kx)$. The stretch is an expansion when $0 < k < 1$ and a compression when $k > 1$.

hyperbola The locus of all points in a plane such that the absolute value of the difference of the distances from any point on the hyperbola to two given points in the plane, the foci, is constant.

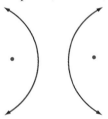

hypotenuse The side opposite the right angle in a right triangle.

image point A point that corresponds to an object point under a mapping.

independent events Events for which the probability that each will occur is not affected by the occurrence of the others.

> In an experiment of rolling a die and flipping a coin, a first event of rolling a 6 and a second event of flipping tails are independent.

independent trials Experiments in which the results of one do not affect the results of others.

independent variable In a relation, a variable whose value may be freely chosen and which determines the value(s) of the dependent variable.

index of summation The variable used in Sigma notation.

> In $\displaystyle\sum_{k=1}^{10} 2k$, the index of summation is k.

inductive reasoning A type of reasoning in which a pattern is observed in a set of data and the pattern is used to make an educated guess, or generalization, about the data.

inequality Two expressions related by an inequality symbol ($>$, $\geq$, $<$, $\leq$, or $\neq$).

> $4x \geq 8$ is an inequality.

infinite geometric series A geometric series that does not end at a specific term, but continues indefinitely.

integer A number in the sequence ..., -3, -2, -1, 0, 1, 2, 3, ...

intercept A point at which a graph crosses or touches the x-axis or y-axis.

interior angle An angle formed inside a polygon by two adjacent sides of the polygon.

invariant point A point that is unaltered by a transformation.

inverse function A function, f^{-1}, defined by $f^{-1}(b) = a$ if $f(a) = b$.

inverse of a relation The relation formed by interchanging the domain and the range of the given relation.

inverse variation A function defined by an equation of the form $xy = k$, where $k \neq 0$.

irrational number A real number that cannot be expressed in the form $\dfrac{a}{b}$, where a and b are integers and $b \neq 0$.

isosceles triangle A triangle with exactly two equal sides.

K

kite A quadrilateral with two pairs of adjacent sides equal.

L

law of cosines The relationship between the lengths of the three sides and the cosine of an angle in any triangle.

$$a^2 = b^2 + c^2 - 2bc \cos A$$

law of sines The relationship between the sides and their opposite angles in any triangle.

$$\frac{\sin A}{a} = \frac{\sin B}{b} = \frac{\sin C}{c}$$

leading coefficient The coefficient of the highest-order term in a polynomial.

linear equation An equation of degree 1. Its graph is a line.

> $y = 5x + 4$ is a linear equation.

linear function A function of the form $f(x) = mx + b$.

line of best fit A line drawn as close as possible to the most points in a scatter plot.

line of symmetry A mirror line that reflects an object onto itself.

locus A set of points determined by a given condition.

logarithm An exponent.

logarithmic equation An equation that has the variable in a logarithm.

$\log_2 x = \log_2 3 + \log_2 5$ is a logarithmic equation.

logarithmic function The inverse of an exponential function. A function of the form $f(x) = \log_a x$ where $a > 0$.

$y = \log_a x$ means $a^y = x$.

logarithmic spiral The plane curve whose vectorial angle is proportional to the logarithm of the radius vector.

lower limit of summation The number below the Σ in Sigma notation.

In $\displaystyle\sum_{k=1}^{10} 2k$, the lower limit is 1.

lune A crescent-shaped figure bounded by two circular arcs.

M

magic square A square arrangement of numbers for which the sum of the numbers in any line (horizontal, vertical, or diagonal) is the same number.

major axis The longer of the two line segments that form the axes of symmetry for an ellipse.

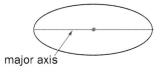

major axis

mapping A pairing of each element in the domain of a function with each element in the range. A correspondence of points between an object and its image.

margin of error The value $\pm z_{\frac{\alpha}{2}}\sqrt{\dfrac{pq}{n}}$ where $(1-\alpha)\%$ of the time the percent of successes in a sample is within $z_{\frac{\alpha}{2}}\sqrt{\dfrac{pq}{n}}$ of the expected probability of success, where p is the probability of success, q is the probability of failure, and n is the size of the sample.

mean The sum of a set of values divided by the number of values. The symbol μ represents the mean of $x_1, x_2, x_3, \ldots, x_n$.

The mean of 4, 5, 8, and 10 is 6.75.

mean deviation The mean of the absolute values of the differences between data items and their mean.

median The middle number of a set of values arranged in order from greatest to least.

The median of 4, 5, 8, and 10 is 6.5.

median of a triangle The line segment joining a vertex to the midpoint of the opposite side.

minor axis The shorter of the two line segments that form the axes of symmetry for an ellipse.

minor axis

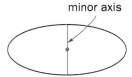

mode The number that occurs most frequently in a set of values.

The mode of 3, 4, 4, 6, and 8 is 4.

monomial A number, a variable, or a product of numbers and variables.

mutually exclusive events Two events in a probability experiment that share no outcomes.

In an experiment of drawing cards from a standard deck of playing cards, drawing a 10 and drawing a queen are mutually exclusive, while drawing a 10 and drawing a heart are not mutually exclusive.

N

natural logarithm   A logarithm in base e.

natural number   A number in the sequence 1, 2, 3, 4, 5, 6, …

nonagon   A polygon with nine sides.

normal curve   The spread of data in a histogram that is bell shaped with properties as follows. It is symmetrical about the mean; the total area under the curve is 1; the area of the curve between $x = a$ and $x = b$ is the probability that a data value will fall between a and b; approximately 68.3% of the data occur within one standard deviation of the mean, approximately 95.4% occur within two standard deviations of the mean, and approximately 99.7% are within three standard deviations of the mean. It is denoted $N(\mu, \sigma^2)$, representing the distribution of data with mean μ and standard deviation σ where

$$f(x) = \frac{1}{\sigma\sqrt{2\pi}} e^{\frac{-(x-\mu)^2}{2\sigma^2}}.$$

normal distribution   The distribution function whose graphical representation is a bell or normal curve.

O

oblique triangle   A triangle that is not right-angled.

obtuse angle   An angle whose measure is greater than 90° but less than 180°.

octagon   A polygon with eight sides.

octal system   The number system using base 8.

odd function   A function that is invariant under a half-turn rotation about (0, 0); that is, $f(-x) = -f(x)$.

$f(x) = x^3 + 2x^2 + 3x - 1$ is an odd function.

odds   The ratio of favourable outcomes to unfavourable outcomes for an event.

ordered pair   A pair of numbers, such as (–3, 6), used to name a point on a graph.

origin   The intersection of the x- and y-axes on a Cartesian coordinate grid. Described by the ordered pair (0, 0).

outcome   The result of a probability experiment.

In an experiment of drawing a card from a standard deck of playing cards, drawing the queen of hearts is one of 52 possible outcomes.

P

palindrome   A number or word that reads the same backwards as forwards.

24 542 and noon are palindromes.

parabola   The graph of a quadratic function for which the domain is the set of real numbers. The locus of all points in a plane that are the same distance from a line in the plane, the directrix, as from a fixed point in the plane not on the line, the focus.

parallel lines   Two lines in the same plane that never meet.

parallelogram   A quadrilateral with opposite sides parallel.

partial sum S_n, the nth partial sum, is the sum of the first n terms in a series.

The 3rd partial sum of the series $48 + 24 + 12 + 6 + 3 + 1\frac{1}{2} + \frac{3}{4} + \dots$ is 84.

Pascal's triangle   The triangular arrangement of numbers with 1 in the first row and 1 1 in the second row, and each number in the succeeding rows is the sum of the two numbers above it in the preceding row.

pentagon   A polygon with five sides.

pentomino A polygon formed by joining five identical squares along whole sides.

perfect square A whole number that can be expressed as the square of a whole number.

25 is a perfect square.

perfect square trinomial A trinomial that can be factored as the square of a binomial.

$$a^2x^2 + 2abx + b^2 = (ax + b)^2$$

perigee of a satellite The closest distance that the orbit of the satellite takes the satellite to Earth.

perimeter The distance around a closed plane figure.

period The magnitude of a periodic function over which it repeats itself.

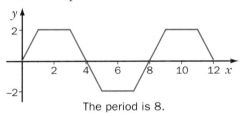

The period is 8.

periodic function A function that repeats itself over an interval of its domain.

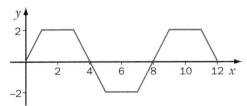

permutation An arrangement of objects in a definite order. The number of permutations of n distinct objects is $n!$ The number of permutations of n objects of which a objects are alike, another b objects are alike, another c objects are alike, and so on, is $\dfrac{n!}{a!\,b!\,c!\ldots}$. The number of permutations of n distinct objects taken r at a time, denoted by $_nP_r$, is $\dfrac{n!}{(n-r)!}$.

perpendicular bisector The line that intersects a line segment at right angles, dividing it into two congruent parts.

perpendicular lines Lines that intersect at right angles.

phase shift The horizontal translation of a trigonometric function.

pigeonhole principle The rule that states that, if n objects are put in p boxes, where $1 \le p < n$, then some boxes contain at least two objects.

Platonic solids Three-dimensional figures with congruent polygon-shaped faces.

point of tangency The point of intersection of a tangent and a circle.

polygon A closed plane figure formed by at least three line segments.

polyhedron A three-dimensional object having polygons as faces.

polynomial An expression of the form $a_n x^n + a_{n-1} x^{n-1} + \ldots + a_1 x^1 + a_0$, where the coefficients $a_n, a_{n-1}, \ldots, a_0$ represent real numbers, a_n is not zero, and the exponents are non-negative integers.

$3x^5 + 4x^4 - 2x^3 + x^2 - 5x - 1$ is a polynomial.

polyomino A polygon formed by joining identical squares along whole sides.

power A product obtained by using a base as a factor one or more times.

5^3 is the power that equals 125.

power function A function of the form $f(x) = ax^n$ where $a \ne 0$ and n is a positive integer.

primary trigonometric ratios The sine, cosine, and tangent ratios.

prime number A number with exactly two factors—itself and 1.

2, 5, and 7 are prime numbers.

principal angle The least non-negative coterminal angle.

probability   The ratio of the number of favourable outcomes to the number of possible outcomes. The study of chance and uncertainty.

probability tree   A tree diagram with probabilities assigned to the branches.

proper divisor   A number that divides evenly into a given number.

proper subset   P is a proper subset of Q if $P \neq Q$.

Pythagorean Theorem   The relation that expresses the area of the square drawn on the hypotenuse of a right triangle as equal to the sum of the areas of the squares drawn on the other two sides.

Q

quadrant   One of the four regions formed by the intersection of the x-axis and the y-axis.

quadratic equation   An equation in the form of $ax^2 + bx + c = 0$, where a, b, and c are real numbers and $a \neq 0$.

quadratic function   A function defined by a quadratic equation of the form $y = ax^2 + bx + c$.

quadrature of a plane figure   The construction of a square of exactly the same area as a figure in a plane, using only a straightedge and compasses.

quadrilateral   A polygon with four sides.

R

radian   The measure of the angle formed by rotating the radius of a circle through an arc equal in length to the radius.

radical equation   An equation that has a variable in a radicand.

$$\sqrt{x+1} + 2 = 4 \text{ is a radical equation.}$$

radical function   A function that has a variable in a radicand.

$$f(x) = \sqrt{x-3} \text{ is a radical function.}$$

radical sign   The symbol $\sqrt{}$, which indicates the principal or non-negative root of an expression.

radicand   An expression under a radical sign.

radius   A line segment that joins the centre of a circle and a point on the circumference.

random sample   A sample in which each member of the population has the same chance of being selected.

range of a relation   The set of all second coordinates of the ordered pairs of a relation. The set of all values of a function $f(x)$.

range of data   The difference between the greatest data item and the least data item.

rational equation   An equation that contains one or more rational expressions.

$$\frac{3}{x-4} = 2 \text{ is a rational equation.}$$

rational function   A function of the form $f(x) = \dfrac{g(x)}{h(x)}$, where $g(x)$ and $h(x)$ are polynomials and $h(x) \neq 0$.

$$f(x) = \frac{1}{x+1} \text{ is a rational function.}$$

rational number   A number that can be expressed in the form $\dfrac{a}{b}$, where a and b are integers and $b \neq 0$.

real numbers   All the rational and irrational numbers.

real zero   An x-intercept of the graph of a function.

reciprocal function   A function, $\dfrac{1}{f}$, defined by $\dfrac{1}{f(a)} = \dfrac{1}{b}$ if $f(a) = b$.

reciprocals   Two numbers that have a product of 1.

$$2 \text{ and } \frac{1}{2} \text{ are reciprocals.}$$

reciprocal trigonometric ratios   The cosecant, secant, and cotangent ratios.

rectangle   A parallelogram with four right angles.

rectangular hyperbola   A hyperbola with perpendicular asymptotes.

recursive formula   A formula that relates each term of a sequence to the term before it.

$$t_n = t_{n-1} + (3n - 1)$$ is a recursive formula.

reflection   A transformation that maps an object onto an image by a reflection in a line.

regression   A method of determining the equation of a curve that fits the distribution of points on a scatter plot.

regression line   An accurate line of best fit, usually determined with a computer or a graphing calculator.

regular polygon   A polygon in which all sides are equal and all angles are equal.

relation   A set of ordered pairs.

relative maximum   A point that does not have the greatest y-coordinate of any point of a function, but no nearby point has a greater y-coordinate. A peak turning point.

relative minimum   A point that does not have the least y-coordinate of any point of a function, but no nearby point has a lesser y-coordinate. A valley turning point.

relatively prime numbers   Numbers that have no common prime number factors.

restriction on a variable   A condition placed on the value(s) of a variable.

rhombus   A parallelogram in which all sides are equal.

right circular cone   A cone with a circular base that is perpendicular to its central axis.

right triangle   A triangle with one right angle.

rotation   A transformation that maps an object onto its image by a turn about a fixed point.

sample space   The set of all possible outcomes of a probability experiment.

scale drawing   A drawing in which all distances are reduced or enlarged by a fixed factor.

scalene triangle   A triangle with no sides equal.

scatter plot   The result of plotting data that can be represented as ordered pairs on a graph.

secant ratio   The reciprocal of the cosine ratio.

sector   A region of a circle bounded by two radii and their intercepted arc.

sector angle   An angle formed by two radii of a circle. Also known as a central angle.

segment of a circle   The region between a chord and an arc subtended by the chord.

sequence   An ordered list of numbers.

series   The sum of the terms in a sequence.

set   Any collection of objects.

Sierpinski's triangle   An equilateral triangle in which the midpoints of the three sides are joined and the equilateral triangle formed is removed. The process is repeated on each remaining equilateral triangle to obtain successive stages.

Sigma notation   The notation used to abbreviate the writing of a series using the Greek letter Σ.

$$\sum_{k=1}^{10} 2k$$ is an example of Sigma notation.

similar triangles   Triangles with corresponding angles equal and corresponding sides proportional.

sine ratio   For an acute angle in a right triangle, the ratio of the length of the opposite side to the length of the hypotenuse.

sinusoidal function   A function that is used to model periodic data.

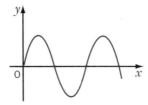

slope   The ratio $\dfrac{\text{rise}}{\text{run}}$. For a non-vertical line containing two distinct points (x_1, y_1) and (x_2, y_2), the slope is $\dfrac{y_2 - y_1}{x_2 - x_1}$.

Snell's Law   The relationship stating that the index of refraction is the ratio of the sine of the angle of incidence to the sine of the angle of reflection.

sphere   The set of all points in space that are the same distance from a given point.

square-based pyramid   A pyramid with a square base.

square root of a number   A number that, when multiplied by itself, gives the original number.

standard deviation   A measure of the spread of data about the mean, specifically, the square root of the sum of the squares of the deviations from the mean divided by the number of data items. The symbol σ represents the standard deviation.

$$\sigma = \sqrt{\dfrac{\sum\limits_{i=1}^{n}(x_i - \mu)^2}{n}}$$

standard error   A measure of error that can be expected in drawing conclusions about a sample based on a population. If p is the probability of success and q is the probability of failure where $p + q = 1$ and n is the size of the sample, then the standard error is $\sqrt{\dfrac{pq}{n}}$.

standard form of a circle   When the equation of the circle is written as $(x - h)^2 + (y - k)^2 = r^2$.

standard form of a hyperbola   When the equation of the hyperbola is written as
$$\dfrac{(x - h)^2}{a^2} - \dfrac{(y - k)^2}{b^2} = 1 \text{ or } \dfrac{(y - k)^2}{a^2} - \dfrac{(x - h)^2}{b^2} = 1.$$

standard form of an ellipse   When the equation of the ellipse is written as $\dfrac{(x - h)^2}{a^2} + \dfrac{(y - k)^2}{b^2} = 1$.

standard form of a parabola   When the equation of the parabola is written as $(x - h)^2 = 4p(y - k)$ or $(y - k)^2 = 4p(x - h)$.

standard form of a quadratic function   A quadratic function written in the form $y = a(x - p)^2 + q$, where $a \ne 0$.

standard normal curve   The normal curve denoted $N(0, 1)$, that is, the curve for a normally distributed set of data with a mean of 0 and a standard deviation of 1.

standard position   The position of an angle when its vertex is at the origin and its initial ray is on the positive x-axis.

statistical sampling   The field of mathematics dedicated to designing accurate and representative experiments to estimate empirically the probability that something will occur.

straight angle   An angle whose measure is 180°.

stretch of a function   A transformation where (x, y) on the graph of $y = f(x)$ is transformed into (x, ay) on the graph of $y = af(x)$, or a transformation where (x, y) on the graph of $y = f(x)$ is transformed into $\left(\dfrac{x}{k}, y\right)$ on the graph of $y = f(kx)$.

subset   If all the elements of P are also elements in Q, then P is a subset of Q. The empty set and the entire set Q are considered subsets of Q.

supplementary angles   Two angles whose sum is 180°.

system of equations   Two or more equations studied together.

T

table of values   A method of organizing values of a relation.

tangent ratio   For an acute angle in a right triangle, the ratio of the length of the opposite side to the length of the adjacent side.

tangent to a circle   A line that intersects a circle at exactly one point.

tangram   An ancient Chinese puzzle in which a square is cut into seven polygons—five triangles, one square, and one parallogram.

terminal arm   The ray of an angle in standard position that is not on the positive x-axis.

transformation   A mapping of points of a plane onto points of the same plane.

translation   A transformation that maps an object onto its image so that each point in the object is moved the same distance in the same direction.

transverse axis   The line segment between the vertices of a hyperbola that is one of its axes of symmetry.

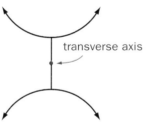

trapezoid   A quadrilateral with one pair of parallel sides.

tree diagram   A diagram illustrating the possible outcomes of an event.

triangle   A polygon with three sides.

trigonometric equation   An equation involving one or more trigonometric functions of a variable.

$\cos x - 2 \sin x \cos x = 0$ is a trigonometric equation.

trigonometric function   A function involving a primary trigonometric ratio or a reciprocal trigonometric ratio.

$y = 4.5\cos\dfrac{x}{4}$ is a trigonometric function.

trigonometric identity   A trigonometric equation that is true for all values of the variable for which both sides of the equation are defined.

trinomial   A polynomial consisting of three terms.

$x^2 + 2xy + y^2$ is a trinomial.

turning point   A relative maximum or relative minimum of a graph.

U

upper limit of summation   The number above the Σ in Sigma notation.

In $\displaystyle\sum_{k=1}^{10} 2k$, the upper limit of summation is 10.

V

variable   A letter or symbol, such as x, used to represent a number.

vector   A directed line segment.

Venn diagram   A diagram that uses overlapping circles inside a rectangle to model statements.

vertex of a cone   The point about which the line is rotated in the generation of a cone.

vertex of a hyperbola   The point on each branch of a hyperbola that is closest to the centre of the hyperbola.

vertex of a parabola   The point where the axis of symmetry of a parabola intersects the parabola.

vertical line test   A test for determining whether a given graph represents a function. If a vertical line intersects the graph more than once, then the relation is not a function.

vertical stretch   A transformation where (x, y) on the graph of $y = f(x)$ is transformed into (x, ay) on the graph of $y = af(x)$. The stretch is an expansion when $a > 1$, and a compression when $0 < a < 1$.

visible-factor number   A natural number that is divisible by each of its non-zero digits.

volume   The number of cubic units contained in a solid.

W

whole numbers   Numbers in the sequence 0, 1, 2, 3, 4, 5, …

X

x-axis   The horizontal line used as a scale for the independent variable in the Cartesian coordinate plane.

x-coordinate   The first value in an ordered pair.

x-intercept   The x-coordinate of a point where a line or curve crosses the x-axis.

Y

y-axis   The vertical line used as a scale for the dependent variable in the Cartesian coordinate plane.

y-coordinate   The second value in an ordered pair.

y-intercept   The y-coordinate of a point where a line or curve crosses the y-axis.

Z

zero of a function   Any value of x for which the value of the function $f(x)$ is 0.

z-score   The number of multiples of the standard deviation that a data item is from the mean, specifically, the deviation from the mean divided by the standard deviation.

$$z_x = \frac{x - \mu}{\sigma}$$

INDEX

Text Credits

xii bottom (screen view) Statistics Canada Internet Site, www.stscan.ca/start.html, 9/20/99; **183** (graph, adapted) NOAA/National Geophysical Data Center; **220-21** (material on CBL™) Reprinted with permission of Texas Instruments; **224** (graph, adapted) Courtesy of Environment Canada; **323** (screen view) Statistics Canada Internet Site, www.stscan.ca/start.html, 9/20/99; **416-417** From *Finite Mathematics*. Author Stewart et al., McGraw-Hill Ryerson Ltd. © 1988. Table page 508-509. Reprinted with permission of McGraw-Hill Ryerson Ltd.; **429** (data used on map) Data obtained from: http://www.unicef.org/statis Source: UNESCO

Photo Credits

v Corel Corporation; **vi** U.S. Navy Photo by Ensign John Gay; **vii** Photo courtest of Wind Power Inc., Pincher Creek, AB; **viii** Corel Corporation; **x left** T. Bonderud/First Light; **xii top** Ian Crysler, **bottom centre** Alan Sirulnikoff/First Light; **xiii top** Digital imagery® copyright 1999 PhotoDisc, Inc., **centre top** John Edwards/Tony Stone Images, **centre bottom** Corel Corporation, **bottom** Corel Corporation; **xv** CORBIS/Kevin R. Morris; **xvi** Canadian Currency Museum; **xvii** Ian Crysler; **xix** Canapress/John MacKay; **xx** Corel Corporation; **xxi** Canapress/John Mahler; **xxiv** © Copyright The British Museum; **xxvi-1** Symmetry Drawing E67 by M.C. Escher. © 1999 Cordon Art - Baarn - Holland. All Rights Reserved.; **2** Canapress/Paul Chiasson; **4-5** Ian Crysler; **7** Greg Stott/Masterfile; **14** Don Ford; **16** Grisel Gonzalez; **30** Al Harvey/The Slide Farm; **41** John Edwards/Tony Stone Images; **44** Canadian Tourism Commission; **50** World Gold Council; **58** Canapress/Todd Korol; **60** Digital imagery® copyright 1999 PhotoDisc, Inc.; **61** Corel Corporation; **63** Corel Corporation; **68-69** Digital imagery® copyright 1999 PhotoDisc, Inc.; **70** Paul Barton/First Light;

72 Agile Design; **74** Corel Corporation; **77** CNRI/Science Photo Library; **84** CORBIS/Kevin R. Morris; **86** Digital imagery® copyright 1999 PhotoDisc, Inc.; **91** Alan Sirulnikoff/First Light; **98** Corel Corporation; **102** Digital imagery® copyright 1999 PhotoDisc, Inc.; **108** Corel Corporation; **116** Alan Sirulnikoff/First Light; **121** Mark Stephenson/First Light; **124 top** National Archives of Canada/Neg no. C17335; **124-25** Canapress/Scott Dunlop; **127** Corel Corporation; **130-31** U.S. Navy Photo by Ensign John Gay; **132 top** Photo Courtesy of David Queen/Buckland and Taylor Ltd., **centre top** Corel Corporation, **centre bottom** Ron Watts/First Light, **bottom left** Musson Cattell Mackay Partnership; **bottom right,** Canadian Tourism Commission; **134** Ian Crysler; **138** Courtesy Sony Canada; **143** NOAO/Digital Stock Corporation; **153** NASA; **154** B. Rondel/First Light; **164 left** Corel Corporation, **right** © 1997 Digital Vision Ltd. All Rights Reserved. ; **inset** Ron Watts/First Light; **172** Terrace Economic Development Corporation; **182-83** NASA **186** Bernd Wittich/Visuals Unlimited; **192** SUI/Visuals Limited; **194** Photo by Boily; **202** CORBIS/BETTMAN; **203** Tek Image/Science Photo Library; **204** Photo courtesy of Wind Power Inc., Pincher Creek , AB; **212** Victoria and Albert Museum, London/Art Resource N.Y.; **220-21** Ian Crysler; **222** Yokohama Convention and Visitor's Bureau; **228** Greg Pease/Tony Stone Images; **234** Science Photo Library; **240-241** Lydia Pawelak/National Ballet of Canada; **244** David Hardy/Science Photo Library; **249** NASA/Langley Research Center; **254** VU/Visuals Unlimited; **258** University of Louisville Department of Physics; **268** MacDonald Dettwiller Space and Advanced Robotics Ltd.; **275** George Hunter/ Comstock; **276** Jeff Greenberg/Visuals Unlimited; **282-83** Metro Zoo; **286** David Nunuk/First Light; **292-93** Corel Corporation; **297** CORBIS/BETTMAN; **302** Michael Philip Manheim/First Light; **306** T. Bonderud/First Light; **311** Corel Corporation; **313** Corel Corporation;

322 Ontario Hydro Services Company (OHSC) Archives, negative no. 90.0454-17; **330-31** Digital imagery® copyright 1999 PhotoDisc, Inc.; **332** Corel Corporation; **334** Photos of Alberta, British Columbia, Manitoba, Saskatchewan, Northwest Territories and Yukon licence plates are from the following website, © 1998-99 Joseph P. Sallmen: http://members.home.com/canp18s (A book based on this site will be published soon.) Nunavut, Andrew Osborne; **338** S. McBrady/Photo Edit; **344** Digital imagery® copyright 1999 PhotoDisc, Inc. ; **350** Corel Corporation; **354** Science Photo Library; **364-65** James L. Shaffer/Photo Edit; **368** CORBIS/BETTMAN; **375** CORBIS/ BETTMAN; **382** Canapress/Chuck Stoody; **387** Canapress/Ryan Remiorz; **388** David Young-Wolff/Photo; **393** Digital imagery® copyright 1999 PhotoDisc, Inc.; **394 top** ©1997 Digital Vision Ltd. All Rights Reserved.; **394-95** NOAO/ Digital Stock Corporation; **400-401** Courtesy of Environment Canada; **402** Dick Hemingway; **404** Alain Ernoult/ Image Bank; **409** Bob Rose/ Comstock; **418** Russ Kinne/Comstock; **424** Elyse Lewin/Image Bank; **428** David Young-Wolff/ Photo Edit; **436-37** Canapress/Carlo Allegri; **438-39** Canapress/Frank Gunn.

Illustration Credits

xvi bottom Bernadette Lau; **xviii** Deborah Crowle; **xxii** Clarence Porter; **xx bottom** Michael Herman; **42** Bernadette Lau; **122** Michael Herman; **143 centre** Deborah Crowle; **179 left** Peter Cook; **284** Deborah Crowle; **286** Peter Cook; **287** Peter Cook; **289** Peter Cook; **296** Peter Cook; **288** Peter Cook; **310 bottom** Deborah Crowle; **321** Deborah Crowle; **331** Bernadette Lau; **358** Bernadette Lau; **373** Bernadette Lau; **383** Michael Herman; **384** Deborah Crowle; **429** Peter Cook; **436** Peter Cook

Technical Art by Tom Dart, Bruce Krever, Alana Perez, Claire Milne of First Folio Resource Group, Inc.